JOURNAL FOR THE STUDY OF THE OLD TESTAMENT
SUPPLEMENT SERIES
98



JSOT Press
Sheffield

# ANCIENT CONQUEST ACCOUNTS

## A Study in Ancient Near Eastern and Biblical History Writing

K. Lawson Younger, Jr

Journal for the Study of the Old Testament
Supplement Series 98

Published by JSOT Press
JSOT Press is an imprint of
Sheffield Academic Press Ltd
The University of Sheffield
343 Fulwood Road
Sheffield S10 3BP
England

Printed in Great Britain
by Billing & Sons Ltd
Worcester

British Library Cataloguing in Publication Data available

ISSN 0309-0787
ISBN 1-85075-252-4

TO MY FATHER AND MOTHER:

KENNETH AND DORIS YOUNGER

עם כבוד ויראה

**(Ex. 20:12; Lv. 19:3)**

# CONTENTS

Preface 11
List of abbreviations 13
Illustration: *Verso of the Narmer Palette* 21

*INTRODUCTION*
*"THE UNDERPINNINGS"*

Chapter One PRELIMINARY ISSUES

Part I: History: Cultivating an Idea 25
Removing 'Old Roots' 26
Nurturing 'New Shoots' 35
Part II: Ideology—Unmasking of the Concept 47
Part III: Method: Obtaining Comprehension 52
Establishing the Framework 52
Performing the Reading 55

*STAGE ONE*
*ANCIENT NEAR EASTERN CONQUEST ACCOUNTS*

Chapter Two ASSYRIAN CONQUEST ACCOUNTS 61

Assyrian Ideology: How Do You Spell 'Torture' 65
Type and Nature 65
Ideological Patterns: The Enemy 67
Literary Structures: The Stereotyping Department 69
Syntagmic Valency 70
Introduction 70
The Syntagms of the Assyrian Texts 72
Syntagmic Analysis 79
Annalistic Texts 79
Tiglath-Pileser I 79
Ashur-Dan II 90
Aššur-nasir-pal II 94
Shalmaneser III 99
Sennacherib 111
Letters to the God 115

Sargon II 115
Summary or Display Texts 120
Aššur-nasir-pal II 120
Adad-nirari III 121
Conclusion 122

Chapter Three HITTITE CONQUEST ACCOUNTS 125

Hittite Ideology: Feeling a Little Vengeful Today? 128
Literary Structures: "And the Sungoddess of Arina, my Lady ..." 130
Syntagmic Analysis 132
Hattušili I 136
Muršili II
Ten Year Annals 140
Detailed Annals 158
The Deeds of Suppiluliuma 160
Conclusion 163

Chapter Four EGYPTIAN CONQUEST ACCOUNTS 165

Past Studies 167
Some Generic Considerations (It Depends on Your Purpose) 168
*Iw.tw* Texts 168
*Nḫtw*: The Daybook Reports 170
*Nḫtw*: The Literary Reports 172
Conclusion 173
Egyptian Ideology (Just Being Better Than Everyone Else!) 175
Royal Ideology 175
The Enemy 177
Administration 185
Diffusion of the Ideology 189
Literary Aspects (Never Any Embellishments Here!) 189
Hyperbole 190
Metonymy 192
Conclusion 194

## *STAGE TWO*
## *ISRAELITE CONQUEST ACCOUNTS*

Chapter Five JOSHUA 9-12 197

Literary Structures (Writing It Just Like Everyone Else) 199
Chapter 9 200
Chapters 10 and 11 204
The Code: Joshua 10:11-15 208
The Hailstones 208
The Long Day 211
The Code: Joshua 10:16-27 220
Chapter 10:28-42 226
Chapter 11 228
Chapter 12 230
Israelite Ideology (What You Can Do Through the Right 'Connections') 232
Type 233
Jural Aspect 236
Conclusion 237

## *STAGE THREE*
## *SYNTHESIS*

Chapter Six IMPLICATIONS AND ENTAILMENTS 241

The Notion of a 'Complete Conquest' 241
The Notion of an 'All Israel' Redaction 247
Sources, Structure and Composition 249
Ideological Aspect 253
An Entailment Concerning 'Holy War' 258
Other Entailments 260
Conclusion 263

CONCLUSION 265

NOTES 267

BIBLIOGRAPHY 333

APPENDIX 359

The Syntagms of Joshua 9-12 359
Text and Translation 361
Notes 377

INDEX 385

Author Index 385
Subject Index 388
Scripture 390
Ancient Texts 391

# PREFACE

Works on Old Testament historiography, the 'Conquest', and the origins of ancient Israel have mushroomed in recent days. To that end this book is just one more addition. But while others have been issuing forth 'new' reconstructions and models—many times ignoring the biblical text—, this work will emit a 'new close reading' of the biblical text. The work will be concerned with the literary techniques employed by the ancient writers in order to come to a better understanding of these ancient texts in their context. It is our conviction that it is in this area that biblical scholars have not always taken into account the results of two important disciplines: the philosophy of history and literary criticism. Obviously, there are exceptions, but many biblical scholars still function in these areas with out-moded literary approaches and a historicist view of history. This work will attempt to wrestle with some of these issues and apply them to biblical study.

I owe particular gratitude to Dr. Philip Davies at the University of Sheffield for his encouragement and enthusiasm, his suggestions were always constructive—as time and reflection have shown. Others who, in one way or another, seasoned the work are: Mark Brett, Danny Carroll, David Clines, Steve Fowl, Kenneth Kitchen, Alan Millard, Stan Porter, John Rogerson, and Donald Wiseman.

Substantial financial assistance was provided by a number of individuals and institutions. I gratefully acknowledge the financial support of the British Government through their Overseas Research grants. I am indebted to a number of members of Christchurch, Fulwood in Sheffield: Dr. and Mrs. Ian Manifold, Mr. and Mrs. Robert Dunigan, and Mr. and Mrs. Steven Tynan. I also gratefully acknowledge the backing that I received from the Tyndale House Fellowship.

My family was a constant source of support and encouragement. Without the sacrificial efforts of my parents, Kenneth and Doris Younger, I could never have begun this study; without the support of my aunt, Mrs. George Bickerstaff, I would not have been able to continue; and without the love and tolerance—throughout the entire work—of my wife, Patti, and my children, Kenneth, Andrew and Rebecca, I could never have completed it.

Finally, I must give thanks to Him who has given me life and purpose.

Longview, November 8, 1989 K.L.Y.

# ABBREVIATIONS AND SYMBOLS

| | |
|---|---|
| *AAA* | *Annals of Archaeology and Anthropology* (University of Liverpool). |
| *ABC* | A.K. Grayson. *Assyrian and Babylonian Chronicles*. Locust Valley, N.Y., 1975. |
| *AEL* | M. Lichtheim. *Ancient Egyptian Literature: A Book of Readings*. Berkeley, Los Angeles, and London, 1973-1980. |
| *AEO* | A.H. Gardiner. *Ancient Egyptian Onomastica*. 3 Vols. Oxford, 1947. |
| *AfO* | *Archiv für Orientforschung*. |
| *AHR* | *The American Historical Review*. |
| *AHw* | W. von Soden. *Akkadisches Handwörterbuch*. Wiesbaden, 1959-1975. |
| *AJSL* | *American Journal of Semitic Languages*. |
| *AKA* | L.W. King (and E.A.W. Budge) *Annals of the Kings of Assyria*. Vol. I. London, 1902. [No subsequent volumes appeared. |
| *ANET*[3] | J.B. Pritchard. Editor. *Ancient Near Eastern Texts Relating to the Old Testament*. 3rd Ed. with supplement. Princeton, N.J., 1969. |
| AnBib | Analecta Biblica. |
| AnOr | Analecta Orientalia. |
| AOAT | Alter Orient und Altes Testament. |
| *ARAB* | D.D. Luckenbill. *Ancient Records of Assyria and Babylonia*. 2 Vols. Chicago, 1926-27. |
| *Arch.* | *Archaeologia*. |
| *ARI* | A.K. Grayson. *Assyrian Royal Inscriptions*. 2 Vols. Wiesbaden, 1972-76. |

| | |
|---|---|
| *ARINH* | F.M. Fales. Editor. *Assyrian Royal Inscriptions: New Horizons in Literary, Ideological and Historical Analysis*. [Orientis Antiqvi Collectio, 17]. Rome, 1981. |
| *ARMT* | *Archives royales de Mari.* |
| *ArOr* | *Archiv Orientální.* |
| *AS* | *Anatolian Studies.* |
| *ASAE* | *Annales du Service des antiquités de l'Egypte.* |
| *Asn.* | Le Gac, *Les Inscriptions D'Aššur-Nasir-Aplu III*. Paris, 1906. |
| *Assur* | *Assur*. [Monographic Journals of the Near East]. Malibu, Ca. |
| *Aspects.* | A. Spalinger. *Aspects of the Military Documents of the Ancient Egyptians*. [Yale Near Eastern Researches, 9]. New Haven and London, 1983. |
| *ASTI* | *Annual of the Swedish Theological Institute.* |
| *BA* | *The Biblical Archaeologist.* |
| *BAL*[2] | R. Borger. *Babylonische-assyrische Lesestücke*. 2nd Ed. [AnOr 54]. Rome, 1979. |
| *BAR* | J.H. Breasted. *Ancient Records of Egypt*. 5 Vols. Chicago, 1906-1907. Reprint New York, 1962. |
| *BASOR* | *Bulletin of the American Schools of Oriental Research.* |
| *BBSt* | L.W. King. *Babylonian Boundary-Stones and Memorial Tablets in the British Museum*. London, 1912. |
| *BES* | *Bulletin of the Egyptological Seminar.* |
| *BIFAO* | *Bulletin de l'Institut Français d'Archéologie Orientale.* |
| *BiOr* | *Bibliotheca Orientalis.* |
| *BJRL* | *Bulletin of the John Rylands Library.* |
| BM | British Museum. |
| *B-McL* | A.E. Brooke and N. McLean, with H. St. John Thackeray. Editors. *The Old Testament in Greek: Vol. I, The Octateuch*. Cambridge, 1906-1940. |

| | |
|---|---|
| BoSt | Boghazköi-Studien. |
| *BoTU* | E. Forrer, *Die Boghazhöi-Texte in Umschrift*. Berlin, 1929. |
| BWANT | Beiträge zur Wissenschaft vom Alten und Neuen Testament. |
| *BZ* | *Biblische Zeitschrift.* |
| *BZAW* | *Beihefte zur Zeitschrift für die Alttestamentliche Wissenschaft.* |
| *CAD* | A.L. Oppenheim et al. *The Assyrian Dictionary of the Oriental Institute of the University of Chicago*. 1956-. |
| *CAH*[3] | *The Cambridge Ancient History*. 3rd Ed. Cambridge, 1973-75. |
| *CBQ* | *Catholic Biblical Quarterly.* |
| *CdÉ* | *Chronique d'Égypte.* |
| *CHD* | H.G. Güterbock and H.A Hoffner. *The Hittite Dictionary of the Oriental Institute of the University of Chicago*. Chicago, 1980-. |
| *CRAI* | *Académie des Inscriptions et Belles-Lettres, Comptes rendus des séances.* |
| *CSSH* | *Comparative Studies in Society and History.* |
| CT | Cuneiform Texts from Babylonian Tablets in the British Museum. |
| *DOTT* | D. Winton Thomas. Editor. *Documents from Old Testament Times*. London, 1958. |
| *EA* | J.A. Knudtzon, et al. *Die El-Amarna-Tafeln*. [Vorderasiatische Bibliothek 2]. Leipzig, 1915. |
| *EAK* | *Einleitung in die assyrischen Königsinschriften*. R. Borger, Vol. I. W. Schramm, Vol. II. |
| *EI* | *Eretz-Israel.* |
| FRLANT | Forschungen zur Religion und Literatur des Alten und Neuen Testament. |

| | |
|---|---|
| *FT* | *Faith and Theology.* |
| *GAG* | W. von Soden. *Grundriss der Akkadischen Grammatik.* [AnOr 33]. Rome, 1952. |
| *GKC* | W. Gesenius. *Hebrew Grammar.* Ed. E. Kautzsch, 2nd Eng. Ed., revised in accordance with 28th German Edition by A.E. Cowley. Oxford, 1966. |
| GM | *Göttinger Miszellen.* |
| *GTJ* | *Grace Theological Journal.* |
| HAT | Handbuch zum Alten Testament. |
| *HED* | J. Puhvel. *Hittite Etymological Dictionary.* [2 Vols. in 1]. Paris, 1984. |
| *HHI* | H. Tadmor and M. Weinfeld. Editors. *History, Historiography and Interpretation.* Jerusalem, 1983. |
| *HKL* | R. Borger. *Handbuch der Keilschriftliteratur.* 3 Vols. Berlin, 1967-1973. |
| HSS | Havard Semitic Studies. |
| *HTR* | *Havard Theological Review.* |
| *HUCA* | *Hebrew Union College Annual.* |
| *HW* | J. Friedrich. *Hethitisches Wörterbuch.* [Indogermanische Bibliothek 2]. Heidelberg, 1952. |
| *IAK* | E. Ebeling, B. Meissner, and E.F. Weidner. *Die Inschriften der Altassyrischen Könige.* [Altorientalische Bibliothek 1]. Leipzig, 1926. [No subsequent volumes appeared]. |
| ICC | International Critical Commentary. |
| *IDB* | *The Interpreter's Dictionary of the Bible.* Ed. by G.A. Buttrick. 4 Vols. New York, 1962. |
| *IEJ* | *Israel Exploration Journal.* |
| *IntB* | *The Interpreter's Bible.* 12 Vols. Nashville, 1951-57. |
| *JANES* | *Journal of the Near Eastern Society.* |
| JAOS | *Journal of the American Oriental Society.* |
| *JARCE* | *Journal of the American Research Center in Egypt.* |

| | |
|---|---|
| *JBL* | *Journal of Biblical Literature.* |
| *JCS* | *Journal of Cuneiform Studies.* |
| *JEA* | *Journal of Egyptian Archaeology.* |
| *JEOL* | *Jaarbericht ban het Vooraziatisch-Egyptisch Genootschap: Ex Oriente Lux.* |
| *JJS* | *Journal of Jewish Studies.* |
| *JNES* | *Journal of Near Eastern Studies.* |
| *JPOS* | *Journal of the Palestinian Oriental Society.* |
| *JRAS* | *Journal of the Royal Asiatic Society.* |
| *JSOT* | *Journal for the Study of Old Testament.* |
| *JSS* | *Journal of Semitic Studies.* |
| *JSSEA* | *Journal of the Society for the Study of Egyptian Antiquity.* |
| *KAI* | H. Donner and W. Röllig. *Kanaanäische und aramäische Inschriften.* 3 Vols. Wiesbaden, 1962-64. |
| KAT | Kommentar zum Alten Testament. |
| *KBL* | L. Koehler and W. Baumgartner. *Lexicon in Veteris Testamenti Libros.* Leiden, 1958. |
| *KBo* | *Keilschrifttexte aus Boghazköi.* |
| *KRI* | K.A. Kitchen. *Ramesside Inscriptions, Historical and Biographical.* Oxford, 1969-. |
| *KUB* | *Keilschrifturkunden aus Boghazköi.* |
| LCL | Loeb Classical Library. |
| *LdÄ* | *Lexikon der Ägyptologie* (Wiesbaden, 1972- ). |
| *L-S* | H.G. Liddell and R. Scott. *A Greek-English Lexicon.* New York, 1878. |
| *MAOG* | *Mitteilungen der Altorientalischen Gesellschaft.* |
| *MDAIK* | *Mitteilungen des deutschen archäologischen Instituts, Abteilung Kairo.* |
| *MDOG* | *Mitteilungen der Deutschen Orient-Gesellschaft.* |

| | |
|---|---|
| *MIO* | *Mitteilungen des Instituts für Orientforschung.* |
| *MVAG* | *Mitteilungen der Vorderasiatischen / Vorderasiatisch Ägyptischen Gesellschaft.* |
| *Nin.A* | R. Borger. *Die Inschriften Asarhaddons Königs von Assyrien.* [Archiv für Orientforschung, Beiheft 9]. (Graz, 1956), pp. 39-64. |
| *OA* | *Oriens Antiquus.* |
| OG | Old Greek. |
| OIP | The University of Chicago, Oriental Institute Publications. |
| *OLZ* | *Orientalistische Literaturzeitung.* |
| *Or* | *Orientalia.* |
| OTL | The Old Testament Library, Westminster Press. |
| *OTS* | *Oudtestamentische Studiën.* |
| *PAPS* | *Proceedings of the American Philosophical Society.* |
| *PEQ* | *Palestine Exploration Quarterly.* |
| *RA* | *Revue d'Assyriologie et d'Archéologie Orientale.* |
| *RHA* | *Revue d'Hittite et Asianique.* |
| *RB* | *Revue Biblique.* |
| *RdE* | *Revue d'Egyptologie.* |
| *RGG* | *Die Religion in Geschichte und Gegenwart.* 1st, 2nd, and 3rd editions. |
| *RKT* | H. and A. Smith. "A Reconstruction of the Kamose Texts." *ZÄS* 103 (1976): 48-76. |
| *RLA* | *Reallexikon der Assyriologie.* Ed. by Ebeling and Meissner et al. |
| *SAAMA* | "Studies on the Annals of Aššurnasirpal II: I. Morphological Analysis." *VO* 5 (1982-83): 13-73. |
| *SAK* | *Studien zur altägyptische Kultur.* |

*SARI* — Jerrold S. Cooper. *Sumerian and Akkadian Royal Inscriptions*. Vol. I. [The American Oriental Society Translation Series, 1] New Haven, Conn.: The American Oriental Society, 1986.

SBL — Society of Biblical Literature.

SBT — Studies in Biblical Theology.

*SSEAJ* — *Society for the Study of Egyptian Antiquities Journal.*

SSI — J.C.L. Gibson. *Textbook of Syrian Semitic Inscriptions.* 3 Vols. Oxford, 1973-79.

SWBAS — The Social World of Biblical Antiquity Series.

*TB* — *Tyndale Bulletin.*

TCL — Musée du Louvre, Département des Antiquités orientales, *Textes cunéiformes.*

TCS — Texts from Cuneiform Sources.

*TDOT* — G. Johannes Botterweck and H. Ringgren. Editors. *Theological Dictionary of the Old Testament.* Revised Edition. Trans. by J.T. Willis. Grand Rapids: 1974-.

*TN* — E. Weidner. *Die Inschriften Tukulti-Ninurtas I. und seiner Nachfolger.* [AfO Beiheft, 12]. Graz, 1959.

*TUAT* — O. Kaiser. Editor. *Texte aus der Umwelt des Alten Testaments.* Gütersloh, 1984.

*TZ* — *Theologische Zeitschrift.*

*UF* — *Ugarit-Forschungen.*

*Urk.* IV — *Urkunden des ägyptischen Altertums, Abteilung IV: Urkunden der 18. Dynastie.* Ed. by K. Sethe and W. Helck. Fascicles 1-22. Leipzig and Berlin, 1906-1958.

*VO* — *Vicino Oriente.*

*VT* — *Vetus Testamentum.*

*VTS* — *Supplements to Vetus Testamentum.*

*Wb.* — *Wörterbuch der ägyptische Sprache.* Ed. by A. Erman and H. Grapow. 7 Vols. Leipzig, 1926-1963.

| | |
|---|---|
| WMANT | Wissenschaftliche Monographien zum Alten und Neuen Testament. |
| *WO* | *Die Welt des Orients.* |
| YOS | Yale Oriental Series. |
| *ZA* | *Zeitschrift für Assyriologie und vorderasiatische Archäologie.* |
| *ZÄS* | *Zeitschrift für ägyptische Sprache und Altertumskunde.* |
| *ZAW* | *Zeitschrift für die Alttestamentliche Wissenschaft.* |
| *ZDMG* | *Zeitschrift der Deutschen Morgenländischen Gesellschaft.* |
| *ZDPV* | *Zeitschrift des deutschen Palästina-Vereins.* |
| *ZThK* | *Zeitschrift für Theologie und Kirche.* |

The Beginning of a High-Redundance Message
(*The Verso of the Narmer Palette*)

# INTRODUCTION:

# "THE UNDERPINNINGS"

# Chapter 1

# PRELIMINARY ISSUES

> Historia est proxima poetis et quodammodo carmen solutum[1]
>
> Quintilianus

## PART I: HISTORY: CULTIVATING AN IDEA

While the number of articles and books devoted to the subject of Old Testament historiography has increased exponentially, there is seldom within these works any discussion of what history is.[2] One rarely finds any kind of definition given, and usually writers work with the assumption that there is a unified view of what history is: i.e., 'modern scientific'.[3] Biblical scholars have generally ignored recent developments in the philosophy of history, developments which have clarified numerous aspects of 'narrative history'. And since most history writing in the Old Testament is 'narrative history', an investigation into these developments promises to yield positive results.

Many may object to the inclusion of theoretical discussions from the realm of the 'philosophy of history'. But the words of M.I. Finley easily counter such objections:

> Historians, one hears all the time, should get on with their proper business, the investigation of the concrete experiences of the past, and leave the 'philosophy of history' (which is a barren, abstract and pretty useless activity anyway) to the philosophers. Unfortunately the historian is no mere chronicler, and he cannot do his work at all without assumptions and judgments.[4]

*Removing 'Old Roots'*

So completely is modern biblical scholarship the grateful recipient of the gifts of the German historiographic tradition that the general tenets of that tradition are immediately assumed to be one and the same with what any right-minded student of the religion of Israel would do almost intuitively.[5] But perhaps a caution should be penned: 'beware of Germans bearing historiographic gifts'![6]

Two biblical scholars' definitions of history will demonstrate this: John Van Seters and George Coats.[7] Van Seters has recently assumed a definition of history proposed by the Dutch historian Johan Huizinga:

> History is the intellectual form in which a civilization renders account to itself of its past.[8]

He uses this definition 'because I regard the question of genre as the key issue in the discussion, whether we are dealing with the biblical writers or the Greek and Near Eastern materials'. Moreover, he feels that 'in conformity with Huizinga's definition, this work examines the development of national histories and the history of the Israelites in particular'.[9] Thus he associates history writing with national identity. 'Only when the nation itself took precedence over the king, as happened in Israel, could history writing be achieved'. After a long survey of ancient Near Eastern material he argues that the 'historiographical genres' of the Egyptians, Hittites, and Mesopotamians (eg. annals, chronicles, king lists) 'did not lead to true history writing'. He subsumes all historical texts under the term 'historiography' as a 'more inclusive category than the particular genre of history writing'.[10]

If one consults Huizinga's essay, the following arguments appear:

> The idea of history only emerges with the search for certain connexions, the essence of which is determined by the value which we attach to them. It makes no difference whether we think of a history which is the result of researches strictly critical in method, or of sagas and epics belonging to former phases of civilization ... We can speak in the same breath of historiography and historical research ... of the local annalist and the designer of an historical cosmology.

> Every civilization creates its own form of history ... If a civilization coincides with a people, a state, a tribe, its history will be correspondingly simple. If a general civilization is differentiated into distinct nations, and these again into groups, classes, parties, the corresponding differentiation in the historical form follows of itself. The historical interests of every sectional civilization must hold its own history to be the true one, and is entitled to do so, provided that it constructs this history in accordance with the critical requirements imposed by its conscience as a civilization, and not according to the craving for power in the interests of which it imposes silence upon this conscience.[11]

It appears that Van Seters has misunderstood Huizinga's definition and invested it with a quite different meaning.[12]

For Huizinga, history writing is not necessarily 'nationalistic'. Van Seters never defines what he means by 'nation', and there are serious doubts whether by any definition of 'nation' history writing is so restricted, especially to 'when the nation itself took precedence over the king'.

In this emphasis on the nation, Van Seters (whether he is aware of it or not) shows a dependence on the German historiographic concept that the political history of the state is primary.[13] Of all the historians for Van Seters to choose, Huizinga is certainly one of the least likely to have been in sympathy with this notion since he saw cultural history as a deeper and more important pursuit than political history.[14]

While for many late 19th century and early 20th century historians (especially in Germany), there was an inseparable connection between 'history' and 'political' or 'national history', modern historians have long ago abandoned such a notion. And yet it persists in biblical studies!

But the argument becomes circular. For Van Seters the question of genre is the key issue. Genre determines what is history, but the definition of history determines what is history's genre.

Biblical scholars have often maintained that a rigid, essentialist genre analysis alone is sufficient to identify (and hence define) history writing.[15] They believe the matter of genre to be all-important because they think that genre is a determinate category with fixed constituents. These scholars seem to conclude that if one can simply understand correctly which genre is being employed, then the correct interpretation will necessarily follow. In this way genre functions as a type of magic wand for interpretation. This essentialist or classificationist view of genre (the classical view of genre) has been thoroughly debunked.[16]

The essentialist believes that there are inherent traits belonging to the genre itself which are part of the genre's very nature. There are three reasons to question an essentialist position: the very notion that texts compose classes has been questioned; the assumption that members of a genre share a common trait or traits has been questioned; and the function of a genre as an interpretative guide has been questioned. Fredric Jameson has gone so far as to conclude that genre criticism has been 'thoroughly discredited by modern literary theory and practice'.[17] J. Derrida argues that no generic trait completely or absolutely confines a text to a genre or class because such belonging falsifies the constituents of a text:

> If ... such a [generic] trait is remarkable, that is, noticeable, in every aesthetic, poetic, or literary corpus, then consider this paradox, consider the irony ... this supplementary and distinctive trait, a mark of belonging or inclusion, does not belong. It belongs without belonging ...[18]

While questioning the essentialist position, Ralph Cohen does not feel that genre criticism has been totally 'discredited'. Instead, he advances a new approach to genre theory. Cohen argues that genre concepts in theory and practice, arise, change, and decline for socio-historical reasons. And since each genre is composed of texts that accrue, the grouping is a process, not a determinate category. He adds:

> Genres are open categories. Each member alters the genre by adding, contradicting or changing constituents, especially those of members most closely related to it. Since the purposes of critics who establish genres vary, it is self-evident that the same texts can belong to different groupings or genres and serve different generic purposes.[19]

Furthermore, classifications are empirical, not logical. They are historical assumptions constructed by authors, audiences and critics in order to serve communicative and aesthetic purposes. Genres are open systems; they are groupings of texts by critics to fulfill certain ends.[20]

Cohen argues that genre theory does not have to be dependent on essentialist assumptions. Rather, because of the fluidity of genre, 'a process theory of genre' is the best explanation of 'the constituents of texts'.[21] He also points out that there is a relationship between genre and ideology. D. LaCapra notes in this regard:

> One obvious point is that the defense or critique of generic definitions typically involves a defense or critique of discursive and social arrangements, since genres are in one way or another inserted into sociocultural and political practices. This point is frequently not made explicit because it would impair the seeming neutrality of classifications and the way they function in scholarship.[22]

Thus there cannot be a neutral, objective classification of texts along the lines advocated by the essentialist approach. And certainly such classifications cannot function as 'interpretive keys'.

Van Seters's discussion of the genre of the Apology of Hattušili illustrates this.[23] He argues that the text is not an apology, but 'comes close to the mark' of an 'endowment document' (p. 120). Because it is a 'special defense of an interested party in a quasi-legal context', and since '... one cannot thereby include all texts recording legal judgments under the rubric of historiography' the text cannot be historiographic (p. 121). He asserts that it is not an apology because one thinks of an apology as:

> implying a legal context with a fairly clearly defined 'jury' and one's status or life at stake. But this work is not directed to such a body as the senate or to any other political organ for a judgment (p. 119).

I have absolutely no idea where Van Seters obtained such a restrictive definition of an apology! Obviously, the most famous apology of all time is Plato's dialogue in defense of Socrates before the tribunal that sentenced Socrates to death. But certainly apologies are not restricted only to the courtroom and to life-threatening circumstances. J.A. Cuddon defines an apology as 'a work written to defend a writer's opinions or to elaborate and clarify a problem';[24] and Harry Shaw offers: 'a defense and justification for some doctrine, piece of writing, cause or action'.[25] But let one apply the magic wand and one can remove the text from the genre of apology and argue that it is not history writing.

This becomes even harder to accept when one considers Van Seters's argument. He claims that an apology implies a 'legal context' and the text of Hattušili is, therefore, not an apology. But on Van Seters's own admission, the Hattušili text is very similar to a legal document (an endowment document), and this becomes even more clear if one compares it to the *Proclamation of Telipinu*. He argues that an edict (specifically the Telipinu text) is a legal text and not a history. Thus, the Hattušili text, since it is a quasi-legal text, is not history writing. What are we to conclude from such a discussion? Is an apology not history writing because it has a legal context? Must a historical text not include an edict because that is legal material? Can a quasi-legal text never be history writing? Such loosely controlled hairsplitting tends to the absurd!

It is ironic in light of Van Seters's definition of apology that in the *Proclamation of Telipinu* the two words Hittite words for 'political assembly' (*panku-* and *tuliya-*) occur.[26] On the basis of this and other arguments, H.A. Hoffner concludes in his analysis of this work that it is an apology!

> The two clearest examples of apologies among the official texts in the Hittite archives are the Telepinu Proclamation and the Apology of Hattušili III.[27]

Thus, the very evidence, which distinguishes a work as an apology according to Van Seters, can be used to support an argument to identify the Telipinu text as an apology. And this is the text which Van Seters wants to compare to the Hattušili text to prove that that text is not an apology! 'This is the form-critic shaking an impotent fist at the refractory ancient who wrote to suit his own selfish ends'.[28]

To sum up: essentialist generic approaches fail because they see genre as a determinate category made up of fixed constituents. Many scholars who follow this type of approach feel that they can distinguish historiography from fiction simply by form. But this is very fallacious because of the variabilitv of literary conventions employed in both.[29] Such approaches to genre cannot succeed in helping to solve the difficulties confronted in the study of ancient Near Eastern and biblical historiography.

Finally, Van Seters views history as secular, unbiased, scientific, and antithetical to religion. Moreover, he implies that true history writing is non-pragmatic and non-didactic. Thus, he argues:

> The Hittites were more interested in using the past than in recording it, and they used it for a variety of purposes. In the Old Kingdom ... there was the strong tendency ... to use the past for didactic purposes. The past could be used to justify exceptional political actions and behavior or it could provide a precedent to support a continuity of royal rights and privileges ... The Hittites' use of the past here as else-where is too pragmatic to give rise to actual history writing.[30]

This view is difficult to accept. Many works of history are didactic or pragmatic. They are designed to teach future generations (so that mistakes of the past will not be repeated!) or to influence present public opinion through propaganda. In her work on Islamic historiography, M. Waldman devotes an entire chapter to the didactic character of that historiography.[31] It seems, therefore, that Van Seters's understanding is totally inadequate for an investigation of ancient Near Eastern or biblical history writing.[32]

Another recent attempt to define history, which in many ways is representative of O.T. scholarship, is that of George Coats. He states:

> History as a genre of literature represents that kind of writing designed to record the events of the past *as they actually occurred* <emphasis mine>. Its structure is controlled, then, not by the concerns of aesthetics, nor by the symbolic nature of a plot, but by the chronological stages or cause-effect sequences of events as the author(s) understood them. It is not structured to maintain interest or to provoke anticipation for a resolution of tension. It is designed simply to record ... History writing marks a movement away from the contexts of the family or tribe, with their storytelling concerns, to the record-keeping responsibilities of the nation. History writing would thus be identified in some manner with the affairs of the royal court, with its archives. It derives from the concern

> to document the past of the people in order to validate the present administration.[33]

Coats's definition is problematic. First, he equates history writing with the nation and its politics:

> History writing marks a movement away from the contexts of the family or tribe, with their storytelling concerns, to the record-keeping responsibilities of the nation.[34]

Second, his idea of recording events 'as they actually occurred' is a recent echo of a notion which is usually attributed to Ranke's influential phrase, 'wie es eigentlich gewesen'.[35] Inspired by the search for the past as it really was, many scholars assumed that an objective knowledge of the past was not only possible but mandatory. Anything less than a complete and impartial account of some event or series of events in the past was bad history (the more the 'objective' detail, the better the history).

This concept (that history writing is rooted in objectivity) has prevailed in biblical studies. For example H. Gunkel concluded:

> Only at a certain stage of civilisation has objectivity so grown that the interest in transmitting national experiences to posterity so increased that the writing of history becomes possible ... ['history' is prosaic and aims] 'to inform us of what has actually happened.[36]

Thus for Gunkel objectivity was one of the major criteria for the development of history writing in a civilization.

Likewise, H. Gressmann believed that 'history' portrays what actually happened, and shows a remarkable moral objectivity toward its subjects.[37] R.A. Oden comments:

> Just as the tradition founded by Herder and Humboldt claimed to be free of ideology, so too Gressmann proclaimed that alone an inves-tigation which pursues 'nur die geschichtlichen Tatsachen als solche' can be free of dogma.[38]

E.H. Carr sarcastically criticized this idea, wrongly attributed to Ranke ('wie es eigentlich gewesen'), stating:

> Three generations of German, British, and even French historians marched into battle intoning the magic words 'wie es eigentlich gewesen' like an incantation—designed, like most incantations, to save them from the tiresome obligation to

> think for themselves ... [According to this view] the facts are available to the historian in documents, inscriptions and so on, like fish on the fishmonger's slab. The historian collects them, takes them home, and cooks and serves them in whatever style appeals to him ... The facts are really not at all like fish on the fishmonger's slab. They are like fish swimming about in a vast and sometimes inaccessible ocean; and what the historian catches will depend, partly on chance, but mainly on what part of the ocean he chooses to fish in and what tackle he chooses to use.[39]

Carr's caution must be heeded.

The historical work is always the historian's interpretation of the events, being filtered through vested interest, never in disinterested purity.[40] Thus, Oden argues:

> ... it is undeniable that the role of the German historiographic tradition, and hence that tradition's manifestations in biblical study, is great, and probably greater than many have been willing to allow. Barry Barnes has recently reminded us that 'those general beliefs which we are most convinced deserve the status of objective knowledge—scientific beliefs—are readily shown to be overwhelmingly theoretical in character.' If this is true of scientific beliefs, it is true as well of the concepts with which biblical scholarship has operated for most of this century. The occasional reminder of how thoroughly theory dependent is biblical criticism can only aid us in our attempt to direct further research.[41]

While the facts/events must be interpreted in light of the significance they have won through their effects so that coherence and continuity are maintained, there is not necessarily a 'logical bond of implication between the cause and effect';[42] and one must remain conscious that it is 'our understanding ... [not the objective facts] as the first sources saw them' which superintends our writing of history. Consequently, R. Nash argues:

> It hardly seems necessary to waste any time critiquing hard objectivism. Why beat a horse that has been dead for several generations? Whatever the value of their own theories may have been, idealists like Dilthey, Croce, and Collingwood unveiled the folly of any quest for history as it really was. The nineteenth-century model of a scientific history was an oversimplified distortion of the historian's enterprise.[43]

Thus a document does not have to be objective or unbiased in order to be in the category of history writing. Let us consider a specific text: the Babylonian Chronicle. Some have argued that this text is an objective, unbiased historical document.[44]

But L.D. Levine has questioned this:

> whatever its record for accuracy, the Chronicle is fully as biased a source as any other. Its particular bias can probably best be described as Babylocentric.[45]

For example, in the case of the battle of Halule, the result was, from the Babylonian point of view, a retreat by the Assyrian army. The Assyrians had, up to the battle, been marching to Babylon. After the battle, the Assyrians were no longer so marching. Thus while the Babylonian Chronicle could not record an Assyrian defeat, it could record a retreat. Apparently, 'retreat, like beauty, is in the eye of the beholder'.[46] Thus an outcome can be viewed by different spectators to mean different things, and neither is necessarily right or wrong. This is what is often called 'objectivity relative to a point of view'. Thus, Millard correctly remarks:

> Undoubted bias need not provoke the modern reader to a totally adverse attitude to a document, nor give rise to allegations that the accounts are untrue or imaginary. Recognition of the unconcealed standpoints of many ancient documents has resulted in fuller understanding of their contents, without any recourse to a devaluation or discrediting of them. The fact that the modern interpreter does not share the beliefs and aims of the writers does not prevent him from respecting them and giving them their due weight.[47]

A third problem with Coats's definition is that it advocates a chronological, sequential approach to history. History writing is linear and developmental. Such an approach to history cannot be maintained in light of the many examples which can be cited from many different civilizations of other ways of recording the past. What of certain historical poems, cross-sectional histories, or histories of particular technologies? What of presentations of history which are non-developmental or employ cyclic patterns?

The fourth problem with Coats's definition is that he believes that the structure of the historical narrative is simply to record. It is 'controlled not by the concerns of aesthetics, nor by the symbolic nature of a plot, but by the chronological stages or cause-effect sequences of events'. Hayden White has recently argued that one of the primary ways of presenting a coherent history is in the form of a narrative:

> I treat the historical work as what it most manifestly is: a verbal structure in the form of a narrative prose discourse. Histories ... combine a certain amount of 'data', theoretical concepts for 'explaining' these data, and a narrative structure for their presentation ... The same event can serve as a different kind of element of many different historical stories ... In the chronicle, this event is simply 'there' as an element of a series; it does not 'function' as a story element. The historian arranges the events in the chronicle into a hierarchy of significance ... Providing the 'meaning' of a story by identifying the *kind of story* that has been told is called explanation by emplotment ... I identify at least four different modes of emplotment: Romance, Tragedy, Comedy and Satire ... For example, Michelet cast all his histories in the Romantic mode, Ranke cast his in the Comic mode, Tocqueville used the Tragic mode, and Burkhardt used Satire ... With the exception of Tocqueville, none of these historians thrust the formal explanatory argument into the foreground of the narrative ... the weight of explanatory effect is thrown upon the mode of emplotment. And, in fact, that 'historism' of which Michelet, Ranke, Tocqueville, and Burkhardt are now recognized to have been equally representative can be characterized in one way as simply substitution of emplotment for argument as an explanatory strategy.[48]

Let us recapitulate. History writing is not nationalistic or based on an unbiased objectivity. In the formulation of a definition of history, these invalid criteria must be repudiated. Moreover, history is artistically constructed and does not necessarily follow a strict chronological format of presentation.

### *Nurturing 'New Shoots'*

Thus far we have investigated what history is not via two definitions which Old Testament scholars have put forth. In this next section we will investigate what history is.

Numerous philosophers of history have pointed out that historical narrative is differentiated from fictional by means of its commitment to its subject-matter ('real' rather than 'imaginary' events) rather than by form.[49]

It is, however, important that this 'real' or 'true' (rather than 'imaginary') narrative be understood culturally. For instance, the mentioning of a deity or deities may be the result of cultural or religious encoding, and should not, therefore, be taken as evidence *per se* that the narrative deals with 'imaginary' or fabricated events. One must allow for the possibility of cultural encoding of the narrative. This is especially true in ancient Near Eastern history writing.

Two examples will perhaps illustrate this point. If I related this historical narrative:

> when my daughter was two months old, she suffered a tachycardia and was on the verge of death. My wife and I prayed to the Lord and by his grace she survived, and to this day is a healthy little girl,

it would be improper to conclude that since prayer and a deity's activity are mentioned in the narrative that this is imaginary and not historical. Another example comes from a passage from prism A of Tiglath-Pileser I:

> The land of Adauš was terrified by my strong belligerent attack, and they abandoned their territory. They flew like birds to ledges on high mountains. But the splendor of Aššur, my lord, overwhelmed them, and they came back down and submitted to me.[50]

Again, it would not be wise to conclude that on the basis of the use of a divine name or figurative language that this text is not historical. Cultural and religious encoding of the story must be taken into consideration.

Another point must be made concerning 'real' as opposed to 'imaginary' events. While the use of direct speech is not acceptable in today's modern canon of history writing unless it is a quote, in ancient history writing direct speech was quite common.

Whybray sees the abundance of direct speech in the Succession Narrative as a problem. He accepts that ancient historians artistically reconstructed *public* speeches. For him the question is:

> whether in the reports of *secret* conversations and scenes the author can be said in any sense at all to have recorded historical events ... it is almost entirely by means of these pri-

> vate scenes that he gives his interpretation of the characters and motives of the principal personages and of the chain of cause and effect ... [thus the Succession Narrative] is not a history either in intention or in fact.[51]

Whybray's sentiments can be compared with another author who has discussed the use of direct speech by Thucydides. At the beginning of his work, Thucydides describes his method of dealing with the two elements that compose his work—the speeches and the deeds. Concerning the speeches, he states:

> in so far as each of the speakers seemed to me to have said the things most relevant to the ever-current issues—I have presented their words, keeping as close as possible to the general sense of what was actually said.[52]

D. Rokeah points out that Thucydides's aim was to present material which would further his description of the Peloponnesian War, and because of this he censored those parts of the speeches (just as he also censored the accounts of the actions) which were not useful for the understanding of matters on his agenda.[53] Furthermore, the style and literary art of the speeches is Thucydides' own.[54] Kieran Egan argues that Thucydides' speeches function in a similar way to the speeches in Greek drama: they 'point up the moral', 'alert our expectations' and 'echo irony and prophecy'.[55] But while many of the speeches were so structured, their content was what Thucydides 'knew or thought he knew from the reports of others, had in fact been used on those occasions; e.g. "my information is that the Athenians did use those arguments at Melos"'.[56]

Thus, direct speeches in a document must be read carefully; and their inclusion in a work—public or secret speeches—does not prejudice the work so that one can conclude that the work is not history writing.[57]

Systematic methods and categories of analysis through which questions of the validity of referents in a historical narrative could be approached are virtually nonexistent.[58] The whole issue of the veracity of the narrative naturally leads into the question of 'story'.

'Story' embraces both historical and fictional narratives.[59] A number of scholars use the term 'story' to describe the OT historical narratives. For example, J. Barr states:

> the long narrative corpus of the Old Testament seems to me, as a body of literature, to merit the title of story rather than that of history.[60]

Barr enumerates some of the ways in which this material possesses the characteristics of history and yet must be differentiated from it. For example, the Old Testament does not make the distinction essential for a modern historian between the legendary elements of stories and those parts which might have a more solid historical foundation. Divine and human actions are inextricably bound together without any sense of impropriety—which may be an admirable thing, but is clearly not history. In short, the narrative portions of the Old Testament are of primary importance, yet they are not history but 'history-like'. Thus for Barr history writing is a secular enterprise.[61]

Such a view is not very helpful. As White has pointed out, there is no difference *in form* between an imaginary story and a historical narrative. And Barr's problem with divine action in the midst of human events is the result of a misunderstanding of the cultural encoding nature of ancient Near Eastern and biblical narrative. If one were to adopt Barr's view, then there would be virtually no history writing in the ancient world (not to mention the medieval world or the Far East) for there are very few ancient historians who do not intermingle divine intervention with human events. They reported occurrences which they could only express in terms of divine intervention (as a considerable number of examples from Assyrian, Egyptian, and Hittite sources demonstrates).[62]

Ronald Clements follows a similar line of argument to that of Barr, although he seems to prefer 'theological or religious narrative' instead of 'story'. To him, history is objective, impartial, political, non-religious, non-pragmatic and non-didactic.[63] Hence, he feels that the purpose of the stories of David's rise was not

> simply to report events in an impartial and objective fashion, such as the critical historian would do. On the contrary, it becomes abundantly plain that the events have been recounted in such a fashion as to justify and legitimate the usurping

> of Israel's throne by David and the subsequent succession of Solomon to this office.[64]

Moreover, what we have is:

> a kind of narrative-theology, rather history-writing in the true sense ... what we are faced with here are first and foremost ancient religious narratives which possess a distinctive historical form.[65]

Like Barr, it is primarily divine activity in human affairs within the narrative which is the problem for Clements. God has divinely elected David and his dynasty to rule and has rejected Saul.

Again, this kind of view of history is deficient. History is not objective, impartial reporting. Simply because there is justification and legitimation of the Davidic dynasty's seizure of power in the narrative, does not exclude the text from the category of history writing. H. Tadmor has shown that through a comparison with the apologies of Esarhaddon and Aššurbanipal one can come to a better understanding of the Davidic material as royal apology[66] (which is certainly within the category of history writing). In the Assyrian texts, divine election plays a major role in the argument of justification and legitimation. Thus, Clements' understanding of history writing is incorrect since many of what he considers unique theological issues in the biblical texts are regularly encountered within the ANE historical texts.

What underlies many views concerning the biblical narrative is the conviction that the Bible's storytelling is partly or wholly fictional. For instance, Robert Alter concludes:

> As odd as it may sound at first, I would contend that *prose fiction* <emphasis mine> is the best general rubric for describing biblical narrative. Or, to be more precise, and to borrow a key term from Herbert Schneidau's speculative, sometimes questionable, often suggestive study, *Sacred Discontent*, we can speak of the Bible as *historicized* prose fiction.[67]

Alter feels that the Bible is different from modern historiography since there is no 'sense of being bound to documentable facts that characterizes history in its modern acceptation'.[68]

Earlier Robert Pfeiffer argued that the bulk of the Old Testament narratives were fictional since it was:

> only in the recital of events on the part of an eyewitness (unless he be lying as in I Sam. 22:10a and II Sam. 1:7-10) may exact historicity be expected in the Old Testament narratives. Their credibility decreases in the ratio of their distance in time from the narrator ...
>
> these are ... popular traditions and tales long transmitted orally ... What holds a simple audience of Bedouins, shepherds, or peasants spellbound in listening to a tale is interest in the plot, curiosity as to the denouement, romantic atmosphere, conscious or unconscious art (as in the Andersen and Grimm fairy tales, respectively), but not in the least the historical accuracy ...
>
> tales that are the product of either some scanty memories of actual events or out of the storehouse of a vivid Oriental imagination ...[69]

Clearly one of the major concerns of both Pfeiffer and Alter is the issue of the eyewitness. According to their view, the most powerful argument for the historicity of a particular text is its dependence on eyewitness accounts. A. Danto has addressed this problem in his discussion of the 'Ideal Chronicler'.[70] The 'Ideal Chronicler' would be an individual who had knowledge of everything that happens, as it happens, the way it happens. He would also record accurate, full descriptions of everything as it occurred. This Chronicler's account would hence be an 'Ideal Chronicle', a cumulative record of 'what really happened'. Danto then poses the question: 'what will be left for the historian to do?' The obvious answer would be 'Nothing'. This 'Ideal Chronicle' is complete and the past, as it is often maintained, is 'fixed, *fait accompli*, and dead' so it cannot change.

But Danto answers differently. He argues that the historian's task is not done. While the 'Ideal Chronicle' is complete in the way in which an ideal witness might describe it, 'this is not enough'.

> For there is a class of descriptions of any event under which the event cannot be witnessed, and these descriptions are necessarily and systematically excluded from the I.C. ['Ideal

> Chronicle']. The whole truth concerning an event can only be known after, and sometimes only *long* after the event itself has taken place, and this part of the story historians alone can tell. It is something even the best sort of witness cannot know.[71]

Hence, without referring to the future, without going beyond what can be said of what happens, as it happens, the way it happens, the historian could not write in 1618, argues Danto, 'the Thirty Years War begins now'. To this the 'Ideal Witness' is blind. So even if we could witness certain events, we could not verify them under *these* descriptions. 'Cut away the future and the present collapses, emptied of its proper content'.[72] Thus, 'any account of the past is *essentially* incomplete' because 'a complete account of the past would presuppose a complete account of the future'.[73]

Two obvious implications to be drawn from his discussion are: 1) a 'full description' cannot adequately meet the needs of historians, and so fails to represent the ideal by which we should judge accounts. 2) not being witness to the event is not such a bad thing if our interests are historical. Thus, whether the author of the biblical text was an eyewitness or not need not effect our decision concerning whether it is history or not. So, the credibility of the biblical accounts does not necessarily decrease 'in the ratio of their distance in time from the narrator'.

What hinders many biblical scholars is a misunderstanding that historians use the same techniques as any literary artist to *arrange* or *fashion* their materials.[74] There seem to be two reasons for the failure of many to realize this. One reason is that what the historian says about his ostensible topic and how he says it are really indistinguishable. D. Levin puts it this way:

> I discovered that some fallacies persist as stubbornly today as if the work of Benedetto Croce, R.G. Collingwood, Carl Becker, and others had not shown them to be indefensible. The notion that none but the romantic histories are 'literary' thrives as vigorously as the discredited conviction that the facts of history can speak for themselves. Too many historians and teachers of literature accept also the dubious corolla-

> ry that good literature—whether history or fiction—always takes liberties with 'the facts'.[75]

Levin then concludes that 'there is no necessary conflict between historical fidelity and literary merit, no easy division of the historian's work into two distinct parts, the one essential and the other ornamental'.[76]

Another reason for the failure to understanding that historians employ the same devices as any literary artist to *arrange* or *fashion* their works is the assumption that historical actuality itself has narrative form which the historian does not create but discovers, or attempts to discover. History-as-it-was-lived, that is, is an untold story. The task of the historian is to find that untold story, or part of it, and to retell it even though in abridged or edited form.[77] While fiction writers fabricate their stories any way they wish, historians discover the story hidden in the data. Thus history needs only to be communicated, not constructed. It is because of this presupposition that some historians have not emphasized literary skill—like my 8th grade history textbook!—, or found it instructive or accurate to compare the historian with the novelist. Louis Mink believes that while no one consciously asserts that past actuality is an untold story, many implicitly hold this presupposition. He argues that this assumption is the legacy of the idea of Universal History—'the idea that there is a determinate historical actuality, the complex referent for all our narratives of "what actually happened", the untold story to which narrative histories approximate'. He contends that this presupposition should be 'abandoned' because:[78]

> 1. If past actuality is a single and determinate realm then narrative histories should aggregate because they each tell a part of that untold story. But in practice they do not. In fact, histories are more like fiction in that they have their own beginnings, middles and ends. Historical narratives can and do displace each other.
> 2. If past actuality is a single and determinate realm then the truth value of the historical narrative should simply be a logical function of the truth or falsity of its individual assertions taken separately: the conjunction is true if and only if each of the individual propositions is true. But while this may be true of chronicle it is not true of history. Historical narratives, like fictional narratives, contain indefinitely

many ordering relations, and indefinitely many ways of *combining* these relations. It is such combination which we mean when we speak of the coherence of a narrative, or lack of it. Historical narrative claims truth not only for each of its statements, but for the complex form of the narrative itself. 3. If past actuality is a single and determinate realm then the term 'event' should presuppose 'both an already existing division of complex processes into further irreducible elements, and some *standard* description of each putative event'. But hardly any concept is less clear than that of 'event'. Uncertainty sets in as soon as we attempt to consider the limits of the application of the concept.[79]

Consequently, the function of narrative form is not just to relate a succession of events but to present an ensemble of interrelationships of many different kinds as a single whole. Historical understanding converts congeries of events into concatenations.[80] While in fictional narrative the coherence of the whole may provide aesthetic or emotional satisfaction, in historical narrative it additionally claims truth. Sternberg elaborates on this point:

> The difference between truth value and truth claim is fundamental. If the title to history writing hinged on the correspondence to the truth—the historicity of the things written about—then a historical text would automatically forfeit or change its status on the discovery that it contained errors or imbalances or guesses and fabrications passed off as verities.[81]

For history writing is not a record of fact—of what 'really happened'—but a discourse that claims to be a record of fact. Nor is fiction writing a tissue of free inventions but a discourse that claims freedom of invention. The antithesis lies not in the presence or absence of truth value, but of the commitment to truth value.[82]

But this is where the problem arises. On the one hand, the analysis and evaluation of historical evidence may in principle resolve disputes about facts or to some extent about the relations among facts; but on the other hand, such procedures cannot resolve disputes about the possible combination of kinds of relations. The same event, under the same description or different descriptions, may belong to different stories (historical or fictional). And its particular significance will vary with its place in these often very different narratives. Also, just as 'evidence' does not dictate which story is to be constructed, so it does not always bear on the preference of one narrative over another. When it comes to the narrative treatment of an ensemble of relationships we credit the imagination or the sensibility or the insight of the individual historian. And we cannot do otherwise. There are no rules for the construction of a narrative as there are for the analysis and evaluation of evidence.[83] Consequently, bad historiography does not yet make fiction; *bad* historiography is bad *historiography*: no more, no less.[84] Because of this and because no past is ever given, history is *always* the imposition of form upon the past. Even mere narration is already the communication of a meaning. Thus history is imaginatively constructed and is always constructed from a particular point of view.[85]

But such an acknowledgement, White argues, need not lead to historical skepticism:

> This fashioning process need not—be it stressed—entail violations of the so-called 'rules of evidence' or the criteria of 'factual accuracy' resulting from simple ignorance of the record or the misinformation that might be contained in it.[86]

Hence, it is evident that all historical accounts are artistically constructed and there is no necessary conflict between rigorous historical method and literary construction.

Thus if history writing is the imposing of an interpretive form on the past, then it is, in a sense, artificial. The form itself is not reality; it is only one figurative way of re-figuring, or better, re-presenting reality. It is always the writer's selective arrangement or presentation of the events. Obviously, different modes may be employed to accomplish this task. Whether 'narrative' is the best way to impose form on the past is moot here since we are not discussing the writing of a history of Israel (i.e., our own reconstruction of Israelite history), but the interpretation and understanding of already extant narratives which have imposed form on the past.[87]

Thus narrativization in historiography always produces figurative accounts. H. White explains this in his typically eloquent style:

> To present the question of narrativization in historiography is to raise the more general question of the 'truth' of literature itself. On the whole, this question has been ignored by the analytical philosophers concerned to analyze the logic of narrative explanations in historiography. And this because, it seems to me at least, the notion of explanation which they brought to their investigation ruled out the consideration of *figurative discourse* as productive of genuine knowledge. Since historical narratives refer to 'real' rather than 'imaginary' events, it was assumed that their 'truth-value' resided either in the literal statements of fact contained within them or in a combination of these and a literalist paraphrase of statements made in figurative language. It being generally given that figurative expressions are either false, ambiguous, or logically inconsistent (consisting as they do of what some philosophers call 'category mistakes'), it followed that whatever explanations might be contained in an historical narrative should be expressible only in *literal language* ...
>
> ... If there is any 'category mistake' involved in this literalizing procedure, it is that of mistaking a narrative account of real events for a literal account thereof. *A narrative account is always a figurative account, an allegory.* To leave this figurative element out of consideration in the analysis of a narrative is not only to miss its aspect as allegory; it is to miss the performance in language by which *a chronicle is transformed into a narrative.* And it is only a modern prejudice against allegory or, what amounts to the same thing, a scientistic prejudice in favor of literalism, that obscures this fact to many modern analysts of historical narrative.[88]

Thus the historical narrative is always figurative. Obviously, there are varying degrees in the use of figurative language. But all historical narratives can be analyzed in terms of the modes of figurative language use that they variously favor. Thus figures of speech are the 'very marrow of the historian's individual style'. Remove them from his discourse, and you destroy much of its impact as an 'explanation' in the form of an 'idiographic' description. The theory of figures of speech permits us 'to track the historian in his encodation of his message'. This means that the clue to the meaning of a given historical discourse is contained 'as much in the rhetoric of the description of the field as it is in the logic of whatever argument may be offered as its explanation'.[89] This, however, as White argues, does not mean that the figurative discourse of the historical narrative is not productive of genuine knowledge and 'truth.' It simply means that the interpreter of the historical text must work that much harder at the interpretive process.

Hence, when we say that a historical narrative is figurative, we are speaking primarily of this impositional nature of the account. This nature manifests itself in three ways:[90] 1) the structural and ideological codes underlying the text's production, 2) the themes or motifs that the text utilizes,[91] and 3) the usage of rhetorical figures in the accounts. The second and third can very often be understood in terms of the old-time standard type of ANE and OT parallels. The first is a different concept for biblical studies: that the biblical narratives are the structures which communicate the historical image. Both of these are utilized as ideological communicators. Obviously, while, at times, it is possible to isolate these aspects, they generally overlap so that a rhetorical figure communicates the ideological codes of the text and vice versa. Consequently, we will not always attempt to differentiate and demarcate these aspects, since to do so would impair the reader.

In conclusion, history might be defined as 'a committedly true account which imposes form on the actions of men in the past'. It must be stressed that a literary mode of cultural production is connected with the rise of history writing.[92] So while it is possible to have an oral account of the past, the fact that in oral cultures there is 'the unobtrusive adaptation of past tradition to present needs' means that 'myth and history merge into one'.[93] In the ancient Near East history writing included such literary categories as king's lists, chronicles, annals, royal apologies, memorial inscriptions, historical poems, narratives, etc. Finally, from a technical standpoint, historiography is 'the principles, theory, and history of historical writing'.[94] Thus historiography, as F.J. Levy comments, 'is interested primarily in the methods previous historians have used to attain their results'.[95]

## PART II: IDEOLOGY — UNMASKING THE CONCEPT

Few concepts play a larger part in present-day discussions of ancient Near Eastern and biblical historical topics than does that of ideology;[96] and yet, it is not always clear what meaning is applied to the term by those who employ it. It is important to remember what David Apter has correctly noted:

> Ideology is not quite like other subjects. It reflects the presuppositions of its observers.[97]

There are at least three different meanings for the notion of ideology:[98]

First, ideology can be defined in the narrow sense as 'false consciousness'. Karl Marx gave prominence to the term 'ideology', and used it for distorted or selected ideas in defense of the *status quo* of a social system (i.e., 'a capitalist ideology').[99] Ideology was the distortion of reality because of a society's 'false consciousness'. This concept of ideology as 'false consciousness' leads back to the problem of establishing the true consciousness which will enable men to understand their role. The reason that they do not possess true consciousness is because 'social being ... determines consciousness'; hence, the truth about man is one and the same for all stages of history, but every stage produces its own illusions. And this has been the state of affairs in history, but is due to disappear when a rational order has been created. Thus the concept of ideology demonstrates that men are not in possession of true consciousness which—if they had it—would enable them to understand the totality of the world and their own place in it.[100]

Second, ideology can be defined in a restrictive sense. In other words, it is only those aspects which are distorted or unduly selective.

> Ideology consists of selected or distorted ideas about a social system or a class of social systems when these ideas purport to be factual, and also carry a more or less explicit evaluation of the 'facts.'[101]

Thus ideology consists *only* of those parts or aspects of a system of social ideas which are distorted or unduly selective from a scientific viewpoint. This definition does not restrict ideology to the conservative type.

Third, ideology can be defined in a 'neutral sense'. Thus Geertz defines ideology as 'a schematic image of social order'.[102] He argues that it is hardly scientific to define ideology as distortion and selectivity because distortion and selectivity are secondary and an empirical question in each case. In this view, ideology embraces both normative and allegedly factual elements; and these elements are not *necessarily* distorted.[103]

In many ways it is the issue of 'distortion' that distinguishes these definitions from one another. Consequently, we will attempt to investigate this issue more fully.

While Marx was the first to emphasize the concept of 'false consciousness' and subsequent 'distortion', he has influenced many (especially Georg Lukács and Karl Mannheim who developed the tradition of the sociology of knowledge). This approach, represented in the Frankfurt School of German sociology, has concentrated mostly on understanding the ideological basis of all forms of social knowledge including the natural sciences.[104] The tradition's most recent advocate is Jürgen Habermas.[105]

Mannheim distinguished between utopias and ideologies. The proponents of utopias contend for the realization of an 'ideal' which they allege has never existed previously within a society; while on the other hand, ideologies work for the realization of an 'ideal' which existed in the past but no longer exists. According to Johnson, Mannheim also used the term 'ideology' to refer to conservative ideas as distortions (although he was not consistent on this point).[106] Thus,

> ideology is by its nature untruthful, since it entails a 'masking' or 'veiling' of unavowed and unperceived motives or 'interests' ... [It] is a manifestation of a 'false consciousness'.[107]

Werner Stark, a follower of Mannheim, puts it this way:

> ideological thought is ... something shady, something that ought to be overcome and banished from our mind ... Both <lying and ideology> are concerned with untruth, but whereas the liar tries to falsify the thought of others while his own private thought is correct, while he himself knows well what the truth is, a person who falls for an ideology is himself deluded in his private thought, and if he misleads others, does so unwillingly and unwittingly.[108]

Putting it more on a linguistic level, Eco argues that ideological manipulation endeavors to conceal the various present options, and must therefore involve a rhetorical labor of code shifting and overcoding (via what he calles 'inventio' and 'dispositio'). Ideology is 'a partial and disconnected world vision'. By disregarding the multiple interconnections of the semantic universe, it also conceals the pragmatic reasons for which certain signs (with all their various interpretations) were produced. This oblivion produces a 'false conscience'.[109]

Thus ideology has the unfortunate quality of being psychologically 'deformed' ('warped', 'contaminated', 'falsified', 'distorted', 'clouded') by the pressure of personal emotions like hate, desire, anxiety, or fear. Ideology is a dirty river such that if one drinks from it, he will be poisoned.[110]

According to this view in which vested interest plays a vital role, ideology is a mask and a weapon; its pronouncements are seen against the background of a universal struggle for advantage; men pursue power and control often in the midst of class conflict. This view that social action is fundamentally an unending struggle for power leads to an unduly Machiavellian view of ideology as a form of higher cunning and, consequently, to a neglect of its broader, less dramatic social functions.[111]

Shils points out the incorrectness of this view. Ideologies, like all complex cognitive patterns, contain many propositions; even though ideologists strive for, and claim to possess, systematic integration, they are never completely successful in this regard. Hence, true propositions can coexist alongside false ones.[112] It follows, therefore, that to understand 'ideology' simply as 'a distortion of reality'[113] is not adequate. There is distortion, but not every element in the ideology is necessarily distorted.

Moreover, because many sociologists have failed to recognize the usage of figurative language within ideological discourse, they have often confused this usage with 'distortion'. Geertz has observed that:

> It is the absence of such a theory <of symbolic language> and in particular the absence of any analytical framework within which to deal with figurative language that have reduced sociologists to viewing ideologies as elaborate cries of pain.

> With no notion of how metaphor, analogy, irony, ambiguity, pun, paradox, hyperbole, rhythm, and all the other elements of what we lamely call 'style' operate—even, in a majority of cases, with no recognition that these devices are of any importance in casting personal attitudes into public form, sociologists lack the symbolic resources out of which to construct a more incisive formulation.[114]

He points out that although very few social scientists seem to have read much of the literature on metaphor, an understanding of it is quite useful in the discussion of ideology. In figurative language there is, of course, a stratification of meaning, in which an incongruity of sense on one level produces an influx of significance on another. The feature of metaphor that has most troubled philosophers (and, for that matter, scientists) is that it is 'wrong':

> It asserts of one thing that it is something else. And, worse yet, it tends to be most effective when most 'wrong'.[115]

The power of a metaphor derives precisely from the interplay between the discordant meanings it symbolically coerces into a unitary conceptual framework and from the degree to which that coercion is successful in overcoming the psychic resistance such semantic tension inevitably generates in anyone in a position to perceive it. When it works, a metaphor transforms a false identification into an apt analogy; when it misfires it is mere extravagance.

Obviously, a metaphor (in the strict sense of that term) is not the only stylistic resource upon which ideology draws. Geertz notes:

> Metonymy ('All I have to offer is blood, sweat and tears'), hyperbole ('The thousand-year Reich'), meiosis ('I shall return'), synecdoche ('Wall Street'), oxymoron ('Iron Curtain'), personification ('The hand that held the dagger has plunged it into the back of its neighbor'), and all the other figures the classical rhetoricians so painstakingly collected and so carefully classified are utilized over and over again, as are such syntactical devices as antithesis, inversion, and repetition; such prosodic ones as rhyme, rhythm, and alliteration; such literary ones as irony, eulogy, and sarcasm.[116]

Moreover, not all ideological expression is figurative. The bulk of it consists of quite literal, flat-footed assertions, which, a certain tendency toward *prima facie* implausibility aside, are difficult to distinguish from properly scientific statements: 'The history of all hitherto existing society is the history of class struggles'; 'the whole of the morality of Europe is based upon the values which are useful to the herd'; and so forth. As a cultural system, an ideology that has developed beyond the stage of mere sloganeering consists of an intricate structure of interrelated meanings—interrelated in terms of the semantic mechanisms that formulate them—of which the two-level organization of an isolated metaphor is but a feeble representation.[117]

Thus there exists in ideological language a subtle interplay of which concepts like 'distortion', 'selectivity', or 'oversimplification' are simply incompetent to formulate. Not only is the semantic structure of the figure a good deal more complex than it appears on the surface, but an analysis of that structure forces one into tracing a multiplicity of referential connections between it and social reality, so that the final picture is one of a configuration of dissimilar meanings out of whose interworking both the expressive power and the rhetorical force of the final symbol derive. This interworking is itself a social process, an occurrence not 'in the head' but in that public world where 'people talk together, name things, make assertions, and to a degree understand each other'.[118]

Hence, it would seem best to advocate a neutral sense for the understanding of the concept of ideology so that:

> ideology is a 'schematic image of social order', 'a pattern of beliefs and concepts (both factual and normative) which purport to explain complex social phenomena' in which there may be simplification by means of symbolic figurative language, code shifting and/or overcoding.

While ideology is often equated with rationalization in the psychological sense because it is assumed to be essentially a defense of vested interests (which is partly true), many people may have ideological ideas that are even contrary to their interests or that are related to their interests in so complex a way that experts would hesitate to attempt to calculate the net effect.[119] So,

> The likelihood that groups and individuals who have vested interests will defend them by means of distorted arguments is too well known to require extended comment. If anything, many people *exaggerate* the relative importance of concern for vested interests as a source of ideology.
> Those who stand to gain from a proposed social change are also, of course, likely to be less than objective in their appraisal of the *status quo* and of the general merit of the proposed change.[120]

## PART III: METHOD: OBTAINING COMPREHENSION
### *Establishing the Framework*

In the interpretive endeavor, it seems important to employ what W.W. Hallo has called the 'contextual approach':[121] in other words, a 'comparative/ contrastive' investigation of 'the literary context, broadly interpreted as including the entire Near Eastern literary milieu to the extent that it can be argued to have had any conceivable impact on the biblical formulation'.[122] For instance, if one compares the conquest account in the book of Joshua with other ancient Near Eastern conquest accounts, one will gain a better understanding of the biblical narrative. Such a method offers controls on the data. It is exactly a lack of controls which has contributed—at least in part—to some of the interpretive problems in Old Testament studies.

Some scholars have voiced the belief that the ancient Near East, while it produced many historical texts, did not produce works of history. Von Rad, for example, felt that only in Israel and Greece did a 'historical sense' arise that could apply causal thinking to sequences of political events.[123]

A similar type of objection is expounded by R.J. Thompson. He argues that because Israel was unique in the ancient Near East (Israel alone developed real historiography), the relevance of the comparative material is questionable.[124] He cites Mowinckel for support of this claim:

> It is a well known fact that Israel is the only people in the whole ancient Near East where annalistic writing developed into real historiography ... neither the Babylonians nor the Assyrians took it beyond short chronicles in annalistic form; ... From Egypt we know some historical legends, but no his-

> toriography, where the historical events are seen in the larger context. Something more of a historical view is found among the Hittites, but even here in fragmentary form, as tendencies, not as realizations. The only exception is Israel.[125]

It is very interesting that the comparative method can be dismissed by a comparative argument! Mowinckel has made an assessment of Israelite historiography by comparing it to ancient Near Eastern historiographies (an assessment which is highly debatable).[126] Thompson has accepted this judgment (uncritically) and turned it into an argument against the comparative method. Such an objection (unfortunately common among O.T. scholars) is groundless.[127]

Another form of this objection is that the influence on Israel during the O.T. period was minimal; Israel developed its own culture and traditions without a great degree of foreign influence. While the degree of influence varied at different periods, this is again a case of using a comparative argument to dismiss the need of a comparative method. This objection should be spurned. There is no question that there are differences between the Hebrew histories and their ancient Near Eastern counterparts, just as there are differences between each ancient Near Eastern culture's history writing. Moreover, it is only through comparison that these differences can be discerned. But there are also many similarities that argue in favor of 'real' history writing among these ancient Near Eastern cultures, and cry out for comparison with the Israelite material as Hallo, Tadmor, Roberts, and others have pointed out.[128]

One area of the ancient world which will not be included in this contextual investigation is Greece. One might wonder—especially in light of Van Seters's recent work—why this area will not be included for he contends:

> it would appear to be self-evident and entirely natural for biblical scholars who treat the subject of the origins of history writing in ancient Israel to give some attention to the corresponding rise of history writing in Greece and to the work of Herodotus in particular (p. 8).

Is it really 'self-evident and entirely natural'. Most biblical scholars believe that there was some contact and subsequent influence between the Hebrews and the Greeks, but that it was minimal in the early biblical period. Van Seters argues that the issue of date cannot be used to avoid such a comparison, but he does so by redating the biblical material by means of such a comparison.[129] This is highly circular argumentation! But going further, he asks the reader to take a 'leap of faith':

> The question of the origin of other shared features, such as the paratactic style of early prose and the anecdotal digressions within chronologies, is hard to answer on the basis of the *extant material* from Phoenicia. But it would appear *most reasonable* that those features clearly shared by Greek and Hebrew historiography also belonged to the Phoenicians, who were the close contact with both regions. It is, of course, doubtful that there was much direct cultural contact between the Greeks and the Hebrews before the fourth century B.C. Once we *admit* that Phoenicia could serve as a bridge between Israel and the Aegean as well as a center for the dissemination of culture in both directions, *nothing stands in the way* of an intensive comparative study of the Bible and early Greek historiography. [emphasis mine][130]

If there were some extant evidence, then perhaps this might be 'reasonable', but by taking the theory and making it fact, Van Seters not only can argue for the legitimacy of his comparison of Greek and Hebrew historiography, but can also argue for the later dating of the biblical material. He has not proved that there was a definite 'conceivable impact on the biblical formulation'.

Moreover, Van Seters uses the same argumentation concerning the extant material to contest H. Cancik's claim that the Hittite texts explain the rise of historiography in both ancient Greece and ancient Israel. He argues against Cancik that 'to see the agent of cultural mediation through "Canaan" is hardly justified. No evidence for this kind of cultural influence is evident at Ugarit or in any extant Canaanite-Phoenician inscriptions' (p. 103). So on the one hand, Van Seters can use the absence of extant material to argue (probably rightly) against Cancik's thesis; while on the other hand, he can choose to ignore the same absence of extant material to advance his own theory.

### *Performing the Reading*

Another important aspect in the interpretation of historical texts is the method of analysis. In other words, how should one read historical texts? Gene Wise has suggested that in the initial stage of analysis the critic must practice 'a willing suspension of disbelief' in order to conduct an 'intricate textual analysis'. He must ascertain the structure of the text and its mode of communication.[131]

It is important to consider the 'willing suspension of disbelief'. The reader of a historical text must curb his skepticism in order not to miscon-strue the obvious. This is not an endorsement of a naive approach which has repudiated criticism. Rather, it is a warning that the modern reader must not dismiss something in the text simply because he finds it unbelievable. He must willingly suspend his disbelief in order to 'participate' in the world of the text. The following will exemplify Wise's point.

Due to overt skepticism, H. Cancik dismisses the 'staff meeting' by Thutmose III before the battle of Megiddo as a fictitious element from the so-called *Königsnovelle*.[132] But how many kings, rulers, or generals down through the ages have taken counsel or held a 'staff meeting' before a major battle? To even consider a 'meeting' of this type as fictitious, one must have some very strong reason beyond a simple suspicion of the presence of a Königsnovelle motif. But, on the contrary, A.J. Spalinger has recently shown that this war council at Yhm prior to the battle of Megiddo originated from war dairy accounts so that the account is, in all likelihood, historical.[133]

To accomplish this 'intricate textual analysis' of which Wise speaks, semiotics appears to offer a viable method. Hence, one seeks to discern and understand the *transmission code(s)* which are used to convey the 'message' of the text.[134] As a text, a piece of writing is understood as 'the product of a person or persons, at a given point in human history, in a given form of discourse, taking its meanings from the interpretative gestures of individual readers using the grammatical, semantic, and cultural codes available to them'.[135] The narrative form of the discourse is a medium for the message, having no more truth-value or informational content than any other formal structure, such as a logical syllogism, a metaphorical figure, or a mathematical equation. The narrative is a vehicle, apparatus, or trellis for the transmission of the message. The strength of this method is that it does not confuse 'literary' questions with 'referential' or 'historicity' questions. The historical writing must be analyzed primarily as a kind of prose discourse before its claims to objectivity and truthfulness can be tested.[136] Thus the dilemma of whether and to what extent the events of a text correspond to the 'truth'[137] (i.e., the question of the veracity or reliability of the text) can be put aside (at least temporally) in order to shift one's attention to the texts themselves.[138]

So while it is perfectly valid, important and necessary to ask questions concerning *which* events were narrated, it is equally valid, important and necessary to ask questions concerning *the way* in which the events were narrated. In fact, it is the latter questions which reveal the text's ultimate meaning and purpose. F.M. Fales puts this way:

> the utilization of the document as source of information on the narrated events must be preceded by an analytical breakdown of the document itself into its ideological and compositional foundations, i.e. into *the complex of ideas* (as indicated by lexical items) and into the *literary structures* (as indicated by the organisation of words into syntagms, etc.) ...[139]

Since reading a text entails 'expanding [étoiler] upon the text rather than gathering it together',[140] R. Barthes proposed anthrology—'the science of the components'[141]—to account for the interweaving of code and message in the system of a text. Thus it is important to distinguish the components of a text in order to understand its meaning.[142]

Robert Scholes has suggested that 'we can generate meaning by situating a text among the actual and possible texts to which it can be related'.[143] Consequently, it is our assertion that by using semiotics in conjunction with a contextual method, it will be possible to achieve a better understanding of the biblical historical narrative. It must be emphasized that we are not arguing that the semiotic approach will give us 'the final, definite, and authoritative interpretation' of any historical text. We are only suggesting that it will reveal certain aspects of the text's make-up which will further the interpretive endeavor. It permits a finer distinctions to be maintained in the analyses.

Obviously this type of approach is very different from the common diachronic method with its concerns for correctly dating various stages in a tradition's development, for separating early traditions from redactional elements, and so forth. Because the inheritance of the nineteenth century has been so powerful for such a long time in biblical study, research has been dominated by these diachronic concerns. Hence this approach has come to be seen as self-evidently correct and as particularly appropriate to the alleged character of the biblical texts. So much is this the case that an initial response to some methods of understanding which accent rather a synchronic analysis has been that these latter methods looked suspiciously *a priori* and theoretical.

But Oden points out that this response is fundamentally mistaken:

> The clash of the traditional, historical approach with newer methods of analysis is not, as the partisans of the former might wish to assert, a clash between an objective, scientific approach on the one hand, and a subjective, theoretical approach on the other. The conflict is rather a conflict between two equally theoretical methods of understanding, neither of which can claim to be working in the first instance from a direct confrontation with the text itself. The pressing question for us is therefore that of which theory is the more coherent.[144]

Consequently we are not arguing that the combination of the contextual method and semiotics is the only method to understand historical texts. We are offering it as a possibly more coherent method to analyze these texts.

Therefore, in line with the contextual method, a thorough examination of ancient Near Eastern conquest accounts will be necessary.[145] In the first stage of the study, conquest accounts from the Assyrians, Hittites and Egyptians will investigated.[146] In the next stage, there will be an examination of the conquest account in Joshua. Throughout a semiotic approach will be employed. Lastly, these two stages of the inquiry will be integrated and an evaluation of the evidence offered.

# STAGE ONE:

# ANCIENT NEAR EASTERN CONQUEST ACCOUNTS

# Chapter 2

# ASSYRIAN CONQUEST ACCOUNTS

> ...not yet general is the consciousness that the analysis of the 'events' narrated in the text must be set aside from the analysis of the literary and thought patterns according to which the events are presented.[1]

Liverani's assessment still correctly describes, for the most part, the situation in the study of Assyrian history writing. Most past studies on the subject[2] can be categorized according to their approach: 1) reconstructional approaches, 2) generic approaches, and 3) 'ideas of history' approaches.

In the reconstructional approach, one concentrates upon the evaluation of the Assyrian royal inscriptions for the historiographic purpose of reconstructing a modern history.[3] Whereas the importance of historical reconstruction should not be underestimated, the need for a thorough literary analysis must be the first concern in a study of a culture's history writing.

With the generic approaches to Assyrian history writing concern has been primarily with classification of the texts in varying degrees of comprehensiveness.[4] On occasion, problems have arisen when improper criteria have been applied in the classification process. For example, J.J. Finkelstein made historicity the crucial test for Mesopotamian history writing in his search for the one genre which best represented the 'intellectual form' in which the Mesopotamians rendered account to themselves of their past.[5] He suggested that:

> the omen texts and the historical information imbedded in them, lie at the very root of all Mesopotamian historiography, and that as a historical genre they take precedence both in time and in reliability over any other genre of Mesopotamian writing that purports to treat of the events of the past ...

> Upon analysis, it would become clear that all genres of Mesopotamian literature that purport to deal with past events, with the exception of omens and chronicles, are motivated by purposes other than the desire to know what really happened, and the authenticity of the information they relate was not in itself the crucial point for their authors.[6]

Thus Finkelstein blatantly mixed literary analysis with historicity questions so that his contention must be judged as incorrect.

While such approaches[7] can be helpful (and this to varying degrees), they are hindered by the limitations of a purely generic approach so that at times they do not really further the interpretation of the texts. For example, does it really help one in interpreting a certain Assyrian historical text to know that it is of the genre:

> commemorative inscription of the annalistic type with collections of annalistic accounts which follow the type (IA2a) (starting with subject (royal name and epithets) followed by the annalistic narration, description of building activities, and blessings—with possible insertions)?[8]

Such a detailed breakdown is more confusing than helpful.

We are not advocating that the brilliant work of scholars who have worked along these lines is insignificant or worthless, nor are we advocating that generic analysis is useless. This is not the case. For example, the distinction between the 'Summary' and purely 'Annalistic' inscriptions is important and helpful.[9] Knowing which type of inscription one is reading enhances the interpretive expectations as one approaches the text. But this is not the end of the interpretive endeavor. By knowing that both types of inscriptions utilize the same syntagms and ideology, one can obtain a better understanding of the accounts. Moreover, generic approaches do not generally separate the 'analysis of the "events" narrated in the text from the analysis of the literary and thought patterns according to which the events are presented'.

Finally, the 'idea of history' approach attempts to identify a culture's concept or sense of history. Such an approach, however, usually assumes that there is a uniformity of thought about the past by a particular culture. But this is never really the case.[10]

All three approaches fail to sufficiently distinguish between historical and literary questions. They do not—to use Liverani's words—'set aside the analysis of the "events" narrated in the text' from the 'analysis of the literary and thought patterns according to which the events are presented'. One of the most important requirements for attaining a suitable level of understanding of the messages of the Assyrian royal inscriptions is an appreciation of the peculiarities of the transmission codes which they employ. Moreover, it is important to realize that the historical *referent* (l'événement), in itself, is but the occasional event which furnishes the trellis for the textual *performance*.[11] Only among some recent semiotic or other modern literary approaches has this differentiation been maintained.

While semiotic approaches and stylistic analyses do not rule out the possibilities of inquiries concerning the *factual* contents of the inscriptions, the événementielle (or referential) items in the texts are not necessarily the primary point to which ultimate significance should be attached.[12]

For example, single elements can be used to describe either positive or negative events. Consequently, Zaccagnini observes that: 'in terms of informatics, the reason according to which the messages of the Neo-Assyrian royal inscriptions are patterned and vehiculated is fundamentally binary'.[13] This is true on the chronological, the ideological, and the morphological axes. Thus the same *referent* (i.e. the same event which is recorded in an *episode*) can be viewed in a completely different way, as concerns its ideological connotations. For instance, the digging of a canal is considered a positive achievement if accomplished by the Assyrian king. However, if the enemy digs a canal, it has negative connotations. This is even clearer in the case of ruin or destruction of a territory or city (a negative event in itself). If caused by the Assyrians, it is viewed positively.

While it is perfectly valid (and important) to ask questions concerning which events were narrated, it is equally valid and important to ask questions concerning the way in which events were narrated. In fact it is the latter questions which reveal the texts' ultimate purpose.

The inscriptions' purpose was very specific. They were:

> an optimal instrument for conveying (ideological) messages to serve for practical purposes: e.g. terror to be inspired upon inner or outer 'subjects'; exaltation of the king, by reasserting the immensity of his power and the uniqueness of his legitimate rulership; asseveration that outside the Assyrian 'cosmogonic' order there is but chaos, ruin, perdition, non-existence; etc.[14]

To this can be added two very important purposes: 1) the glorification of the gods of Assyria, especially, Aššur; and 2) the preservation of the message for a future ruler.[15] The Assyrian ideology is an important part of the super-structure undergirding the historical texts. The referents make up the construction of the narrative. But, of course, this is true of all historical narratives because of their figurative nature. A. Leo Oppenheim stated it this way:

> In all instances, we have to keep foremost in our mind that even strictly historiographic documents are literary works and that they manipulate the evidence, consciously or not, for specific political and artistic purposes. Even these few texts that are patently more reliable than others, whose aim is mainly literary, cater to preconceived ideological requirements. In short, nearly all these texts are as wilfully unconcerned with the 'truth' as any other 'historical text' of the ancient Near East.[16]

If the dilemma of whether and to what extent the events of the text correspond to the truth (i.e., the question of the veracity of the text) is put aside, then one's attention shifts to the texts themselves.[17] Only after identifying the literary and ideological structures used in composing the historical narratives, is it possible to gain a proper understanding of the text. Fales explains:

> that 'the utilization of the document as a source of information on the narrated events must be preceded by an analytical breakdown itself into its ideological and compositional foundations, i.e. into the *complex of ideas* (as indicated by lexical items) and into the *literary structures* (as indicated by the organisation of words into syntagms, etc.) which led to the writing of the document along preconceived lines and slants'.[18]

Thus there are two constituents on which we will concentrate in our analysis of the Assyrian historical text: ideology and literary structures. While these are separate in many ways, they nevertheless intertwine to create the historical account.

At this point, it must be emphasized—as discussed in the previous chapter—that the figurative nature of the accounts includes not only these ideological and structural aspects, but also the use of motifs and rhetorical figures. It is our purpose in this chapter to delineate the Assyrian ideology and literary structures (especially the texts' syntagmic configuration), since other studies have dealt with these other aspects.

## ASSYRIAN IDEOLOGY: *How Do You Spell 'Torture'?*

### *Type and Nature*

M. Liverani has offered the most comprehensive study on Assyrian ideology.[19] He argues that Assyrian ideology was of the 'imperialistic type'; in other words, 'an ideology of unbalance'.[20] He argues that this type of ideology has the aim:

> of bringing about the exploitation of man by man, by providing the motivation to receive the situation of inequality as 'right', as based on qualitative differences, as entrusted to the 'right' people for the good of all ... Ideology has the function of presenting exploitation in a favourable light to the exploited, as advantageous to the disadvantaged. It provides those who surrender their wealth, their work, their life, with a counterpart of a non-physical but moral, religious, cultural character.[21]

Furthermore, an imperialistic ideology is characterized by three 'roles'; namely, the beneficiaries, the agents, and the victims. The authors and beneficiaries of the imperialistic ideology (i.e., the Assyrian ruling class) need motivation which provides them with greater credibility and effectiveness. Hence, 'an effective, victorious, enduring imperialism is generally a self-convinced and even fanatical imperialism'.[22]

The agents of the ideology (i.e., the whole of the Assyrian population which provided the human material for the war and production machines) are the receivers of its ideological propaganda. This propaganda must achieve the 'arduous aim of prompting them to perform an active role, not a passive one; that of the ruler, not the ruled, without reaping the annexed benefits'.[23]

Finally, the victims of the imperialistic ideology (i.e., the external populations that were conquered) perceive it (in the first instance) as a *ideology of terror*, or as Olmstead described the policy of the Assyrians in the ninth century B.C. 'calculated frightfulness'.[24] H.W.F. Saggs points out:

> There are frequent references in the Assyrian annals to the pouring out upon the enemy of 'šaḫurrātu', 'nammurratu', or 'ḫattu' by the Assyrian king, or the covering of the enemy land by 'ḫurbašu' or by the king's 'puluḫtu', and I would maintain that this represented a definite conscious use by the Assyrians not of terrorism for sadistic purposes, but of psychological warfare ... In the absence of mass media of communication, terror, spreading from village to village and town to town, was the only means of softening up an enemy population in advance.[25]

Even in the occupation and process of de-culturation the 'ideology of terror' enhanced the maintenance of control. The process is accomplished by the breaking down of the foreign ideologically active centers (temples, palaces), the deportation of certain sections of populations, the impositioning of linguistic unification, and the provincial administration.

With regard to the diffusion of the ideology, Liverani argues that the religious character of the imperial ideology is not 'an additional element that deserves a special section in the analysis; it is in fact the very form of that ideology in its general terms'.[26] In other words, the religious character is not autonomous from the ideology. Thus he states:

> I believe on the contrary that if we consider the divinities and the acts of cult as hypostatic expressions of social values, the problem vanishes. The 'holiness' of a war cannot result from an analysis, since indeed there cannot be a 'lay' war. The war is always a holy one if fought by us, always a wicked one if fought by the enemy; therefore 'holy' means only that it answers our social values, it means Assyrian. A king is not legitimate because of the approval of Aššur; a king, while he rules in Assyria, is always legitimate, and his legitimacy is

expressed in religious terms (in fact the less obvious it is, the more it is emphasized).[27]

Liverani's model of ideology at this point is too simplistic. Religion is a much more sophisticated system. It is a social value system. And, as Harry Johnson has observed, by definition, the conception of cognitive distortion and selectivity requires that a distinction be made between ideology and 'religious' ideas (more precisely, nonempirical existential ideas).[28] One reason for this is that a given value system may be compatible with more than one set of cognitive ideas, and these need not be ideological. Therefore, it is scientifically desirable to distinguish between a value system itself and ideology.[29]

The diffusion of the ideology was accomplished through the written message which was complemented by the visual and oral messages. In some cases the written texts were to be orally divulged in a ceremony: for example, Sargon's Letter to the God Aššur (giving account of his eighth campaign).

At this point, it is important to remember that there are interconnections between war, trade, power centers, and ideology. Economic concerns played a significant role in the Assyrian ideology. And since 'exchanges are peacefully resolved wars and wars are the result of unsuccessful transactions',[30] tribute—to a significant degree in the Neo-Assyrian empire—took the place of long distance trade.[31]

Finally, Liverani attempts to discuss the aspects of this imperialistic ideology in relationship to the diversity of space, time, men, and goods. These aspects have been explored by others who are part of the *Lessico ideologico assiro*, as well as others. We will now examine one of these aspects attempting to summarize and evaluate the findings.

### *Ideological Patterns: The Enemy*

Recently both Zaccagnini and Fales have written articles on the enemy in the Assyrian inscriptions analyzing the 'ethnographic description' and 'the moral judgement aspects' of this topic, respectively.[32]

Zaccagnini points out that the Assyrian ethnographic vision of the enemy is dualistic. Consequently, the historical texts are written from the point of view of the Assyrian political ideology in which everyone has a precise role: the king of Aš-šur, the people of Assyria, the foreign kings, the foreign peoples, the dynamics of the encounter and opposition between the respective cultures, etc.[33] The ethnographic remarks concerning the enemy are in most cases confined to derogatory, incidental and repetitive notations. Except for descriptions of foreign landscapes, the descriptions are rarely concerned with foreign people, their culture, or their way of life. When these are encountered in the texts, the purpose of their inclusion is 'not to record and describe the diversities of the 'other cultures', but to celebrate the Assyrian self-legitimation as a hegemonic, unique power over the rest of the world'.[34] This ethnocentrical vision is not unique in the pre-classical Near East. F.M. Fales emphasizes that:

> there is only one Enemy—with a capital letter—appearing in and out of Assyrian royal inscriptions. With this seeming paradox, I mean to state that the many topoi as regards antagonists to Assyrian kingship may—to a very large extent—be considered as tassels of a single coherent political ideology of *nakrūtu*, shared among the collective authorship of annalistic texts; and that the different figures of opponents that appear in the texts themselves, the various Ursas and Teummans, Marduk-apal-iddinas and Inib-Tešubs, are as little observed with a chronicler's individualizing interest as much as they are, instead, described as separate manifestations of a unitary ideology of enmity.[35]

Operating with this ideology of the *nakrūtu*, the Assyrian scribes described the various individual historical figures through pre-established categories which were tied to a binary moral framework: 'negativity' as opposed to 'positivity'. Thus the *nakrūtu* is the product of the decision to take the 'wrong path', when a 'right path' is existent and visible to all. With this being the case, only attitudes of hubris, lunacy, or downright wickedness could lead to this decision.[36]

Consequently, Fales suggests that discussion concerning the *nakrūtu* can be divided into two groupings: 1) the foreigner who errs by not doing what he was supposed to do; and 2) the foreigner who errs by doing what he was not supposed to do. In the first grouping there are two subsections:

a) The enemy violates the oaths/pacts; he does not respect them; he sins; he betrays; he has no reverential fear; he fails to perform the normal acts of submission (seizing the feet of the king, sending to ask for the royal health, etc.).
b) The enemy is forgetful of past kindness; he has no judgement, no common sense; his mind is altered.

In the second grouping there are three subsections:

a) The enemy is insubmissive; insolent; proud; haughty; he trusts in human or natural factors to oppose Assyria victoriously.
b) The enemy speaks words of suspicion, hostility; he lies; he is false, treacherous. He plots against Assyria.
c) The enemy is wicked; hostile, rebellious; murderous; an outlaw, especially in relation to his actions.[37]

## LITERARY STRUCTURES:
## *'The Stereotyping Department'*

Fales rightly observes that very little research has been hitherto dedicated to this aspect of the Assyrian royal inscriptions. It seems that Assyriologists have believed that since the style of the Assyrian royal inscriptions has been given the (currently accepted) definition of *Kunstprosa*, the artistic (i.e. literary) elements are in fact irrelevant, and the material can be 'altogether assimilated to unstructured prose accounts, such as one finds, for example, in epistolary texts'.[38]

One reason for this lies in the presuppositions and outlook of the Twentieth Century interpreter. Thus Grayson urges:

> ... we must shake off our presuppositions and outlook if we ever hope to understand an alien and archaic civilization. Ancient Mesopotamian society was not a 'primitive' culture, nor was it 'unsophisticated' or 'barbaric'; it was a civilization as highly developed as our own but along totally different lines (without the horrors of the industrial revolution) and with completely different attitudes.[39]

With this in mind, we will attempt to isolate the particular literary structure of syntagmic patterning, since some of the other features have already been dealt with elsewhere[40] and since this is unquestionably the predominant stylistic structure of the Assyrian conquest accounts.

## *Syntagmic Valency*[41]

### *Introduction*

This section is interested in investigating the syntagmic valency of the transmission code. Since the texts of our study are in prose, 'the syntagm is a natural candidate as a unit of classification'.[42] By *syntagm* we mean the individual elements configured within an episode, i.e., the individual functions or syntactic entities.

In the case of the Assyrian royal inscriptions, precise and easily recognizable structural elements were used along preconceived lines and slants. There are two ways of analyzing these syntagms in the Assyrian texts: 1) one can investigate their use within a particular episode within the different recensions of a king's 'annals'; or 2) one can examine their use in the various episodes of a particular historical text. Utilizing the first way, F.M. Fales has argued that the accounts of the Egyptian campaigns in Aššurbanipal's inscriptions were:

> the product of a *literary* form of text-writing: scholastic and canonical in the sense of its being discernible from one account to the next, and preconceived in the sense that it acted as a *filter* through which both the narrated fact and the basic ideological tenets were passed.[43]

Concerning the syntagmic structures in the different recensions, he concludes that:

> there is no doubt that series of elements (words making up a syntagm or chains of syntagms), endowed with similar characteristics as for length and rhythm in a general way, and with further similarities of a syntactical and/or semantic character, are present.[44]

He identifies eight features which at an experimental level correspond to the basic range of stylistic means by which effects and results of variation were achieved from one to the other version of the Egyptian campaign story of Aššurbanipal where the minimally similar themes are treated by all versions.

Fales believes that these features take part in 'one homogeneous compositional process'; in other words, they are not set more or less haphazardly side by side in a relatively free build up of the text, but represent 'a key to an organized way of writing, or stylistic code'. They witness to a 'scribal competence'.[45] Thus he concludes:

> It does not therefore seem rash to posit an overall literary competence at work in this material: a competence summing up the 'title' to write, the background work in order to write, and the entire complex of ready-at-hand literary instruments that we have analyzed. Only in such a way, i.e. by positing a scribal competence, do we feel that a correct account may be taken of the many individual literary performances to be brought forth from Ashurbanipal's inscriptions (and perhaps also those of other kings?): performances which show the intriguing characteristic of being somehow always different, but at the same time clearly the offshoots of a single plant.[46]

While Fales has admirably shown the syntagmic features at work in the story of the Egyptian campaign in the versions of Aššurbanipal, we are interested in employing the second way in order to investigate the syntagmic patterns in the episodic structure of the Assyrian royal inscriptions (obviously, this type of syntagmic analysis is more applicable to the biblical narrative than the first type). The *episodes* of the Assyrian royal inscriptions manifest a typical structural pattern where particular elements are used to build the narrative; and it is the patterning of these elements which provides the *trellis* for the historical referents. The same elements occur throughout the *episodes*. The sequential order may be altered, but in either case the *episodes* consist exactly of the same amount of structural elements (1 + 2 + 3 + ... + n = 1 + 4 + 2 + ... n). This type of structure is a type of iterative scheme.[47] Eco describes the scheme as:

> A series of events repeated according to a set scheme iteratively, in such a way that each event takes up again from a sort of virtual beginning, ignoring where the preceding event left off.
> If we examine the iterative scheme from a structural point of view, we realize that we are in the presence of a typical *high-redundance message*.[48]

This redundance can often be used as a vehicle to express ideology or re-inforce the message. In the case of the Assyrian texts, we believe that they often employ an iterative code producing a high-redundance message which communicates the Assyrian ideology.

Moreover, it must be stressed that the individual episodes (the campaign in certain instances), and not the entire text, must serve as the basic unit of analysis. L.D. Levine observes:

> For questions of sources and compositional technique, the episode and the campaign must serve. For questions of historical worth and historiographic intent, both the individual campaigns *and* the entire manuscript must be examined.[49]

In order to show the peculiarities of the syntagmic structures of the Assyrian royal inscriptions, it is necessary to analyze particular texts. Individual episodes from these texts are extracted in order to exegete their syntagmic configurations. The analysis is divided into the following categories: Annalistic Texts, Letters to the God, and Summary or Display Texts.

Methodologically, our approach is more concerned with the stylistic analysis of the surface of the narrative than with the 'deep structure'. This latter aspect, however, is not forgotten or neglected. Instead, it manifests itself to a very high degree in the former. This is why the Assyrian ideology and literary structures cannot be divorced one from the other. Both are part of the figurative nature of the Assyrian accounts.

In the Assyrian historical accounts, it is clear that we are dealing with a series of narratives of homologous structure, the product of a single scribal environment over a short period of years (for individual kings). In our identifications of the syntagms, we seek to be precise enough to render possible even the re-writing in Assyrian of the texts themselves.

This type of morphological analysis has been carried out on the Annals of Aššur-nasir-pal II by a group of Italian scholars.[50] In many ways this work is foundational to the following analysis.

### *The Syntagms of Assyrian Texts*[51]

*FUNCTIONS*

A — *Spatio-Temporal Coordinates*

$A^1$ = spatial collocation; $A^2$ = temporal collocation; $A^{1,2}$ = spatio-temporal collocation; a = spatio-temporal reference within a campaign (esp. at the beginning of stages, insertions, or other narrative sections. Some examples:

$a^1$ :: *ištu* / *ultu X ... at-tu-muš* (this value only at the beginning of a unit) $A^2$ :: *ina N palê(BAL$^{MEŠ}$)-ya* // *ina li-me N* // *ina ištēt šatti*.

B — *Disorder*[52]

This the enunciation of a state of disorder which induces the Assyrian king to act. The disorder is usually given in the form of a report (*ṭēmu*), and the typical verb employed to describe the situation is nabalkutu 'to rise against', 'to rebel (*ittabalkit*)'. As regards the numerous instances in which function B is absent, it is clear that the absence is due to the obvious and given existence of disorder. This is part of the Assyrian royal ideology. This function may be formulated as 'the interruption' of current relations which are usually manifested in the following syntagms: *maddattu kudurru ša Aššur bēliya iklû* (i.e., the withholding of tribute); the 'crossing over' of boundaries (*ebēru*); the killing of the legitimate rulers and replacement by usurpers; and the carrying out of military deeds against the Assyrians.

C — *Divine Aid*[53]

The description of divine aid has been sub-divided into:

$C^1$ = enunciation of normal divine favor towards the Assyrian king (*ina tukulti DN* :: 'trusting in god N');

$C^2$ = the obtaining of an explicit divine guarantee, evidently by means of an oracle (*ina qibīt DN* :: 'according to the word of god N');

$C^3$ = tools or concrete aid provided by the divinity (*$^{d}$uri-gal ālik pāniya* :: 'the (divine) banner that precedes me') and (*ina idāti ṣīrāti ša DN* :: 'with the lofty arms (strength) of god X').

D — *Gathering of the Troops*

Most commonly this syntagm is expressed by the fixed formulation: *narkabāti ummānāti dekû* :: 'to assemble chariots and troops'.

E — *Move from place to place*[54]

$E^{\phi}$ = a non-connotated modality; $E^{D}$ = a difficult road; $E^{!}$ = the motive of priority. This function is divided according to verbal usage:

| | | | |
|---|---|---|---|
| $E^1$ | *etēqu* | $E^9$ | *nabalkutu* |
| $E^2$ | *alāku* | $E^{10}$ | *aṣû* |
| $E^3$ | *namāšu* | $E^{11}$ | *redû* |
| $E^4$ | *arādu* | $E^{12}$ | *elû* |
| $E^5$ | *erēbu* | $E^{13}$ | *šakānu* |
| $E^6$ | *ebēru* | $E^{14}$ | *ešēru* |
| $E^7$ | *qarābu* | $E^{15}$ | *rakābu* |
| $E^8$ | *ṣabātu* | $E^{16}$ | *nagāšu* |

F — *Presence*

$F^1$ = the (terrifying) presence of the god and/or of the Assyrian king expressed through symbolic expressions. For example: in the case of the god (usually *Aššur*): *melammū* or *pulḫu melammū* followed by *saḫāpu* 'to overwhelm'; in the case of the monarch: *melammū* (+ *šar-*

*rūtiya*) and the verb *palāḫu* 'to fear'; there are often elements that allude to military strength — always with the use of verbs corresponding to 'fear' :: *ištu pān kakkēya dannūti taḫāzya šitmuri idātiya gitmālūti palāḫu* or *ištu pān namurrat kakkēya šurībāt bēlūtiya adāru*. In a parallel way the verbs expressing 'fear' follow those corresponding to 'overwhelming' and 'pouring out'.

$F^2$ = the siege of the enemy city. It is most often characterized by the use of the verb lamû 'to surround'. On occasion the expression is specified by *ina gipiš ummānāte tāḫāziya šitmuri* and *ina mitḫuṣ tidūki*.

f = the passing of the night. The terminology of the nightly stage is absolutely stereotyped: it is always *bâtu* 'to pass the night' preceded by the term (*ušmāna*) *šakānu* 'to encamp' [and sometimes *târu* 'to return (to camp)'.[55]

G — *Flight*

This syntagm reflects the flight of the enemy when faced by the presence of the Assyrian king. There can be either $G^-$ = non-flight (only codified when the text explicitly refers to it), or $G^\Delta$ = a flight in difficult places. The logical and terminological sequence can be outlined as follows:

$G^{-1}$ = Most often this is expressed by the verb *takālu* ('to trust') in connection with such phrases as: *ana dūrāni dannūti u ummānāte ma'dūte*, *ina gipiš ummānāti*, *ana ummānāt GN rapšāti*, *ina gipiš narkabāti ummānāti idāti*, *ana ummānāte ma'dūte*; and *ana emūqu ramānīšunu ittatkilū* :: 'they trusted in their own strength'.

$G^{\Delta 1}$ = the moment of 'fearing' (*palāḫu*), 'hiding oneself' (*qarāru*).

$G^{-2}$ = In non-flight this is the action of 'assembling' (*dekû*) the troops.

$G^{\Delta 2}$ = the moment of the 'abandoning' *uššuru*.

$G^{-3}$ = In non-flight, this is the action of a battle (*ana tarṣi tebû*).

$G^{\Delta 3}$ = the flight in the true sense of the word is indicated by the term *naparšudu* 'to fly (escape)'; but it is most often indicated by the term *elû* 'to go up'; and sometimes by *maqātu* 'to throw oneself into a river' and *erēbu* 'to enter' a fortified place.

$G^{-4}$ = In non-flight, this is represented as that of hostilely 'occupying' the crossing or land.

$G^{\Delta 4}$ = In flight this is represented by the term 'occupying' (*ṣabātu*) protected places with the goal of there 'resting/staying'.

The stereotyped motivations of flight are those of 'saving one's life' (*ana šūzub napišti*). The motivation of non-flight is that of making battle (*ana epēš qabli u tāḫāzi*; *tāḫāza ēpušū*).

H — *Pursuit*

This is the logical sequel to G and is similar in its structure to that of E. Its most common lexical identification is seen in the expression *arkīšu*(*nu*) 'after him/them'. The verbs employed are: *alāku*, *ṣabātu*, *redû*, *elû*, *še'û*, and *šadê ḫâtu* 'to explore' + *saḫāpu*. It can be difficult $^\Delta$.

I — *Combat*

The terminology is simple: *ittišunu maḫāṣu* or the equivalent *mitḫuṣa šakānu*.

L — *Outcome of the Combat*

The outcome of the combat (i.e., the concrete results of victory) is usually expressed by either a character of destruction ($L^1$) or one of acquisition ($L^2$). There is an indicator of destruction of the enemy attributable to natural causes in addition to the Assyrian military action ($L^3$). Common syntagms are:

$L^{1\text{ל}}$ = e.g., commonly *abikta šakānu* 'to bring about the defeat'.
$L^{2\text{ב}}$ = e.g., seen in the expression *šallata* (*ma'atta* or *kabitta*) *šalālu*.
$L^3$ = e.g., *sitāte ḫurru u nadbaku ša šadê akālu* (usually preceded by *dāmu* šadê ṣarāpu* or *pagrē ina šadê tabāku*.

Function L is essential and often culminating in the narrative chain. However, commonly there are sequences within the function L. The most characteristic sequence is: $L^{2\text{א}\zeta}$ $L^{1\text{ב}\beta}$ $L^{2\text{ב}\gamma\varepsilon}$ $L^{1\text{אבג}\zeta}$. This type of sequence fits in cases of siege and, hence, it is normally the outcome of $F^2$.

$L^{2\text{א}\zeta}$ = an initial/generic statement of the conquest of the city. It is usually a stereotyped expression such as *āla kašādu* 'to conquer the city'.

$L^{1\text{ב}\beta}$ = a description of the massacre of the enemy combatants. It is expressed by a generic formulation: *dīkta ma'atta dâku* :: 'to make a great havoc'.

$L^{2\text{ב}\gamma\varepsilon}$ = a description of the booty in terms of prisoners and goods. The simple term *šallatu* (which alone could refer to $^{\gamma}$ only, especially if accompanied by $^{\chi}$, or otherwise to a generic booty $^{\gamma+\delta+\varepsilon}$ to be codified hence as $L^{2\phi}$) may be accompanied by other fairly generic terms such as *bušû* or *makkūru*. Often there is a listing such as *šallatu* + *bušû* + *alpē* + *ṣēnē*. The basic verb *šalālu* may be substituted by *našû*, *aṣû*, *arādu*, or *târu*. Special expressions include: *lītē ṣabātu* 'to take hostages' [also: $L^{2\text{ה}\gamma}$ *ana ḫubtani lu aḫtabbatšunu* :: 'I took prisoners']; *kī lītūte ištēn ina libbišunu balṭu ul ēzib*; *ṣābē balṭūti ṣabātu* 'to take alive'; *nasāḫu* 'to deport'; and *sisē ekēmu* 'to take possession of horses'. $L^{2\text{ה}\gamma\varepsilon 1}$ = *ilānišunu áš-ša-a* :: 'I took away their gods'.

$L^{1\text{אבג}\zeta}$ = a description of the physical destruction of the settlement (normally in the last position in the sequence). It is almost always centered on *napālu* + *naqāru* + *ina išāti šarāpu* with such variants as *napālu* + *naqāru* + *ina tilli u karmi turru*. Occasionally one finds *ana tilli u karmi turru*. In certain instances this syntagm will be identified in the following way: $L^{1\text{א}\zeta}$ = *napālu*; $L^{1\text{ב}\zeta}$ = *naqāru*; $L^{1\text{ג}\zeta}$ = *ina išāti šarāpu* // *qamû*; $L^{1\text{ד}\zeta}$ = *ana tilli u karmi uter*.

The verbal extensions of the Assyrian syntagms are represented by superscripted Hebrew letters. The following are the Assyrian verbal extensions for both $L^1$ and $L^2$:[56]

| $L^1$ | | | $L^2$ | | |
|---|---|---|---|---|---|
| א | *napālu* | 'raze' | א | *kašādu* | 'capture, conquer' |
| ב | *naqāru* / *qatû* | 'destroy' | ב | *šalālu* | 'plunder' |
| ג | *šarāpu* / *qamû* | 'burn' | ג | *ṣabātu* | 'take, capture' |
| ד | *târu* / *šemû* | 'turn' | ד | *târu* | 'return' |
| ה | *nakāsu* | 'cut' | ה | *ḫabātu* | 'plunder' |
| ו | *arādu* | 'bring down' | ו | *arādu* | 'bring down' |
| ז | *petû* | 'open' | ז | *kanāšu* | 'to subdue' |
| ח | *našû* | 'lift' | ח | *našû* | 'carry' |
| ט | *nasāḫu* ( *ab ālu*) | 'tear' | ט | *nasāḫu* | 'deport' |
| י | *tabāku* | 'pour out' | י | *ekēmu* | 'to take prisoner' |
| כ | *dâku* | 'kill' | כ | *aṣû* | 'take out' |
| ל | *abikta šakānu* | 'to inflict a defeat' | ל | *elû* (Š) | 'cause to go up' |
| | *dīktašuna lu adûk* | 'massacre' | | | |
| מ | *nadû* | 'cast, lay' | | | |
| נ | *malû* | 'fill' | | | |
| ס | *eṣēdu* | 'harvest' | | | |
| ע | *alāku* Š + *arbūtu* | 'to make a devastation' | | | |
| פ | *parāru* | 'scatter, burst' | | | |
| צ | *maqātu* / *nâlum* | 'fell;' 'lay low' | | | |
| ק | *ṣarāpu* | 'dye' | | | |
| ר | *akālu* | 'devour' | | | |
| שׂ | *nazāru* | 'curse, execrate' | | | |
| שׁ | *kašāṭu* | 'cut off' | | | |
| ת | *elû* | 'hang' | | | |

M — *Submission*

The personal submission of the enemy king ($M^{\alpha}$) or of the enemy people ($M^{\beta\gamma\zeta}$) together with the delivery of the tribute ($M^{\delta\epsilon}$) are distinguished from the taking of booty ($L^2$) insofar as the former occur spontaneously, perhaps through fear, but without Assyrian recourse to military action. The usual act of submission is 'seizing the feet' *šēpē ṣabātu* of the Assyrian king [the negative 'not to seize the feet' indicates non-submissions].

N — *Exemplary Punishment* ———————— *The Ideology of 'Terror'*

This function is distinct from the 'normal massacres' which the Assyrians would inflict. Exemplary punishments were generally carried out upon those enemies who have shown a stiffer resistance. The more specific punishment of flaying alive seems to have been reserved for Assyrian traitors and usurpers (see: p. 66, n. 35). Obviously N is mostly preceded by or intermingled with the 'normal massacres' of type $L^1$. These punishments were designed as deterrences, instilling fear in the enemy peoples and provided the military with the upper hand in psychological warfare.

Consequently, the use of corpses or parts of corpses in the narratives transmit the message quite eloquently. Extensions include:

$N^a$ = flaying alive :: *kâṣu*; with a spreading out of the skin on the city walls :: *maška ḫalāpu*.

$N^b$ = Impalement :: *ina ziqpi zaqāpu*; normally with *ṣābē balṭūti* 'soldiers (that are) still alive'.

$N^c$ = cutting or excising :: *nakāsu* (usually the head *qaqqadu*); *batāqu* (usually the hands, noses, ears and so on); and *napālu* (the eyes).

$N^d$ = burning alive :: *ina išāti/maqlūti šarāpu* (usually *batulē batulāte* 'young boys and girls').

$N^e$ = Smashing :: *makāku* 'to scatter.'

$N^f$ = heaping or piling up heaps :: *asīta raṣāpu* (of corpses [*pagrū*] or of heads [*qaqqadū*]); detached heads were sometimes hanged (*ina gupni e'ēlu*).

$N^g$ = Removal of corpses.

O — *Consequences*

This function establishes an understanding of the new relationship between the Assyrian king and the vanquished enemy. The generic affirmation of belonging to Assyria ($O^{\phi}$) is more often than not rendered explicit with reference to the imposition of taxes or corvée ($O^1$), to the installation of an Assyrian governor ($O^2$), or it could be expressed by a figurative phrase ($O^3$). The terminology of $O^{123}$ is based on the expression *elišunu šakānu* 'to place upon them (= the defeated)'. The extensions are:

$O^1$ = the parallelisms of *ušātir elišunu aškun* and *udannin elišunu aškun*. With reference to the supplying of goods the object is defined a *maddattu* or *biltu* (or in the hendiadys *biltu u tāmartu*). With reference to the provision of work the term is *kuddurru*. Quite often the expression *eli ša pān* 'more than before' is added.

$O^2$ = the imposition of an Assyrian governor is stereotypically narrated as *(PN) šaknu ša ramāniya elišun / ana muḫḫišunu aškun*.

$O^3$ = The basic verb is *šakānu* which governs objects like *lītu u danānu*; *mātu ša pā ištēn*; *pulḫu u melammu Aššur*; *nīr bēlūtiya kabta elišunu ukîn* :: 'I imposed on them the heavy yoke of my lordship'.

$O^4$ = Summary statement of rulership: *GN ana pāṭ gimriša apil* :: 'I ruled over GN in its entirety'.

$O^5$ = Annexation: *ana miṣir mātiya utir* :: 'I annexed (it) to the borders of my land'.

$O^6$ = Setting up a puppet ruler: *PN ... ina* $^{\text{GIŠ}}$*kussî bēlūtišu ušešib*.

$O^{\phi}$ = *āla/GN ana ramāniya ṣabātu* :: 'I took the city for myself'. This is related, on the one hand, to the expression of $O^2$ through the phrase *ana ramāniya* and, on the other hand, to the acquisitive sphere of $L^2$ by the verb *ṣabātu*. = belonging to Assyria: *pān Aššur bēliya ušadgilšunuti* :: 'I made them vassals of Aššur, my lord'.

P — *Acts of Celebration*

There are three functions within P:

$P^1$ = the erection of a statue or stela of the Assyrian king. The terminology of $P^1$ is rich but stereotyped. As a rule there is a subdivision into three periods: (1) the stela/statue is 'made' (always *epēšu*); (2) it is 'inscribed' (always *šaṭāru*); and (3) it is erected (*uzuzzu* Š, *šakānu*, *zaqāpu*).

$P^2$ = the foundation or restoration of cities. The terminology primarily emphasizes the work of reconstruction (*ana aššuti ṣabātu*), but also of improvement (*eli ša pān*) and of accuracy and completeness (*raṣāpu* + *šuklulu*).

$P^3$ = the offerings to the deity. The terminology is comprised by such phrases as *kakkē ullulu* 'to wash the weapons', *niqê ṣabātu* 'to make libations' and so on.

Q — *Return*

It is significant that function Q is not very common. The interest of the narration culminates and disappears with the victory and the acts of celebration. The description of the return journey is omitted as obvious and lacking ideological interest. Nevertheless, there are two types of 'returns' which are encountered:

q = the return to the base camp during a campaign (*ana ušmāni târu* + *bâtu* 'to return to camp + to pass the night', obviously followed by //.

Q = statements that booty and prisoners were brought back to Assyrian cities (here the return is only alluded to).

R — *Supplemental Royal Activities on the Campaign*

The Extensions are: $R^1$ = killing wild beasts; $R^2$ = capturing wild beasts; $R^3$ = cutting down trees.

S — *Summary Statement*

T — *Geographic note*

*Connotations and Extensions*

α = (enemy) king
β = (enemy) troops
γ = civilians
Δ = difficulty of route (used with EGHQ)
δ = animals
ε = inanimate goods
ζ = cities
η = 'the rest'
γ = leaders
λ = withholding tribute
χ = numerical quantification (used especially in LM)
φ = non-connotated or non-specified function
! = motive of priority (used especially in E)

* = comparison
° = listing (more than 2 elements, used especially in LM)
\- = indication of the non-materialization of the function.

## *Syntagmic Analysis*

### *ANNALISTIC TEXTS*

### 1. *Tiglath-Pileser I*[57]

A.K. Grayson states that the Annals of Tiglath-Pileser I (1114-1076 B.C.) represent the 'first true annalistic text' among the Assyrian royal inscriptions.[58] The Aššur prism (prism A) is divided into paragraphs (the scribe indicated these by drawing horizontal lines across the column and beginning the first line of each new paragraph in the margin). Furthermore, each military campaign is introduced by a paragraph which contains the royal name and epithets distinctive of that particular paragraph. Thus, Grayson concludes that the inscription is:

> a collection of individual campaign reports and we may assume that separate accounts of single campaigns also existed by this time although none are actually attested until the reign of Ashur-nasir-apli II (883-859 B.C.).[59]

Although Tiglath-Pileser's annals appear to be chronological, they are neither numbered or dated (by a *palû* or by an eponym year) as in the annals of later kings. The Aššur prism records the events of the first five years as the summary near the end of the prism makes clear: 'I conquered altogether 42 lands ... from my accession year to my fifth regnal year (5th *palû*)'.

Furthermore, the Aššur prism of Tiglath-Pileser, as Tadmor observes, reveals this new literary genre <i.e. 'annals'> in all its complexity:

> metaphorical language, poetic comparisons, epic hyperbolae, as well as specific 'topoi' such as the royal hunt of lions, his putting draft animals to the plow, and his having stored more barley than his fathers. These features, arranged in a chronological narrative, are combined here for the first time in a high style that was imitated by Tiglath-Pileser's immediate successors, but was not used again until the historical inscriptions of the Sargonids.[60]

In the text of the prism, there are twenty *episodes* concerned with Tiglath-Pileser's military campaigns. One is impressed by the repetitive, yet refined, nature of these episodes. The prism is a testimony to the literary flowering under Tiglath-Pileser's reign. A comparison of the episodes exhibits how much the ancient writer sought to alternate their formulations, although, because of the number of campaigns, he often repeated numerous lines verbatim.[61] A examination of episodes 9 and 19 reveals the following:

*Episode 9*
(III.73-87)

| | |
|---|---|
| $I^2$ | **III**$^{73 māt}$Sa-ra-uš $^{māt}$Am-ma-uš $^{74}$ša iš-tu u$_4$-um ṣa-a-te ka-na-a-ša $^{75}$la-a i-du-ú ki-ma tíl(DU$_6$) a-bu-be $^{76}$áš-ḫu-up |
| $I^1$ | it-ti um-ma-na-te-šu-nu DAGAL$^{MEŠ}$(-te) $^{77}$i-na $^{KUR}$Aru-ma al-ta-na-an-ma |
| L$^{1ל}$ | $^{78}$dab-da-šu-nu áš-kun |
| $N^f$ | šal-ma-at $^{79}$muq-tab-li-šu-nu i-na gi-sal-lat KUR-i ki-ma ser-ma-ṣe $^{80}$lu-me-ṣi |
| L$^{2}$אζ | URU$^{MEŠ}$-ni-šu-nu ak-šud |
| L$^{2}$חγε1 | $^{81}$ilāni(DINGIR$^{MEŠ}$)-šu-nu áš-ša-a |
| L$^{2}$בγε | šal-la-su-nu $^{82}$bu-ša-šu-nu nam-kur-šu-nu ú-še-ṣa-a |
| L$^{1}$אבגζ | $^{83}$URU$^{MEŠ}$-ni-šu-nu i-na išāti(IZI$^{MEŠ}$) áš-ru-up $^{84}$ap-púl aq-qur |
| L$^{1}$דζ | a-na tīli(DU$_6$) ù kar-mi $^{85}$ú-tir |
| $O^3$ | ni-ir bēlu(EN)-ti-ya kabta(DUGUD) $^{86}$eli(UGU)-šu-nu ú-kin |
| $O^{\phi}$ | pa-an Aššur bēli(EN)-ya $^{87}$ú-šad-gil-šu-nu-ti |

I overwhelmed the lands Sarauš (and) Ammauš, which from ancient times had not known submission, (so that they looked) like ruin hills (created by) the Deluge.
I fought with their extensive army in Mt. Aruma, and
I brought about their defeat.
The corpses of their men-at-arms I laid out on the mountain ledges like grain heaps.
I conquered their cities.
I carried away their gods.
I carried off their booty, possessions and property.
I burned, razed, and destroyed their cities.
I turned (them) into ruin hills and heaps.
I imposed on them the heavy yoke of my lordship.
I made them vassals of Aššur, my lord.

*Episode 19*
(V.99-VI.21)

| | |
|---|---|
| $I^2$ | **V**$^{99}$ $^{URU}$Ḫu-nu-sa URU dan-nu-ti-šu-nu $^{100}$ki-ma tíl(DU$_6$) a-bu-be áš-ḫu-up |

| | |
|---|---|
| $I^{1}$ | **VI**[1]it-ti um-ma-na-a-ti-šu-nu gab-ša-a-te [2]i-na URU ù KUR-e šam-riš lu am-da-ḫi-iṣ |
| $L^{\text{1ל}}$ | [3]a-bi-ik-ta-šu-nu lu-ú áš-kun |
| $N^{f}$ | [4]ṣābē(ERÍN$^{\text{MEŠ}}$) muq-tab-li-šu-nu i-na qe-reb ḫur-šá-ni [5]ki-ma šu-be lu uš-na-il |
| $N^{c}$ | qaqqadē(SAG.DU$^{\text{MEŠ}}$)-šu-nu [6]ki-ma zi-ir-qi ú-ni-ki-is |
| $L^{\text{1ד}\beta}$ | [7]damē(ÚŠ$^{\text{MEŠ}}$)-šu-nu ḫur-ri ù ba-ma-a-te šá KUR-i [8]lu-šar-di |
| $L^{\text{2א}\zeta}$ | URU šu-a-tu ak-šud |
| $L^{\text{2ח}\gamma\varepsilon 1}$ | [9]ilāni(DINGIR$^{\text{MEŠ}}$)-šu-nu áš-ša-a |
| $L^{\text{2ב}\gamma\varepsilon}$ | šal-la-su-nu buša-šu-nu nam-kur-šu-nu [10]ú-še-ṣa-a |
| $L^{\text{1אבג}\zeta}$ | URU i-na išāti(IZI$^{\text{MEŠ}}$) áš-ru-up [11]3 durāni$^{\text{MEŠ}}$-šu-nu GAL$^{\text{MEŠ}}$ ša i-na a-gur-ri [12]ra-áš-bu ù si-ḫir-ti URU-šu [13]ap-púl aq-qur |
| $L^{\text{1ד}\zeta}$ | a-na tīli(DU$_6$) ù kar-mi [14]ú-tir |
| $L^{\text{1ש}\zeta}$ | ù NA$_4^{\text{MEŠ}}$ ṣi-pa i-na muḫ-ḫi-šu [15]az-ru |
| $P^{1}$ | {biriq(NIM.GÍR) siparri(UD.KA.BAR) e-pu-uš |
| | {[16]ki-ši-ti KUR.KUR$^{\text{MEŠ}}$ ša i-na $^{d}$A-šur bēli(EN)-ya [17]ak-šu-du URU šu-a-tu {a-na la ṣa-ba-ti [18]ù dūra-šu la-a ra-ṣa-pi i-na muḫ-ḫi [19]al-tu-ur |
| | {bītu(É) ša a-gur-ri i-na muḫ-ḫi-šu [20]ar-ṣip |
| | {biriq(NIM.GÍR) siparri(UD.KA.BAR) ša-a-tu-nu [21]i-na lib-bi ú-še-ši-ib |

I overwhelmed the city Hunusu, their stronghold, (so that it looked) like a ruin hill (created by) the Deluge.
Violently I fought with their mighty army in city and mountain.
I inflicted on them a decisive defeat.
I laid low their men-at-arms in the mountains like sheep.
I cut off their heads like sheep.
I made their blood flow into the hollows and plains of the mountains.
(Thus) I conquered that city.
I took their gods; (and)
I carried off their booty, possessions (and) property.
I burned the city.
The three great walls which were constructed with baked bricks and the entire city I razed (and) destroyed.
I turned (it) into a ruin hill and a heap.
I strewed 'ṣipu'-stones over it.
I made bronze lightning bolts (and)
I inscribed on them (a description of) the conquest of the lands which by Aššur, my lord, I had conquered, (and) a warning) not to occupy that city and not to rebuild its wall.
On that (site) I built a house of baked brick.
I put inside it those bronze lightning bolts.

The episodes can be charted:

| Episode 9 | Episode 19 |
|---|---|
| $I^2$ | $I^2$ |
| $I^1$ | $I^1$ |
| $L^{\text{1ל}}$ | $L^{\text{1ל}}$ |
| $N^f$ | $N^f$ |
| - | $N^e$ |
| - | $L^{\text{1ך}\beta}$ |
| $L^{\text{2א}\zeta}$ | $L^{\text{2א}\zeta}$ |
| $L^{\text{2ח}\gamma\varepsilon 1}$ | $L^{\text{2ח}\gamma\varepsilon 1}$ |
| $L^{\text{2כ}\gamma\varepsilon}$ | $L^{\text{2כ}\gamma\varepsilon}$ |
| $L^{\text{1אבג}\zeta}$ | $L^{\text{1אבג}\zeta}$ |
| $L^{\text{1ד}\zeta}$ | $L^{\text{1ד}\zeta}$ |
| - | $L^{\text{1ש}\zeta}$ |
| $O^3$ | - |
| $O^\phi$ | - |
| - | $P^1$ |

As can be seen from the above chart, the two episodes are practically identical in structure. Yet, the episodes occurred in different years of Tiglath-Pileser's reign (separated by at least two years), and the referents of the episodes are entirely different (different geographical regions and different ethnic groups). Stereotyped syntagms have been used to pattern the structure. The referents have been *attached* to the narrative's trellis.

The variations in the structure can be easily explained in terms of expansion, amplification, replacement, ellipsis, or deletion. For example, in the first line of episode 9, there is expansion (another place-name ${}^{māt}$*Am-ma-uš*) and amplification (the phrase: *ša iš-tu* $u_4$*-um ṣa-a-te ka-na-a-ša la-a i-du-ú* :: 'which from ancient times had not known submission'). In the second line of episode 19 there is expansion and amplification (*gab-ša-a-te i-na URU ù KUR-e šam-riš* :: 'Violently ..... mighty ... in city and mountain'). In the third line of the episodes there is replacement (*dab-da-šu-nu* (9) = *abi-ik-ta-šu-nu* (19)). But in a number of instances there is exact duplication [e.g. *ilāni-šu-nu áš-ša-a* (lines III.81 and VI.9) or *a-na tīli ù kar-mi ú-tir* (III.84 and VI.13)].

There are other episodes in this text of Tiglath-Pileser I which deserve attention (episodes 2, 4, 6, and 7).

*Episode 2*
(I.89-II.15)

| | |
|---|---|
| $a^2$ | $^{89}$i-na $u_4$-mi-šu-ma |
| B | a-na $^{\text{māt}}$Kad-mu-ḫi la-a ma-gi-ri $^{90}$ša bilta(GUN) ù ma-da-at-ta a-na $^{\text{d}}$A-šur |
| $E^2$ | bēli(EN)-ya $^{91}$ik-lu-ú lu al-lik |
| $L^{2\aleph\zeta}$ | $^{\text{māt}}$Kad-mu-ḫu $^{92}$a-na si-ḫir-ti-ša lu-ú ak-šud |
| $L^{2\beth\gamma\epsilon}$ | $^{93}$šal-la-su-nu bu-ša-šu-nu nam-kur-šu-nu $^{94}$ú-še-ṣa-a |
| $L^{1\aleph\beth\gimel\zeta}$ | URU$^{\text{MEŠ}}$-ni-šu-nu i-na išāti(IZI$^{\text{MEŠ}}$) **II**$^{1}$áš-ru-up ap-púl aq-qur |
| $G^{\Delta 3\eta}$ | si-te-et $^{2\text{māt}}$Kad-mu-ḫi ša i-na pa-an $^{\text{GIŠ}}$kakkē(TUKUL$^{\text{MEŠ}}$)-ya $^{3}$ip-par-ši-du a-na $^{\text{URU}}$Še-ri-eš-še $^{4}$ša šēpē(GÌR.II$^{\text{MEŠ}}$) am-ma--a-te ša $^{\text{íd}}$Idiglat $^{5}$lu e-be-ru |
| $G^{\Delta 4}$ | URU a-na dan-nu-ti-šu-nu $^{6}$lu iš-ku-nu |
| $H^{\Delta}$ | $^{\text{GIŠ}}$narkabāti(GIGIR$^{\text{MEŠ}}$) ù qu-ra-di-ya$^{\text{MEŠ}}$ $^{7}$lu al-qi KUR-a mar-ṣa ù gir-ri-te-šu-nu $^{8}$pa-áš-qa-a-te i-na aq-qúl-lat erê$^{\text{MEŠ}}$ $^{9}$lu aḫ-si-ḫu-la a-na me-te-iq $^{10\text{GIŠ}}$narkabāti(GIGIR$^{\text{MEŠ}}$)-ya ù um-ma-na-te-ya lu-ti-ib $^{11\text{íd}}$Idiglat lu e-bir |
| $L^{2\aleph\zeta}$ | $^{\text{URU}}$Še-ri-še $^{12}$URU dan-nu-ti-šu-nu ak-šu-ud |
| $N^{f}$ | $^{13}$ṣābē(ERÍN$^{\text{MEŠ}}$) muq-tab-li-šu-nu i-na qe-reb tam-ḫa-ri $^{14}$ki-ma ser-ma-ši lu-ú-mi-ṣi |
| $L^{1\daleth\beta}$ | $^{15}$damē(ÚŠ$^{\text{MEŠ}}$)-šu-nu ḫar-ri ù ba-mat ša KUR-i $^{16}$lu-šar-di |

At that time:
I marched to the insubmissive land of Kadmuhu which had withheld tribute and impost from Aššur, my lord.
I conquered the land of Kadmuhu in its entirety.
Their booty, property, (and) possessions I brought out.
Their cities I burned, razed (and) destroyed.
The remainder of the land of Kadmuhu, who had fled from my weapons (and) had crossed over to the city Šerešše which is on the opposite bank of the Tigris, made that city their stronghold.
I took my chariots and warriors (and)
I hacked through the rough mountain range and difficult paths with copper picks (and) I made a good way for the passage of my chariots and troops. I crossed the Tigris (and)
I conquered Šerešše, their stronghold.
I laid out in the midst of the battle (the corpses of) their men-at-arms like grain heaps.[62]
I made their blood flow in the watercourses and the plains of the mountains.

*Episode 6*
(III.7-31)

| | |
|---|---|
| $E^2$ | **III**$^{7}$i-na šit-mur qar-du-ti-ya-ma ša-nu-te-ya $^{8}$a-na $^{\text{māt}}$Kad-mu-ḫi lu-(ú) al-lik |
| $L^{2\aleph\zeta}$ | nap-ḫar $^{9}$URU$^{\text{MEŠ}}$-ni-šu-nu ak-šud |

| | |
|---|---|
| $L^{2\text{ב}\gamma\epsilon}$ | šal-la-su-nu $^{10}$bu-ša-šu-nu ù nam-kur-šu-nu ana la-a mi-na áš-lul |
| $L^{1\text{אבג}\zeta}$ | $^{11}$URU$^{\text{MEŠ}}$-ni-šu-nu i-na išāti(IZI$^{\text{MEŠ}}$) áš-ru-up $^{12}$ap-púl aq-qur |
| $G^{\Delta 3\eta}$ | ù si-te-et $^{13}$um-ma-na-te-šu-nu ša i-na pa-an $^{\text{GIŠ}}$kakkē (TUKUL$^{\text{MEŠ}}$)-ya $^{14}$iz-zu-te ip-la-ḫu-ma ti-ib tāḫāzi(MÈ)-ya $^{15}$dan-na e-du-ru a-na šu-zu-ub $^{16}$nap-ša-te-šu-nu |
| $G^{\Delta 4}$ | gab-'a-a-ni dan-nu-te $^{17}$ša KUR-e eqla(A.ŠÀ) mar-ṣa lu iṣ-ba-tu |
| $H^{\Delta}$ | $^{18}$a-na šik-kat ḫur-ša-a-ni ša-qu-ú-te $^{19}$ù gi-šal-lat KUR-i pa-áš-qa-a-te $^{20}$ša a-na ki-bi-is amelu(LÚ) la-a na-tu-ú $^{21}$ar-ki-šu-nu lu e-li |
| I | $^{\text{GIŠ}}$kakka(TUKUL$^{\text{MEŠ}}$) qabla(MÚR) $^{22}$ù tāḫāza(MÈ) it-ti-ya lu e-pu-šu |
| $L^{1\text{כ}}$ | $^{23}$a-bi-ik-ta-šu-nu lu-(ú) áš-kun |
| $N^{f}$ | šal-mat $^{24}$qu-ra-di-šu-nu i-na gi-šal-lat KUR-i $^{25}$ki-ma ra-ḫiṣi lu-ki-mir |
| $L^{1\text{ד}\beta}$ | damē(ÚŠ$^{\text{MEŠ}}$)-šu-nu $^{26}$ḫur-ri ù ba-ma-a-te ša KUR-i $^{27}$lu-šar-di |
| $L^{2\text{ד}\gamma\epsilon}$ | šal-la-su-nu bu-ša-šu-nu $^{28}$ù nam-kur-šu-nu it-ti gab-'a-a-ni $^{29}$ša KUR-e dan-nu-te [...]-ri-da |
| $O^{4}$ | $^{30\text{māt}}$Kad-mu-ḫu a-na paṭ gim-ri-ša a-píl-ma |
| $O^{5}$ | $^{31}$a-na mi-ṣir māti(KUR)-ya ú-tir |

With my valorous onslaught I went a second time[63] to the land of Kadmuhu.
I conquered all their cities.
I carried off without number their booty, possessions, and property.
I burned, razed (and) destroyed their cities.
Now the remainder of their troops, which had taken fright at my fierce weapons and had been cowed by my strong and belligerent attack, in order to save their lives took to secure heights in rough mountainous terrain.
I climbed up after them to the peaks of high mountains and perilous mountain ledges where a man could not walk.
They waged war, combat, and battle with me; (and)
I inflicted a decisive defeat on them.
I piled up the corpses of their warriors on mountain ledges like the Inundator (i.e. Adad).
I made their blood flow into the hollows and plains of the mountains.
I bro[ught do]wn their booty, possessions and property from the secure heights of the mountains.
(Thus) I ruled over the entire land of Kadmuhu; and
I annexed (it) to the borders of my land.

The readout of the components of the structure of these two episodes is:

| Episode 2 | Episode 6 |
|---|---|
| $a^{2}$ | - |
| B | - |
| $E^{2}$ | $E^{2}$ |
| $L^{2\text{א}\zeta}$ | $L^{2\text{א}\zeta}$ |
| $L^{2\text{ב}\gamma\varepsilon}$ | $L^{2\text{ב}\gamma\varepsilon}$ |
| $L^{1\text{אבג}\zeta}$ | $L^{1\text{אבג}\zeta}$ |
| $G^{\Delta 3\eta}$ | $G^{\Delta 3\eta}$ |
| $G^{\Delta 4}$ | $G^{\Delta 4}$ |
| $H^{\Delta}$ | $H^{\Delta}$ |
| - | I |
| - | $L^{1\text{ל}}$ |
| $L^{2\text{א}\zeta}$ | - |
| $N^{f}$ | $N^{f}$ |
| $L^{1\text{ד}\beta}$ | $L^{1\text{ד}\beta}$ |
| - | $L^{2\text{ד}\gamma\varepsilon}$ |
| - | $O^{4}$ |
| - | $O^{5}$ |

Episode 2 begins with a chronological marker which is very common in the inscription (*i-na* $u_4$*-mi-šu-ma* :: 'at that time'). This marker is absent from the account in episode 6. There is identical structure in a number of the following components ($E^{2}$, $L^{2\text{א}\zeta}$, $L^{2\text{ב}\gamma\varepsilon}$, $L^{1\text{אבג}\zeta}$, $G^{\Delta 3\eta}$, $G^{\Delta 4}$, $H^{\Delta}$, etc.). The two accounts then have variant expansion in the next three components followed by identical structure in the next two ($N^{f}$ and $L^{1\text{ד}\beta}$). Episode 6 rounds out the account with three components which are absent in episode 2.

*Episode 4*
(II.63-84)

| | |
|---|---|
| $C^{3}$ | **II**$^{63}$i-na šu-mur $^{\text{GIŠ}}$kakkē(TUKUL$^{\text{MEŠ}}$)-ya iz-zu-te šá Aššur bēlu(EN) |
| D | $^{64}$da-na-na ù me-til-lu-ta iš-ru-ka $^{65}$i-na 30 $^{\text{GIŠ}}$narkabāti (GIGIR$^{\text{MEŠ}}$)ya a-li-kàt i-di $^{66}$ga-mar-ri-ya ir-ḫu-te qu-ra-di-ya $^{67}$ša mit-ḫu-uṣ tap-di-e li-tam-du $^{68}$lu al-qi |
| $E^{2}$ | a-na $^{\text{māt}}$IŠ.diš sap-ṣu-te $^{69}$la-a ma-gi-ri lu al-lik |
| $E^{1\Delta}$ | KUR$^{\text{MEŠ}}$ $^{70}$dan-nu-ti eqil(A.ŠÀ) nam-ra-ṣi $^{71}$ṭâba(DUG$_{10}$.GA) i-na $^{\text{GIŠ}}$narkabāti(GIGIR$^{\text{MEŠ}}$)-ya ù mar-ṣa i-na šēpē(GIR.II)-ya $^{72}$lu e-te-ti-iq |
| $E^{\Delta}$ | i-na $^{\text{KUR}}$A-ru-ma $^{73}$eqli(A.ŠÀ) pa-áš-qi ša a-na me-tiq $^{\text{GIŠ}}$narkabāti(GIGIR$^{\text{MEŠ}}$)ya $^{74}$la-a na-tu-ú $^{\text{GIŠ}}$narkabāti(GIGIR$^{\text{MEŠ}}$) lu-ú e-zib |

| | |
|---|---|
| E[8Δ] | [75]pa-an qu-ra-di-ya[MEŠ] aṣ-bat |
| E[1Δ] | [76]ki-ma šib-bi ir-ḫi-ku-ma i-na qi-šal-lat KUR-i [77]pa-áš--qa-a-te šal-ṭí-iš e-te-ti-iq |
| I[2] | [78mât]IŠ.diš ki-ma tíl(DU₆) a-bu-be áš-ḫu-up |
| L[1צβ] | [79]ṣābē(ERÍN[MEŠ]) muq-tab-li-šu-nu i-na qe-reb tam-ḫa-ri [80]ki-ma šu-be uš-na-il |
| L[2בγε] | šal-la-su-nu [81]bu-ša-a-šu-nu nam-kur-šu-nu áš-lu-ul |
| L[1בζ] | [82]nap-ḫar URU[MEŠ]-ni-šu-nu i-na išāti(IZI[MEŠ]) aq-mu |
| O[1] | [83]li-i-ti[MEŠ] bilta(GUN) ù ma-da-at-ta [84]eli(UGU)-šu-nu ú-kin |

With the onslaught of my fierce weapons by means of which Aš-šur, the lord, gave me strength and authority I took with thirty of my chariots escorting my aggressive personal carriers,[64] my warriors trained for successful combat.
I marched to the land of Išdiš (where) rebellious (and) insubmissive people (lived).
Mighty mountains and rough country, in my chariot where (the road) was good, and on foot where difficult, I passed over.
In Mt. Aruma, a difficult area which was impassable for my chariots, I abandoned my chariotry.
I took the lead of my warriors.
I climbed victoriously over the perilous mountain ledges with the aggressiveness of a viper.[65]
The land of Išdiš I overwhelmed (so that it looked) like ruin hills (created by) the Deluge.
Their warriors I laid low in battle like sheep.
Their booty, possessions, and property I carried off.
I burned all their cities.
I imposed upon them (the obligation to provide) hostages, tribute, and taxes.

*Episode 7*
(III.35-65)

| | |
|---|---|
| C[2] | III[35]i-na e-mu-qi ṣi-ra-a-te ša [d]A-šur bēli(EN)-ya [36]a-na [mât]Ḫa-ri-a ù um-ma-na-at [37mât]Pap-ḫe-e[MEŠ] DAGAL-ti ḫur-ša-ni [38]ša-qu-ti ša a-šar-šu-nu šarru(ŠÀR) ia-um-ma [39]la i-ba-'u [d]A-šur bēlu(EN) a-na a-la-ki [40]iq-ba-a |
| D | [GIŠ]narkabāti(GIGIR[MEŠ]) ù um-ma-na-te-ya [41]lul-te-šìr |
| E[8] | bir-ti [KUR]Et-ni [42]ù [KUR]A-ia eqil(A.ŠÀ) nam-ra-ṣi lu-aṣ-bat |
| E[Δ] | [43]KUR[MEŠ] ša-qu-te ša ki-ma zi-qip patri(GÍR) [44]ú šam-ṭu ša a-na me-tiq [GIŠ]narkabāti(GIGIR[MEŠ])-ya [45]la-a na-ṭu-ú [GIŠ]narkabāti(GIRIR[MEŠ]) i-na la-a ba-ni [46]lu e-mi-id |
| E[1Δ] | KUR[MEŠ] pa-áš-qu-te [47]lu e-te-tiq |
| G[-2] | kul-lat [mât]Pap-ḫe-e[MEŠ] [48]um-ma-na-te-šu-nu DAGAL[MEŠ]-(te) lu-ul-taq-ṣi-ru-ma |
| G[-4] | [49]a-na epiš [GIŠ]kakkē(TUKUL[MEŠ]) qabli(MÚR) ù ta-ḫa-zi [50]i-na [KUR]A-zu dáp-níš lu iz-zi-zu-ni-ma |
| I[1] | [51]i-na KUR-e eqil(A.ŠÀ) nam-ra-ṣi it-ti-šu-nu [52]am-da-ḫi-iṣ |

L$^{1ל}$ dab-da-šu-nu áš-kun
N$^{f}$ [53]šal-ma-at qu-ra-di-šu-nu i-na ba-mat KUR-i [54]a-na gu-ru-na-a-te lu-ú-ki-ri-in
L$^{1ךβ}$ [55]damē(ÚŠ$^{MEŠ}$) qu-ra-di-šu-nu ḫur-ri ù ba-ma-a-te [56]ša KUR-i lu-šar-di
F$^{2}$ a-na URU$^{MEŠ}$-ni [57]ša i-na gi-šal-lat KUR-i ša-ak-nu šam-riš [58]lu as-niq
L$^{2אζ}$ 25 URU$^{MEŠ}$-ni ša $^{māt}$Ḫa-ri-a [59]ša i-na šēp(GÍR) $^{KUR}$A-ia $^{KUR}$Šu-i-ra $^{KUR}$Et-ni [60]$^{KUR}$še-e-zu $^{KUR}$še-el-gu $^{KUR}$Ar-za-ni-bi-ú [61]$^{KUR}$ú-ru-su ù $^{KUR}$A-ni-it-ku [62]šà-al-'a-ni ak-šud
L$^{2בγε}$ šal-la-su-nu [63]bu-ša-šu-nu ù nam-kur-šu-nu áš-lul
L$^{1אבגζ}$ [64]URU$^{MEŠ}$-ni-šu-nu i-na išāti(IZI$^{MEŠ}$) áš-ru-up [65]ap-pu-ul aq-qur

With the exalted strength of Aššur, my lord, against the land Haria and the army of the extensive land of Paphe in high mountains, where no king had ever gone, Aššur, the lord, commanded me to march.
I put my chariotry and army in readiness; (and)
I took a rugged route between Mt. Etnu and Mt. Aya.
In the high mountains, which are like the blade of a dagger and which were not suitable for the passage of my chariots, I put the chariots on (the soldiers') necks.
(Thus) I passed through the difficult mountain range.
All of the Paphe, their extensive army, joined together; and they took up aggressively a position to wage war, combat, and battle in Mt. Azu.
I fought with them in rough mountainous terrain, (and)
I brought about their defeat.
I built up mounds with the corpses of their warriors in the plains of the mountain; (and)
I made the blood of their warriors flow into the hollows and plains of the mountain.
I stormed[66] against the cities which were on mountain ledges; (and)
I conquered 25 cities of the land Haria which lies at the foot of Mounts Aya, Šuira, Etnu, Šezu, Šelgu, Arzanibiu, Urusu and Anitku.
Their booty, possessions, and property I carried off.
Their cities I burned, razed (and) destroyed.

*Episode 2a*
(II.16-35)

a$^{2}$ i-na u$_{4}$-mi-šu-ma
L$^{1צβ}$ um-ma-na-at [17]$^{māt}$Pap-ḫe-e$^{MEŠ}$ ša a-na šu-zu-ub [18]ù ni-ra--ru-ut-te ša $^{māt}$Kad-mu-ḫi [19]il-li-ku-ni it-ti um-ma-na-at [20]$^{māt}$Kad-mu-ḫi ki-ma šu-be lu-uš-na-il

| | |
|---|---|
| $N^{f}$ | [21]pa-gar muq-tab-li-šu-nu a-na gu-ru-na-te [22]i-na gi-šal-lat KUR-i lu-ki-ri-in |
| $N^{g}$ | [23]šal-mat qu-ra-a-di-šu-nu $^{íd}$Na-a-me [24]a-na $^{íd}$Idiglat lu-ú-še-ṣi |
| $L^{2\text{א}\theta}$ | [25]$^{I}$Ki-li-$^{d}$TE.ŠUB mār(DUMU) Ka-li-$^{d}$TE.ŠUB [26]ša $^{I}$Er-ru-pi i-sa-siú-šu-nu [27]šarra(ŠÀR)-šu-nu i-na qe-reb tam-ḫa-ri qa-ti [28]ik-šu-ud |
| $L^{2\text{ה}\gamma\epsilon+1}$ | aššati(DAM$^{MEŠ}$)-su mārē(DUMU$^{MEŠ}$) [29]nab-ni-it lib-bi-šu el-la-su 3 šu-ši (60) [30]ruq-qi erê$^{MEŠ}$ 5 nir-ma-ak siparri(UD.KA.BAR) [31]it-ti ilāni(DINGIR$^{MEŠ}$-šu-nu ḫurāṣu(KUG.GI$^{MEŠ}$) ù kaspu(KÙ.BABBAR$^{MEŠ}$) [32]ù du-muq-nam-kur-ri-šu-nu áš-ša-a |
| $L^{2\text{ב}\gamma\epsilon}$ | [33]šal-la-su-nu bu-ša-a-šu-nu ú-še-ṣa-a |
| $L^{1\text{אבג}\zeta}$ | [34]URU ša-a-tu ù ekallu(É.GAL)-šu i-ti išāti(IZI$^{MEŠ}$) [35]áš-ru--up ap-púl aq-qur |

At that time:
I laid low the army of Paphe which had come to the aid and assistance of the land of Kadmuhu together with the army of Kadmuhu like sheep.
I built up mounds with the corpses of their men-at-arms on mountain ledges.
I allowed the river Name to carry the bodies of their warriors out to the Tigris.
I captured in the midst of the battle their king Kili-Tešub, son of Kali-Tešub, who is called Errupi.
His wives, his sons, his clan, 180 copper kettles, 5 bronze bathtubs, together with their gods, their gold and silver, the best of their property I carried off.
I brought out their booty (and) possessions.
I burned, razed (and) destroyed that city and its palace.

If we add Episode 19 (see above) to the comparison, the chart of these episodes is:

| Episode 4 | Episode 7 | Episode 2a | Episode 19 |
|---|---|---|---|
| - | - | - | $a^{2}$ |
| $C^{3}$ | $C^{2}$ | - | - |
| D | D | - | - |
| $E^{2}$ | $E^{8}$ | - | - |
| $E^{1\Delta}$ | - | - | - |
| $E^{\Delta}$ | $E^{\Delta}$ | - | - |
| $E^{8\Delta}$ | - | - | - |
| $E^{1\Delta}$ | $E^{\Delta}$ | - | - |
| - | $G^{-2}$ | - | - |
| - | $G^{-4}$ | - | - |
| $I^{2}$ | - | - | $I^{2}$ |

| | | | |
|---|---|---|---|
| - | $I^{1}$ | - | $I^{1}$ |
| $L^{1\text{צ}\beta}$ | $L^{1\text{ל}}$ | $L^{1\text{צ}\beta}$ | $L^{1\text{ל}}$ |
| - | $N^{f}$ | $N^{f}$ | $N^{f}$ |
| - | - | $N^{c}$ | $N^{c}$ |
| - | $L^{1\text{ר}\beta}$ | - | $L^{1\text{ר}\beta}$ |
| - | $F^{2}$ | - | - |
| - | $L^{2\text{א}\zeta}$ | $L^{2\text{א}\beta}$ | $L^{2\text{א}\zeta}$ |
| - | - | $L^{2\text{ח}\gamma\varepsilon 1}$ | $L^{2\text{ח}\gamma\varepsilon 1}$ |
| $L^{2\text{ב}\gamma\varepsilon}$ | $L^{2\text{ב}\gamma\varepsilon}$ | $L^{2\text{ב}\gamma\varepsilon}$ | $L^{2\text{ב}\gamma\varepsilon}$ |
| $L^{1\text{בג}\zeta}$ | $L^{1\text{אבג}\zeta}$ | $L^{1\text{אבג}\zeta}$ | $L^{1\text{אבג}\zeta}$ |
| - | - | - | $L^{1\text{ד}\zeta}$ |
| - | - | - | $L^{1\text{ט}\zeta}$ |
| $O^{1}$ | - | - | - |
| - | - | - | $P^{1}$ |

Again, one can see the use of stereotyped syntagms. As before, variations in the patterning can be explained in terms of expansion, amplification, replacement, ellipsis, or deletion. Thus the annals of Tiglath-Pileser I illustrate the employment of stereotyped syntagms to pattern the campaign accounts of Assyrian monarch. While there is variation (this obviously breaks the monotony), the repetition of certain key components maintains a structural unity in the narrative, and creates an iterative scheme and a *high-redundance message*.

Through the analysis it becomes obvious that several syntagms are constantly present and more detailed, while others appear less frequently and are only briefly expounded. For example, while the journey to the place of combat (E) is usually present and often connotates, the return journey (Q) is seldom mentioned. Another example can be seen in the case of the actual combat (I) which is infrequent, while the subsequent massacre and acquisition of booty ($L^1$, $L^2$) is incessant! This disparity in the utilization of various syntagmic functions demonstrates clearly what was considered to be more or less significant and functional for the attainment of the Annals' objectives (i.e., persuasion, deterrence and celebration).[67]

## 2. *Ashur-Dan II*[68]

This text includes six episodes of military campaigns which the scribe delineated by drawing a line on the tablet. There are echoes of Tiglath-Pileser I in the inscription.

*Episode 1*
(6-15)

| | |
|---|---|
| $A^{2}$ | $^{6}$[i-na šur-rat ŠAR$_{4}$-ti-ya i-na maḫ-r]i-e palê(BAL$^{\text{MEŠ}}$)-ya |
| [ ] | ša i-na $^{\text{GIŠ}}$kussî(GU.ZA) ŠAR$_{4}$-te $^{7}$[ra-bi-iš ú-ši-bu ...] |
| B | ṣābē(ERÍN$^{\text{MEŠ}}$) $^{\text{māt}}$Ya-ú-sa-a-ya e-li-ú |
| $G^{-1}$ | $^{8}$[... a-na e-mu]-qan(?) ra-ma-ni-šú-nu it-ta-at-ki-lu $^{9}$[....-šu]-nu ú-bi-ul |
| $C^{1}$ + D | i-na túkulti($^{\text{GIŠ}}$TUKUL-ti) Aš-šur bēli(EN)-ya $^{10}$[... $^{\text{GIŠ}}$narkabāti(GIGIR$^{\text{MEŠ}}$) ummānāte(ERÍN.ḪI.A$^{\text{MEŠ}}$)-ya a]d-ki |
| $L^{2\text{ה}\zeta}$ | iš-tu $^{\text{URU}}$Ekal(É.KAL)-pi-i-nari(ÍD) [...] $^{11}$[...m]aš-kan-na--te$^{\text{MEŠ}}$-šu-nu aḫ-bu-ut |
| $L^{1\text{ב}\beta}$ | $^{12}$[... di-ik-ta-šu-nu ma-'a-at-t]a a-duk |
| $L^{1\text{ב}\eta}$ | si-ta-te-šu-nu ú-qa-at-[ta] |
| $L^{2\text{ב}\delta}$ | $^{13}$[nap-šat-su-nu ... alpē(GU$_{4}$$^{\text{MEŠ}}$)-šu-nu $^{\text{UDU}}$ṣi-ni$^{\text{MEŠ}}$-šu-nu a-na la-a ma-[ni] $^{14}$[áš-lu-ul . . . |
| $L^{1\text{ג}\zeta\gamma}$ | URU$^{\text{MEŠ}}$-šu-nu mārē(DUMU$^{\text{MEŠ}}$)-šu-nu i-na išāti(IZI[$^{\text{MEŠ}}$]) $^{15}$[áš-ru-up |
| $L^{2\text{ל}\epsilon}$ | šal-la-su-nu kabit(DUGUD-ta) i]š-tu libbi(ŠÀ) $^{\text{māt}}$A-ri-mi ú-še-li [...] |

[In my accession year (and) in] my first regnal year,
after [I nobly ascended] the royal throne,
[...] the troops of the Yausu came up(stream);
[...] They trusted in their own strength;
they brought their [...]
With the support of Aššur, my lord, I mustered [... my chariots (and) troops].
I plundered their depots from the city Ekal-pi-nari [...to...].
I inflicted [upon them a decisive defeat].
Those that survived I slaughtered.
[I carried off] their [herds] (and) flocks without number.
I burned their cities (and) their citizens.
I brought up from the Arameans [valuable booty].

*Episode 2*
(16-22)

| | |
|---|---|
| B | $^{16}$[... sa] iš-tu tar-ṣi $^{\text{I.d}}$Šul-ma-nu-ašaridu(ŠAG) ŠAR$_{4}$ [māt Aš-šur abi-ya] $^{17}$<i-na libbi(ŠÀ) nišē$^{\text{MEŠ}}$ māt Aš-šur ...] .. ù du-a-ki ig-muru-ú-n[i] $^{18}$.. kul-lat(?) //VAT 8890:1// [mārē (DUMU$^{\text{MEŠ}}$)-šu-nu mārāti (DUMU.MUNUS]$^{\text{MEŠ}}$)-šu-nu a-na kaspi(KÙ.BABBAR$^{\text{MEŠ}}$) ipšuru(BÙR$^{\text{MEŠ}}$)-ú-[ni] |

| | |
|---|---|
| $C^{2}$ + | $^{19}$[... i-na qi-bit Aš-šur b]ēli(EN)-ya a-na ḫu-ub-ta-ni lu |
| $L^{2\text{ה}\gamma}$ | aḫ-tab-[bat-su-nu] |
| $L^{1\text{ל}}$ | $^{20}$[di-ik-ta-šu-nu] ma-'a-[at-ta] lu a-duk |
| $L^{2\text{ב}\delta\varepsilon}$ | šal-la-su-nu buša(NÌ.ŠU$^{MEŠ}$)-šu-nu $^{21}$[makkur(NÌ.GA$^{MEŠ}$)-šu- -nu alpē(GU$_{4}^{MEŠ}$)-šu-nu $^{UDU}$]ṣini$^{MEŠ}$-šú-nu áš-lu-la |
| Q | a-na URU-ya [Aš-šur ub-la] |
| [ ] | $^{22}$[....]-li $^{māt}$Ru-qu-ḫu $^{íd}$Za-ba ša $^{māt}$..[...] |

[... which] from the time of Shalmaneser, king of [Assyria, my fore-father], had destroyed [the people of Assyria by ...] and murder;
They had sold all /VAT 8890:1/ their [sons and daughters];
By the command [of Aššur], my lord, I took prisoners.
I inflicted [upon them] a decisive <defeat[.
I carried off their booty, possessions, [property, herds, (and)] flocks;
[I brought (them)] to my city [Aššur ....]
The land Ruqahu, the River Zab of the land [...]

*Episode 3*
(23-32)

| | |
|---|---|
| B | $^{23 māt}$ú-lu-zu //VAT 8890:6// [...] $^{māt}$Y[a-ḫa-a-nu $^{māt}$A-ru-mu ša ku-tal $^{māt}$Pi-[....] $^{24}$[... ša iš-tu ṭar-ṣi $^{I}$Aš-šur-rabi] ŠAR$_{4}$ māt Aš-šur a-na abi(AD)-ya URU$^{MEŠ}$-ni ša šid-di [māti(KUR)-ya] $^{25}$[...] a-na ra-ma-ni-šu-nu ú-ṣab-bi-tu-ú-ni |
| D | $^{GIŠ}$narkabāti(GIGIR$^{MEŠ}$) [ummānāte(ERÍN.ḪI.A$^{MEŠ}$)-ya i-na tukulti($^{GIŠ}$TUKUL-ti)] $^{26}$ša Aš-šur bēli(EN)-ya //VAT 8890:9// [ad-ki] |
| $L^{1\text{ל}}$ | di-ik-ta-šu-nu ma-'a-at-ta a-[duk] |
| $L^{1\text{אגבג}\zeta}$ | $^{27}$[URU$^{MEŠ}$-šu-nu] ap-pu-ul aq-qur i-na išāti(IZI$^{MEŠ}$) áš-ru-pu |
| $H^{\eta}$ | $^{28}$[si-ta-at ummānāte(ERÍN.ḪI.A$^{MEŠ}$)-šu-nu ša] iš-tu pa-an $^{GIŠ}$kakkē(TUKUL$^{MEŠ}$)-ya ip-par-ši-du-ú-[ni] $^{29}$[iš-tu ...] a-di $^{URU}$Ḫal-ḫa-la-uš ša $^{māt}$Sa-[...]-zi $^{30}$[arki(EGIR)-šu-nu] ar-di$_{12}$ |
| $L^{1\text{ל}}$ | [di-i]k-ta-šu-nu ma-'a-at-ta a-duk |
| $L^{2\text{ב}\gamma\varepsilon}$ | $^{31}$šal-la-su-nu [buša(NÌ.ŠU$^{MEŠ}$)-šu-nu áš-lu-la ...] |
| $L^{2\text{ט}\eta}$ | si-ta-te-šu-nu a-su-ḫa i-na [...$^{32}$... |
| $O^{\phi}$ | ... a-na mi-ṣi]-ir māt Aš-šur am-nu-šu-nu-[ti] |

The lands of Uluzu ..., [..Y]ahanu, the land of the Arameans, which is behind the land Pi[...] which from the time of Aššur-ra[bi (II), king of Assyria, my forefather, the cities of the district of [my land, ...] they captured for themselves.
[I mustered] chariots and troops.
[.....] I inflicted upon them a decisive defeat.
I destroyed, ravaged, (and) burnt their [cities].
I pursued [the remainder of their troops which] had fled from my weapons [from ...] to the city Halhalaus of the land Sa[..]zi.

I inflicted upon them a decisive defeat.
(and) [I carried off] their booty and [possessions].
The rest of them I uprooted;[69]
(and) [I settled them] in [...].
(and) I counted them [within] the borders of Assyria.

*Episode 4*
(33-41)

| | |
|---|---|
| $E^2$ | $^{33}$[i-na] qi-bit Aš-šur [bēli(EN)-ya a-na $^{māt}$Ka]d-mu-ḫi lu allik(GIN-ik) |
| $L^{1}$אבגζ | $^{URU}$ša-ra-[... $^{34}$... ap-pu-ul a]q-qur i-na išāti(IZI$^{MEŠ}$) áš-ru-up |
| $L^{2}$א$\alpha$ | $^{I}$Ku-un-da-ab-ḫa-li-e $^{35}$[ŠAR$_4$ $^{māt}$Kad-mu-ḫi i-n]a qabal-(MÚR) ekalli (É.GAL)-šu qa-a-ti lu ik-šu-su |
| $Q^e$ | $^{36}$[... sip]arru(ZABAR$^{MEŠ}$) anāku(AN.NA$^{MEŠ}$) abān(ZÁ) KUR-e šu-qu-[ru] $^{37}$[...]$^{MEŠ}$-šu šalla-su kabit(DUGUD)-ta a-na UR[U-ya] $^{38}$[Aš-šur ub-la |
| $O^6$ | .... -sil-la amēla da-gil pa-ni ša ra-ma-n[i-ya] $^{39}$[i-na $^{GIŠ}$kussî (GU.ZA) be-lu-ti-šu ú-še-šib |
| $Q^a$ | $^{I}$Ku-un-da-ab-ḫa-li-e ŠAR$_4$ $^{māt}$Kad-mu-ḫi $^{40}$[a-na māt Aš-šur ub-la |
| $N^{A\alpha}$ | i-na $^{URU}$Ar]ba-ili(DINGIR) lu a-ku-[uṣ] mašak(KUŠ)-šu $^{41}$[dūra ša $^{URU}$...] -na-áš ú-ḫa-al-lip |

[By] the command of Aššur, [my lord], I marched [to the land of Ka]dmuhu.
The city of Sara[... I destroyed], ravaged, (and) burnt.
I captured Kundabhale, [the king of the land of Kadmuhu] inside his palace.
[....] bronze, tin, precious stones of the mountains, [....], his valuable booty [I brought] to [my] city [Aššur].
[On the throne I set ...-s]illa, a man loyal to me.
Kundabhale, king of the land of Kadmuhu, [I carried off]
[(and) in the city] Arbail I flayed (him and) I draped his skin [over the wall of the city ...]nash.

*Episode 5*
(42-45)

| | |
|---|---|
| $C^2$ + D | $^{42}$[i-na qi-bit Aš-šur bēli(EN)-ya di-ku-ut um-ma-na-te-ya] áš-kun |
| $L^{2}$א | $^{māt}$Mu-uṣ-ra-a-ya $^{43}$[ša it-ti-ya ik-ki-ru-ú-ni] ak-šud |
| $L^{1}$אבגζ | URU$^{MEŠ}$-šú-nu ap-pu-ul aq-qur $^{44}$[i-na išāti(IZI$^{MEŠ}$) áš-ru-up] |
| $L^{2}$ב$e$ | [šal-la-su-nu a-na l]a mi-ni ú-še-ṣa-a |
| Q | $^{45}$[a-na URU-ya Aš-š]ur ub-la |

[By the command of Aššur, my lord,] I mustered [my troops].
I conquered the land of the Muṣri[70] [which had rebelled against me].
I destroyed, ravaged, (and) [burnt] their cities.

I brought forth [their booty without] number (and)
I carried (it) [to my city Aš]šur.

*Episode 6*
(R.1-8)

| | |
|---|---|
| B | **R**$^{1}$[...]-e ša Aš-šur bēli(EN)-ya ša iš-tu $^{2}$[tar-ṣi ....] ma-da-tu a-na Aš-šur bēli(EN)-ya $^{3}$[ik-lu-ú |
| $C^{1,3}$ | i-na tukulti($^{GIŠ}$TUKUL-ti) Aš-šur bēli(EN)-ya ù $^{d}$urigalli(-URI$_{3}$.GAL) a-lik pa-ni-ya $^{4}$[... |
| $O^{\phi}$ | a-na šal-la-a]t ra-ma-ni-ya lu am-nu |
| $P^{2}$ | $^{5}$[......] EN uzna(GEŠTU) rapaš(DAGAL)-ta iqîš(NÀ.BA) $^{6}$[.... bē]lu(EN)-ti-ya ša da-ra-a-te $^{7}$[...] ilāni(DINGIR$^{MEŠ}$-ni)-ya bīt(É) Aš-šur bīt(É) $^{d}$Šamaš(UTU) $^{8}$[...uš-še] ekal(É.GAL)-lim-ya ad-di |

[....] of Aššur, my lord, which since [the time of .... had withheld] tribute from Aššur, my lord.
[With the support of Aššur], my [lord] and the divine standard which goes before me [... to] my own [...] I counted.
[....who] granted wisdom [....of] my durable dominion [...of] my gods, the temple of Aššur, the temple of Šamaš, [....the foundations] of my palace I laid.

*Episode 7*
(R.9-14)

| | |
|---|---|
| $C^{2}$ + $E^{2}$ | [$^{9}$i-na qi-bit Aš-šur bēli(EN)-ya a-na $^{māt}$Kir-r]i-ú-ri lu a-lik |
| $L^{2\aleph\zeta}$ | $^{URU}$Šu-ḫu $^{URU}$[...] $^{10URU}$Si-me-ir-ra $^{māt}$Lu[...] URU$^{MEŠ}$-ni ša $^{māt}$Kir-ri-ú-ri $^{11}$[...][lu ak-šud] |
| $L^{2\beth\delta\epsilon}$ | šal-la-su-nu buša(NÌ.ŠU)$^{MEŠ}$-šu-nu makkur(NÌ.GA)$^{MEŠ}$-šu-nu $^{12}$[alpē(GU$_{4}$$^{MEŠ}$)-šu-nu $^{UDU}$ṣi-ni$^{MEŠ}$-šu-nu] ú-še-ṣa-a |
| Q | a-na URU-ya Aš-šur ub-la |
| $P^{3}$ | $^{13}$[ilāni(DINGIR$^{MEŠ}$-ni)-šu-nu] ki-i kiš-šu-te a-na Aš-šur bēli(EN)-ya lu a-qiš |
| $L^{2\text{ח}\delta\epsilon}$ | $^{14}$[...] ša-aš-šá-a |
| $P^{3}$ | a-na Aš-šur bēli(EN)-ya lu a-qiš |

By the command of Ašš[ur, my lord,] I marched [to the land of Kirr]iuru.
I conquered the cities of Šuhu, [...], Simerra, the land of Lu[...], cities of the land of Kirriuru [...].
I brought forth their booty, possessions, property, [herds (and) flocks];
I took (them) to my city Aššur.
I gave [their gods] as gifts to Aššur, my lord.
I carried off [....]
I gave (it/them) to Aššur, my lord.

These seven episodes can be charted:

| Episode 1 | Episode 2 | Episode 3 | Episode 4 | Episode 5 | Episode 6 | Episode 7 |
|---|---|---|---|---|---|---|
| $A^2$ | - | - | - | - | - | - |
| B | B | B | - | - | B | - |
| $G^{-1}$ | - | - | - | - | - | - |
| - | - | - | $E^2$ | - | - | $E^2$ |
| $C^1$ | $C^2$ | - | - | $C^2$ | $C^{1,3}$ | $C^2$ |
| D | - | D | - | D | - | - |
| $L^{2\text{ה}\zeta}$ | $L^{2\text{ה}\gamma}$ | - | - | $L^{2\text{א}}$ | - | $L^{2\text{א}\zeta}$ |
| $L^{1\text{ב}\beta}$ | $L^{1\text{ל}}$ | $L^{1\text{ל}}$ | - | - | - | - |
| $L^{1\text{ב}\eta}$ | - | $L^{1\text{אבג}\zeta}$ | $L^{1\text{אבג}\zeta}$ | $L^{1\text{אבג}\zeta}$ | - | - |
| - | - | $H^{\eta}$ | - | - | - | - |
| - | $L^{1\text{ל}}$ | - | - | - | - | - |
| $L^{2\text{ב}\delta}$ | $L^{2\text{ב}\delta\epsilon}$ | $L^{2\text{ב}\gamma\epsilon}$ | - | - | - | $L^{2\text{ב}\delta\epsilon}$ |
| $L^{1\text{ב}\zeta\gamma}$ | - | - | - | - | - | - |
| $L^{2\text{ל}\epsilon}$ | - | $L^{2\text{ב}\eta}$ | $L^{2\text{אב}}$ | $L^{2\text{ב}\epsilon}$ | - | $L^{2\text{ה}\delta\epsilon}$ |
| - | - | - | $Q^{e}$ | - | - | - |
| - | - | $O^{\phi}$ | $O^{6}$ | - | $O^{\phi}$ | - |
| - | Q | - | $Q^{a}$ | Q | - | Q |
| | | | $N^{A\alpha}$ | . | | |
| | | | | | $P^2$ | $P^3$ |

Again, the use of key components maintains the structural unity of the narrative, and produces an iterative scheme. This can be seen especially in the use of C {Note how often the national deity ordered the conquest of the various lands—the Assyrian justification (cf. Josh. 1)}, $L^{1\text{אבג}\zeta}$, $L^{2\text{ב}\delta\epsilon}$, O, and Q.

### 3. *Aššur-nasir-pal II*[71]

The annalistic narrative sections of Aššur-nasir-pal II's inscriptions reveal the use of stereotyped syntagms in the creation of an iterative scheme. The analysis of the Italian team (*SAA-MA*) has already disclosed the use of these syntagms. Here we are looking at three episodes which manifest the iterative scheme and its consequent high-redundance message.

*II.39-43*

| | |
|---|---|
| $a^1$ | [39]ištu(TA) uš-ma-ni an-ni-te-ma at-tu-muš |
| $E^2$ | a-na URU$^{\text{MEŠ}}$ šá ṣīr $^{\text{KUR}}$Ni-ṣir šá a-šat-šú-nu ma-am-ma la-a e-mu-ru a-lik |

| | |
|---|---|
| $L^{2\text{א}\zeta}$ | $^{URU}$La-ar-bu-sa $^{40}$URU dan-nu-ti-šú šá $^{I}$Ki-ir-ti-a-ra 8 URU$^{MEŠ}$ šá li-me-tu-šú akšud(KUR-ud) |
| $G^{D1}$ | ṣābē(ERÍN$^{MEŠ}$) ig-dur-ru |
| $G^{D4}$ | KUR-ú mar-ṣu iṣ-ṣab-tú |
| | KUR-ú kīma(GIN$_7$) zi-qip patri(GÍR) parzilli(AN.BAR) $^{41}$še-e-su na-a-di |
| H | šarru itti ummānāti(ERÍN.ḪI.A$^{MEŠ}$)-šú arki(EGIR)-šú-nu e-li |
| $L^{1\text{מ}\beta}$ | ina qé-reb KUR-e pag-ri-šú-nu ad-di |
| $L^{1\text{ב}\beta}$ | 172 ṣābē(ERÍN$^{MEŠ}$) ti-du-ki-šú-nu a-duk |
| $L^{1\text{י}\beta}$ | ṣābē(ERÍN$^{MEŠ}$) $^{42}$ma'aduti(ḪI.A$^{MEŠ}$) ina ka-a-pi šá KUR-e at-bu-uk |
| $L^{2\text{ד}\gamma e}$ | šal-la-su-nu bušá$^{MEŠ}$-šú-nu alpē(GU$_4$)$^{MEŠ}$-šú-nu $^{UDU}$ṣi-ni-šú-nu utira (GUR-ra) |
| $L^{1\text{גב}\zeta}$ | URU$^{MEŠ}$-ni ina išāti(IZI$^{MEŠ}$) $^{43}$ašrup(GIBÍL-up) |
| $N^{b}$ | qaqqadē(SAG.DU$^{MEŠ}$)-šú-nu ina $^{GIŠ}$gu-up-ni šá KUR-e e-'e-il |
| $N^{d}$ | $^{LÚ}$ba-tul$^{MEŠ}$-šú-nu $^{MÍ}$ba-tu-la-ti-šú-nu a-na maqlute(GIBÍL-te) ašrup (GIBÍL) |
| Q + f | ina uš-ma-ni-ia utira(GUR-ra) be-dàk |

I departed from this camp.
I marched to the cities in the plain of Nisir which no one had ever seen.
I conquered Larbusa, the fortified city of Kirtiara (and) 8 cities in its environs.
The (enemy) troops were afraid (and)
they took to a rugged mountain.
The mountain has a peak sharp like the point of an iron dagger.
The king went up after them with his army.
I threw down their corpses on the mountain.
I massacred 172 of their troops; (and)
I poured out many troops on the mountain ledges.
I brought back booty, possessions, herds and flocks.
I burned their cities.
I hung their heads on the mountain trees.
I burned their adolescent boys (and) girls.
I returned to my camp (and) spent the night.

*II.53-60*

| | |
|---|---|
| $E^{13}$ | ištu(TA) šēp(GÌR) $^{KUR}$Si-ma-ki $^{GIŠ}$narkabāti(GIGIR$^{MEŠ}$) dannūtu(KALAG-tu) pit-ḫal-lu ašarid(SAG-RID)-su i-si-ya a-si-kin |
| $E^{11}$ | mu-šu a-di $^{54}$na-ma-ri ar-te-di |
| $E^{6}$ | $^{ÍD}$Tur-na-at e-te-bir |
| $E^{7}$ | ina mit-ḫar sa-an-te a-na māt(KUR) $^{URU}$Am-ma-li URU dan-nu-ti-šú šá $^{I}$A-ra-áš-tu aq-ṭí-ib |
| $F^{2}$ | $^{55}$ina mit-ḫu-ṣi ti-du-ki URU a-si-bi aktašad(KUR-ad) |
| $L^{1\text{צ}\beta}$ | 800 ME ṣābē(ERÍN$^{MEŠ}$) mun-daḫ-ṣi-šú-nu ina $^{GIŠ}$kakkē-(TUKUL$^{MEŠ}$) ú-šam-qit |

| | |
|---|---|
| L[1נβ] | pag-ri$^{\text{MEŠ}}$-šú-nu sūqī(SILA) URU-šú-nu ú-mal-li |
| L[1קβ] | damē(ÚŠ$^{\text{MEŠ}}$)-šú-nu $^{56}$bītatišunu(É.ḪI.A$^{\text{MEŠ}}$-šú-nu) as-ru-up |
| L[2גβ] | $^{\text{LÚ}}$ṣābē(ERÍN$^{\text{MEŠ}}$) ma'dūte(ḪI.A$^{\text{MEŠ}}$) balṭūte(TI.LA$^{\text{MEŠ}}$) ina qati(ŠU-ti) ú-ṣa-bi-ta |
| L[2בγε] | šal-la-su-nu ma'atta(ḪI.A$^{\text{MEŠ}}$) áš-lu-la |
| L[1אבגζ] | URU a-púl a-qur ina išāti(IZI$^{\text{MEŠ}}$) ašrup(GIBÍL-up) |
| L[2אζ] | $^{\text{URU}}$Ḫu-du-un $^{57}$u 30 URU$^{\text{MEŠ}}$-ni šá li-me-tu-šú-nu akšud (KUR-ud) |
| L[1ל] | diktašunu(GAZ-šú-nu) a-duk |
| L[2בγε] | šal-la-su-nu alpē(GU$_4$$^{\text{MEŠ}}$)-šú-nu $^{\text{UDU}}$ṣi-ni-šú-nu áš-lul |
| L[1אבגζ] | URU$^{\text{MEŠ}}$-šú-nu a-púl a-qur ina išāti(IZI$^{\text{MEŠ}}$) áš-ru-up |
| N[d] | $^{\text{LÚ}}$ba-tul$^{\text{MEŠ}}$-šú-nu $^{58\text{MÍ}}$ba-tu-la-ti-šú-nu ana maqlūte(GIBÍL-te) ašrup(GIBÍL) |
| L[2אζ] | $^{\text{URU}}$Ki-ṣir-tu URU dan-nu-ti-šú-nu šá $^{\text{I}}$Ṣa-bi-i-ni a-di 10 URU$^{\text{MEŠ}}$ šá li-me-tu-šú-nu akšud(KUR-ud) |
| L[1ל] | diktašunu(GAZ-šú-nu) a-duk |
| L[2בγε] | šal-la-su-nu $^{59}$áš-lul |
| L[1אבגζ] | URU$^{\text{MEŠ}}$ šá $^{\text{URU}}$Ba-ra-a-a šá $^{\text{I}}$Ki-ir-ti-a-ra šá $^{\text{URU}}$Du-ra-a-a šá $^{\text{URU}}$Bu-ni-sa-a-a a-di ni-rib šá $^{\text{KUR}}$Ḫaš-mar a-púl a-qur ina išāti(IZI$^{\text{MEŠ}}$) ašrup(GIBÍL-up) |
| L[1דζ] | $^{60}$ana tīli(DU$_6$) u kar-me utēr(GUR-er) |

From the foot of Mount Simaki I took with me strong chariots, cavalry (and) crack troops.
I continued travelling through the night until dawn.[72]
I crossed the Turnat River.
At first light I approached the land[73] of the city of Ammali, the fortified city of Araštu.
In a clash of arms I besieged the city (and) conquered (it).
I felled with the sword 800 of the combat troops.
I filled the streets of their city with their corpses.
I dyed their houses red with their blood.
I captured many troops alive (and)
I carried off much booty.
I razed, destroyed (and) burned the city.
I conquered the city Hudun and 30 cities in its environs.
I massacred them.
I carried off their booty, herds and flocks.
I razed, destroyed and burned their cities.
I burned their adolescent boys (and) girls.
I conquered the city Kisirtu, the fortified city of Sabini, together with ten cities of its environs.
I massacred them.
I carried off booty.
I razed, destroyed (and) burned the cities of the Bareans, of the man Kirtiara, of the Dureans, (and) of the Buniseans, as far as the pass of Mount Hašmar.

*II.103-112*

| | |
|---|---|
| a$^1$ | ina tukulti($^{GIŠ}$TUKUL-ti) Aššur bēli(EN)-ya ištu(TA) $^{URU}$Tu-uš-ḫa-an a-tú-muš |
| E$^{13}$ | $^{GIŠ}$narkabāti(GIGIR$^{MEŠ}$) DAN-tu pit-ḫal-lu ašarid(SAG)-su i-si-ya a-si-kin |
| E$^6$ | ina rak-su-te $^{104ÍD}$Idiglat e-te-bir |
| E$^{11}$ | kal mu-ši-ti ar-te-di |
| E$^7$ | a-na $^{URU}$Pi-tu-ra URU dan-nu-ti-šú-nu šá $^{māt}$Di-ir-ra-a-ia aq-ṭí-ib |
| H$^D$ | URU marṣi(GIG) dan-niš |
| | $^{105}$2 dūrāni(BÀD$^{MEŠ}$-ni) la-a-bi |
| | kir-ḫu-šu kīma(GIN$_7$) ubān(ŠU-SI) KUR-e šá-kin |
| C$^3$ + | ina idāti(DA$^{MEŠ}$) ṣīrāti(MAḪ$^{MEŠ}$) šá Aššur bēli(EN)-ya ina gi-biš |
| I | ummānāti(ERÍN.ḪI.A$^{MEŠ}$)-ya tāhāzi(MÈ-ia) šit-mu-ri $^{106}$it-ti-šú-nu am-da-ḫiṣ |
| | ina 2 u$_4$-me la-am $^d$Šamaš na-pa-ḫi kīma(GIN$_7$) $^d$Adad šá riḫṣi (GÌR.BAL) eli(UGU)-šú-nu áš-gu-um |
| | nab-lu eli(UGU)-šú-nu ú-šá-za-nin |
| | ina šip-ṣi$^{107}$u da-na-ni mun-daḫ-ṣi-a kīma(GIN$_7$) $^d$Ze-e($^{MUŠEN}$) eli(UGU)-šú-nu i-še-'e |
| $\mathrm{L}^{2\text{א}\zeta}$ | URU aktašad(KUR-ad) |
| $\mathrm{L}^{1\text{צ}\beta}$ | 800 ME ṣābē(ERÍN$^{MEŠ}$) mun-daḫ-ṣi-šú-nu ina $^{GIŠ}$kakkē-(TUKUL$^{MEŠ}$) ú-šam-qit |
| $\mathrm{L}^{1\text{ה}\beta}$ | qaqqadē(SAG.DU$^{MEŠ}$)-šú-nu $^{108}$unikis(KUD-is) |
| $\mathrm{L}^{2\text{ג}\beta}$ | ṣābē(ERÍN$^{MEŠ}$) balṭīti(TI.LA$^{MEŠ}$) ma'adīti(ḪI.A$^{MEŠ}$) ina qāti(ŠU) uṣabita (DIB-ta) |
| $\mathrm{L}^{1\text{ג}\eta}$ | si-ta-ti-šú-nu ina išāti(IZI$^{MEŠ}$) ašrup(GIBÍL-up) |
| $\mathrm{L}^{2\text{ב}\gamma e}$ | šal-la-su-nu kabitta(DUGUD-ta) aš-lul |
| N$^f$ | a-si-tu šá balṭūti(TI.LA$^{MEŠ}$) šá qaqqadē(SAG.DU$^{MEŠ}$) $^{109}$ina pu-ut abulli(KÁ.GAL)-šú ar-ṣip |
| N$^b$ | 700 ME ṣābē(ERÍN$^{MEŠ}$) ina pu-ut abulli(KÁ.GAL)-šú-nu a-na $^{GIŠ}$zi-qi-pi ú-za-qip |
| $\mathrm{L}^{1\text{אב}\zeta}$ | URU a-púl a-qur |
| $\mathrm{L}^{1\text{ד}\zeta}$ | ana tīli(DU$_6$) u kar-me utēr(GUR-er) |
| N$^d$ | $^{LÚ}$ba-tul$^{MEŠ}$-šú-nu $^{110MÍ}$ba-tu-la-ti-šú-nu ana maqlūte(GIBÍL-te) ašrup(GIBÍL) |
| $\mathrm{L}^{2\text{א}\zeta}$ | $^{URU}$Ku-ú-ku-nu šá pi-i ni-rib šá KUR-e $^{KUR}$Ma-at-ni ak-šud |
| $\mathrm{L}^{1\text{צ}\beta}$ | 700 ME ṣābē(ERÍN$^{MEŠ}$) ti-du-ki-šú-nu ina $^{GIŠ}$kakkē(TU-KUL$^{MEŠ}$) ú-šam-qit |
| $\mathrm{L}^{2\text{ב}\gamma e}$ | $^{111}$šal-la-su-nu ma'attu(ḪI.A) aš-lul |
| $\mathrm{L}^{2\text{א}\zeta}$ | 50 URU$^{MEŠ}$-ni šá $^{māt}$Di-ra-a akšud(KUR-ud) |
| $\mathrm{L}^{1\text{ל}}$ | dikta(GAZ$^{MEŠ}$)-šú-nu a-duk |
| $\mathrm{L}^{2\text{ב}\gamma e}$ | šal-la-su-nu aš-lul |
| $\mathrm{L}^{2\text{ג}\beta}$ | 50 ṣābē(ERÍN$^{MEŠ}$) balṭūti(TI.LA$^{MEŠ}$) ú-ṣa-bi-ta |
| $\mathrm{L}^{1\text{אבג}\zeta}$ | URU$^{MEŠ}$ ap-púl a-qur ina išāti(IZI$^{MEŠ}$) ašrup(GIBÍL-up) |
| $\mathrm{L}^{1\text{י}}$ | me-lam bēlu(EN)-ti-ya eli(UGU)-šú-nu at-bu-uk |

With the assistance of Aššur my lord, I departed from Tušhan.
I took with me strong chariots, cavalry, (and) crack troops.
I crossed the Tigris by means of a bridge of rafts.[74]
I travelled all night (and)
I approached the city of Pitura, the fortified city of the Dirraens.
The city was very difficult.
It was surrounded by 2 walls;
its citadel was like a mountain summit.
With the exalted strength of Aššur my lord (and) with a fierce battle I fought with them.
For two days, before sunrise, I thundered against them like Adad-of-the-Devastation, (and)
I rained down flames upon them.
With the might and power of my combat troops I flew against them like the Storm Bird.
I conquered the city.
I felled with sword 800 of their combat troops (and)
I cut off their heads.
I captured many troops alive.
I carried off valuable booty.
I piled up a heap of live (men and) of heads before his gate.
I impaled 700 troops on stakes before their gate.
I razed (and) destroyed the city.
I turned the city into ruin hills.
I burned their adolescent boys (and) girls.
I conquered the city Kukunu which is at the entrance to the pass of Mount Matni.
I felled with the sword 700 their fighting men.
I carried off much booty.
I conquered 50 cities of the Dirraens.
I massacred them.
I carried off their booty.
I captured 50 soldiers alive.
I razed, destroyed (and) burned the cities.
I poured out against them my lordly radiance.

| II.39-43 | II.53-60 | II.103-112 |
|---|---|---|
| $a^1$ | - | $a^1$ |
| E | - | - |
| - | $E^{13}$ | $E^{13}$ |
| - | $E^{11}$ | $E^{11}$ |
| - | $E^6$ | $E^6$ |
| - | $E^7$ | $E^7$ |
| - | $F^2$ | - |
| $G^{\Delta 1}$ | - | - |
| $G^{\Delta 4}$ | - | - |
| H | - | $H^{\Delta}$ |

| | | |
|---|---|---|
| - | - | $C^{3+I}$ |
| $L^{2\text{א}\zeta}$ | - | $L^{2\text{א}\zeta}$ |
| - | $L^{1\text{צ}\beta}$ | $L^{1\text{צ}\beta}$ |
| $L^{1\text{מ}\beta}$ | $L^{1\text{ב}\beta}$ | $L^{1\text{ה}\beta}$ |
| - | $L^{2\text{ג}\beta}$ | $L^{2\text{ג}\beta}$ |
| $L^{1\text{ג}\zeta}$ | - | $L^{1\text{ג}\eta}$ |
| - | $L^{2\text{ב}\gamma\epsilon}$ | $L^{2\text{ב}\gamma\epsilon}$ |
| - | $L^{1\text{אבג}\zeta}$ | $L^{1\text{אבג}\zeta}$ |
| - | $L^{2\text{א}\zeta}$ | - |
| $L^{1\text{ב}\beta}$ | $L^{1\text{ל}}$ | $L^{1\text{צ}\zeta}$ |
| - | $L^{2\text{ב}\gamma\epsilon}$ | - |
| - | $L^{1\text{אבג}\zeta}$ | - |
| $L^{1\text{י}\beta}$ | - | $L^{1\text{י}}$ |
| $N^{b}$ | - | $N^{b}$ |
| $N^{d}$ | $N^{d}$ | $N^{d}$ |
| - | $L^{2\text{א}\zeta}$ | $L^{2\text{א}\zeta}$ |
| - | $L^{1\text{ל}}$ | $L^{1\text{ל}}$ |
| $L^{2\text{ד}\gamma\epsilon}$ | $L^{2\text{ב}\gamma\epsilon}$ | $L^{2\text{ב}\gamma\epsilon}$ |
| - | - | $L^{2\text{ג}\beta}$ |
| - | $L^{1\text{אבג}\zeta}$ | $L^{1\text{אבג}\zeta}$ |
| - | $L^{1\text{ד}\zeta}$ | $L^{1\text{ד}\zeta}$ |
| Q + f | - | - |

4. *Shalmaneser III*[75]
(Marble Slab Inscription)[76]

There are numerous inscriptions from the reign of Shalmaneser III which preserve the different recensions of his annals. It would be impossible to present an analysis of them all. Thus we have chosen to show particular episodes from the Marble Slab inscription to demonstrate the use of syntagmic patterning in the creation of an iterative scheme in this king's royal texts.

*Episode 19*
(III. 37b-45a)

| | |
|---|---|
| $A^{2}$ | ina XVII palê(BAL$^{\text{MEŠ}}$)-ya |
| $E^{6}$ | $^{\text{íd}}$Puratta $^{38}$e-bir |
| M | ma-da-tú šá ŠAR$_4$$^{\text{MEŠ}}$-ni ša māt Ḫat-te $^{39}$am-ḫur |
| $E^{12}$ | a-na KUR-e $^{\text{KUR}}$Ḫa-ma-ni e-li |
| $R^{3}$ | $^{40\text{GIŠ}}$gušūrē(ÙR$^{\text{MEŠ}}$) $^{\text{GIŠ}}$e-ri-ni a-ki-si |
| Q | a-na $^{41}$URU-ya Aš-šur ub-la |
| $a^{1,2}$ | ina ta-ya-ar-ti-ya $^{42}$ša issu $^{\text{KUR}}$Ḫa-ma-ni |

$R^{1x}$ 1 šu-ši 3 $^{\text{GUD}}$rīmāni(AM$^{\text{MEŠ}}$) $^{43}$dan-nu-te šu-ut qar-ni gít-ma-lu-te ina $^{\text{URU}}$Zu-qar-ri $^{41}$ša šēpē(GÌR.II) am-ma-a-te ša $^{\text{íd}}$Puratti a-duk

$R^{2x}$ 4 balṭūte(TI.LA$^{\text{MEŠ}}$) $^{45}$ina qa-te aṣ-bat

In my 17th regnal year:
I crossed the Euphrates.
I received the tribute of the kings of the land of Hatti.
I went up to Mt. Hamanu (Amanus).
I cut down logs of cedar and juniper.
I brought (them) to my city Aššur.
On my return from the Mt. Hamanu (Amanus):
I killed 63 mighty wild bulls, with horns, perfect specimens[77] in the area of the town of Zuqarri on the opposite bank of the Euphrates River.
I caught 4 alive with (my) hands!

*Episode 21*
(IV. 15b-22a)

$A^2$ ina XIX palê(BAL$^{\text{MEŠ}}$)-ya
$E^6$ $^{16}$17-šú $^{\text{íd}}$Puratta e-bir
M ma-da-tú ša ŠAR$_4$$^{\text{MEŠ}}$-ni $^{17}$ša māt Ḫat-te am-ḫur
$E^{12}$ a-na $^{\text{KUR}}$Ḫa-ma-ni e-li
$R^3$ $^{18\text{GIŠ}}$gušūrē(ÙR$^{\text{MEŠ}}$) $^{\text{GIŠ}}$e-ri-ni $^{\text{GIŠ}}$burāši(ŠIM.LI) a-ki-si
Q $^{19}$a-na URU-ya Aš-šur ub-la
$a^{1,2}$ ina ta-ya-ar-ti-ya $^{42}$ša issu $^{\text{KUR}}$Ḫa-ma-ni
$R^{1x}$ 10 $^{\text{GUD}}$rīmāni(AM$^{\text{MEŠ}}$) dan-nu-te šu-ut $^{21}$qar-ni gít-ma-lu-te 2 $^{\text{GUD}}$būrē(AMAR$^{\text{MEŠ}}$) ina $^{\text{URU}}$Zu-qar-ri $^{22}$ša šēpē(GÌR.II) am-ma-a-te ša $^{\text{íd}}$Puratti a-duk

In my 19th year:
I crossed the Euphrates River for the 17th time.
I received the tribute of the kings of the land of Hatti.
I went up to Mt. Hamanu (Amanus).
I cut down logs of cedar and juniper.
I brought (them) to my city Aššur.
On my return from the Mt. Hamanu (Amanus):
I killed 10 mighty wild bulls, with horns, perfect specimens (and) 2 calves (as hunted game)[78] in the area of the town of Zuqarri on the opposite bank of the Euphrates River.

These two episodes can be charted as follows:

| Episode 19 | Episode 21 |
|---|---|
| $A^2$ | $A^2$ |
| $E^6$ | $E^6$ |
| M | M |
| $E^{12}$ | $E^{12}$ |
| $R^3$ | $R^3$ |

| Q | Q |
|---|---|
| $a^{1,2}$ | $a^{1,2}$ |
| $R^{1\kappa}$ | $R^{1\kappa}$ |
| $R^{2\kappa}$ | - |

One can easily see that these two episodes are identical except for the very last syntagm ($R^{2\kappa}$)!

Episodes 5, 11, 12, and 22 also demonstrate the syntagmic patterning:

*Episode 5*
(I. 48b - II.9a)

| | |
|---|---|
| $A^2$ | ina IV palê(BAL$^{\text{MEŠ}}$)-ya |
| $E^6$ | $^{49\text{íd}}$Puratta ina mi-li-šá e-bir |
| H | arkī(EGIR) $^{50\text{I}}$A-ḫu-ni mār(DUMU) A-di-ni ar-te-di |
| $G^{\Delta 4}$ | $^{51\text{KUR}}$ši-tam-rat ú-ba-an KUR-e ša a-ḫat Col. II $^{1\text{íd}}$Puratti a-na dan-nu-ti-šú iš-kun |
| $L^{2\kappa\zeta}$ | $^{2}$ú-ba-an KUR-e a-si-bi ak-ta-šad |
| $L^{2\mho\alpha\beta}$ | $^{3\text{I}}$A-ḫu-ni mār(DUMU) A-di-ni a-di ilāni(DINGIR$^{\text{MEŠ}}$-ni)-šu $^{4\text{GIŠ}}$narkabāti (GIGIR$^{\text{MEŠ}}$)-šu sīsê(ANŠE.KUR.RA$^{\text{MEŠ}}$)-šú 20 lim 2 lim $^{5}$ummānāti(ERIN.ḪI.A$^{\text{MEŠ}}$)-šú a-su-ḫa-šu |
| Q | a-na URU-ya $^{6}$Aš-šur ub-la |
| $a^2$ | ina šattim-ma ši-a-te |
| $E^9$ | $^{\text{KUR}}$Kúl-la-ar $^{7}$at-ta-bal-kát |
| $E^4$ | a-na māt Za-mu-a ša bīt(É)-a-ni $^{8}$at-ta-rad |
| $L^{2\kappa\zeta}$ | URU$^{\text{MEŠ}}$-ni ša $^{\text{I}}$Ni-iq-di-ma $^{9}$[$^{\text{I}}$Ni-iq-di-ma] akšud(KUR-ud) |

In my fourth regnal year:
I crossed the Euphrates at its flood stage.
I pursued after Ahuni of Bit-Adini.
He made Shitamrat, a mountain peak on the bank of the Euphrates, into his fortress.
I besieged (and) I conquered the mountain top.
I uprooted Ahuni of Bit-Adini together with his gods, his chariots, his horses (and) 22,000 of his troops.
I brought them to my city, Aššur.
In that same year:
I crossed over the Kullar border.
I descended into the interior of the land of Zamua.
I conquered the cities of Niqdima.

*Episode 10*
(II. 35-44)

| | |
|---|---|
| $A^2$ | $^{35}$ina IX palê(BAL$^{\text{MEŠ}}$)-a ina šanê gir-ri-ya |
| $L^{2\kappa\zeta}$ | $^{36\text{URU}}$Ga-na-na-te akšud(KUR-ud) |

| | |
|---|---|
| E$^{12}$ | $^{I\,d}$Marduk-bēl-ú-sa-te $^{37}$a-na šu-zu-ub napšāti(ZI$^{MEŠ}$)-šú a-na KUR-e $^{38}$e-li |
| H | arkī(EGIR)-šú ar-di |
| L$^{1\aleph\alpha\beta}$ | $^{I\,d}$Marduk-bēl-ú-ṣa-te $^{39}$a-di ṣābē(ERÍN$^{MEŠ}$) bēl(EN) ḫi-aṭ-ṭi šá it-te-šú $^{40}$ina $^{GIŠ}$kakki(TUKUL) ú-šam-qit |
| P$^{3}$ | niqê(SISKUR$^{MEŠ}$) $^{41}$ina $^{URU}$Bābili(KÁ.DINGIR.RA.KI) $^{URU}$Bár-sip$_{4}$(BÁR.SAP.KI) $^{42\,URU}$Ku-te-e ēpuš(DÙ-e) |
| E$^{4}$ | a-na māt Kal-di ú-ri-id |
| L$^{2\aleph\zeta}$ | $^{43}$URU$^{MEŠ}$-ni-šú-nu akšud(KUR-ud) |
| M | man(!)-da-tú šá ŠAR$_{4}$$^{MEŠ}$-ni $^{44}$šá māt Kal-di ina $^{URU}$Babili(KÁ. DINGIR.RA.KI) am-ḫur |

In my ninth regnal year; in my second campaign:
I conquered the city of Gananate.
Marduk-bel-usate went up into the mountains in order to save his life.
I pursued after him.
Marduk-bel-usate together with the warriors of rebellion who were with him I felled (laid low) with the sword.
I made offerings in the cities of Babylon, Borsippa, (and) Cuta.
I descended to the land of Kaldu.
I conquered their cities.
I received tribute of the kings of the land of Kaldu in the city of Babylon.

*Episode 11*
(II. 45 - 50)

| | |
|---|---|
| A$^{2}$ | $^{45}$ina X palê(BAL$^{MEŠ}$)-ya |
| E$^{6}$ | 8-šú $^{íd}$Puratta e-bir |
| L$^{2\aleph\zeta}$ | $^{46}$URU$^{MEŠ}$-ni ša $^{I}$Sa-an-ga-ra $^{URU}$Gar-ga-miš-a-a [akšud(KUR-ud)] |
| E$^{3}$ | $^{47}$issu URU$^{MEŠ}$-ni ša $^{URU}$Gar-ga-miš-a-a at-tu-muš |
| E$^{7}$ | $^{48}$a-na URU$^{MEŠ}$-ni ša $^{I}$A-ra-me aq-ṭí-rib |
| L$^{2\aleph\zeta}$ | $^{49\,URU}$Ar-ne-e URU ŠAR$_{4}$-ti-šu a-di 1 me $^{50}$URU$^{MEŠ}$-ni ša li-me-tu-šú akšud(KUR-ud) |

In my tenth regnal year:
I crossed the Euphrates River for the eighth time.
<I conquered> the cities of Sangara of Karkamiš.
I moved on from the cities of Karkamiš; (and)
I drew near to the cities of Arame.
I conquered the city of Arnê, his royal city, together with 100 of the towns of its neighborhood.

*Episode 12*
(II. 51-57)

| | |
|---|---|
| A$^{2}$ | $^{51}$ina XI palê(BAL$^{MEŠ}$)-ya |
| E$^{6}$ | 9-šu $^{⌈íd}$Puratta e-bir |

| | |
|---|---|
| $L^{2ζ}$ | $^{52}$97 URU$^{MEŠ}$-ni šá $^{I}$Sa-an-ga-ra $^{53}$1 me URU$^{MEŠ}$-ni šá $^{I}$A-ra-me akšud(KUR-ud) |
| $E^{8}$ | $^{54}$ši-di $^{KUR}$Ḫa-ma-ni aṣ-bat |
| $E^{9}$ | $^{KUR}$Ya-ra-qu $^{55}$attabalkat |
| $E^{4}$ | a-na URU$^{MEŠ}$-ni šá $^{KUR}$A-ma-ta-a-a $^{56}$at-ta-rad |
| $L^{2ζ}$ | $^{URU}$Ab-ši-ma-ku $^{57}$a-di 89 URU$^{MEŠ}$-ni akšud(KUR-ud) |

In my eleventh regnal year:
I crossed the Euphrates for the ninth time.
I conquered 97 cities of Sangara (and) 100 cities of Arame.
I took (the way) along Mt. Hamanu (Mt. Amanus).
I passed over the land of Yaraqu.
I went down to the cities of the land of Hamath; (and)
I conquered the city of Absimaku together with 89 towns.

*Episode 22*
(IV. 22b - 34)

| | |
|---|---|
| $A^{2}$ | ina XX palê(BAL$^{MEŠ}$)-ya |
| $E^{6}$ | $^{23}$20-šú $^{íd}$Puratta e-bir |
| D | ŠAR$_{4}$$^{MEŠ}$-ni ša māt Ḫat-ti $^{24}$kalâ-šú-nu it-ti-ya ad-ki |
| $E^{9}$ | $^{KUR}$Ḫa-ma-nu attabalkat |
| $E^{4}$ | $^{25}$ana URU$^{MEŠ}$-ni ša $^{I}$Ka-te-i $^{KUR}$Qa-ú-a-a $^{26}$at-ta-ra-da |
| $L^{2אζ}$ | $^{URU}$Lu-sa-an-da $^{URU}$A-bar-na-ni $^{27URU}$Ki-su-at-ni URU$^{MEŠ}$-ni dannūte (KAL$^{MEŠ}$) a-di $^{28}$URU$^{MEŠ}$-ni a-na la ma-ni issu rēš URU$^{MEŠ}$-ni-šú $^{29}$a-di qa-na URU$^{MEŠ}$-ni-šú ak-šu-ud |
| $L^{1ל}$ | dīkta(GAZ)-šú-nu $^{30}$a-duk |
| $L^{2בγε}$ | šal-la-su-nu áš-lu-la |
| $P^{1}$ | II ṣa-lam ŠAR$_{4}$-ti-ya $^{31}$ēpuš ta-na-ti kiš-šu-ti-a ina libbi al-ṭu-ur $^{32}$ištēn ina rēš URU$^{MEŠ}$-ni-šú šanû ina qa-ni URU$^{MEŠ}$-ni-šú $^{33}$ina rēš tam-di áz-qu-up |
| $O^{3}$ | li-i-ti ù da-na-ni $^{34}$eli(UGU) $^{URU}$Qa-ú-e al-ta-ka-an |

In my 20th regnal year:
I crossed the Euphrates River for the 20th time.
I summoned the kings of the land of Hatti (for corvée work), all of them.
I passed over Mt. Hamanu (Amanus).
I went down to the cities of Kati of Que.
I conquered the cities of Lusanda, Abarnani, Kisuatni fortified cities together with towns without number from the beginning of his towns to the end of his towns.
I massacred them.
I carried off their spoils.
I made two stelae of my royalty.
I wrote on them the praise of my power.
I erected the first at the beginning of his cities and the second at the end of his cities, where the sea begins.
I achieved victory and triumph over Que.

The readout of these episodes is:

| Episode 5 | Episode 10 | Episode 11 | Episode 12 | Episode 22 |
|---|---|---|---|---|
| $A^2$ | $A^2$ | $A^2$ | $A^2$ | $A^2$ |
| $E^6$ | - | $E^6$ | $E^6$ | $E^6$ |
| H | - | - | - | - |
| $G^{\Delta 4}$ | - | - | - | - |
| $L^{2\aleph\zeta}$ | $L^{2\aleph\zeta}$ | $L^{2\aleph\zeta}$ | $L^{2\aleph\zeta}$ | - |
| $L^{2\beth\alpha\beta}$ | $E^{12}$ | - | - | - |
| Q | H | - | - | - |
| $a^2$ | $L^{1\aleph\alpha\beta}$ | - | - | D |
| - | $P^3$ | - | $E^8$ | - |
| $E^9$ | - | $E^3$ | $E^9$ | $E^9$ |
| $E^4$ | $E^4$ | $E^7$ | $E^4$ | $E^4$ |
| $L^{2\aleph\zeta}$ | $L^{2\aleph\zeta}$ | $L^{2\aleph\zeta}$ | $L^{2\aleph\zeta}$ | $L^{2\aleph\zeta}$ |
| - | - | - | - | $L^{1\text{ל}}$ |
| - | - | - | - | $L^{2\beth\gamma\epsilon}$ |
| - | M | - | - | - |
| - | - | - | - | $P^1$ |
| - | - | - | - | $O^3$ |

Finally, episodes 8 and 9 can also be cited.

*Episode 8*
(II. 26 - 30)

$A^2$ $^{26}$ina VII palê(BAL$^{MEŠ}$)-ya
$E^2$ a-na URU$^{MEŠ}$-ni šá $^{I}$Ḫa-bi-ni $^{27URU}$Tíl-Abne(NA$_4$$^{MEŠ}$)-a-a al-lik
$L^{2\aleph\zeta}$ $^{URU}$Tíl-Abne(NA$_4$$^{MEŠ}$) $^{28}$URU dan-nu-ti-šú a-di URU$^{MEŠ}$-ni šá li-me-tu-šú $^{29}$akšud(KUR-ud)
$E^2$ a-di rēš $^{íd}$E-ni ša $^{íd}$Idiqlat $^{30}$a-šar mu-ṣa-ú ša mē$^{MEŠ}$ šak-nu al-lik

In my seventh regnal year:
I marched against the cities of Habini of Til-Abne.
I conquered Til-Abne, his mighty city, together with the towns of its neighborhood.
I went up to the source of the Tigris from whence the water comes.

*Episode 9*
(II. 31 - 34)

$A^2$ $^{31}$ina VIII palê(BAL$^{MEŠ}$)-ya
B $^{I.d}$Marduk-zākir-šumi ŠAR$_4$ māt Kar-du-ni-áš $^{32I.d}$Marduk-bēl-ú-sa-te aḫu-šú it-ti-šú ib-bal-kit
$E^2$ $^{33}$a-na tu-ur gi-mil-li lu al-lik

| | |
|---|---|
| $L^{2אζ}$ | ${}^{34\text{URU}}$mê$^{\text{MEŠ}}$-túr-na-at $^{\text{URU}}$La-ḫi-ru akšud(KUR-ud) |

In my eighth regnal year:
(During the period of) Marduk-zakir-šumi, the king of Karduniaš,
Marduk-bel-usate, his brother, rebelled against me.
I marched in order to avenge.
I conquered the cities of Mêturnat (and) Lahiru.

Thus the scansion reveals:

| Episode 8 | Episode 9 |
|---|---|
| $A^2$ | $A^2$ |
| - | B |
| $E^2$ | $E^2$ |
| $L^{1אζ}$ | $L^{1אζ}$ |
| $E^2$ | - |

Obviously, the two episodes are patterned along similar lines.

Finally, within the recensions of Shalmaneser III, it is interesting to compare particular episodes. One particular episode is seen in a number of recensions: the 18th *palû* campaign against Hazael. Here we will compare the texts of the Marble Slab, the Aššur Annal Fragment, the Bull inscriptions, and the Kurba'il Statue.[79]

*The Marble Slab*[80]

| | |
|---|---|
| $A^2$ | ina XVIII palê(BAL$^{\text{MEŠ}}$)-ya |
| $E^6$ | 16-šú ${}^{46\text{íd}}$Puratta e-bir |
| $G^{-1}$ | $^{\text{I}}$Ḫa-za-'i-ilu(DINGIR) šá māt Imēri-šú $^{47}$a-na gi-piš ummā-nāti (ERÍN.ḪI.A$^{\text{MEŠ}}$)-šu it-ta-kil-ma |
| $G^{-2}$ | $^{48}$ummānāti(ERÍN.ḪI.A$^{\text{MEŠ}}$)-šu a-na ma-'a-diš id-ka-a |
| $G^{-4}$ | ${}^{49\text{KUR}}$Sa-ni-ru $^{\text{KUR}}$ú-ba-an KUR-e ša pu-ut ${}^{50\text{māt}}$Lab-na-ni a-na dan-nu-ti-šu iš-kun |
| $L^{1צβχ}$ | $^{51}$16 lim 20 ṣābē(ERÍN$^{\text{MEŠ}}$) ti-du-ki-šu ina $^{\text{GIŠ}}$kakkē(TU-KUL$^{\text{MEŠ}}$) $^{52}$ú-šam-qit |
| $L^{2יεχ}$ | 1 lim 1 me 21 $^{\text{GIŠ}}$narkabāti(GIGIR$^{\text{MEŠ}}$)-šú $^{53}$4 me 70 pit-ḫal-lu-šú it-ti uš-ma-ni-šú Col. IV $^{1}$e-kim-šu |
| $G^{\Delta 3}$ | a-[na š]u-zu-ub napšati(ZI$^{\text{MEŠ}}$)-šú $^{2}$e-li |
| H | arkī(EGIR)-šu ar-te-di |
| $F^2$ | ina $^{\text{URU}}$Di-ma-áš-qi $^{3}$URU ŠAR$_4$-ti-šu e-ser-šu |
| $L^{1ה}$ | $^{\text{GIŠ}}$kirê(KIRI$_6$$^{\text{MEŠ}}$)-šú a-ki-s[i] |
| $L^{1ג}$ | $^{4}$ku-ri-la-šu ina išāti(IZI$^{\text{MEŠ}}$) áš-ru-up |
| $E^2$ | a-di KUR-e ${}^{5\text{KUR}}$Ḫa-ú-ra-ni al-lik |
| $L^{1אבגζ}$ | URU$^{\text{MEŠ}}$-ni a-na $^{6}$la ma-ni ap-púl aq-qur ina išāti(IZI$^{\text{MEŠ}}$) áš-ru-up |
| $L^{2בγe}$ | $^{7}$šal-la-su-nu áš-lu-la |

E$^{2}$ a-na KUR-e $^{8KUR}$Ba-a'-li-ra-'a-si ša pūt(SAG) tam-di $^{9}$ša pu-ut māt ṣur-ri al-lik
P$^{1}$ ṣa-lam ŠAR$_{4}$-ti-ya $^{10}$ina lìb-bi ú-te-ziz
M ma-da-tu šá $^{I}$Ba-'-li-ma-AN-zēr $^{11I}$Ṣur-ra-a-a ša $^{I}$Ia-a-ú mār(DUMU) $^{I}$Ḫu-um-ri-i $^{12}$am-ḫur

a$^{1,2}$ ina ta-ya-ar-ti-ya
E$^{12}$ a-na $^{13KUR}$Lab-na-na lu e-li
P$^{1}$ ṣa-lam ŠAR$_{4}$-ti-ya $^{14}$it-ti ṣal-me ša $^{I}$Tukul-ti-apil-é-šár-ra $^{15}$ŠAR$_{4}$ rabî(GAL-i) a-lik pa-ni-ya ú-še-ziz

In my 18th regnal year:[81]
I crossed the Euphrates for the 16th time.
Hazael of Damascus trusted in his numerous troops; and mustered his army in great numbers.
He made Mt. Senir (Saniru), a mighty peak, which (lies) opposite the Lebanon, his fortress.
I felled (laid low) 16,000 of his fighting men with the sword.
I took away from him 1,121 of his chariots, 470 of his cavalry-horses together with his camp.
In order to save his life he ran away.
I pursued after him.
I enclosed him in Damascus, his royal city.
I cut down his orchards.
I burned his shocks.
I went to the mountains of Haurani.
Cities without number I destroyed, I devastated, I burned with fire.
I carried off their spoils.
I went to the mountains of Ba'li-ra'si at the side of the sea and (lies) opposite Tyre.
I erected a stela of my royalty there.
I received the tribute of Ba'limanzir,[82] the Tyrian, and of Jehu,[83] the son of Omri.

On my return:
I went up on Mt. Lebanon.
I set up a stela of my royalty with the stela of Tiglath-Pileser (I), the great king who went before me.

*The Aššur Annal Fragment*[84]

A$^{2}$ $^{1}$ina XVIII palê(BAL$^{MEŠ}$)-ya
E$^{6}$ 16-šú $^{íd}$Puratta $^{2}$e-bir
G$^{-1}$ $^{I}$Ḫa-za-'-ilu(DINGIR) šá māt Imēri-šú $^{3}$a-na gi-piš ummānā-ti(ERÍN. ḪI.A$^{MEŠ}$)-šú $^{4}$it-ta-kil-ma
G$^{-2}$ ummānāti(ERÍN.ḪI.A$^{MEŠ}$)-šú $^{5}$a-na ma-'a-diš id-ka-a
G$^{-4}$ $^{6KUR}$Sa-ni-ru ubān KUR-e $^{7}$šá pu-ut $^{māt}$Lab-na-na a-na dan-nu-ti-šú $^{8}$iš-kun
I$^{1}$ it-ti-šú am-daḫ-ḫi-iṣ

| | |
|---|---|
| $L^{\text{1ל}}$ | $^{9}$dabdâ(BAD$_5$.BAD$_5$)-šú áš-kun |
| $L^{\text{1צβχ}}$ | 16 lim $^{10}$ṣābē(ERÍN$^{\text{MEŠ}}$) ti-du-ki-šú ina $^{\text{GIŠ}}$kakkē(TUKUL$^{\text{MEŠ}}$) $^{11}$ú-šam-qit |
| $L^{\text{2יεχ}}$ | 1 lim 1 me 21 $^{\text{GIŠ}}$narkabāti(GIGIR$^{\text{MEŠ}}$)-šú $^{12}$4 me 70 pit-ḫal-lu-šú it-ti uš-ma-ni-šú $^{13}$e-kim-šú |
| $G^{\Delta 3}$ | a-na šu-zu-ub $^{14}$napšāti(ZI$^{\text{MEŠ}}$)-šú e-li |
| H | arkī(EGIR)-šú ar-te-di |
| $F^{2}$ | $^{15}$ina $^{\text{URU}}$Di-maš-qi URU ŠAR$_4$-ti-šú e-ser-šú |
| $L^{\text{1ה}}$ | $^{16\text{GIŠ}}$kirê(KIRI$_6$$^{\text{MEŠ}}$)-šú ak-kis |
| $E^{2}$ | a-di KUR-e $^{17\text{māt}}$Ḫa-ú-ra-ni a-lik |
| $L^{\text{1אבגζ}}$ | URU$^{\text{MEŠ}}$-ni $^{18}$a-na la ma-ni a-púl a-qur $^{19}$ina išāti(IZI$^{\text{MEŠ}}$) ašrup (GIBÍL-up) |
| $L^{\text{2בγε}}$ | šal-la-su-nu $^{20}$a-na la ma-ni áš-lu-la |
| $E^{2}$ | $^{21}$a-di KUR-e $^{\text{māt}}$Ba-a'-li-ra-'a-si $^{22}$šá pūt(SAG) tam-di$_4$ a-lik |
| $P^{1}$ | ṣa-lam ŠAR$_4$-ti-ya $^{23}$ina lìb-bi az-qup |
| $a^{2}$ | ina u$_4$-me-šú-ma |
| M | $^{24}$ma-da-tu šá $^{\text{māt}}$Ṣur-ra-a-a $^{25\text{māt}}$Ṣi-du-na-a-a šá $^{\text{I}}$Ia-ú-a $^{26}$mār(DUMU) $^{\text{I}}$Ḫu-um-ri-i am-ḫur |

In my 18th regal year:
I crossed the Euphrates for the 16th time.
Hazael of Damascus trusted in the mass of his troops; and mustered his troops in great number.
He made Mt. Senir,[85] a mountain peak, opposite the Lebanon, his fortress.
I fought with him.
I brought about his defeat.
I laid low 16,000 of his troops with the sword.
I took away from him 1,121 chariots, 470 cavalry-horses together with his camp.
In order to save his life he went up/away.
(But) I followed after him.
I besieged him in Damascus, his royal city.
I cut down his orchards.[86]
I went up to the mountains of the land of Hauran.
Cities without number I destroyed, razed (and) burned with fire.
I plundered their booty without number.
I went up to the mountains of the land of Ba'lira'si[87] which is on the seashore.
I erected there a stela of my majesty.

At that time:
I received the tribute of the Tyrians, the Sidonians, and of Jehu, son of Omri.[88]

*The Bull Inscriptions*[89]

Schramm understands the inscription to be the Recension D of Shalmaneser III's annals. The text extends through the eighteenth regnal year. The part which should have contained the accession year and the first regnal year is destroyed. Interestingly, the account of the eighteenth *palû* follows immediately after the introduction and before the beginning of the missing annals of the accession and first years.

| | |
|---|---|
| $A^2$ | $^{41}$ina XVIII palê(BAL$^{\text{MEŠ}}$)-ya |
| $E^6$ | 16-šú $^{\text{íd}}$Puratta $^{42}$e-bir |
| $G^{-1}$ | $^{\text{I}}$Ḫa-za-ʾ-ilu(DINGIR) šá māt Imēri-šú $^{43}$a-na gi-piš ummānāti(ERÍN. ḪI.A$^{\text{MEŠ}}$)-šú $^{44}$it-ta-kil-ma |
| $G^{-2}$ | ummānāti(ERÍN.ḪI.A$^{\text{MEŠ}}$)-šú a-na ma-ʾa-diš $^{45}$id-ka-a |
| $G^{-4}$ | $^{\text{KUR}}$Sa-ni-ru ubān KUR-e $^{46}$šá pu-ut $^{\text{māt}}$Lab-na-na a-na dannu-ti-šú $^{47}$iš-kun |
| $I^1$ | it-ti-šú am-daḫ-ḫi-iṣ |
| $L^{1}$כ | dabdâ(BAD$_5$.BAD$_5$)-šú $^{48}$áš-kun |
| $L^{1}$צβχ | (16 lim ṣābē(ERÍN$^{\text{MEŠ}}$) ti-du-ki-šú $^{49}$ina $^{\text{GIŠ}}$kakkē(TUKUL$^{\text{MEŠ}}$) ú-šam-qit |
| $L^{2}$'εχ | $^{50}$1 lim 1 me 31 $^{\text{GIŠ}}$narkabāti(GIGIR$^{\text{MEŠ}}$)-šú $^{51}$4 me 70 pit-ḫal-lu-šú it-ti $^{52}$uš-ma-ni-šú e-kim-šú |

In my 18th regal year:[90]
I crossed the Euphrates for the 16th time.
Hazael of Damascus trusted in the mass of his troops; and mustered his troops in great number.
He made Mt. Senir, a mountain peak, opposite the Lebanon, his fortress.
I fought with him.
I brought about his defeat.
I laid low 16,000 of his troops with the sword.
I took away from him 1,131* chariots, 470 riding horses together with his camp.

*Kurba'il Statue*[91]

The Kurba'il Statue is somewhat contemporary with the Marble Slab and according to Schramm belongs to Recension E.[92] This text is not a typical annal inscription, but is addressed to the god Adad of Kurba'il. Nevertheless, it includes accounts of the 18-20 regnal years and must be considered in the analysis.

| | |
|---|---|
| $A^2$ | $^{21}$ina 18 palê(BAL$^{\text{MEŠ}}$)-ya |
| $E^2$ | 16-šú $^{\text{íd}}$Puratta e-bir |

| | |
|---|---|
| $G^{-1}$ | $^{I}$Ḫa-za-’-ilu(DINGIR) šá $^{māt}$Imēri-šú a-na gi-piš $^{22}$ummānāti (ÉRÍN. ḪI.A$^{MEŠ}$)-šú it-ta-kil-ma |
| $G^{-2}$ | ummānāti(ÉRÍN.ḪI.A$^{MEŠ}$)-šú a-na ma-’a-diš id-ka-a |
| $G^{-4}$ | $^{KUR}$Sa-ni-ru $^{KUR}$Ú-ba-an KUR-e šá pu-tu $^{māt}$Lab-na-na $^{23}$a-na dannu(KAL)ti-šú iš-kun |
| $I^{1}$ | it-ti-šú am-da-ḫi-iṣ |
| $L^{1\text{לְ}}$ | dabdâ(BAD$_5$.BAD$_5$)-šú aš-kun |
| $L^{1\text{צ}\beta\chi}$ | 16 lim $^{LÚ}$mun-daḫ-ḫi-ṣi-šú $^{24}$ina $^{GIŠ}$kakkē(TUKUL$^{MEŠ}$) ú-šam-qit |
| $L^{2\text{י}\epsilon\chi}$ | 1 lim 1 me 21 $^{GIŠ}$narkabāti(GIGIR$^{MEŠ}$)-šú 4 me 70 pit-ḫal-lu-šú it-ti uš-ma-ni-šú $^{25}$e-kim-šú |
| $G^{\Delta 3}$ | a-na šu-zu-ub napšāti(ZI$^{MEŠ}$)-šú e-li |
| H | arkī(EGIR)-šú ar-te-di |
| $F^{2}$ | ina $^{uru}$Di-ma-áš-qi $^{26}$URU ŠAR$_4$-ti-šú e-ser-šú |
| $L^{1\text{ה}}$ | $^{GIŠ}$kirê(KIRI$_6$)-šú ak-kis |
| $E^{2}$ | a-di KUR-e $^{māt}$Ḫa-ú-ra-ni a-lik |
| $L^{1\text{אבגב}\zeta}$ | $^{27}$URU$^{MEŠ}$-ni a-na la ma-ni ap-púl a-qur ina išāti(IZI$^{MEŠ}$) ašrup (GIBÍL-up) |
| $L^{2\text{ב}\gamma\epsilon}$ | $^{28}$šal-la-su-nu a-na la ma-ni áš-lu-la |
| $E^{2}$ | adi(EN) KUR-e $^{KUR}$Ba-a’-li-ra-si šá pūt(SAG) tam-di a-lik |
| $P^{1}$ | $^{29}$ṣa-lam ŠAR$_4$-ti-ya ina lìb-bi az-qup |
| $a^{2}$ | ina u$_4$-me-šú-ma |
| M | ma-da-tu šá $^{māt}$Ṣur-ra-a-a $^{māt}$Ṣi-du-na-a-a šá $^{I}$Ia-ú-a $^{30}$mār (DUMU) $^{I}$Ḫu-um-ri-i am-ḫur |

In my eighteenth year:
I crossed the Euphrates for the sixteenth time.
Hazael of Damascus had trusted in massing his troops; and he had mustered his army in strength.
He made Mount Saniru a peak of the mountains of the Anti-Lebanon, his stronghold.
I fought with him;
(and) I brought about his defeat.
I felled with the sword 16,000 of his men-of-arms.
I took from him 1,121 of his chariots, 470 of his cavalry-horses, together with camp.
He fled for his life.
(But) I pursued him.
I besieged him in Damascus, his capital city.
I cut down his orchards.
I marched as far as the mountains of Hauran.
I destroyed, devastated, (and) burned with fire countless cities.
I carried away their booty without number.
I marched to the mountains of Ba’li-rasi which is over against the sea;
I erected a stela of my sovereignty there.

At that time:

> I received the tribute of Tyre and Sidon, and of Jehu (Ia-ú-a), son of Omri (Ḫu-um-ri-i).

These yield the following patterns (the superscripted letter represents the recension to which the text belongs according to Schramm).

| Aššur Annal[d] | Bull Inscription[d] | Marble Slab[e] | Kurba'il Statue[e] |
|---|---|---|---|
| $A^2$ | $A^2$ | $A^2$ | $A^2$ |
| $E^6$ | $E^6$ | $E^6$ | $E^6$ |
| $G^{-1}$ | $G^{-1}$ | $G^{-1}$ | $G^{-1}$ |
| $G^{-2}$ | $G^{-2}$ | $G^{-2}$ | $G^{-2}$ |
| $G^{-4}$ | $G^{-4}$ | $G^{-4}$ | $G^{-4}$ |
| $I^1$ | $I^1$ | - | $I^1$ |
| $L^{1\text{ל}}$ | $L^{1\text{ל}}$ | - | $L^{1\text{ל}}$ |
| $L^{1\text{צ}\beta\chi}$ | $L^{1\text{צ}\beta\chi}$ | $L^{1\text{צ}\beta\chi}$ | $L^{1\text{צ}\beta\chi}$ |
| $L^{2\text{י}\epsilon\chi}$ | $L^{2\text{י}\epsilon\chi}$ | $L^{2\text{י}\epsilon\chi}$ | $L^{2\text{י}\epsilon\chi}$ |
| $G^{\Delta 3}$ | - | $G^{\Delta 3}$ | $G^{\Delta 3}$ |
| H | - | H | H |
| $F^2$ | - | $F^2$ | $F^2$ |
| $L^{1\text{ה}}$ | $L^{1\text{ה}}$ | $L^{1\text{ה}}$ | $L^{1\text{ה}}$ |
| - | - | $L^{1\text{ג}}$ | - |
| $E^2$ | - | $E^2$ | $E^2$ |
| $L^{1\text{אבג}\zeta}$ | - | $L^{1\text{אבג}\zeta}$ | $L^{1\text{אבג}\zeta}$ |
| $L^{2\text{ב}\gamma\epsilon}$ | - | $L^{2\text{ב}\gamma\epsilon}$ | $L^{2\text{ב}\gamma\epsilon}$ |
| $E^2$ | - | $E^2$ | $E^2$ |
| $P^1$ | - | $P^1$ | $P^1$ |
| $a^2$ | - | - | $a^1$ |
| M | - | M | M |
| - | - | $a^{1,2}$ | - |
| - | - | $E^{12}$ | - |
| - | - | $P^1$ | - |

One can see from this readout that the Marble Slab is the most complete account and hence most at variance with the other three. The Marble Slab is missing $I^1$, $L^{1\text{ל}}$, and $a^1/a^2$; and adds $L^{1\text{ג}}$, $a^{1,2}$, $E^{12}$, and $P^1$. Even though the Aššur Annal and the Kurba'il statue are different recensions, in this episode they are almost exactly the same.

## 5. *Sennacherib*[93]

It is important to understand that a 'campaign', as it is reported in Sennacherib's annals, does not necessarily end with the events described in the original document. In fact, it was possible to produce an account of a campaign before that campaign had been completed.[94] With regard to the principles underlying the composition of his 'annals', events are assigned to a particular campaign relative according to the writer's point of view rather than strict chronological grounds. High-redundancy is achieved in the text as in previous inscriptions via the use of the iterative scheme.

*Second Campaign* (I. 65-80a)[95]

| | |
|---|---|
| $A^{2}$ | $^{65}$i-na 2-e gir-ri-ya |
| $C^{1}$ | $^{d}$Aš-šur be-lí ú-tak-kil-an-ni-ma |
| $B + E^{2}$ | $^{66}$a-na māt(KUR) ($^{LÚ}$)Kaš-ši-i ù māt(KUR) ($^{LÚ}$)Ia-su-bi-gal-la-a-a $^{67}$ša ul-tu ul-la a-na šarrāni(LUGAL$^{MEŠ}$-ni) abbī(AD$^{MEŠ}$)-ya la kit-nu-šú $^{68}$lu al-lik |
| $E^{15\Delta}$ | qé-reb ḫur-šá-a-ni zaq-ru-ti $^{69}$eqel(A.ŠÀ) nam-ra-ṣi i-na sīsî(ANŠE. KUR.RA) ar-kab-ma |
| $E^{14\Delta}$ | $^{70GIŠ}$narkabāt(GIGIR) šēpī(GÌR.II)-ya i-na ti-ik-ka-(a-)te ú-šá-áš-ši $^{71}$áš-ru šup-šu-qu i-na šēpī(GÌR.II)-ya |
| $E^{16}$ | ri-ma-niš at-tag-giš |
| $L^{2\text{א}\zeta}$ | $^{72URU}$Bīt(É)-$^{I}$Ki-lam-za-aḫ $^{URU}$Ḫa-ar-diš-pi $^{73URU}$Bīt(É)-$^{I}$Ku-bat-ti ālāni(URU$^{MEŠ}$)-šú-nu bīt(É) dūrāni(BÀD$^{MEŠ}$-ni) $^{74}$dan-nu-ti al-me akšud(KUR-ud) |
| $L^{2\text{ב}\phi}$ | niši(UN$^{MEŠ}$) sīsî(ANŠE.KUR.RA$^{MEŠ}$) $^{75ANŠE}$parî(KUNGA$^{MEŠ}$) imēri(ANŠE$^{MEŠ}$) alpi(GU$_4$$^{MEŠ}$) ù ṣe-e-ni $^{76}$ul-tu qer-bi-šú-un ú-še-ṣa-am-ma |
| $O^{\phi}$ | šal-la-tiš am-nu |
| $L^{1\text{אבג}\zeta}$ | $^{77}$ù ālāni(URU$^{MEŠ}$)-šú-nu ṣeḫruti(TUR$^{MEŠ}$) ša ni-ba la i-šu-ú $^{78}$ap-pul aq-qur |
| $L^{1\text{ד}\zeta}$ | ú-še-me kar-míš |
| $L^{1\text{ג}\zeta}$ | bīt(É) ṣēri(EDIN) kul-ta-ri $^{79}$mu-šá-bi-šú-nu i-na $^{d}$Girá-(GIŠ.BAR) aq-mu-ma |
| $L^{1\text{ד}\zeta}$ | di-tal-liš $^{80}$ú-še-me |

In my second campaign:
Aššur, my lord, encouraged me, and
I indeed marched against the land of the Kassites and the land of the Yasubigalli who from old had not been submissive to the kings, my fathers.
In the midst of the high mountains I rode on horseback across difficult terrain; and
I had my chariot carried up by the tie-bar where it was too steep.

Like a wild bull I crashed through.
The cities of Bit-Kilamzah, Hardišpi, (and) Bit-Kubatti, their cities, their fortifications, I besieged (and) I captured.
People, horses, mules, asses, cattle, and sheep from their midst I brought out;
I counted as spoil.
And their small cities which are without number I destroyed, I devastated,
I turned into ruins.
The houses of the steppe, the tents, in which they dwell I burned with fire;
and turned them into ashes.

*The Fifth Campaign* (III. 75 - IV. 11)

| | |
|---|---|
| A$^{2}$ | $^{75}$i-na 5 gir-ri-ya |
| B | ba-ḫu-la-te $^{URU}$Tu-mur-ri $^{76URU}$Šá-(a)-ru-um $^{URU}$E-za-(a)-ma $^{URU}$Kib-šú $^{URU}$Ḫal-BU gíd-da $^{77URU}$Qu-u-a $^{URU}$Qa-na ša kīma (GIM) qin-ni arî(TU$_{8}$)$^{MUŠEN}$ a-šá-red $^{78}$iṣṣūrāti(MUŠEN.ḪA) ṣe-er zuq-ti $^{KUR}$Ni-bur šadî(KUR-i) mar-ṣi $^{79}$šu-bat-sún šit-ku-na-at-ma la kit-nu-šú a-na ni-(i)-ri |
| f | $^{80}$i-na šēpī(GÌR.II) $^{KUR}$Ni-bur ka-ra-ši ú-šá-áš-kin-ma |
| E$^{8}$ | $^{81}$it-ti $^{LÚ}$qur-bu-ti šēpī(GÌR.II)-ya na-as-qu-ti Col. IV $^{1}$ù ($^{LÚ}$)ṣābī (ERM$^{MEŠ}$) taḫāzi(MÈ)-ya la ga-mì-lu-ti $^{2}$a-na-ku kīma(GIM) ($^{GU4}$)rīmī(AM) eq-di pa-nu-uš-šú-un as-bat |
| E$^{\Delta}$ | $^{3}$ḫar-ri na-ḫal-li na-at-bak šadî(KUR-i) me-le-e $^{4}$mar-ṣu-ti i-na $^{GIŠ}$kussî(GU.ZA) áš-ta-am-di-iḫ $^{5}$a-šar a-na $^{GIŠ}$kussî-(GU.ZA) šup-šu-qu i-na šēpī(GÌR.II)-ya áš-taḫ-ḫi-it $^{6}$kīma(GIM) ar-me |
| E$^{12}$ | a-na zuq-ti šá-qu-(ú)-ti ṣe-ru-uš-šú-un $^{7}$e-li |
| E | a-šar bir-ka-a-a ma-na-aḫ-tu i-šá-a $^{8}$ṣe-er abān(NA$_{4}$) šadî (KUR-i) ú-šib-ma mê(A$^{MEŠ}$) $^{KUŠ}$na-a-di ka-ṣu-te $^{9}$a-na ṣu-(um)-me-ya lu áš-ti |
| H | i-na ubānāt(ŠU.SI$^{MEŠ}$) $^{10}$ḫur-šá-a-ni ar-de-šú-nu-ti-ma |
| L$^{1}$ל | áš-ta-kan $^{11}$taḫ-ta-šú-un |
| L$^{2}$אζ | ālāni(URU$^{MEŠ}$)-šú-nu akšud(KUR-ud)-ma |
| L$^{2}$בγε | áš-lu-la šal-la-sún |
| L$^{1}$אגבζ | ap-pul aq-qur i-na $^{d}$Girá(GIŠ.BAR) aq-mu |

In my fifth campaign:
the warriors of Tumuru, Sarun, Ezama, Kibšu, Halbuda, Qua, (and) Qana, whose abodes like the nest of eagles, foremost of birds, were set on the peak of Mt. Nibur, a steep mountain, (these people) had not been submissive to my yoke.
I pitched my camp at the foot of Mt. Nibur. And
with my chosen body-guard and battle-experienced soldiers, I, like a strong wild-ox, took off before them.

The difficult ravines and streams of the mountains I traversed in a sedan chair. Where it was too steep for my chair, I advanced on foot like a young buck (gazelle or mountain goat).
I mounted the high peaks in pursuit of them.
Wherever my knees found a resting-place, I sat down on the mountain rock;
I drank cold water from water-skins to quench my thirst.
To the summits of the mountains I pursued them; and
brought about their defeat.
Their cities I conquered; and
carried off their spoil.
I destroyed, devastated, (and) burned with fire.

*The Seventh Campaign* (IV. 54-81)[96]

$A^{2}$ $^{54}$i-na 7-e gir-ri-ya
$C^{1}$ $^{d}$Aš-šur be-lí ú-tak-kil-an-ni-ma
$E^{2}$ $^{55}$a-na māt(KUR) E-lam-ti lu al-lik
$L^{2\text{א}\zeta}$ $^{URU}$Bīt(É)-$^{I}$Ḫa-’i-i-ri $^{56URU}$Ra-ZA-a ālāni(URU$^{MEŠ}$) ša mi-ṣir māt (KUR) Aš-šur$^{ki}$ $^{57}$ša i-na tar-ṣi abī(AD)-ya E-la-mu-ú e-ki-mu da-na-niš $^{58}$i-na me-ti-iq gir-ri-ya akšud(KUR-ud)
$L^{2\text{ב}\gamma\epsilon}$ áš-lu-la šal-la-sún
$E^{5}$ $^{59}$ṣābī(ERÍN$^{MEŠ}$) šu-lu-ti-ya ú-še-rib qé-reb-šú-un
$O^{5}$ a-na mi-ṣir $^{60}$māt(KUR) Aš-šur$^{ki}$ ú-tir-ra-ma
$O^{2}$ qāti(ŠU.II) $^{LÚ}$ráb(GAL) $^{URU}$bīrti(ḪAL.ṢU) Dēri(BÀD. DINGIR)$^{ki}$ $^{61}$am-nu
$F^{2}$ + $^{URU}$Bu-bé-e $^{URU}$Dun-ni-$^{d}$Šamaš(UTU) $^{URU}$Bīt(É)-$^{I}$Ri-si-ia $^{62URU}$Bīt(É)-Aḫ
$L^{2\text{א}\zeta}$ la-me-e $^{URU}$Du-ru $^{URU}$Dan-nat-$^{I}$Su-la-a-a $^{63URU}$Ši-li-ip-tu $^{URU}$Bīt(É)-$^{I}$A-ṣu-si $^{URU}$Kār-$^{I}$Zēru(NUMUN)-iqīša(BA-šá) $^{64URU}$Bīt(É)-($^{I}$)Gi-iṣ-ṣi $^{URU}$Bīt(É)-Kàt-pa-la-ni $^{URU}$Bīt(É)-$^{I}$Im-bi-ia $^{65URU}$Ḫa-ma-(a)-nu $^{URU}$Bīt(É)-$^{I}$Ar-ra-bi $^{URU}$Bu-ru-tu $^{66URU}$Dim-tú-ša-$^{I}$Su-la-a-a $^{URU}$Dim-tú-ša-$^{I.d}$Mār(DUMU)-bīti(É)-ēṭir(KAR-ir) $^{67URU}$Ḫar-ri-áš-la-ke-e $^{URU}$Rab-ba-a-a $^{68URU}$Ra-a-su $^{URU}$Ak-ka-ba-ri-na $^{URU}$Tīl(DU$_6$)-$^{I}$Ú-ḫu-ri $^{69URU}$Ḫa-am-ra-nu $^{URU}$Na-di-tu a-di ālāni(URU$^{MEŠ}$) $^{70}$ša né-re-bi ša $^{URU}$Bīt(É)-$^{I}$Bu-na-ki $^{URU}$Tíl(DU$_6$)-$^{d}$Ḫu-um-bi $^{71URU}$Dim-tú-ša-$^{I}$Du-me-ilu(DINGIR) $^{URU}$Bīt(É)-$^{I}$Ú-bi-ia $^{72URU}$Ba-al-ti-li-šir $^{URU}$Ta-qab-li-šir $^{73URU}$Ša-na-qi-da-te $^{URU}$Ma-ṣu-tú-šap-li-ti $^{74URU}$Sa-ar-ḫu-de-ri $^{URU}$A-lum-ša-GAŠAN-bīti(É) $^{75URU}$Bīt(É)-$^{I}$Aḫḫi(PAB$^{MEŠ}$)-idinna(SUM-na) $^{URU}$Il-ṭe-ú-ba $^{76}$34 ālāni (URU$^{MEŠ}$) dan-nu-ti a-di ālāni(URU$^{MEŠ}$) ṣeḫruti (TUR$^{MEŠ}$) $^{77}$ša li-me-ti-šú-nu ša ni-ba la i-šu-ú $^{78}$al-me akšud(KUR-ud)
$L^{2\text{ב}\gamma\epsilon}$ áš-lu-la šal-la-sún
$L^{1\text{אבג}\zeta}$ ap-pul aq-qur $^{79}$i-na $^{d}$Girá(GIŠ.BAR) aq-mu
$L^{1\text{בג}\zeta}$ qu-tur naq-mu-ti-šú-nu $^{80}$kīma(GIM) imbari(MURU$_9$,IM. DUGUD) kab-ti pa-an šamê(AN-e) rap-šu-ti $^{81}$ú-šak-ti-im

In my seventh campaign:

Aššur, my lord, encouraged me, and
I (indeed) marched against the land of Elam.
I conquered in the course of my campaign (the cities of) Bit-Ha'iri (and) Raza, cities on the border of Assyria, which during the time of my father, the Elamite had seized by force; and
I carried off their spoil.
I caused soldiers, my garrison, to enter into their midst.
I returned them to the border of Assyria.
I assigned (them) into the hands of the commander of the fort of Der.
(The cities of) Bubê, Dunni-Šamaš, Bīt-Risia, Bīt-Ahlame, Duru, Dannat-Sulaya, Šiliptu, Bīt-Asusi, Kār-Zēru-iqīša, Bīt-Gissi, Bīt-Katpalani, Bīt-Imbia, Hamanu, Bīt-Arrabi, Burutu, Dim-tu-ša-Sulaya, Dim-tu-ša-Mar-bīti-ētir, Harriašlakê, Rabbaya, Râsu, Akkabarina, Til-Uhuri, Hamranu, Naditu together with the cities of the mountain passes of Bīt-Bunaki, Til-Humbi, Dim-tu-ša-Dume-ilu, Bīt-Ubia, Baltilišir, Taqablišir, Šanaqidate, Masutu-šapliti, Sarhuderi, Alumša-GAŠAN(Belet or Sarrat?)-biti, Bīt-Ahhi-idinna, Ilteuba, 34 strong cities together with the cities surrounding their environs, which were countless, I besieged, I conquered;
I carried off their spoil;
I destroyed, I devastated, (and) I burned with fire.
I covered the face of the wide heavens with the smoke of their conflagration[98] like a heavy fog.

These episodes can be charted as follows:

| 2nd Campaign | 5th Campaign | 7th Campaign |
|---|---|---|
| $A^2$ | $A^2$ | $A^2$ |
| $C^1$ | - | $C^1$ |
| B | B | - |
| $E^2$ | [f] | $E^2$ |
| - | $E^8$ | - |
| $E^{15\Delta}$ | $E^{\Delta}$ | - |
| $E^{14\Delta}$ | $E^{\Delta}$ | - |
| $E^{16}$ | $E^{12}$ + E | - |
| - | H | - |
| - | $L^{1\text{ל}}$ | - |
| $L^{2\text{א}\zeta}$ | $L^{2\text{א}\zeta}$ | $L^{2\text{א}\zeta}$ |
| $L^{2\text{ב}\phi}$ | $L^{2\text{ב}\gamma\epsilon}$ | $L^{2\text{ב}\gamma\epsilon}$ |
| - | - | $E^5$ |
| $O^{\phi}$ | - | $O^5 + O^2$ |
| - | - | $F^2$ |
| - | - | $L^{2\text{א}\zeta}$ |
| - | - | $L^{2\text{ב}\gamma\epsilon}$ |
| $L^{1\text{אבג}\zeta}$ | $L^{1\text{אבג}\zeta}$ | $L^{1\text{אבג}\zeta}$ |

| | | |
|---|---|---|
| L$^{\text{1דζ}}$ | - | - |
| L$^{\text{1גζ}}$ | - | L$^{\text{1גζ}}$ |
| L$^{\text{1דζ}}$ | - | - |

Thus one can see the use of stereotyped syntagms in the episodes of the royal annals of Sennacherib. This patterning of the syntagms gives the accounts coherence, while the variation within the episodes prevents monotony.

### *LETTERS TO THE GOD*

## *Sargon's Letter to the God*[98]

*Lines (269-276)*

a$^{1}$ [269]TA URU$^{\text{MEŠ}}$-ni dan-nu-ti ša $^{\text{māt}}$Sa-an-gi-bu-te at-tu-muš
E$^{7}$ a-na $^{\text{māt}}$Ar-ma-ri-li-i na-gi-i aq-ṭi-rib
L$^{\text{1אζ}}$ [270]$^{\text{URU}}$Bu-bu-zi bir-tu $^{\text{URU}}$Ḫu-un-du-ur ša 2 BÀD$^{\text{MEŠ}}$-ni la-mu-ú pi-i di-im-ti tu-bal-e ma-ḫi-re ru-uk-ku-su [271]$^{\text{URU}}$Ai-ia-le-e $^{\text{URU}}$Ṣi-ni-iš-pa-la-a $^{\text{URU}}$Ṣi-ni-ú-nak $^{\text{URU}}$Ar-na $^{\text{URU}}$Sar-ni-i [272]7 URU$^{\text{MEŠ}}$-ni dan-nu-ti a-di 30 URU$^{\text{MEŠ}}$-ni ša li-mé--ti-šu-nu ša i-na šēpē(GÌR II) $^{\text{KUR}}$Ú-bi-anda KUR-e na-du-ú [273]se-ḫer-šu-nu ap-pul-ma
L$^{\text{1בζ}}$ qaq-qa-reš am-nu
L$^{\text{1גζ}}$ GIŠ.ÙR$^{\text{MEŠ}}$ ta-aṣ-lil-ti-šu-nu i-na $^{\text{d}}$BIL.GI aq-mu-ma
L$^{\text{1דζ}}$ di-tal-li-iš ú-še-mi
L$^{\text{1ז}}$ [274]qi-ra-a-te-šu-nu na-kam-a-ti ú-pat-ti-ma
L$^{\text{1ד}}$ ŠE.PAD$^{\text{MEŠ}}$-šu-nu ma-'a-at-tu ša la ni-i-bi um-ma-ni-ia ú-šá-a-kil
L$^{\text{1ג}}$ [275]EBUR tuk-lat UN$^{\text{MEŠ}}$-šú ù $^{\text{u}}$pu-e nap-šat bu-li-šu ab-ri-iš a-qu-ud-ma
L$^{\text{1ע}}$ ar-bu-ti-iš ú-šá-li-ka ta-mer-tu-uš
L$^{\text{1ה}}$ [276]$^{\text{GIŠ}}$KIRI$_{6}$$^{\text{MEŠ}}$-šú-nu a-kis-ma
L$^{\text{1ש}}$ $^{\text{GIŠ}}$TIR$^{\text{MEŠ}}$-šú-nu ak-šiṭ
L$^{\text{1ג}}$ nap-ḫar $^{\text{GIŠ}}$gup-ni-šu-nu a-na gu-ru-un-ni ag-ru-un-ma i-na $^{\text{d}}$BIL.GI aq-mu

From the strong cities of the land of Sangibutu I moved on.
I approached the district of Armarilî.
Bubuzi, the fortress of Hundur, that was surrounded by two walls, erected ... along the moat of the ... of the tower, Ayyalê, Sinišpalâ, Siniunak, Arna, Sarnî, seven strong cities, together with thirty towns of their neighborhood, which lie at the foot of Mt. Ubianda, uncultivated mountains, I destroyed in their entirety; and
I leveled to the ground.
The beams of their roofs I set on fire; and

I made like a flame.
Their overflowing granaries I opened; and
their great food supplies beyond counting I let my army devour.
The harvest, the nourishment of its people, and the chaff, the life of its cattle I burned like brush; and
I made its plain like a devastation.
Their orchards I cut down; and
their forests I felled.
All of their tree trunks I gathered into heaps; and
I set on fire.

*Lines (277-279)*

| | |
|---|---|
| a$^{1,2}$ | $^{277}$i-na me-taq-ti-ya |
| E$^{2}$ | a-na $^{\text{URU}}$Ar-bu URU É AD-šu ša $^{\text{I}}$Ur-sa-a u $^{\text{URU}}$Ri-ya-ar URU-šú ša $^{\text{md}}$XV-dure$_{8}$ a-lik |
| L$^{\text{1אζ}}$ | $^{278}$7URU$^{\text{MEŠ}}$-ni ša li-mé-ti-šu-nu ša ŠEŠ$^{\text{MEŠ}}$-šú NUMUN LUGAL-ti-šú i-na lìb-bi-šu-nu šu-šu-bu-ma dun-nu-nu ma-ṣar-tu $^{279}$URU$^{\text{MEŠ}}$-ni šu-a-tu-nu ap-pul |
| L$^{\text{1בζ}}$ | qaq-qa-reš am-nu |
| L$^{\text{1ג}}$ | É $^{\text{d}}$Ḫal-di-a DINGIR-šu ab-re-eš a-qu-ud-ma |
| L$^{\text{1א}}$ | ú-šal-pi-ta sa-a-gi-su |

On my march I came to Arbu, the city of the house of Rusa's father, and Riyar, Sardure's city.
Seven cities of their neighborhood, where his brothers, (members) of the royal family have their residence, and whose guard was very strong, those cities I destroyed; (and)
I made level to the ground.
The house (temple) of Haldi, his god, I set on fire like brush; and
I destroyed his shrine (sanctuary).

*Lines (280-296)*

| | |
|---|---|
| a$^{1}$ | $^{280}$TA $^{\text{māt}}$Ar-ma-ri-ya-li-i at-tu-muš |
| E$^{9}$ | $^{\text{KUR}}$Ú-i-zu-ku KUR ŠIM.LI ša ši-pik-šu NA$_{4}$DÚR.MI.NA at-ta-bal-kàt |
| E$^{7}$ | a-na $^{\text{māt}}$A-ya-di aq-ṭi-rib |
| G$^{\Delta 1}$ | $^{281\text{URU}}$An-za-li-a $^{\text{URU}}$[K]u-a-yá-in $^{\text{URU}}$Qa-al-la-ni-a $^{\text{URU}}$Bi-it-aiai $^{\text{URU}}$Alu-ar-za $^{\text{URU}}$Qi-ú-na $^{\text{URU}}$Al-li-i $^{282\text{URU}}$Ar-zu-gu $^{\text{URU}}$Šík-ka--nu $^{\text{URU}}$Ar-diú-nak $^{\text{URU}}$Da-yazu-na $^{\text{URU}}$Ge-e-ta $^{\text{URU}}$Ba-a-ni-ú $^{283\text{URU}}$Bir-ḫi-lu-za $^{\text{URU}}$Dee-zi-zu $^{\text{URU}}$Di-li-zi-a $^{\text{URU}}$A-ba-in-di $^{\text{URU}}$Du-a-in $^{\text{URU}}$Ḫa-as-ra-na $^{284\text{URU}}$Pa-ar-ra $^{\text{URU}}$A-ya-su-un $^{\text{URU}}$A-ni-áš-ta-ni-a $^{\text{URU}}$Bal-du-ar-za $^{\text{URU}}$Sar-ú-ar-di-i $^{285\text{URU}}$Su-ma-at-tar $^{\text{URU}}$Šá-al-zi-i $^{\text{URU}}$Al-bu-ú-ri $^{\text{URU}}$Ṣiqar-ra $^{\text{URU}}$Ú-a-yá-is la-bi-ru $^{286}$30 URU$^{\text{MEŠ}}$-šú dan-nu-ti ša i-na a-ḫi A.AB.BA gal-la-ti ti-bi-ik KUR$^{\text{MEŠ}}$ GAL$^{\text{MEŠ}}$ sa-ad-ru-ma šu-uṣ-bu-tú ki-ma us-si $^{287\text{URU}}$Ar-giš-ti-ú-na $^{\text{URU}}$Qa-al-la-ni-a bi-ra-ti-šu dan-na-ate ru-uk-ku-sa bi-ru-uš-šu-un $^{288}$el-en $^{\text{KUR}}$Ar-ṣi-du ù $^{\text{KUR}}$Maḫ-un-ni-a kak-ka-biš a-ṣa-ma a-na 4 UŠ ṬA.ÀM |

in-na-at-ta-lu SUḪ-[šu-u]n $^{289\,\text{LÚ}}$qura-di-šu a-šá-re-tú um-ma-ni-šu le-'u-tu ta-ḫa-zi na-áš ka-ba-bi as-ma-ri-i tu-kul-ti māti-šú šu-lu-ú qé-reb-šin $^{290}$ki-šit-ti $^{\text{māt}}$Ar-ma-ri-ya-li-i na-ge-e i-te-e-šu-nu e-mu-ru-ma it-ru-ra iš-da-a-šu-un

$G^{\Delta 2}$ $^{291}$URU$^{\text{MEŠ}}$-ni-šu-nu it-ti mar-ši-ti-šu-nu ú-maš-še-ru-ma

$G^{\Delta 3}$ a-na qé-reb bi-ra-a-ti šu-a*-ti*-na ki-ma iṣ-ṣu-re ip-par-šu

H $^{292}$um-ma-ni ma-'a-at-ta-tu a-na URU$^{\text{MEŠ}}$-ni-šu-nu ú-še-li-ma

$L^{\text{2בγe}}$ NÍG.ŠU-šú-nu a-na mu-'u-de-e iš-lu-lu NÍG.GA-šu-un

$L^{\text{1אζ}}$ $^{293}$BÀD$^{\text{MEŠ}}$-ni-šu-nu dan-nu-ti a-di 87 URU$^{\text{MEŠ}}$-ni ša li-me-ti-šu-nu ap-pul-ma

$L^{\text{1בζ}}$ qaq-qa-reš ú-šak-ši-id

$L^{\text{1גζ}}$ $^{294}$i-na É$^{\text{MEŠ}}$ qer-bi-šu-nu $^{\text{d}}$BIL.GI ú-šá-aṣ-bit-ma

$L^{\text{1דζ}}$ GIŠ.ÙR$^{\text{MEŠ}}$ ta-aṣ-lil-ti-šu-nu di-tal-li-iš ú-še-mi

$L^{\text{1ז}}$ $^{295}$qi-ra-te-šu-nu na-kam-a-te ú-pat-ti-ma

$L^{\text{1ר}}$ ŠE.PAD$^{\text{MEŠ}}$ la ni-i-bi um-ma-ni ú-šá-a-kil

$L^{\text{1ה}}$ $^{296\,\text{GIŠ}}$KIRI$_6$$^{\text{MEŠ}}$-šu-nu ak-kis-ma

$L^{\text{1ש}}$ $^{\text{GIŠ}}$TIR$^{\text{MEŠ}}$-šu-nu ak-šiṭ

$L^{\text{1ג}}$ kul-lat $^{\text{GIŠ}}$gup-ni-šu-nu ú-paḫ-ḫer-ma
i-na $^{\text{d}}$BIL.GI aq-mu

I departed from the land of Armariyalî.
I crossed Mt. Wizuku, the juniper mountain, whose core is breccia.
I approached the land of Ayadu.
Anzalia, Kuayin, Qallania, Bitaya, Aluarza, Qiuna, Allî, Arzugu, Šikkanu, Ardiunak, Dayazuna, Geta, Baniu, Birhiluza, Dezizu, Dilizia, Abaindi, Duain, Hasrana, Parra, Ayasun, Aniaštania, Balduarza, Saruardî, Sumattar, Šalzî, Alburi, Siqarra, Old Uayis—thirty of its strong cities, which were lined up on the shore of the 'gallu' sea, at the foot of great mountains, in an uninterrupted row; Argištiuna, Qallania, its strong fortresses, erected among them, which rise above Mt. Arsidu and Mt. Mahunnia like stars—their foundations were visible for 240 (...) each way—his warriors, his picked army, powerful in battle, bearing shield and lance, the support of his land, were stationed therein; They saw the conquest of Armariyali, their neighboring district; and their legs trembled.
Their cities they abandoned with their possessions; and
they fled like birds into the midst of those fortresses.
I sent up large numbers of troops against their cities; and
they carried off large quantities of their property, their goods.
Their strong walls, together with 87 towns of their neighborhood
I destroyed;
I leveled to the ground.
I set on fire the houses within them; and
their roof beams I left in flames.
I opened up their well-filled granaries. And

food beyond counting I let my army devour.
Their orchards I cut down; and
their forests I felled.
All their tree trunks I gathered; and
I set on fire.

*Lines (297-305)*

a[1] $^{297}$TA $^{\text{mät}}$A-ya-di at-tu-muš
E[6] $^{\text{íd}}$Al-lu-ri-a $^{\text{íd}}$Qa-al-la-ni-a $^{\text{íd}}$In-na-aiai ÍD$^{\text{MEŠ}}$ e-te-bir
E[7] $^{298}$a-na $^{\text{URU}}$Ú-a-yá-is na-gi-i tuk-la-te-šu še-pit mi-iṣ-ri ša $^{\text{mät}}$Ur-ar-ti ša pat-ti $^{\text{mät}}$Na-'i-ri aq-ṭi-rib
G[-2] $^{299\text{URU}}$Ú-a-ya-is URU dan-nu-ti-šu bir-tu-šu GAL-tu ša UGU kul-lat bira-a-te-šu dun-nu-na-at-ma nu-uk-ku-lat ep-še-es-sa $^{300\text{LÚ}}$ERÍN$^{\text{MEŠ}}$ ti-duki-šu ek-du-ti $^{\text{LÚ}}$da-aiai-li mu-še-ri-bu ṭè-em KUR.KUR$^{\text{MEŠ}}$ limé-ti-šú šu-šu-bu qer-bu-uš-šu $^{301\text{LÚ}}$EN.NAM$^{\text{MEŠ}}$-šu a-di ki-iṣ-ri-šunu i-na lìb-bi ú-še-li-ma it-ti BÀD-šu dan-nu mun-daḫ-se u-šal-mi
L[2א] $^{302}$ša $^{\text{URU}}$bir-ti šu-a-ti ku-tal-la-šá ak-šu-ud
L[1הβ] $^{\text{LÚ}}$qu-ra-di-šu i-na IGI KÁ.GAL-šú ki-ma as-le ú-nap-pi-iṣ
L[1ש] $^{303\text{GIŠ}}$KIRI$_6$$^{\text{MEŠ}}$-šú ak-šiṭ-ma
L[1ה] $^{\text{GIŠ}}$TIR$^{\text{MEŠ}}$-šú ak-kis
L[1ג] kul-lat $^{\text{GIŠ}}$gup-ni-šu nak-su-ti ú-paḫ-ḫer-ma
i-na $^{\text{d}}$BIL.GI aq-mu
L[1גζ] $^{304\text{URU}}$Bar-zu-ri-a-ni $^{\text{URU}}$Ú-al-tu-qu-ya $^{\text{URU}}$Qu-ut-ta $^{\text{URU}}$Qi-ip-pa $^{\text{URU}}$Asa-pa-a $^{305}$5 É BÀD$^{\text{MEŠ}}$-ni dan-nu-ti a-di 40 URU$^{\text{MEŠ}}$-ni ša li-méti-šu-nu i-na $^{\text{d}}$BIL.GI aq-mu

From Ayadi I departed.
I crossed the rivers Alluria, Qallania, (and) Innayya.
I drew near to the district of Uayis, his mainstay, on the lower border of Urartu (and) on the border of Nairi.
The city of Uayis, his fortification, his great fortress, which was stronger than any other of his fortresses, and whose workmanship was well performed—his powerful battle troops, the scouts (whose task it is to) bring in reports about the countries adjacent to his, were stationed therein; He manned it with his governors together with their troops. And he surrounded the combat troops with strong walls.
I took that fortress from the rear;
I slaughtered its warriors in front of its gate like lambs.
Its orchards I cut down;
its forests I felled.
I gathered all of its severed tree trunks; and
I set (them) on fire.
Barzuriani, Ualtuquya, Qutta, Qippa, Asapâ, five strong walled cities, together with 40 towns of their neighborhood, I set on fire.

These lines can be charted as follows:

| 269-276 | 277-279 | 280-296 | 297-305 |
|---|---|---|---|
| $a^1$ | $a^{1,2}$ | $a^1$ | $a^1$ |
| - | $E^2$ | $E^9$ | $E^6$ |
| $E^7$ | - | $E^7$ | $E^7$ |
| - | - | $G^{\Delta 1}$ | $G^{-2}$ |
| - | - | $G^{\Delta 2}$ | - |
| - | - | $G^{\Delta 3}$ | - |
| - | - | H | - |
| - | - | $L^{2\text{ב}\gamma\epsilon}$ | $L^{2\text{א}}$ |
| $L^{1\text{א}\zeta}$ | $L^{1\text{א}\zeta}$ | $L^{1\text{א}\zeta}$ | - |
| $L^{1\text{ב}\zeta}$ | $L^{1\text{ב}\zeta}$ | $L^{1\text{ב}\zeta}$ | - |
| $L^{1\text{ג}\zeta}$ | $L^{1\text{ג}}$ | $L^{1\text{ג}\zeta}$ | - |
| $L^{1\text{ד}\zeta}$ | $\{L^{1\text{א}}\}$ | $L^{1\text{ד}\zeta}$ | - |
| $L^{1\text{ז}}$ | - | $L^{1\text{ז}}$ | - |
| $L^{1\text{ר}}$ | - | $L^{1\text{ר}}$ | - |
| $L^{1\text{ג}}$ | - | - | - |
| $L^{1\text{ע}}$ | - | - | - |
| $L^{1\text{ה}}$ | - | $L^{1\text{ה}}$ | $L^{1\text{ה}\beta}$ |
| $L^{1\text{ש}}$ | - | $L^{1\text{ש}}$ | $L^{1\text{ש}}$ |
| - | - | - | $L^{1\text{ה}}$ |
| $L^{1\text{ג}}$ | - | $L^{1\text{ג}}$ | $L^{1\text{ג}}$ |
| - | - | - | $L^{1\text{ג}\zeta}$ |

The use of stereotyped syntagms in the episodes of Sargon's Letter to the God is evident. The employment of this patterning of the syntagms in a different literary type (Letter to the God) demonstrates that the usage is not confined to the 'annals' alone.

This iterative scheme is not limited only to cases in which combat is present, but also in cases of submission and the paying of tribute. The following chart demonstrates this through a scansion of some lines which contain descriptions of submissions:

| 31-36 | 37-38a | 38b-41 | 306-308 |
|---|---|---|---|
| - | - | - | $a^1$ |
| $E^4$ | - | $E^4$ | - |
| - | $E^7$ | - | $E^7$ |
| $F^1$ | - | $F^1$ | - |
| $E^2$ | - | - | $E^2$ |
| M | M | M | M |

### *SUMMARY OR DISPLAY TEXTS*[99]

The texts in this category are commemorative inscriptions without episodic narration. When military campaigns are included in the narration, early and later military activities tend to be condensed into one geographically, but not chronologically, coherent narrative. This type of inscription is usually much shorter than any edition of the royal annals, especially as it was often inscribed upon a surface with limited space, such as a commemorative stela or a slab. For this reason, Summary or Display Texts do not witness the iterative scheme, but do manifest many of the other rhetorical devices used in the Assyrian military accounts. The following Summary Texts illustrate this point.

*Aššur-nasir-pal II*
(The 'Standard' Inscription)[100]

| | |
|---|---|
| $a^{2} + C^{1}$ | e-nu-ma Aššur bēlu(EN) na-bu-ú $^{7}$šumi(MU)-ya mu-šar-bu-ú šar$_{4}$-ti-a $^{\text{GIŠ}}$kakka(TUKUL)-šú la pa-da-a a-na i-da-at bēlu-(EN)-ti-a lu-ú it-muḫ |
| $L^{1\gamma\beta}$ | ummānāti(ERÍN.ḪI.A$^{\text{MEŠ}}$) $^{\text{māt}}$Lu-ul-lu-me-e $^{8}$rapšate(DA-GAL)$^{\text{MEŠ}}$ ina qé-reb tam-ḫa-ri ina $^{\text{GIŠ}}$kakkē(TUKUL$^{\text{MEŠ}}$) lu ú-šam-qit |
| $C^{1}$ | ina re-ṣu-te šá $^{\text{d}}$Ša-maš $^{9}$u $^{\text{d}}$Adad(IŠKUR) ilāni(DINGIR$^{\text{MEŠ}}$) tik-li-a |
| I | ummānāt(ERÍN.ḪI.A$^{\text{MEŠ}}$) mātāti(KUR.KUR) Na-i-ri $^{\text{māt}}$Ḫab-ḫi $^{\text{māt}}$Šu-ba-re-e u $^{\text{māt}}$Ni-rib kīma(GIM) $^{\text{d}}$Adad(IŠKUR) ra-ḫi-ṣi eli(UGU)-šú-nu áš-gu-um |
| $L^{2\iota}$ | $^{10}$šar$_{4}$ šá ištu(TA) e-bir-tan $^{\text{íd}}$Idiglat(ḪAL.ḪAL) a-di $^{\text{KUR}}$Lab-na-na u tâmti(A.AB.BA) rabīte(GAL-te) $^{\text{māt}}$La-qe-e ana si-ḫír-ti-šá $^{\text{māt}}$Su-ḫi a-di $^{\text{uru}}$Ra-pi-qi ana šēpē(GÌR II)-šú $^{11}$ú-šík-ni-šá |
| $L^{2\kappa}$ | ištu(TA) rēš(SAG) e-ni $^{\text{íd}}$Su-ub-na-at a-di $^{\text{māt}}$U-ra-ar-ṭí qāt(ŠU)-su ikšud(KUR-ud) |
| $O^{5}$ | ištu(TA) $^{\text{KUR}}$né-re-be šá $^{\text{māt}}$Kìr-ru-ri a-di $^{\text{māt}}$Gíl-za-ni $^{12}$ištu (TA) e-bit-tan $^{\text{íd}}$Za-ba šupalê(KI.TA) a-di $^{\text{uru}}$Tīl(DU$_{6}$)-ba-a-ri šá el-la-an $^{\text{māt}}$Za-ban ištu(TA) $^{\text{uru}}$Tīl(DU$_{6}$)-šá-ab-ta-a-ni a-di $^{\text{uru}}$Tīl(DU$_{6}$)-šá-Za-ab-da-a-ni $^{13\text{uru}}$Ḫi-ri-mu $^{\text{uru}}$Ḫa-ru-tu $^{\text{KUR}}$bi-ra-a-te šá $^{\text{māt}}$Kar-du-ni-áš ana mi-iṣ-ri māti-a ú-ter |
| $O^{\phi}$ | ištu(TA) $^{\text{KUR}}$né-rib-šá $^{\text{KUR}}$Ba-bi-te a-di $^{\text{māt}}$Ḫaš-mar $^{14}$a-na niši (UKU$^{\text{MEŠ}}$) māti(KUR)-ya am-nu |

$O^{2}$ ina mātāti(KUR.KUR$^{\text{MEŠ}}$) šá a-pì-lu-ši-na-ni $^{\text{LÚ}}$šak(GAR)-nu-te-ya al-ta-kan

$O^{\phi}$ ur-du-ti ú-pu-šú

When Aššur, the lord who called me by name (and) made my kingship great, entrusted his merciless weapon in my lordly arms, I felled with the sword in the midst of battle the wide-spread troops of the Lullume.
With the aid of Šamaš and Adad, my divine helpers, I thundered like Adad, the destroyer, against the armies of the lands of Nairi, Habhi, the Shubare, and Nirib.
The king who subdued at his feet (the area) from the opposite bank of the Tigris to Mount Lebanon and the Great Sea, the entire lands of Laqe (and) Suhi including the city of Rapiqu.
He conquered from the source of the Subnat River to Urartu.
I annexed within the borders of my land (the area) from the passes of Mount Kirruru to the land of Gilzanu, from the opposite bank of the Lower Zab to the city of Til-Bari which is upstream from Zaban, from Til-Sha-Abtani to Til-Sha-Zabdani, the cities of Hirimu, Harutu, fortresses of Karduniash (Babylonia).
I counted as people of my land (the inhabitants) from the pass of Mount Babite to Mount Hashmar.
In the lands over which I ruled I appointed my governors.
They did obeisance.

Not only are a number of common syntagms employed in the narrative, but there is also the usual hyperbole.

*Adad-nirari III*

(The Tell Al Rimah Stela)[101]

D $^{\text{4GIŠ}}$narkabāti(TUKUL$^{\text{MEŠ}}$) ṣābē(ERÍN.ḪI.A$^{\text{MEŠ}}$) karāšē-(KARAŠ$^{\text{MEŠ}}$) lu ad-ki

E ana $^{\text{māt}}$Ḫat-te alāka(GIN-ra) lu aq-bi

$a^{2}$ ina ištēt(DIŠ-et) šatti(MU.AN-ti)

$L^{2i}$ $^{\text{5māt}}$Amurru(MAR.TU)$^{\text{KI}}$ $^{\text{māt}}$Ḫat-te a-na si-ḫir-ti-šá ina šēpē(GÌR II$^{\text{MEŠ}}$)-ya lu ú-šak-niš

$O^{1}$ biltu(GU.UN) ma-da-tu $^{6}$a-na arkat(EGIR) $u_4$-me eli(UGU)-šú-nu lu ú-kin

$M^{e}$ 2 lim biltu(GU.UN) kaspu(KÙ.BABBAR) 1 lim biltu(GU.UN) erû 2 lim biltu(GU.UN) parzillu(AN.BAR) $^{7}$3 lim lu-bùl-ti bir-me u $^{\text{TÚG}}$kitê (GADA$^{\text{MEŠ}}$) ma-da-tu ša $^{\text{I}}$Ma-ri-'i ša $^{\text{māt}}$Imeri-šú im-ḫur

M $^{8}$ma-da-tu šá $^{\text{I}}$Ia-'a-su $^{\text{māt}}$Sa-me-ri-na-a-a $^{\text{māt}}$Ṣur-a-a $^{\text{māt}}$Ṣi-du-na-a-a $^{9}$im-ḫur

I mustered (my) chariots, troops and camps;
I ordered (them) to march against Hatti-land.
In a single year:[102]
I made the entire lands of Amurru and Hatti kneel at my feet.
I imposed tribute and tax for future days upon them.
He (sic) received 2000 talents of silver, 1000 talents of copper, 2000 talents of iron, 3000 multi-colored garments and (plain) linen garments as tribute from Mari'[103] of the land of Damascus. He received the tribute of Ia'asu the Samaritan,[104] of the Tyrian (ruler), and of the Sidonian (ruler).

$E^2$ ana tam-tim rabîte(GAL-te) šá šùl-me $^{d}$Šam-ši lu a-lik
$P^1$ ṣa-lam bēlu(EN)-ti-ya $^{10}$ina $^{uru}$Ar-ma-di ša qabal(MÚR) tam-tim lu-u az-qu-pu
$E^{12}$ ana $^{KUR}$Lab-na-ni $^{11}$lu e-li
$R^3$ $^{GIŠ}$gušūrē(ÙR) 1 me $^{GIŠ}$e-ri-ni dan-nu-te ḫi-ši-iḫ-ti ekalli(É.GAL) ekurrāti(É.KUR)-ya $^{12}$lu ak-kis
M ma-da-te šá šarrāni(ŠAR$_4$$^{MEŠ}$-ni) šá $^{māt}$Na-'i-ri kalê(MEŠ)-šú-nu lu-u im-ḫur

I marched to the great sea where the sun sets;
(and) I erected a stela of my royal self in the city of Arvad which is in the midst of the sea.
I climbed the Lebanon mountains;
(and) I cut down timbers: 100 mature cedars, material needed for my palace and temples.
He received tributes from all the kings of Nairi.

This inscription has been identified as a 'summary inscription'.[105] It telescopes all the wars in the west into one 'single year'—a figure also employed in the Sheikh Hammad stela.[106] A similar figure of quick victory in 'one single year', or even 'half a year', occurs earlier in the inscriptions of Samsu-iluna and in the Akkadian version of Suppiluliuma's treaty with Mattiwaza (*BoST* 8, 14:46).[107]

While the Summary Texts do not evince an iterative scheme in the narrative, they do use many of the stereotyped syntagms. Moreover, other rhetorical devices are employed in them so that their figurative nature is very clear.

## CONCLUSION

Through our analyses, we have been able to reveal some of the ideological and literary structures underlying Assyrian history writing. In particular, we have demonstrated that stereotyped syntagms are utilized as components to build up the text's transmission code.

Furthermore, this code provides the trellis for the historical account. The patterning of syntagms produces an 'iterative scheme' which, in turn, produces a 'high-redundance message' expressing the ideology of the inscriptions. Thus the figurative nature of these accounts is heavily reinforced.

The monotonous iteration of the typical syntagms instilled in the ancient public a sense of forced anticipation of the obvious outcome of the event itself; and hence, of the relentless efficacy of the action of the Assyrian king both in its operative aspects (whether in his bellicose, destructive nature or in his economic-acquisitive nature) and in its institutional implications.

Our analysis has revealed some of the narrative's literary structures. The use of syntagmic patterning in the narration of each campaign—whatever its level of awareness—reflects the Assyrian concept of a *girru* (campaign). The real sense of a campaign is to be found in its desire for the restoration of order. The enemy has brought about disorder and chaos, and the Assyrian king must reinstate order, righteousness and life. The decisive moment, therefore, is set in function M: the submission of all the surrounding minor political centers to the Assyrian king. This submission can be obtained in three ways:

1) the antagonist decides immediately that it is convenient to submit, and thus the basic sequence is: E → M.
2) the antagonist decides to face the Assyrian king, and is irreparably defeated, and then submits; the basic sequence is: E → IL → M.
3) Through flight, the antagonist endeavors to evade submission or combat but nevertheless is caught, defeated, and made to submit; the basic sequence is E → GH → IL → M.

The these can be graphically summed up as follows:[108]

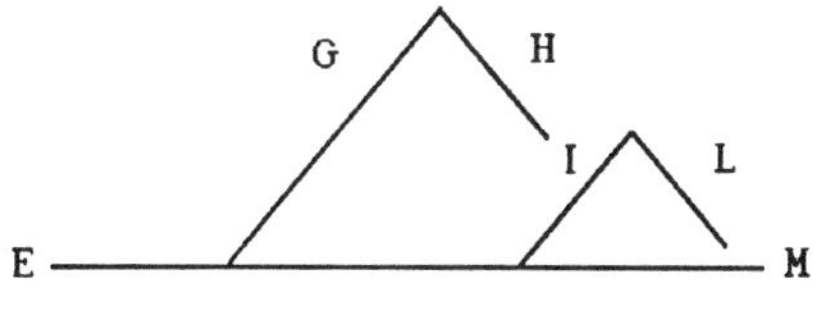

The fact that all three ways lead inevitably to the same outcome demonstrates that—from the Assyrian point of view—the object in whatever case is attained. But some differences do exist (especially for the enemy) based on the manner of his submission. While there is similarity between the listings of booty ($L^{2\delta\varepsilon}$) and the listings of tribute ($M^{\delta\varepsilon}$), there is a substantial difference between the fate of the enemy who resists and is suppressed ($L^1$) and that of the enemy who submits and is granted his life. Thus, whatever happens, the Assyrians always obtain the material goods; but for the enemies, it is far more convenient to submit than futilely offer resistance.[109]

Within the episodes several functions are constantly present and more detailed, while others appear less frequently and are only briefly expounded. For example, while the journey to the place of combat (E) is always present and often connotated, the return journey (Q) is practically ignored. Or again, the actual combat (I) is normally passed over, while the subsequent massacre ($L^1$) is incessantly described. This disparity among the functions demonstrates what was considered to be more or less significant for the attainment of the objectives (whether of persuasion or deterrence and/or celebration). The Annals were configured and promulgated with these objectives in view.[110]

The fact that this configuring can be observed in different episodes with different historical referents (i.e. different characters, geographical locations, regnal years, etc.) within the same text, as well as in texts from different kings from different periods and from different genres, argues for the legitimacy of syntagmic valency. Its employment in such different categories as Sargon's Letter to the God and the dedication text of the Kurba'il statue demonstrates that the usage is not confined to the 'Annals' alone. While the Summary/Display Texts do not show the iterative scheme (due to their lack of episodic narration), they do evince these same ideological and literary structures as found in the other Assyrian texts. The wide selection of inscriptions investigated shows that there was a common transmission code which was characteristic of the Assyrian royal inscriptions.

# Chapter 3

## HITTITE CONQUEST ACCOUNTS[1]

> By stressing the scientific character of their work, historians of the nineteenth and twentieth centuries have conveyed the impression that what they have written is strictly scientific and literally so. Nothing could be farther from the truth.[2]

There have been a number of contributions to the study of Hittite history writing. Most of these have taken a generic approach being concerned chiefly with classification of the texts. One prime example of this method is H.G. Güterbock's comprehensive work[3].

Some of these contributions have been interested in the Hittites' 'sense of history'. For example, Annelies Kammenhuber argued that there was a 'historical sense' among the Hattians and Hittites that can be documented from an early period.[4] She believed that this 'Hattian-Hittite historical sense' was superior to the Sumerian and Babylonian 'historical sense' because the latter lacked any real sense of history as such.[5] Moreover, she concluded that Hittite history writing 'strictly speaking' ('im engeren Sinne') is found in only two forms: 1) 'chronikliteratur', and 2) the self-presentation of individual kings.[6] These forms have 'an interest in history' beyond any religious expression that the text might also contain. Thus she understands Hittite history writing as being far superior to Israelite history writing since it, like that in Mesopotamia, was primarily concerned with ethic and eschatology.[7]

Hoffner strongly criticizes this idea pointing out the similarities between the Hittite and Mesopotamian views.

> It seems to me, therefore, gratuitous to speak of a praiseworthy 'historischer Sinn' of the Hittites, which was clearly superior to the concepts of the neighboring contemporary

> peoples and which one must attribute to the symbiosis between Hattians and Indo-European Hittites.[8]

Another illustration of this type of work can be seen in H. Cancik's exploration of 'historical truth' in the Hittite texts.[9] He concludes that there was a similar degree of historical consciousness and notions of causality in Hittite and Israelite history writing, but not in Mesopotamia. While many of his observations are helpful, this type of approach is plagued from the start by numerous problems. Such studies often assume that there was continuity and development in the civilization so that concepts of 'truth' and 'historical consciousness' are traceable.[10] But Hoffner correctly counters:

> What we may learn, therefore, is not a single uniform 'view' of history writing held by the Hittites, but many individual viewpoints held by some of the Hittites who undertook to write down portions of their past as they conceived it.[11]

Finally, a few works have attempted to understand Hittite historiographic techniques. For instance, Cancik compared Hittite and Old Testament prose on the basis of a historiographic narrative style (Erzählstrukturen, Erzählformen).[12] The analysis of Cancik of particular texts (such as Muršili II's annals) is very helpful. But the work is again damaged by Cancik's presuppositions and generalizations concerning other ancient Near Eastern history writing, and by his thesis concerning the direct influence of Hittite historiography on Israelite and Greek history writing.[13]

M. Liverani has published an article which disputes the 'prima lettura' understanding of the treaty between Suppiluliuma and Sunaššura (Kizzuwatna).[14] He argues that the symmetry in the treaty (col. I, 1.17-18 and I, 1.30-31) is expressive of a formula of reciprocity used in relationships of subordination.[15] Thus in Liverani's opinion, Kizzuwatna had no real choice. The Hittites used the occasion of the treaty to send a message destined for the Hurrians. Kizzuwatna, therefore, was exploited for the purpose of establishing a communication between the Hittites and the Hurrians.[16]

Liverani also makes an important point: Hittite history writing is not impartial, objective and unbiased. It is highly selective (like any history writing) making precise moral evaluations and presenting the data in a positive or negative light. In short, Hittite historical texts were written from a particular *Tendenz*.[17] This is important because it is too often assumed by ancient Near Eastern and biblical scholars that 'history' is objective reporting and that 'political propaganda' is tendentious reporting. But a 'narrative' is a form of explanation that imposes a structure or a pattern on the 'facts.' It is not a coherent structure that we 'find' embedded within the mass of 'facts,' and it is always constructed from a particular point of view. This point of view is usually quite different in different cultures and in different ages. So while the past might not change, our manner of organizing it does.[18]

Liverani has also looked at the *Proclamation of Telipinu*.[19] He argues that the underlying pattern of the text is the pattern of the 'restorer of order'. In this pattern, the characteristic qualities of time are viewed in terms of a 'rotation'. The sequence of qualities of time is: 'good' → 'bad' → 'good'; but the subject seems to have moved one step further in the sequence. The happy past is pushed back into a more remote past, a veritable mythical age, and its function of ideal model of a corrected situation is underscored. The phase of corruption and chaos is over (i.e., moved from the present to a nearby past, just finished; while the second stage of order and prosperity is moved ahead from the future to the present). It would seem, therefore, that the cycle had undergone a rotation of one degree. This pattern is a public one (i.e., it establishes contact between two different groups: namely, between the king and his subjects). Furthermore, the pattern is a characteristic of the 'edict of reform.'[20] Hence, the political authority arranges for his subjects a rotation of one degree in their existential cycle. Whether the rotation really takes place (apart from an initial enthusiasm) or not, is another matter. In this text, Telipinu terms himself a 'restorer of order' and conveys in essence a message of this type: 'The negative present in which all of you used to live is over beginning now; all the hopes you had are fulfilled beginning from now'. It is a blatant use of propaganda. Telipinu's rotation is of the make-believe type[21] since he has pushed back the happy past into a more remote past, a veritable mythical age (the kingship of 'Labarna') and since he proclaims the introduction of a mechanism for the succession to the throne which was already in use. Thus Liverani sees in the *Proclamation of Telipinu* the final request of the old *panku-* in connection with a strengthening of the royal Despot and the solidarity between the king and the immediate family of the royal house.[22]

Finally, H.G. Güterbock has recently readdressed the subject.[23] He reevaluates some of the earlier work and attempts to offer a new survey of the Hittite historical texts. For example, he clarifies his earlier statements concerning the use of the 'umma' formula. He emphasizes that he only spoke of historical texts which have the form of edicts, but did not derive all Hittite historiography from edicts. He points out that the 'umma' formula 'puts the historical accounts on the same level as any other pronouncement of the king'.[24] This fact observed by Güterbock is important because it shows that formulae are not necessarily always indicators of literary type or genre.

In this chapter we will not attempt to offer a survey of Hittite historical texts nor will we endeavor to classify them according to genre. Other studies have already worked hard on accomplishing these things. Most of these contributions have taken some sort of generic approach, although a few have been interested in the Hittites' 'sense of history'. As in the previous chapter, our interest are primarily in the literary and ideological structures which undergird the Hittite accounts.

In our probe into Hittite history writing, we will investigate the literary and ideological aspects in the writing of their history. We will also carry out syntagmic analysis on numerous Hittite historical accounts in order to demonstrate the simulated nature of these accounts.

## HITTITE IDEOLOGY: *Feeling a little vengeful Today?*

Very little has been written on the subject of Hittite ideology. A. Goetze, writing in 1928, proposed a model to explain Hittite expansionist ideology: 'At the Taurus the stream of immigrants came to a halt, but its seems that the tendency to press on further to the southeast remained alive in them'.[25] Gurney feels that in this sentence we see an attempt 'to explain Hittite imperialism in terms of almost natural causes: the Hittites were like an irresistible flood which no dam could hold'.[26] Their ideology was a type of 'manifest destiny'. H. Otten seems to understand Hittite ideology in this way stating: 'the attainment of maritime boundaries was the natural goal of Hittite power from the earliest times'.[27]

Gurney, however, rejects this view of Hittite ideology arguing that 'Hittite history is the history of a city-state and its rulers, not a tribe which saw its kismet in an empire ruling all Anatolia and Syria'.[28] Furthermore, while it is true that successive kings are said to have 'made them borderlands of the sea' and that this refrain is even repeated in a prayer, this view that the Hittites believed it to be their natural fate to have maritime boundaries does not, according to Gurney, explain the onward expansion into Syria and the Babylonian adventure.[29]

Thus for Gurney there are three bases for Hittite imperialistic[30] ideology which explain what impelled the Hittite kings, both of the Old and New Kingdoms, to conquer their neighbors, expand their boundaries, and acquire dominion over distant territories:

1). A geographic-economic basis. The fact that both Mesopotamia and Anatolia are lacking in indispensable raw materials and that Syria possessed the ports to allow access to trade to acquire these materials meant that the possession of Syria assured supremacy in the world in antiquity.[31] Thus Gurney concludes: 'Here, no doubt, is the underlying economic cause which explains the early Hittite expansion and especially the direction that it took'.[32]

2). Expansion for its own sake. Gurney states: 'The phraseology of the early texts, with the frequent simile of the 'raging lion', suggests that those old kings saw no further than this, that for them expansion was an ideology in its own right, a true sport of kings'.[33]

3). The motive of vengeance. For Gurney this was a major driving force in the Hittite imperialistic ideology.

> In the fourteenth century the natural drive to control the wealth of Syria was intensified by the motive of vengeance. The challenge of invasion and suffering called forth a furious

> response and a determination to emulate the ancient kings. Suppiluliuma and his successors felt that the gods were on their side in avenging the wrongs that had been done to them. The word 'kattawatar' 'vengeance' appears significantly in the account of a campaign against Isuwa. The preambles to the treaties harp on the 'sins' that had been committed by neighbouring kings, their violation of oaths and other insulting behaviour. Retaliation followed as of right.[34]

While these were the grounds of the Hittite imperialistic ideology, Gurney points out that it was not a limitless expansionist ideology. The Hittite kings were in many ways realists because they knew where to stop. Apparently, this spilled over into the dissemination of their imperialism for the Hittites (according to Gurney) maintained their 'characteristic humanity, sense of justice and respect for the gods' so that their 'overlordship was generally acceptable'.[35]

## LITERARY STRUCTURES

> *'And the sungoddess of Arinna, my lady; the mighty stormgod, my lord; Mezzulla (and) all of the gods ran before me ...'*

There are numerous Hittite conquest accounts which included more than one episode or campaign. The earliest text which we will examine which fits this qualification is the Anitta Text.[36] It is too fragmentary to subject to a full syntagmic analysis, but in light of the much recent discussion concerning this text, a few observations are in order.

Since the Babylonian type of script was employed in the extant copy, some have assumed that Anitta and his father Pithana were not Hittites, but Hattic (or protohittite)[37] and that the language originally used in the work was Hattic and later translated into Old Hittite.

However, E. Neu points out in his new edition that translations from Hattic are always marked by a certain awkwardness (*Holprigkeit*), which betrays them as translations, and that the Anitta text does not manifest any of these.[38] Furthermore, Güterbock points out that there is evidence for contact between central Anatolia and Mari at this time so that the use of the Babylonian type of script is not really a problem at all.[39]

Hoffner concludes: 'there is no cogent reason to exclude this text from the corpus of Hittite historical texts'.[40]

Güterbock notes that the Anitta text is one of two exceptions to the usual opening which employs the 'umma' formula:[41]

> Its introduction is still a crux, since it only consists of his name, patronymic, and title followed apparently by 'qibi', the imperative 'speak', which is common in letters but makes little sense without saying 'to whom' the reader should speak. Here it almost sounds as if the command were addressed to Anitta![42]

It is important, however, to remember that the text states that it was inscribed on the gate (common in Mesopotamia and Anatolia).[43] But this mention of an inscription comes very early in the text, and the narrative continues after this, as though the author had added the accounts of the most important events to an existing short text.[44] Van Seters runs with this idea, stating:

> On closer examination, however, it may be noted that the text has the appearance of being a compilation of various earlier texts and inscriptions. This is indicated most clearly by the reference to a royal inscription containing the words of the first part of the account (lines 33-35). Also, two sets of curses follow two accounts of military campaigns. The last part of the text seems to be a rather haphazard collection of royal deeds. If indeed the text was a compilation of inscriptions it would be easier to explain its form in terms of Mesopotamian antecedents. Several features of this text may also be found in Assyrian royal inscriptions. References to military campaigns and to temple building are known from inscriptions of the time of Shamshi-Adad I and Yahdun-lim, king of Mari, near contemporaries of Anitta ... What is exceptional is the way in which various inscriptional accounts have been combined to give the appearance of a primitive annals text, even though the events are not clearly dated. Yet it may be this rather unartistic compilation that ultimately gave rise to the Hittite annals.[45]

While it is probably true that the Anitta text has utilized other sources in the composition, it may not be fair to judge the text as an 'unartistic compilation'. First, the fragmentary nature of the text does not allow us to know enough of the narrative to make such evaluations as 'haphazard' or 'primitive compilation'. Such assessments are a bit premature.

Second, the two curses[46] may be as a dividing technique utilized to produce symmetry within the accounts. That there are links between sections is apparent from phrases like *ta-a-an nam-ma* $^{i}$*Pi-i-u-us-ti-is* LUGAL [$^{\text{uru}}$]*Ha-at-ti u-*[ :: 'For a second time then Piyusti, king of Hatti, c[ame]' (line 36) which seems to link to LUGAL *H[a-at-ti* :: 'king of Hatti' (line 14). Also the mentioning of 'All the lands from Zalpuwa from the sea' (lines 31-32; 39ff); and the taking of the accursed cities 'in the night by force' (lines 18, 48); and finally the descriptions of the building activities and the hunt (lines 55-63) are in between the two campaigns against Salatiwara (52-54 and 64-67). Also the use of historical retrospect can be observed in the narrative by the use of the adverbs '*karu*' and '[*app]ezziyana*' :: 'previously' and 'but later' (lines 39-42); and in the inclusion of events from the reign of the author's immediate predecessor.[47] But obviously a document from the time which the Anitta Text purports to come is not going to be on the same level of development in historiographic technique as say the Annals of Muršili II. The Anitta Text is a very interesting work which hopefully someday we will be able to completely understand.

## *Syntagmic Analysis*

### *Syntagms of the Hittite Texts*

These are roughly the syntagmic functional equivalents to the Assyrian functions previously discussed.

A — *Spatio-Temporal Coordinates*

$A^{2}$ MU-*an-ni-ma* :: 'In the following year'

$A^{2}$ *ma-aḫ-ḫa-an-ma ḫa-me-eš-ḫa-an-za* :: 'So when it became spring'

$A^{2}$ *nam-ma* :: 'Meanwhile // At that same time'

$A^{2}$ *nam-ma a-pi-e-da-ni* MU$^{\text{ti}}$ :: 'Then that very same year'

$A^{1,2}$ [43][*nam-ma* $^{\text{d}}$UT$^{\text{ši}}$ EGI]R-*pa ú-wa-nu-un* :: '[After this, my sun, came back again'

$A^{2}$ [43]*lu-uk-kat-ti-ma* :: 'On the next day'

B — *Disorder*

[30]*ŠA* KUR $^{\text{uru}}$*Tur-mi-it-ta-mu* $^{\text{uru}}$*Ka-aš-ka-aš ku-u-ru-ri-ya-aḫ-ta* :: 'The Kaskaens of the region of Turmitta made war with me'

*nu-mu x x x* [31]*nam-ma* $^{\text{uru}}$*Ka$_4$-aš-ka$_4$-aš ú-it-pit* :: 'Furthermore, the Kaškaens came'

*nu* KUR $^{uru}$*Tur-mi-it-ta* GUL-*an-ni-iš-ki-u-an da-*[*a-iš*] :: 'and began to attack the region of Turmitta'
*nu* KUR UGU *ša-ra-a da-a-aš* :: 'and seize (and plunder) the Upper Land'
*nu-za-kán* $^{ḫur.sag}$*A-ri-in-na-an-da-an e-ip-pir* :: 'and they occupied Mt. Arinnanda'

B$^1$ *nu-mu* ERÍN.MEŠ Ú-UL *pi-eš-ki-it* :: 'and they were not giving me troops (as an act of rebellion)'

C — *Divine Aid*

C $^{16}$*nu-za* $^{d}$U NER.GÁL EN-YA *pa-ra-a ḫa-an-da-an-da-a-tar te-ik-ku-uš-ša-nu-ut* :: 'the mighty stormgod, my lord, showed his godly miracle'
$^{17}$*nu* $^{giš}$*kal-mi-ša-na-an ši-ya-a-it* :: 'He hurled a meteor'
*nu* $^{giš}$*kal-mi-ša-na-an am-me-el* KARAŠ.ḪI.A-*YA* $^{18}$*uš-ki-it* :: 'My army saw the meteor'
*nu* $^{giš}$*kal-mi-ša-na-aš pa-it* :: 'And the meteor went'
$^{19}$*nu* KUR $^{uru}$*Ar-za-u-wa GUL-aḫ-ta* :: 'and struck the land of Arzawa'
$^{20i}$*U-uḫ-ḫa-*LÚ-*na gi-nu-uš-šu-uš a-še-eš-ta* :: 'Uhhaziti fell on (his) knees'
*na-aš ir-ma-li-ya-at-ta-at* :: 'and became ill'

C$^1$ *nu-mu* $^{d}$UTU $^{uru}$*A-ri-in-na* $^{39}$[*GAŠAN-YA*] $^{d}$U NER.GÁL EN-YA $^{d}$*Me-iz-zu-ul-la-aš* DINGIR.MEŠ *ḫu-u-ma-an-te-eš pi-ra-an hu-i-e-ir* :: 'and the sungoddess of Arinna, [my lady]; the mighty stormgod, my lord, Mezzulla, (and) all the gods ran before me'
*nu-uš-ši* DINGIR.MEŠ *kat-ta-an ti-i-e-er* :: 'And the gods stood by him'

C$^2$ [$^{d}$UTU $^{uru}$TÚL-*na*] $^{8d}$U $^{uru}$*Ḫa-at-ti* $^{d}$U KI.KAL.BAD $^{d}$IŠTAR LIL :: '[the sun goddess of Arinna, the storm god of Hatti, the storm god of the Army, and Ištar of the Battlefield'

D — *Gathering of Troops*

$^{8}$*nu-za* ERÍN.MEŠ ANŠU.KUR.RA.MEŠ *ni-ni-in-ku-un* :: 'I mustered troops and charioteers'

E — *Move from place to place*

$^{32}$*nu-uš-ši* $^{d}$UT$^{ši}$ *pa-a-un* // *i-ya-an-ni-ya-nu-un* :: 'I, my sun, went to it (the region)' // 'I marched'
Main verbs = *iyannai-* 'to march'; *pai-* 'to go'; and *uwa-* 'to come'

F — *Presence*

*nu* GIM-*an I-NA* $^{ḫur.sag}$*La-wa-ša a-ar-ḫu-un* :: 'and as I arrived at Mt. Lawasa'
*nu-mu-uš-ša-an I-NA* $^{uru}$*Pal-hu-iš-ša* EGIR-*an* LÚ.KÚR $^{uru}$*Pi-eš-ḫu-ru-uš* $^{3}$MÈ-*ya ti-ya-at* :: 'And I positioned myself behind Palhuissa (in order to) fight (against) the enemy of the city of Pishuru'

F$^{1}$ $^{28}$*ma-aḫ-ḫa-an-ma* LÚ.MEŠ $^{uru}$*Az-zi a-ú-e-ir* URU.AŠ.AŠ.ḪI.A BAD-*kán ku-it za-aḫ-ḫi-ya-az* $^{29}$*kat-ta da-aš-ki-u-wa-an te-eḫ-ḫu-un* :: 'When the people of the city of Azzi saw that fighting (their) strong cities I subjugated them'

$^{36}$[*ma-aḫ-ḫ*]*a-an-ma* KUR $^{uru}$*Ka-aš-ka ŠA* $^{uru}$*Ha-li-la* U *ŠA* $^{uru}$*Du-ud--du-uš-ka ḫar-ni-in-ku-u-ar* $^{37}$[*iš-t*]*a-ma-aš-ta* :: 'But when the land of Kaška heard of the destruction of Halila (and) Dudduska'

F$^{3}$ *nu-za* BAD KARAŠ $^{48}$*I-NA* $^{id}$*As-tar-pa wa-aḫ-nu-nu-un* :: 'I pitched camp at the river Astarpa'

G — *Flight*

G$^{\Delta 1}$ *nu-mu* $^{i}$*Uḫ-ḫa*-LÚ-*iš Ú-UL ma-az-za-aš-ta* :: 'and Uhhaziti could not withstand me'

$^{67}$[*nu-uš-ša-an* $^{i}$*Ta-pa-la-zu-na*]-*u-liš ku-iš* DUMU $^{i}$*U-uḫ-ḫa*-LÚ *INA* $^{uru}$*Pu-ra-an-da še-ir e-ešta* $^{68}$[*na-aš na-aḫ-šar-ri-ya-a*]*t-ta-at* :: 'Tapalazunauli, the son of Uhhaziti, who was in Puranda, was afraid'

G$^{-2}$ *nu* KUR $^{uru}$*Ka-aš-ka ḫu-u-ma-an an-da wa-ar-ri-eš-še-eš-ta* :: 'the entire land of the Kaskaens came together to help'

G$^{-3}$ $^{38}$[*na-at-m*]*u* MÈ-*ya ú-it* :: '[and] came against me for battle'

*nu-mu-kán* $^{i}$SUM-*ma*-$^{d}$KAL-*an* DUMU-*ŠU* $^{23}$*QA-DU* ERÍN.MEŠ ANŠU.KUR.RA.MEŠ *me-na-aḫ-ḫa-an-da para-a na-eš-ta* :: '(but) he sent his son, Piyama-KAL, together with troops and charioteers to engage me'

G$^{\Delta 3}$ *na-aš-mu nam-ma za-aḫ-ḫi-ya* $^{22}$*me-na-aḫ-ḫa-an-da Ú-UL ú-it* :: 'he did not come against me to fight'

*na-an-ša-an nam-ma Ú-U*[*L ú-e-mi-ia-zi*] :: 'but again he did not [engage] him'

*nu-mu* ERÍN.MEŠ $^{uru}$[*Ḫu-wa-ar-ša-na-ša-na-aš-ša*] $^{27}$U ERÍN. MES $^{uru}$[....... *pi-ra-an ar-ḫa par-še-ir*] :: '[And the troops of Huwarsanasanassa] and the troops of [.....fled before me]'

*nu* KUR-*e-an-za ḫu-u-ma-an-za* URU.AŠ.AŠ.ḪI.A BAD $^{37}$EGIR-*pa e-ip-pir* :: '(But) the whole country withdrew to the fortress towns'

H — *Pursuit*

$^{74}$[*nu-uš-ši* $^{d}$UT$^{ši}$ ERÍN$^{meš}$ ANŠU.KUR.R]A$^{meš}$ EGIR-*an-da ú-i-ya-nu-un* :: 'then I, my sun, sent troops and charioteers after him'

*nam-ma-an* EGIR-*an-pit AṢ-BAT* :: 'Then I pursued him'

I — *Combat*

*nu ŠA* $^{uru}$*Ka-aš-ka ku-i-e-eš* SAG.DU.MEŠ KUR.KUR.MEŠ $^{uru}$*Ha-li-la-aš* $^{33uru}$*Du-ud-du-uš-ka-aš-ša e-šir na-aš* GUL-*un* :: 'and I attacked Halila and Dudduska which were major cities of the Kaskaens'

*na-an* $^{d}$UTU$^{ši}$ MÈ-*ya-nu-un* // *za-aḫ-ḫi-ya-nu-un* :: 'And I, my sun, fought against it (the entire land)'

$^{65}$[*na-an-kán an-da*] *ḫa-at-ki-eš-nu-nu-un* :: 'And I pressed against it'

$^{75}$[*na-at* $^{i}$*Da-pa-la-zu-na-wa-li-i*]*n* KAŠ-*ši* EGIR-*an-da ta-ma-aš-šir* :: 'And they pressed Tapalazunauli on the road from behind'

L — *Outcome of Combat*

$L^{1}$ = *destruction*

- $L^{1}$ל = *na-an-kán ku-e-nu-un* :: 'I defeated it'
- $L^{1}$ב = *ḫar-ni-in-ku-un* :: 'I destroyed'
- $L^{1}$ג = *wa-ar-nu-nu-un* :: 'I burned'
  $^{35}$[$^{uru}$*Ḫa*]*-li-la-an-ma* $^{uru}$*Du-ud-du-uš-ka-an-an ar-ḫa wa-ar-nu-nu-un* :: 'I completely burned down Halila (and) Dudduska'
- $L^{1}$ד = *dan-na-at-ta-aḫ-ḫu-un* :: 'I made ... empty (of humanity)'
  $^{šad}$*Aš-ḫar-pa-ya-an-ma dan-na-at-ta-aḫ-ḫu-un* :: 'I made Mt. Asharpaya empty (of humanity)'
- $L^{1}$ב = BA.$UG_{6}$ // BA.BAD // *akiš-* :: 'he died'
  *nu* $^{l}$[$^{ú}$KUR] $^{9}$*pa-an-ga-ri-it* BA.BAD :: '(so that) the en[emy] died in multitudes'

$L^{2}$ = *acquisition*

- $L^{2}$אζ = *taraḫḫun* :: 'I conquered'
  $^{40}$[*nu-za* ŠAK]UR $^{uru}$*Kaš-ka* ERIM.MEŠ *NA-RA-RU tar--aḫ-ḫu-un* :: '(So) I conquered the auxiliary troops of the land of Kaska'
- $L^{2}$ = *IK-ŠU-UD* :: 'He captured'
  $^{6}$*nu* $^{lú}$KUR $^{uru}$*Ka-aš-ka pa-a-an-ku-un* EREM.MEŠ *ŠU-TI I-NA* [ŠA.KUR-*TI*] $^{7}$*IK-SU-UD* :: '(But) the Kaska enemy, all of their tribal troops, he met in [the country]'
- $L^{2}$גγ = *da-aḫ-ḫu-un* :: 'I took (as captives)' [*da-* = 'take']
- $L^{2}$ו = *ÌR-aḫ-ta-at* :: 'I subjugated' [*ÌR-naḫ(ḫ)-* = 'subjugate']
- $L^{2}$ד = *te-eḫ-ḫu-un* :: 'I subjugated' [*dai-* = 'subdue']
- $L^{2}$ט = *ḫulliya-* 'to overturn'

M — *Submission*

*na-at-mu* GÌR.MEŠ-*aš kat-ta-an* $^{47}$*ḫa-a-li-ya-an-da-at* :: 'And they bowed themselves down at (my) feet'

O — *Consequences*

- O♦ *na-aš-za* ERÍN.MEŠ ANŠU.KUR.RA.ḪI.A *i-ya-nu-un* :: 'And I made them troops and charioteers'
- $O^{1}$ $^{42}$[*nu-mu* ERÍN.MEŠ]*pi-eš-ki-u-an da-a-ir* :: '[And] (again) they began to provide [me troops]'
- $O^{2}$ *nu-kán* ERÍN.MEŠ *ašandulanni dalaḫḫun* :: 'I garrisoned troops'
- $O^{6}$ *nu* KUR ... *ANA 'PN' AD-DIN* // *pi-eḫ-ḫu-un* :: 'I gave the land ... to PN'

P — *Acts of Celebration*

*nu-za* EZEN MU$^{ti}$ *a-pi-ya i-ya-nu-un* :: 'and I celebrated the New-year festival there'

$P^3$ *I-NA* É $^{d}$*Me-iz-zu-ul-la pi-eḫ-ḫu-un* :: 'I gave to the temple of Mezzulla'

Q — *Return*

$Q^1$ $^{41}$*nu-za* $^{d}$UT$^{ši}$ *ku-in* NAM.RA *I-NA* É LUGAL *ú-wa-te-nu-un* :: 'And those of the inhabitants which I, my sun, brought into the royal palace'

$Q^2$ *nam-ma-kán* NAM.RA.MEŠ $^{uru}$KÙBABBAR-*ši pa-ra-a* $^{45}$*ne-eḫ-ḫu-un* :: 'Finally, I sent forth the captive inhabitants to Hattuša'

$Q^3$ *na-aš* $^{uru}$KÙBABBAR-*ši ar-ḫa ú-da-aḫ-ḫu-un* :: 'and I brought them forth to Hattuša'

S — *Summary*

*nu ki-i I-NA* MU 1.KAM *i-ya-nu-un* :: 'And I did (all) this in one year'

Y — *Report* (oral and/or written)

With delineation by superscription.

*Special Symbols* — generally the same extensions as the Assyrian with the following being most common:

χ $^{42}$*na-aš* 1 x 10000 5 LI-IM 5 x 100 NAM.RA *e-eš-ta* :: 'were 15,500 people'

Φ *nu-uš-ša-an kap-pu-u-wa-u-wa-ar* $^{44}$NU.GAL *e-eš-ta* :: 'the number does not exist'

η *nu-kán a-pí-ya* $^{55}$[*ku-i-*]*e?-eš?* [....] *iš-par-te-ir* :: 'And those who had escaped'

## *The 'Concise' Annals of Hattušili I*[48]

The Annals of Hattušili I (both the 'Concise' and 'Extensive' accounts) are the oldest examples of what may be called annals among the Hittites. The term 'annals' is used here in the same sense as for the later Assyrian annals discussed in the previous chapter. The Hittite word for this type of work is '*pišnadar*' (it is usually written as 'LU-*natar*',[49] which means literally 'manliness', hence 'Manly Deeds'. According to Güterbock the Hittite term is not the same as 'res gestae', but rather has the connotation of 'virtues'.[50] Interestingly, the 'Concise' account of the 'Manly Deeds' of Hattušili I were written in both Hittite and Akkadian.[51]

This 'Concise' account was only a selected account of his most important achievements, leaving out the routine years of his reign and the campaigns that he did not deem to be significant. Kempinski and Košak argue that this is clearly understood when consideration is given to the purpose of the selection, namely, 'that it was to be engraved on the small golden statue presented to the Sungoddess of Arinna (*KBo* 10:2 rev. III 21-24)'.[52]

Furthermore, through a comparison of the 'Concise' and 'Extensive' Annals, the former's selectivity becomes obvious. Firstly, some important events in the reign are excluded. For example, the important episode of the conflict with Purušhanda (see *CTH* 9:6 and the Extensive Annals) is not mentioned by the writer of the 'Concise' Annals.[53] Secondly, there appears to be the combining of events from different years. The incorporation of conquest of Uršu and Alalah in the 'second year' in the 'Concise' Annals may have been a device of the narrator to emphasize a dramatic event by telescoping several different episodes into one year.[54] Finally, the 'Concise' Annals utilizes a literary comparison between Hattušili I and Sargon the Great at the end of the text as a type of climax to the king's 'manly deeds'.[55]

While priority for each version (Hittite and Akkadian) of the 'Concise' Annals has been claimed, Hoffner concludes:

> It is therefore probably the wisest course to give up any attempt to show absolute priority of either version. Even if the text was first drawn up in Akkadian, unless the composer was a native speaker of that language, it was thought out in Hittite and translated mentally into Akkadian. The text is clearly a Hittite composition in the fundamental sense.[56]

For the purposes of our study, it will be sufficient to analyze the Hittite version. There are five episodes which we will present to demonstrate the stereotyped syntagmic structure of the account.

*Episode 1 (I.4-8)*

| | |
|---|---|
| E | $^{4}$[(*IN*)*A* $^{uru}$*Š*]*anawitta pait* |
| L$^{1ɔ}$ | *ša-an na-at-ta* $^{5}$[*ḫarnikt*]*a* |
| | *nu*(-)*utne-ššet ḫarnikta* |
| O$^{2}$ | $^{6}$[*nu-kán* ERÌN$^{meš}$] 2 ASRA *ašandulanni da*[*la*]*ḫḫun* |
| O$^{7}$ | $^{7}$[*nu kwe k*]*we ašawar ešta* |
| | $^{8}$[*n-(at)*] ANA ERÌN$^{meš}$ *ašanduli pi-eḫ-ḫu-un* |

He went to Sanawitta;
and he did not destroy it;
but he did destroy the countryside (around it).
And I left troops for garrison duty at two places.
[And wh]atever sheepfolds were there,
I gave them to the troops in the garrison.

*Episode 2 (I.9-14)*

E $^{9}$[EGIR-*an-d*]*a-ma I-NA* $^{uru}$*Za-al-pa pa-a-u*[*n*]
L$^{1ב}$ $^{10}$[*na-a*]*n ḫar-ni-in-ku-un*
L$^{2א e1}$ *nu-uš-ši* DINGIR$^{meš}$-*ŠU ša-ra-a da-aḫ-ḫu-un*
O$^{7}$ $^{1}$1U 3 $^{giš}$GIGIR$^{meš}$ *MA-AD-NA-NU A-NA* $^{d}$UTU $^{uru}$TÚL-*na pí-eḫ-ḫu-un*
$^{12}$ 1 GUD KÙ.BABBAR 1 GEŠPU KÙ.BABBAR *I-NA* É $^{d}$IŠKUR *pí-eḫ-ḫu-un*
$^{13}$*a-aš-še-er-ma-kán ku-i-e-eš* [DINGIR$^{meš}$] *na-aš I-NA* É $^{d}$*Me-iz-zu-ul-la* $^{14}$*pí-eḫ-ḫu-un*

[Thereaf]ter I went to Zalpa;
and destroyed it.
Its gods I took away;
and (its) 3 'madnanu'-chariots I gave to the sungoddess of Arinna.
I gave one silver bull (and) one 'fist' of silver to the temple of the stormgod;
but those [gods] who remained,
I gave to the temple of Mezzulla.

*Episode 3 (I.15-21)*

A$^{2}$ $^{15}$MU.IM.MA-*an-ni-ma*
E *I-NA* $^{uru}$*A-la-al-ḫa pa-a-[un]*
L$^{1ב}$ $^{16}$*na-an ḫar-ni-in-ku-un*
E EGIR-*an-da-[ma] I-NA* $^{uru}$*Wa-ar-šu-wa* $^{17}$*pa-a-un*
$^{uru}$*Wa-ar-šu-wa-az-ma I-NA* $^{uru}$*I-ka-ka-li* $^{18}$*pa-a-un*
$^{uru}$*I-ka-ka-la-az-ma I-NA* $^{uru}$*Ta-aš-ḫi-ni-ya* $^{19}$*pa-a-un*
L$^{1ב}$ *nu ki-e* KUR.KUR$^{meš}$ *ḫar-ni-in-ku-un*
L$^{2א}$ *a-aš-šu-ma-aš-ši* $^{20}$*ša-ra-a da-aḫ-ḫu-un*
Q *nu É-ri-mi-ti a-aš-ša-u-i-it* $^{21}$*ša-ra-a šu-un-na-aḫ-ḫu-un*

In the next year:
I went to Alalha.
And I destroyed it.
Afterwards I went to Warsuwa (A: Ursum);
I went from Warsuwa (Ursum) to Igakali.
From Igakali I went to Tashiniya.
And I destroyed these countries.
I took (their) goods away from them;
and I filled my house up to the brim with their goods.

*Episode 6 (I.46-II.1)*

| | |
|---|---|
| A$^{2}$ | $^{46}$[MU.IM.MA-*an-ni-ma* |
| E | *I-N]A* $^{uru}$*Ša-na-aḫ-ḫu-it-ta* MÈ-*ya pa-a-un* |
| I | $^{47}$[*nu* $^{uru}$*Ša-na-aḫ-ḫu-it]-ta-an I[NA]* ITU.5.KAM *za-aḫ-ḫi-eš-ki-nu-un* |
| L$^{1ɔζ}$ | $^{48}$[*na-an I-NA* ITU.6.KAM] *ḫar-ni-in-[ku]-un* |
| L$^{1α}$ | *nu-za* LUGAL.GAL $^{49}$[ZI-*an waršiJyanunun* |
| F | *nu-kán* ŠA KUR.KUR.MEŠ $^{50}$[EGIR-*panda* $^{d}$UTU-*uš tiyat* |
| - | LU-*na-tar-na* $^{51}$[*ku-it* ................ |
| P$^{3}$ | *na-at] A-NA* $^{d}$UTU $^{uru}$*A-ri-in-na* $^{52}$[*pí-eḫ-ḫu-un* |
| L$^{2υ}$ | [...]$^{53}$[... $^{giš}$GIGIR.MEŠ ŠA KUR $^{uru}$]*Ap-pa-ya* $^{54}$[*ḫu-ul-li-ya--nu-un*] |
| L$^{2λ}$ | [*nu* GUD.ḪI.A UDU.ḪI.A *ANA* $^{uru}$*Takš]an[n]aya* **II**$^{1}$*piran šara daḫḫun* |

In the next year:
I went to Sanahhuitta to fight.
I continually fought Sanahhuitta for five months.
And I destroyed it in the sixth month.
And I, the Great King, satisfied my soul.[57]
The sungod afterwards took up his position in the midst of the countries.
(The manly) deeds, which ....
And I gave it to the sungoddess of Arinna.
I overturned the chariots of the land of Appaya.
And I took the cattle and sheep of Taksanaya away.

*Episode 9 (II.54-III.12)*

| | |
|---|---|
| E | $^{54}$LUGAL.GAL *tabarnaš INA* $^{uru}$*Zippašna* $^{55}$*[p]aun* **III**$^{1uru}$*Ḫaḫḫan-ma-za-kán* UR.MAḪ *maḫḫan* $^{2}$*arḫa tarkuwalliškinun* |
| L$^{1ɔζ}$ | $^{3}$*nu* $^{uru}$*Zippaššanan ḫarninkun* |
| L$^{2λ}$ | $^{4}$DINGIR$^{meš}$-*ma-aš-ši ša-ra-a da-aḫ-ḫu-un* |
| P$^{3}$ | $^{5}$*na-aš A-NA* $^{d}$UTU $^{uru}$TUL-*na pí-e-da-aḫ-ḫu-un* |
| E | $^{6}$*nu I-NA* $^{uru}$*Ḫa-aḫ-ḫa pa-a-un* |
| L$^{21}$ | *nu-kán I-NA* $^{uru}$*Ḫa-aḫ-ḫa* $^{7}$KA.GAL$^{ḪIA}$-*aš* 3 ŠU *an-da* MÈ-*in te-eḫ-ḫu-un* |
| L$^{1ɔζ}$ | $^{8}$*nu* $^{uru}$*Ḫa-aḫ-ḫa-an ḫar-ni-in-ku-un* |
| L$^{2λe1}$ | *a-aš-šu-ma-aš-ši* $^{9}$*ša-ra-a da-aḫ-ḫu-un* |
| Q | *na-at* $^{uru}$*Ha-at-tu-ši* $^{10}$URU-*ri-mi-it ar-ḫa u-da-aḫ-ḫu-un* $^{1}$12 TA-PAL $^{GIŠ}$MAR.GÍD.DA$^{MEŠ}$ *IŠ-TU* KÙ.BABBAR $^{12}$*ta-a-iš-ti-ya-an e-eš-ta* |

The Great King, Tabarna, went to Zippasna.
But I kept looking angrily at Hahha like a lion;
and I destroyed Zippassana.
I took its gods away from it;
and I gave them to the sungoddess of Arinna.

Then I went to Hahha.
And three times I carried the battle to the city-gates of Hahha.
And I destroyed Hahha.
I took their goods away from it;
and I brought it forth to Hattuša, my city.
Two complete wagons were loaded with silver.

These syntagms yield the following readout:

| Episode 1 | Episode 2 | Episode 3 | Episode 6 | Episode 9 |
|---|---|---|---|---|
| - | - | $A^2$ | $A^2$ | - |
| E | E | E | E | E |
| - | - | - | I | - |
| $L^{1ג}$ | $L^{1ג}$ | $L^{1ג}$ | $L^{1גζ}$ | $L^{1גζ}$ |
| - | - | - | $L^{1\alpha}$ | - |
| $O^2$ | - | - | F | - |
| - | $L^{2\mathfrak{a}el}$ | - | - | $L^{2\mathfrak{a}el}$ |
| $O^7$ | $O^7$ | - | $O^7$ | $O^7$ |
| | | E | - | E |
| | | - | $L^{1ט}$ | $L^{21}$ |
| | | $L^{1ג}$ | - | $L^{1גζ}$ |
| | | $L^{2\mathfrak{a}}$ | $L^{2\mathfrak{a}}$ | $L^{2\mathfrak{a}}$ |
| | | Q | - | Q |

*The Ten Year Annals of Muršili II*[58]

The Annals of Muršili (his 'Ten Year Annals' and his 'Detailed' or 'Comprehensive Annals') are by far and away the best preserved and most developed historiographic texts of the Hittite Empire.[59] Another work which comes from the time of Muršili II is the Deeds of Suppiluliuma. Since both of the Deeds of Suppiluliuma and the 'Detailed Annals' are fragmentary, we will concentrate our analysis on the 'Ten Year Annals'. A work like Muršili's 'Ten Year Annals' must have been conceived as a whole and written at one time, which obviously could not have been earlier than the tenth year of his reign. It is unlikely that it was then all written from memory; there must have been some records on which the writers could draw.[60] The use of archival records can be seen in a number of texts. For example, Muršili says concerning his father Suppiluliuma:

> Then my father asked for the tablet of the treaty again, (in which there was told) how formerly the Stormgod took the people of Kurustama, sons of Hatti, and carried them to Egypt and made them Egyptians; and how the Stormgod concluded a treaty between the countries of Egypt and Hatti ...[61]

According to Cancik's analysis, the basic organization of the Ten Year Annals is a prologue, an epilogue which consciously resumes the prologue, and a symmetrical central section bisected by a 'Binnenschluss' (an internal conclusion) which occurs at the end of the account of year four. Within the central section episodes of two types alternate: (1) terse, report-like narratives ('Berichte') of Kaška campaigns, and (2) more literary descriptions ('Geschichten') of the protracted Arzawa war and other matters. In the literary descriptions ('Geschichten') one finds extensive use of speeches, letters, speculations about hypothetical courses of action either by the king or his opponent, portrayal of simultaneous happenings in different locations. In the terse, report-like narratives ('Berichte') one finds only stereotyped formulas. Cancik thinks that this alternation is a conscious literary technique, which proves that Muršili's 'Ten Year Annals' were the end-product of an editorial process of selection and arrangement of narrative material from a larger corpus of written records.

There is no debate that the 'Ten Year Annals' is a literary unity. The epilogue and the prologue presuppose one another (note especially the emphasized last sentences):

'Prologue'

**Vs I**$^{1}$[*UM-MA* $^{d}$UTU]$^{ši}$ $^{i}$*Mur-ši-li* LUGAL KUR *Ḫa-at-ti* UR.SAG $^{2}$[DUMU $^{i}$*Šu-up]-pi-lu-li-u-ma* LUGAL.GAL UR.SAG

Thus (speaks) 'my sun', Muršili (II), king of the land of Hatti, hero, son of Suppiluliuma (I), great king, hero:

$^{3}$*ku-it-ma-an-za-kán A-NA* $^{GIŠ}$GU.ZA *A-BI-YA na-wi e-eš-ḫa-at nu-mu a-ra-aḫ-ze-na-aš* $^{4}$KUR.KUR.MEŠ LÚ.KUR *ḫu-u-m-a-an-te-eš ku-u-ru-ri-ya-aḫ-ḫi-ir*
*nu-za A-BU-YA ku-wa-pí* DINGIR$^{li}$*-iš* DÙ*-at*
$^{5}$ $^{i}$*Ar-nu-wa-an-da-as-ma-za-kán ŠEŠ-YA A-NA* $^{GIŠ}$GU.ZA *A-BI-ŠU e-ša-at* EGIR*-an-ma-aš* $^{6}$*ir-ma-li-ya-at-ta-at-pít ma-aḫ-ḫa-an-ma* KUR.KUR.MEŠ LÚ.KUR $^{i}$*Ar-nu-wa-an-da-an ŠEŠ-YA ir-ma-an* $^{7}$*iš-ta-ma-aš-šir*

*nu* KUR.KUR.MEŠ LÚ.KUR *ku-u-ru-ri-ya-aḫ-ḫi-eš-ki-u-wa-an da-a-ir*
[8]*ma-aḫ-ḫa-an-ma-za* $^{i}$*Ar-nu-wa-an-da-aš ŠEŠ-YA* DINGIR$^{lì}$-*iš ki-ša-at*
*nu* KUR.KUR.MEŠ LÚ.KUR *Ú-UL-ya ku-i-e-eš ku-u-ru-ri--ya-aḫ-ḫi-eškir*
[9]*nu a-pu-u-uš-ša* KUR.KUR.MEŠ LÚ.KUR *ku-u-ru-ri-ya-aḫ-ḫi-ir*
*nu a-ra-aḫ-ze-na-aš* KUR.KUR LÚ.KUR *ki-iš-ša-an* [10]*me-mi-ir*
*A-BU-ŠU-wa-aš-ši ku-iš* LUGAL KUR *Ḫat-ti e-eš-ta nu-wa-ra-aš* UR.SAG-*li-iš* LUGAL-*uš e-eš-ta*
[11]*nu-wa-za* KUR.KUR.MEŠ LÚ.KUR *tar-aḫ-ḫa-an ḫar-ta*
*nu-wa-ra-aš-za* DINGIR$^{lì}$-*iš* DU-*at*
DUMU-*ŠU-ma-wa-aš-ši-za-kán* [12]*ku-is A-NA* $^{GIŠ}$GU.ZA *A-BI-ŠU e-ša-at*
*nu-wa a-pa-a-aš-ša ka-ru-u* LÚ.KALA-*an-za e-eš-ta*
[13]*nu-wa-ra-aš ir-ma-li-ya-at-ta-at*
*nu-wa-za a-pa-a-aš-ša* DINGIR$^{lì}$-*iš ki-ša-at*
[14]*ki-nu-un-ma-wa-za-kán ku-iš A-NA* $^{GIŠ}$GU-ZA *A-BI-ŠU e-ša-at*
*nu-wa-ra-aš* DUMU-*la-aš*
[15]*nu-wa* KUR *Ḫat-ti* ZAG.ḪI.A KUR *Ḫa-at-ti-ya-wa Ú-UL-TI-nu-zi*

When I did not yet sit on my father's throne,
All the neighboring enemy countries began to fight (against) me.
When my father became god,
Arnuwanda (II), my brother, sat down on the throne of his father.
But then he became ill.
As soon as the enemy countries heard that Arnuwanda, my brother, (was) ill,
the enemy lands became hostile.
But when Arnuwanda, my brother, had become god,
then the enemy countries, which had not yet become hostile,
(now) those enemy countries also became hostile.
The neighboring enemy countries spoke thus:
"His father, who was the king of the land of Hatti, who was a mighty king,
(he) kept (the) enemy countries in submission.
Now he has become god;
Moreover, his son, who (afterwards sat on his father's throne),
who also was in his early days a military hero,
nevertheless, he has become ill;
and he also has become god.
And now the one who is sitting on the throne of his father
he is a child!
And he will not be able to maintain (lit. 'keep alive') the land of Hatti and the boundaries of Hatti!"

[16]*A-BU-YA-ma-kán I-NA* KUR [uru]*Mi-it-ta-an-ni ku-it an-da a-ša-an-duli-eš-ki-it*
[17]*na-aš-kán a-ša-an-du-li an-da iš-ta-an-da-a-it*
*ŠA* [d]UTU [uru]*A-ri-in-na-ma-kán* GAŠAN-*YA* [18]EZEN.ḪI.A *ša-ku-wa-anda-ri-eš-ki-ir*

But because my father was garrisoned in the interior of the land of Mitanni,
and lingered in garrison,
the festivals of the sungoddess of Arinna, my lady, remained unperformed.

[19]*ma-aḫ-ḫa-an-ma-za-kán* [d]UT[ši] *A-NA* [GIŠ]GU.ZA *A-BI-YA e-eš-ḫa-at*
*nu-mu a-ra-aḫ-ze-na-aš* KUR.KUR LÚ.KUR [20]*ku-i-e-eš ku-u-ru-ri-ya-aḫ-ḫi-ir nu A-NA* KUR LÚ.KUR *na-wi ku-it-ma-an*
*ku-e-da-ni-ik-ki* [21]*pa-a-un*
*nu A-NA ŠA* [d]UTU [uru]*A-ri-in-na-pít* GAŠAN-*YA* SAG.UŠ-*aš A-NA* EZEN.ḪI.A EGIR-*an ti-ya-nu-un*
[22]*na-aš-za i-ya-nu-un*
*nu A-NA* [d]UTU [uru]*A-ri-in-na* GAŠAN-*YA ŠU-an ša-ra-a e-ip-pu-un*
[23]*nu ki-iš-ša-an AQ-BI*
[d]UTU [uru]*A-ri-in-na* GAŠAN-*YA*
*a-ra-aḫ-ze-na-aš-wa-mu-za* KUR.KUR LÚ.KUR *ku-i-e-eš* [24]DUMU-*la-an ḫal-zi-eš-šir*
*nu-wa-mu-za te-ip-nu-uš-kir*
*nu-wa tu-el ŠA* [d]UTU [uru]*A-ri-in-na* [25]GAŠAN-*YA* ZAG.ḪI.A *da-an-na ša-an-ḫi-iš-ki-u-an da-a-ir*
*nu-wa-mu* [d]UTU [uru]*A-ri-in-na* GAŠAN-*YA* [26]*kat-ta-an ti-ya*
*nu-wa-mu-kán u-ni a-ra-aḫ-ze-na-aš* KUR.KUR LÚ.KUR *pi-ra-an ku-en-ni*
[27]*nu-mu* [d]UTU [uru]*A-ri-in-na me-mi-an iš-ta-ma-aš-ta*
*na-aš-mu kat-ta-an ti-ya-at*
[28]*nu-za-kán A-NA* [GIŠ]GU.ZA *A-BI-YA ku-wa-pi e-eš-ha-at*
*nu-za ki-e a-ra-aḫ-ze-na-aš* [29]KUR.KUR.MEŠ LÚ.KUR *I-NA* MU 10.KAM *tar-aḫ-ḫu-un*
*na-at-kán ku-e-nu-un*

When I, my sun, sat down on the throne of my father,
I did not yet go to any enemy country of the neighboring enemy countries which had begun the war against me
until I had taken care of the established festivals of the sungoddess of Arinna, my lady.
And I performed them myself.
I grasped the hand of the sungoddess of Arinna, my lady.
And I spoke thus:
'Oh sungoddess of Arinna, my lady!

The neighboring enemy countries who call me 'a child'
and insult me;
they have begun to seek to take your boundaries!
Oh, sungoddess of Arinna, my lady -- stand beside me, and defeat the aforementioned neighboring enemy countries before me'.
*And the sungoddess of Arinna heard my word,*
*and she stood beside me.*
*And when I had sat down on the throne of my father,*
*I conquered these enemy countries in ten years;*
*and defeated them.*

'Conclusion'

[44]*nu-za-kán A-NA* $^{GIŠ}$GU.ZA *A-BI-YA ku-wa-pi e-eš-ḫa-at*
*nu ka-ru-u* MU 10.KAM [45]LUGAL-*u-iz-na-nu-un*
*nu-za ki-e* KUR.KUR LÚ.KUR *I-NA* MU 10.KAM *am-me-e-da-az ŠU-az* [46]*tar-aḫ-ḫu-un*
DUMU.MEŠ LUGAL-*ma-za BE-LU*$^{MEŠ}$-*ya ku-e* KUR.KUR LÚ.KUR *tar-aḫ-ḫi-eš-kir*
[47]*na-at-ša-an Ú-UL an-da*
*pa-ra-a-ma-mu* $^{d}$UTU $^{uru}$TÚL-*na* GAŠAN-*ya* [48]*ku-it pí-eš-ki-iz-zi*
*na-at a-ni-ya-mi na-at kat-ta te-eḫ-ḫi*

*After having sat myself on the throne of my father,*
*I have ruled already 10 years.*
*These enemy countries I conquered in 10 years by my (own) hand.*
*The enemy countries which the royal princes and the generals have conquered,*
*are not (preserved) herein.*
But what the sungoddess of Arinna, my lady, assigns to me,
that I will carry out,
and I will accomplish.

Obviously, the writer of the 'Annals' has been selective in his narration. But this is the natural job of every historian. The 'Detailed' or 'Comprehensive' Annals cover the ten years and also continue for several more. In instances where an episode is preserved in both, the 'Detailed Annals' often give the activities of the princes and generals as well as other details.

Hoffner disagrees with Cancik that there is an internal conclusion ('Binnenschluss') at the end of year four. He feels that the end of year four is not described differently from the ends of other years, nor does year five begin remarkably differently. Hoffner feels that the central section is a seamless whole. Hoffner is correct in this criticism. A comparison of the end of the account of year four and the beginning of year five with the end of year nine and the beginning of year ten demonstrates that there is no reason to posit an internal conclusion for the four year.

*Years 4-5*

| | |
|---|---|
| $L^{2K\zeta}$ | $^{36}$*nu-za ma-aḫ-ḫa-an* KUR $^{uru}$*Ar-za-u-wa ḫu-u-ma-an tar-aḫ-ḫu-un* |
| E | $^{37}$*nam-ma* $^{uru}$KÙBABBAR-*ši ar-ḫa ú-wa-nu-un* |
| $a^2$ | *nu-kán I-NA* KUR $^{uru}$*Ar-za-u-wa ku-it* $^{38}$*an-da gi-im-ma-an-da-ri-ya-nu-un* |
| [S] | *nu ki-i I-NA* MU 1.KAM DÙ-*nu-un* |

Thus when I had conquered all of the land of Arzawa,
I came back to Hattuša.
And since I had spent the winter inside the land of Arzawa,
I did (all) this in one year.

| | |
|---|---|
| $a^2$ | $^{39}$MU.KAM-*an-ni-ma* |
| E | *I-NA* $^{šad}$*Aš-ḫar-pa-ya pa-a-un* |

In the following year:
I went into the mountains of Asharpaya.

*Years 9-10*

| | |
|---|---|
| $L^{2K\zeta}$ | *nu-za ma-aḫ-ḫa-an* $^{uru}$*Ya-a[ḫ-ri-e]š-ša-an* $^{33}$[KUR $^{uru}$*Pi-ig-ga--i-na-ri-ešša-ya tar-aḫ-ḫu-un* |
| E | *nam-ma* $^{uru}$KÙBABBAR-*ši* EGIR-*pa ú-wa-nu-un* |
| [S] | $^{34}$*nu ki-i I-NA* MU 1.KAM DÙ-*nu-un* |

Now when I had conquered Yahressa (and) Piggainaressa,
then I came back to Hattuša.
I did (all this) in one year.

| | |
|---|---|
| $a^2$ | $^{35}$MU-*an-ni-ma* |
| E | *I-NA* KUR *Az-zi pa-a-un* |

In the following year:
I went to the land of Azzi.

Thus there is no internal conclusion. Hoffner also questions the differences in style between the alternating sections. He feels that they are minimal and could be outgrowths of the content. He states:

> A question should be raised: What are the boundaries of the alternating units? Cancik's first stereotyped section comprises two regnal years (para. 7-11). When only two types of narrative are distinguished, it is a simple matter to argue

that they 'alternate', even if the types of paragraphs are represented schematically as AABABBAAAABAA.[62]

The text of the 'Ten Year Annals' divides naturally into twenty-six episodes. We will now investigate the use of syntagmic patterning in this text of Muršili II.

*Episode 1*
(KBo III.4 Vs I.30-35)

| | |
|---|---|
| B | [30]*ŠA* KUR $^{uru}$*Tur-mi-it-ta-mu* $^{uru}$*Ka-aš-ka-aš ku-u-ru-ri-ya-aḫ-ta* |
| | *nu-mu za-aḫ-ḫi-ya* [31]*nam-ma* $^{uru}$*Ka$_4$-aš-ka$_4$-aš ú-it-pit* |
| | *nu* KUR $^{uru}$*Tur-mi-it-ta* GUL-*an-ni-iš-ki-u-an da-*[*a-iš*] |
| E | [32]*nu-uš-ši* $^{d}$UT$^{ši}$ *pa-a-un* |
| I | *nu ŠA* $^{uru}$*Ka-aš-ka ku-i-e-eš* SAG.DU.MEŠ KUR.KUR.MEŠ $^{uru}$*Ḫa-li-la-as* [33]$^{uru}$*Du-ud-du-uš-ka-aš-ša e-šir na-aš* GUL-*un* |
| $L^{2αγδ}$ | *na-aš IŠ-TU* NAM.RA GUD.ḪI.A UDU.ḪI.A [34][*š*]*a-ra-a da-aḫ-ḫu-un* |
| Q | *na-aš* $^{uru}$KÙBABBAR-*ši ar-ḫa ú-da-aḫ-ḫu-un* |
| $L^{1αζ}$ | [35]$^{uru}$*Ḫa-li-la-an-ma* $^{uru}$*Du-ud-du-uš-ka-an-an ar-ḫa wa-ar-nu-nu-un* |
| | The Kaskaeans of the region of Turmitta made war with me. Furthermore, the Kaskaeans came to me in order to fight, and began to attack the region of Turmitta. |
| | I, my sun, went to it (the region), |
| | and I attacked Halila and Dudduska which were major cities of the Kaskaeans. |
| | I took out from them the inhabitants (as captives), cattle (and) sheep; |
| | and I brought them forth to Hattuša. |
| | I completely burned down Halila (and) Dudduska. |

*Episode 3*
(KBo III 4 Vs I.43-48)

| | |
|---|---|
| $A^{2}$ | [43][*nam-ma* |
| E | $^{d}$UT$^{ši}$ EGI]R-*pa ú-wa-nu-un* |
| B | *nu-mu ŠA* KUR $^{uru}$*Iš-ḫu-pí-it-ta ku-it* $^{uru}$*Ka-aš-ka-aš* [44][*ku-u-ru-ri-yaaḫ-ḫa-an ḫar-t*]*a* |
| $B^{1}$ | *nu-mu* ERÍN.MEŠ *Ú-UL pí-eš-ki-it* |
| E | *nu* $^{d}$UT$^{ši}$ *I-NA* KUR $^{uru}$*Iš-hu-pí-it-ta* [45][*pa-a-un* |
| I | *nu* $^{uru}$*X*]-*hu-mi-es-se-na-an* GUL-*un* |
| $L^{2αγδ}$ | *na-an IŠ-TU* NAM.RA GUD UDU [46][*ša-ra-a da-ah-hu-un*] |
| Q | *na-an* $^{uru}$KÙBABBAR-*ši ar-ḫa ú-da-aḫ-ḫu-un* |
| $L^{1αζ}$ | URU-*an-ma ar-ḫa* [47][*wa-Xr-nu-nu-un* |
| $L^{2'}$ | *nu-za ŠA*] KUR $^{uru}$*Iš-ḫu-pí-it-ta* $^{uru}$*Ka-aš-ka da-a-an* EGIR-*pa* ÌR-*aḫ-ḫu-un* |
| O | [48][*nu-mu* ERÍN.MEŠ *pí-eš-ki-u-an da-a-i*]*r* |

[S] *nu ki-i I-NA* MU 1.KAM *i-ya-nu-un*

[After this, my sun, ca]me back again;
and because the Kaskaeans of the region of Ishupitta had [started a war] against me,
and were not giving me troops
[I], my sun, [went] to the region of Ishupitta.
I attacked [the city of ....]humessena.
[I took out] from it the inhabitants (as captives), cattle (and) sheep;
I brought them forth to Hattuša.
I completely [burned] down the city.
I again subjugated the Kaskaeans of the region of Ishupitta for a second time.
[and (again) they] beg[an to provide me troops].
And I did (all) this in one year.

*Episode 4*
(KBo III 4 Vs I.49-52)

| | |
|---|---|
| $A^2$ | $^{49}$(MU-*an-ni-ma*) |
| E | [*I-NA* KUR $^{uru}$UGU$^{ti}$] *pa-a-un* |
| B | *nu-mu* KUR $^{uru}$*Ti-pi-ya ku-it ku-u-ru-ri-ya-aḫ-ḫa-*[*an*] *ḫar-ta* |
| $B^1$ | $^{50}$[*nu-mu* ERÍN.MEŠ *Ú-UL pí-eš-ki-it*] |
| I | *nu* $^{d}$UT$^{ši}$ $^{uru}$*Kat-ḫa-id-du-wa-an* GUL-*un* |
| Q | $^{51}$(*na-an I*)[*Š-TU* NAM.RA GUD UDU $^{uru}$KÙBABBAR-*ši ar-ḫa ú-da-aḫḫu-un* |
| $L^{1\alpha\zeta}$ | $^{52}$[URU-*an-ma ar-ḫa wa-ar-nu-nu*]-*un* |

In the following year I went [to the Upper Land].
Because the region of Tipiya had begun to make war against me,
[and had not provided me troops],
I, my sun, attacked the city of Kathaidduwa.
And I brought out from it the inhabitants (as captives), cattle (and) sheep to Hattuša.
[The city] I burn[ed down completely].

The similarity between the episodes is striking with the syntagms forming a iterative scheme and high-redundance message. Note in particular the syntagms B, I, $L^{2\alpha\gamma\delta}$, Q, and $L^{1\alpha\zeta}$.

| Episode 1 | Episode 3 | Episode 4 |
|---|---|---|
| - | $A^2$ | $A^2$ |
| - | E | E |
| B | B | B |
| - | $B^1$ | $B^1$ |
| E | E | - |

| | | |
|---|---|---|
| I | I | I |
| $L^{2\alpha\gamma\delta}$ | $L^{2\alpha\gamma\delta}$ | $L^{2\alpha\gamma\delta}$ |
| Q | Q | Q |
| $L^{1\alpha\zeta}$ | $L^{1\alpha\zeta}$ | $L^{1\alpha\zeta}$ |
| - | $L^{2'}$ | - |
| - | O | - |
| - | [S] | - |

The syntagms repeat in stereotyped fashion to form an iterative high-redundance message. This usage of the syntagms continues:

*Episode 5*
(KBo III 4 Vs I.53-Bo II 43 Vs II.24)

| | |
|---|---|
| $A^2$ | $^{53}$(*nam-ma*) |
| E | [*IŠ-TU* KUR $^{uru}$*Ti-pí-ya* EGIR-*pa I-NA* $^{uru}$KÙBABBAR-*ši ú-wa*]-*nu-un* |
| B | *nu* KUR $^{uru}$*Iš-ḫu-pí-it-ta ku-it* $^{54}$[*ku-ru-ur eš-ta*] |
| I | [*nu* .....] (*na-at-z*)[*a da*]-*a-an* EGIR-*pa tar-aḫ-ta* |
| " | *nu-kán a-pi-ya* $^{55}$[*ku-i-*]*e?-eš*? [....] *iš-par-te-ir* |
| ? | $^{56}$($^{i}$*Nu-un*)-[*na-ta-aš* .....] x |
| ? | *na-aš-kán I-NA* KUR $^{uru}$*Ka-aš-ka* x $^{57}$[.....] |
| ? | (*nu-kán*) [......*iš-pa*]*r-za-aš-ta* |
| ? | $^{58}$(*nu an*)[.....] (*an-tu-u*)[*h-še-eš*] SAG.DU.MEŠ BAL $^{59}$[......] |
| ? | (*na-aš-k*)[*an* ..... |
| I | *nu* $^{d}$]UT$^{ši}$ $^{uru}$*Kam-ma-ma-an* $^{60}$[GUL-*un* |
| $C^1$ | *nu-mu* $^{d}$UTU $^{uru}$*A-ri-in-na*] (GAŠAN-*Y*)[*A* $^{d}$U NER.GÁL EN-YA $^{d}$*Me-iz-z*]*u-ul-*[*la-aš*] **Bo II 43 Vs II** $^{20}$DINGER.MEŠ [*ḫu-u-ma-an-te-eš pí-ra-an ḫu-u-ie-ir*] |
| $L^{2\zeta}$ | $^{21}$[*nu-za* [$^{uru}$*Kam-ma-ma-an tar-aḫ-ḫu-un* |
| $L^{2\gamma\delta}$ | *na-an IŠ-TU* NAM.RA] $^{22}$GUD UDU [*ša-ra-a da-aḫ-ḫu-un* |
| Q | *na-an* $^{uru}$*Ḫa-at-tu-ši*] $^{23}$*ar-ḫa* [*ú-da-aḫ-ḫu-un* |
| $L^{1\alpha\zeta}$ | URU-*an-ma ar-ḫa wa-ar-nu-nu-un*] |
| [S] | $^{24}$*nu ki-*[*i I-NA* UM 1.KAM *i-ya-nu-un*] |

(Next) I ca[me back to Hattuša from the region of Tipiya].
And because the region of Ishupitta [was hostile],
[.....] he(?) attacked it again for a second time.
And those who had escaped,
Nun[natas .....]
And he [....] in the land of the Kaskaeans.
And he escap[ed ......]
And [......] people, the heads of the revolt,
and [?]
[and I], my sun, [attacked] the city of Kammaman.
[and the sungoddess of Arinna], my lady; [the mighty storm-god, my lord; Me]zzull[a (and) [all] the gods [ran before me].

And [I conquered the city of Kammanman].
[And I took out from it the inhabitants (as captives)], cattle (and) sheep.
[And I brought it] to [Hattuša].
[I burned down the city completely].
[I did (all)] thi[s in one year].

*Episode 9*
(KBo III 4 Vs II.15-49)

$A^2$ + E — [15]*ma-aḫ-ḫa-an-ma i-ya-aḫ-ḫa-at*
*nu* GIM-*an I-NA* $^{íd}$*La-wa-ša a-ar-ḫu-un*
C — [16]*nu-za* $^{d}$U NER.GÁL EN-*YA pa-ra-a ḫa-an-da-an-da-a-tar te-ik-ku-uš-ša-nu-ut*
[17]*nu* $^{giš}$*kal-mi-ša-an ši-ya-it*
*nu* $^{giš}$*kal-mi-ša-na-an am-me-el* KARAŠ.ḪI.A-*YA* [18]*uš-ki-it*
KUR $^{uru}$*Ar-za-u-wa-ya-an uš-ki-it*
*nu* $^{giš}$*kal-mi-ša-na-aš pa-it*
[19]*nu* KUR $^{uru}$*Ar-za-u-wa* GUL-*aḫ-ta*
*ŠA* $^{i}$*U-uḫ-ḫa*-LÚ-*ya* $^{uru}$*A-pa-a-ša-an* URU-*an* GUL-*aḫ-ta*
$G^{\Delta 3}$ — [20]$^{i}$*Uḫ-ḫa*-LÚ-*na gi-nu-uš-šu-uš a-še-eš-ta*
*na-aš ir-ma-li-ya-at-ta-at-pát*
[21]*nu ma-aḫ-ḫa-an* $^{i}$*U-uḫ-ḫa*-LÚ-*iš* GIG-*at* [*ir-ma-li-ya-at-ta-at*]
*na-aš-mu nam-ma za-aḫ-ḫi-ya* [22]*me-na-aḫ-ḫa-an-da Ú-UL ú-it*
$G^{-3}$ — *nu-mu-kán* $^{i}$SUM-*ma*-$^{d}$KAL-*an* DUMU-*ŠU* [23]*QA-DU* ERÍN.MEŠ ANŠU. KUR.RA.MEŠ *me-na-aḫ-ḫa-an-da pa-ra-a na-iš-ta*
[24]*na-aš-mu I-NA* $^{íd}$*A-aš-tar-pa I-NA* $^{uru}$*Wa-al-ma-a* MÈ[*za-aḫ-ḫi*]-*ya ti-ya-at*
I — [25]*na-an* $^{d}$UT$^{ši}$ *za-aḫ-ḫi-ya-nu-un*
$C^1$ — *nu-mu* $^{d}$UTU $^{uru}$*A-ri-in-na* GAŠAN-*YA* [26]$^{d}$U NER.GÁL *BE-LI-YA* $^{d}$*Me-iz-zu-ul-la-aš* DINGIR.MEŠ-*YA ḫu-u-ma-an-te-eš pí-ra-an ḫu-u-i-e-ir*
$L^{2\aleph\zeta}$ — [27]*nu-za* $^{i}$SUM-*ma*-$^{d}$KAL-*an* DUMU $^{i}$*Uḫ-ḫa*-LÚ *QA-DU* ERÍN.MEŠ-*ŠU* ANŠU.KUR.RA.MEŠ-*ŠU tar-aḫ-ḫu-un*
$L^{1}$ל — [28]*na-an-kán ku-e-nu-un*
H — *nam-ma-an* EGIR-*an-pít AṢ-BAT*
E — *nu-kán I-NA* KUR $^{uru}$*Ar-za-u-wa* [29]*par-ra-an-da pa-a-un*
*nu I-NA* $^{uru}$*A-pa-a-ša A-NA* URU$^{li}$ [30]*ŠA* $^{i}$*U-uḫ-ḫa*-LÚ *an-da-an pa-a-un*
$G^{\Delta 3}$ — *nu-mu* $^{i}$*Uḫ-ḫa*-LÚ-*iš Ú-UL ma-az-za-aš-ta*
$G^{\Delta 4}$ — [31]*na-aš-mu-kán ḫu-u-wa-iš*
*na-aš-kán a-ru-ni par-ra-an-da* [32]*gur-ša-u-wa-na-an-za pa-it*
*na-aš-kán a-pí-ya an-da e-eš-ta*
$G^{\Delta 4}$ — [33]KUR $^{uru}$*Ar-za-u-wa-ma-kán ḫu-u-ma-an par-aš-ta*
*nu ku-i-e-eš* NAM.RA *I-NA* $^{šad}$*A-ri-in-na-an-da* [34]*pa-a-ir*

*nu-za-kán* [šad]*A-ri-in-na-an-da-an e-ip-pir*
*ku-i-e-eš-ma* NAM.RA.ḪI.A [35]*pa-ra-a I-NA* [uru]*Pu-u-ra-an-da pa-a-ir*
*nu-za-kán* [uru]*Pu-ra-an-da-an e-ip-pir*
[36]*ku-i-e-eš-ma-kán* [*ku-iš-ma-kán*] NAM.RA.MEŠ *a-ru-ni par-ra-an-da IT-TI* [i]*Uḫ-ḫa*-LÚ *pa-a-ir* [*pa-it*]
[37]*nu* [d]UT[ši] *I-NA* [šad]*A-ri-in-na-an-da A-NA* NAM.RA EGIR-*an-da pa-a-un*
I [38]*nu* [šad]*A-ri-in-na-an-da-an za-aḫ-ḫi-ya-nu-un*
$C^1$ *nu-mu* [d]UTU [uru]TUL-*na* GAŠAN-*YA* [39d]U NER.GÁL *BE-LI-YA* [d]*Me-iz-zu-ul-la-aš* DINGIR.MEŠ-*YA* *ḫu-u-ma-an-te-eš pí-ra-an* [40]*ḫu-u-i-e-ir*
$L^{2\kappa\zeta}$ *nu-za* [šad]*A-ri-in-na-an-da-an tar-aḫ-ḫu-un*
$Q^{1A}$ [41]*nu-za* [d]UT[ši] *ku-in* NAM.RA *I-NA* É LUGAL *ú-wa-te-nu-un*
$\chi$ [42]*na-aš* 1 x 10000 5 LI-IM 5 x 100 NAM.RA *e-eš-ta*
$Q^1$ [uru]KÙBABBAR-*aš-ma-za* EN.MEŠ ERÍN.MEŠ ANŠU.KUR.RA.MEŠ-*ya* [43]*ku-in* NAM.RA.MEŠ *ú-wa-te-it*
$\Phi$ *nu-uš-ša-an kap-pu-u-wa-u-wa-ar* [44]NU.GÁL *e-eš-ta*
$Q^2$ *nam-ma-kán* NAM.RA.MEŠ [uru]KÙBABBAR-*ši pa-ra-a* [45]*ne-eḫ-ḫu-un*
$Q^1$ *na-an ar-ḫa ú-wa-te-ir*
$L^{2\kappa\zeta}$ [46]*nu-za ma-aḫ-ḫa-an* [šad]*A-ri-in-na-an-da-an tar-aḫ-ḫu-un*
$a^2$ [47]*nam-ma* EGIR-*pa*
E *I-NA* [íd]*A-aš-tar-pa ú-wa-nu-un*
f *nu-za* BÀD KARAŠ [48]*I-NA* [íd]*Aš-tar-pa wa-aḫ-nu-nu-un*
P *nu-za* EZEN MU[ti] *a-pi-ya i-ya-nu-un*
[S] [49]*nu ki-i I-NA* MU 1.KAM *i-ya-nu-un*

So I marched,
and as I arrived at Mt. Lawasa,
the mighty stormgod, my lord, showed his godly miracle.
He hurled a meteor.
My army saw the meteor.
(And) the land of Arzawa saw (it).
And the meteor went;
and struck the land of Arzawa.
It struck Apasa,[63] the capital city of Uhhaziti.
Uhhaziti fell on (his) knees;
and became ill.
When Uhhaziti became ill;
so he did not come against me to fight;
(but) sent his son, Piyama-KAL,[64] together with troops and charioteers to engage me.
He took his stand to fight with me at the river Astarpa at Walma.
And I, my sun, fought with him.
The sungoddess of Arinna, my lady; the mighty stormgod, my lord; Mezzulla, (and) all the gods ran before me.

And I conquered Piyama-KAL, the son of Uhhaziti, together with his troops and charioteers.
And I defeated him.
Then I pursued him,
and I entered into the land of Arzawa.
I entered into Apasa, into the capital city of Uhhaziti;
and Uhhaziti could not withstand me.
He fled before me;
and went across the sea by ship.[65]
And he remained there.
The whole country of Arzawa fled;
and certain ones of the inhabitants went to the mountains of Arinnanda;
and they occupied Mt. Arinnanda.
But certain others of the inhabitants went forth to Puranda;
and they occupied Puranda.
And certain other inhabitants went across the sea with Uhhaziti.
Then I, my sun, went after the inhabitants to Mt. Arinnanda,
and I fought (them) at Mt. Arinnanda.
The sungoddess of Arinna, my lady; the mighty stormgod, my lord; Mezzulla (and) all the gods ran before me.
Thus, I conquered Mt. Arinnanda.
And those of the inhabitants which I, my sun, brought into the royal palace were 15,500 people.
(And) those of the inhabitants which the generals of Hattuša, the troops (and) the charioteers brought (home)
the number does not exist.
Finally, I sent forth the captive inhabitants to Hattuša;
and they brought them forth.
When I had conquered Mt. Arinnanda,
I then came again to the river Astarpa.
I pitched camp at the river Astarpa;
and I celebrated the New-year festival there.
And I did (all) this in one year.

*Episode 11*
(KBo III 4 Vs II.57-65)

| | |
|---|---|
| D | [57][*nu* $^{d}$UT$^{ši}$ ERÍN.MEŠ $^{uru}$*Ḫa-at*]*-ti kar-ap-pu-un* |
| E | *nu INA* $^{uru}$*Pu-ra-an-da* MĚ-*ya* [*za-aḫ-ḫi-ya*] *pa-a-un* |
| G$^{-3}$ | [58]*nu-kán* $^{i}$*Ta-*[*pa-la-zu-na*]*-wa-liš IŠ-TU* ERÍN.MEŠ ANŠU. KUR.RA. MEŠ $^{uru}$*Pu-ra-an-da-za kat-ta ú-it* |
| | [59][*na-aš-m*]*u za-aḫ-ḫi-ya me-na-aḫ-ḫa-an-da ú-it* |
| | *na-aš-mu-kán ANA* A.ŠÀ A.KAR-*ŠU* [60]*an-da* MÈ-*ya ti-ya-at* |
| I | *na-an* $^{d}$UT$^{ši}$ MÈ-*ya-nu-nu-un* |

$\mathrm{C}^{1}$ $^{61}$*nu-mu* $^{d}$UTU $^{uru}$*A-ri-in-na* [GAŠAN-*YA*] $^{d}$U NER.GÁL *BE-LI-YA* $^{62d}$*Me-iz-zu-ul-la-aš* DINGIR.MEŠ-*ya* *ḫ*[*u-u-ma-an-t*]*e-eš* *pí-ra-an ḫu-u-i-e-ir*
$\mathrm{L}^{2\text{א}\zeta}$ *nu-za* $^{i}$*Da-pa-la-zu-na-u-wa-li-in* $^{63}$[....] *QA.DU* ERÍN.MEŠ-*ŠU* ANŠU. KUR.RA.MEŠ-*ŠU tar-aḫ-ḫu-un*
$\mathrm{L}^{1\text{ל}}$ *na-an-kán ku-e-nu-un*
H $^{64}$*nam-ma-an* EGIR-*an AṢ-BAT*
E *nu pa-a-un*
$\mathrm{F}^{2}$ $^{uru}$*Pu-ra-an-da-an an-da wa-aḫ-nu-nu-un*
I $^{65}$[*na-an-kán an-da*] *ḫa-at-ki-eš-nu-nu-un*
$\mathrm{L}^{2\text{ג}}$ *nu-uš-ši-kán u-i-d*[*a-a-a*]*r ar-ḫa da-aḫ-ḫu-un*

So I, my sun, mustered the troops of Hatti,
and went to Puranda to fight.
Tapalazunauli came down from Puranda with troops and charioteers.
And he came for battle against me.
he positioned himself for battle with me on his plain.
And I, my sun, fought against him;
and the sungoddess of Arinna, my lady; the mighty stormgod, my lord; Mezzulla; and all the gods ran before me.
And I conquered Tapalazunauli ... together with his troops and his charioteers.
And I defeated him.
Then I pursued him;
and I entered,
(and) I surrounded Puranda.
And I pressed against it;
and I deprived him of water.

*Episode 14*
(KBo III 4 Vs II.79-86)

I $^{79}$*ma-*[*aḫ-ḫa-an-ma-k*]*án* $^{uru}$*Pu-ra*]*-an-da-an an-da ḫa-at-ki-*[*e*]*š-nu-nu-un* $^{80}$[...... *za-aḫ-ḫi-ya-nu*]*-un*
$\mathrm{C}^{1}$ $^{81}$[*nu-mu* $^{d}$UTU $^{uru}$*A-ri-in-na* GAŠAN-*YA* $^{d}$U NER.GÁL EN-*Y*]*A* $^{d}$*Me-iz-zu-ul-la-*[*aš*] $^{82}$[DINGIR.MEŠ-*ya* *ḫu-u-ma-an-te-eš pí-ra-an ḫu-u-i-e-ir*
$\mathrm{L}^{2\text{א}\zeta}$ *nu*]*-za* $^{uru}$*Pu-ra-an-da-a*[*n tar-a*]*ḫ-ḫu-un*
$\mathrm{Q}^{1}$ $^{83}$[*nu-za ku-in* NAM.RA *I-NA* É LUGAL *ú-wa-te-nu-un*
$\chi$ *n*]*a-aš* 1 x 10000 5 LI-IM [N x ] 100 NAM.RA $^{84}$[*e-eš-ta*
$\mathrm{Q}^{1A}$ $^{uru}$KÙBABBAR-*aš-ma-za* EN.MEŠ ERÍN.MEŠ ANŠU.KUR. RA.MEŠ]*-ya ku-i*[*n* NAM.RA] GUD UDU $^{85}$[*ú-wa-te-it*
$\Phi$ *nu-uš-ša-an kap-pu-u-wa-u-wa-ar* NU.GÁL *e-e*]*s-t*[*a*]
$\mathrm{Q}^{2}$ $^{86}$[*na-an-kán* $^{uru}$KÙBABBAR-*ši pa-ra-a ne-eḫ-ḫu-un*
$\mathrm{Q}^{1}$ *na-an ar-ḫa*] *ú-wa-te?-ir*

When I pressed against Puran[da],
[....] I fought [against it].

And the sungoddess of Arinna, my lady; the mighty storm-god, my lord; Mezzulla; (and) all the gods ran before me.
And I conquered Puranda.
And those of the people which I brought into the royal palace were 15,000 people.
(And) those of the inhabitants, cattle, (and) sheep which the generals of Hattuša, the troops (and) the charioteers brought (home)
[the number does not ex]ist.
[Finally, I sent them forth to Hattuša].
[And they brought them] forth.

*Episode 19*
(KBo III 4 Rs III.47-56)

| | |
|---|---|
| a$^2$ | $^{47}$*nu ku-it-ma-an A-BU-YA I-NA* KUR $^{uru}$*Mi-it-tan-ni e-eš-ta* |
| B | *nu* LÚ.KUR $^{uru}$*A-ra-u-wa-an-na-aš* $^{48}$*ku-iš* KUR $^{uru}$*Ki-iš-ši-ya-a* GUL-*an-ni-eš-ki-it* |
| | *na-at me-ik-ki ta-ma-aš-ša-an* $^{49}$*ḫar-ta* |
| E | *nu* $^d$UT$^{ši}$ *I-NA* KUR $^{uru}$*A-ra-u-wa-an-na pa-a-un* |
| I | *nu* KUR $^{uru}$*A-ra-u-wa-an-na* $^{50}$GUL-*un* |
| C$^1$ | *nu-mu* $^d$UTU $^{uru}$TUL-*na* GAŠAN-*YA* $^d$U NER.GÁL *BE-LI-YA* $^d$*Me-iz-zuul-la-as* $^{51}$DINGIR.MEŠ-*ya ḫu-u-ma-an-te-es pí-ra-an ḫu-u-i-e-ir* |
| L$^{2κζ}$ | *nu-za* KUR $^{uru}$*A-ra-u-wa-an-na ḫu-u-ma-an tar-aḫ-ḫu-un* |
| Q$^{1A}$ | $^{52}$*nu-za IŠ-TU* KUR $^{uru}$*A-ra-u-wa-an-na ku-in* NAM.RA.MEŠ *I-NA* É LUGAL *ú-wa-te-nu-un* |
| χ | $^{53}$*na-aš* 3 LI-IM 5 x 100 NAM.RA *e-eš-ta* |
| Q$^1$ | $^{uru}$KÙBABBAR-*aš-ma-za* EN.MEŠ ERIN.MEŠ ANŠU.KUR.RA.MEŠ-*ya* $^{54}$*ku-in* NAM.RA.MEŠ GUD UDU *ú-wa-te-it* |
| Φ | *nu-kán kap-pu-u-wa-u-wa-ar* NU.GÁL *e-eš-ta* |
| L$^{2κζ}$ | $^{55}$*nu-za ma-aḫ-ḫa-an* KUR $^{uru}$*A-ra-u-wa-an-na tar-aḫ-ḫu-un* |
| Q | *nam-ma* EGIR-*pa* $^{uru}$KÙBABBAR-*ši* $^{56}$*ú-wa-nu-un* |
| [S] | *nu I-NA* MU 1.KAM *ki-i i-ya-nu-un* |

While my father had been in the land of Mitanni,
the enemy of Arawanna who the land of Kissiya had continually attacked had greatly pressured it.
Then I, my sun, went to the land of Arawanna.
And I attacked the land of Arawanna.
And the sungoddess of Arinna, my lady; the mighty storm-god, my lord; Mezzulla; (and) all the gods ran before me.
And I conquered all of the land of Arawanna.
And the captives which I brought from the land of Arawanna into the palace were 3,500 people.
Those of the inhabitants, cattle (and) sheep which the generals of Hattuša, the troops (and) the charioteers brought (home)

their number does not exist.
And when I had conquered the land of Arawanna,
I came back to Hattuša.
And (all) this I did in one year.

*Episode 26*
(KBo III 4 Rs IV.35-43)

| | |
|---|---|
| $a^2$ | $^{35}$MU-*an-ni-ma* |
| E | *I-NA* KUR *Az-zi pa-a-un* |
| $G^{\Delta 2}$ | *nu-mu nam-ma* ERÍN.MEŠ ANŠU.KUR.RA.MEŠ *ŠA* KUR *Az-zi* $^{36}$*za-aḫ-ḫi-ya Ú-UL ti-ya-at* |
| $G^{\Delta 3}$ | *nu* KUR-*e-an-za ḫu-u-ma-an-za* URU.AŠ.AŠ.ḪI.A BAD $^{37}$EGIR-*pa e-ip-pir* |
| I | *nu* 2 URU.AŠ.AŠ.ḪI.A BAD-*pít* $^{uru}$*A-ri-ip-ša-a-an* $^{uru}$*Du-uk-kam-ma-an-na* $^{38}$*za-aḫ-ḫi-ya-nu-un* |
| $C^1$ | *nu-mu* $^{d}$UTU $^{uru}$TUL-*na* GAŠAN-*YA* $^{d}$U NER.GÁL *BE-LI-YA* $^{d}$*Me-iz-zu-ul-la-aš* $^{39}$DINGIR.MEŠ-*ya ḫu-u-ma-an-te-eš pí-ra-an ḫu-u-i-e-ir* |
| $L^{2\Delta\zeta}$ | *nu-kán* $^{uru}$*A-ri-ip-ša-a-an* $^{40uru}$*Du-uk-ka-am-ma-an-na za-aḫ--ḫi-ya-za kat-ta da-aḫ-ḫu-un* |
| $Q^{1A}$ | *nu-za* $^{d}$UT$^{ši}$ $^{41}$*ku-in* NAM.RA *I-NA* É LUGAL *ú-wa-tenu-un* |
| χ | *na-aš* 3 LI-IM NAM.RA *e-eš-ta* |
| $Q^1$ | $^{42uru}$KÙBABBAR-*aš-ma-za* EN.MEŠ ERÍN.MEŠ ANŠU.KUR.RA.MEŠ-*ya ku-in* NAM.RA GUD UDU *ú-wa-te-it* |
| Φ | $^{43}$*na-aš-ša-an Ú-UL an-da e-eš-ta* |

In the following year I went to the land of Azzi.
The troops (and) charioteers of the land of Azzi did not position themselves to fight against me.
(But) the whole country withdrew to the fortress towns.[66]
But I fought only against the two fortresses Aripsa (and) Dukkamma.
And the sungoddess of Arinna, my lady; the mighty storm-god, my lord; Mezzulla, (and) all the gods ran before me.
I took Aripsa (and) Dukkamma through battle.
Those captives which I, my sun, brought forth into the palace,
were 3,000 people.

The captives, cattle (and) sheep which the generals of Hattuša, the troops, (and) the charioteers brought forth were numberless.

| Episode 5 | Episode 11 | Episode 14 | Episode 19 | Episode 26 | Episode 9A* | Episode 9B* |
|---|---|---|---|---|---|---|
| $A^2$ | [D] | - | $a^2$ | $A^2$ | $A^2$ | $A^2$ |
| E | E | - | E | E | E | E |
| B | - | - | B | [$G^{\Delta 2}$] | [C] | - |
| - | $G^{-3}$ | - | - | $G^{\Delta 3}$ | $G^{\Delta 3}$ | $G^{\Delta 3}$ |
| I + $^{\eta}$ | - | - | - | - | $G^{-3}$ | $G^{\Delta 4}$ |
| I | I | I | I | I | I | I |
| $C^1$ | $C^1$ | $C^1$ | $C^1$ | $C^1$ | $C^1$ | $C^1$ |
| $L^{2\kappa\zeta}$ | $L^{2\kappa\zeta}$ | $L^{2\kappa\zeta}$ | $L^{2\kappa\zeta}$ | $L^{2a\zeta}$ | $L^{2\kappa\zeta}$ | $L^{2\kappa\zeta}$ |
| - | $L^{1ל}$ | - | - | - | $L^{1ל}$ | - |
| - | H | - | - | - | H | - |
| - | - | $Q^1$ | $Q^{1A}$ | $Q^{1A}$ | - | $Q^{1A}$ |
| - | - | $\chi$ | $\chi$ | $\chi$ | - | $\chi$ |
| - | - | $Q^{1A}$ | $Q^1$ | $Q^1$ | - | $Q^1$ |
| - | [E] | $\Phi$ | $\Phi$ | $\Phi$ | - | $\Phi$ |
| - | [$F^2$] | $Q^2$ | - | - | - | $Q^2$ |
| $L^{1a\zeta}$ | [I] | $Q^1$ | - | - | - | $Q^1$ |
| $L^{2a\gamma\delta}$ | $L^{2a}$ | | $L^{2\kappa\zeta}$ | | | $L^{2\kappa\zeta}$ |
| Q | | | Q | | | $a^2$ |
| | | | | | | E |
| | | | | | | f |
| | | | | | | P |
| [S] | | | [S] | | | [S] |

As with the first group of episodes, one can see from the readout that certain syntagms are used in a stereotyped manner. Furthermore, the accounts use the same syntagmic pattern to produce an iterative scheme which in turn produces a high-redundance message. Finally one can see the syntagmic patterning in episodes 7, 18 and 20.

*Episode 7*
(KBo III 4 Vs II.1-6)

| | |
|---|---|
| $a^2$ | **Vs II** $^1$*nam-ma* |
| E | [*pa-ra*]-*a I-NA* $^{uru}$*Iš-ḫu-pi-it-ta pa-a-un* |
| I | *nu* $^{uru}$*Pal-ḫu-iš-ša*-[*an*] $^2$GUL-*un* |
| F | *nu-mu-uš-ša-an I-NA* $^{uru}$*Pal-ḫu-iš-ša* EGIR-*an* LÚ.KUR $^{uru}$*Pi-eš-ḫu-ru-uš* $^3$MÈ-*ya ti-ya-at* |
| I | *na-an za-aḫ-ḫi-ya-nu-un* |

C[1] *nu-mu* $^{d}$UTU $^{uru}$*A-ri-in-na* GAŠAN-*YA* $^{4d}$U NER.GÁL *BE-LI-YA* $^{d}$*Me-izzu-ul-la-aš* DINGIR.MEŠ-*ya ḫu-u-ma-an-te-eš pí-ra-an ḫu-i-e-ir*
L[1ל] $^{5}$*nu-kán* LÚ.KUR *Pi-iš-ḫu-ru-un I-NA* $^{uru}$*Pal-ḫu-iš-ša* EGIR-*an ku-e-nu-un*
L[1גζ] $^{6}$*nam-ma* URU-*an ar-ḫa wa-ar-nu-nu-un*

Meanwhile, I had gone forth to the city of Ishupitta.
And I attacked the city of Palhuissa.
And I positioned myself behind Palhuissa (in order to) fight (against) the enemy of the city of Pishuru.
And I fought (with) it.
And the sungoddess of Arinna, my lady; the mighty storm-god, my lord; Mezzulla; (and) all the gods ran before me.
And the enemy of Pishuru I defeated behind Palhuissa.
Moreover, I burned down the city completely.

*Episode 18*
(KBo III 4 Rs III.39-46)

A[2] $^{39}$MU.KAM-*an-ni-ma*
E *I-NA* $^{šad}$*Aš-ḫar-pa-ya pa-a-un*
B *nu-za* $^{šad}$*Aš-ḫar-pa-ya-an ku-iš* $^{40}$URU *Ka-aš-ka-aš e-ša-an ḫar-ta*
*nu ŠA* KUR $^{uru}$*Pa-la-a* KAS.MEŠ *kar-aš-ša-an ḫar-ta*
I $^{41}$*nu u-ni ŠA* $^{šad}$*Aš-ḫar-pa-ya* $^{uru}$*Ka-aš-kan za-aḫ-ḫi-ya-nu-un*
C[1] *nu-mu* $^{d}$UTU $^{uru}$TUL-*na* GAŠAN-*YA* $^{42d}$U NER.GÁL *BE-LI-YA* $^{d}$*Me-iz-zu-ul-la-aš* DINGIR.MEŠ-*ya ḫu-u-ma-an-te-eš pí-ra-an* $^{43}$*ḫu-u-i-e-ir*
L[2א] *nu-za* $^{šad}$*Aš-ḫar-pa-ya-an ku-iš* $^{uru}$*Ka-aš-ka-aš e-ša-an ḫar-ta* $^{44}$*na-anza-an tar-aḫ-ḫu-un*
L[1ל] *na-an-kán ku-e-nu-un*
L[1ר] $^{šad}$*Aš-ḫar-pa-ya-an-ma dan-na-at-ta-aḫ-ḫu-un*
Q $^{45}$*nam-ma ar-ḫa ú-wa-nu-un*

In the following year I went into the mountains of Asharpaya.
And the Kaskaeans who had continued to occupy Mt. Asharpaya
and the ways to the land of Pala they had cut off,
I fought against these Kaskaeans of Mt. Asharpaya.
And the sungoddess of Arinna, my lady; the mighty storm-god, my lord; Mezzulla (and) all of the gods ran before me.
And the Kaskaeans who had continued to occupy Mt. Asharpaya I conquered.
and I defeated.
I made Mt. Asharpaya empty (of humanity).
Then I came back;

*Episode 20*
(KBo III 4 Rs III.57-66)

| | |
|---|---|
| $A^{2}$ | **III** $^{57}$MU-*an-ni-ma* |
| E | *I-NA* KUR $^{uru}$*Zi-ḫar-ri-ya pa-a-un* |
| B | *nu-za A-NA PA-NI A-BI A-BI-YA* $^{58}$*ku-iš* $^{uru}$*Ka-aš-ka-aš* $^{šad}$*Ta-ri-ka-rimu-un* ŠU.DIM$_4$-*az e-ša-at* |
| | $^{59}$*nam-ma-aš-za* $^{uru}$KÙBABBAR-*ši ḫar-ga-aš ki-ša-at* |
| $G^{-3}$ | *nu u-e-ir* $^{uru}$KÙBABBAR-*ša-an* GUL-*ḫi-ir* |
| | $^{60}$*na-an me-ik-ki dam-me-eš-ḫa-a-ir* |
| E | *nu* $^{d}$UT$^{ši}$ *pa-a-un* |
| I | *nu-za* $^{šad}$*Ta-ri-ka-ri-mu-un* $^{61}$*ku-iš* $^{uru}$*Ka-aš-ka-aš e-ša-an ḫar-ta na-an* GUL-*un* |
| $C^{1}$ | *nu-mu* $^{d}$UTU $^{uru}$TUL-*na* $^{62}$GAŠAN-*YA* $^{d}$U NER.GÁL *BE-LI-YA* $^{d}$*Me-iz-zu-ul-la-aš* DINGIR.MEŠ-*ya ḫu-u-ma-an-te-eš* $^{63}$*pí-ra-an ḫu-u-i-e-ir* |
| L$^{2א}$ | *nu-za ŠA* $^{šad}$*Ta-ri-ka-ri-mu* $^{uru}$*Ka-aš-kán* $^{64}$*tar-aḫ-ḫu-un* |
| L$^{1כ}$ | *na-an-kán ku-e-nu-un* |
| L$^{1ד}$ | $^{šad}$*Ta-ri-ka-ri-mu-un-ma* $^{65}$*dan-na-at-ta-aḫ-ḫu-un* |
| L$^{1ג}$ | KUR $^{uru}$*Zi-ḫar-ri-ya-ya ḫu-u-ma-an ar-ḫa wa-ar-nu-nu-un* |
| Q | $^{66}$*nam-ma* EGIR-*pa* $^{uru}$KÙBABBAR-*ši ú-wa-nu-un* |
| [S] | *nu ki-i I-NA* MU 1.KAM DU-*nu-un* |

The following year
I went to the land of Ziharriya.
Certain Kaskaeans who at the time my grandfather had occupied the mountains of Tarikarimu by force,
—then there was calamity for Hattuša—
they came (and) attacked Hattuša.
And they greatly pressured it
Then I, my sun, went;
and I attacked those Kaskaeans who had continually occupied the mountains of Tarikarimu.
And the sungoddess of Arinna, my lady; the mighty storm-god, my lord; Mezzulla; (and) all the gods ran before me.
I conquered the Kaskaeans of the mountains of Tarikarimu.
And I defeated them.
I made the mountains of Tarikarimu empty (of humanity).
I completely burned down the land of Ziharriya.
And I came back to Hattuša.
This I did in one year.

| Episode 7 | Episode 18 | Episode 20 |
|---|---|---|
| $A^{2}$ | $A^{2}$ | $A^{2}$ |
| E | E | E |
| - | B | B |
| - | - | [Edit C] |
| [I] | - | $G^{-3}$ |

| | | |
|---|---|---|
| F | - | E |
| I | I | I |
| $C^1$ | $C^1$ | $C^1$ |
| - | $L^{2\text{א}}$ | $L^{2\text{א}}$ |
| $L^{1\text{ב}}$ | $L^{1\text{ב}}$ | $L^{1\text{ב}}$ |
| - | $L^{1\text{ד}}$ | $L^{1\text{ד}}$ |
| $L^{1\text{גז}}$ | - | $L^{1\text{ג}}$ |
| - | Q | Q |

Thus the Ten Year Annals of Muršili II evince an iterative scheme through the use of stereotyped syntagms.

### *The Detailed Annals*[67]

Another document from the reign of Muršili II utilizes these stereotyped syntagms: The Detailed Annals. Because of the limits of space, we will only cite one very clear example.

*KBo IV 4 Rs III.43-51*

| | |
|---|---|
| $A^2$ | [43]*lu-uk-kat-ti-ma* |
| E | *I-NA* [uru]*Tap-ti-na pa-ra-a i-ya-aḫ-ḫa-at* |
| | *ma-aḫ-ḫa-an-ma* [44]*I-NA* [uru]*Tar-ku-ma a-ar-aḫ-ḫu-un* |
| $L^{1\text{גז}}$ | *nu* [uru]*Tar-ku-ma-an ar-ḫa wa-ar-nu-nu-un* |
| $M^1$ | [45]*nu-mu* LÚ.MEŠ [uru]*Tap-ti-na* LÚ.MEŠ [uru]*Hur-ša-ma* LÚ.MEŠ |
| | [uru]*Pí-ku-ur-zi* [46]*me-na-aḫ-ḫa-an-da ú-e-ir* |
| $M^2$ | *na-at-mu* GIR.MEŠ-*aš kat-ta-an* [47]*ḫa-a-li-ya-an-da-at* |
| Y | *nu ki-iš-ša-an me-mi-ir* |
| $Y^1$ | *BE-LI-NI-wa-an-na-aš* [48]*li-e ḫar-ni-ik-ti* |
| $Y^2$ | *nu-wa-an-na-aš-za* ÌR-*an-ni da-a* |
| $Y^3$ | [49]*nu-wa-an-na-aš-za* ERÍN.MEŠ ANŠU.KUR.RA.ḪI.A *i-ya* |
| $Y^4$ | *nu-wa-ad-da* [50]*kat-ta-an la-aḫ-ḫi-ya-an-ni-iš-ga-u-e-ni* |
| $M^3$ | *na-aš-za* ÌR-*an-ni* [51]*da-aḫ-ḫu-un* |
| $M^4$ | *na-aš-za* ERÍN.MEŠ ANŠU.KUR.RA.ḪI.A *i-ya-nu-un* |

On the next day: I marched towards the city of Taptina.
When I arrived at the city of Tarkuma,
I burned Tarkuma down completely.
Then the people of the cities of Taptina, Hursama, (and) Pikurzi came before me.
And they bowed themselves down at (my) feet.
And they spoke thus:
"Our lord! Do not destroy us!
Take us into servitude;

and make us troops and charioteers.
And we will go on the campaign."
So I took them into servitude.
And I made them troops and charioteers.

Compare the following passage:[68]

*KBo IV 4 Rs IV.28-37*

$a^2$ $^{28}$*ma-aḫ-ḫa-an-ma* LÚ.MEŠ $^{uru}$*Az-zi a-ú-e-ir* URU.AŠ.AŠ.ḪI.A BAD-*kán ku-it za-aḫ-ḫi-ya-az* $^{29}$*kat-ta da-aš-ki-u-wa-an te-eḫ-ḫu-un nu* LÚ.MEŠ $^{uru}$*Az-zi ku-i-e-eš* $^{30}$URU.AŠ.AŠ.ḪI.A BAD NA *pí-e-ru-nu-uš* ḪUR.SAG. MEŠ-*uš pár-ga-u-e-eš na-ak-ki-i* $^{31}$AŠ-RI.ḪI.A EGIR-*pa ḫar-kir*

$G^{\Delta 1}$ *na-at na-aḫ-ša-ri-ya-an-da-ti*

$M^1$ *nu-mu* LÚ.MEŠ ŠU.GI KUR$^{TI}$ $^{32}$*me-na-aḫ-ḫa-an-da ú-e-ir*

$M^2$ *na-at-mu* GIR.MEŠ-*aš kat-ta-an ḫa-a-li-i-e-ir*

Y $^{33}$*nu-mu me-mi-ir*

$Y^1$ *BE-LI-NI-wa-an-na-aš li-e ku-it-ki ḫar-ni-ik-ti*

$Y^2$ $^{34}$*nu-wa-an-na-aš-za BE-LI-NI* ÌR-*an-ni da-a*

$Y^3$ *nu-wa A-NA BE-LI-*[*NI*] ERÍN.MEŠ ANŠU.KUR.RA.-ḪI.A $^{35}$*pí-eš-ki-u-wa-an ti-i-ya-u-e-ni*

$Y^5$ [NAM.R]A $^{uru}$*Ḫa-at-ti-ya-wa-an-na-aš-kán ku-iš* $^{36}$*an-da nu-wa-ra-an pa-ra-a pí-i-y*[*a-u-*]*e-ni*

$L^{-1}$ *na-aš nam-ma* $^{d}$UTU$^{ši}$ *Ú-UL* $^{37}$*ḫar-ni-in-ḫu-un*

$M^3$ *na-aš-za* ÌR-*an-ni da-aḫ-ḫu-un*

$M^4$ *na-aš-za* ÌR-*ah-hu-un*

When the people of the city of Azzi saw that fighting (their) strong cities I subjugated them:
—the people of Azzi, who have strong cities, rocky mountains, (and) high difficult terrain—
they were afraid!
And the elders of the land came before me,
and they bowed themselves down at (my) feet.
And they spoke:
"Our lord! Do not destroy us!
Lord, take us into servitude,
and we will begin to provide to (your) lordship troops and charioteers.
The Hittite fugitives which (are) with us, we will provide these."
Then I, my sun, did not destroy them.
I took them into servitude;
and I made them slaves.

This yields the following readout:

| Rs III.43-51 | Rs IV.28-37 |
|---|---|
| $A^2$ | $a^2$ |
| E | $G^{\Delta 1}$ |
| $L^{1a\zeta}$ | - |
| $M^1$ | $M^1$ |
| $M^2$ | $M^2$ |
| Y | Y |
| $Y^1$ | $Y^1$ |
| $Y^2$ | $Y^2$ |
| $Y^3$ | $Y^3$ |
| $Y^4$ | - |
| - | $Y^5$ |
| - | $L^{-1}$ |
| $M^3$ | $M^3$ |
| $M^4$ | $M^4$ |

One can see from this readout that the two accounts are practically the same in their syntagmic structure.

### *The Deeds of Suppiluliuma*[69]

The Deeds[70] of Suppiluliuma were composed by his son Muršili II in order to commemorate the great achievements of his father. The text is preserved on a number of fragmentary tablets. Even so the use of stereotyped syntagms can be observed. We offer four 'episodes' to demonstrate the synthetic patterning.[71]

1). *Fragment 10) D Col. i 2-10* (pp. 62-63)

| | |
|---|---|
| $A^2$ | [2]*ma-aḫ-ḫa-a[n-m]a A-BU-YA i-y[a* ... |
| I | [3]*nu nam-ma* LÚ.KUR [uru]*Ḫa-ia-ša I-N[A* KUR .... *Ú-UL*] [4]*ú-e-mi-ia-zi* |
| E | *nu A-BU-YA A-NA* LÚ.KUR [[uru]*Ḫa-ia-ša* EGIR-*an-da*] [5]*i-ya-at-ta-at* |
| I | *na-an-ša-an nam-ma Ú-U[L ú-e-mi-ia-zi*] |
| | [6]*nu* LÚ.KUR [uru]*Ka-aš-ka pa-a-an-ku-un* EREM.MEŠ *ŠU-TI I-NA* [ŠÀ.KUR-TI] [7]*IK-ŠU-UD* |
| $C^2$ | *nu-uš-ši* DINGIR.MEŠ *kat-ta-an ti-i-e-er* |
| $C^1$ | [[d]UTU [uru]TÚL-*na*] [8d]U [uru]*Ḫa-at-ti* [d]U KI.KAL.BAD [d]IŠTAR LÍL |
| $L^{1\text{כ}}$ | *nu* L[Ú.KUR] [9]*pa-an-ga-ri-it* BA.BAD |
| $L^{2\text{ג}}$ | [lú.meš]ŠU.DIB-*an-na me[-ek-ki-in IṢ-BAT*] |
| $Q^1$ | [10]*na-an* EGIR-*pa I-NA* [uru]*Ša-mu-ḫa ú-wa-te-[et*] |

But when my father mar[ched forward],
he [did not] engage the Hayašaean enemy in [the country of ....]
So my father went [after the Hayašaean] enemy,
but again he did not [engage] him.
(But) the Kaška enemy, all of their tribal troops, he met in [the country].
And the gods stood by him:
[the sun goddess of Arinna, the storm god of Hatti, the storm god of the Army, and Ištar of the Battlefield,
(so that) the en[emy] died in multitudes.
He also [took] many prisoners;
and brought them back to Samuha.

2). *Fragment 14) F col. iii. 38-46* (p. 68)

| | |
|---|---|
| Y | $^{38}$[*UM-MA A-BU-YA*] *A-NA A-BI A-BI-Y*[*A* ... |
| [DS] | $^{39}$[*A-NA* LÚ.KUR $^{uru}$*Ar-z*]*a-u-wa-wa am-mu-uk* IGI-*a*[*n-da u-i-ia* |
| D | *nu-kán A-BI A-BI-YA* $^{40}$[*A-BU-YA A-NA*] LÚ.KUR $^{uru}$*Ar-za-w-wa me-n*[*a-aḫ-ḫa-an-da ú-i-ya-at* |
| a$^{2}$ + E | $^{41}$[*nu-kán ma-aḫ-ḫa-an*] *A-BU-YA ḫ*[*a-an-t*]*e-ez-zi-i*[*n* ... |
| ? | $^{42}$[......] *I-NA* x[.....*i*]*a-aš-ha* x [...... |
| C$^{2}$ | $^{43}$[*nu A-NA A-BU-YA* DINGIR].MEŠ *p*[*í-ra-a*]*n ḫu-u-i-e-*[*er*] |
| C$^{1}$ | $^{44}$[$^{d}$UTU $^{uru}$TÚL-*na* $^{d}$U] $^{uru}$*Ḫ*[*a-at-t*]*i* $^{d}$U K[I.KAL.BAD $^{d}$IŠTAR LÍL] |
| L$^{1}$ל | $^{45}$[*nu-kán A-BU-YA* LÚ.KUR] $^{uru}$[*A*]*r-za-wa-an* x-x-x [*ku-en-ta*(?)] |
| L$^{1}$כ | $^{46}$[................] *nu* EREM.MEŠ LÚ.KUR *pa-an-*[*ga-ri-it* BA.BAD] |

[Thus (spoke) my father] to my grandfather:
["Oh my lord!] Against the Arza]waean [enemy send] me!"
[So my grandfather sent my father] against the Arzawaean enemy.
[And when] my father [had marched for (?)] the first [day?,
[he came? to the town of ? ]-ašha.
[The gods] ran before [my father:]
[the sun goddess of Arinna, the storm god of Hatti, the storm god of the Army, and Ištar of the Battlefield,
[(so that) my father slew the] Arzawaean [enemy].
and the enemy troops [died in] multi[tudes ......

3). *Fragment 15) F col. iv / / G col. i. 5-10* (p. 75)

| | |
|---|---|
| B | $^{5}$[..... *A-NA A-BU-YA me-mi-an*] *ú-te-er* LÚ.KUR-*wa* [*ku-iš*] $^{6}$[*I-NA* $^{uru}$*A-ni-ša pa-ra-a pa-a*]*-an-za e-eš-ta nu-w*[*a* ....] $^{7}$[*ki-nu-un-wa-ra-aš* ŠA.PAL $^{uru}$*x-iš-ša* |
| E | *nu-uš-ši A-BU-YA pa-it*] |

$C^2$ [*nu A-NA*] *A-BU-YA* DINGIR.MEŠ *p*[*í-ra-an ḫu-u-e-er*]

$C^1$ $^{8}$[$^{d}$UTU $^{uru}$*A-ri-in-na* $^{d}$U $^{uru}$]*Ḫa-at-t*]*i* $^{d}$U [KI.KAL.BAD] $^{9}$[$^{d}$GAŠAN LÍL-*ya*]

$L^{1}$ל [*nu-kán u-ni pa*]-*an-ku-un ŠU-TI* [*ku-en-ta*]

$L^{1}$כ $^{10}$*nu* EREM.MEŠ LÚ.K[UR *pa-an-ga-ri-i*]*t* BA.BAD [ ]

they brought word to my father below the town of [.....]:
"The enemy who had gone forth to (the town of) Aniša,
is now below (the town of) [...]-iššа."
(So) my father went against him.[72]
And the gods ran before my father:
the Sun Goddess of Arinna, the Storm god of Hatti, the Storm god of the Army, and the Lady of the Battlefield.
(Thus) he slew the aforementioned whole tribe,
and the enemy troops died in multitudes.

4). *Fragment 50) BoTU 45 col. i or iv (?). 11-18* (pp. 117-118)

E $^{11}$[..... *na*]*m-ma-aš a-pé-e-da-ni* UD-*ti i-ia-an-ni-eš-pát*

$G^{-3}$ $^{12}$[....]LÚ.KUR-*ma pa-an-ga-ri-it ú-it*

$a^2$ $^{13}$[....] GIM-*an-ma lu-uk-kat-ta* $^{d}$UTU-*uš-kán u-up-ta-at*

I $^{14}$[... *z*]*a-aḫ-ḫi-ia i-ya-an-ni-iš*
$^{15}$[.....] *za-aḫ-ḫi-ia-at*

$C^2$ *nu A-NA A-BU-YA* DINGER.MEŠ $^{16}$[*pí-ra-an ḫu-u-e-er*]

$C^1$ [$^{d}$UTU $^{uru}$*A-ri*]-*in-na* $^{d}$U $^{uru}$*Ḫa-at-ti* $^{d}$U KI-KAL.BAD $^{17}$[$^{d}$..... $^{d}$.....]
$^{d}$IŠTAR. LÍL $^{d}$ZA.BA$_4$.BA$_4$-*ya*

$L^{1}$כ $^{18}$[..... *pa-an-ga*]-*ri-it* BA.BAD

Then he marched forth on that very day [.......].
But the enemy came in multitudes.[73]
But when it became light and the sun rose,
he went .... to battle
[and] he fought [.........]
And the gods [ran before] my father:
[The sungoddess of Ari]nna, the stormgod of Hatti, the stormgod of the Army, [the god X, the god Y], Ištar of the Battlefield and Zababa,
[(so that) the enemy troops] died in [multi]tudes.

These four 'episodes' evince the following pattern:

| Fragment 10 | Fragment 1 | Fragment 15 | Fragment 50 |
|---|---|---|---|
| $A^2$ | Y | - | E |
| I | [DS]+D | B | $G^{-3}$ |
| - | $a^2$ | - | $a^2$ |
| E | E | E | - |
| I | - | - | I |
| $C^2$ | $C^2$ | $C^2$ | $C^2$ |
| $C^1$ | $C^1$ | $C^1$ | $C^1$ |

| | | | |
|---|---|---|---|
| - | $L^{1ל}$ | $L^{1ל}$ | - |
| $L^{1כ}$ | $L^{1כ}$ | $L^{1כ}$ | $L^{1כ}$ |
| $L^{גמ}$ | | | |
| $Q^{1}$ | | | |

As can be seen from this chart, an iterative scheme of stereotyped syntagms was used to create the accounts of Suppiluliuma's conquests. Consequently, the figurative nature of the accounts and the ideology underlying them are re-inforced.

## CONCLUSION

Through our investigation of the ideological and figurative aspects of the Hittite conquest accounts, we have seen that there are parallels with the Assyrian accounts. The Hittite imperial ideology was very similar to the Assyrian ideology, although it placed less emphasis on 'an ideology of terror' than its Assyrian counterpart. The stereotyped use of syntagms in the historical narrative episodes was also observed in the Hittite texts as it was in the Assyrian.[74] This produced an iterative scheme and high-redundance message reinforcing the text's ideology.

# Chapter 4

## EGYPTIAN CONQUEST ACCOUNTS

> The Egyptians who live in the cultivated parts of the country, by their practice of keeping records of the past, have made themselves much the best historians of any nation ...[1]
>
> Herodotus

Egypt has been almost totally neglected in discussions of ancient Near Eastern history writing. This is especially true in the context of Israelite history writing. There are two reasons for this neglect.

First, it is assumed that the Egyptians did not have a concept or idea of history and consequently did not produce any historical pieces of any real merit. This assumption is due in part to the conclusion which L. Bull reached in his article on the Egyptian idea of history:

> In the writer's view it seems fair to say that ancient Egypt cannot have had an 'idea of history' in any sense resembling what the phrase means to thinkers of the present age or perhaps of the last 2,400 years.[2]

As a result of such a view, other scholars of ancient Near Eastern and biblical history have dismissed Egypt from consideration. Thus, H. Gese maintains:

> we shall leave Egypt completely out of account, since at first glance the Egyptian evidence seems to be quite irrelevant to our question.[3]

But John Van Seters correctly points out the error in Bull's thinking:

> But what is significant is that the statement is more a remark about the theoretical impossibility of historiography among the Egyptians than a conclusion based upon the data

> collected. Bull asserts that the Egyptians *cannot* have had an 'idea of history' by emphasizing their static view of life.[4]

Thus, while Bull does not deny that the Egyptians had a great interest in, and reverence for, the past, he has denied the theoretical possibility of history writing among the Egyptians. This must be rejected.

Although the Hebrews and Greeks did develop continuous histories, this kind of generalization leads to a neglect of true history writing among the Egyptians and of the comparison of this with Israelite history writing. Moreover, it is not legitimate to compare ancient Near Eastern history writing to a twentieth century historicist or positivist model. And, as Van Seters points out, there are numerous historical genres which are observable in ancient Egyptian literature and which demand comparison with the biblical material.[5]

Another reason for the neglect of Egypt in discussions of ancient Near Eastern history writing is the tendency in Old Testament studies to look first to Canaanite and Mesopotamian literary sources for some of the origins of concepts found in the Old Testament, so that, too often, the Egyptian material has been overlooked or not given due consideration. R.J. Williams astutely elucidates the reason for this propensity:

> By the very nature of their training, Old Testament scholars are more likely to have acquired a first-hand knowledge of the Canaanite and cuneiform sources than they are to have mastered the hieroglyphic and hieratic materials of Egypt. For this reason they have had to depend to a greater degree on secondary sources for the latter. It is not surprising, then, that Israel's heritage from Western Asia in such areas as mythology, psalmody, theodicy, proverb collections, legal 'codes' and practices, suzerainty treaties and royal annals has been more thoroughly investigated. Yet Egypt's legacy is by no means negligible, and greater appreciation of this fact has been achieved during the past half century.[6]

There can be little doubt that the Egyptians' influence on the historical literature of ancient Israel was much more than is usually considered;[7] and therefore, the inclusion of an analysis of Egyptian conquest accounts in our study is both legitimate and necessary.

## PAST STUDIES

In the past, Egyptologists have generally been more concerned with the writing of histories of ancient Egypt (and hence with different methods in obtaining a reconstruction of particular periods, aspects of society, etc.) than with the analysis of the literary characteristics of Egyptian history writing. This was, no doubt, due in part to the opinions of scholars like Bull. Consequently, in 1964, M. Lichtheim concluded that due to the nature of the material most histories of Egypt up to that point had concentrated on the political history.[8] But she predicted that future studies would concentrate on the social and economic history of Egypt. She has been proven correct.[9]

Obviously, there have been some exceptions to these reconstructional tendencies. For example, E. Otto argued that in ancient Egyptian history writing there was a tension between the world of facts and a historical ideal.[10] For Otto 'History writing then stands in strained relationship between the world of facts and the ideal image of history'. The situating of the historical texts between reality and the ideal picture is 'dictated by an over-riding individuality of the spirit of the age (*Zeitgeist*)'. Furthermore, there is 'a discrepancy between the ideal and reality, i.e., between that which should be, and that which is'. This 'discrepancy was much too great for the ancient Egyptians' so that they were inclined 'to confine the content of reality to a minimum'.[11] Thus Otto differentiated three spheres: the historical ideal (*Geschichtsbild*), history writing (*Geschichtsschreibung*), and historical reality (*geschichtlicher Realität*).[12] He felt that the two factors which distinguished these are the notion of time and the function of the king.

While there is little argument that ideological, chronological and figurative factors undergird the Egyptian historical accounts, Otto's three-fold division and his linking of the Egyptians' historical conception to the *Zeitgeist* must be rejected because of their historicist presuppositions. However, Otto correctly maintained that one should not deny that the Egyptians had any interest in history. The Egyptians seemed to be aware of their long history and tried to come to terms with it. In this regard, Van Seters correctly comments:

> No Near Eastern society was more meticulous in its record keeping, as represented in the annals and king lists, and yet more ideological in its presentation of past events as they centered upon the king.[13]

## SOME GENERIC CONSIDERATIONS
### *(It Depends on Your Purpose)*

There have been a number of studies on different individual genres of history writing in ancient Egypt. For example, A. Hermann, as well as S. Hermann have studied the Egyptian genre of the 'so-called' *Königsnovelle*.[14] The king-lists tradition has been treated by H.W. Helck.[15] D. Redford[16] has recently dealt with not only the king-lists, annals[17] and day-books, but also the Egyptian sense of history. E. Otto has published a study on Late Egyptian biographies.[18] And Van Seters has tried to categorize the different literary genres.[19] Some very helpful studies have come from the pen of A. Spalinger.[20] For example, in his important work *Aspects of the Military Documents of the Ancient Egyptians*, he examines the different genres of the Egyptian military accounts. Since a large percentage of the these come from the time of the Empire (1500-1200 B.C.), our study will concentrate on this period.

### *Iw.tw Texts*

The *iw.tw* formula originates in conquest accounts from the reign of Thutmose II, under the influence of the Middle Kingdom epistolary style.[21] The *iw.tw* genre thus appears to have been a fairly standardized form. It was often used as a type of report which related the whereabouts and/or actions of the enemy. In fact, it came to be used as the prime method of recording the announcement to the Pharaoh of the hostilities of the enemy, and not the military action of the king. Furthermore, it is reasonable to expect that considerable time elapsed between the announcement and the Pharaoh's response.

While the *iw.tw* texts contain a great degree of figurative language (or as Spalinger puts it 'much that is pure verbiage'[22]), they nevertheless were an attempt to present a factual report of a specific military venture. Moreover, they were, for the most part, employed as relatively short accounts of campaigns in which the Pharaoh did not personally lead his army. Detail was kept to a minimum.

Thus the purpose of the *iw.tw* texts was two-fold:

> 1). The purpose of these compositions was therefore not to narrate the day-to-day progress of a military campaign. The Pharaoh is depicted far less as a military commander and more as the supreme ruler of his land. The message report served the purpose of highlighting the rebels' moves against his might ... these compositions glossed over the sequence of events leading up to the defeat of the enemy. Indeed, the precise background information on the war is for all practical purposes ignored.
> 2). However, the *iw.tw* texts could also serve as brief resumes of a war which would be recorded in a more lengthy composition. That is to say, they served as simple statements on a war, relating the date, the name of the enemy, and the eventual success of the Pharaoh.[23]

It should be noted that the *iw.tw* texts are often connected with the Nubian wars which were not as important as the Libyan or Asiatic campaigns.

Hence, the intention of the ancient authors of these *iw.tw* military inscriptions was not to present a matter-of-fact narrative of a particular war. Rather, it was to state the occurrence of a campaign and the restitution of the status *quo ante bellum* by means of the Pharaoh's decision to send his troops in reaction to a message of enemy hostility. Consequently, in the *iw.tw* texts, the Pharaoh looms far more as a figure of permanent stability and omnipotence, in the role of leader of his land, rather than as commander-in-chief of the army (here the Egyptian ideology of kingship comes into play). These texts provided the mundane equivalent of the better known campaign reports, such as the Karnak *Annals* of Thutmose III, the Kadesh Inscriptions of Ramesses II, or the Medinet Habu texts of Ramesses III. In other words, unlike those more detailed accounts, the *iw.tw* stelae related the military activity of the Pharaoh briefly, and within a set format which allowed for little freedom of expression or introduction of unique information. Thus the rise of the Egyptian Empire and its concomitant series of military campaigns formed the impetus for this new type of literary composition.[24]

In his analysis of the *iw.tw* texts, Spalinger demonstrates that up to the passage describing the defeat of the despised enemy forces a single set pattern was employed, but that the conclusion to the text could be approached in a variety of ways.[25] Hymns of praise to the victorious Pharaoh were often placed after the announcement of the overthrow of the enemy, rather than an account of the return of the Egyptian army to Egypt (although this remained common). The *iw.tw* texts can be divided into three parts corresponding to each phase of the military encounter: the background; the reaction; and the result. Spalinger studies the vocabulary which is used in the accounts and concludes that the *iw.tw* texts were unified 'with respect to lexical vocabulary; indeed they are quite repetitious'.[26] The *iw.tw* texts not only conform to a standard literary pattern, but are also written with a set list of common lexical items. Hence, like the Hittite and Assyrian accounts which utilize stereotyped syntagms in order to build the narrative, the Egyptian accounts construct the description of the military engagement. Spalinger's charts of the lexical data (which we cannot repeat) show that the Egyptian *iw.tw* texts build an iterative scheme which in turn produces a high-redundance message which is a vehicle for the Egyptian ideology.[27] In this regard the *iw.tw* texts are artificial, synthetic and simulated as their Assyrian and Hittite counterparts.

### *Nḫtw: The Daybook Reports*

Unlike the *iw.tw* texts, this new form was based on the scribal war diary.[28] When the king went out on a campaign, he took his war scribes with him, and they jotted down the days' accounts, in hieratic. Even when the king was not present at a besieging of a city, the account was still written down, as an aside in the *Annals* of Thutmose III reveals:

> Now all that his majesty did to this town and to that wretched enemy together with his wretched army was recorded on (each) day in its name, in the name of the expedition and the names of the (individual) infantry-commanders.[29]

We are told that the official war reports 'are recorded on a roll of leather in the temple of Amun to this day'.[30] The 'to this day' refers to the days following the battle of Megiddo.[31] Thus the *Annals* have the Day-book Reports as their core.

While this is true, it is often difficult to determine the original report. From other sources it is known that the scribes had a terse style because they had to record the events as quickly as they occurred.[32] This style, which Noth and Grapow noticed and labelled *Tagebuchstil*,[33] consists of a series of 'bare' infinitives, i.e., infinitives without a subject.[34] Hence the Daybooks formed the core of the narrative to which the literary embellishment of the scribes was added. Spalinger isolates five New Kingdom texts that have the War Reports as their core: The Tomb Biography of Ahmose son of Ebana, the *Annals* of Thutmose III (*Stück* I), the Memphis and Karnak Stelae of Amenhotep II, the Bubastis Fragment of Amenhotep III, and the Kadesh Inscriptions of Ramesses II.[35]

It must be stressed at this point that the particular Daybooks which were employed in the construction of the military narratives were different from the Daybooks which were used to record the goods and tribute brought back to Egypt.[36] The word *ḫrwyt*, 'daybook', referred to both the daybook excerpts and the tribute and booty lists. In either case, the scribe was held to truth and accuracy.[37]

The fact that the Daybook was the historical 'core' has certain implications for the accounts which have it as their core. For example, Aharoni claimed that the story contained on the Karnak and Memphis Stelae of Amenhotep II 'jumps from place to place without any connecting text'.[38] To him the two texts compress or telescope events; hence, the dates on the stelae cannot be accepted. Spalinger's analysis of the two stelae, however, argues against this understanding.

> The Egyptian scribes had at their disposal a complete diary of their king's campaigns, which they could embellish with any literary account they wished. The narrative, however, follows the diary reports, not the other way around. It is the journal that provides the exact arrangement for the scribe. With that document as the core of the narrative, very little historical manipulation (either intentional or not) occurred.

> Aharoni has therefore misunderstood the historical core of these two inscriptions.[39]

Thus conquest accounts with the Daybook as their core are less likely to manipulate the historical data as some other type.[40]

Moreover, two accounts based on the same diary as their core do not necessarily have to yield the exact same narrative. The literary ability and creativity of the authors must be brought into consideration since they embellished the accounts in accordance to their point of view. The Karnak and Memphis stelae of Amenhotep II clearly demonstrate this, as also the Kadesh Inscriptions of Ramesses II.[41]

Finally, it is clear that the scribes were careful in the constructing of the accounts. Switches from third to first person should not necessarily be understood as sloppy scribal editing. For example, with respect to the so-called 'poem' of Ramesses II commemorating his victory at Kadesh, Gardiner argued that the composition was defective because the scribe often shifted from third person to first and back again.[42] Spalinger convincingly shows that the 'Poem' preserves a regular and quite organized structure and that the supposed 'lapses' in the use of the personal pronouns are the result of the blending in the text of literary traditions (i.e., highly rhetorical 1st person speeches and Daybook accounts).[43] Thus he concludes that the 1st person accounts of Ramesses II 'were blended into the narrative very effectively'.[44]

### *Nḫtw: The Literary Reports*

These are accounts which do not have the Daybook Reports as their core. While the scribes could record the actions of the Egyptian army (without) Pharaoh in a short account (an *iw.tw* text), and they could describe in a longer account the actions of the Pharaoh in battle which was based on the Daybook Reports, they also had a third option: they could narrate the account without any reference to a Daybook Report and with a heavier dependence on the Egyptian literary tradition (rhetoric and poetics).

In the 18th Dynasty, there are five texts which do not utilize the War Diaries: the Armant Stela of Thutmose III, his Gebel

Barkal Stela, the Tombos Stela of Thutmose I, the Kamose Stelae, and Thutmose III's *Annals—Stücke* V-VI. These five can be further divided: the Armant Stela and the Gebel Barkal Stela are 'address' (*sḏd*) texts;[45] the Tombos Stela of Thutmose I is a highly rhetorical text;[46] and the Kamose Stelae and *Stücke* V-VI of Thutmose III's *Annals* are primary narratives based on the literary tradition (by and large less rhetorical than the Tombos Stela).[47] In a recent study of the Gebel Barkal Stela, Irene Shirun-Grumach has isolated a number of the individual poems interspersed between the narrative.[48] The Kamose Stela, while not based on a Day-book account, shows great creativity in its well-developed narrative. Spalinger concludes:

> the composition bears the mark of a highly trained author or authors who employed many literary images and turns of phrase (outside the literary opening). Whether or not Kamose himself had a direct role in the creation of the work is another point. However, it must be noted that in lines 36ff is preserved his command to the treasurer Neshi, wherein the Pharaoh directly orders the carving and erection of his monument. Hence, one may hypothesize that Kamose's orders were part of his involvement in the actual composition of the narrative.[49]

The tradition of the literary record continued into the Ramesside period: the Karnak Wall Scenes of Seti I; the Kadesh Reliefs of Ramesses II; the inscriptions of Merenptah: the Athribis Stela, the Karnak War Inscription, and the Israel Stela; and the inscriptions of Ramesses III: Year 5, Year 8 and Year 11 texts.[50] Again, as with the texts of this category from the 18th Dynasty, the degree of usage of poetics dictates the difference between each inscription.

Thus these texts are separated from the first two categories above primarily on their lack of the employment of the Day-book Reports or the *iw.tw* formula and their greater use (to varying degrees) of rhetoric and poetics.

## *Conclusion*

The Egyptians had names and titles for their literary compositions. The title which the Egyptians gave to their military documents was that of *nḫtw*. Interestingly, the Kadesh Poem of Ramesses II, the Year 5 and the Year 11 inscriptions of Ramesses III are the only texts so labelled. Thus, 'even though the Poem with its straightforward narrative style interspersed with daybook accounts presents an entirely different approach from its Ramesses III counterparts, all three texts belong to the same literary genre'.[51]

The term *nḫtw* seems to be a singular (perhaps a collective noun) which means something like 'strengths', 'powers', and/or 'victories'.[52] It had a nuance of 'military power' or 'military ability',[53] and in the Armant Stela of Thutmose III, the inscription itself is called a 'summary of the occurrences of *ḳnt* and *nḫtw* which this good god did'.[54]

That two internally different inscriptions could be considered by the Egyptians to belong to the same genre is dramatically shown in the *Annals* of Thutmose III. In the opening phrases of *Stück* I, it is stated that Amun gave to Thutmose his *nḫtw* which the latter drew up on his temple walls (*Urk.* IV, 647.5-6).[55] Later in *Stücke* V-VI, it is stated that 'His majesty commanded the causing that one record the *nḫtw* which his father (= Amun) gave to him' (*Urk.* IV, 684.9ff); and again 'now his majesty commanded that one record the *nḫtw* which he had done from the twenty-third year to the forty-second' (*Urk.* IV, 734.13-14).[56] But note Spalinger's description of *Stücke* V-VI:

> The format of this section (V-VI) of Thutmose's *Annals* avoids any connected narrative the length or extent of *Stück* I, the Megiddo campaign. The authors of *Stücke* V-VI have preferred instead to employ short descriptive sentences and lists of impost and booty. They have often interpolated the return voyage and subsequent events before the tribute lists ... It is clear that the separate reports of booty lists and the military narratives were considered to belong to one genre—the king's personal deeds, his *nḫtw*.... *Stücke* V-VI of Thutmose's *Annals* is therefore a combination of such brief descriptive narrative sections plus lists of tribute and booty, all combined with some daybook excerpts.[57]

Moreover, the Egyptians gave their military texts another specification: *sḏd* 'narrations' (hence, the 'narrations of the *nḫtw*'). Thus one encounters in the Israel Stela of Merenptah the title:

'Recitation of his victories (*nḫtw*)'. And in the Armant Stela one finds that it is specifically written in order to 'relate' (*sḏd*) the king's powers for 'millions of years'.[58]

It has been demonstrated that there were three major categories of military inscriptions among the many Egyptian inscriptions. First, the *iw.tw* texts were used primarily for short accounts, especially in those cases when the Pharaoh himself was not a participant. Second, in a longer account, in which the actions of the Pharaoh in battle were recorded, a report based on the Daybook Records might be utilized. Finally, the scribes could narrate the account without any reference to a Daybook Report and with a heavier dependence on the Egyptian rhetoric and poetics.

Thus while there are numerous differences in their military accounts, the Egyptians themselves saw these, in the final analysis, as reporting the *nḫtw* of the Pharaoh. Even so, the Egyptians were able (any one of them who was literate) to look at the different military texts and could determine which type of account was being presented.

## EGYPTIAN IDEOLOGY
## *(Just Being Better Than Everyone Else!)*

### *Royal Ideology*

For a long time, it has been recognized that the ideology of kingship had a great influence on Egyptian history writing. S. Morenz states:

> Strictly speaking, the only acceptable subject <of historiography> is the Egyptian sacrosanct ruler, through whom or in relation to whom all essential things happen, no matter whether he is appointed by God, who controls his actions, or is free to decide for himself matters of war and peace. To this extent Egyptian history is written as a dogma of sacrosanct monarchy.[59]

Even so, it is quite clear throughout Egyptian history that royal power becomes continually weaker; the king submits himself more and more profoundly to the might and will of the gods, and his dependence on other human and earthly possessors of power increases.[60]

Thus, at the beginning of the Middle Kingdom, as the Egyptian ideological foundations of kingship were reformulated, divine authority took precedence over the monarchy.[61] In order to legitimate his rule, the king alludes to his 'election' by a god. In order to justify his actions the monarch claims to be acting according to the 'commands' of the god. Hence, even one of the most important rulers of the New Kingdom, Thutmose III legitimates his claim to the throne by an oracular pronouncement of the god Amun and ascribes his victories to that god's agency.[62] In a very similar way to his father, Amenhotep II asserts:

> He Himself <Amun-Re> caused him <Amenhotep> to appear as
> King upon the throne of the living,
> He assigned to him the Black Land (Kmt) as his retinue,
> The Red Land as his serfs;
> He bestowed on him a heritage forever,
> A kingship for all time.
> He gave to him the throne of Geb,
> The mighty rulership of Atum,
> The Two Lords' portions,
> The Two Ladies' shares,
> Their years of life and of dominion.[63]

Hornung notes that this movement culminates in the 'theocracy' of the Twenty-first Dynasty, in which the oracular decisions of Amun regulate everything that happens down to relatively insignificant administrative and political matters.[64]

At the ideological level, the Pharaoh was *the protector of Egypt*. During the 18th Dynasty, this concept was extended to cover relations with Western Asia. Thus one finds, for example, Amenhotep II stating concerning himself:

> He has taken all of Egypt,
> South and North are in his care.
> The Red Land brings him its dues,
> *All countries have his protection*;
> His borders reach the rim of heaven,
> The lands are in his hand in a single knot.[65]

This concept of the Pharaoh being *the protector* continues into the 19th dynasty. Thus Ramesses II describes himself as:

a husband to the widow and *protector* of the orphan;
he is an intervener for the needy,
    valiant shepherd in sustaining mankind;
he is an excellent wall for Egypt,
    a buckler for millions,
        protector of multitudes;
he has rescued Egypt when it was plundered,
    marching against the Asiatics to repel them.
He causes all lands to be under his feet,
    King of Upper and Lower Egypt: Usimare-setepenre,
    Son of Re': Ramesses-miamun.[66]

K.A. Kitchen has noted concerning the extension of the royal ideology that:

> when beginning his first Syrian campaign, Tuthmosis III took the line that his opponents were 'rebel'; victory here as anywhere was ordained by Amun, and these lands and their products belonged to Amun who cared not to give 'his' timber to the Asiatics. Similarly, the diplomatic presents from foreign rulers (even of major powers) were termed *inw*—as tribute was, generally.[67]

This concept of the Pharaoh as *the protector of Egypt* can be clearly seen in an inscription of Merenptah:

Then spoke they, the Lords of Heliopolis,
    concerning their son, Merenptah Satisfied by Truth:
'Grant him a lifespan like Re',
    that he may intervene for who(ever) is oppressed by any foreign country.'
Egypt has been assigned to him, to be his given portion;
    she is his forever, that he may protect her people.
Re' has turned again to Egypt,
    The Son is ordained as her Protector.[68]

While this was the ideology which could justify Egyptian intervention in the political situations among its neighbors, the practical outworking was more complex as the Amarna correspondence shows. This royal ideology, however, greatly influenced the generating of the Pharaoh's conquest accounts.

### *The Enemy*

From Egyptian literature (e.g. *Merikare* and *The Admonitions of Ipuwer*) it is quite evident that the Egyptians had 'an intense hatred for their foreign neighbors'.[69] Without much variation over the years, both Egyptian art and literature record the relationship between Egypt and her neighbors. Many of the motifs continue for millennia. O'Connor explains it in these terms:

> Another important continuity was the Egyptian attitude to foreigners. By the New Kingdom centuries of successful military and quasi-military commercial activities in neighbouring regions had established an Egyptian self-image as *a culturally superior group* whose foreign activities were encouraged by their gods ... A potent factor in sustaining the sense of Egyptian *superiority* was its supernatural validity, which made reverses abroad, however serious, mere incidents in a cosmic drama in which Egypt and its gods would ultimately triumph. Mythic and real struggles were inextricably fused; the state, personified by the king, ritually aided the gods in their implicitly always successful struggle against supernatural enemies and disorder, while the gods promised the state ultimate victory over its foreign enemies, who were themselves part of that threatening chaos. <emphasis mine>[70]

Thus the enmity between Egypt and her neighbors was rooted in the Egyptian sense of superiority, an attitude that was validated by the religious system.

This had its outworking in the Egyptian vocabulary used to describe the enemy. The characterization of Egypt's enemies as those of 'bad character' (*nbdw ḳd*) is encountered on a number of occasions in the writings of the 18th dynasty.[71] For example, in the Gebel Barkal Stela, Thutmose III is described as:

| | |
|---|---|
| [18]*nṯr nfr* | *i͗ṯ m ḫpš.f* |
| [19]*ḥw-rsyw* | *ḥsk mḥtyw* |
| [20]*ssḥ tpw nbdw-ḳd* | |

| | |
|---|---|
| The good god, | who conquers with his arm, |
| Who smites the southerners, | who beheads the northerners. |
| Who scatters the heads of those of bad character.[72] | |

The term *nbdw* has been associated with the root *nbd*, which means 'evil, bad'.[73] Not only is this root attested as early as the Old Kingdom, it is the name of the divinity 'the Evil One'.[74] Thus Hoffmeier argues:

> apparently related to the same root is the word *nbd* meaning 'plait' and *ndbt* meaning 'tress of hair.' One wonders if the Egyptians, who loved word plays, saw a connection between 'those of evil character' (i.e. the enemies of the cosmic order) and those whom pharaoh grasped by their long locks of hair when he smashed their heads. The link with hair is clear since the words *nbd* 'plait,' *Nbd* 'the Evil One,' and *nbdw ḳd* are all written with the hair determinative , (D-3 of Gardiner's sign list). The idea of hair may enter the picture because many of the foreign peoples, Libyans and Asiatics specifically, had long and sometimes braided hair.[75]

Since the enemy was *by nature* evil, he was often described as vile or wretched (e.g., *ḫrw pf ẖsỉ n Ḳdšw*: 'that vile/wretched enemy of Kadesh').[76] The root *ẖs(y)* means 'weak, feeble, humble'. hence also 'mean of conduct'; and it is connected with the terms *ẖst* 'cowardice', *ẖsy* 'coward', and *ẖsyt* 'wrongdoing, crime'.[77] So whether the Egyptian scribes wanted to describe the ruler of Kadesh, the town of Kadesh itself, the King of Hatti, the chief of the Libyans, or the Nubians, etc. the vocabulary was basically the same: *the enemy was wicked and evil.*[78]

The utter contempt which the Egyptians had for their enemies can be seen in two speeches of the Egyptian king Kamose to the Hyksos ruler, Apophis:[79]

*First Speech*

> [1]*smi ẖs m hnw dmỉ.k*
> *tw.k ṯf.ti r.gs mšʿ.k*
> *r.k hns*
> *m ỉr.k wi m wr*
> *ỉw.k m ḥḳʾ*
> *r dbh* [2]*n.k tʾ nmt hrt.k n.s*
> *mʾ sʾ.k bỉn mšʿ.i m sʾ.k*
> *nn ỉwr hmtw Ht-wʿrt*
> *nn sn ỉbw.sn* [3]*m-ẖnw ẖt.sn*
> *sḏmt hmhmt nt pʾy.i mšʿ*

> A vile report is in the interior of your town.
> You are driven back with your army!
> Your speech is vile,
> when you make me as 'a chieftain,'
> while you are 'a ruler;'
> so as to want for yourself what is wrongly seized, through which you shall fall!
> Your back sees misfortune, since my army is after you.

The women of Avaris will not conceive,
for their hearts will not open in their bodies,
when the battle cry of my army is heard.[80]

Second Speech

*ḥn pw*
[10]*mk.wi ỉi.kwi*
*mʿr.i*
*spt m-ʿ.i*
*mnḫ sp.i*
*w'ḥ Imn ḳn nn w'h.i tw*
*nn di.i* [11]*dgs.k 'ḥt iw nn.wi ḥr.k*
*whm ib.k ỉr.f °m ẖs*
*mk swr.i m ỉrp n k̄'mw.k*
[12]*m ʿth n.i °mw n ḥ'ḳ.i*
*ḫbi.i st.k ḥmst*
*šʿd.i mnw.k*
*grm.n.i hmwt.k r wnwt*
[13]*nḥm.i t' nt-ḥtri*
*°m 'ḳ* [16]*wh m ỉb.k iry.f*
*°m ẖs wn ḥr ḏd*

It is an attack!
Behold, I have come;
I am successful.
What is left over is in my hand.
My situation is fortunate.
As the mighty Amun lives, I will not tolerate you,
I will not let you walk the fields without being upon you.
O wicked of heart,[81] wretched Asiatic!
Behold, I am drinking the wine of your vineyard,
which Asiatics of my capturing press for me.
I am leveling your dwelling places;
I am cutting down your trees;
As I have carried off your women to the holds (of the ships);
and I am taking away (your) chariotry.
O Asiatic, fit to perish! May your heart fail!
O wretched Asiatic ...

Another passage which illustrates the Egyptians' contempt towards their enemies is found in the Merenptah Stela. In the description of the Libyan chief we can detect the paragon of the enemy personified. Here we see the development from simple *name calling* to a detailed description of the divine reasons behind the enemy's downfall:[82]

*The despised, fallen chief of the Libu* fled in the dead of night alone,
no plume on his head, his feet bare.

His wives were seized in his (very) presence,
and his food supplies were snatched away,
he had no skin of water to sustain him.
The faces of his brothers were furious, (ready) to kill him,
and his commanders fought among themselves.
Their encampments have been burned, and reduced to ashes,
and all his goods became food for the (Egyptian) troops.
he reached his country (racked) with misery,
those left in his land were (too) angry to receive him:
*'Ruler whom an evil fate has deprived of the plume!'*,
—so all say of him, those of his town.
*he is in the power of the gods, the lords of Memphis,*
*the Lord of Egypt has cursed his name—*
*Mauriyu*[83] *is an abomination to Memphis* (lit. 'White Wall'),
from son to son of his family for ever!
*Baienre Meryamun* shall pursue his children,
*Merenptah Satisfied by Truth* is his appointed fate!
He has become a proverb for the Libu,
generation shall tell generation of his victories:
"It was never done to us since Re('s reign)!",
—so says every old man, addressing his son.

Woe to the Libu,
—they have ceased living pleasantly,
in roaming about in the meadow(s).
In a single day their wandering was ended,
In a single year the Tjehenu were consumed.
*Seth*[84] has turned his back on their chief.
plundered are their settlements at his word.
There is no carrying loads(?), these days,
hiding away is best, safe in a cave.[85]

The great Lord of Egypt, —power and victory are his,
who can fight, knowing his (bold) stride?
*A mindless fool is (any)one who takes him on,*
*there's no doubting tomorrow('s fate) for (any) who attacks his border.*

"As for Egypt," they say, "since the time of the Gods,
(she is) the sole Daughter of the Sun-god (Pre),
and his son occupies the throne of the Sun."
None who attacks her people will succeed,
the eye of every god pursues who(ever) would rob her.

"It is she who shall vanquish her foes",
—so say they who gaze at their stars,
all who know their spells by observing the winds.

A great wonder has happened for Egypt,
her attacker was delivered as a prisoner into her power,

through the counsels of the king,
triumph(ant) over his foes in Pre's presence.
*Mariyu, the evil-doer,*
*condemned(?) by every god who is in Memphis,*
*by whom he stood trial in Heliopolis,*
*—the Ennead found him guilty of his crimes.*
*Said the Lord-of-All:*
*"Give the (victory-)sword to my Son,*
*upright, gracious and mild,*
*Baienre Meryamun"*, <emphasis mine>.

To the Egyptians, the enemy was arrogant. He trusted in his many troops and not in Amun-Re'.[86] He arrogantly rebelled against the order of the Egyptian pharaoh and the Egyptian deities. The Egyptians' concept of the enemy was to regard them as cowardly, vain, and boastful. Thus one reads:

*'Iḫny p' 'b'w m-ẖnw mš'.f*
Ikheny, the boaster, was in the middle of his army.[87]

One of the most common expressions of the Egyptians' concept of the enemy's homeland speaks of the cowardly army of rebels holing up in a remote locality—a hidden valley.[88] The word *int* came to have a frozen use. The Asiatic and Nubian territories were remote and strange to the Egyptians, especially at the beginning of the 18th Dynasty. It was at that time that the Egyptian armies penetrated up to the fourth cataract of the Nile and permanently took control of Nubia. Hence one reads:

*gm.n.f ḫrww nb n Nḥsyw m int št'[t]*
It was in an inaccessible valley that he found all the Nubian enemies.[89]

Moreover, in discussing a fragmentary text in which a rebellion against Egypt is related, Spalinger notes that one of the standard opening phrases occurs: a foreign land *fell* into a state of active hostility against Egypt.[90] This was a stereotyped introduction to an ensuing narrative which was used as a common literary topos by the writers of military inscriptions. Consequently, one sees that the astrologer, Amenemhat, described the beginning of the war of Thutmose I against Mitanni in terms similar to these. The military aggression of the foreign monarch is painted as having been dependent upon (presumed) arrogance. The typical verb used by the scribes is *w'*, 'to fall into', a lexical item which occurs quite frequently in

Egyptian military texts. Spalinger lists some of the occurrences:

a. *r-ntt Kš ḫst w'.ti r.bštw* '... to the effect that vile Kush has fallen into hostility'. Thutmose II Assuan-Philae Text: *Urk.* IV, 138.13.
b. *sbit w'.(w) r ḥwtf rhyṯ Kmt*: 'Rebels have fallen into robbing the people of Egypt.' Thutmose II Assuan-Philae Text: *Urk.* IV, 138.15.
c. *w'.f r tr n rḳt*: 'He has fallen into an occasion of conspiracy'. Thutmose II Assuan-Philae Text: *Urk.* IV, 139.3.
d. *isṯ š" - m Yrḏ nfryt-r pḥw t' w'.(w) r bšt' ḥr ḥm.f*: 'Now (the land) from Yrḏ to the upper reaches of Asia fell into hostility against his majesty'. Thutmose *Annals, Stück* I: *Urk.* IV, 648.6-7.
e. *iw.sn w'.(w) r 'š'*: 'They have become numerous'. Thutmose III *Annals, Stück* I: *Urk.* IV, 650.2.
f. *... nw pḥw t' 'š' st r š'w n wḏb w'.(w) r 'ḥ' ḥn' ḥm.f*: '... of the upper reaches of Asia—they were more numerous than the sand of the seashore —fell into attacking his majesty'. Thutmose III *Annals, Stück* V: *Urk.* IV, 710.6-9.
g. *t'w fnḫw wn.w w'.w r tkk t'šw.i*: 'The Phoenician lands which had fallen into attacking my boundaries'. Thutmose III Dedication Inscription: *Urk.* IV, 758.7.
h. *ḫ'swt bšt'w wn.w w'.(w) r tk t'š.f*: 'Rebellious foreign lands that were falling into attacking his boundary'. Ramesses II: Undated War Scene: *KRI* II, 154.3.
i. *ḫ'swt bšt'w wn.(w) w'.(w) tk t'š.f*: 'Rebellious foreign lands that were falling into attacking his boundary'. Ramesses II: Undated War Scene: *KRI* II, 166.14.[91]

The reason why these enemy countries 'fell' into rebellion was due again to their evil nature. By nature they could only conspire and plot rebellion. Thus, for example, 'he planned hostility in his heart'[92] or 'they planned hostility'[93] or 'they have made a conspiracy'.[94]

Enemy rulership meant anarchy and chaos—hence, it was necessary that pharaoh, the good god, should re-establish order and stability. This is illustrated by a section[95] of Thutmose III's *Annals*:

*[9]isṯ 'ḥ' nw 'š' m rnpwt iw Rṯ[nw w' r]*
*[10]ḥ'ḏ' s nb ḥr rk? r [sn-nw.f?] ...*
*[11]ḫpr.n.is m-h'w k'w*
*iw'yt ntt im [12]m dmi n š'rh'n*
*isṯ š"-m yrḏ' [13]nfryt pḥww t' w'(.w) r bštw ḥr ḥm.f*

> Now for a long period of years Ret[jenu had fallen into]
> a state of anarchy,[96] every man showing hostility
> towards/overpowering(?) his neighbor [...].
> For it happened in a later period,[97]
> that the garrison[98] which had been there was (now) in the
> town of Sharuhen;[99]
> Now (the land) from *Yrḏ'* to the upper reaches of the Earth had
> begun to fall[100] into hostility (i.e., rebel) against his majesty.[101]

Thus the king of Egypt in accomplishing ultimate victory over his foreign enemies in Retjenu, who were themselves part of 'the threatening chaos', brought stability and order and *ma'at*.

The *iw.tw* texts illustrate this outlook starkly. It was not the fault of the Egyptians or their king that hostility broke out. Some wretched foreigner had disrupted the status quo which had been set up at the 'first beginning'. Hence in the *iw.tw* texts, the king is the passive component of war. He acts only after he has received news of foreign unrest. His army is dispatched only after others have stirred up trouble, and then only to reestablish the status quo.[102] The very strict patterning of the vocabulary of the *iw.tw* texts (e.g., *iw.tw*, *h'ỉ*, *k'ỉ*, *sḥwy*, *sḥwy mš'*, *sbỉ*, *gmỉ*, *ḫ'yt ''t*)[103] created such a format that a high-redundance message was produced which was a vehicle to reinforce the Egyptian ideology.

Furthermore, since the enemy was 'evil,' there was every reason to annihilate him (if not literally, then figuratively!). Thus:

> He enters into the mass of men,
> his blast of fire attacked them like a flame.
> he makes them non-existent,
> while they are prostrated in their blood.
> It is his uraeus-serpent that overthrows them for him,
> his royal serpent which subdues his enemies.[104]

Here the ideological and the figurative aspects obviously overlap.

The Egyptians' hatred for foreigners during the New Kingdom period is a possible explanation for why the Egyptians adopted an expansionist foreign policy. During the Hyksos period, Egypt suffered oppression by a foreign power,[105] and the desire to drive out the foreigners was kindled. Thus the incentive to establish an empire derived primarily from political and military reasons rather than from the desire for material gain *per se*.[106] Not only does this appear to be the case for the expansion northwards, but it also may explain the expansion southward. The rulers of the independent Nubian Kingdom, which came into existence in the centuries preceding the New Kingdom, were close allies of the Hyksos kings.[107] Therefore, the reason for the retribution upon Nubia and its subsequent subjugation was the same as that for the Levant.[108]

### *Administration*

This imperialistic ideology also had its outworking in the administration of the conquered territories. The two regions over which Egypt gained control and which we possess enough information to assemble some type of model were Nubia and the Levant. Interestingly, while there are some similarities in the way in which these two were administered,[109] it is clear that, on the whole, they were quite different. Hence, while Egypt possessed 'an empire by any standard definition of the term, in that it exercised authority over other nation-states or nations for its own benefit', it is very clear that 'two types of imperial rule must be differentiated'.[110]

In Nubia, the Egyptians attempted and accomplished 'an almost perfect Egyptianization'.[111] The country was governed using the Egyptian administrative of technique dividing the land into two regions: Wawat and Kush (thus corresponding to Upper and Lower Egypt). The Viceroy of Nubia ('King's Son of Kush') headed a purely Egyptian bureaucratic régime and was directly responsible to the king. Under the Viceroy there was a separate military commander who oversaw the militia.[112] In Nubia, local chiefs are almost never featured except as occasional rebel leaders; and then they are without any command of resources or a culture remotely comparable with those of Egypt. Although the administration was backed by these Egyptian armed forces garrisoned in the numerous fortresses throughout the area, the success of the Egyptianization policy was largely due to the new settlements which were established in great number especially in Lower Nubia.[113] The pattern of these settlements was a replica of that in Egypt. P.J. Frandsen has recently argued that while the evidence is extremely sparse, it appears that 'the Nubian economy was structurally integrated into the Egyptian which roughly speaking was a system of redistribution'.[114] He maintains that:

> since, after all, it was an old enemy territory, and since—with the exception of gold—the products of Nubia were, by and large, of a kind unobtainable in Egypt (ivory, ebony, ostrich feathers, leopard skins, etc.) the control of this area assumed a more overt, occasionally repressive—and ideologically more intensive form ...
> Above all, the integration of the economy into the Egyptian redistributive economy—reveals, in my opinion, nothing short of a conscious effort on the part of the Egyptians to push also the non-material borderline southwards to the 4th cataract.[115]

Thus an Egyptianization policy was carried out on Nubia which manifested itself in the restructuring of the political and administrative institutions, the acculturation of at least the upper strata of Nubian society, the transformation of the settlement pattern, and an ideological expansion amounting almost to propaganda.

In contrast to this Egyptianization policy in Nubia, the Egyptian rule in Syria and Palestine seems to have had the maintenance of ordered relations between separate societies as its primary objective so that trade would not be hindered. While the Egyptians' original intention might have been complete subjugation of the Levant, the outcome was a relationship between societies based on a system of international law.[116] In Syria the Egyptians made no serious attempt to displace the local rulers of the city-states in favor of any thoroughly Egyptian administrative network. The population already had an evolved social and political structure, and a mature culture and ethos, such as to leave no real vacuum to be filled by an alien structure and culture. In this situation individual vassals, in return for political and social stability, swore allegiance to the reigning king. The Canaanite rulers might keep their their small feudal levies of 'knights' (*maryannu*) and men-at-arms, and continue to trade and quarrel with their neighbors; but they were bound to pharaoh by an oath.[117] Although no treaties and fealty oaths have been discovered so far in ancient Egypt, Lorton is probably correct when he states:

> documents were [probably] as important to the Egyptian system as to the Asiatic ... Since the oath was the constitutive element of the agreement, and since the documents were only evidentiary, the terms 'oath' and 'treaty' have been used interchangeably here.[118]

Moreover, there is indirect evidence that the Egyptians used loyalty oaths. For example, Thutmose III made the Canaanites swear an oath of allegiance:[119]

> [14]*ỉsṯ st ʿḥʿ ḥr ỉnbw.sn*
> *ḥr rdit iʾw n ḥm.i*
> [15]*sỉ tw rdỉt n.sn ṯʾw n ʿnḫ*
> [16]*ʿḥʿ.n rdỉ.n ḥm.i di.tw sḏf.sn tryt m ḏd*
> [17]*nn wḥm.n r bin ḥr Mn-ḫpr-Rʿ ʿnḫ* ḏt
>
> Moreover, they stood on their walls
> in order to give praise to my majesty,
> seeking that the breath of life might be given to them.
> Then my majesty caused them to swear their oath of allegiance, saying:
> Never again will we commit evil against Menkheperreʿ, may he live forever!

Hence the Egyptian adminstration of Syria and Palestine in certain general respects resembled that of a feudal society. The Egyptians retained, by and large, the existing political and administrative organization to which they added only a small top administration to oversee the preservation of Egyptian suzerainty.[120] Since this was the case, the Egyptians kept in all probability a close watch on the flow of tribute to Egypt from the different petty rulers as a practical test of their loyalty.

Although Egypt's administration of Syria and Palestine was different from that of Nubia, this does not mean that there were no attempts at Egyptianization in the Levant. For example, in the area of land holding, there were royal and temple lands which would have served in the Egyptianization endeavour. Also there were Egyptian 'inspectors' who estimated the yield of Palestinian harvests, just as in Egypt, and there were Palestinian territories which were assigned to the domains of the Egyptian temples.[121] Thus this Egyptian administration was:

> applied to the princedoms of Syria-Palestine, and was to last right through to the end of the LBA—witness the octraca from Lachish itself concerning harvest-tax in a Year 4 (? of Merenptah), and the Palestinian revenues for some temples even under Ramesses III.[122]

Whereas in Nubia the overall control was in the hands of the Viceroy, Syria-Palestine was apparently divided into three provinces: Amurru with its capital at Simyra, Upe with its capital at Kumidi, and Kana'an with its capital at Gaza. Each province was administered by a provincial official (*rabiṣu*).[123]

But in contradistinction to what happened in Nubia, there were no deliberate attempts to impose Egyptian cults upon the people of the Levant. The cultural atmosphere was more one of constant 'give and take between Egypt and Syria'.[124] And yet the Egyptians obviously were the ones who benefitted the most from the political and economic arrangements in the Levant.

Having established that there were two distinct types of imperial rule in the Egyptian empire, the question of how to account for the two types must be raised. Unquestionably, one reason had to do with the geography of the two regions. Nubia was more geographically suited for the type of administration which was instituted there. Another reason may have been the difference in the Egyptians' outlook toward the peoples of these two areas. Trigger asserts that Egypt did not 'alter the internal social or political arrangements' of the Asiatic states because:

> the Egyptians were well aware that in some crafts, such as weaving and metal-working, the Levantines were more skilled than they were and Asiatic deities soon found an honoured place in the Egyptian pantheon. By contrast, the Egyptians had *no respect for* the technology, religion or customs of the Nubians. Like European colonists in Africa more recently, they dismissed the local technology and failed to appreciate religious practices or patterns of kinship and reciprocity that were based on principles that were radically different from their own. <emphasis mine>[125]

Thus it seems that there were at least two reasons for the differences in the different types of rule in the Egyptian empire. On the one hand there was the practical reason of geography.[126] On the other hand there was the ideological reason which was linked to the difference in the Egyptians' outlook towards the peoples of these two different regions.[127]

### *Diffusion of the Ideology*

With regard to the diffusion of the Egyptian imperialistic ideology, it is very clear that the message was communicated by the visual, oral and written modes. The publication of the texts on the outside walls of temples, on stelae set up in key locations throughout the empire, and the very nature of the hieroglyphs themselves demonstrate that the messages of the texts were intended for the public and that some attempt at a high-redundance message was being undertaken. Since the temple-centered towns probably formed the backbone of urbanism in Egypt during the Empire period (ca. 1500-1200 B.C.),[128] the diffusion of these messages was greatly enhanced.[129]

## LITERARY ASPECTS
## *(Never Any Embellishments Here!)*

Like their counterparts in Hittite and Assyrian conquest accounts, Egyptian conquest accounts are figurative accounts. In the case of the Egyptian conquest accounts, this is most manifest in the area of rhetoric. On the one hand, the Egyptian ideology of kingship dictated this. But, on the other hand, the type of account employed demanded it. Even in their most sober cases, Egyptian conquest accounts utilize a high percentage of rhetorical figures; and it is this fact that has led some scholars to the conclusion that either the Egyptians did not have a concept of history or that certain accounts which exhibit a high degree of figures were of such inferior quality that they were not really history writing.[130] Of course, neither conclusion is necessary. When the figurative nature of the accounts is acknowledged, then each account can be understood and appreciated on its own merits. Unfortunately, before coming to grips with the use of rhetoric within the accounts, too many scholars have dismissed the accounts altogether.

Caution must be used as one approaches the texts. For example, since Year 33 in Thutmose III's *Annals*[131] parallels with the more literary narratives of the Armant and Gebel Barkal Stelae of Thutmose III,[132] one might suspect that a sober war report is not included here. But since the language is freely flowing, one must entertain the possibility that the policy of the composers was to use terse phrases for unimportant accounts and a smoothly written narrative for the more detailed ones.[133] In such a situation, narrative embellishments would be used to heighten significance within the account [*not all that different than a modern TV newscast!*].

In the case of Year 33, there was, of course, a very important event. That year witnessed Thutmose's famous Euphrates campaign. Similarly, Year 35 employs common lexical items in the normal order for such inscriptions. It also contains more high-blown language and turns of phrase.[134]

*Hyperbole*

One method of embellishment which the Egyptian scribes utilized was hyperbole. A few examples of the hyperbolic function of certain Egyptian syntagms will illustrate this:

(1) *n sp ir.t(w) mitt* :: 'Never had the like been done ...'[135] This is a very common phrase which may be reminiscent of the concept of 'permanent revolution' which Hornung has seen in Egyptian thought.[136] The phrase is first used by Thutmose I in the description of his hunt of elephants in Niy.[137] It is subsequently used by Thutmose III[138] and by Amenhotep III at Konosso.[139] Its equivalent is also seen in the 'Israel Stela' of Merenptah: 'Never has it been done to us since the time of Re'.[140] A similar expression is 'whose like has (never) existed in the whole world':

> who has widened his frontiers as far as he wished,
> who rescued his infantry and saved his chariotry
> when all foreign countries were in rage,
> who makes them non-existent,
> being alone by himself,
> no one else with him,
> valiant warrior, hero,
> whose like has (never) existed in the whole world.[141]

In Egyptian conquest accounts, it is often only a matter of degree which separates the 'so-called' sober accounts from the 'so-called' bombastic accounts. Surely the preceding quote from Ramesses II is as 'bombastic' as any passage in the Medinet Habu composition of Ramesses III. Thus it was not only the so-called 'jaded Egyptians of the Silver Age of Egypt's might' who relished complicated imagery and intricate literary motifs.[142]

(2) *irr st m tm m wn* :: 'who makes them non-existent'. This is a common syntagm in the military accounts. For example:

[1]*'ḳ m wmt*
*wn th i hh.f r.s m sḏt*
[2]*ir.st m tm wn*
    *ḥdbw ḥr snfw.sn*

He enters into the mass of men,
(6)his blast of fire attacked them like a flame.
he makes them non-existent,
    while they are prostrated in their blood.[143]

[5]*mš' 'š' n Mṯn*
*sḫrw m km n 't*
[6]*sbyw rssy*
*mỉ ntyw n ḫpr*
[7]*mỉ r-'(wy) n imy sḏt*

The great army of Mitanni,
it is overthrown in the twinkling of an eye.
It has perished completely,
as though they had never existed.
Like the ashes (lit. 'the end') of a fire.[144]

*Ynnw'm ir m tm m wn*
Yanoam is made nonexistent.[145]

These three examples demonstrate the use of this hyperbolic syntagm.

(3) *ir ẖ'yt ''t* :: 'A Great Slaughter was made'. This is commonly encountered in the *iw.tw* texts.[146] Thus one reads:

*irw ẖ'yt ''t im.sn*
*n rẖ ṯnw š'd ḏrwt iry*
A great slaughter was made among them:
The number of hands cut off was not known thereof.[147]

*iry ẖ'yt im.sn*
*n rẖ ṯnw*
A slaughter was made among them:
The number was unknown.[148]

*ir ḫ'yt [m] sw nb*
Who makes a slaughter among all men.[149]

*ir š't.sn ḫt int̲.sn*
who makes their slaughter throughout their valley.[150]

*'ḥ'.n ir ḫ'yt "t im.sn*
Then a great heap of corpses was made among them.[151]

Thus it is clear just from these few examples that hyperbole played a major role in the construction of the Egyptian conquest accounts.

### *Metonymy*

Another figure which one regularly encounters in the Egyptian historical account is that of metonymy. One specific example which relates to conquest accounts is that figure of the Pharaoh trampling or treading on his enemies and their land.[152] In treading on the enemy, the king shows himself as victorious over the vanquished enemy, and that the enemy is now subject to him. In other words, for an Egyptian monarch to tread on the land of his enemies meant that Egypt was staking its claim over it. Quite a few conquest accounts support this view.[153] The most impressive example of this metonymy is seen in the Poetical Stela of Thutmose III where Amun-Re' first states:

6*di.i ḫr rkw.k h̲r t̲bwt.k*
*titi.k šntyw h̲'kw-ib*
7*ḫnd.k ḫ'swt nbt ib.k 'w*

I made your opponents fall under your soles,
so that you trampled the rebels and disaffected persons.
You trod all foreign lands with joyful heart.

and then at the beginning of each strophe in the poetic section of the text the deity speaks the refrain: *ii.n.i di.i titi.k* :: 'I came to make you trample'. Thus:

13*ii.n.i di.i titi.k wrw D̲'hy*
*sš.i st h̲r rdwy.k ḫt ḫ'swt.sn*
*di.i m".sn ḥm.k m nb stwt*
*sḥd̲.k m-ḥr.sn m snn.i*

I came to make you trample the chiefs of Djahy,
I spread them under your feet throughout their lands;
I caused them to see your majesty as lord of light rays,

so that you shone before them in my likeness.

[14]*ii.n.i di.i titi.k imyw S̱tt*
*sḳr.k tpw ᶜmw nw Rṯnw*
*di.i m".sn ḥm.k ᶜpr m-ḫkrw.k*
*šsp.k ḫᶜw ᶜḥᶜ ḥr wrryt(.k)*

I came to make you trample those of Asia,
so that you smote the Asians' heads of Retjenu;
I caused them to see your majesty equipped in your panoply,
as you displayed your weapons on your chariot.

[15]*ii.n.i di.i titi.k tᶜ-iᶜbty*
*ḫnd.k nᶜwt m ww tᶜ-nṯr*

I came to make you trample the eastern land,
as you trod down those in the regions of god's land;[154]

Later, in a text of Ramesses III it is stated: *sḫr.n.f tᶜw ptpt.n.f tᶜ nb ẖr rd.wy.fy* :: 'he overthrew lands and trampled every land under his feet'.[155] These texts seem to indicate that by the process of defeating one's enemies and treading his turf one could claim possession of it. Hence the terms for treading and trampling are metonymies being put for the subjugation and possession of a land.[156]

Another example is *iw* :: 'to come'. In numerous instances this is a metonymy being put for the mustering and arrival of the enemy in preparation for war with the Egyptian forces.[157]

A final example is seen in the usage of *spr* 'to arrive'. It is used as a metonymy being put for the army's attack of the enemy.[158] Two examples demonstrate this figure:

*ᶜḥᶜ.n mšᶜ pn n ḥm.f spr r Kš ẖst*
Then the army of his majesty arrived at wretched Kush.[159]

*spr ḥm.f r.sn mi ḥwt bik*
His majesty reached them (the enemy) like the stroke of a falcon.[160]

Obviously, there are many more figures which one could delineate. But our purpose here has been primarily to emphasize the fact that the Egyptian conquest account was a figurative account (obviously, to varying degrees).

## CONCLUSION

In this chapter, the three major categories of the Egyptian military inscriptions have been delineated. In the first category, it was shown that the *iw.tw* texts were used primarily for short accounts especially in those cases when the Pharaoh himself was not a participant. These stereotyped inscriptions produced a high-redundance message which reinforced the Egyptian ideology. In the second category, a longer account, in which the actions of the Pharaoh in battle were recorded, would be based on the Daybook Records. The third category shows that the scribes could narrate an account without any reference to a Daybook Report and with a heavier dependence (to varying degrees) on rhetoric and poetics.

We then discussed Egyptian ideology showing that the person of the king played a major role in that ideology. It was a binary and imperialistic system in which the enemy was viewed as vile, wretched and evil. He was the cause of disorder and rebellion. The Pharaoh was the means by which order was restored to the status quo. The *iw.tw* texts played a significant role in the diffusion of this ideology since they employed a high-redundance message. In the administration of the empire the Egyptians employed two different systems: one for Nubia in which there was an Egyptization policy, and another for Syria and Palestine in which international law was the administrative policy.

Finally, we demonstrated that the Egyptian texts (whether *iw.tw* texts, *Nḫtw* texts based on Daybook Reports, or *Nḫtw* texts based on the Literary Reports) are fashioned by utilizing a high degree of literary devices. We have been able to isolate some of the rhetoric use in the accounts.

In all, it is best to remember that the Egyptian scribes were selective with their material and constructed their accounts from their particular point of view. Beginning to understand that point of view has been one of the objectives in our survey.

# STAGE TWO:

# THE ISRAELITE CONQUEST ACCOUNT:

# JOSHUA 9-12

# Chapter 5

## THE CONQUEST ACCOUNT OF JOSHUA 9–12

> We should neither exempt biblical literature from the standards applied to other ancient Near Eastern literatures, nor subject it to standards demanded nowhere else.[1]

Joshua 9–12 forms a unit in which the Israelite Conquest is narrated. This is evident for a number of reasons. In the first place, the first two verses of chapter nine give an introductory statement which forecasts the content of the narrative:

> [1]ויהי כשמע כל המלכים אשר בעבר הירדן בהר ובשפלה ובכל חוף הים הגדול אל מול הלבנון החתי והאמרי הכנעני הפרזי החוי היבוסי
> [2]ויתקבצו יחדו להלחם עם יהושע ועם ישראל פה אחד
>
> [1]When all the kings west of the Jordan who were in the hill country, the Shephelah, and all along the sea coast of the Great Sea as far as Lebanon—the Hittites, the Amorites, the Canaanites, the Perizzites, the Hivites, and the Jebusites—heard about these things, [2]they came to together and united to fight unanimously against Joshua and Israel.

Thus we know the story's setting and the major emplotment.

Second, the outworking of this story is manifested by the use of a key phrase in 9:1 (ויהי כשמע כל המלכים) linking up the narrative unit. It is reiterated in 9:3 (וישבי גבעון שמעו)—a partial resolution in a central area, in 10:1 (ויהי כשמע אדני צדק מלך ירושלם)—introducing a partial resolution in the south, and in 11:1 (ויהי כשמע יבין מלך חצור)—introducing a partial resolution in the north.

Third, the introductory statement of 9:1–2 receives its final resolution in chapter 12 where in verse one we are told:

> ואלה מלכי הארץ אשר הכו בני ישראל
> these are the kings of the land which the Israelites smote.

and verse seven:

ואלה מלכי הארץ אשר הכה יהושע ובני ישראל בעבר הירדן ימה

These are the kings which Joshua and the Israelites smote on the west side of the Jordan.

The introductory statement and the concluding summaries and lists presuppose one another. In this one recalls a similar structure in the 'Ten Year Annals' of Muršili II. There is no debate that the 'Ten Year Annals' is a literary unity. The prologue and epilogue presuppose one another (see chapter 3). Thus chapters 9–12 form a unit in which the conquest of 'all the kings west of the Jordan' (9:1; 12:7)—and then some—is enumerated. The unit, therefore, affords comparison with the ancient Near Eastern material.

While there are other conquest accounts before and after this section, this unit, nonetheless, is the major narration of the conquest in the book. Thus we have for reasons of economy and clarity of analysis chosen to restrict the comparison to Joshua 9-12. Moreover, while a full scale comparison of the conquest accounts in Joshua 10 and Judges 1 would be very interesting and is very important, it will not be carried out, again for reasons of economy and clarity. We will, however, include many comments on the relation between the two.

There is only one major difference which needs to be noted before a full scale analysis of Joshua 9–12 can proceed. In many ancient Near Eastern conquest accounts (such as in the Assyrian texts) direct speech is generally minimal, whereas in the biblical accounts it is commonplace. This only obscures in some ways the similarity in syntagmic structure between the biblical and ancient Near Eastern material. For example, in the Assyrian texts it will be stated 'By the command of Aššur, my lord, I did such and such'. The actual command is not stated; its exact content is unknown. In the biblical account, however, the actual command is given. This feature creates a more sophisticated surface to the narrative, but does not necessarily add significant information. Hence there is, in fact, an essential similarity of content between the ancient Near Eastern and biblical materials.

## LITERARY STRUCTURES
### (*Writing it just like everyone else*)

As we have already noted, the nature of the figurative aspect manifests itself in three ways: 1) the structural and ideological codes which are the apparatus for the text's production, 2) the themes or motifs that the text utilizes, and 3) the usage of rhetorical figures in the accounts. The second and third can very often be understood in terms of the old-time standard type of ANE and OT parallels. The first is a different concept for biblical studies: that the biblical narratives are the structures which communicate the historical image. All of these are utilized as ideological communicators. Obviously, while, at times, it is possible to isolate these aspects, they generally overlap so that a rhetorical figure communicates the ideological codes of the text and vice versa. Consequently, we will not always attempt to differentiate and demarcate these aspects, since to do so would impair the reader. However, we will attempt to give proper indication when it is possible.

Thus, when we say that a historical narrative is figurative, we are primarily speaking of the impositional nature of the account. Consequently we are interested in the figurative or metaphoric usage that P. Stambovsky identifies as Depictive Imagery. This utilization facilitates presentationally the (phenomenological) apprehension of meanings and occurrences, and is a component of sequential discourse.[2]

While the syntagmic iterative scheme is encountered primarily in chapters 10 and 11, the over-all transmission code in chapters 9–12 is very similar to what we have witnessed already in the ancient Near East. [For the text, translation, and syntagmic identification, see the Appendix]. This iterative scheme is not ornamental. It is an important literary convention for communicative purposes. We are not arguing that it is exclusively a historiographic code; it may well be encountered in fictive literature as other literary devices are. The ancient authors (just like their modern counterparts) utilized literary conventions as they fashioned their accounts.

*Chapter 9*

The function of the submission of the 'Enemy' (usually denoted M) is a common feature of the ancient Near Eastern historical texts. Often this submission follows on the heels of a recognition of the 'splendor', 'valor', or 'heroic deeds' of the victorious monarch and his army (or, as in some cases, the deity). Chapter 9 of Joshua in many ways follows in this pattern.

It is the syntagm $A^2$ which reveals that chapter 9 is linked to chapters 10-12. It is used in verse one to introduce the entire conquest narrative of chapters 9-12, and a second time in verse 3 to introduce the specific account of the treaty agreement between Israel and Gibeon. Hence verses 1 and 2 produce a general introduction to the account, with 9:3, 10:1 and 11:1 introducing the particular, detailed accounts.

The semantic equivalent to syntagm $A^2$ is used to introduce similar types of accounts in the Assyrian material. For example:

> Tarharqa, the king of Egypt and Nubia, in Memphis *heard of the coming of my expeditionary force*; and in order to make armed resistance and to make battle with me he mustered his warriors.[3]

and also:

> 4,000 Kasku (and) Urumu, insubmissive troops of Hatti-land—who had seized by force the cities of the land of Subartu which were vassals of Assur, my lord—*heard of my coming* to the land of Subartu. *The splendor of my valor overwhelmed them. Fearing battle they seized my feet (submitted to me).* Together with their property and 120 chariots (and) harnessed horses I took them; and I reckoned them as people of my land.[4]

These examples illustrate the accounts in chapters 9–11. In the first, like Tarharqa, the reaction of Adoni-Zedeq and Jabin is to muster armies against Joshua; but in the second, like the Kašku and Urumu, the reaction of the Gibeonites is to submit to Israel and to become integrated into its society.

The fact that there was some type of treaty between the Gibeonites and the Israelites has not really been questioned.[5] One reason for this is the fact that the tradition is attested convincingly in the tragic account of II Samuel 21:1–14. Another reason is that it is clear that the Gibeonites did serve in some capacity in ancient Israel.[6]

But the Gibeonite ruse in Joshua 9, unlike the treaty, has been regarded with almost complete skepticism. Many scholars feel that most of the components of the story are etiological in origin and are, therefore, unhistorical; they simply explain the origin of an institution.[7] For M. Noth, the ruse was introduced into the account as an 'etiological explanation' of the Gibeonites' service to the altar of YHWH in the sanctuary at Gilgal.[8] J. Liver claims that the account contains a historical tradition, but that the deceit was integrated into the text by an editor contemporaneous with Saul in order to justify Saul's attack upon the Gibeonites.[9]

In the present form of the biblical account, the Gibeonites resort to a ruse in order to gain a treaty with Israel.[10] While there were, no doubt, numerous kings, who for reasons of expedience, entered with deceitful motives into alliance with Assyrian kings, there does not appear to be an exact parallel to the biblical account in the Assyrian material *per se*. However, one example of submission which may have been tied up with deception is the famous character of Gyges (Assyrian: *Gūgu*). According to recension E,[11] Gyges, king of distant Lydia, a land which had remained outside the political horizons of Aššurbanipal's forefathers, was being overrun by Cimmerian invaders. In the midst of being pressed by his enemies, Gyges dispatched a rider to go from Lydia to Nineveh with a plea from him for Assyrian help against the enemy. After describing the devastating invasion, the rider relates the circumstances which brought him to the court of Aššurbanipal. His master, the Lydian king, had seen in a dream the *nibît šumi*, i.e., 'the written name' of Aššurbanipal[12] and had heard a voice ordering him to subject himself to Assyria in order to defeat those who were threatening his country. The god Aššur himself had revealed this formula for overcoming the Cimmerians. Thus Gyges desired a vassal relationship to Aššurbanipal. As a result of this dream, Aššurbanipal agreed to accept Lydia into the Assyrian fold. Awe-struck by the dream, Gyges undertook a yearly tribute to Assyria. However, he did not remain a loyal vassal. Prism A relates the death of Gyges:

> The riders which he constantly sent to inquire of my well-being broke off. I was informed that he had become unfaithful to the word of Aššur, the god, my begetter, and that he trusted in his own strength; he had become proud. He had sent troops to aid Psammetichus, king of Egypt, who had thrown off my yoke. I prayed to Aššur and Ištar: 'let his corpse be cast before his enemy; his bones carried off (i.e. scattered about).' That which I implored of Aššur, came about. Before his enemies his corpse was cast; his bones were carried off. The Cimmerians, whom he had defeated by invoking my name, rose up and swept over his entire land. After his demise, his son inherited his throne. (As a result of) the harsh treatment which the gods, my support, had given his father, his begetter—in response to my prayer—he sent his messenger, laid hold of my royal feet and said: 'You are the king singled out by god. You cursed my father and so, misfortune befell him. Unto me, your reverent servant, be gracious, so that I may bear your yoke.[13]

One might suggest that the dream itself was a type of ruse to gain support from the Assyrian monarch. Gyges expediently entered into relationship with Assyria for political gain. Once the enemies of Gyges were eliminated there was no reason to continue the deceptive stratagem. Yet the strategy of shifting alliance was Gyges's undoing as the Assyrian text so stresses.[14]

While the Assyrian account is helpful, there are two Hittite texts that also illustrate Joshua 9. One is found in the Ten Year Annals of Muršili (*KBo* III 4 Rs III.10-22):[15]

> But as I came back out of the land of the Seha River,
> I would have had to fight in the heart of Seha River(-land) Manapa-Datta who was the ruler (of that region). (However), when Manapa-Datta heard concerning me:
> "The king of Hatti comes!"
> He was afraid, and did not come forth to meet me. He sent forth his mother, the old men, (and) the old women to meet me. They came to me. They bowed down at (my) feet. Now because women bowed down at my feet I gave to the women as they wished. And so I did not go into the Seha River(-land). The fugitives of Hattuša, who were in the Seha River(-land), they handed over to me (freely). The fugitives which they handed over to me were 4,000 people. And I sent them forth to Hattuša. And they brought them forth. But Manapa-Datta and the land of the Seha River I took into servitude.

Manapa-Datta was a cunning ruler. He sent forth his mother, the old men and women of his country to meet the mighty Hittite army knowing (or at least trusting very strongly) that the Hittite ruler would not attack them and would grant to them their request (which apparently meant a treaty). So Muršili took them into servitude. This is a ruse of the rank of the Gibeonites. By craftiness Manapa-Datta saved his country from sure destruction.

Another text comes from Muršili's 'Detailed Annals'.[16] Here Muršili had been waging war against the Azzi, who like the Kaska[17] were a traditional enemy of the Hittites and were ruled by elders, not by a monarch (note the similarity to the Gibeonites in our context). Muršili had captured and plundered numerous towns when the text states:

> When the people of the city of Azzi saw that fighting (their) strong cities I subjugated them: —the people of Azzi, who have strong cities, rocky mountains, (and) high difficult terrain— they were afraid!
> And the elders of the land came before me, and they bowed themselves down at (my) feet. And they spoke:
>> "Our lord! Do not destroy us! Lord, take us into servitude, and we will begin to provide to your lordship troops and charioteers. The Hittite fugitives which (are) with us, we will provide these."
>
> Then I, my sun, did not destroy them. I took them into servitude; and I made them slaves.

It is certainly possible to accuse the people of Azzi of only going through the motions of submitting themselves to Muršili in order to get rid of him. For, when Muršili had returned home for the winter, the Azzians subsequently broke the oath. But they later yielded and became his slaves when he yet again threatened an attack. Whenever a treaty is entered into, there is always the possibility of insincerity on the part of one of the participants so that deceptive stratagems may play a role in the treaty-making process (the twentieth century gives ample witness to this!). Thus the possibility that the Gibeonite ruse is historical must be, at least, permitted.

Since submissions to the different ancient Near Eastern kings are regularly encountered in the texts, it appears that they are part of the *transmission code* of these texts. This means that through analogy chapter 9 might be considered as an integral part of the Joshua conquest narratives.[18]

One final example which illustrates this comes from Egyptian sources. In Ramesses III's account of his victory over the Libyans in the text of the 5th year at Medinet Habu,[19] we see the Libyan groups (Meshwesh, Libu, Temeh, and Tejhenu) crying out:

> ... we were trapped, they drew us in, like in a net. The gods caused us to succeed, indeed, (merely) to offer us up, to overthrow us for Egypt! (So,) let us make a *brt* (a treaty) with [the Egyptians (?) before they de]stroy us ...

These groups are then described in an address to the pharaoh:

> ...your terror seizes them, cowed, miserable and straying. They all make a *brt* (a treaty), bringing their tribute [on their backs ..., and coming with prai]se to adore [him = the king].[20]

One must keep in mind that this in no way proves the historicity of the account in Joshua 9. One is free to question the veracity of the historical referents in Joshua[21] as one might also question the referents in the Assyrian, Hittite, and Egyptian accounts above. The point which the comparison makes is that the account in Joshua 9 functions plausibly in its present context because it basically follows the same transmission code as observed in the ancient Near Eastern conquest accounts. Thus there is no compelling reason to break up this narrative of Joshua and dismiss it as history writing.

## *Chapters 10 and 11*

In these two chapters, the biblical text utilizes an iterative code both in a general manner and in a dense form. The following readout visualizes this (cf. also the Appendix):

| *Chapter 10* | *Chapter 11* |
|---|---|
| $A^{2}$ (10:1) | $A^{2}$ (11:1a) |
| $G^{\Delta 1}$ (10:2) | - |
| $G^{-2X}$ (10:3–4) | $G^{-2X}$ (11:1b–3) |
| $G^{-2}$ (10:5a) | $G^{-2}$ (11:4) |
| $G^{-3}$ (10:5b) | $G^{-3}$ (11:5) |
| B (10:6) | - |
| $E^{12}$ (10:7) | - |

| | |
|---|---|
| $C^2$ (10:8a) | $C^2$ (11:6a) |
| $C^{\aleph}$ (10:8b) | $C^{\aleph}$ (11:6b) |
| $^{C}L^{\aleph}$ (10:8c) | $^{C}L^{\aleph}$ (11:6c) |
| N (10:8d) | N (11:6d) |
| $E^{\zeta}$ (10:9) | $E^{\zeta}$ (11:7a) |
| - | $L^{1\beta}$ (11:7b) |
| $C^4$ (10:10) | $C^4$ (11:8a) |
| $L^{1\text{צ}\beta}$ (10:10b) | $L^{1\text{צ}\beta}$ (11:8b) |
| H (10:10c) | H (11:8c) |
| $L^{1\text{צ}\beta}$ (10:10d) | $L^{1\text{צ}\beta}$ (11:8d) |
| - | $L^{1h}$ (11:8) |
| $G^{\Delta 3}$ (10:11a) | - |
| $C^4$ (10:11b) | $C^4$ (11:9a) |
| N (10:11c) | N (11:9b) |

---

$a^2 + C^4$ (10:12a)
+ N (10:12b–14)

---

[Q (10:15) Inclusio]***

---

$G^{\Delta 3}$ (10:16a)
$G^{\Delta 4}$ (10:16b)
$L^{2\alpha}$ (10:17–18)
H (10:19a-d)
$C^4$ (10:19e)
$L^1$ (10:20a)
$G^{\Delta 3}$ (10:20b)
$G^{\Delta 4}$ (10:20c)
Q (10:21a)
[ ] (10:21b)
N (10:22–25)
$L^{1\text{צ}\alpha}$ (10:26a)
$L^{1\text{ב}\alpha}$ (10:26b)
N (10:26c-d)
$N^g$ (10:27a-c)
$N^f$ (10:27d-e)

---

| | |
|---|---|
| $A^2$ (10:28a) | $a^2$ (11:10a) |
| $L^{2\aleph\zeta}$ (10:28a) | $L^{2\aleph\zeta}$ (11:10b) |
| $L^{1\text{צ}\zeta a}$ (10:28b) | $L^{1\text{צ}\zeta\alpha}$ (11:10c-d) |
| - | $L^{1\text{צ}\zeta}$ (11:11a) |
| $L^{1\text{ב}\tau}$ (10:28c) | $L^{1\text{ב}\zeta}$ (11:11b) |
| $L^{1\eta}$ (10:28d) | $L^{1\eta}$ (11:11c) |
| - | $L^{1\text{ג}\zeta}$ (11:11d) |
| N (10:28e) | - |
| $A^2$ (10:29a) | - |
| $L^{1\zeta}$ (10:29b) | - |

| | |
|---|---|
| $C^{4}$ (10:30a) | - |
| $L^{2\text{א}\zeta}$ (10:30b) | $L^{2\text{א}\zeta\alpha}$ (11:12a) |
| $L^{1\text{צ}\zeta}$ (10:30c) | $L^{2\text{צ}\zeta\alpha}$ (11: 12b) |
| - | $L^{1\text{ב}\zeta}$ (11:12c) |
| $L^{1\eta}$ (10:30d) | - |
| N (10:30e) | - |
| - | $C^{2}$ (11:12d) |
| $A^{1,2}$ (10:31a) | < $L^{1\text{-ג}\zeta}$ > (11:13a) |
| F (10:31b) | < $L^{1\text{ג}\zeta}$ > (11:13b) |
| $L^{1\zeta}$ (10:31c) | - |
| $C^{4}$ (10:32a) | - |
| $L^{2\text{א}\zeta}$ (10:32b) | $L^{2\text{ב}\delta\epsilon}$ (11:14a) |
| $L^{1\text{צ}\zeta}$ (10:32c) | $L^{1\text{צ}\zeta}$ (11:14b) |
| $L^{1\text{ב}\zeta}$ (10:32d) | - |
| N (10:32e) | - |
| $a^{2}$ (10:33a) | - |
| $G^{-3}$ (10:33a) | - |
| $L^{1\text{צ}\alpha\beta}$ (10:33b) | $L^{1\eta}$ (11:14c) |
| $L^{1\eta}$ (10:33c) | $L^{1\eta}$ (11:14d) |
| $A^{1,2}$ (10:34a) | - |
| F (10:34b) | - |
| $L^{1\zeta}$ (10:34c) | - |
| $C^{4}$ (10:35a) | $C^{2}$ (11:15) |
| $L^{2\text{א}\zeta}$ (10:35b) | - |
| $L^{1\text{צ}\zeta}$ (10:35c) | - |
| $L^{1\text{ב}\zeta}$ (10:35d) | - |
| N (10:35e) | - |
| $A^{1,2}$ (10:36a) | - |
| $L^{1\zeta}$ (10:36b) | - |
| - | $L^{2\text{ג}\zeta}$ (11:16) |
| $L^{2\text{א}\zeta}$ (10:37a) | $L^{2\text{א}\alpha}$ (11:17b) |
| $L^{1\text{צ}\zeta\alpha}$ (10:37b) | $L^{1\text{צ}\alpha}$ (11:17c) |
| $L^{1\eta}$ (10:37c) | $L^{1\text{ל}}$ (11:18) |
| N (10:37d) | - |
| - | $G^{-6}$ (11:19a) |
| - | $G^{\Delta 6}$ (11:19b) |
| $L^{1\text{ב}\zeta}$ (10:37e) | - |
| - | $L^{2\text{ג}\zeta}$ (11:19c) |
| - | $C^{4}$ (11:20a) |
| - | $^{C}L^{1\text{ב}}$ (11:20b) |
| - | $^{C}L^{1\eta}$ (11:20c) |
| - | $C^{2}$ (11:20d) |
| $A^{1,2}$ (10:38a) | $a^{2}$ (11:21a) |
| $L^{1\zeta}$ (10:38b) | $L^{1\eta}$ (11:21b-c) |
| $L^{2\text{א}\zeta\alpha}$ (10:39a) | - |
| $L^{1\text{צ}\zeta}$ (10:39b) | - |
| $L^{1\text{ב}\zeta}$ (10:39c) | $L^{1\text{ב}}$ (11:21d) |

| | |
|---|---|
| $L^{1\eta}$ (10:39d) | $L^{1\eta}$ (11:22a) |
| N (10:39e) | $L^{-\eta}$ (11:22b) |
| $L^{1צ\zeta}$ (10:40a) | - |
| $L^{1\eta}$ (10:40b) | - |
| $L^{1ב\zeta}$ (10:40c) | - |
| $C^2$ (10:40d) | - |
| $L^{1צ\zeta}$ (10:41) | - |
| $L^{2א\zeta\alpha}$ (10:42a) | $L^{2ג}$ (11:23a) |
| $C^4$ (10:42b) | $C^4$ (11:23b) |
| [Q (10:43) inclusio]*** | $O^5$ (11:23c) |
| | $O^7$ (11:23d) |

The syntagms are employed in the two conquest accounts to form an iterative scheme. If the two expansions in chapter 10 (i.e. the 'miracles' and 'the capture and killing of the 5 kings') are temporarily laid aside, then it is abundantly clear that the two accounts exhibit this iterative scheme. The synthetic or simulated nature of the narrative account is evident from the continued use of the hyperbolic stereotyped syntagms throughout the two chapters. Consequently, the figurative nature of the account is reinforced.

The stereotyped syntagmic account in chapter 10 is very similar to an account found in Muršili's *Comprehensive Annals*.[22] Note the sequence in the narrative:

> As soon as I heard such words (i.e., a reported plot by one Pitaggatalli to prevent the entry of the Hittite army into the city of Sapidduwa), I made Altanna into a depot and left the baggage there; but the army I ordered to advance in battle order. And because (the enemy) had outposts, if I had tried to surround Pitaggatali, the outposts would have seen me, and so he would not have waited for me and would have slipped away before me. So I turned my face in the opposite direction towards Pittapara. But when night fell, I turned about and advanced against Pitaggatalli. I marched the whole night through, and daybreak found me on the outskirts of Sapidduwa. And as soon as the sun rose I advanced to battle against him; and those 9,000 men whom Pitaggatalli had brought with him joined in battle with me, and I fought with them. And the gods stood by me: the proud stormgod, my lord, the sungoddess of Arinna, my lady, the stormgod of Hatti, the protective deity of Hatti, the stormgod of the army, Ištar of the field, and Yarriš. And I destroyed the enemy.

The account continues and, while fragmentary,[23] it narrates the pursuit of Pittaggatalli by the Hittite army. Moreover, in the case of Pittapara, Muršili pursues him in person; and the booty is brought back to the Altanna camp.

In the case of the two expansions in chapter 10, while they are not part of the iterative scheme *per se*, they do make a significant contribution to the build up of the narrative and evince a similar transmission code to other ancient Near Eastern conquest accounts. In these expansions the figurative nature of the account is manifested primarily on the motif level; and it is on this level that the similarity between the ancient Near Eastern texts' and the biblical narrative's codes is most evident.

### *The Code: Joshua 10:11–15*

#### *1. The Hailstones*

A comprehension of the transmission code underlying ancient Near Eastern conquest accounts enhances our understanding of the biblical account of the 'miracles' of Joshua, i.e., the hailstones and the long day.[24] One text which is particularly helpful in understanding the 'stones from heaven' is that of the Ten Year Annals of Muršili (*KBo* III 4 Vs II.15-49):[25]

> So I marched, and as I arrived at Mt. Lawasa, the mighty stormgod, my lord, showed his godly miracle.[26] He hurled a meteor.[27] My army saw the meteor; (and) the land of Arzawa saw (it). And the meteor went; and struck the land of Arzawa. It struck Apasa, the capital city of Uhhaziti. Uhhaziti fell on (his) knees; and became ill. When Uhhaziti became ill; he did not come against me to fight; (but) he sent his son, Piyama-KAL, together with troops and charioteers to engage me. He took his stand to fight with me at the river Astarpa at Walma. And I, my sun, fought with him. The sungoddess of Arinna, my lady; the mighty stormgod, my lord; Mezzulla, (and) all the gods ran before me. And I conquered Piyama-KAL, the son of Uhhaziti, together with his troops and charioteers. And I defeated him. Then I pursued him, and I entered into the land of Arzawa. I entered into Apasa, into the capital city of Uhhaziti; and Uhhaziti could not withstand me. He fled before me; and went across the sea by ship. And he remained there. The whole country of Arzawa fled; and certain of the inhabitants went to the mountains of Arinnanda; and they oc-

> cupied Mt. Arinnanda. But certain others of the inhabitants went forth to Puranda; and they occupied Puranda. And certain other inhabitants went across the sea with Uhhaziti. Then I, my sun, went after the inhabitants to Mt. Arinnanda, and I fought (them) at Mt. Arinnanda. The sungoddess of Arinna, my lady; the mighty stormgod, my lord; Mezzulla (and) all the gods ran before me. Thus, I conquered Mt. Arinnanda. And those of the inhabitants which I, my sun, brought into the royal palace were 15,500 people. (And) those of the inhabitants which the generals of Hattusa, the troops (and) the charioteers brought (home) the number does not exist. Finally, I sent forth the captive inhabitants to Hattusa; and they brought them forth. When I had conquered Mt. Arinnanda, I then came again to the river Astarpa. I pitched camp at the river Astarpa; and I celebrated the New-year festival there. And I did (all) this in one year.

This passage is especially helpful in understanding Jos. 10:11 where 'YHWH hurled large hailstones down on them from the sky, and more of them died from the hailstones than were killed by the swords of the Israelites'. The Hittite phrase *para ḫandandatar* ('miracle') is very interesting. H. Wolf concludes that this phrase means

> divine power usually displayed as an out-pouring of grace to strengthen, deliver, or encourage its recipient. It is a means of preserving divine order and justice, and it can be accompanied by miracles.[28]

In the context of the miracles of Joshua 10, one can also see how YHWH's work is an outpouring of divine grace to strengthen the Israelites and to carry out justice in the destruction of the Amorite alliance. Just as Muršili and his army arrive, the stormgod sends his 'miracle' and there is confusion and discouragement among the enemy. Joshua and his army march and come upon the Amorites suddenly and YHWH throws them into confusion and there is a great victory. Just as the stormgod 'hurled his meteor', so YHWH 'hurled stones' (השליך עליהם אבנים). Just as the stormgod's meteor killed the people of Arzawa, so YHWH killed many Amorites.[29] Just as Muršili fights a great field battle and then pursues the enemy, so Joshua fights a great field battle and pursues the enemy. Just as Muršili conquered the entire region of Arzawa in one campaign ('one year'), so Joshua 'conquered the entire region in one campaign' (10:42). Thus it would seem that the similarity between the text of Joshua and that one of Mursili is due to a common ancient Near Eastern transmission code. The national deity could fight on behalf of his people and this might involve the employment of natural phenomenon.

Another passage which is beneficial in this discussion is found in Sargon's Letter to the God:[30]

> Metatti, (the ruler) of Zikirtu, together with the kings of his neighboring regions I felled their assembly (of troops). And I broke up their organized ranks. I brought about the defeat of the armies of Urartu, the wicked enemy, together with its allies. In the midst of Mt. Uauš he came to a stop. I filled the mountain ravines and wadis with their horses. And they, like ants in straits, squeezed through narrow paths. In the heat of my mighty weapons I climbed up after him; and *I filled ascents and descents with the bodies of (their) fighters. Over 6 'double-hours' of ground from Mt. Uauš to Mt. Zimur, the jasper mountain, I pursued them at the point of the javelin.* The rest of the people, who had fled to save their lives, whom he had abandoned that *the glorious might of Aššur, my lord, might be magnified, Adad*, the violent, the son of Anu, the valiant, *uttered his loud cry against them*; *and with the flood cloud and hailstones (lit. 'the stone of heaven' [$NA_4$ AN-e]), he totally annihilated the remainder.*[31] Rusa, their prince, who had transgressed against Samaš and Marduk, who had not kept sacred the oath of Aššur, the king of the gods, became afraid at the noise of my mighty weapons; and his heart palpitated like that of a partridge fleeing before the eagle. Like a man whose blood is pouring out from him, he left Turuspâ, his royal city. Like a roaming fugitive *he hid in the recesses of his mountain.* Like a woman in confinement he became bedridden. Food and water he refused in his mouth. And thus he brought a permanent illness upon himself. *I established the glorious might of Aššur, my lord, for all time to come upon Urartu. I left behind a terror never to be forgotten in the future* <emphases mine>.

It can be clearly seen that in the midst of a factual account of the battle there is some type of divine intervention which is very similar to that of the Joshua account—in fact, the mechanics of this intervention are revealed:[32] *i-na ur-pat re-eḫ-si u $NA_4$ AN-e* = אבנים מן השמים. Furthermore, the comparison is strikingly similar in narrative flow. The confederation under the direction of Rusa, including Metatti and other puppet kings, is broke up (*ú-par-ri-ra ki-iṣ-ri-šu-un* = ויהמם יהוה לפני ישראל :: 'YHWH threw them into confusion before Israel'). There is a great slaughter which takes place during the pursuit on the ascent and descent of the mountain (= 10:10 'smote them in a great victory at Gibeon, and who pursued them on the road of the ascent of Beth Horon ... on the descent of Beth Horon to Azekah'). The pursuit was over a great distance, 6 'double-hours' (Jos. 10: 'from Gibeon to Azekah'). During the descent the divine intervention occurred so that the remainder (*si-ta-at UN*$^{MEŠ}$, *re-e-ḫa*) were totally annihilated (= 'during their flight from Israel on the descent of Beth Horon, YHWH hurled large hailstones ... so that more of them died from the hailstones than were killed by the swords of the Israelites'). The Urartian king, Rusa, hid in the recesses of his mountain [*šá-ḫa-at KUR-šú*] (the five kings hid themselves in a cave). And finally, the land of Urartu and its allies were subdued, 'the glorious might of Aššur was established for all time' (in this single campaign of Sargon) (= 10:40–42).

Thus, on the basis of the evidence from the ancient Near East, it appears that the narrative of the miracle of the hailstones is a notable ingredient of the transmission code for conquest accounts.[33]

*2. The Long Day*

Not only can a comparison of ancient Near Eastern conquest accounts and the biblical account help us to gain a better understanding of the miracle of the hailstones, but it can also help us achieve sagacity into the performance of the heavenly signs. The text of Joshua 10:12–14/15 is very often seen by biblical scholars as a type of separate alternative tradition to the narrative of 10:1–11.[34] However, the use of אז and the preterite (ידבר) should be understood as a type of flashback—simply introducing a section of the text which narrates material which chronologically belongs between verse 9 and 10. אז functions very much like its Assyrian semantic counterpart *ina ūmīšuma* in the Assyrian royal annalistic inscriptions where it lacks strict chronological significance.[35] Hence, the biblical writer relates the principal incident which is connected to the battle (namely, the hailstones) first, before he then proceeds to the special point to be cited from the book of Yashar.[36]

The phenomenon of the 'sun standing still' in Joshua 10:12--14 has perplexed many interpreters. It would be foolhardy to believe that a definite explication can be given here. What seems to be clear is that celestial bodies participated in the battle which YHWH fought for Israel. Some modern interpreters have attempted to understand the poem (10:12b–13a) as poetic hyperbole.[37] For example, J. Bright understood the poem to be a prayer that the sun not dissipate the early morning mist in the valley before the surprise attack can take place.[38] Other scholars have tried to understand the event against the background of eclipses of the heavenly bodies which occurred in Joshua's time. Thus Sawyer dates the text exactly to an eclipse of the sun which lasted four minutes on 30 September 1131 B.C. beginning at 12:40 p.m.[39] J. Dus (following Heller) argued that the heroic song was a polemical curse against the cities of the Sun and Moon god, and that Israel's enemies in this encounter were in fact the cities of Gibeon and Aijalon.[40] R. de Vaux correctly points out the problems with this interpretation:

> there is nothing to indicate the presence of these cults at Aijalon and Gibeon and, secondly, Gibeon was not an enemy town. On the contrary, Joshua was fighting to defend it.[41]

In 1968, J.S. Holladay offered a study of the passage with some further comparative analysis. He concluded in his analysis that the poem is:

> a) intimately related to the geographical area occupied by the Gibeonite confederacy; b) concerned that both the sun and the moon 'stand', whatever that may mean, with the very strong possibility being that the sun is understood to be rising in the east, over Gibeon, and the moon is setting in the west, over the Aijalon valley, and c) this latter phenomenon is somehow to be connected with the question of the defeat of 'the enemy' by the nation (Israel).[42]

He argued that through a comparison with ancient Mesopotamian (especially Assyrian) astrological texts in which the position of the sun with the moon have positive and negative implications for the present and future, we can see that:

> Within this context, the meaning of Josh 10:12c–13b could hardly be more clear. The first stich is a prayer (or incanta-

> tion) that the sun and moon will 'stand' (*dmm* = *izuzzum*) in opposition (= *šitqulu*; hence the very necessary reference to Gibeon on the east and the valley of Aijalon on the west) on a day favorable to 'the nation' (most probably the fourteenth of the month) rather than to her enemies (the result if the moon were to 'flee' from the approaching sun, thus delaying conjunction until the unfavorable fifteenth of the month). The second and third stichoi, then, simply report a favorable outcome to the prayer, 'the nation' in effect gaining its ascendancy over 'its enemies' during those few fateful minutes of opposition when the great lunar and solar orbs 'stood' in the balance.[43]

In support of this Holladay cites numerous astrological texts to demonstrate his point that the sun and the moon serve as 'signs'. Firstly, the appearance of the sun and moon together on the fourteenth day was understood by the late Assyrian astronomical texts as a 'good sign':

> On the fourteenth day the Moon was seen with the Sun. When the Moon and the Sun are seen with one another on the fourteenth, there will be silence, the land will be satisfied; the gods intend Akkad for happiness. Joy in the heart of the people.[44]

> When Sin and Shamash are 'balanced' (*šitqulu*) [on the fourteenth of the month], the land will be secure, trustworthy speech will be established in the mouth of the people, the king of the land (on) the throne will grow old.[45]

On the other hand, an appearance of the sun with the moon on another day was interpreted as a bad omen. For example if on the thirteenth day:

> There will not be silence; there will be unsuccessful traffic in the land; the enemy will seize on the land.[46]

Or on the fifteenth day:

> When the Moon and Sun are seen with one another on the fifteenth day, a powerful enemy will raise his weapons against the land. The enemy will destroy the gate of my city.[47]

Thus Holladay felt that these passages elucidate the poem in Joshua 10, especially the usage of the terms דמם and עמד.

In a recent article, Halpern endorses this interpretation of these verses in Joshua and argues that this is a case in which the writer of the prose (i.e., the historian) has misinterpreted the poetry which he is quoting:

> The poem, situated 'in the day when YHWH gave the Amorites over before the children of Israel,' reports a request for a favorable omen—that the sun should be visible in the east while the moon remained visible in the west—and the granting of that omen (Josh 10:12–13). The prose interprets the poetry, not unreasonably, to mean that the sun stood still.[48]

While this view has some obvious merit, it has not, however, been without its critics. R. de Vaux argues that:

> One can accept Joshua's asking for a favourable omen and the fact that the sun and the moon were in their respective positions at the required time, but the consequence was that they *remained* there until revenge had been taken on the enemy. There is no parallel to this situation in any of the Assyrian texts.[49]

One of P.D. Miller's objections is that 'the עד of verse 13a and, therefore, the understanding of the whole line is not clearly explained by Holladay's interpretation.'[50] Furthermore, he points out, the examples which Holladay cites do not indicate that the good or bad fortune will take place while the astronomical phenomena are happening but that they are indicators that such things will happen in the immediate future.[51]

Similarly, Weinfeld argues that the phrase 'until the nation avenged itself on its enemies' (v. 13) is organically connected with the poetic section which precedes it in verse 12 so that the sun needs stop from its course in order to lengthen, as it were, the day and thus enable the fighting nation to take vengeance on its foes.[52] He feels that the prose narrator correctly understood the phrase when he comments 'thus the sun stopped in the middle of the sky and delayed going down about a complete day. God, who does battle here for Israel performs an extraordinary act in order that the warriors will be able to complete their victory while it is still day'.[53]

Weinfeld asserts that this is paralleled by the battle of Saul and Jonathan against the Philistines in I Samuel 14, except that there the extraordinary act is on the part of the people following the swearing in of the leader: 'For Saul had laid an oath upon the troops: "Cursed be the man who eats any food before night falls and I take revenge on my enemies"' (v. 24). He also points out a passage from the Iliad in support of his thesis where Agamemnon declares:

> Zeus, most glorious, most great, the one of the dark clouds, that dwellest in the heaven, grant that the sun set not, neither darkness come upon us, until I have cast down in headlong ruin the hall of Priam ... burned with consuming fire.[54]

Thus the address to the sun and the moon implies that they both stood, or were visible in the heavens at the time; and inasmuch as it was spoken to the Lord, involves a prayer that the Lord and Creator of the world would not suffer the sun and the moon to set till Israel had taken vengeance upon its foes.[55]

Taking these criticisms into consideration, it may be preferable to understand this phenomenon as containing a polemic. It is very possible that the Canaanite view would have understood the appearance of the sun and moon together on the fourteenth day in their 'stations' as a favorable sign. Ironically, it was Joshua, who in answer to his a prayer to YHWH, received control over these elements as YHWH fought for Israel.

Addressing more directly the sentences in verses 13b–14, Tadmor argues that there was a literary convention in which a king's military prowess was concentrated in one single year.[56] This was a convention of the heroic epic:

> Another unit of time typical of the heroic-epic narration is one day ... One is also reminded of some typical biblical examples: Joshua defeats the Kings of Canaan and Saul the Philistines within a single day. In the case of Joshua, until the heroic feat is accomplished, the sun stands still and thus the framework of a single—albeit long—day is preserved (Josh. 10:12–14, I Sam. 14:23–24).[57]

Because of the figurative nature of the accounts of the ancient Near East, it seems that this might very well be the explanation of כיום תמים (10:13). One passage which is unquestionably the closest parallel to Joshua in this sense comes from the Annals of Tiglath-Pileser I (V.44-53):

> With the support of Aššur, my lord, I took my chariots and warriors, (and) I set off for the desert. I marched against the 'aḫlamu' Arameans, enemies of Aššur, my lord. *I plundered from the edge of the land of Suhu to Carchemish of Hatti-land in a*

> *single day*. I massacred them. I carried back their booty, possessions, and goods without number.

One can see how the phrase *ina ištēn ūme* :: 'in a single day' is used here in a hyperbolic sense for the distance between Suhu (on the middle Euphrates) to Carchemish (in northern Syria) is very great to traverse in a single day. This certainly seems to be a possible explanation for the phrase in verse 14 כיום חמים which might very well be a hyperbole.

Another example of this type of figure can be seen in the inscription of Puzur-In-Sušinak:58

> **Col. I** Puzur-In-Sušinak, the governor of Susa, the viceroy of the land of Elam, the son of Simpi-išhuk; When (the land of Kimaš) and Hurtum rebelled against him, he went and he captured his enemies; and he vanquished Hubsana, ...
>
> [After two lines whose reading and interpretation is difficult, there is a list of more than seventy place-names which for the most part are unknown; This enumeration occupies the end of column I, column II to IV and the first four lines of column V.]
>
> **Col. V** *In one day*,[59] he subdued (these towns) to his feet; and when the king of Simaški came, he seized the feet of Puzur-In-Sušinak. [Puzur]-In-Sušinak granted his request and [... Lacuna ...].

Here Puzur-In-Sušinak claims to have conquered seventy towns *in one day*. It seems best to understand this as hyperbole.

Finally, a passage from an inscription of Seti I should be added to this discussion.[60] As Seti I moved north to confirm his hold on Canaan, he received a report which stated:

> On this day, His Majesty was informed as follows: "The despicable foe who hails from the town of Hammath has gathered a large force, capturing the town of Beth-Shan. And in league with the people of Pahil, he has prevented the chief of Rehob from getting out ....."

Seti reacted quickly to this report:

> ..... So His Majesty dispatched the 1st Division of Amun, 'Mighty of Bows,' against the town of Hammath; the 1st Division of Re', 'Abounding in Valor,' against the (captured) town of Beth-Shan, and the 1st Division of Seth, 'Strong of Bows,' against the town of Yenoam. *In the space of a single day*, they had fallen to the power of His Majesty![61]

It would appear that the victory of Seti I is put forth in hyperbolic terms: three cities in a day.

But arguing along different lines, A. Soggin, after discussing the numerous different opinions concerning this passage, states:

> Thus it seems more prudent to regard the phenomenon as one of the numerous miracles of which the Bible tells us (such as are found elsewhere in the ancient world), remembering that in the biblical message a miracle is always a 'sign' of an extraordinary divine intervention which imparts a grace unmerited by man and inconceivable in any other way.[62]

Therefore, we offer another passage from the ancient Near East which might prove to be helpful[63] in understanding the text of Joshua. This is a section from the Gebal Barkal Stela of Thutmose III.[64]

> (33)[.............] My [majesty speaks]: Hear, O people of the South-land who are at the Holy Mount, which was called 'Thrones-of-the-Two-Lands' (Karnak) among the people (the Egyptians(?)). It was not known that you might learn/witness the miracle[65] of [Amun-Re'] before the face of all the Two Lands (Egypt).

> (34)[It was evening, when the enemy troops came near[66]]. [The guards] were about to come to meet in the night to make the regular (change of) watch. There were two hour-watchers;[67] then a star came from the south of them. The like had never happened. It beamed[68] towards them from its position.[69] Not one remained standing there.

> (35)[(Then) I slaughtered them (the enemy), like they had never existed, prostrating (them) in their blood, casting (them) down][70] in heaps. Now [the royal serpent] was behind them, with fire to their faces. No one of them found his hand, nor looked back. They had not their horses, which were scattered in [plain(?)].

> [............................] ... in order to cause all foreign peoples to see the glory of my majesty. I came south with joyful heart, having triumphed for my lord, [Amun-Re, lord of Karnak]. It is he who commanded these victories, who gave the terror [of me] [....]

In this text we have some type of astrological phenomenon (possibly a comet or supernova?) which aids the Egyptians against their enemies in battle. This phenomenon is called a 'miracle'. A star[71] comes from the south and beams toward the enemy on a level with it (remaining stationary as the sun and moon in Joshua?) so that not one (of the enemy) remained standing there; and we are told that 'the like had never happened' (*n ḫpr mitt*). This is very similar to Jos. 10:14: ולא היה כיום ההוא לפניו ואחריו :: 'there has never been a day like that day before or after'). Moreover, it was Amun-Re who commanded these victories for Thutmose (line 222); whereas, כי יהוה נלחם לישראל :: 'Surely YHWH fought for Israel!' Furthermore, the enemies are completely destroyed, incapable of fighting the victorious Egyptians who have this phenomenon working in their behalf; just as the Israelites have 'complete victory', destroying the Amorite allies who are unable to fight back.

In the Egyptian text, moreover, it is apparently this same star which is used as a personification of the Pharaoh in first 'Euphrates Song' of the Stela which states:[72]

> His radiant splendor[73] is between the Two Bows,
> like a star he crosses the sky.[74]
> He enters into the mass of men,
> his blast of fire attacked them like a flame.
> he makes them non-existent,
>     while they are prostrated in their blood.
> It is his uraeus-serpent that overthrows them for him,
>     his royal serpent which subdues his enemies.

Thus in the Egyptian text as in the Hebrew text of Joshua 10 there is the aid of celestial bodies in the battle against the nation's enemies—a motif reminiscent of Judges 5:20. It should be emphasized here that these are celestial bodies under the direction of YHWH.

Consequently, the text in Habakkuk 3 also illuminates Joshua 10 as it states concerning YHWH:

> His glory covered the heavens,
>     and his praise filled the earth.
> His splendor was like the sunrise;
>     rays flashed from his hand ...
>
> *Sun and moon stood still in the heavens*
>     at the glint of your flying arrows,
>     at the lightning of your flashing spear.
> In wrath you strode through the earth,
>     and in anger you threshed the nations ...

P.D. Miller argues that according to this verse one should understand that it is YHWH who commands the sun and the moon to stand still, not Joshua.[75] But to support this Miller must advocate a textual error, 'a mem (for min, which is common with naqam) was lost by haplography from the original form of the text'.[76] While the likelihood of this seems doubtful, the text of Habakkuk definitely supports Miller's contention that according to Israel's understanding cosmic elements (under the control of YHWH) were involved in her wars as 'YHWH fought for Israel'—just as the star was involved in warfare in behalf of the Egyptians in the Gebal Barkal Stela above.

To summarize, in the ancient Near East, one encounters within conquest accounts narration of divine intervention. That it is found in the context of the Israelite conquest of Palestine should be no surprise. From the ancient Near Eastern accounts we can learn the following concerning the biblical text.

First, in the ancient Near East, there were accounts of divine intervention in which hailstones or meteors fell upon the enemy. We cited Hittite and Assyrian examples of this. The biblical account, with respect to this, continues the same transmission code.

Second, through an understanding of astrological omen techniques in the ancient Near East one can better understand the biblical command concerning the sun and the moon in 10:12–13a. It seems preferable to understand this phenomenon as containing a polemic. If the Canaanites viewed the appearance of the sun and moon together on the fourteenth day in their 'stations' as a favorable sign, then it would truly be ironic that YHWH in fighting for Israel answered Joshua's request.

Third, the phraseology of 10:13b–14 may very well be figurative as can be seen from numerous ancient Near Eastern texts in which phrases such as 'in a single day', 'in a single year', etc. are simply hyperbole.

Fourth, through comparison with other ancient texts one can discern a literary technique in which a deity is implored to maintain daylight long enough for there to be victory—a kind of ANE daylight-savings time!

Finally, one can seen that in the ancient Near East divine intervention may come in the form of a miracle/sign. On the one hand, the truthfulness of such utterances is to be sought in the subjective sphere of religious intuition, and not in a literal interpretation of the words. On the other hand, the ancient text may simply be recording something which it is not now possible to identify and explain by scientific means.

Thus—to re-emphasize the main point of our discussion—'the miracles' of Joshua 10 are very much within the ancient Near Eastern transmission code for conquest accounts. There is no reason to dismiss them from being a integral part of the text, i.e., as secondary additions. Furthermore, by comparing the biblical account with its ancient Near Eastern counterparts one is able to better decode and elucidate the former.

### *The Code: Joshua 10:16–27*

The story of the capture and execution of the five kings in Joshua 10:16–27 has been understood by numerous biblical scholars to be an element from a different independent tradition from the preceding verses.[77] Noth maintains that verses 16–27 are purely etiological, invented to explain the cave at Makkedah, or rather the great stones at the mouth of the cave which are said to have been there 'unto this day' (v. 27).[78] One of the main reasons why Noth maintained this isolation of 10:16–27 from 1–14 was because of the evidence of verse 15 which rounds out the battle account by removing Israel from the Makkedah area, the place where the following verses locate the nation.[79] Following Noth's thinking, Butler argues that the passage is a 'narrative fragment transformed into a secondary etiology to illustrate holy war technique'.[80] Therefore this section is viewed as etiological and hence fabricated, secondary, non-historical, etc.

But this is all very unnecessary. When one peruses ancient Near Eastern conquest accounts one quickly realizes that it is very common in the transmission code of these accounts to narrate an open field battle in which the enemies are defeated and from which the king, kings, and/or people flee and take refuge in some place (whether high mountain, mountain cave, or across the sea). In some instances the kings are captured; in other they are not. A few examples will demonstrate this. Concerning Rusa, the king of Urartu, Sargon states that after he had defeated him he fled and:

> like a roaming fugitive he hid in the recesses of his mountain. Like a woman in confinement he became bedridden ...[81]

Aššurbanipal states concerning the Elamite king:

> Ummanaldaši, king of Elam, heard of the entrance of my army into the midst of Elam, and he abandoned Madaktu, his royal city, and fled and went up into the mountains.[82]

and concerning Arabian fugitives:

> None of those who had gone up and entered the mountains to find refuge escaped. Not one survivor slipped through my hands. My hands captured them in their hiding-places.[83]

Esarhaddon stated concerning fugitives in general (*Nin.A*: Col. V.10-14):

> Whoever had fled into the sea in order to save himself did not escape my net; and he did not save his life. The speedy runner, who fled to the stepped ledges of far-off mountains, I caught and tied their wings like a bird from the mountain caves. I caused their blood to flow like a flood in the mountain wadis.

And Sennacherib states (Col. I.16-19):

> And the mighty princes feared my battle array; they fled their abodes, and like bats (living in) cracks (caves), they flew alone to inaccessible places.

Two examples from Egypt must also be mentioned. First Amun-Re‘ states in a speech to Thutmose III:

> You crossed the water of the Euphrates of Nahrin,
> in victory and in power which I had ordained for you,
> hearing your war-shout they hid in *holes*.
> I deprived their nostrils of the breath of life.
> I caused the dread of your majesty to pervade their hearts.
> My uraeus-serpent on your brow destroyed them.[84]

Also in a fragmentary text of Ramesses II at Karnak:

> [The good god] has come back after he had triumphed over the chiefs [of] all forei[gn lands]. He has trampled underfoot the rebellious foreign lands who have attacked his boundaries. He [is like Montu?]. He received the mace like Horus in [his] panop[ly], his [bow] being with him like Bastet. His

arrow is [like (that of) the son of] Nut. No foreign country can stand before him ... Terror of him is in their hearts. All [rebellious?] foreign lands ... having become at peace ... He has made an end of them. He who stands on the battle-field, ignoring [the bearers of the bows]. *They spend the time in the caves (mgrt) hiding like jackals—the fear of you is in their hearts.*[85]

The very word *mgrt*  is a semitic loan word for cave (cf. Hebrew מערה).

Thus it is more than evident from these few examples that the narrative in Joshua 10:16–27 is in full accord with other ancient Near Eastern conquest accounts in that kings who were defeated in open battle often would flee and take refuge in some hiding place such as a cave, and that such kings were sometimes captured and put to death.[86] Furthermore, defeated armies were generally pursued in order to cut off the retreat. For example, in the Annals of Sennacherib:

In pursuit of them, I despatched my chariots and horses after them. Those among them who had escaped, who had fled for their lives, wherever they (my charioteers) met them, they cut them down with the sword. [Col. VI.32-35]

Thutmose III tells us that if his troops had cut off the enemy troops from entering Megiddo, he would have immediately captured the city:[87]

Then his majesty overwhelmed them at the head of his army. When they saw his majesty overwhelming them, they fled headlong [to] Megiddo with faces of fear. They abandoned their horses, their chariots of gold and silver, so as to be hoisted up into the town by their garments. For the people had shut the town behind them, And they now [lowered] [87]garments to hoist them up into the town.

*Now if his majesty's troops had not set their hearts to plundering the possessions of the enemies, then they would have [captured] Megiddo at that very moment,* when the wretched enemy of Kadesh together with the wretched enemy of this town were being pulled up hurriedly, so as to admit them into their town. For the fear of his majesty had entered [88][their bodies], and their arms became weak, as his uraeus overwhelmed them.

As it was for the Canaanites in the days of Thutmose III, it very well may have been for the Canaanites in Joshua's day who fled to their cities. Also the fact that Joshua executed these kings and hung them on trees is paralleled by numerous instances where Assyrian monarchs hung the corpses of the foreign leaders on trees.[88] Thus, Sennacherib states concerning the rulers of Ekron:

> the governors (and) nobles who had sinned I put to death;
> and I hung their corpses on poles around the city (Col. III.8-10).

The number five (which Noth and Gray feel is evidence for the passage 16–27 being etiological) is a clear link to the description of the alliance related in verses 1–5 (see also note 90). The fact that other cities are mentioned or that another city-state comes to the aid of one of the cities is nothing to become alarmed about. It is hardly the type of thing to lead one to the conclusions of Noth and Gray since one can see this same phenomenon in ancient Near Eastern accounts. Thus, in the Annals of Tiglath-Pileser I, one reads:

> (Thus) I crossed the Euphrates. The king of the land Tumme, the king of Tunube, the king of Tuali, the king of Dardaru, king of Uzulu, the king of Unzamunu, the king of Andiabu, the king of Piladarnu, the king of Adurginu, the king of Kulibarzinu, the king of Sinibirnu, the king of Himua, the king of Paiteru, the king of Uiram, the king of Sururia, the king of Abaenu, the king of Adaenu, the king of Kirinu, the king of Albaya, the king of Ugina, the king of Nazabia, the king of Abarsiunu, the king of Dayenu, altogether 23 kings of the lands of Nairi, combined their chariotry and army in their lands; and they advanced to wage war and combat. With the onslaught of my fierce weapons I approached them. I destroyed their extensive army like the inundation of Adad. The corpses of their warriors I laid out like grain heaps on the open country, the plains of the mountains and the environs of their cities. I seized in battle 120 of their chariots with the equipment. 60 kings of the lands of Nairi, together with those who had come to their aid, I chased at arrow point as far as the Upper Sea.

Notice that the number of kings is different (23 ≠ 60). But in ancient Near Eastern warfare there were always vassal 'kinglets' who were among the more powerful 'kings' so that depending on how one counted the number of 'kings' would vary. Hence, the number of cities involved also varied (see more on this point below, p. 230). Furthermore, an army might come to the aid of its ally and be defeated, but its land not be invaded (or perhaps invaded at a later time). For example,

Tiglath-Pileser I relates that when he defeated the land of Kadmuhu (the first time), he 'laid low the army of the land of Paphê which had come to the aid and assistance of the land of Kadmuhu and he captured in the midst of the battle their (Paphê's) king Kili-Tešub' (Col. II.16-35). But he did not apparently invade the land immediately after the battle. Later we are told that he invaded Paphê and defeated its army and conquered its land, but he does not mention the king of Paphê by name (Col. III.35-65). Again, the biblical text of Joshua has a transmission code which is very similar to that of other ancient Near Eastern conquest accounts. Horam, the king of Gezer, came to the aid of Lachish, but was defeated—'no survivors were left'. Yet, there is no mention of an Israelite conquest of Gezer at this time. The kings who organized the alliance against Israel were captured and executed just as those in the above mentioned ancient Near Eastern texts.

So there is no compelling reason to conclude that the passage (verses 16-27) is etiological.[89] The heaping of stones at the cave can hardly merit the account the label of an etiology. The heaping up of the enemy and/or stones, dust etc. for a symbol was a common practice. Thus, Shalmaneser I states:

> I gathered (some of) its [the city of Arina's] dust (and) at the gate of my city, Aššur, I made a heap (of it) for posterity (lit. *ana aḫrât ūme*).[90]

Sargon relates that he slew the warriors of a certain city and piled them up in the gate of the city.[91]
Sennacherib shows the etiological force of a memorial heap!:[92]

> In order that no one might ever forget the might of Aššur my lord, that all peoples might magnify the praises of his warriorship, in the ground where I had brought about the defeat of the king of Babylon and Ummanmenanu the king of Elam—all of their lands together with Parsuas, Anzan, Pasiru, Ellipi, (and) all of Chaldea, as much as there was, all the Arameans—(in this ground) I harvested their skulls like shrivelled grain and I piled (them) up into heaps.

Lastly, the phrase עד עצם היום הזה 'until this selfsame day' does not necessarily signal that the preceding narrative is an etiology.[93] This phrase is closely parallel to a phrase in the Annals of Thutmose III which states:

> *[iw s]n smn ḥr rdit snn nt dḥr m ḥwt-nṯr nt 'Imn m hrw pn*
> They are recorded on a scroll of leather in the temple of Amun to this day.[94]

The reference is to the time of the writing of the account and its depositing in the temple of Amun. The biblical phrase simply refers to the time at which the account was written. It does not (in this instance) refer to the creation of 'a narrative which seeks to explain why something has come to be, or why it has become such and such'.[95] There is certainly no 'mythical causality principle' present in 16–27.[96] But even if the phrase עד עצם היום הזה (or some other element in 16–27) were etiological, it would only explain the preservation, not the creation of the story.[97] It would not automatically mean that the story was fabricated and unhistorical. Nevertheless, Soggin argues that:

> there was a cave half closed by great rocks which did not seem to have got there naturally; nearby, there were several trees; and they stood, moreover, in a region where according to tradition Israel had conquered several enemy armies and executed their kings. This was sufficient material to provide a localization for the story. This must be emphasized, in disagreement with Kaufmann, who does not think that a cave surrounded by trees, which is a very common phenomenon, is a sufficient factor to give rise to an aetiological legend. But it must be noted that whereas each of these elements individually is quite common, for them all to be found together in one place is exceptional.[98]

This is persistence in spite of all odds! First, what in the text would lead one to the conclusion that the cave and the great rocks were not there naturally? Second, what elements does Soggin mean other than the cave, rocks and trees—which are in fact very common—to merit him making the assertion that to be 'found together in one place is exceptional?' If he means to include the 'tradition' of Israel's conquest in the region as an element, then the argument is circular and must immediately be dismissed.

Since Joshua 10:16–27 follows a transmission code very similar to other ancient Near Eastern conquest accounts, and since there are no other compelling reasons to conclude otherwise, it is best to treat it as non-etiological.

### *Chapter 10:28–42*

We have analyzed this section separately because within it, the iterative scheme is manifested in its greatest denseness. This section is composed of eight episodes utilizing eleven syntagms.

| 28 | 29-30 | 31-32 | 33 | 34-35 | 36-37 | 38-39 | 40-42 |
|---|---|---|---|---|---|---|---|
| $A^2$ | $a^{1,2}$ | $a^{1,2}$ | $a^{1,2}$ | $a^{1,2}$ | $a^{1,2}$ | $a^{1,2}$ | - |
| - | - | F | [ $G^{-3}$ ] | F | - | - | - |
| - | $L^{1\zeta}$ | $L^{1\zeta}$ | - | $L^{1\zeta}$ | $L^{1\zeta}$ | $L^{1\zeta}$ | - |
| - | $C^4$ | $C^4$ | - | $C^4$ | - | - | - |
| $L^{2\aleph\zeta}$ | $L^{2\aleph\zeta}$ | $L^{2\aleph\zeta}$ | - | $L^{2\aleph\zeta}$ | $L^{2\aleph\zeta}$ | $L^{2\aleph\zeta\alpha}$ | - |
| $L^{1\aleph\zeta\alpha}$ | $L^{1\aleph\zeta}$ | $L^{1\aleph\zeta}$ | $L^{1\aleph\beta\alpha}$ | $L^{1\aleph\zeta}$ | $L^{1\aleph\zeta\alpha}$ | $L^{1\aleph\zeta}$ | $L^{1\aleph\zeta}$ |
| $L^{1\beth\zeta}$ | - | $L^{1\beth\zeta}$ | - | $L^{1\beth\zeta}$ | - | $L^{1\beth\zeta}$ | - |
| $L^{1\eta}$ | $L^{1\eta}$ | - | $L^{1\eta}$ | - | $L^{1\eta}$ | $L^{1\eta}$ | $L^{1\eta}$ |
| N | N | N | - | N | N | N | - |
| - | - | - | - | - | $L^{1\beth\zeta}$ | - | $L^{1\beth\zeta}$ |
| ↓ | ↓ | ↓ | ↓ | ↓ | ↓ | ↓ | $C^4$ |
| | | | | | | | $L^{1\aleph\zeta}$ |
| | | | | | | | $L^{2\aleph\zeta\alpha}$ |
| | | | | | | | $C^4$ |
| | | | | | | | Q |
| A1 | A2 | B | C | B′ | A′2 | A′1 | |

Not only do these syntagms build a structural pattern that creates the iterative scheme, but they are also arranged in a 'palistrophe'.[99] This structural pattern cannot be fortuitous. Thus the *iterative scheme* creates a *high-redundance message* with a chiastic presentation. And this section is in turn linked with the high-redundance message of chapters 10 and 11.

Thus the account is simulated or artificial in its structure. The writer/historian has used the same techniques as any literary artist to arrange or fashion his materials. The narrative only approaches a representation of the reality which it purports to describe. But, of course, this is the case with *any* historical narrative.[100] Thus M. Fishbane correctly perceives that:

> in the Hebrew Bible historical narrative is always narrative history, and so is necessarily mediated by language and its effects. It is thus language in its artistic deployment that produces the received biblical history.[101]

The seven episodes of 10:28–39, like any historical account, are figurative. These episodes are even more so because of the hyperbolic nature of the various syntagms. For example, the syntagms (ויחרם אותה ואת כל הנפש אשר בה :: 'they completely destroyed it and everyone in it') and (לא השאיר בה שריד :: 'he left no survivors') are obviously hyberbole. This is also true for these: (לא נותר כל נשמה :: 'Not sparing anything that breathed'), (לא השאירו כל נשמה :: 'Not sparing anything that breathed'), and (עד השמדם אותם :: 'until they exterminated them'). That these are figurative is clear from numerous ancient Near Eastern texts. For example,

1). The Gebal Barkal Stela of Thutmose III:[102]

> The great army of Mitanni,
> it is overthrown in the twinkling of an eye.
> It has perished completely,
> as though they had never existed.
> (7)Like the ashes (lit. 'the end') of a fire.

2). The Merenptah 'Israel' Stela:[103]

> Yanoam made nonexistent;[104]
> Israel is wasted, his seed is not.

3). The Meša Inscription:[105]

וארא בה ובבתה
וישראל אבד אבד עלם

> But I saw my desire over him and his house,
> and Israel has utterly perished forever.

ואלתחם בקר
ואחזה
ואהרג את כל העםם מ[ה]קר
רית לכמש ולמאב

> And I fought against the town;
> and I took it.
> I killed all the inhabitants of the town,
> as an offering of propitiation[106] to Kemoš and Moab.

ויאמר לי כמש
לך אחז נבה על ישראל
ואהלך בללה
ואלתחם בה מבקע השחרת עד הצהרם
כי לעשתר כמש החרמתה

Then Kemoš said to me:
"Go, seize Nebo from Israel."
So I went by night;
and fought against it from the break of dawn until noon;
and I took it;
and I killed everyone in it, seven thousand men and women, both natives and aliens, and female slaves;
because I had dedicated (החרמתה) it to ʿAštar-Kemoš.

4). Sennacherib:[107]
The soldiers of Hirimme, dangerous enemies, I cut down with the sword; and not one escaped.

5). Muršili II (KBo III 4 Rs III.44; 64-65):[108]
I made Mt. Asharpaya empty (of humanity) ...
I made the mountains of Tarikarimu empty (of humanity).

Thus it is evident that the syntagms (ויחרם אותה ואת כל הנפש אשר בה :: 'they completely destroyed it and everyone in it'), (לא השאיר בה שריד :: 'he left no survivors'), etc. are to be understood as hyperbole. Just like other ancient Near Eastern conquest accounts, the biblical narrative utilizes hyperbolic, stereotyped syntagms to build up the account.

Finally, concerning Joshua 10:40–43, it is important to point out that the use of summary statements within conquest accounts is quite common. For a further discussion of the figurative nature of these summary type of syntagms, see: pp. 230-31 and 251-53 below.

*Chapter 11*

Chapter 11 clearly is a new episode in the conquest account of Joshua 9–12. Israel has gained a victory over the Amorite alliance in the south and now faces the Canaanite coalition of the north. The chart of the syntagmic structure of the chapter given above shows that the syntagmic patterning is continued in this chapter. Hence the two chapters (10 and 11) combine to create a larger iterative scheme. The forming of the Canaanite coalition in the north is parallel to the Amorite alliance in the south. Just as Adoni-Zedeq took the initiative in the south and organized the alliance, so Jabin did in the north.

The chapter contains three sections (1-9), (10-20), and (21-22) with the last two set off by the use of the temporal indicator בעת ההיא. This type of quotation formula is used as a type of flashback so that the materials of these episodes can be linked together. In all three, stereotyped syntagms are utilized in order to build up the iterative structure.

While the chapter does not contain any 'miracles' corresponding to those in chapter 10, divine intervention, nevertheless, is present. As previously stressed, the mention of divine intervention is a common part of the ancient Near Eastern transmission code. A particularly relevant text in this regard is that of Zakkur.

| *Joshua 10:8* | *Joshua 11:6* | *Zakkur*[109] |
| --- | --- | --- |
| ויאמר יהוה אל<br>יהושע<br>אל תירא מהם<br>כי בירך נתתים<br>לא יעמד איש<br>מהם בפניך | ויאמר יהוה אל<br>יהושע<br>אל תירא<br>מפניהם אנכי<br>נתן את כלם<br>חללים לפני<br>ישראל כי מחר<br>כעת הזאת את<br>סוסיהם תעקר<br>ואת מרכבתיהם<br>תשרף באש | [וירבר[12]]<br>בעלשמין אלי<br>[ב]יד חזין<br>וביד עררן<br>[ויאמר] [13][לי]<br>בעלשמין אל<br>תזחל כי אנה<br>המל[כתך] [ואנ]ה<br>[14][אק]ם עמך<br>ואנה אחצלך<br>מן כל [מלכיא]<br>[אל זי] [15]מחאו<br>עליך מצר |
| YHWH said to Joshua:<br>'Do not be afraid of them; I have delivered them into your hand. Not one man of them will be able to withstand you'. | [6]YHWH said to Joshua:<br>'Do not be afraid of them, because by this time tomorrow I will hand all of them over to Israel, slain. You are to hamstring their horses and burn their chariots'. | And Ba'alshamayn spoke to me through the hand of seers and the hand of envoys and Ba'alshamayn said to me:<br>'do not be afraid because I have made you king, and I will stand with you, and I will deliver you from all these kings who have raised a siege against you'. |

### *Chapter 12*

Chapter 12 continues the code with the following structure:

| | | | |
|---|---|---|---|
| Introduction (General) | | | $L^{1\aleph\alpha}$ (12:1a)<br>$L^{2T}$ (12:1b) |
| A | List | Transjordanian | $L^{\circ\chi}$ (12:2-5) |
| | Moses | | $L^{1\aleph}$ (12:6a)<br>$O^{5}$ (12:6b) |
| B | Joshua | Cisjordanian | $L^{1\aleph}$ (12:7a)<br>$O^{5}$ (12:7b-8) |
| | List | | $L^{\circ\chi}$ (12:9-24)[110] |

Summarizing statements and lists of defeated lands following accounts of military campaigns are common in the Assyrian royal inscriptions. Moreover, though a comparison of the list contained in Sennacherib's annals[111] (after his seventh campaign) with the list in the Walters Art Galley inscription[112] one can quickly see that these lists are partial. They are very selective.[113] [Cities which occur in both lists are italicized].

*Annals*

I conquered in the course of my campaign (the cities of) *Bīt-Ha'iri* (and) *Raza*, cities on the border of Assyria, which during the time of my father, the Elamite had seized by force; and I carried off their spoil.
I caused soldiers, my garrison, to enter into their midst. I returned them to the border of Assyria. I assigned (them) into the hands of the commander of the fort of *Dēr*.

*Walters Art Galley*

I conquered in the course of my campaign (the cities of) *Bīt-Ha'iri* (and) *Raza*, cities on the border of Assyria, which during the time of my father, the Elamite had seized by force; and I carried off their spoil.
I stationed in them archers (and) shield bearers. I returned them to the border of Assyria. I assigned (them) into the hands of the commander of the fort of *Dēr*.

(The cities of) *Bubê, Dunni-Šamaš, Bīt-Risia, Bīt-Ahlame, Dūru, Dannat-Sulaya, Šiliptu, Bīt-Aṣusi, Kār-Zēru-iqīša, Bīt-Giṣṣi, Bīt-Katpalani, Bīt-Imbia, Hamanu, Bīt-Arrabi, Burutu, Dim-tu-ša-Sulaya, Dim-tu-ša-Mār-bīti-ēṭir, Harriašlakê, Rabbaya, Râsu, Akkabarina, Til-Uhuri, Hamranu, Naditu* together with the cities of the mountain passes of *Bīt-Bunaki, Til-Humbi, Dim-tu-ša-Dume-ilu, Bīt-Ubia, Bal-tilišir, Taqablišir, Šanaqidāte,* Masutuš-šapliti, *Sarhuderi, Alum-ša-GAŠAN(Bēlet or Šarrat?)-bīti, Bīt-Ahhi-idinna, Ilteuba,* 34 strong cities together with the cities surrounding their environs, which were countless, I besieged, I conquered, I carried off their spoil;
I destroyed, I devastated, (and) I burned with fire.
I covered the face of the wide heavens with the smoke of their conflagration like a heavy fog.

(The cities of) *Bīt-arrabi,* Alumqasti, *Bubê, Dunni-Šamaš,* Ekalšalla, *Burutu, Bīt-Risia,* Dūr-Dannu-Nergal, Bīt-Lišeru, *Bīt-Ahlame, Alum-ša-Bēlit-bīti,* Ibrat, Kuṣurtain, *Dūru, Dannat-Sulaya, Šiliptu, Bīt-Aṣusi, Kār-Zēru-iqīša, Bīt-Giṣṣi, Bīt-Katpalani, Dim-tu-ša-Sulaya, Dim-tu-ša-Mār-bīti-ēṭir, Harriašlakê, Rabbaya, Râsu, Til-U[huri], Hamranu, Til-Humbi, Dimtu-ša-Dume-ilu, Bīt-Ubia, Balt[ilišir], Taqablišir, Šanaqidate, Sarhuderi, Bīt-Ahhi-idinna, [Ilteuba],* Muthuṣe .., Damtē, Dim-tu-ša-Bēlit-bīti, *Akkabrina, Bīt-[Imbia],* Masuttu, Bīt-Unziya, Bīt-Kisiya, Dim-tu-ša-Šullume, [.....], Dim-tu-ša-Nabâ-šarhi-ilī, Apdinu, Til-raqu, Alum-šarri, [....], the strong fortresses of Rāzi and the smaller cities surrounding [their] environs, [which were countless], *Hamanu, Naditu* as far as the pass of *Bīt-Bunakki* I conquered, I carried off their spoil; I destroyed, I devastated, I burned with fire and turned (them) into a ruin heap.

Thus for a city to be contained in one list and lacking in another (both lists describing the same campaign) does not constitute an error or interpolation, or mean that there are different sources for the lists. It means only that lists of conquered cities in the ancient Near East were often selective or partial. Hence, the inclusion of Megiddo in the list of chapter 12 means only that the account of the conquest of the north is selective and does not include the account of that city's capture; just like the account of this Elamite campaign of Sennacherib was selective and does not include the account of the conquest of the city of Til-raqu (a city which is in the Walters Art Galley list, but for which there is not a conquest account).

Another instance of this phenomenon can be cited from the Kadesh inscriptions of Ramesses II. A list of the Hittite allies is given three times (in the Poem twice: 1-6, 43-47, and in the

Bulletin once: 42-58). In two occurrences of the list 18 allies are mentioned, but in Poem 1-6 only fourteen are named. The reason for this remains obscure and in all probability it is attributable to the selective nature of ancient lists.[114]

One final example is found in Sargon's Letter to the God (lines 87-89):

> The cities of Ištaippa, Saktatuš, Nanzu, Aukanê, Kabani, Gurrusupa, Raksi, Gimdakrikka, Barunakka, Ubabara, Sitera, Tastami, (and) Tesammia—12 of their mighty cities, strongholds—together with 84 cities of their environs, all (of these) I captured.

Notice that the number of cities named is 13 while the round number of 12 has been give for the total.

Not only are lists commonly encountered in ancient Near Eastern conquest accounts but summary statements as well. For example, consider the following inscription of Thutmose III (Armant Stela):[115]

> Year 22, the second month of winter, day 10: Summary of the deeds of valor and victory which this good god performed on every excellent occasion of activity from the beginning since the first generation (of men). That which the Lord of the gods, the Lord of Hermonthis, did for him was to magnify his victories, so that his conquests might be related for millions of years to come, apart from the deeds of activity which his majesty did in both seasons, for if one were to mention each occasion by name, they would be too numerous to put into writing.

Thus, it is entirely natural to have summary statements and lists in historical narratives. They are obvious parts of the transmission code of conquest accounts. Chapter 12 is a natural part of the narration as seen by our comparison with the ancient Near Eastern conquest accounts. Consequently, there is no reason to posit these as the work of redactors.

## ISRAELITE IDEOLOGY
## (*What you can do through the right 'connections'*)

With regard to the functions of ideologies, Shils believes that ideologies are often accepted by persons who are predisposed and who are often inclined to express their views with aggressive affect, who feel a strong need to distinguish between comrades and enemies, or who might have been raised in a salvationary, apocalyptic culture.[116] By making these people believe that:

> they are in contact with the ultimate powers of existence, ideology will greatly reinforce their motivation to act. They will gain courage from perceiving themselves as part of a cosmic scheme: actions that they would not dare to envisage before will now have the legitimacy which proximity to the sacred provides.[117]

One can clearly see the function of ideology in Joshua 9–12. Shils's description aptly fits the Israelites in the book of Joshua. They are in contact with the Ultimate Power of existence and they have motivation and courage to act. The constant reiteration for Joshua and the Israelites to be 'strong and of good courage', and even more importantly in the context of 9–12, 'Do not be afraid of them' demonstrates this ideological aspect.

### *Type*

If one compares the ideology which is present in the ancient Near Eastern conquest accounts with the biblical text, one quickly see a number of similarities.

First, the Hebrew account seems to evince a similar view of the 'enemy' as that observed in Assyrian and Egyptian accounts. The Israelites strongly distinguish between comrades and enemies. There is but one Enemy—with a capital letter—so that whether one is looking at Adoni-zedeq, Jabin, Sihon, Og, or the Anakim, they are viewed through the same unitary ideology of enmity. It is a negative vs. a positive, hence binary, relationship. In the conquest accounts of Joshua 9–12 there is definitely a 'them' vs. 'us' outlook which seems to be attributable to this Israelite ideology. They are all a Common Threat to Israelite well-being. They seek Israel's destruction. And what is most important, they are in opposition to YHWH. They reject Him, His law and ethic.

Second, Israel's ideology is one of 'terror'. The destruction of the populations of enemy cities is a practice of an ideology of 'calculated frightfulness'. The execution and hanging of kings on trees must also be considered in the light of ancient Near

Eastern ideologies of conquest. Such practices did 'soften up' the opposition. The elimination of the population also enhances the speed of de-culturation and hence colonization. This is conquest for *Lebensraum*.

Third, like in Hittite and Egyptian ideology, there is a stress on revenge. This is most clearly seen in the use of the term נקם. Wayne Pitard has convincingly shown that נקם means as a verb 'to avenge, to give recompense, retribution, to be avenged, avenge oneself', and as a noun 'vengeance, recompense, retribution'.[118] It is a vengeance which is a just recompense, a just payment for a crime, and not simply brutal revenge. It is a plain statement of retributive justice, which is so central to the legal conceptions of the Hebrew Bible. YHWH as Judge pronounces recompense and his decree is always completely warranted. This just vengeance is exactly what is called for in the *lex talionis*. In Joshua 10:13, although not in a strict legal context, נקם has the nuance of 'just recompense for a crime'.[119]

For generations, the Hittites suffered under the hands of their neighbors. Thus, feeling that the gods were on their side, they responded with a determination to avenge these wrongs. Likewise, the Egyptians suffered under the hand of the Hyksos. This instilled in them a deep drive for revenge which motivated them to expansions both to the north and to the south. In both cases, innocent nations were conquered, nations who had not been party to the oppressions. Thus, Israel too had been oppressed, and the drive to conquer was motivated by a desire for vengeance. And like the Hittites and Egyptians, the Israelites' God fought for them and awarded to them just recompense.

It is also evident that ideology is connected with the figurative aspect encountered in Joshua 9–12. No doubt, the extensive use of hyperbole is linked to the Israelite ideology. Victory must be described in black and white terms since there is only a 'them' vs. 'us' relationship.

There may, however, be a possible difference between the Israelite ideological view as preserved in Joshua 9–12 and that of the other ancient Near Eastern conquest accounts. In those cultures the ideology underlying the texts has its origin in the 'establishment' of the particular culture, i.e., in the elite power structures of the culture. In the case of the biblical ideology, we may be looking at an ideology which was generated by mal-integration in the existing society, i.e., an ideology which contends 'strenuously for a purer, fuller, or more ideal realization of particular cognitive and moral values than exist in the society in which the ideology obtains currency'.[120]

On the other hand, can one conclude that since the text of Joshua 9–12 manifests the same transmission code as other texts of ancient Near Eastern history writing, it is the product of the same underlying ideology?[121] The indications from this study seem to point to an affirmative answer. The similarities to the other ancient Near Eastern ideologies are too great to conclude otherwise.

One may object that the case of the ban, the נקם and the fanatical desire to gain complete conquest so that a 'new' and 'better' society can be achieved argue against this conclusion. However, the implementation of the נקם was selective,[122] and there is every indication that the concept of the נקם was not unique to Israel. The concept of total war (i.e., the destruction of the population as well as the military) was a practice which one encounters on numerous occasions in the ancient Near Eastern conquest accounts. Two examples will document this:

1) Once again, the Meša Inscription:[123]

> And I fought against the town;
> and I took it.
> I killed *all* the inhabitants of the town,
> as an offering of propitiation to Kemoš and Moab.
>
> Then Kemoš said to me:
> "Go, seize Nebo from Israel."
> So I went by night;
> and fought against it from the break of dawn until noon;
> and I took it;
> and *I killed everyone in it*, seven thousand men and women,
> both natives and aliens, and female slaves;
> because *I had dedicated* (החרמתה) it to 'Aštar-Kemoš.

In this text one can clearly see that total warfare was not a concept unique to Israel. In fact, even the נקם is observable in the final line quoted.

2) The Annals of Aššur-nasir-pal II:[124]

> I crossed over to Mt. Kashiyari (and) I approached the city of Kinabu, the fortified city of Hulaya. I besieged with the mass of my troops (and) my fierce battle array; I conquered the city. I slew with the sword 800 of their combat troops; I burned 3,000 captives from them. *I did not leave one of them alive as a hostage*. I captured Hulaya, their city ruler, alive. I made a pile of their corpses. I burned their young boys (and) girls. I flayed Hulaya, their city ruler; (and) I draped his skin over the wall of the city of Damdammusa. I razed, destroyed, (and) burned the city.

This is definitely an ideology of total war! Thus it would appear that the conquest account in Joshua 9–12 evinces the same basic ideology as one sees in other ancient Near Eastern conquest accounts.

### *Jural Aspect*

Finally, there is a jural ideology of war present in the biblical account. This notion is also seen in the ancient Near East.[125] The nation of Israel is the tool through which YHWH judges the Amorites (10:12–14).[126] There are numerous examples from the ancient Near East in which the events of the past (including wars) are seen as the judgment of the gods. In a recently published inscription, Nabopolassar states:

> He (Marduk) had Nergal, the strongest among the gods, walk at my side; he killed my enemies, he felled my foes. *The Assyrian, who had, because of the wrath of the gods, ruled the land of Akkad and who had oppressed the people of the land with his heavy yoke*—I, the weak, the powerless, who constantly seeks after the lord of lords, with the mighty strength of Nabû and Marduk my lords, I chased them (the Assyrians) out of the land of Akkad and caused (the Babylonians) to throw off their yoke <emphasis mine>.[127]

Here one can clearly see the jural ideology of war in an ancient Near Eastern context.[128]

According to a Babylonian boundary stone,[129] Marduk, the king of the gods, gave Nebuchadnezzar (I) a command, and he took up arms to avenge Akkad. J.J.M. Roberts correctly points out that this 'clearly implies that the Elamites had sinned against Marduk and his land in the past'.[130] Thus later in the inscription it is stated:

> By the command of Ishtar and Adad,
> the gods who are arbiters of battle,
> he (Nebuchadnezzar) turned evil against the king of Elam,
> and destruction overtook him.
> And King Nebuchadnezzar triumphed,
> he captured the land of Elam,
> he plundered its possessions.[131]

Hence, there is a common jural ancient Near Eastern ideology of war underlying the biblical text.

## CONCLUSION

In conclusion, it appears that the text of Joshua 9-12 is structured on a transmission code similar to that of other ancient Near Eastern royal inscriptions. Since the account utilizes similar literary and ideological aspects to the ancient Near Eastern conquest account, as well as similar syntagmic structuring, this conclusion seems justified. The code is observable in the narrative of the Gibeonite vassalage (ch. 9), the conquest accounts of the south and north (ch. 10 and 11) and the summary and lists (ch. 12). Moreover, we have also been able to come to a better understanding of how to interpret the biblical account.

# STAGE THREE:

# SYNTHESIS

## Chapter 6

# IMPLICATIONS AND ENTAILMENTS

It is now time to explore some of the implications of this study. In the foregoing chapters, our analyses have demonstrated that the conquest account in Joshua 9–12 shares a similar transmission code with its ancient Near Eastern counterparts. In its literary and ideological aspects, the biblical text evinces the same general characteristics that one encounters in ancient Near Eastern works. Consequently, while it remains possible that this section of Joshua is a composite of many separate traditions, this may not be the best explanation. It is more likely that the section is a narrative unity exhibiting a typical ancient Near Eastern transmission code commonly employed in the history writing of conquest accounts.[1] This, of course, does not exclude possible textual corruptions (some of which we point out in the Appendix) or glosses by the hand of (a) so-called Deuteronomistic editor(s). But it seriously questions the prevailing opinion that the section is a composite of many different independent *traditions*.[2]

Thus on the basis of the similarity between the conquest account in Joshua 9–12 and other ancient Near Eastern conquest accounts, we would suggest that it is unnecessary to posit so many various traditions for the make-up of these chapters.[3] It is time to re-evaluate some of the conclusions of past studies.

### THE NOTION OF A 'COMPLETE CONQUEST'

Joshua 10:40–42 states:

40 ויכה יהושע את כל הארץ ההר והנגב והשפלה
והאשרות ואת כל מלכיהם
לא השאיר שריד
ואת כל הנשמה החרים

כאשר צוה יהוה אלהי ישראל
[41]ויכם יהושע מקדש ברנע ועד עזה ואת כל
ארץ גשן ועד גבעון
[42]ואת כל המלכים האלה ואת ארצם לכד
יהושע פעם אחת
כי יהוה אלהי ישראל נלחם לישראל

40. Thus Joshua took the whole region, (including) the hill country, the Negev, the Shephelah, and the mountain slopes, together with their kings.
He left no survivors.
He totally destroyed all who breathed,
just as YHWH the God of Israel had commanded.
41. Joshua smote them from Kadesh-Barnea, to Gaza, and from the whole land of Goshen to Gibeon.
42. All these kings and their lands Joshua conquered in a single campaign because YHWH the God of Israel fought for Israel.

If one were to interpret this paragraph literally, then there would be no question that Joshua and the Israelites conquered every bit of southern Palestine. This would be evident from the very first words of the text: 'Thus Joshua took the whole region (כל הארץ)'. Moreover, it states that Joshua conquered 'all these kings and their lands: (כל המלכים האלה ואת ארצם)'.

This is the way many Old Testament scholars read the account in Joshua. It portrays a *complete* conquest of the land of Palestine as compared to the *partial* conquest portrayed in Judges 1. B. Childs lays out the problem:

> First, critical scholars have long since pointed out the tension—it is usually called a contradiction—in the portrayal of the conquest of the land. On the one hand, the conquest is pictured in the main source of Josh. 1–12 as a unified assault against the inhabitants of the land under the leadership of Joshua which succeeded in conquering the entire land (11:23; 18:1; 22:43). On the other hand, there is a conflicting view of the conquest represented by Judges 1 and its parallels in Joshua (15:13–19, 63; 16:10; 17:11–13; 19:47) which appears to picture the conquest as undertaken by individual tribes, extending over a long period beyond the age of Joshua, and unsuccessful in driving out the Canaanites from much of the land. Any number of variations on these two options are possible, such as the theory proposed by G. Mendenhall of an internal social-political upheaval ... Usually the description of the conquest which portrays a complete conquest of the

> whole land under Joshua is assigned to the Deuteronomic redaction of the book.[4]

The usual solution which Old Testament scholars have adopted is to posit two different sources or traditions for the different portrayals. The account in Judges 1 is the older and more reliable account. Hence (to quote a traditional commentator) G. Moore states:

> Which of these two conflicting representations of the Israelite invasion is the truer, cannot be for a moment in question. All that we know of the history of Israel in Canaan in the succeeding centuries confirms the representation of Jud. that the subjugation of the land by the tribes was gradual and partial; that not only were the Canaanites not extirpated, but that many cities and whole regions remained in their possession; that the conquest of these was first achieved by the kings David and Solomon. On the other hand, the whole political and religious history of these centuries would be unintelligible if we were to imagine it as beginning with such a conquest of Canaan as is narrated in the Book of Joshua.[5]

Childs has a different solution:

> How then is one to explain the peculiar features within Josh. 1–12 which present the conquest in the Deuteronomic idiom but as total, unconditional, and of short duration? In my opinion, this feature of the book of Joshua is not to be dismissed as a variant historical tradition, but understood as *a unique theological perspective of the Deuteronomic editor* which the final canonical shape has preserved as normative. The Deuteronomic editor of Joshua fashioned his material into *a highly theological pattern* which not only disregarded strictly historical method, but which also shifted the emphasis to a different focal point from that ordinarily represented by the Deuteronomic tradition.[6]

These interpretations do not take fully into consideration the figurative nature of the account in Joshua 9–12. They have not realized the use of hyperbole in the narrative.[7] Once one admits this element into the interpretive process, there is no reason to maintain that the account in Joshua 9–12 portrays a *complete* conquest.

One point which must be stressed in the analysis of any 'conquest account' is the fact that the terms 'conquer' and 'conquest'[8] can have a number of nuances which are not always present in every context in which they are used. When, for example, one speaks of 'the "conquest" of France' during World War II, or says that 'Germany "conquered" France', the meaning is something like 'the German army defeated the French army in battle and occupied France'. But it did not subjugate the French people, nor did it bring about the colonization of France by Germany. Another example can be seen in these statements of Shalmaneser III:

> I descended to the land of Kaldu. I conquered their cities. I received tribute of the kings of the land of Kaldu in the city of Babylon.

Shalmaneser's claim to have 'conquered' (*akšud*) the land of Kaldu must be understood in a very different way than his 'conquest' of Til Barsip which he renamed Kār Shalmaneser, colonized and which remained a permanent Assyrian city. In the case of Kaldu, he temporarily gained possession of these cities. But it was, nevertheless, a 'conquest'.[9] In this way too, the biblical account in Joshua 10–11 must be understood. The Israelites may very well have 'conquered' the land as generally described in the narrative. But this 'conquest' was in many instances temporary, not permanent. It did not mean the complete subjugation of the land. This is clear from statements such as 'Joshua waged war against all these kings for a long time' (11:18); 'When Joshua was old and well advanced in years, YHWH said to him, "You are very old and there are still very large areas of land to be taken over. (Thus) this is the land that remains"' (13:1b–2a);[10] 'Judah could not dislodge the Jebusites, who were living in Jerusalem ...' (15:63); 'They did not dislodge the Canaanites living in Gezer' (16:10); 'Yet the Manassites were not able to occupy these towns, for the Canaanites were determined to live in that region' (17:12); etc.

The phrase 'all the land' must be understood as hyperbole. The claims to conquest have been overstated.[11] This is a very similar situation in the vast majority of ancient Near Eastern conquest accounts.

For example, in his Ten Year Annals of Muršili II states:

> Thus when I had conquered all the land of Arzawa ... And I conquered all the land of Arawanna ... I conquered all the land of Tipiya.[12]

While Mursili did gain control over these lands, the use of the term *ḫuman-* (all) should be understood as a hyperbole or possibly as a synecdoche. We would prefer hyperbole considering the use of stereotyped syntagms in these contexts of Muršili's Annals (see chapter 3).

An example from Egypt which can be cited is the 'Bulletin' of Ramesses II recording the Battle of Kadesh. Note the hyperbole:

> *All* his ground was ablaze with fire; he burned *all* the countries with his blast. His eyes were savage as he beheld them; his power flared up like fire against them. He took no note of the *millions* of foreigners; *he regarded them as chaff.* Then his majesty charged into the force of the Foe from Hatti together with the many countries that were with them. His majesty was like Seth, great-of-strength, like Sakhmet in the moment of her rage. His majesty slew *the entire force* of the wretched Foe from Hatti, together with his great chiefs and all his brothers, as well as *all* the chiefs of *all* the countries that had come with him, their infantry and their chariotry falling on their faces one upon the other. His majesty slaughtered and slew them in their places; they sprawled before his horses; and his majesty was *alone, none other with him.*
>
> My majesty caused the forces of the foes from Hatti to fall on their faces, one upon the other, as crocodiles fall, into the water of the Orontes. I was after them like a griffin; I defeated *all the foreign countries, I alone.* For my infantry and my chariotry had deserted me; *not one of them* stood looking back. As I live, as Re loves me, as my father Atum favors me, everything that my majesty has spoken I did it in truth,[13] in the presence of my infantry and my chariotry.[14]

These two paragraphs stand in the midst of a fairly straightforward narrative. But the hyperbole is obvious.[15]

Or consider the hyperbolic language of the Merenptah ('Israel') Stela:[16]

| | | | | |
|---|---|---|---|---|
| a | *wrw [nbw] pḫd(w) ḥr ḏd šrm* | | All the rulers are prostrate saying: 'Shalom!'[17] | |
| b | *bn wꜥ ḥr f(t) tp.f m-tꜣ-pḏt 9* | | Not one dare raise his head among the Nine Bows: | |
| a | *ḫf.n. Ṯḥnw* | *Ḫtꜣ ḥtp* | Tjehenu (Libya) is plundered, | Hatti is pacified. |
| b | *ḥꜣḳ pꜣ Kꜣnꜥn m bin nb* | | carried off is Canaan with every evil. | |
| a | *inw ꜣIsḳꜣrn* | *mḥw m Kꜣḏꜣr* | Brought away is Ashkelon, | Gezer seized, |
| b | *Ynwꜥm iri m tm wn* | | Yanoam made nonexistent; | |
| a | *Ysrꜣr fk.t bn pr.t.f* | | Israel is wasted, his seed is not.[18] | |
| b | *Ḫꜣr ḫprw m ḫꜣr.t n tꜣ-mri* | | Hurru is become a widow for Egypt. | |

| | | |
|---|---|---|
| a | *t'w nbw dmḏ(w) st m ḥtpw* | All lands in their entirety are (now) at peace, |
| b | *p' nty nb m sm'.w tw tw ḥr wʿ.f* | and everyone who roamed has been subdued;[19] |

Thus when the figurative nature of the account is considered, there are really no grounds for concluding that Judges 1 presents a different view of the conquest from that of Joshua or that it must be an older account. If scholars had realized the hyperbolic nature of the account in Joshua, if they had compared it with other ancient Near Eastern accounts of *complete* conquest, if they had differentiated a little more closely in the past between occupation and subjugation, the image of the conquest as represented in Joshua would have emerged in far clearer focus than it has, and as a result there would have been no need to regard the first narratives of Judges as historical at the expense of their counterparts in Joshua.

Furthermore, it would have meant that one would not have had to sacrifice one account at the expense of the other. While G.E. Wright correctly points out some of the errors of those who discredit the account in Joshua, he does so by reverse argumentation: Judges 1 is a composite, error filled account. While Judges 1 does have numerous problems, there is no reason to represent it in this fashion. It does preserve much information which is quite ancient.

The fact is that both Joshua and Judges are selective in their presentation of the events. But before one passes judgment on these texts because of this selectivity, let us remind him that *all* history writing is selective being written from a particular point of view.[20] The writer of the conquest account in Joshua expressly states that the work is selective: 'Joshua made war a long time with all those kings' (11:18–19). This statement is not a later editorial comment, but a simple declaration of the nature of the material described. Because he only describes part of the conquests, he adds that there were many more battles which he cannot mention.[21] But this is a common practice in ancient Near Eastern conquest accounts. For example, Tiglath-Pileser I states:

> This is apart from many other expeditions against enemies which are not connected with (this enumeration of) my triumphs (Col. VI.49-50).[22]

Thus, we must question not only Moore's solution, but also Childs'. The account of the conquest in Joshua does not contain a view of a complete conquest which is 'a highly theological pattern' resulting from 'a unique theological perspective of the Deuteronomic editor'.

But there is more evidence which needs to be marshalled. The use of hyperbolic syntagms, such as 'no survivors', argues against the notion of a complete, total conquest. Auld misses the hyperbolic nature when he states:

> Verse 20 reads rather oddly in the RSV translation—if their opponents were entirely wiped out then there could hardly have been a remnant to escape. The Hebrew is certainly ambiguous; but it gives me the impression that Israel completed all it could immediately after the battle and only when no more could be done (because any enemies still alive were now behind walls) did they return to their chief outside Makkedah.[23]

All of this is unnecessary if one recognizes that the syntagm is hyperbolic. The use of the stereotyped syntagms in the narrative of Joshua 10–12 builds an iterative scheme. Thus the account is simulated or synthetic. It is not meant to be interpreted in a wooden, literal sense.

## THE NOTION OF AN 'ALL ISRAEL' REDACTION

In the previous section we looked at the figure 'all the land' and its implications for the concept of a complete conquest. Another figure encountered in the text of Joshua is 'all Israel'. This phrase is often understood by biblical scholars as a reference to a 'pan-Israelite redaction'. For example, Gray believes that:

> The sporadic, local penetration and gradual consolidation of the components of the historical Israel in Palestine, noticed in Jg. 1 and Jos. 15:63; 16:10 and 17:12, contrasts strongly with the general representation of the occupation as a conquest by *all Israel* which proceeded practically without check under Joshua's leadership in fulfillment of the ineluctable purpose of God, who enervated the opposition usually without a struggle. *It is therefore obvious that Jos. 2–11 is generally the stylisation of the occupation as a conquest by a compiler familiar with the ideal of a united Israel of twelve tribes, as*

> *in the J source of the Pentateuch, which was realised only under David over two centuries after the decisive penetration of Palestine by the Rachel group and the dynamic activity of Ephraim.*[24]

Miller and Tucker state:

> It was generally assumed that all Israel was directly involved in all these significant events, but evidence tends to suggest that in fact 'all Israel' did not exist until after the individual tribes had settled in Palestine.[25]

And E.J. Hamlin recently has commented:

> References to 'all Israel' (vv. 15, 31, 43) reflect a view that the whole of the Israelite tribal league as it later became, was working together in the conquest of this part of the land. Yet, as we have seen, the Joshua group probably included only a part of what later became 'all Israel'. This suggests an idealized rather than a sober factual account.[26]

But the use of 'all Israel' is nothing more than a commonly encountered synecdoche found in ancient Near Eastern conquest accounts in the form: 'all [a people's name].' Thus one could read a verse like Joshua 10:29:

> ויעבר יהושע וכל ישראל עמו ממקדה לבנה
> Then Joshua and all Israel with him moved on from Makkedah to Libnah;

and interpret 'all Israel' to mean literally 'every Israelite (man, woman and child from the families and clans of every tribe)' moved on from Makkedah to Libnah with Joshua. However, in the light of both the context of the book of Joshua and a comparison of ancient Near Eastern conquest accounts, it seems better to understand this as a synecdoche. A few examples from ancient Near Eastern materials will help demonstrate this. From the Annals of Muršili one reads:

> *nu KUR* $^{uru}$*Ka-aš-ka ḫu-u-ma-an an-da wa-ar-ri-eš-še-eš-ta*
> The entire land of the Kaskaeans came together to help.

> *KUR* $^{uru}$*Ar-za-u-wa-ma-kán ḫu-u-ma-an par-aš-ta*
> The whole country of Arzawa fled.

> *nu-kán KUR* $^{uru}$*Ar-za-u-wa ku-it ḫu-u-ma-an* 5$^{5}$*x x x x x I-NA* $^{uru}$*Pu-ra-an-da ša-ra-a pa-a-an e-eš-ta*
> And because the whole land of Arzawa x x x x (?) had gone over to the area of Puranda.

> *nu KUR-e-an-za ḫu-u-ma-an-za URU.AŠ.AŠ.ḪI.A BAD* [37]*EGIR-pa e-ip-pir*
> (But) the whole country withdrew to the fortress towns.

One may think that we are pointing out the obvious. But the number of commentators who misunderstand this figure is plethora. For instance, Noth felt that chapters 10–11 were two war narratives which originally were of merely local importance. Secondarily they were elevated to a status involving 'all Israel' and 'Joshua'. Thus he attributed the expression 'all Israel' to this secondary stage in the compilation of the book.[27] But in light of the foregoing discussion of the figurative aspect in these chapters, Noth's hypothesis appears less plausible.

Just as the references in the Annals of Tiglath-Pileser I[28] to 'all the Paphu (*kullat* $^{m\bar{a}t}$*Pap-ḫe-e*)' are figurative (probably a synecdoche), so also the idea conveyed in the phrase 'all Israel' is figurative (probably equivalent to 'Israel' as represented in the Merenptah Stela).[29] Therefore, the proposal of a pan-Israelite redaction is unnecessary. Furthermore, Hamlin's evaluation that 'this suggests an idealized rather than a sober factual account' is especially questionable.

## SOURCES, STRUCTURE AND COMPOSITION

According to many biblical scholars, a particular text is history writing only if it is dependent on accounts of eyewitnesses and the distance between the account and its author is not too remote. Thus it is not surprising to find in a recent commentary on the text of Joshua the following:

> Joshua and Judges are about the past; but if the main thrust of Noth's arguments is valid then it is a past viewed from a great distance. The Israelite and Judean monarchy lasted for a little over four hundred years. If Deuteronomy or Joshua through to Kings is a unit then it was written after the last king had fallen. And the rest of the chapters of the story were more distant from its writer or writers than Elizabeth I and Shakespeare and the founding fathers of the new world across the Atlantic are from us. Memory of the past they may be—but historical record hardly.[30]

Similarly, Miller and Tucker conclude that:

> It is a sound principle of historical reconstruction that—all other things being equal—the older the document, or the nearer it is to the events under consideration, the more reliable it is ... the ideal source is one which comes from the time of the events ... By these principles the book of Joshua has severe limitations as evidence upon which to base historical reconstruction. Much of the material is too late to be very reliable ...[31]

But our study has questioned such assumptions. Let us closely scrutinize the statement of Miller and Tucker that:

> the older the document, or the nearer it is to the events under consideration, the more reliable it is ... the ideal source is one which comes from the time of the events.

In 1945 as the Second World War ended, a history of that war was published.[32] This was a massive account of almost 1,000 pages and over 200 photographs. According to Miller and Tucker, this volume should be 'more reliable' than later histories of the War and 'an ideal source'. However, one finds that this is not always the case. For example, concerning the causes of the war, the volume states:

> The Treaty of Versailles has been criticized as both too severe and too lenient—events have proved that it was too lenient. It failed to recognize the psychology of Europe which for three hundred years has been a 'breeding ground' for war. In its compromises, with its diplomatic exchanges, it placed too great faith in the pledges of the war-mongers.[33]

Few historians today would agree with this interpretation of the treaty. Moreover, while the author of the volume, is able to present the events of the War in the right order and is generally reliable, he cannot interpret them in terms of their relationship to the Cold War, the nuclear age, etc.

Thus the implication is that not being witness to the event is not such a bad thing if our interests are historical.[34] Whether the author of the biblical text was an eyewitness or not need not effect our decision concerning whether it is history or not. Furthermore, the credibility of the biblical accounts does not necessarily decrease 'in the ratio of their distance in time from the narrator'.[35]

There are numerous points at which our study concerning the literary fashioning of the ancient historical narrative has implications for the understanding of the structure and composition of the narrative. The use of hyperbole in 9:1 is one example. Miller and Tucker argue that:

> His statement envisages an alliance of all the rulers of the diverse and independent city states of Palestine. But the summary is not entirely consistent with the material which follows. The remainder of ch. 9 reports how one city sought and won peace with Israel, ch. 10 tells of the defeat of a coalition of five cities in the southern hill-country, and ch. 11 gives an account of the destruction of Hazor and her allies in the north. This statement, in short, is more grandiose than the sum of the individual stories. The editor has a tendency to exaggerate and simplify events, and does so in similar transitional passages throughout the book (cp. 10:40–42; 11:16–20).[36]

But if the passage is understood as hyperbole the problem disappears (cf. our discussion of Tiglath-Pileser I's war against Nairi in chapter 5).

Another example of the figurative aspect can be seen in the use of syntagmic structure. It is through the syntagmic analysis that we further comprehend the figurative aspect of the conquest account. The iterative scheme created by the usage of stereotyped syntagms reveals the representative or simulated nature of the account.[37]

This has ramifications on understanding the structure and composition of Joshua 9–12. For example, Miller and Tucker comment concerning 1:1-15:

> This report of victory in the north has something of the appearance of an appendix: it must have circulated independently, probably as the traditions of one or more northern tribes, before it was made a part of the account of the conquest by all Israel under Joshua. The transition is abrupt, the only link with the preceding narrative being the note that 'Jabin, king of Hazor, heard of all this', i.e. Israel's victories.[38]

However, in light of the syntagmic patterning in Joshua and other ancient Near Eastern conquest accounts, the section 11:1–15 is simply an episode constructed on a common transmission code of the ancient Near East. It exhibits a high degree of similarity to chapter 10.[39] Noth attributes 10:40–42 to the work of the *Sammler*;[40] and Butler sees this as the theological conclusion of the Compiler.[41] Such conclusions are unnecessary. It is quite natural to have a summary statement in the ancient Near Eastern royal inscriptions. For example, Tiglath-Pileser I states:[42]

> Altogether 42 lands and their kings from the other side of the Lower Zab in distant mountainous regions to the other side of the Euphrates—the Hatti-land and the Upper Sea in the west—from my accession year to my fifth regnal year—I conquered. I subdued them to one authority. I took hostages from them. I imposed on them tribute and tax. This is apart from many other expeditions against enemies which are not connected with (this enumeration of) my triumphs. I pursued my enemies[43] by chariot in favorable terrain and on foot in rough terrain. I prevented the enemies from setting foot in my land.
>
> My heroic victories, my successful battles, (and) the suppression of the enemies (and) foes of Aššur, which An and Adad granted me, I wrote on my steles and clay inscriptions.

In this regard, the Armant Stela of Thutmose III also demonstrates the use of summaries in the transmission code of ancient conquest accounts:

> Year 22, the second month of winter, day 10: Summary of the deeds of valour and victory which this good god performed on every excellent occasion of activity from the beginning since the first generation (of men). That which the Lord of the gods, the Lord of Hermonthis, did for him was to magnify his victories, so that his conquests might be related for millions of years to come, apart from the deeds of activity which his majesty did in both seasons, for if one were to mention each occasion by name, they would be too numerous to put into writing.[44]

Therefore, the use of summary statements in a historical account should not lead modern interpreters to necessarily conclude that such statements are the product of redactional work as biblical scholars have often envisioned it.

Therefore, syntagmic analysis reveals the figurative nature of the account. Since the iterative code employing stereotyped language is figurative (and hence in a sense synthetic), the interpretation of the text must take this into account. For example, the repetitive patterning of stereotyped syntagms creates an almost artificial or simulated account so that the individual syntagms must be interpreted figuratively. Consequently, as noted above, such syntagms as 'there were no survivors', 'all the land', etc. in all probability are hyperbolic. This explodes the position which contrasts Joshua 10–11 and Judges 1 and concludes that the latter is history writing and the former is not.

## IDEOLOGICAL ASPECT

Israelite ideology had certain similarities with the 'Imperialistic' ideologies of the ancient Near East—Assyrian, Hittite, Egyptian. In the previous chapter we described the areas of similarity: a similar view of the enemy, calculated terror, the high use of hyperbole, a jural aspect, and the use of stereotyped syntagms to transmit the high-redundance message of the ideology. It would seem that a similar ideology is underlying both the ancient Near Eastern and biblical texts. If this is true, then it may signal difficulties with the 'peasant revolt' theory of Israelite origins.

Norman Gottwald has probably presented the most powerful case for regarding Israel in this period as an egalitarian society throwing off the oppressive rule of the Canaanite city-states:

> Joshua 10:16–43 is noteworthy because it stands out from its later Deuteronomic mold in emphasizing that the royal-aristocratic establishment was what Israel opposed and not the populace in its entirety ... I am not, therefore, claiming that those particular five cities were all taken in one blow by defeating their kings in coalition, in contrast to their having been taken one by one, as the subsequent account reports. My point is that, in spite of the two different historical horizons in the traditions about the aftermath of the battle of Gibeon, when separately examined they attest a common early emphasis upon the kings and their armies as the enemies of Israel and not the populace of the cities 'in toto'. Both accounts are extremely patterned, highly legendary in their stylization, but they show that the sociopolitical situation they are ideologizing was a confrontation between Israel and the royal aristocratic statist system of rule centered in the cities.[45]

In the light of our study, however, it would appear that Gottwald is incorrect. The account in Joshua 9–12 is no more an 'ideologizing of a confrontation between Israel and the royal aristocratic statist system of rule centered in the cities' than any of the Assyrian, Hittite, or Egyptian accounts are.[46] These accounts describe 'total warfare' which often included the population[47] using many of the same syntagms and figures that are encountered in the biblical account.[48] Thus we see no reason to posit that the Israelite conquest was a confrontation between Israel and the royal elite of the city-states (at least not in these chapters).[49]

W. Brueggemann has recently analyzed Joshua 11 using a sociological and literary method.[50] He follows the analysis of Gottwald in considering 'the city-states to be monopolies of socio-economic, political power which are managed in hierarchal and oppressive ways' and which are in direct opposition to Israel, which is 'an egalitarian, peasant movement that is hostile to every concentration, surplus, and monopoly'.[51] He feels that the strongest evidence that this was the situation behind the text of Joshua 11 is threefold mentioning of 'horses and chariots' (vv. 4,6,9).

> Yahweh's hostility to horses and chariots bespeaks Yahweh's hostility to the social system which requires, legitimates, and depends upon them. Israel, in its early period of tribal-peasant life, did not have horses and chariots and greatly feared them. The struggle reflected in Joshua 11 is how this community, so vulnerable and helpless, can exist and function against the kings and their powerful tools of domination.[52]

In addition, Brueggemann argues that the tension between monopoly and liberated structures is observable in the narrative form itself, asserting:

> The Bible is not content simply to describe the royal status quo which seems beyond challenge. The Bible also offers tales of liberation which show Israel challenging, countering and overcoming this formidable royal power. The narrative form lends itself to the articulation of another kind of power which the royal world neither knows nor credits. The narrative mode challenges royal rationality even as the narrative substance challenges royal policy ... The different sociology of these texts needs to be correlated with the different mode of literary expression in which it is reported. Thus the positive assertion of royal power is characteristically reported in lists, inventories, and memos. By contrast, the alternative power of Yahweh does not come articulated in such controlled modes of expression, but in narratives of a playful kind which allow for surprise and inscrutability. The modes of power are

> matched to ways of speech and to the different epistemologies and rationalities practiced by the speech forms.
>
> ... The contrast between the descriptions of royal domination and narratives of alternative forms of power reflects Israel's alternative reading of the historical process ... That is, the mode of discourse correlates with ways of reality and modes of power. How Israel speaks is related to what Israel trusts in and hopes for. That contrast between descriptive inventory and imaginative narrative leads to a warning that Israel should not imitate or be seduced by such royal modes of power (cf. Deut. 17:14–20) or royal modes of communication ... Israel knows it is not to emulate royal modes of power, knowledge, or language. Israel also knows that alternative modes of power, knowledge, and language are available which permit freedom and justice.[53]

If our analysis of the transmission code of Joshua 9–12 is correct, then there are serious problems with Brueggemann's assertions. The historical narrative in which Joshua 9–12 is cast utilizes a common transmission code observable in numerous ancient Near Eastern conquest accounts, employing the same ideology. Since the ideology which lies behind the text of Joshua is one like that underlying other ancient Near Eastern conquest accounts—namely, imperialistic—, then 'egalitarian, peasant' Israel is employing a transmission code (a 'communicative mode') which is self-contradictory [This is, of course, assuming that Brueggemann is correct in his assertions concerning modes of communication].

Finally, we see no reason to posit the type of interpretation to 'horses and chariots' that Brueggemann does. It is simply the result of the difference in technology which is here used to magnify YHWH's (and thus Israel's) victory over the Canaanite coalition. Not only did Israel win a victory over a much larger army, but also one which had superior military might.[54] The phenomenon of one army being technically and/or numerically superior to another army is so common that one must wonder why such an interpretation would ever arise.

The inscriptions of Seti I are very informative on this point. On the lowest register on the east side of the Great Hypostyle Court at Karnak the account of Seti's first campaign northward is preserved in which he encountered the Shasu nomads in the Sinai and outside of Gaza. The Shasu are pictured 'without chariots or horses and are armed with epsilon tang-type axes which may indicate the backward state of their military preparedness'.[55] In another register which appears to be a continuation of the campaign, Seti is shown defeating the Canaanite enemy outside the city of Yenoam (located almost adjacent to the southern tip of the Sea of Galilee, east of the Jordan). The Canaanite enemy of Seti have 'horses and chariots this time, evidence of military ability far superior to the Shasu'.[56] In yet another register, Seti is pictured as fighting against the city of Kadesh. In this scene the Asiatics have horses and chariots too. But in a register containing the account of the Seti I's Libyan war, the Libyans have no chariots or horses, and are likened 'to jackals which spend the day in their holes, presumably stressing that the Libyans would only attack at night'.[57] Thus the fact that an army lacked 'chariots and horses' was only an indication of its lack of military expertise, not YHWH's 'hostility to the social system which requires, legitimates, and depends upon them'.[58]

In some conflicts, a weaker army may lose; in others it wins. There are many cases when an army of superior numbers and strategic position is defeated. For example, the Urartian king Rusa and his allies had superiority in numbers and position against Sargon and the Assyrians and lost; the Canaanites had the superior position against the Egyptians under Thutmose III at Megiddo and lost; and the Persians had numeric and technical superiority over the Greeks and lost. Natural phenomena and the element of surprise are very often the causes of decisive victories. Therefore, we hesitate to endorse Brueggeman's interpretation which seems to build so much on so little.

While our reading effects most directly the 'Peasant Revolt' model of Israelite origins, it has implications for a number of other recent models in which Israel is indigenous to the land. These theories are usually based on archaeological evidence since the biblical data is considered to be very unreliable. Unfortunately, this conclusion is usually based on a superficial, literal reading of the text. The work of such scholars as Finkelstein,[59] Lemche,[60] Coote and Whitelam,[61] and Callaway[62] fall under this assessment.

Thus, for example, Lemche considers the traditions of Israel's early history to be so late in origin as to be useless for historical reconstruction: '... I propose that we decline to be led by the Biblical account and instead regard it, like other legendary materials, as essentially ahistorical, that is, as a source which only exceptionally can be verified by other information'. His alternative reconstruction is based entirely on what one can deduce from archaeological materials 'of the social, economic, cultural and political developments in Palestine towards the close of the second millennium'. He feels that all of this indicates that there was a very gradual (re)tribalization process from the 14th century BC on and that Israel is the product of this evolutionary process.

Coote and Whitelam also explicitly reject the biblical narratives as a source for the reconstruction of Israel's early history. Rather, the historian's task is 'to explain the archaeological record in the context of comparative history and anthropology'. The origin of Israel is to be found in the context of an economic decline which occurred at the end of the LBA, resulting from a breakdown of the interregional trade on which Canaan's urban economy ultimately depended and spurred a combination of processes.

> At this time, the settlement into villages in the hill country of various groups such as peasants, bandits, and pastoral nomads 'was given political and incipient ethnic form in the loosely federated people calling themselves Israel'.[63]

Without discussing the archaeological merits of the individual models, it becomes apparent that with the biblical text considered as secondary data, subjective archaeological reconstructions dominate. None of these hypothetical models give adequate account for the biblical traditions which are usually seen as late fabrications on the grounds of a literal reading!

Our study has shown that regardless of the text's date of origin when it receives the same scrutiny as one would give any ancient text (e.g., Assyrian, Hittite, or Egyptian), the biblical text's commonality with these other ancient accounts demands full consideration. And when this is done, one comes to a very different conclusion than these reconstructions!

AN ENTAILMENT CONCERNING 'HOLY WAR'

Many of the terms and concepts of so-called 'holy war' which many biblical scholars have attributed to Israelite origin must be re-evaluated in light of a comparison with ancient Near Eastern conquest accounts. For example, 'panic', 'terror', or 'fear' are described by numerous biblical scholars as 'the regular instruments of God in Holy War'.[64] Gray tells us:

> Indeed most of the conflicts in the settlement of Israel in Palestine are represented as being settled by this psychological factor rather than by bitter hand-to-hand fighting.[65]

And Butler states:

> Yahweh sent the enemy into a panic before the unexpected reinforcements. This panic, Heb. המם is a technical term in holy war narratives, binding Exod 14; Josh 10; Judg 4; and 1 Sam 7 together.[66]

Along similar lines D.J. McCarthy studied the Hebrew term חפר and stated:

> it is suggestive that the word is so associated with things which inspire fear, one of the *essential* elements in the theory of the holy war <emphasis mine>.[67]

One cannot help but wonder why such scholars would argue that 'fear' and 'panic' are essential elements in 'holy war', when fear and panic are common in every war. The theme of panic, terror or fear which is brought upon the enemy by the national deity, just before or in the midst of the battle, is so common in ancient Near Eastern conquest accounts that we could quote *ad nauseam*.[68] For instance, Thutmose III states that it was Amun-Re 'who commanded these victories who gave the terror [of me ...] ... He put the fear of me in [all] foreign peoples'.[69] In the Poetical Stela, Amun-Re' states to Thutmose (*Urk*. IV, 610.3-4, 9):

> I gave you valor and victory over all foreign lands.[70] I placed your might (and) fear in all lands, the dread of you as far as heaven's four supports. I magnified your awe in all bodies. I caused your majestic war-cry to traverse victoriously the Nine Bows. I caused the dread of your majesty to pervade their hearts.

Thus Müller is correct when he states:

> When we come to consider the religious or theological significance of the idioms using the qal of חמם, we must conclude that there is nothing specifically biblical in the notion of military intervention on the part of the deity or in the motif of an ensuing panic. The *mysterium tremendum* of the power sublimated in the deity everywhere evinces its destructive nature in battle, at the same time inspiring those fighting on the side of the deity with demonic frenzy.[71]

Thus we see no sound reason to understand 'fear and panic' as motifs which are unique to Israelite 'holy war'.

Some other typical thoughts about 'holy war' are seen in this discussion.

> It seems much more likely that the account <ch. 6—destruction of Jericho> has been shaped to a great extent by the institution and ideas of the holy war. (For laws concerning such warfare, see Deut. 20). In the holy war, no battle could begin without religious ceremonies in which the will of God was determined and the army consecrated. The soldiers were not professionals but ordinary Israelite men summoned to fight by the sound of the trumpet; their leader had to be called by the LORD. The presence of the LORD at the head of the army was often symbolized by the Ark. While the enemies trembled before the army (cp. 2:9; 5:1), the Israelites were encouraged to stand firm and have no fear. The victory was usually accomplished by a miracle accompanied by a war-cry; the enemy was thrown into panic. All the spoils of battle belonged to the LORD; except in special circumstances (for example, the agreement with Rahab) all living things were to be killed and all property destroyed except what was taken to the LORD's treasury. While it is not always possible to separate historical fact from theological ideas in the holy-war traditions, it is known that such stories reflect a military institution (with non-professional soldiers and divinely ordained leaders) which was practised in the period before the monarchy. Some features of the institution were revived for a time by Josiah (640-609 B.C.).[72]

But is this really the case in light of our comparison? In the ancient Near East (for that matter, for the vast part of history), religious ceremonies in which the will of God was determined and the army consecrated were performed. In Assyria, divination would often determine whether a campaign would even take place and also why a particular outcome had occurred.[73] The king of each country was chosen by the deity to lead the nation in its wars (eg. Esarhaddon, Hattušili III, etc.). The presence of the deity was often at the head of the army. Moreover, in Assyria the 'weapon of Aššur' was probably some sort of standard which represented the god. The enemy was usually 'afraid' of the on-coming army and, as shown in the previous chapter, divine intervention was not unusual. The panic-stricken flight of the enemy was a common motif in the ancient Near Eastern conquest account (very few lack it). Thus we must object to this way of defining 'holy war'.[74]

Butler, however, argues that pursuit is not only a motif of holy war, but that it is the theme around which the Compiler has tied all his varied material.[75] One must wonder how a motif of pursuit is in any way an indication that the account narrates 'a holy war' as opposed to a 'secular war'.

With regard to 'holy wars' in the ancient Near East (in particular those of Assyria), H. Tadmor has very perceptively recognized and stated:

> Every war of Assyria, led by her monarch—and in theory the high priest of Ashur—was on a theological as well as on a practical-cultic level a 'holy war', ordered by Ashur and approved by oracles, celestial and terrestrial. A defeat of 'Assyria's (or Ashur's) mighty armies'—to use the ideological cliché of the period—was rendered in the traditional terms of theodicy: either the oracles must have been misinterpreted—and some astrologer or haruspex would pay dearly—or the king must have committed some cultic offence to incur the divine wrath. How else could Ashur's armies, headed by the king, an eternal victor, be overcome by the distant Nubians?[76]

And H.E. von Waldow concludes:

> The question is: Did ancient Israel really know the category of holy wars as opposed to other wars that were not holy? The answer should be no.[77]

Therefore, we follow Craigie[78] in advocating that in the description of certain wars in the biblical narrative the label 'holy war' is best not employed. There is a need for a complete rethinking on this subject.

## OTHER ENTAILMENTS

Our study has ramifications for the interpretation of the text of Joshua. For example, E.J. Hamlin has recently made a number of assertions concerning the nature or kind of writing used in Joshua 10:28-39. Two of these are:

> (1) The stereotyped expressions already referred to in the descriptions of the conquest of each of the six cities indicate a symbolic, theological kind of writing, rather than factual reporting.
> (2) The lack of any report of casualties on the Israelite side, or survivors on the Amorite side, suggests that we are dealing with teaching material rather than a careful report of the actual battles.[79]

Hamlin has obviously missed the mark. The reading of one ancient Near Eastern conquest account would have quickly shown Hamlin the errors in his statements.

First, the syntagmic patterning which Hamlin calls 'stereotyped expressions' hardly indicates 'a symbolic, theological kind of writing'. Our study has shown that numerous ancient Near Eastern texts exhibit this phenomenon because it is an important component in the transmission code which they employ. One would hardly label such texts (as for example, Tiglath-Pileser's Annals) 'symbolic, theological writing'. This would be absurd! Since the text in Joshua utilizes the same code, it is equally fatuous to brand it as 'a symbolic, theological kind of writing'.

Second, in the ancient Near Eastern conquest accounts, reports of casualties within one's own army are rare.[80] Numbers for such groups as the dead or prisoners of the enemy are more often included than the survivors (although the group 'survivors' does occur). Furthermore, it is very common in the these texts to describe the total annihilation of the enemy. Thus, Hamlin has no grounds whatever to conclude that this is 'teaching material'. To tag these verses of Joshua with such a phrase is very inane.[81]

Another entailment of our study concerns the date of composition for these chapters of Joshua. Through motif comparison, Van Seters has recently argued that the book of Joshua was modelled after ancient Near Eastern inscriptions, particularly the Assyrian royal inscriptions so that one can conclude that it is the product of the Deuteronomist at a very late stage as a fabrication to explain 'how the people got into the land'.[82]

While there is abundant evidence for a common ancient Near Eastern transmission code for conquest accounts (as we have been arguing throughout), evidence is not sufficient to allow for the dating of documents by this criterion.

Van Seters lists a number of common motifs: a confident inspiring oracle, the crossing of a river (at flood), a few major battles given, capture and execution of kings, terror and fear of Assyria—foreign people submitting, coalitions of foreign lands, repopulation of conquered regions, summary, Hatti-land (as a designation of Syria-Palestine), and omens (esp. positions of heavenly bodies).[83] Van Seters argues that since the majority of these are encountered in the *late* Neo-Assyrian royal inscriptions, therefore the Joshua material is late and highly fabricated.

But is it really possible to date texts on the basis of common motifs? This must be deemed a very difficult procedure since there are no controls on determining the *terminus a quo* and the *terminus ad quem* for the use of such motifs in one culture let alone establishing their use in another culture. Moreover, most of these 'motifs' occur in earlier texts or can easily be explained as West Semitic influence (Aramaization) in the Assyrian royal inscriptions.[84]

For example, crossing a river at flood stage is first found in the Annals of Aššur-nasir-apli II (883-859 B.C.):[85]

> I moved on from the land of Bit-Adini; (and) I crossed the Euphrates, which was in flood, in rafts (made of inflated) goatskins.

It is also found numerous times in the inscriptions of Shalmaneser III.[86] It is found in an inscription of Samsi-Adad V;[87] and it is found in an inscription of Adad-nirari III[88] which states:

> I ordered to march to the land of Hatti. I crossed the Euphrates in its flood.

Lastly, it occurs numerous times in the inscriptions of Sargon II, Esarhaddon, and Aššurbanipal.[89] Thus—in just the Assyrian Annals—one can trace the motif of crossing a river at flood stage throughout the period 883-645 B.C. But, the motif can also be seen in the historical writings of other cultures.

For example, in both the Karnak and Memphis Stelae of Amenhotep II, the king crossed the 'turbulent' Orontes River. These narratives are based on the war diary of Amenhotep II:

*'bd 1 šmw sw 26 ḏ't ḥm.f mšdt 'Irnṯ m hrw pn*
*st ḏ'.n [ḥm.f mšsdt] 'Ir[nt]w ḥr ḫtr m hsmk mi pḥty Mnṯw W'sty*

10.26: The crossing by his majesty of the Orontes Ford on this day. Now [his majesty] crossed the Or[ontes Ford] on a horse in turbulence like the strength of Montu the Theban.[90]

*ḏ'.n ḥm.f 'Irntw ḥr mwm hsmk mi Ršp*

it was upon the turbulent water that his majesty crossed the Orontes like Reshep.[91]

Therefore, from the evidence presented here, it is apparent that the use of this motif for dating purposes is unjustified.

On the basis of our study, it seems that it is only possible to date the composition of the conquest account in Joshua 9–12 in very general terms. The transmission code of the ancient Near Eastern conquest accounts dates roughly 1300-600 BC. But such general dating really does not say very much. The analysis contained in this study is helpful mainly in understanding and interpreting the composition, not in determining the narrative's date.

## CONCLUSION

By making a semiotic analysis of ancient Near Eastern conquest accounts from numerous different genres, it has been possible to formulate interpretive expectations which have aided the process of interpreting the biblical text. Genres such as the Assyrian Annalistic texts, Summary inscriptions and 'Letters to the God', as well as the Hittite Annalistic texts, and the Egyptian *iw.tw* and other military narratives have all provided insight into the writing of conquest accounts in the ancient Near East.[92] Through the identification of some of the figurative, syntagmic and ideological aspects which make up the transmission code of these texts, it has been possible to advance the interpretation of Joshua 9–12.

# CONCLUSION

As we have presented the results of our investigation into the techniques of writing conquest accounts in the ancient Near East and Joshua, we have clearly recognized that they are not final and that much more work remains to be done. We have only 'scratched the surface'.

This study has shown that one encounters very similar things in both ancient Near Eastern and biblical history writing. While there are differences (e.g., the characteristics of the deities in the individual cultures), the Hebrew conquest account of Canaan in Joshua 9–12 is, by and large, typical of any ancient Near Eastern account. In other words, there is a common denominator, a certain commonality between them, so that it is possible for us to speak, for purposes of generalization, of a common transmission code that is an intermingling of the texts' figurative and ideological aspects.

Since the modern historian must first deal with the ancient inscriptions as they are preserved today before even attempting a historical analysis of the events they narrate, we chose the semiotic method as our interpretive guide in our comparative approach to the material. Hence, we did not feel that it was necessary at this time to engage the question of the historicity of the names, places, or numbers present in many of these compositions. Unquestionably, such a task is worthwhile and necessary; but the main goal of our sketch has been to avoid explicit 'historical' conclusions and to concentrate on the texts as texts. In fact, the questions as to the veracity of the reports of numbers killed, the numbers of prisoners taken, etc., are common to classicists, medievalists, and modern historians.[1]

The fact that ancient Near Eastern and biblical conquest accounts have figurative and ideological superstructures means that the interpreter of such texts must work hard at the process of interpretation. The simulated nature of the accounts must be fully considered. In this we would stress the tentativeness of our own interpretations of the various texts studied herein.

We do not wish to give the reader the impression that we believe that none of the data in the ancient texts is trustworthy or that all is rhetoric and stereotyped vocabulary. It is simply that the use of a common transmission code underlying the ancient texts must be taken into account; the commonality of such set language does not negate the fact that a war took place, that someone won or that the army performed certain specific actions. The use in the biblical narrative of such stereotyped syntagms as 'YHWH gave the city into Israel's hand', 'Joshua put the city and everyone in it to the sword', 'he left no survivors', or 'he conquered all the land' does not invalidate them any more than the use of such syntagms as 'a great slaughter was made' or 'his majesty dispatched' invalidates the Egyptian accounts. The fact that there are figurative and ideological underpins to the accounts should not make us call them into question *per se*—it should only force us to be cautious!

So what can be said concerning the author of the biblical narrative in Joshua 9–12? Is this the work of the Deuteronomistic historian? We simply cannot divine the identity of this writer, so that we are not able to give a *annu kēnu*—'an affirmative yes!'

At the end of the day, the goal of this study is quite modest. The area of ancient Near Eastern and biblical history writing is very large and much further work remains and needs to be done. Certainly this is the case in the area of our study on conquest accounts. This contribution is just a start.[2]

# NOTES

## NOTES TO CHAPTER ONE
(pp. 25-58)

1. 'History is akin to the poets and is, so to speak, *a prose poem* <emphasis mine>' (*Institutio Oratoria* X. i. 31) (in this context *solutum* means free of metrical restrictions).

2. One notable exception is the work of B. Halpern in which he devotes two chapters to this topic and makes a real contribution to its understanding (*The First Historians*, pp. 3-35). For him 'history is the undertaking of rendering an account of a particular, significant, and coherent sequence of past human events ... histories purport to be true, or probable, representations of events and relationships in the past ... a selective approximation. History, in sum, is a literally false but scientifically more or less useful coherence imposed by reason on reality' (pp. 6-7).

3. E.g., G. Garbini, *History and Ideology in Ancient Israel*.

4. M.I. Finley, *The Use and Abuse of History*, p. 61. H. White correctly points out that 'those historians who draw a firm line between history and philosophy of history fail to recognize that every historical discourse contains within it a full-blown, if only implicit, philosophy of history' (*Tropics of Discourse*, pp. 126-127).

5. See in this regard, R.A. Oden, Jr., 'Intellectual History and the Study of the Bible', in *The Future of Biblical Studies*, pp. 1-18.

6. Obviously, the German historiographic tradition had its impact on German Old Testament scholars (for the German tradition itself, see: G. Iggers, *The German Conception of History*; for its impact on German OT scholarship, see: R.A. Oden, Jr., 'Hermeneutics and Historiography: Germany and America', in *Seminar Papers of the SBL*, pp. 135-157).

7. John Van Seters, *In Search of History*; and George Coats, *Genesis*. We have chosen to examine these two scholars basically for two reasons: 1) because they offer detailed definitions which requires interaction, and 2) because they are representative of opinions concerning history writing which make up a large segment of Old Testament scholarship.

8. Van Seters, *In Search of History*, p. 1. He is quoting J. Huizinga, 'A Definition of the Concept of History', in *Philosophy and History: Essays Presented to Ernst Cassirer*, p. 9. For Huizinga's concept of history, see: R.L. Colie, 'Huizinga and the Task of Cultural History', *AHR* 69 (1963-64): 607-630.

9. *Ibid.*, p. 354.

10. He states: 'most historical texts of the ancient Near East do not really fit this nationalistic sense of history writing, ... For the sake of discussion, all historical texts may be subsumed under the term *historiography* as a more inclusive category than the particular genre of history writing' (pp. 1-2). There is also a transformation between these two: 'One must pay close attention to the matter of the genre and function of historical texts, for it is in *the transformation of such limited forms of historiography into a particular form of literature* that the origin of history is to be found' (p. 6). So Van Seters's genre analysis becomes a hunt for the point of transformation into the nationalistic form.

11. Huizinga, 'A Definition of the Concept of History', pp. 5-7.

12. See our review of Van Seters in *JSOT* 40 (1988): 110-117. Huizinga was a 'cultural historian', a fact of which Van Seters seems to be unaware. See: Colie, *AHR* 69 (1963-64): 608; and also B. Halpern, *JBL* 104/3 (1985): 507. For a more accurate reading of Huizinga, see W.W. Hallo, 'Biblical History in its Near Eastern Setting: The Contextual Approach', in *Scripture in Context: Essays on the Compartative Method*, p. 6.

13. Emphasis on the political history of the nation was an emphasis common throughout the period of German historicism. German historians from Johann Herder on lay emphasis on the nation/state (howbeit with variations) (Iggers, *The German Conception of History*, pp. 35ff). For example, Hegel stated: 'It is the state which first presents a subject-matter that is not only adapted to the prose of History, but involves the production of such History in the very progress of its own being'. (*Vorlesungen über die Philosophie der Geschichte*, p. 83). In the opinion of F. Meinecke, historicism found its highest achievement in Ranke (*Entstehung des Historismus*, p. 642).

14. 'De Taak van Cultuurgeschiedenis <The Task of Cultural History>', In *Verzamelde Werken*, Vol. 7, p. 46. See also Colie, *AHR* 69 (1963-64): 614-622.

15. E.g., H. Gunkel maintained that genre analysis alone could differentiate history from legend or saga ('Die Grundprobleme der israelitischen Literaturgeschichte', in *Reden und Aufsätze*, pp. 29-38; and 'Die israelitische Literatur', in *Die Kultur der Gegenwart: Die orientalischen Literaturen*, p. 52. Gunkel felt genre was the key data because it gives one access to history's general process. So, the origin of any

genre was to be sought in the people's overall social life (Oden, 'Hermeneutics and Historiography', p. 146).

16. Either by assimilating classification within other more essential functions of genre (Hirsch—determination of meaning; Todorov—relation of single texts to others), or by going beneath classification to some larger or more fundamental dimension of the task of defining genre (Gadamer—genre history; Ricoeur—production of text). See: Mary Gerhart, 'Generic Studies: Their Renewed Importance in Religious and Literary Interpretation', *JAAR* 45 (1977): 309-325.

17. Jameson, *The Political Unconscious*, p. 105. See also G.N.G. Orsini, 'Genres', in *Princeton Encyclopedia of Poetry and Poetics*, pp. 307-309.

18. J. Derrida, 'The Law of Genre', *Critical Inquiry* 7 (1980): 64-65.

19. Ralph Cohen, 'History and Genre', *New Literary History* 17 (1986): 204. Along these same lines Hans-Georg Gadamer has argued that genres can no longer be regarded as timeless a priori categories since they are history-bound (much more than literary critics usually acknowledge). Thus their rise and decline are intrinsic to text-interpretations (*Truth and Method*, pp. 250ff).

20. *Ibid.*, pp. 210, 212.

21. *Ibid.*, p. 217.

22. D. LaCapra, 'Comment', *New Literary History* 17/2 (1986): 221.

23. For another example of misuse, see: our article in *JSOT* 40 (1988): 116.

24. J.A. Cuddon, *A Dictionary of Literary Terms*, p. 52.

25. Harry Shaw, *Dictionary of Literary Terms*, p. 27.

26. Hoffmann, *Der Erlass Telipinus*, pp. 76ff; concerning these two terms see G. Beckman, 'The Hittite Assembly', *JAOS* 102 (1982): 435-442). But obviously, the text does not have to be addressed to the *panku-* or a specific political assembly in order to be an apology. On the propagandistic and apologetic character of the Hattusili text see A. Archi, 'The Propaganda of Hattusili III', *Studi Micenei ed Egeo-Anatolici* 14 (1971): 185-216; and H.M. Wolf, *The Apology of Hattusilis Compared with Other Political Self-Justifications of the Ancient Near East.*

27. H.A. Hoffner, 'Propaganda and Political Justification in Hittite Historiography', in *Unity and Diversity*, p. 51.

28. Halpern, *JBL* 104 (1985): 508.

29. M. Sternberg puts it this way: 'Equally fallacious, because unmindful of convention and its variability, are the attempts to distinguish fictional from historiographic writing by their form ... one

simply cannot tell fictional from historical narrative—still less, fiction from history within narrative—since they may be equally present in both, equally absent, equally present and absent in varying combinations. So, to the possible disappointment of shortcut seekers, ... there are simply no universals of historical vs. fictive form' (*The Poetics of Biblical Narrative*, pp. 26, 29-30).

30. Van Seters, pp. 122-123.

31. M. Waldman, *Toward A Theory of Historical Narrative: A Case Study in Perso-Islamicate Historiography*, chapter 3. G.W. Trompf points out the didactic character of the Hebrew concept of historical recurrence ('Notions of Historical Recurrence in Classical Hebrew Historiography', *Studies in the Historical Books of the Old Testament*, pp. 213-229).

32. Rogerson points out that Van Seters's definition of history has to be stretched in order to sustain his thesis (*JTS* 37/2 (1986): 451-454).

33. Coats, *Genesis*, p. 9.

34. Coats, p. 9. Note the influence of the German 'historicist' view. Historicism is a widely used term. See the discussion of Lee and Beck, 'The Meaning of "Historicism"', *AHR* 59 (1954): 568-577. We are following Iggers's discussion (*The German Conception of History*, pp. 4-10, 29, 270, 287-290).

35. This phrase was used by Ranke in the preface to his *Geschichten der romanischen und germanischen Völker von 1494 bis 1514* (1824), p. vii. Iggers and von Moltke note: 'Indeed Ranke's oft quoted dictum, 'wie es eigentlich gewesen', has generally been misunderstood as asking the historian to be satisfied with a purely factual recreation of the past. Ranke's writings make it clear that he did not mean this. In fact the word 'eigentlich' which is the key to the phrase just quoted has been poorly translated into English. In the nineteenth century this word was ambiguous in a way in which it no longer is. It certainly had the modern meaning of 'actually' already, but it also meant 'characteristic, essential,' and the latter is the form in which Ranke most frequently uses this term. This gives the phrase an entirely different meaning, and one much more in keeping with Ranke's philosophical ideas. It is not factuality, but the emphasis on the essential that makes an account historical' ('introduction', in Leopold von Ranke, *The Theory and Practice of History*, ed. by Iggers and von Moltke, pp. xix-xx). Thus Ranke's emphasis on understanding of the uniqueness of historical characters and situations led him to reject speculation. To understand the unique individuality in history required a reconstruction of the past "wie es eigentlich gewesen", beginning with a strict dedication to the relevant facts. Hence, his insistence on strict method' (p. xlii). Our the point is that Coats' definition reflects Ranke's phrase although embedded now with some of its popular misconceptions.

36. *Legends of Genesis*, pp. 1-2. Along similar lines, see: I. Guidi, 'L'historiographie chez les Sémites', *RB* 15 (1906): 509-519.

37. Gressmann, *Die älteste Geschichtsschreibung und Prophetie Israels*, pp. XIII-XV.

38. R.A. Oden, 'Hermeneutics and Historiography', p. 143.

39. E.H. Carr, *What is History?*, pp. 9 and 23. See also F. Braudel, 'The Situation of History in 1950', in *On History*, p. 11.

40. Jürgen Habermas has shown how all knowledge is related to matters of interest, and that any imagined objectivity is likely to be an exercise in self-deception (*Knowledge and Human Interests*). See, however, R. Nash's balanced critique, *Christian Faith and Historical Understanding*, pp. 82ff.

41. Oden, 'Hermeneutics and Historiography', p. 148. He is quoting Barry Barnes, *Scientific Knowledge and Sociological Theory*, p. 10. See also the comments of Keith Whitelam, *JSOT* 35 (1986): 54.

42. P. Ricoeur, 'Explanation and Understanding: On Some Remarkable Connections Among the Theory of the Text, Theory of Action, and Theory of History', in *The Philosophy of Paul Ricoeur*, p. 156.

43. Ronald Nash, *Christian Faith and Historical Understanding*, p. 82.

44. A.K. Grayson, *ABC*, pp. 11-14; 'Problematical Battles in Mesopotamian History', in *Studies in Honor of Benno Landsberger on His Seventy-fifth Birthday*, p. 342; and Van Seters, *In Search of History*, pp. 80-85.

45. L.D. Levine, *JCS* 34 (1982): 50.

46. *Ibid.*, p. 50.

47. A.R. Millard, 'The Old Testament and History: Some Considerations', *FT* 110 (1983): 41.

48. White, *Metahistory: The Historical Imagination in Nineteenth Century Europe*, pp. ix, 7-8, 142-143.

49. E.g., H. White, *History and Theory* 23 (1984): 21.

50. Prism A. Col. III lines 66-71.

51. R.N. Whybray, *The Succession Narrative*, pp. 16, 19.

52. Thucydides: *Peloponnesian War*, Book I.22.1-3. The translation is that of D. Rokeah, 'Speeches in Thucydides: Factual Reporting or Creative Writing?' *Athenaeum* 60 (1982): 386-401, esp. p. 395. Cp. A.W. Gomme, *A Historical Commentary on Thucydides*, Vol. I, p. 140.

53. *Ibid.*, pp. 388-389.

54. Gomme, *A Historical Commentary on Thucydides*, Vol. I, p. 160.

55. Kieran Egan, 'Thucydides, Tragedian', in *The Writing of History: Literary Form and Historical Understanding*, pp. 78, 82.

56. Gomme, p. 145. Cp. Egan's opinion on this passage (p. 82). But also see: Rokeah's arguments (*Athenaeum* 60 (1982): 386-401).

57. Otherwise, the majority of Egyptian historical texts, as well as Hittite historical texts, are not examples of history writing. For instance, the secret dialogue between Thutmose III and his captains concerning the particular route to take to Megiddo in Thutmose's Annals—according to Whybray's position—prejudices the work so that it is not history writing in the modern sense. The whole issue of the place and understanding of direct speech in ancient history writing is in much need of investigation.

58. Waldman laments this same situation in Islamic historiographic studies (*Toward A Theory of Historical Narrative: A Case Study in Perso-Islamicate Historiography*, p. 3).

59. E.g., Ricoeur uses 'story' to mean 'historical text', in particular, narrative discourse (*The Philosophy of P. Ricoeur*, pp. 152 and 161).

60. James Barr, 'Story and History in Biblical Theology', in *Scope and Authority of the Bible*, p. 5. Also see: R.J. Coggins, 'History and Story in Old Testament Study', *JSOT* 11 (1979): 36-46; and Hans Frei, *The Eclipse of Biblical Narrative*, p. 10 and passim.

61. Cp. von Rad felt that the way God's activity was depicted distinguished 'history writing' from saga. In saga, the activity of God is 'confined to sensational events'. In history writing, the historian 'depicts a succession of occurrences in which the chain of inherent cause and effect is firmly knit up—so firmly indeed that [the] human eye discerns no point at which God could have put in his hand. Yet secretly it is he who has brought all to pass' (G. von Rad, *The Problem of the Hexateuch and Other Essays*, pp. 166-204).

62. See: Weinfeld, 'Divine Intervention in War in Ancient Israel and in the Ancient Near East', in *HHI*, pp. 121-147; and Millard, *FT* 110 (1983): 34-53.

63. Ronald Clements, 'History and Theology in Biblical Narrative', *Horizons in Biblical Theology* 4-5 (1982-83): 51-55.

64. *Ibid.*, p. 54.

65. *Ibid.*, p. 55.

66. H. Tadmor, 'The Autobiographical Apology in the Royal Assyrian Literature', in *HHI*, p. 36-57. One wonders how Clements treats any historical text which seeks to justify or legitimate (e.g., The Apology of Hattušili or the inscription of Bar-Rakib, etc.).

67. Robert Alter, *The Art of Biblical Narrative*, p. 24. Alter quotes H. Schneidau, *Sacred Discontent*, p. 215. A. Cook has recently complain-

ed that 'attention to this element <fiction> runs the risk of implicitly slighting the predominantly historiographic thrust of these writings' ('"Fiction" and History in Samuel and Kings', *JSOT* 36 (1986): 27).

68. Ibid., p. 24. Cp. Sternberg, *The Poetics of Biblical Narrative*, p. 32.

69. R. Pfeiffer, *Introduction to the Old Testament*, pp. 27-29.

70. A. Danto, *Analytical Philosophy of History*, pp. 149ff.

71. *Ibid.*, p. 151.

72. A.N. Whitehead, *Adventures of Ideas*, p. 246.

73. Danto, p. 17.

74. H. White, *History and Theory* Beiheft 14 (1975): 60.

75. D. Levin, *In Defense of Historical Literature*, p. viii.

76. *Ibid.*, p. 14.

77. L. Mink, 'Narrative Form as a Cognitive Instrument', in *Literary Form and Historical Understanding*, p. 137.

78. *Ibid.*, pp. 135-141, 148.

79. *Ibid.*, p. 146.

80. This is one of the things which differentiates history from science. See: Louis O. Mink, 'The Autonomy of Historical Understanding', in *Philosophical Analysis and History*, pp. 160-192.

81. Sternberg, *The Poetics of Biblical Narrative*, pp. 24-25.

82. *Ibid.*, p. 25. Intentionality is the issue. Halpern recognizes this and roots the intentionality in the *author*: 'As readers, we identify what is historiography and what is not based on our perception of the author's *relationship to the evidence*' (*The First Historians*, p. 8). On the other hand, Alan Cooper argues for a *reader* based understanding of history: 'history is nothing but our relation to the work through time or, more concretely, the work mediated through the history of its interpretation' ('Reading the Bible Critically and Otherwise', in *The Future of Biblical Studies*, p. 66). We would prefer grounding intentionality in the text itself!

83. L. Mink, 'Narrative Form as a Cognitive Instrument', p. 145.

84. Sternberg, *The Poetics of Biblical Narrative*, p. 25.

85. White argues that this is the key to historical interpretation; namely, 'to recognize that there is no such thing as a single correct view of any object under study but that there are many correct views, each requiring its own style of representation. This would allow us to entertain seriously those creative distortions offered by minds capable of looking at the past with the same seriousness as ourselves but with

different affective and intellectual orientations' (*Tropics of Discourse*, p. 47).

86. H. White, *History and Theory* Beiheft 14 (1975): 60.

87. Concerning the fact that narratives are prominent, although not universal, ways of history writing, see: W.H. Dray, 'On the Nature and Role of Narrative in Historiography', *History and Theory* 10 (1971): 157; M. Mandelbaum, 'A Note on History as Narrative', *History and Theory* 6 (1967): 417; and *idem*, *Anatomy of Historical Knowledge*, pp. 25-26.

88. H. White, *History and Theory* 23 (1984): 24-25. In no way, in affirming this poetic feature of history writing, are we denying the factual nature of narrative emplotment in history (see in this regard, W.H. Dray, *History and Theory* 27 (1988): 286).

89. H. White, *History and Theory* Beiheft 14 (1975): 53-54.

90. P. Stambovsky delineates the three fundamental ways that metaphor functions in historiography (corresponding to Mandelbaum's historiographic forms: explanatory, sequential, and interpretive). Thus he sees in the following three categories: 1) *heuristic imagery* which advances deliberative, analytic understanding and falls within the domain of explanatory discourse; 2) *depictive imagery* which presentationally facilitates the (phenomenological) apprehension of meanings and occurrences, and which is a component of sequential discourse; and 3) *cognitive imagery* which is operative on the meta-historical plane and orchestrates interpretive discourse ('Metaphor and Historical Understanding', *History and Theory* 27 (1988): 125-134). Our interest is primarily in number 2, *depictive imagery*.

91. Concerning the figurative nature of the biblical motifs, S. Talmon argues: 'In its literary setting, which by definition is secondary, a motif constitutes a concentrated expression of the essence which inheres in the original situation ... A motif stands for the essential meaning of a situation or an event, not for the facts themselves' ('*Har* and *Midbar*: An Antithetical Pair of Biblical Motifs', in *Figurative Language in the Ancient Near East*, p. 122).

92. M. Brett, 'Literacy and Domination: G.A. Herion's Sociology of History Writing', *JSOT* 37 (1987): 20-24. And also, Goody and Watt, 'The Consequence of Literacy', *CSSH* 5 (1963): 304-345.

93. Goody, *Literacy in Traditional Societies*, pp. 34, 48. See also along these lines, M. Noth, 'Geschictsschreibung im A.T.', *RGG*[3], II, pp. 1498-1504; J.J.M. Roberts, *CBQ* 38 (1976): 3, n. 15; and Van Seters, *In Search of History*, pp. 209-227. For the implications of this for those who assume a great degree of reliability in oral tradition, see: M. Brett, *JSOT* 37 (1987): 37, n. 9.

94. *Webster's 3rd New International Dictionary*, Vol. I, p. 1073. Here we are attempting to maintain a distinction which will help clarify our discussion. For two examples of this use of the term, see: W.W. Hallo, 'Sumerian Historiography', in *HHI*, pp. 1-12; and M. Lichtheim, 'Ancient Egypt: A Survey of Current Historiography', *AHR* 69 (1963-64): 30-46.

95. Levy, 'Editor's Foreword' To *The Theory and Practice of History*, p. vi.

96. E.g., G. Garbini, *History and Ideology in Ancient Israel.*

97. D. Apter, 'Ideology and Discontent', in *Ideology and Discontent*, p. 16.

98. Harry M. Johnson, 'Ideology and the Social System', in *International Encyclopedia of the Social Sciences*, p. 76-77.

99. Cf. G. Lichtheim, 'The Concept of Ideology', *History and Theory* 4 (1965): 173.

100. *Ibid.*, pp. 174-177.

101. Johnson, 'Ideology and the Social System', p. 77.

102. Clifford Geertz, 'Ideology as a Cultural System', in *Ideology and Discontent*, p. 63.

103. Cf. J. Gould, 'Ideology', in *A Dictionary of the Social Sciences*, pp. 315-317.

104. See: J. Friedman, 'Ideology', in *The Social Science Encyclopedia*, pp. 375-376.

105. Georg Lukács, *Geschichte und Klassenbewusstsein: Studien über marxistische Dialektik*; Karl Mannheim, *Ideology and Utopia*; Jürgen Habermas, *Theorie und Praxis: Sozialphilosophische Studien*; and *Knowledge and Human Interests*. On Mannheim's derivation from Weber and dependence on the early Lukács, see: G. Lichtheim, 'The Concept of Ideology', pp. 186-192.

106. Johnson, p. 77. It must be stressed that not everyone who assumes the Marxist definition of 'false consciousness' applies it only to the Right. E.g., U. Eco, *A Theory of Semiotics*, pp. 290-297.

107. Shils, 'Ideology: The Concept and Function of Ideology', in *International Encyclopedia of the Social Sciences*, Vol. 7, p. 73. The concept of ideology as a mask is rooted back in Nietzsche's thought of 'unmasking'. For him all thought is ideological and must be 'unmasked' (see G. Lichtheim, 'The Concept of Ideology', p. 183).

108. W. Stark, *The Sociology of Knowledge*, p. 48.

109. Eco, *A Theory of Semiotics*, pp. 297 and 312, n. 54. Garbini clearly sees ideology in the sense of false consciousness and distortion (*History and Ideology in Ancient Israel*, p. xvi).

110. Stark, pp. 90-91. See also, Mannheim, *Ideology and Utopia*, pp. 55-59.

111. Cf. Geertz, 'Ideology as a Cultural System', pp. 52-54. This view is evident among recent structural Marxists (e.g., Althusser, 'Ideology and Ideological State Apparatuses', in *Lenin and Philosophy*, pp. 35-51), with in their extreme functionalism where ideological *apparatuses* are conceived as instruments that exist to maintain the coherence of a mode of production, a system of economic exploitation that generates its own self-maintenance by way of the production of appropriate mentalities, political structures and socialized subjects who are only mere agents of the system (see: Friedman, 'Ideology', in *The Social Science Encyclopedia*, p. 375).

112. Shils, p. 73.

113. If we level ideology to only distortion of reality/false consciousness, are we not then faced ultimately with a type of Nietzsche's nihilism?

114. Geertz, 'Ideology as a Cultural System', p. 57.

115. W. Percy, 'Metaphor as Mistake', *The Sewanee Review* 66 (1958): 79-99. Cf. U. Eco's discussion of metaphor. Although Eco, himself, follows the Marxist notion of ideology as 'false consciousness', he also recognizes its 'rhetorical labor' (*A Theory of Semiotics*, pp. 290-297).

116. Geertz, 'Ideology as a Cultural System', p. 74, n. 30.

117. *Ibid.*, p. 74, n. 30.

118. *Ibid.*, p. 60.

119. One example that we can cite: While the 'New Right' was gaining power in the U.S. during the election of 1980, many older, very conservative southerners refused to vote Republican because of ideological hangovers from the days of Reconstruction. One old Texan remarked, 'I would rather vote for a dead dog than a Republican!' Yet through the election of the Republican candidate, Ronald Reagan, that man stood to gain much more because of his social position than if the Democratic candidate Jimmy Carter had been elected.

120. Johnson, p. 80.

121. W.W. Hallo, 'Biblical History in its Near Eastern Setting: The Contextual Approach', in *Scripture in Context: Essays on the Comparative Method*, p. 2. Also K.A. Kitchen, *Ancient Orient and the Old Testament*.

122. *Ibid.*, pp. 1-26.

123. Von Rad, *The Problem of the Hexateuch and Other Essays*, pp. 166-204. See also: M. Noth, 'Geschichtsschreibung im A.T.', *RGG*[3], p. 1500. But Van Seters correctly points out one of the errors in such thinking: 'there is an implied comparison here on the level of 'historical thinking' between a Near Eastern mythological perspective and an Israelite 'historical' perspective that at least prejudices any comparative approach on the literary level' (Van Seters, *In Search of History*, pp. 209-248, esp. p. 218, n. 33).

124. R.J. Thompson, *Moses and the Law in a Century of Criticism Since Graf*, pp. 118-120.

125. Mowinckel, 'Israelite Historiography', *ASTI*, II, p. 8. See also B. Maisler, 'Ancient Israelite Historiography', *IEJ* 2 (1952): 82-88; U. Cassuto, 'The Rise of Historiography in Israel', in *EI* 1 pp. 85-88. <Hebrew>; idem, in *Biblical and Oriental Studies*, vol. 1, pp. 7-16.

126. E.g., his judgment concerning Egyptian history writing is quite wrong.

127. See: B. Albrektson, *History and the Gods*; and Van Seters, *In Search of History*, esp. p. 59. While Albrektson overstates the case, he nevertheless does undermine the argument against the comparative approach.

128. Hallo, 'Scripture in Context', pp. 1-24; Tadmor, 'The Autobiographical Apology ...', in *HHI*, p. 56; J.J.M. Roberts, *CBQ* 38 (1976): p. 13; Thus Millard concludes: 'where comparisons are possible they should be made, otherwise the Hebrew writings have to be treated in a vacuum, and the results of that can be, in fact often have been, extremely misleading' (*TB* 36 (1985): 75).

129. Van Seters, p. 8. We agree with his debunking of the idea that Greek and Hebrew thought were entirely in contrast.

130. *Ibid*., pp. 53-54. Parataxis can be found on different levels in many different languages and in many different periods. Thus it does not follow that because one finds parataxis in Greek and Hebrew history writing there is a necessary link between the two. While the existence of parataxis might explain certain problems, one cannot use parataxis to argue for dating as Van Seters does. Van Seters has not delineated exactly what he sees as the demarcations of parataxis in Greek and/or Hebrew literature. B. Long has attempted to define the parameters of parataxis in the Hebrew historical narrative (*I Kings*, pp. 19-30). Even so, exact relationships and dating remain very moot.

131. Gene Wise, *American Historical Explanations*, p. 171. Wise is advocating a 'New Critic' reading. In this connection, Karel van der Toorn insists that we practice 'self-restraint' when dealing with ancient cultures in order to sweep away the generalizations and mis- (or pre-) conceptions we invariably bring to our disciplines (*Sin and Sanction in Israel and Mesopotamia: A Comparative Study*, p. 9ff).

132. H. Cancik, *Grundzüge der hethitischen und alttestamentlichen Geschichtsschreibung*, p. 130.

133. Spalinger, *Aspects of the Military Documents of the Ancient Egyptians*, pp. 107, 116, 134-141.

134. It must be kept in mind that every narrative discourse consists, not of one single code monolithically utilized, but rather of a complex set of codes, the interweaving of which by the author—for the production of a story infinitely rich in suggestion and variety of affect, not to mention attitude toward and subliminal evaluation of its subject-matter—attests to his talents as an artist, as master rather than as the servant of the a single code available for his use. This explains the 'density' of the various ANE and biblical historical texts (see further: White, *History and Theory* 23 (1984): 18ff).

135. Robert Scholes, *Semiotics and Interpretation*, p. 16. With reference to biblical studies, see A. Cooper, 'The Life and Times of King David According to the Book of Psalms', in *The Poet and the Historian: Essays in Literary and Historical Biblical Criticism*, pp. 117-131.

136. H. White, 'Historicism, History, and the Figurative Imagination', *History and Theory* Beiheft 14 (1975): 52.

137. R. Barthes, *La Plaisir de Text*, p. 49. Hence, one can overcome the 'fallacy of referentiality'. See also: U. Eco, *A Theory of Semiotics*, p. 65.

138. H. White's criticism at this point is valid. He argues that a discourse should be regarded 'as an apparatus for the *production* of meaning, rather than as only a vehicle for the transmission of information about an extrinsic referent' (*History and Theory* 23 (1984): 19). However, semiotics remains a practical means of analysis, especially in light of the overemphasis in biblical studies on referentiality. So our utilization is in many ways pragmatic.

139. F.M. Fales, 'A Literary Code in Assyrian Royal Inscriptions: The Case of Ashurbanipal's Egyptian Campaigns', in *ARINH*, p. 170.

140. R. Barthes, *S/Z*, p. 20.

141. R. Barthes, *Eléments de Sémiologie*, p. 130.

142. H. White, *History and Theory* 23 (1984): 20.

143. Scholes, p. 30.

144. Oden, 'Hermeneutics and Historiography', p. 149.

145. Two areas with which this book will not deal are: 1) the idea of history in the ANE and the Bible. Numerous scholars have written on this subject [e.g., E.A. Speiser, 'Ancient Mesopotamia', in *The Idea of History in the Ancient Near East*, pp. 35-76; and 'The Biblical Idea of History in its Common Near Eastern Setting', *Biblical and Oriental Studies*, pp. 187-210. M. Burrows, 'Ancient Israel', in *The Idea of His-*

*tory in the Ancient Near East*, pp. 99-131. H. Gese, *ZThK* 55 (1958): 127-145. J. Krecher und H.-P. Müller, *Saeculum* 26 (1975): 13-44. B. Albrektson, *History and the Gods*. N. Wyatt, *UF* 11 (1979): 825-832].

But Van Seters points out that these studies are often flawed by the notion of a uniform idea of history in a particular culture (*In Search of History*, pp. 57-58). Cf. Hoffner's important comment: 'What we may learn, therefore, is not a single uniform 'view' of history writing held by the Hittites, but many individual viewpoints held by some of the Hittites who undertook to write down portions of their past as they conceived it' [*Or* (1980): 288]. So also it appears to be the case with other nations.

Moreover, these studies are flawed by their selectivity (See: Van Seters, p. 57 and p. 238; and note G.A. Press's remarks, *The Development of the Idea of History in Antiquity*, p. 142). [A vivid example of this problem is Gese's study in which the selectivity of the ANE and biblical materials does not present an accurate picture of any of the cultures' ideas of history]. Often similarities are oversimplified [e.g., A. Malamat, *VT* 5 (1955): 1-12].

and 2) a reconstruction of Israelite History. Since a thorough investigation of the ANE and biblical accounts must be completed before the issue of a reconstruction of Israelite history can be addressed, the main concern must be with how to read and interpret these texts. Thus, in our discussion of the Joshua conquest account, we will offer no reconstruction; not only because of the pragmatics of space, but also because a historiographic inquiry is primarily a literary study, while a reconstruction is, of necessity, concerned with questions of historicity.

146. The kinds of ANE texts that we will be investigating are ANE conquest accounts—obviously including many literary genres (e.g. Analistic texts, Display/Summary inscriptions, Letters to the God, etc.). Our primary concern is with texts that contain more than one episode or campaign, although we will not neglect scrutiny of single campaign texts (like the Kadesh Inscription of Ramesses II). By investigating this broad category (genre?!) we will be better able to understand Joshua's main conquest account (chs. 9-12).

## NOTES TO CHAPTER TWO
(pp. 61-124)

1. M. Liverani, 'Memorandum on the Approach to Historiographical Texts', *Or* 42 (1973): 181. Obviously, different heuristic methods can be put forth, but stylistic analysis seems to be a method best suited for this study. Hence our interest in the syntagmic aspect of Assyrian history writing (see pp. 72-78 above). In his statement Liverani is following the work of linguists like Roland Barthes and Umberto Eco

(U. Eco, *A Theory of Semiotics*, pp. 64-65; Barthes, *Le Plaiser du Texte*, p. 120).

2. For a more comprehensive review of past studies, see: A.K. Grayson, 'Histories and Historians of the Ancient Near East: Assyria and Babylonia', *Or* 49 (1980): 143-148.

3. The earliest study on Assyrian history historiography was concerned with this. See: A.T.E. Olmstead, 'Assyrian Historiography', The University of Missouri Studies, Social Studies Series III/1 (1916). While very different from Olmstead, W.W. Hallo has also examined the Assyrian texts with reconstructional goals in mind. ['Assyrian Historiography Revisited', *EI* 14 (1978): 1-7]. He also has worked along these lines in Sumerian historiography [W.W. Hallo, 'Sumerian Historiography', in *HHI*, pp. 9-20].

4. E.g. S. Mowinckel's article ['Die vorderasiatischen Königs- und Fürsteninschriften: Eine stilistische Studie', in *Eucharisterion Gunkel*, pp. 278-322] had numerous weaknesses, in particular, the very limited corpus of royal inscriptions which he utilized in the study [See: W. Baumgartner, *OLZ* 27 (1924): 313-318]. More comprehensive studies are: H.G. Güterbock, 'Die historische Tradition und ihre literarische Gestaltung bei Babyloniern und Hethitern bis 1200', *ZA* 42 (1934): 1-91; 44 (1938): 45-149; A.K. Grayson, 'Histories and Historians of the Ancient Near East: Assyria and Babylonia', *Or* 49 (1980): 140-194; J. Renger, 'Königsinschriften. B. Akkadisch', in *RLA* 6 (1980): 65-77; and John Van Seters, *In Search of History*, pp. 55-99.

5. J.J. Finkelstein, 'Mesopotamian Historiography', *PAPS* 107 (1963): 461-472). Finkelstein is following Huizinga's definition (see our discussion in the previous chapter).

6. *Ibid.*, pp. 463 and 469.

7. There have been numerous studies of particular genres of Assyrian and/or Babylonian historical texts. To name a few: W. Röllig, 'Zur Typologie und Entstehung der babylonischen und asyrischen Königslisten', in *lišan mitḫurti. Festschrift W. von Soden*, (1969), pp. 265-277; Grayson, *ABC* (1975); W.W. Hallo, *IEJ* 16 (1966): 231-242; R. Borger, *BiOr* 28 (1971): 3-24. See A.K. Grayson, *Or* 49 (1980): 143-148 for a complete list. For the Sumerian royal inscriptions, see most recently, D.O. Edzard, 'Königsinschriften. A. Sumerisch', in *RLA* 6 (1980): 59-65; cf. also W.W. Hallo, *HUCA* 33 (1962): 1-43.

8. A.K. Grayson, *Or* 49 (1980): 151. The very fact that—according to Grayson, 'the Assyrian commemorative inscriptions reveal considerable experimentation by the scribes, down through the years, with the view to include more and more details about the military enterprises of the king' (p. 154)—means that we are dealing with a very 'open' genre.

9. H. Tadmor, 'The Historical Inscriptions of Adad-Nirari III', *Iraq* 35 (1973): 141. Tadmor distinguishes between these two types designating one as 'annals' and the other as 'summary inscriptions'. The 'summary inscriptions' are called 'display inscriptions' by Olmstead (1916) and Grayson (1980) in their respective articles.

10. E.A. Speiser proposed that 'Mesopotamian man' had a unified concept of history stemming from the ancient Sumerians and running through the subsequent civilizations of Assyria and Babylonian ['Ancient Mesopotamia', in *The Idea of History in the Ancient Near East*, 35-76; and 'Geschichtswissenschaft', in *RLA* 3, pp. 216-220]. More recently, through a generic analysis, J. Krecher suggests that there were a variety of ideas about the past in ancient Mesopotamia [J. Krecher, and H.-P. Müller, 'Vergangenheitsinteresse in Mesopotamien und Israel', *Saeculum* 26 (1975): 13-44]. While the study is much more controlled than Speiser's, it is far too brief to deal adequately with the material. Furthermore, one must question whether it is possible to understand the ideas of history in a particular civilization simply through analysis of its genres. For some brief comments on the idea of history in ancient Mesopotamia, also see: W.G. Lambert, *Or* 39 (1970): 170-179; and *OTS* 17 (1972): 65-72.

11. Carlo Zaccagnini, 'An Urartean Royal Inscription in the Report of Sargon's Eighth Campaign', in *ARINH*, p. 261.

12. We are not using the term événementielle as it is understood in the 'Annalistes'. In the discussion of the French 'Annales' school, 'histoire événementielle' is usually viewed negatively, being opposed to quantitative history (e.g., François Furet, 'Quantitative History', in *Historical Studies Today*, 54-60; and E. LeRoy Ladurie, *The Mind and Method of the Historian*, pp. 8, 308).

13. Zaccagnini, pp. 260-262.

14. *Ibid.*, p. 262.

15. This point is not to be underestimated since a large number of Assyrian royal inscriptions were designated for the gods or a future king (e.g., cylinders deposited within buildings). These inscriptions carefully carved in inaccessible spots and addressed to the deity are attempts at manipulation of the deity. They report the king's victories and his piety and demand blessings in return. See: A. Leo Oppenheim, *Ancient Mesopotamia*, pp. 147-148; and A.K. Grayson, *Or* 49 (1980): 151.

16. Oppenheim, *Ancient Mesopotamia*, pp. 143-144. It must be stressed here that Oppenheim was not in the semiotic or literary camp.

17. R. Barthes, *Le Plaisir du Texte*, pp. 35-50. This does not mean questions of veracity are unimportant. It is a question of priority.

Concerning the 'veracity' of ancient writers, see: A. Millard, *FT* 110 (1983): 34-53.

18. F.M. Fales, 'A Literary Code in Assyrian Royal Inscriptions: The Case of Ashurbanipal's Egyptian Campaign', in *ARINH*, p. 170.

19. M. Liverani, 'The Ideology of the Assyrian Empire', in *Power and Propaganda: A Symposium of Ancient Empires*, pp. 297-317. Liverani's conception of ideology is influenced by U. Eco. Eco argues that one must understand ideology in the Marxist sense as 'false consciousness' so that ideology is 'a message which starts with a factual description, and then tries to justify it theoretically, gradually being accepted by society through a process of overcoding' (U. Eco, *A Theory of Semiotics*, p. 290).

20. Imperialism has acquired so many meanings that its use proves to be problematic. For example, to classical Marxists it means the triumph of (mostly Western European) monopoly finance capital over a still larger array of non-European peoples at the end of the 19th century. For some 'underdevelopment theorists', the term is simply synonymous with capitalism in general, not just its monopolistic stage.

Michael Twaddle discusses imperialism and concludes: 'Probably imperialism is best defined in some median manner. Imperialism is probably best separated analytically from both 'capitalism' and 'colonialism' and *treated principally as the pursuit of intrusive and unequal economic policy in other countries supported by significant degrees of coercion*' [Emphasis mine] ('Imperialism', in *The Social Science Encyclopedia*, pp. 377-379). Hence, we are not linking imperialism in this discussion to capitalism (certainly as an economic system of the 19th and 20th centuries).

21. Liverani, 'The Ideology of the Assyrian Empire', p. 298.

22. *Ibid.*, p. 299. It is wise to keep in mind at this point that while it is well known that the likelihood of a group or individual who has a vested interest will defend it by means of distortion, it is easy to overestimate the importance of this as a source of ideology.

23. *Ibid.*, p. 299. With regard to lower class ideologies, Liverani states: 'The identification of ideologies belonging to the lower social classes or to marginal groups (such as peasants and nomads) is problematical, due to the shortage of evidence. Such ideologies, as far as they have not been absorbed and crushed by the official ideology, ought to be characterized by greater simplicity and by non-involvement in the problem of the empire'.

24. A.T.E. Olmstead, *JAOS* 38 (1918): 209-263; 41 (1921): 345-382. H. Tadmor notes that the annals of Shalmaneser III refrain from describing the atrocities which Aššur-nasir-pal II systematically narrate. He wonders 'whether the absence of atrocities reflects an actual change of Assyrian policy toward the West, or whether it is a refine-

ment in the character of historical writing' ('Assyria and the West: The Ninth Century and its Aftermath', in *Unity and Diversity*, p. 36).

25. H.W.F. Saggs, 'Assyrian Warfare in the Sargonid Period', *Iraq* 25 (1963): 149, 154.

26. Liverani, 'The Ideology of the Assyrian Empire', p. 301.

27. Ibid., p. 301.

28. Harry L. Johnson, 'Ideology and the Social System', in *International Encyclopedia of the Social Sciences*, p. 78.

29. *Ibid.*, p. 78. Moreover, Ninian Smart argues that the distinction between church and state, religion and ideology, must be maintained in order to facilitate scientific analysis (*Religion and the Future of Western Civilization*, pp. 19-21, 208-237, and 274-306). Finally, it is important to remember at this point that one should not confuse ontological and epistemological questions.

30. C. Lévi-Strauss, *The Elementary Structures of Kinship*, p. 67.

31. M.B. Rowton, 'War, Trade and the Emerging Power Center', *Mesopotamien und Seine Nachbarn*, p. 191. He also points out that in Akkadian the terms *girru* and *ḫarranu* both have the following meanings: road/route, trading expedition and military expedition.

32. Zaccagnini, 'The Enemy in the Neo-Assyrian Royal Inscriptions: The 'Ethnographic' Description', and Fales, 'The Enemy in Assyrian Royal Inscriptions: 'The Moral Judgement'', in *Assyrien und seine Nachbarn*, pp. 409-424; and 425-435.

33. Zacagnini, 'The Enemy', p. 418.

34. *Ibid.*, p. 418.

35. Fales, 'The Enemy', p. 425. While the Assyrian ideology tended to picture the enemy in a 'them' versus 'us' manner, they did distinguish between 'pure' enemies and rebels (see our discussion of function *N*, pp. 84-85). D. Luckenbill noted that: 'The Assyrian kings always distinguished between enemies and rebels. Enemies were given a chance to submit and become tributaries, but rebels ("sinners" is a literal translation of the term employed), those who "sinned against Aššur and the great gods," were usually exterminated with the utmost savagery' (*The Annals of Sennacherib*, p. 5).

36. *Ibid.*, pp. 427, 430.

37. *Ibid.*, pp. 428-430.

38. Fales, *ARINH*, p. 171. For the definition of *Kunstprosa*, see: K. Hecker, *Untersuchungen zur akkadischen Epik*, p. 135, n. 2.

39. Grayson, *Or* 49 (1980): 194.

40. For example, H. Tadmor has recently discussed the use of temporal and genelogical formulae ('History and Ideology in the Assyrian

Royal Inscriptions', in *ARINH*, pp. 13-33). On the one hand, he discusses the temporal formulae which express the military and pious 'erga' of the king upon his accession to the throne; while on the other hand, he discusses the Assyrian genealogical formulae demonstrating that the Assyrian king's reign could be legitimated either by the use of a formula of his royal descent or by an account of his divine election. However, Tadmor seems to imply that since these are literary or ideological conventions, they must purposefully distort historical reality (pp. 24-25). Obviously, such an understanding is certainly not correct since all historical narratives employ ideological and literary conventions. Hence, ideology does not always distort reality, at least in the way Tadmor seems to imply. This does not mean that we believe that the Assyrian accounts do not distort reality (which they do on occasions) or that Tadmor's analysis of the individual examples is necessarily incorrect. We are simply pointing out that caution must be employed and generalization avoided (even if only implied). Along these lines see the arguments of N. Abercrombie, Hill, and Turner, *The Dominant Ideology Thesis*. They argue that one must know in advance the ideology in order to conclude that it is distorting reality.

41. By valency we mean: 'Broadly, the capacity of something to unite, react, or interact with something else' (*The American Heritage Dictionary of the English Language*, p. 1414).

42. F.M. Fales, 'A Literary Code', in *ARINH*, p. 172.

43. *Ibid.*, p. 171.

44. *Ibid.*, p. 173.

45. *Ibid.*, pp. 171-176.

46. *Ibid.*, pp. 201-202.

47. U. Eco, *The Role of the Reader*, p. 117.

48. *Ibid.*, pp. 117, 120.

49. L.D. Levine, 'Preliminary Remarks on the Historical Inscriptions of Sennacherib', in *HHI*, pp. 69. He points out that a 'campaign', as reported in the annals of Sennacherib, does not necessarily end with the events described in the original document; and that it was possible to produce an account of a campaign before that campaign had been completed (pp. 72-73). Finally, with regard to the principles underlying the composition of the 'annals', events may be assigned to a particular campaign relative to the writer's point of view rather than strict chronological grounds (p. 73).

50. E. Badalì, et al., 'Studies on the Annals of Aššurnasirpal II: I. Morphological Analysis', *Vicino Oriente* 5 (1982-83): 13-73 [henceforth: *SAAMA*].

51. In the labelling of these syntagms, we are, for the most part, following *SAAMA*, pp. 18-41. Interestingly, R. Borger has also noted

a number of these syntagms in his analysis of the style and vocabulary of Tiglath-Pileser I's prisms (*EAK* I, p. 125-28). His isolations and identifications are incorporated in this analysis. It is also important to note that Borger has shown the utilization of many of these syntagms in a number of Assyrian kings prior to Tiglath-Pileser I (e.g., esp. in the inscriptions of Shalmaneser I and Tukulti-Ninurta I). This may have implications on the beginning of 'annal' writing in Assyria!

52. In the case of Aššurnasirpal II, the sequence ABC²DE is typical and recurrent (I.74-77, 101-104; II.23-27, 49-51). As regards the numerous cases in which function B is absent, one may remark that from an ideological point of view the lack of an explicitly enunciated disorder does not mean that there was no disorder. Rather, since every action of the Assyrian king was aimed at the re-establishment of order, the absence of an explicit B would be due to the obvious and given existence of such disorder.

53. 'On the level of syntax, function C is never expressed by a principal sentence (except in I 44-45), but rather by a circumstantial expression annexed to sentences that enunciate the function which follows (D or E or some other one). This signifies that the acquisition of the divine assent is a prerequisite of the most operative technical and military preparation for the campaign and that the link between the ideological and operative levels (C and D) is solidly acknowledged and recorded' (*SAAMA*, p. 24).

54. 'Normally function E describes any movement in space of the protagonist (= the Assyrian king), apart from the specific functions of pursuit (H) and return (Q)' (*SAAMA*, p. 25).

55. 'Here we are dealing with stages of a purely functional character, stages which take place in the course of one's moving from one place to another (Ef // qf), or in the proximity of the cities where tributes are to be collected (EfM). Rarely are they followed by violent actions (EfL)' (*SAAMA*, p. 30).

56. Here we are attempting to improve the analysis of *SAAMA*.

57. Text: King, *AKA*, pp. 27ff; Borger, 'Textkritisches zur Prisma-Inschrift Tiglatpileser's I.', *AfO* 25 (1974-77), pp. 161-165. Translation: Grayson, *ARI* II, p. 3ff. Studies: Borger, *EAK* I, p. 129ff; and H. Tadmor, 'Observations on Assyrian Historiography', p. 209ff.

58. See: A.K. Grayson, 'Assyrian Royal Inscriptions: Literary Characteristics', in *ARINH*, p. 38; and H. Tadmor, 'Observations on Assyrian Historiography', p. 209.

59. A.K. Grayson, *ARI*, II, p. 3.

60. Tadmor, 'Observations on Assyrian Historiography', p. 209.

61. Borger feels that, since the writer's intentions were deliberate, there naturally sprung forth a great number of essential variants, omissions and additions (*EAK*, I, p. 125).

62. *ser-ma-ši*. See: *AHw* p. 1030a; and *ARI* II p. 7, n. 33.

63. Following the reading of C.

64. Grayson feels that *gamarriya* is a variant of *magarriya* (*ARI*, p. 8, n. 40). If this is true, metathesis would be the probable explanation. On the other hand, the scribe's writing of *magarru* may be flawed (cf. *CAD* G p. 24).

65. For *šib-bu* see: *AHw* p. 1226. Cf. Tukulti-Ninurta Epic IV. 42.

66. *CAD* S p. 135. Cf. *AKA* p. 67, iv. 88; and Tukulti-Ninurta I.

67. *SAAMA*, p. 72.

68. Text: following the reconstruction by Weidner, *AfO* 3 (1926): 151-161; and *AfO* 22 (1968-69): 75ff. Translation: Grayson, *ARI* II, pp. 74-78. Concerning Ashur-Dan's policy see A.K. Grayson 'Studies in Neo-Assyrian History: The Ninth Century B.C.', *BiOr* 33 (1976): 136.

69. VAT 8890.16 reads: *às-su-ḫa i-na*.

70. We follow the identification of Muṣri as put forward by H. Tadmor ('Que and Musri', *IEJ* 11 (1961): 143-150, esp. p. 146). This Muṣri is to be placed not too far from Qummani. It was conquered in the 12th century B.C. (by Tiglath-Pileser I), revolted, and was reconquered by Ashurdan II. By the Sargonid period, it was an integral part of Assyria proper.

71. Text: King, *AKA*, pp. 254-387; Le Gac, *Asn.*, pp. 1-122. Translations: Grayson, *ARI* II, pp. 117-147. Studies: Schramm, *EAK* II, pp. 18-31.

72. Cp. Joshua 10.

73. Le Gac, *Asn.*, p. 62, n. 4.

74. See *AHw* sub *raksu* 1e (p. 948a).

75. For a full discussion of the inscriptions of Shalmaneser III, see W. Schramm, *EAK* II, pp. 70-105. See also the remarks of A.K. Grayson, 'Studies in Neo-Assyrian History', *BiOr* 33 (1976): 134-145.

76. (Aššur Text #32) Text: F. Safar, 'A Further Text of Shalmaneser III from Assur', *Sumer* 7 (1951): 3-21; E. Michel, *WO* 2/1 (1954): 27-45. Translation: R. Borger, *TUAT* 1/4 pp. 366-367 (partial). According to Schramm, this is the main exemplar of Recension E (*EAK* II, p. 77).

77. *CAD* G p. 111.

78. *CAD* B p. 341.

79. The 18th *palû* is also recorded on the Black Obelisk (E. Michel, *WO* II/2 (1955): 153-154), and on the right side of a stela fragment

(J.A. Brinkman, *JNES* 32 (1973): 40-46 (too wanting to merit inclusion). In the case of the Black Obelisk, the account is so abbreviated, it is not necessary to include in our comparison.

80. E. Michel, *WO* 2/1 (1954): 38-39; D. Wiseman, in *DOTT*, pp. 46-50.

81. According to Assyrian chronology this would have been 841.

82. See Flavius Josephus, *Against Apion* I 124: τουτον διεδεξατο βαλεζωρος ὑιος, βιωσας ἐτη με' ἐβασιλευσεν ἐτη ἑξ :: '(Ithobal) was succeeded by his son Balezor, who lived forty-five years and reigned six'. Hence, Phoenician: בעלעזר.

83. P.K. McCarter argues that 'it is probable that the name written *Ia-ú-a* or *Ia-a-ú* in Shalmaneser's records is in fact the hypocoristicon "Yaw"' ... Thus, the references in Shalmaneser's annals to "Yaw, son of Omri" (as we should now read it) are ambiguous so far as the name of "Yaw" is concerned. It may be Jehu who is meant, as scholars have surmised, or it may be Jehoram ... the title "son of Omri" is decidedly in favor of Jehoram ... Accordingly, it was this last of the Omrides, Jehoram, who paid tribute to Shalmaneser in 841' (*BASOR* 216 (1974, erch. 1975): 6). On the other hand, E.R. Thiele argues that 'both Jehoram and Jehu were rulers in Israel in 841, so either of these kings could have been the Hebrew ruler mentioned by Shalmaneser' (*BASOR* 222 (1976): 19). However, M. Weippert disagrees with McCarter's identification. arguing that *Ia-ú-a mār* [I]*Ḫu-um-ri-i* does not have to be identified with Jehoram (Joram II Kgs. 1:17). He concludes that 'Salmanassars [I]*Ia-ú-a* kann daher als *Yaw-hu'a* "YHWH ist es!" interpretiert werden' (*VT* 28 (1978): 115). Furthermore, he argues 'Dazu kommt, dass McCarter mit *Yaw(a') für *Yawram einen kaum gebräuchlichen Namenstyp rekonstruiert hat' (p. 116). Thus for him, 'das Jahr der schlacht bei Qarqar (853) ist zugleich das Todesjahr Ahabs, das Jahr des Tributs Jehus (841) sein 1. Regierungsjahr'. Weippert's arguments seem to be strong and we must add that McCarter has not adequately addressed the spelling of Jehoram in the II Kings passage (Joram): the ה has remained in the shortened form, hence why is it missing in the Assyrian translation?

Finally, Na'aman argues against McCarter's proposal stating: 'The recent proposal of McCarter (1974) to interpret the name "*Ia-ú-a* / *Ia-a-ú*" in these passages as a shortened form of Jehoram (based on a hypocoristic PN Yaw!) is unsound. Furthermore, hypocoristic names are rare exceptions in the Assyrian royal inscriptions; such a solution is "a priori" inadequate. It is preferable to adhere to the original interpretations which consider the above cuneiform spellings as attempts to approximate the pronunciation of the biblical name Jehu. Ungnad showed that the name "*mār PN*" (e.g. "*mār Ḫumri*") actually denotes *(ša) bīt PN* "(which is) of the house PN" (Ungnad, 'Jaua, mâr Humri', *OLZ* 9 (1906): 224-226). The Assyrians often denoted countries by the name of the founder of the ruling dynasty at the time of their first acquaintance with it (e.g. "Bīt Baḫiani, Bīt Agusi, Bīt Ḫumri"), regardless of which dynasty was in power at the time. Thus the name "*mār Ḫumri*" for Jehu poses no problem. Accordingly, the synchronization between Jehu and Shalmaneser III in 841 B.C.E. remains valid' (N. Na'aman, *Tel Aviv* 3 (1976): 102, n. 26). See also A.R. Millard, *JNES* 38 (1979): 311.

84. (III R 5, 6). E. Michel, *WO* 1/4 (1949): 265-268. *text #22. See R. Borger for additional bibliography and translation: *TUAT* 1/4, pp.365-366. Schramm understands this text as Recension D.

85. Borger comments: 'Gemeint ist der Antilibanon oder der Hermon. Die von Salmanassar verwendete Namensform lautet Saniru' (*TUAT*, p. 366, n. 6a). Cf. Deut. 3:9: שניר.

86. D. Wiseman correctly states: 'Note that the Assyrian makes no claim to the capture of the city' (*DOTT*, p. 49). This is informative of the situation in Sennacherib's campaign against Jerusalem. Concerning that account, D. Luckenbill's words still are on the mark: 'The Assyrian account of the investment of the city is very full and detailed, a sure sign that the victory claimed was not at all decisive' (*The Annals of Sennacherib*, p. 11).

87. Borger notes that the location is unclear, although apparently in the neighborhood of Tyre (according to the 'Marble Slab' inscription of Shalmaneser, E. Michel, *WO* 2/1 (1954): 27ff). However, Wiseman states that this is 'the headland by the Nahr-el-Kelb (Dog River), north of Beirut, where inscriptions and stelae of Shalmaneser III and later kings have been discovered cut in the rock face of the pass' (*DOTT*, p. 49).

88. See note 83 above.

89. A. Billerbeck and F. Delitzsch, 'Die Palasttore Shalmanassars II von Balawat', *Beiträge zur Assyriologie und semitischen Sprachwissenschaft* 6 (1908): 129-155, esp. pp. 150-151.

90. According to Assyrian chronology this would have been 841.

91. Kinner-Wilson, *Iraq* (1962): 96-115.

92. W. Schramm, *EAK* II, p. 78.

93. Text: Borger, *BAL*$^2$ pp. 68ff. See also: D.D. Luckenbill, *The Annals of Sennacherib*, [OIP 2], Chicago, 1924. Studies: L.D. Levine, 'Sennacherib's Southern Front: 704-689 B.C.', *JCS* 34 (1982): 28-58. Idem, 'Preliminary Remarks on the Historical Inscriptions of Sennacherib', in *HHI*, pp. 58-75; Liverani, 'Critique of Variants and the Titulary of Sennacherib', in *ARINH*, pp. 225-258; ;and J. A. Brinkman, *Prelude to Empire*, pp. 54-70.

94. L.D. Levine, 'Preliminary Remarks on the Historical Inscriptions of Sennacherib', in *HHI*, pp. 69-73.

95. L.D. Levine feels that Sennacherib's 2nd campaign was a logical extension of his 1st. He suggests that the 'first' and the 'second' campaigns of the Annals should be combined and understood as one campaign; and this for historical-geographical and historiographic reasons (see *JCS* 34 (1982): 29-40, esp. pp. 37-38; and 'The Second Campaign of Sennacherib', *JNES* 32 (1973): 312-317). For a different understanding of the first two *girrū*, see J.A. Brinkman, 'Merodach-Baladan II', in *Studies Presented to A. Leo Oppenheim*, pp. 31-35. There may well be grounds for maintaining separate campaigns (see now especially, Brinkman, *Prelude to Empire*, pp. 58-60). Here we are treating only the first episode of the second campaign for comparative reasons.

96. L.D. Levine argues that the *sixth* and *seventh* campaigns of the annals should be combined and viewed as one campaign (*JCS* 34 (1982): 46-47). He marshalls three reasons for this conclusion: 1) the *sixth* campaign does not end with any statement about returning to Assyria, as does the *seventh*. 2) According to the annals, events beginning in the summer of 694 and ending over a year later, in the summer of 693, are all assigned to the *sixth* campaign, while the events of the *seventh* campaign are all contained in a short three month period immediately following upon the last event of the *sixth*. 3) The Nebi Yunus inscription (Luckenbill, *Annals*, pp. 86-89) separates the first half of the *sixth* campaign from the second half of that campaign (and combines the second half of the *sixth* with the *seventh*?); as such it represents a divergent historiographic tradition within the royal chancery. A divergent tradition is also evident in the Walters Art Gallery Inscription [A.K. Grayson, 'The Walters Art Galley Sennacherib Inscription', *AfO* 20 (1963): 84], where yet another system of splitting up the campaigns was used. Levine concludes: 'The historical continuum was, and is, subject to various legitimate attempts at periodization, depending upon the goals of the inquiry' (p. 47). However, for the comparative purposes of our investigation we are isolating it as a separate episode.

97. *CAD* N I, p. 336.

98. Text: Most recently see, W. Mayer, *MDOG* 115 (1983), pp. 65-132. Earlier publication: F. Thureau-Dangin, *Une Relation de la Huitième Campagne de Sargon* [TCL 3], Paris, 1912. Additions: B. Meissner, 'Die Eroberung der Stadt Ulhu auf Sargons 8. Feldzug', *ZA* 34 (1922): 113-122; E.F. Weidner, 'Neue Bruchstücke des Berichtes über Sargons achten Feldzug', *AfO* 12 (1937-1939): 144-148. Studies: H. Rigg, 'Sargon's 'Eighth Military Campaign", *JAOS* 62 (1942): 130-138; A.L. Oppenheim, 'The City of Aššur in 714 B.C.', *JNES* 19 (1960): 133-147; L.D. Levine, 'Geographical Studies in the Neo-Assyrian Zagros - II', *Iran* 12 (1974): 99-124; A.A. Çilingiroğlu, 'The Eighth Campaign of Sargon II', *Anadolu Araştirmalari* 4-5 (1976-1977): 252-269; W. Mayer, 'Die Finanzierung einer Kampagne', *UF* 11 (1979): 571-595;

and *MDOG* 112 (1980), pp. 13-33. C. Zaccagnini, 'An Urartean Royal Inscription in the Report of Sargon's Eighth Campaign', in *ARINH*, pp. 260-279.

99. E. Schrader labelled these as 'Prunkinschriften' (*Zur Kritik der Inschriften Tiglath-Pileser II*, p. 13), and Olmstead called them 'Display Inscriptions' (*Assyrian Historiography*, p. 3). H. Tadmor prefers the label 'Summary Inscriptions' ('The Historical Inscriptions of Adad-Nirari III', *Iraq* 35 (1973): 141). He traces this to an earlier label of Schrader's: 'Übersichtsinschriften'. A.K. Grayson argues that the designation 'Display' is inaccurate since, like the annals, while some of these texts were intended for display, others were buried in the foundation or other parts of buildings (*Or* 49 (1980): 152). Even so Grayson uses the term for convenience. J. Reade has suggested that inscribed bricks may have been the original form of the display inscription ('Twelve Ashur-nasir-pal Reliefs', *Iraq* 34 (1972): 122; see also: S. Paley, *King of the World: Ashur-nasir-pal II of Assyria 883-859 B.C.*, p. 115). Summary Texts could be used as sources for later annals [H. Tadmor, 'The Campaigns of Sargon II of Assur: A Chronological-Historical Study', *JCS* 12 (1958): 36ff].

100. Lines 6-14. S.M. Paley, *King of the World*, pp. 115-144 and W. de Filippi, The Royal Inscriptions of Aššur-Nasir-Apli II (883-859 B.C.), pp. 4-17. See also: King, *AKA* 212-221; Le Gac, *Asn*. pp. 152-170; Grayson, *ARI* II, pp. 164-167 (no. CI 13); Schramm, *EAK* II, pp. 39-42.

101. Text and translation: Stephanie Page, 'A Stela of Adad-Nirari III and Nergal-Ereš from Tell Al Rimah', *Iraq* 30 (1968): 139-153. The stela was discovered at Tell al Rimah where it stood in 'position inside the cella of a Late Assyrian shrine, set beside the poduim, a placing that is unparalleled among the find spots of other royal stelae' (p. 139). It is dedicated *ana* $^{d}$*Adad*. See also now R. Borger, *TUAT* 1/4, p. 368.

102. Here, Adad-nirari III claims that he subjugated the lands of Amurru and Hatti (= Northern Syria) within 'a single year'. It is obvious that several campaigns to Syria (= war against Arpad [806], the Sea-shore [802], and the defeat of Damascus [796] were telescoped into one by using the figure (*ina ištēt šatti*) (cf. Tadmor, *Iraq* 35 (1973): 62, 143 and 'History and Ideology in the Assyrian Royal Inscriptions, in *ARINH*, p. 18, n. 17).

103. Page identifies $^{I}$*Ma-ri-'i* $^{māt}$*Imeri-šú* as Ben-hadad, the son of Hazael (*Iraq* 30 (1968): 149-150). The inscribed ivory from Arslan Tash states: הזאל למראן showing that Hazael, king of Damascus had the title *mr'(n)*. Since Hazael had the title, it is likely that his son Ben-hadad also held it on becoming monarch. Hazael ruled 'all the days of Jehoahaz' (II Kings 13:22), which implies that he died either in the same year as Jehoahaz or later. (This verse, like so

many, is suspected of corruption by enthusiastic commentators for no compelling reason). Since *Ia'asu* is probably Joash, *Mari'* may be either Hazael, or more probably his son Ben-hadad (II Kings 13:25).

Page suggests that since no verse in the Old Testament records either Adad-nirari's intervention in Damascus or tribute given to the Assyrian monarch by Joash (or Jehoahaz for that matter), the Israelite king (Joash) took his chance by siding with the Assyrians when the Assyrians appeared at the gate of Damascus. Joash's gift was then recorded by the Assyrian scribes (p. 150).

104. Many scholars date the year of Jehoash's tribute to 805-802 B.C. See for example: A. Jepsen, 'Ein neuer Fixpunkt für die Chronologie der israelitischen Könige?', *VT* 20 (1970): 359-361; and J. Alberto Soggin, 'Ein ausserbiblisches Zeugnis für die Chronologie des J$^e$hô'aš/Jô'aš, König von Israel', *VT* 20 (1970): 366-368. Jepsen points out that *ina ištēt šatti* translates more correctly ('verbessert'): 'In einem einzigen Jahr'. He interprets this literally and states: 'Es gibt daher keinen Grund, den in der Inschrift bezeugten Zug nicht in das Jahr dieses Eponymen, d.h. in das Jahr 802 zu setzen. Solange nicht neue assyrische Quellen diesen Heerszug eindeutig anders datieren, wird man ihn nur mit der Angabe der Eponymenchronik für das Jahr 802 kombinieren können. (Ein früheres Jahr kommt schwerlich in Frage, s.u.)' (p. 359). Thus he argues that the campaign mentioned in this text should be dated to the year 802 rather than 798.

However, if *ina ištēt šatti* (line 4) is figurative, then the Assyrian sources are not necessarily in favour of a date of 805-802 B.C. Millard, after considering the evidence of the various inscriptions of Adad-nirari III concludes: 'the campaigns of 805-803 B.C. were limited to subduing the rebel states of north Syria—the campaign of 802 B.C. being directed to the Sea-Land, or possibly referring to the subjugation of Arpad noted in the Rimah Stele. Accordingly, southern Syria was the aim of the later effort noted as 'to Mansuate' in 796 B.C. ... 796 B.C. being the occasion when the Assyrians overcame Damascus and received the tribute of her dependents, Samaria, Philistia, and Edom' ('Adad-Nirari III, Aram, and Arpad', *PEQ* 105 (1973): 163, and 162). Thus according to this interpretation, Jehoash paid his tribute in 796 B.C. See further, W. Pitard, *Ancient Damascus*, pp. 160-189.

105. Tadmor, *Iraq* 35 (1973): 143.

106. See: A.R. Millard and H. Tadmor, 'Adad-Nirari III in Syria: Another Stele Fragment and the Dates of His Campaigns', *Iraq* 35 (1973): 57-64.

107. Tadmor, *Iraq* 35 (1973): 143, n. 17.

108. Adapted from *SAAMA*, p. 70.

109. *Ibid.*, p. 72

110. *Ibid.*, p. 72

NOTES TO CHAPTER THREE
(pp. 125-163)

1. We are following H.A. Hoffner, Jr. in restricting the term 'Hittite' to 'the immediate subjects of that sequence of kings beginning with Anitta of Kuššar (reigned c. 1750 B.C.) and concluding with Suppiluliuma II (reigned c. 1200 B.C.)' ['Histories and Historians of the Ancient Near East: The Hittites', *Or* 49 (1980): 283].

2. C.W. Ceram, *The Secret of the Hittites*, p. 119.

3. 'Die historische Tradition und ihre literarische Gestaltung bei Babyloniern und Hethitern bis 1200. Zweiter Teil: Hethiter', *ZA* 44 (1938): 45-149. After classifying the historical texts into native and non-native Hittite compositions, Güterbock subdivided the native ones into two divisions: 1) products of the 'official history writing' ('offizielle Geschichtsschreibung'), and 2) literary works based upon an oral tradition which existed alongside the official history writing (p. 101). Liverani feels that Güterbock's work shows 'di dipendere da modelli storiografici [allora dominanti in Germania] ispirati alla obbiettività, al non-impegno' ('Storiografia Politica Hittita—I. Šunaššura, ovvero: Della Reciprocità', *OA* 12 (1973): 295, n. 60).

Other examples of generic approaches include: Annelies Kammenhuber, 'Die hethitische Geschichtsschreibung', *Saeculum* 9 (1958): 136-155; A. Archi, 'La storiografia ittita', *Athenaeum* 47 (1969): 7-20; and H.A. Hoffner, Jr., 'Propaganda and Political Justification in Hittite Historiography', in *Unity and Diversity*, pp. 49-62; and *Or* 49 (1980): 283-332 [the most comprehensive study on the subject of historiography to date. We will utilize this work throughout our discussion]. See also, Van Seters, *In Search of History*, pp. 100-126.

4. Kammenhuber, *Saeculum* 9 (1958): 146.

5. She states: 'Wie schon die Sumerer, so hatten auch die semitischen Babylonier *keinen Sinn für Geschichte* als solche' <emphasis mine> (p. 146).

6. *Ibid.*, p. 146. Kammenhuber's literary analysis has been shown to be contradictory (see: Hoffner, *Or* 49 (1980): 312-322; and also Liverani's criticism, *OA* 12 (1973): 295, n. 60; and Van Seters, *In Search of History*, p. 113.

7. *Ibid.*, p. 146.

8. Hoffner, *Or* 49 (1980): 322.

9. H. Cancik, *Mythische und historische Wahrheit* (1970).

10. See for example Speiser's arguments in 'Ancient Mesopotamia', in *The Idea of History in the Ancient Near East*, pp. 35-76.

11. Hoffner, *Or* 49 (1980): 268. The reason for this is the fact that we possess only a small portion of the ancient historiographic endeavors

which were undertaken during the some five centuries of the Hittite period. Furthermore to conclude as Cancik does that this 'historical consciousness concerning truth and causality' was found in Hatti and Israel, but not in Mesopotamia or Egypt, must be rejected. This in no way diminishes the importance of individual statements in the Hittite texts concerning these issues. But it does mean that generalizations of this sort cannot be maintained.

12. *Grundzüge der hethitischen und alttestamentlichen Geschichtsschreibung* (1976).

13. Van Seters violently objects to these, *In Search of History*, pp. 100-126.

14. Liverani, 'Storiografia politica Hittita—I. Šunaššura, ovvero: della reciprocità', *OA* 12 (1973): 267-297. For the 'prima lettura' interpretation, see A. Goetze, *CAH*[3] II, pp. 6-7.

15. *Ibid.*, pp. 267-271. He is following the arguments of C. Levi-Strauss, 'Reciprocity and Hierarchy', *American Anthropologist* 46 (1944): 266-268. One must question, however, if Levi-Strauss' analysis which is based on the moiety system of tribal relationships in South American Indians is applicable to the relationship between nations in ancient Anatolia and Syria in the late 2nd millennium B.C. In the context of Levi-Strauss' discussion, a moiety is one of two basic complementary tribal subdivisions; especially, one (as a phratry) of two unilateral usually exogamous groups. Certainly, such a tribal arrangement is not clearly present in the context of the treaty between Suppiluliuma and Šunaššura. Furthermore, it is important to note that Levi-Strauss states that there are numerous indications that the present relations between the moieties which he studied are not very ancient. Hence, one must be doubly cautious in the use of such a model in the interpretation of the relations between nations of the 2nd millennium B.C. For a thorough analysis of the use of anthropology in the interpretation of ANE and biblical texts, see: J. Rogerson, *Anthropology and the Old Testament*, Sheffield, 1984.

16. *Ibid.*, p. 297.

17. *Ibid.*, p. 295.

18. In this regard, Levin has pointed out that not only do all historians have to select, but that they do so from evidence which is itself a selection (*In Defense of Historical Literature*, p. 11).

19. 'Storiografia Politica Hittita—II. Telipinu, Ovvero: Della Solidarietà', *OA* 16 (1977): 105-131.

20. *Ibid.*, p. 130. He states: 'L'andamento della storia istituzionale dello stato hittita che Telipinu fornisce (compattezza → disgregazione → ricompattezza) non è altro che un'applicazione del generale sche-

matipo (bene → male → bene) che caratterizza tutti gli editti di "riforma."'

21. Or in Liverani's words: 'storia "già fatta" o storia da farsi' (p. 105 and in passim).

22. *Ibid.*, p. 105ff, esp. p. 128. Concerning the *panku-*, see: M. Marazzi, *WO* 15 (1984): 99; F. Starke, 'Der Erlass Telipinus', *WO* 16 (1985): 102; and esp. G. Beckman who states: 'It has been widely held that during the earliest period of Hittite history the king was elected by the nobility, meeting in assembly for this purpose. Examination of the available attestations of the two Hittite words for political assembly, *panku-* and *tuliya-*, which differ only in their syntactic employment, demonstrates that the Hittite assembly was not the gathering of a class, but rather primarily a judicial body, subject even in this area to the will of the monarch. It is further suggested that this assembly was composed of the members of the higher state bureaucracy, and not the nobility *per se*, although the actual relationship between the two groups remains to be elucidated. No evidence for an elective system of kingship is found ... Thus the attested functions of the Hittite assembly, like those of its divine counterpart, are judicial, and even here are constrained in most instances by the will of the monarch ... a judicial character, namely of witnessing agreements and royal proclamations of great importance, and of trying criminal offenders of particularly high status' ('The Hittite Assembly', *JAOS* 102 (1982): 435, 440, and 442).

23. H.G. Guterbock, 'Hittite Historiography: A Survey', in *HHI*, pp. 21-35.

24. *Ibid.*, p. 22.

25. Goetze, 'Das Hethiter Reich', *Der Alte Orient* 27, Heft 2, p. 13.

26. O.R. Gurney, 'The Hittite Empire', in *Power and Propaganda: A Symposium on Ancient Empires*, p. 153.

27. H. Otten, 'Aitiologische Erzählung von der Überquerung des Taurus', *ZA* 21 (1963): 160ff.

28. Gurney, p. 153.

29. *Ibid.*, p. 163.

30. Again, we are using the term 'imperialism' as 'the pursuit of intrusive and unequal economic policy in other countries supported by significant degrees of coercion'.

31. Cf. Goetze, *CAH*[3] II, Part 2, 1.

32. Gurney, p. 163.

33. *Ibid.*, p. 163. He adds: 'Paradoxically, perhaps, it did not lead to an empire. All that had been gained was immediately lost again and

the Hittites were thrown back on to their plateau', One wonders if this attitude did not continue throughout the period of the Hittite kingdom.

34. *Ibid.*, pp. 163-164. Cf. the vengeance motif in Joshua 10:13.

35. *Ibid.*, p. 164. If Gurney is correct, then there may be an important difference between the Hittite and Assyrian imperialistic ideologies. With regard to control, the Hittites may have depended less on a policy of 'calculated frightfulness' than the Assyrians. Clearly the latter depended heavily in the de-culturation process on their 'ideology of terror'. But on the other hand, this could simply be the result of our knowledge of the administration of the two empires which corresponds proportionally to the material preserved from each.

36. E. Neu, *Der Anitta-Text*, pp. 10-15. Anitta of Kuššar reigned ca. 1750 B.C. according to H.A. Hoffner, *Or* 49 (1980): 283. Neu lists the texts as A = KBo III 22 = BoTU 7; B = KUB XXVI 71 = BoTU 30; C = KUB XXXVI 98 + 98a + 98b (p. 3). Güterbock has offered a new translation and added some comments in his article on Hittite historiography in *HHI*, pp. 22-25. See also Van Seters's comments, *In Search of History*, pp. 105-107; and F. Starke, 'Halmasuit im Anitta-Text', *ZA* 69 (1979): pp. 47-120.

37. A. Kammenhuber, *Saeculum* 9 (1958): 148. She feels that Pithana and Anitta were 'protohattische Fürsten'.

38. E. Neu, *Der Anitta-Text*, 132ff.

39. Güterbock, 'Hittite Historiography', pp. 24-25. But note his earlier position, *ZA* 44 (1938): 139-143.

40. Hoffner, *Or* 49 (1980): 292.

41. The other text is the text of Suppiluliuma II which uses the words: 'I am Suppiluliuma, the Great King ...' (see: Kümmel, *TUAT* II/5 p. 494 and bibliography).

42. Güterbock, 'Hittite Historiography', p. 22. It is possible that the Akkadogram *qibima* should be understood as an artificial representation standing for the Hittite equivalent.

43. Cf. for a much later example, the Azitawadda inscription.

44. Güterbock, 'Hittite Historiography', p. 23.

45. Van Seters, *In Search of History*, pp. 106-107.

46. We would understand lines 20-35 as one curse. There may have been a third and final curse in the missing lines at the end of the tablet.

47. See Hoffner, *Or* 40 (1980): 292-293.

48. *CTH* 4. We use the term 'concise' to differentiate the bilingual text of Hattušili I from the recently published text (*CTH* 13) which Kempinski and Košak call the 'extensive' annals of Hattušili I (A. Kempinski and S. Košak, '*CTH* 13: The Extensive Annals of Hattušili I', *Tel Aviv* 9 (1982): 87-116). They call *CTH* 4 the 'Six-year Annals'. However, the term 'concise' may be more precise since this text obviously condenses some of the material from the reign of Hattušili. Furthermore, Melchert argues for a reduction in the year count within the text from six to five (C. H. Melchert, 'The Acts of Hattušili I', *JNES* 37 (1978): 1-22). For the texts of the 'concise' annals: F. Imparati and C. Saporetti, 'L'autobiografia di Hattušili I', *Studi Classici e Orientali* 14 (1965): 40-85. See Houwink ten Cate for a discussion of the priority of the text, ('The History of Warfare According to Hittite Sources: The Annals of Hattušiliš I', *Anatolica* 10 (1983): 91-109); and Hoffner, *Or* 40 (1980): 294.

49. See J. Friedrich, *HW*, p. 45. For the Hittite reading see E. Neu and H. Otten, *Indogermanische Forschungen* 77 (1972): 181-190. One can compare the Hebrew גבורה, as in I Kings 16:27: As for the other events of Omri what he did וגבורתו אשר עשה (and his 'manly deeds' which he achieved), are they not written in annals of the kings of Israel (למלכי ישראל רברי הימים)?

50. Güterbock, 'Hittite Historiography', p. 31.

51. This is also the case for another work of this king, 'The Political Testament of Hattušili': see F. Sommer and A. Falkenstein, *Die hethitisch-akkadische Bilingue des Hattušili I.*

52. Kempinski and Košak, *Tel Aviv* 9 (1982): 109. In this regard, cf. the discussion of the Egyptian *iw.tw* texts in the next chapter 4.

53. Kempinski and Košak speculate 'that the divine judgment on a quarrel between Hatti and Purušhanda was not fit to be inscribed on the statue dedicated to the Sungoddess of Arinna, perhaps because the judgment was passed by another deity, or for some other theological or political reason' (*Ibid.*, p. 110, n. 5).

54. *Ibid.*, p. 110. Kempinski and Košak state: 'That the conquest of Syria took place in stages over many years (and was certainly not accomplished in a single year) can be adduced from the Extensive Annals where the campaign around Hatra and Sukzija alone took at least two years ("he [the Hurrian] wintered in Sukzija" II 36)'. The 'Concise' Annals do not use precise chronological phrases, but instead only generally mark off the episodes with the phrases: *ana balāṭ* :: 'in the next year', and MU.IM.MA-*an-ni-ma* :: 'in the following year'. A. Goetze suggested that the Hittite scribe may have misunderstood the Sumerian MU.IM.MA (= Akkadian *šaddaqda* :: 'the previous year') and thought that it was the equivalent to the Akkadian *ana balāṭ* :: 'in the next year' (*JCS* 16 (1962): 24ff). Hoffner adds that if this is

the case, 'the same mistake was not made in all copies of the Hittite version, for *KBo* X 3 i 15 ("D") has MU-*an-n*[*i-ma*], just as Muršili II in his Ten-Year Annals' (*Or* 49 (1980): 295, n. 47). Thus the text does not employ a strict chronology.

55. This episode may have also been included in the last column of the 'Extensive' Annals which unfortunately is not preserved.

56. Hoffner, *Or* 49 (1980): 294. We would certainly lean towards the Hittite version.

57. See: Kümmel, *TUAT* II/5 p. 461.

58. A. Goetze, *Die Annalen des Muršiliš*, pp. 14-137; H. Otten, 'Neue Fragmente zu den Annalen des Muršili', *MIO* 3 (1955): 161-165.

59. See H. Cancik, *Grundzüge der hethitischen und alttestamentlichen Geschichtsschreibung*, pp. 4-22.

60. Güterbock, 'Hittite Historiography', p. 32. One could speculate that there were individual campaign reports.

61. See Güterbock, 'The Deeds of Suppiluliuma as Told by His Son, Muršili II', *JCS* 10 (1956): 98.

62. Hoffner, *Or* 40 (1980): 313.

63. *Apasa*. 'Ephesus or perhaps some site in the vicinity of Izmir', *Repertoire Geographique des Texte Cuneiformes*, p. 26. See also J. Garstang and O.R. Gurney, *The Geography of the Hittite Empire*, p. 88.

64. *Piyama*-KAL. The deity's name is uncertain. KAL reflects the standard reading of the cuneiform (see: Kümmel, *TUAT*, II/5 p. 475, n. 22a).

65. *gur-ša-u-wa-na-an-za*. The word is an hapax. Friedrich suggested a 'ship' (*HW*, p. 59). Kümmel suggests that it may be an island on the coast of Asia Minor (*TUAT*, II/5 p. 475, n. 31a).

66. Puhvel, *HED*, p. 235.

67. For the text, see A. Goetze, *Die Annalen des Muršiliš*, pp. 128-131. *KBo* IV 4 Rs III.43-51. Also for this context see: E. von Schuler, *Die Kaškäer. Ein Beitrag zur Ethnographie des Alten Kleinsasien*, pp. 28ff.

68. See: Goetze, *Die Annalen des Muršiliš*, p. 138-139. *KBo* IV 4 Rs IV.28-37.

69. H.G. Güterbock, 'The Deeds of Suppiluliuma as Told by His Son, Muršili II', *JCS* 10 (1956): 41-50; 59-68; 75-85; 90-98; 107-130.

70. Hittite: *Suppiluliumaš* LÚ-*nannaš* (the Genitive plural of LÚ-*natar*)— hence, 'the manly deeds of Suppiluliuma'.

71. A number of other episodes in the narrative show the same syntagms (e.g. Fragment 43, p. 115). However, they are too fragmentary

to include here. Coincidentally, the Kaškaean enemy consisted of 12 tribes!

72. Following the reading of the text of G (line 3ff).

73. Note the irony conveyed by the use of the term *pangarit* in lines 12 and 18.

74. Occasionally, the opinion is voiced that Hittite historiography, particularly the annals, served as the basis for the development of Assyrian annalistic writing. But this is exaggerated, if not misleading. Each developed independently of the other (see: P. Machinist, 'Assyrians and Hittites in the Late Bronze Age', in *Mesopotamien und seine Nachbarn*, p. 267).

## NOTES TO CHAPTER FOUR
(pp. 165-194)

1. See: A. de Selincourt (tr.), *Herodotus: The Histories*, p. 131.

2. L. Bull, 'Ancient Egypt', in *The Idea of History in the Ancient Near East*, p. 32. In a similar way, R.A. Wilson argued that the Egyptians' concept of history was so primitive that it never led to a type of 'real' history writing (as compared to the Greeks) (*The Culture of Ancient Egypt*, p. 314). While Wilson was not denying the possibility of history writing among the Egyptians, the essence of the argument, nevertheless, leads to almost the same conclusion.

3. H. Gese, 'Geschichtliches Denken im Alten Orient', *ZThK* 55 (1958): 128. See also, H. Cancik, *Grundzüge der hethitischen und alttestamentlichen Geschichtsschreibung*, p. 3. Both base their arguments on Bull's assessment.

4. Van Seters, *In Search of History*, pp. 127-128.

5. *Ibid.*, pp. 128-187.

6. R.J. Williams, 'A People Come Out of Egypt: An Egyptologist Looks at the Old Testament', *VTS* 28 (1974): 321-32.

7. For example, a number of motifs relating to warfare and enemies in the OT have been influenced by their Egyptian counterparts; see now, J.K. Hoffmeier, 'Some Egyptian Motifs Related to Warfare and Enemies and Their Old Testament Counterparts', in *Egyptological Miscellanies: A Tribute to Professor Ronald J. Williams*, pp. 53-70.

8. M. Lichtheim, 'Ancient Egypt: A Survey of Current Historiography', *AHR* 69 (1963-1964): 30-41, esp. 40.

9. For example, B.C. Trigger, B.J. Kemp, D. O'Connor, and A.B. Lloyd, *Ancient Egypt: A Social History*. Cambridge, 1983.

10. E. Otto, 'Geschichtsbild and Geschichtsschreibung in Ägypten', *WO* 3/3 (1964/1966): 161-176.

11. *Ibid.*, p. 161.

12. *Ibid.*, p. 163.

13. Van Seters, *In Search of History*, p. 129.

14. A. Hermann, *Die ägyptische Königsnovelle*; S. Herrmann, 'Die Königsnovelle in Ägypten und in Israel', *Wissenschaftliche Zeitschrift der Karl-Marx Universität Leipzig* 3 (1953/54): 51-62; and '2 Samuel VII in the Light of the Egyptian Königsnovelle—Reconsidered', in *Pharaonic Egypt*, pp. 119-128.

15. W. Helck, *Untersuchungen zu Manetho und den ägyptischen Königslisten*.

16. Donald B. Redford, *Pharaonic King-Lists, Annals and Day-Books*. See also the review of E. Hornung, *BiOr* 45 (1988): 108.

17. Redford demonstrates that the Egyptian word *gnwt*, which is commonly translated 'annals', developed over the centuries of Egyptian history into a broad category which included cosmogonic myths that narrated the 'historical' reigns of the gods (*Pharaonic King-lists*, pp. 67-96). The 'so-called' *Annals* of Thutmose III were not called *gnwt*; but were classified as a *wḏ*. They were built, in part, upon the day-book tradition.

18. E. Otto, *Die biographischen Inschriften der ägyptischen Spätzeit*.

19. Van Seters, *In Search of History*, pp. 127-187.

20. See bibliography.

21. Grapow, *Studien*, pp. 61-63. He posited two areas from which the *iw.tw* formula originated. (1) the Egyptian scribes evolved the phrase *iw.tw r ḏd n ḥm.f* :: 'One came to say to his majesty' from similar phrases common in literary texts of the Middle Kingdom in order to introduce the military action as quickly as possible. (2) the scribes utilized the MK epistolary style for the recording of a military campaign: *iw.tw r ḏd* :: 'One came to say'. The scribe was faced with providing 'a terse account of the military venture of the king with all the concomitant facts included. Recorded mainly on stelae, which do not allow for a lengthy or verbose description, the *iw.tw* reports quickly became rather bland and often stereotyped ... they recorded the military activity of the king briefly, within a set format' (*Aspects of the Military Documents of the Ancient Egyptians* {Henceforth: *Aspects*}, p. 1).

22. Spalinger, *Aspects*, p. 20.

23. *Ibid.*, p. 20.

24. Spalinger discusses the Kamose Stelae in the context of the development of the *iw.tw* form stating: 'the tradition of the Kamose Stelae, with their 1st person narration and literary style, was abandoned by the Egyptian scribes together with the form behind the royal boun-

dary stelae. Instead, the Egyptians developed from the classical epistolary form a message report which was employed as brief accounts of campaigns in which the Pharaoh rarely participated at the head of his army ... For small historical narratives, the *iw.tw* report served well. For longer texts, and those wars in which the king personally led his army, the style of the Kamose Stelae was abandoned' (p. 47).

25. *Ibid.*, p. 48ff.

26. *Ibid.*, p. 49.

27. See *Ibid.*, pp. 70-75. Spalinger does not, of course, conclude that this is a high-redundance message. This is our interpretation of his data. Furthermore, we are not arguing that the *iw.tw* texts are exact equivalents to the phenomenon in the Assyrian and Hittite annalistic tradition. But it is evident that the *iw.tw* texts followed a very strict style of stereotyped syntagms; and it is because of this that we label they as forming a high-redundance message, the apparatus for disseminating the Egyptian royal ideology.

28. Redford, however, rejects completely the idea of a scribal war diary/daybook—a 'Kriegstagebuch'. He argues against the leather roll as evidence of a war journal and also the autobiographical statement of the scribe Tjaneny (*Pharaonic King-lists, Annals, and Day-books*, pp. 121-126).

29. *Urk.* IV, 661.14-662.2. Lit. 'On the day in its name, in the name of the journey, and in the names of the commanders of [troops]'. In the Theban tomb biography of 'the Army Scribe' Tjaneni, who served under Thutmose III (*Urk.* IV.1004), we read: 'I was the one who set down the victories which he achieved over every foreign country, put into writing as it was done'. See: Wilson, *ANET*, p. 237, n. 39.

30. *Urk.* IV, 662.5-6.

31. Spalinger, *Aspects*, p. 140.

32. *Ibid.*, p. 123. For other examples of the terse style, see P. Anastasi I (1,6) and (2,5-6) in Gardiner, *Egyptian Hieratic Texts I*, pp. 6 and 12.

33. Noth, 'Die Annalen Thutmose III. als Geschichtsquelle', *ZDPV* 66 (1943): 156-174; and Grapow, *Studien zu den Annalen Thutmosis des Dritten und zu ihnen verwandten historischen Berichten des Neuen Reiches*.

34. Redford correctly points out that it is a mistake to use the occurrence of this infinitival construction as a mechanical criterion (*Pharaonic King-lists*, p. 122).

35. *Aspects*, pp. 126-128. He notes that two later inscriptions also are of this type: the Piye Stela and the Dream Stela of Tanwetamani (p. 128).

36. See note 28.

37. Amenemope xxi.9ff states: *m-ỉr ỉr n.k h'rw n 'ḏ' st štmw ° n mwt st 'nḫyw " n sḏf-tryt st n smtr n wḥmw* :: 'do not make false journal entries, for that is a serious capital offence. They (involve) serious oaths of allegiance (?), and are destined for criminal investigation'. See in connection with the 'oaths of allegiance', D. Lorton, *The Juridical Terminology of International Relations in Egyptian Texts through Dyn. XVIII*, p. 132.

38. Aharoni, 'Some Geographical Remarks Concerning the Campaigns of Amenhotep II', *JNES* 19 (1960): 177-178.

39. Spalinger, *Aspects*, p. 148.

40. This does not mean that there will not be problems in the interpretation of the data. For example, while Daybook Reports were employed in the writing of *Stück* I of the *Annals*, there is still a problem concerning the actual date of the battle of Megiddo. For the two differing opinions see: Helck, *MDAIK* 28 (1972): 101-102; and Spalinger, *MDAIK* 30 (1974): 221-229.

41. Spalinger, *Aspects*, p. 152. The fact that poetic and narrative accounts (or if one prefers rhetorical and less rhetorical accounts) could originate from the same time period (if not even from the same author), should caution certain biblical critics from making quick hypothetical conclusions concerning the cases where a narrative and a poem about the same general subject occur side by side.

42. Gardiner, *The Kadesh Inscriptions of Ramesses II*, p. 20, n. to P 110.

43. Spalinger, *Aspects*, pp. 166-173.

44. *Ibid.*, p. 173.

45. *Ibid.*, pp. 200-206.

46. Breasted comments: 'This important inscription offers no sober narrative of the events which it commemorates, but is written in that fulsome style so often found in victorious hymns of the Pharaohs. This is a style so overloaded with far-fetched figures and unfamiliar words that it is often quite unintelligible' (*BAR* II, pp. 28-29).

47. The division is more one of degree: the more poetic texts as opposed to the less rhetorical. Thus in *Stücke* V-VI in the midst of tribute and booty lists, one finds the more detailed account of Year 33 (the Mitanni campaign during which Thutmose crossed the Euphrates and erected his stela (Faulkner, *JEA* 32 (1946): 39-42). This can be seen to reflect a 'literary perspective containing more verbiage than facts. In fact, that section of *Stücke* V-VI parallels other records of Thutmose III of a nature more eloquent than sober (the Gebel Barkal and Armant Stelae)' (Spalinger, *JARCE* 14 (1977): 44). Thus 'Thutmose III interrupts the consistent, almost repetitious account of *Stück*

V of the *Annals* to tell of his sailing on the Euphrates and the erecting of a stela there. In fact, the latter half of Thutmose's *Annals* presents a rather formalized arrangement of the wars of Thutmose except for one or two narrative sections. Significantly, the land of Naharain is mentioned in the latter sections (e.g. *Urk*. IV.710-711.2; year thirty-four) almost as if the Egyptian scribes wished to stress the importance of their monarch's military campaigns in that area'. (Spalinger, 'A New Reference To An Egyptian Campaign of Thutmose III in Asia', *JNES* 37 (1978): 40.

48. I. Shirun-Grumach, 'Die Poetischen Teile der Gebel-Barkal-Stele', in *Scripta Hierosolymitana: Egyptological Studies*, pp. 117-186. In connection with the Gebel Barkal Stela, one must also add the Poetical Stela.

49. Spalinger, *Aspects*, p. 199.

50. *Ibid.*, p. 234-236.

51. *Ibid.*, p. 224.

52. See *Wb* II, p. 317.5; *CDME* p. 139.

53. Spalinger, *Aspects*, p. 228.

54. *Urk*. IV, 1244.15. Cp. the Hittite word *pišnadar* which means literally 'manliness', hence 'Manly Deeds'. Grapow felt that Thutmose III's *Annals* were nothing more than elaborate *Heldentaten* (See: Grapow, *Studien*, p. 6).

55. Concerning the god giving victories to Pharaoh, see Morenz, *Egyptian Religion*, p. 61, n. 24.

56. The concluding lines of *Stücke* V-VI state: 'Now, his majesty commanded the establishment of this inscription (*wḏ*) upon this temple' (*Urk*. IV, 734.13-16). Thus, *Stücke* V-VI could not have been finished before Year 42. Spalinger argues: 'Now, if the connections between the two major divisions of the Annals are as close as I have described, then might one not maintain that they were composed at the same time? After all, Years 24 and 40 on *Stück* I were written in the style of the later reports of *Stücke* V-VI and the reference to Year 40 would imply a date after Year 39.... Now, if *Stück* I of the *Annals* was drawn up as a unit on this north wall and thereby included the reports for Years 23, 24 and 40, then it must have been composed at a time contemporary with *Stücke* V-VI as well as with the decision of Thutmose III to dishonor his stepmother <Hatshepsut>. This new policy of the Pharaoh occurred significantly at the time when Thutmose III ceased from actively campaigning abroad. This complex analysis of the *Annals* of Thutmose III derives from the inherent difficulties in elucidating the date of composition of Egyptian inscriptions. To the Egyptian scribes, *Stück* I and *Stücke* V-VI belonged together. Even though all their king's deeds were not inscribed on the temple walls

of Karnak and even though all the *Annals*—not to mention *Stücke* V-VI alone— were written in quite different styles, the Egyptian composers had piously fulfilled their purpose' (Spalinger, *JARCE* 14 (1977): 52).

57. Spalinger, *JARCE* 14 (1977): 48 and 50-51.

58. *Urk*. IV, 1244.18.

59. S. Morenz, *Egyptian Religion*, p. 11. He also notes that once the king has departed from the path of order, the deity punishes this violation in accordance with an almost biblical theodicy. Egypt is, of course, not unique in this emphasis on the monarchy being the subject of historical writing.

60. E. Hornung, *Der Eine und die Vielen*, p. 186.

61. *Ibid*., p. 188.

62. For example, see: the Poetical Stela: *Urk*. IV, 610-619 (lines 23-25).

63. The Great Sphinx Stela at Giza: *Urk*. IV, 1276.17-21.

64. Hornung, *Der Eine und die Vielen*, p. 188.

65. The Great Sphinx Stela at Giza: *Urk*. IV, 1276-1283, line 5ff.

66. Beth-Shan Stela of Ramesses II. See J. Černý, 'Stela of Ramesses II from Beisan', in *EI* 5 (1958): 75-82. (lines 15-17).

67. See K.A. Kitchen, 'Interrelations of Egypt and Syria', in *La Siria del Tardo Bronzo*, p. 82.

68. *KRI* IV, 17.2-4; 19.1.

69. J.K. Hoffmeier, 'Some Egyptian Motifs', p. 53.

70. David O'Connor, 'New Kingdom and the Third Intermediate Period, 1552-664 B.C.', in *Ancient Egypt: A Social History*, pp. 194-195.

71. *Urk*. IV, 84.3; 613.16. *Wb*. II, 247.5.

72. See: A.H. Gardiner, *AEO I*, p. 134.

73. *Wb* II, 247,4-5.

74. *CDME*, p. 130.

75. Hoffmeier, 'Some Egyptian Motifs', p. 55.

76. Thutmose III, *Annals*: *Urk*. IV,645.20 and in passim.

77. *CDME*, p. 204.

78. Cf. the common epithet 'vile Kush'. Also see D. Lorton, 'The So-Called 'Vile' Enemies of the King of Egypt (in the Middle Kingdom and Dyn. XVIII', *JARCE* 10 (1973): 65-70.

79. Text: L. Habachi, *The Second Stela of Kamose*, pp. 31-44. W. Helck, *Historisch-Biographische Texte der 2. Zwischenzeit und neue Texte der 18. Dynastie*, pp. 82-97. Translation: J.A. Wilson, *ANET*, pp. 554-555. Studies: H. and A. Smith, *RKT*, 48-76; Barta, *BiOr* 32 (1975): 287-290; Gitton, *BiOr* 31 (1974): 249-251; Spalinger, *Aspects*, pp. 193-199.

80. Smith and Smith point out that lines 1-3 comprise a taunting speech of Kamose to Apophis. It is formally proved by the alternation of second person singular pronouns (*ḏmi.k, tw.k tf.ti, mšʿ.k, r.k, ỉr.k, ỉw.k, n.k, ḥrt.k, sʾ.k*) with first person singular pronouns (*wỉ, mšʿ.i*), and by the prophesying character of the sentence containing the two future negatives *nn ỉwr, nn sn* (*RKT*, p. 51).

81. Habachi states: '*Whm* must be the mason's error for *whỉ*' (p. 36, n. d). Also *CDME*, s.v. *whỉ* :: 'be undone of heart', Kamose 11 (p. 65).

82. *KRI* IV, 14.10-16.10.

83. The name of the Libyan ruler.

84. Lichtheim comments: 'The god Seth was viewed as the protector of the foreign peoples to the east and west of Egypt. Here the god has turned against Libya' (*AEL* II, p. 78, n. 7).

85. Cf. Joshua 10:16ff.

86. Gebel Barkal Stela states:

> There is no flight (since) they trust in many troops,
> (since) there is no limit in men and horses.
> They have come stout-hearted,
> no terror is in their hearts.

87. Amenhotep III, Assuan Philae Road Stela: *Urk*. IV, 1666.13.

88. See Spalinger, *Aspects*, pp. 52-55.

89. Thutmose IV, Konosso Stela: *Urk*. IV, 1547.20. See: Spalinger, *Aspects*, p. 54).

90. Spalinger, *JARCE* 14 (1977): 50.

91. *Ibid*., pp. 50-51. See also *Aspects*, pp. 56-58. In the latter half of Dynasty XVIII the Egyptian scribes preferred the more common lexical item *ḳ'y* 'to plan', in place of *wʾ*. For *ḳ'y*, see: (1) Thutmose II—*Urk*. IV, 138.14; (2) Thutmose IV—*Urk*. IV, 1542.12; (3) Amenhotep III—*Urk*. IV, 1666.4 and 1959.17; (4) Amenhotep IV—*Urk*. IV, 1963.11; Seti I—*KRI* I, 102.14/15; (6) Ramesses III—*KRI* III, 26.1 and 69.14; and (7) Psammetichus III—Sauneron and Yoyotte, *BIFAO* 52 (1950): 174 and p. III.

92. Amenhotep III, Assuan Philae Stela: *Urk*. IV, 1666.4.

93. Seti I, Nubian War Texts: *KRI* I 102.14-15.

94. Ramesses III, Medinet Habu Wall Text: *KRI* V 12.3.

95. Following Redford, 'The Historical Retrospective at the Beginning of Thutmose III's Annals', in *Festschrift Elmar Edel*, pp. 338-342.

96. Or 'criminal activity'. Cf. H. Goedicke, *The Report about the Dispute of a Man with his Ba*, pp. 162ff.

97. Redford, *Festschrift Elmar Edel*, p. 340, n. 12.

98. The phrase, 'the garrison which was there', appears to refer to Egyptian troops in Asia, see: Redford, *Festschrift Elmar Edel*, p. 339, n. 6.

99. Where the troops had been before this is difficult to say. Byblos is perhaps a possibility (See: Helck, *AfO* 22 (1969): 27. The town of Sharuhen is mentioned in the inscription of Ahmose, son of Ebana (Wilson, *ANET*, p. 233; see also Goedicke, *JARCE* 11 (1974): 31-41). The traditional identification of Sharuhen is Tell el-Far'ah (Wilson, *ANET*, p. 233, n. 12). But recently an identification of Sharuhen with Tell el-'Ajjul has been suggested: A. Kempinski, 'Tell el 'Ajjul Beth-Aglayim or Sharuhen', *IEJ* 24 (1974): 145-152; and J.R. Stewart, *Tell el-'Ajjul: The Middle Bronze Remains* (1974), pp. 62-63; and James M. Weinstein, 'The Egyptian Empire in Palestine: A Reassessment', *BASOR* 241 (1981): 6, 18.

100. Spalinger states: 'At the beginning of *Stück* I and before the historical narration, this phrase serves a similar function to that of the *w'* clauses in the message reports' (*Aspects*, p. 57).

101. See: Redford, *Festschrift Elmar Edel*, p. 341; and Helck, *Beziehungen*, p. 120.

102. This concept of passivity has been amply covered by Hornung, especially in his *Geschichte als Fest*.

103. See Spalinger, *Aspects*, p. 232.

104. Thutmose III, Gebel Barkal Stela, *Urk*. 17, 1230.1-4.

105. The Egyptian attitude toward the Hyksos and their Egyptian allies can be seen in the following words of Kamose: 'I destroyed their towns, burning their abodes which are made into desert mounds forever, because of the damage which they have done within Egypt, who set themselves to hearken to the summons of the Asiatics, after they had wronged Egypt their mistress' (See Habachi, *The Second Stela of Kamose*, (lines 17-18).

106. This is the case whether one feels that the Hyksos were 'Hurrian' or 'Semitic'! For an example of one who argues that the Hyksos were not of Semitic stock but were Hurrians and feels that this explains why the Egyptian expansion already under Thutmose I had Mitanni as its military goal, see: Helck, *Die Beziehungen Ägyptens zu Vorderasien im 3. und 2. Jahrtausend v. Chr.*$^2$, pp. 110-116; and OA 8 (1969): 310-311). For arguments against this view, see: Van Seters,

*The Hyksos: a New Investigation*, pp. 181-185; and D. Redford, 'The Hyksos Invasion in History and Tradition', *Or* 39 (1970): 1-51.

107. This is clear from the captured letter of the Hyksos ruler Apophis to the ruler of Kush as recorded in the Second Stela of Kamose (lines 18-24).

108. Trigger, *Nubia Under the Pharaohs*, p. 103.

109. For example, the military architecture utilized the forts along the 'Ways of Horus' in northern Sinai was similar to that used in fortifications in Nubia. And in both places the sites served as administrative and cultic centers. See: E. Oren, 'The 'Ways of Horus' in North Sinai'. In *Egypt, Israel, Sinai: Archaeological and Historical Relationships in the Biblical Period* (Ed. by A.F. Rainey. Tel Aviv, 1987), pp. 69-119.

110. P.J. Frandsen, 'Egyptian Imperialism', in Power and Propaganda: A Symposium on Ancient Empires, p. 177. Also see Hayes, *CAH* II[3], pp. 346-353; R. Giveon, *The Impact of Egypt on Canaan*; and D. Redford, *Akhenaten: The Heretic King*, pp. 23-27, and 193-203.

111. *Ibid.*, p. 169.

112. T. Säve-Söderbergh, *Ägypten und Nubien*, pp. 12-25.

113. P.L. Shinnie states: 'This period marks the real beginning of urban development in the region, and though its impact on native life is hard to assess, it seems to have been considerable. These towns served as centres from which Egyptian influences penetrated the countryside and the number of them (there were towns at Sesibi, Kawa, and Napata, in addition to those already mentioned) meant that the whole rural population could now be in touch with centres of a sophisticated urban culture' ('Urbanism in the Ancient Sudan', in *Glimpses of Ancient Egypt*, p. 124).

114. Frandsen, 'Egyptian Imperialism', p. 171. Concerning the Egyptian economy as redistribution, see Janssen, *SÄK* 3 (1975): 183-185.

115. *Ibid.*, pp. 173-174. But according to Frandsen, this exploitation may not have been any different than that in any other area (even Egypt itself): 'Contrary to the usual idea of a unilateral exploitation of Nubia on the part of its conqueror I am suggesting that Nubia was no more exploited than any other region of considerable economic potentialities in Egypt itself'.

116. *Ibid.*, p. 175.

117. Redford remarks: 'The Egyptian term 'to cause (the vassal) to eat the *tryt*' (whatever that was) may originally have indicated some kind of ritual that accompanied the swearing ceremony; but the oath itself was a simple promise, taken in the king's name, to be loyal and not rebel. Because the obligation was personal, each new pharaoh upon

his accession had to reimpose the oath, employing his own throne-name' (*Akhenaten: The Heretic King*, p. 25).

118. D. Lorton, *The Juridical Terminology of International Relations in Egyptian Texts Through Dynasty XVIII*, p. 178.

119. The Gebel Barkal Stela (*Urk.* IV, 1235.14-18). For more indirect evidence, see Weinfeld, 'The Loyalty Oath in the Ancient Near East', *UF* 8 (1976): 413; and W. Helck, *Die Beziehungen*², p. 246. For the Egyptian use of the term *bryt* in the political context, see Kitchen, 'Egypt, Ugarit, Qatna and Covenant', *UF* 11 (1979): 453-464, esp. pp. 453-457. For a very interesting interpretation of the data, see M. Liverani, 'Le lettere del faraone a Rib-Adda', *OA* 10 (1971): 253-268.

120. D. Lorton, *The Judicial Terminology*, p. 176.

121. See K.A. Kitchen, 'Interrelations of Egypt and Syria', p. 80. See also, the group of Hieratic Ostraca from Tel Sera': O. Goldwasser, 'Hieratic Inscriptions From Tel Sera' in Southern Canaan', *Tel Aviv* 11 (1984): 77-93. Goldwasser states concerning one of the texts: 'This appears to constitute the documentation of the *šmw* (harvest tax) paid by one of the city-states in the Negev to an Egyptian religious institution, and it may provide the explanation for the mixed character of our finds, namely texts of an *administrative* nature written on *votive* bowls' (p. 86).

122. *Ibid.*, p. 81. Frandsen disagrees arguing that the evidence which Kitchen uses 'applies in fact only to the Egyptian domains' (p. 188, n. 63). But we see nothing in the texts which contradicts Kitchen's interpretation. Moreover, the evidence from Tel Sera' seems to support Kitchen's view (see previous note).

123. According to W. Helck: 'Ganz anders war der Aufbau der Verwaltung in den ägyptischen Besitzungen in Asien. Dabei dürfen wir wohl die Zustände, wie sie durch die Amarnabriefe bekannt sind, auch für die Zeit Thutmosis' III. annehmen: Es bestanden 3 Provinzen: Kanaan mit der Hauptstadt Gaza, Upe mit Kumidi, Amurru mit Simyra an der Eleutherosmündung. Dort amtierten ägyptische „Vorsteher der nördlichen Fremdländer" (akkadisch „*rabiṣu*" genannt), jedoch blieb die Verwaltung der einzelnen Stadt-staaten fast vollständig in der Hand der einheimischen Fürsten' (*Geschichte des alten Ägypten*, p. 157); *MDOG* 92 (1960): 5; and *Beziehungen*², p. 256.

124. *Ibid.*, p. 83. See also Frandsen, 'Egyptian Imperialism', p. 177. Obviously, many Egyptian customs were adopted. But there was also a great degree of Asiatic influence on Egypt too. Kitchen enumerates and discusses some of the areas of 'give and take' (see, pp. 83-94).

125. Trigger, *Nubia Under the Pharaohs*, pp. 109-110. While the Egyptians may have had some respect for the Asiatic peoples, when it came to conquest accounts, the Asiatics were, nevertheless, character-

ized as 'vile, evil, wretched ...' because the Egyptian ideology dictated these categories.

126. This pragmatic reason is mentioned by Drower who states: '... to introduce into Syria the whole machinery of Egyptian government would have put too great a strain on manpower, even had it been wise' (*CAH* II[3], p. 468).

127. See Frandsen, 'Egyptian Imperialism', p. 179.

128. Kemp, 'The Early Development of Towns in Egypt', *Antiquity* 51 (1977): 185-200. And 'Fortified Towns in Nubia', in *Settlement and Urbanism*, p. 654.

129. The outer walls at Abydos and Luxor which record the battle of Kadesh are certainly two examples among many which could be cited.

130. In the former case, L. Bull, 'The Egyptian Idea of History', pp.1-34. In the latter case, Van Seters, *In Search of History*, pp. 156-157.

131. *Urk.* IV, 697.3, despite the opening lacuna.

132. Grapow, *Studien*, pp. 21-22 and 57-58. *Urk.* IV, 1232.5 (Gebel Barkal Stela) is similar to *Urk.* IV, 697.12 and *Urk.* IV, 1247.4 (the Armant Stela) is similar to *Urk.* IV, 697.14; see also *Urk.* IV, 1232.11-12 and 1245.20-1246.2 and Sethe's part restoration in *Urk.* IV, 697.3-5. See also the Seventh Pylon text: *Urk.* IV, 188.15-189.15.—Spalinger, *JARCE* 14 (1977): 53, n. 28.

133. Spalinger, *JARCE* 14 (1977): 46-47.

134. *Ibid.*, p. 49.

135. See Gardiner, *Gram*, p. 81, § 106.

136. 'Politiche Planung und Realität im alten Ägypten', *Saeculum* 22 (1971): 48-58; esp. pp. 57-58.

137. *Urk.* IV.103-104. See also Gardiner, *AEO* I, pp. 158-159.

138. *Urk.* IV.1233.13ff; and University Museum of the University of Pennsylvania number 39-12-3 (line x + 2) (see: A. Spalinger, 'A New Reference to an Egyptian Campaign of Thutmose III in Asia', *JNES* 37 (1978): 35-41).

139. *Urk.* IV.1662.12.

140. *KRI* IV, 15.7.

141. Beth-Shan Stela of Ramesses II. See J. Černý, 'Stela of Ramesses II from Beisan', in *EI* 5 (1958): 75-82. (lines 11-13).

142. As depicted by Wilson, 'The Language of the Historical Texts Commemorating Ramses III', in *OIC* 7 (1930): 24-25. Spalinger cites the Tombos Inscription of Thutmose I (*Urk.* IV, 82.9-86) as support (*Aspects*, p. 45).

143. Thutmose III, Gebel Barkal Stela: I.20-II.4.

144. Thutmose III, Gebal Barkal Stela (lines 5-7): G.A. Reisner and M.B. Reisner, *ZÄS* 69 (1933): 24-39.

145. Merenptah, 'Israel' Stela: *KRI*, IV, 19.5-7.

146. Spalinger, *Aspects*, p. 77.

147. Hatshepsut, Deir El Bahri Fragment: Naville, *The Temple of Deir El Bahari VI*, pl. 165.

148. Thutmose III, List of Southern Lands: *Urk.* IV, 795.9-10.

149. Thutmose III, Gebel Barkal Stela: *Urk.* IV, 1230.9.

150. Amenhotep II, Karnak Eighth Pylon: *Urk.* IV, 1333.15.

151. Piye Stela: *Urk.* III, 10.14 (also found 3 more times in this stela).

152. For this figure see Hoffmeier, 'Some Egyptian Motifs', pp. 63-64.

153. Hoffmeier cites numerous examples from Egyptian art and from Middle Egyptian texts. For example, 'Sinuhe hails Senusret I as "one who extends the borders" (*swsh t'š*) by smiting (*hwi*) and trampling (*ptpt*) the enemies (A.M. Blackman, "Middle Egyptian Stories," *Bibliotheca Aegyptiaca II*, (1932) B71-73)' (p. 64).

154. 'God's land' was a vague designation of regions south and east of Egypt and included the land of Punt.

155. H.H. Nelson, *Medinet Habu*, Vol. I, plate 36.

156. Hoffmeier notes that this idea of trampling the enemy and his territory strikes a familiar note when we consider several Old Testament passages. In Joshua 1:3 God tells the Israelites: 'Every place that the sole of your foot will tread upon I will give it to you'. He concludes: 'This seems to have been the rationale of campaigning Egyptian kings. For the trampling of one's foes, consider the following references: "He (God) tramples kings under foot" (Psalm 60:12); "With God we shall do valiantly, it is he who will tread down our foes" (Psalm 108:13); "Through thee we push down our foes; through thy name we shall tread down our assailants" (Psalm 44:5) (p. 64). Cf. also Isa. 63:6' (p. 65).

157. See Spalinger's list for this term, *Aspects*, pp. 49-52.

158. See Grapow, *Studien*, pp. 45,49, and 70.

159. Thutmose II, Assuan Philae Inscription: *Urk.* IV, 140.6.

160. Amenhotep III, Assuan Philae Stela: *Urk.* IV, 1666.7. Here is a clear reference to the encounter between the enemy and the Pharaoh. Cf. also Ramesses II in the Kadesh 'Poem': 'I entered into the ranks fighting like the pounce of a falcon' (*KRI* II 86.1/5; P. 280).

## NOTES TO CHAPTER FIVE
(pp. 197-237)

1. W.W. Hallo, *Scripture in Context*, p. 5.

2. See: P. Stambovsky, *History and Theory* 27 (1988): 125-134.

3. Aššurbanipal: Prism A (Rassam) I.78-80. M. Streck, *Aššurbanipal*, I, pp. 56-60 {first campaign}.

4. Annals of Tiglath-Pileser I, (II.100-II.6). See *AKA*, pp. 48-49.

5. J.M. Grintz concludes that in broad terms the treaty which Israel made with the Gibeonites was one of the protégé type, 'since the Gibeonite cities had not been captured in fighting ...' ('The Treaty of Joshua with the Gibeonites', *JAOS* 86 (1966): 125). See also Boling, p. 271.

6. On the general historicity of the treaty see F.C. Fensham, 'The Treaty Between Israel and the Gibeonites', *BA* 27 (1964): 96-100; J.M. Grintz, *JAOS* 86 (1966): 113-126; B. Halpern, *CBQ* 37 (1975): 308-310; and Soggin, p. 111ff.

7. A. Alt, 'Josua', *BZAW* 66 (1936): 19ff; K. Möhlenbrink, *ZAW* 56 (1938): 241ff.

8. Noth, *Das Buch Josua*, pp. 53-59, esp. 53. From the very first sentence of his discussion Noth asserts that the story is an etiology because of the ending phrase עד היום הזה, and acknowledges that in this he is following Gressmann and Alt. See our discussion of this phrase as a 'quick indicator' of an etiology (pp. 224-25 above and note 93 below).

9. J. Liver, 'The Literary History of Joshua IX', *JSS* 8 (1963): 227-243. See also Soggin, pp. 111-115. B. Halpern opts cautiously for this stating: 'Though reason exists to regard the Gibeonite ruse as fictitious—Saulide invention seems its most likely provenance—this judgment remains at best an informed hypothesis. It should be noted, therefore, that if in spite of other indications the ruse is historical, the compulsion remains for Jerusalem and the south to attack' (*CBQ* 37 (1975): 315, n. 43).

10. P. Kearney has argued that the ruse is the product of the Deuteronomist who fabricated it and inserted it into the narrative in order to historize the episode ['The Role of the Gibeonites in the Deuteronomic History', *CBQ* 35 (1973): 1-19]. While this is an obvious possibility, the material that we are investigating here seems to indicate that such an understanding may not be the best explanation. The use of craftiness and deception is not only encountered in ANE accounts of submissions, but is so much a part of political life that the biblical account of the Gibeonite ruse certainly could be historical.

11. Prism E: A.C. Piepkorn, *Historical Prism Inscriptions of Ashurbanipal*, pp. 8-17 + M. Cogan and H. Tadmor, 'Gyges and Ashurbanipal', *Or* 46 (1977): 65-84. For the order of the recensions, see H. Tadmor, 'The Last Three Decades of Assyria', in *The Proceedings of the 25th International Congress of Orientalists*, pp. 240-242. R. Gelio has traced this episode through the different recensions ('La Délégation Envoyée par Gygés, Roi de Lydie: un Cas de Propagande idéologique', in *ARINH*, pp. 203-224).

12. C.J. Gadd called the dream 'the fiction of an ambassador' (*Ideas of Divine Rule in the Ancient East*, p. 25, n. 5), a designation which A.L. Oppenheim violently rejects ('The Interpretation of Dreams in the Ancient Near East', p. 202). Oppenheim points out that typologically the dream of Gyges corresponds to the dreams of the allies of Hattuši-li. Moreover, he asserts that the dream-story was inserted into the annals solely to exemplify and to extol the power of the mere name of the Assyrian king (p. 202). But in either case, the account of the dream is a type of ruse. Finally, Gelio has recently argued that if the question whether the dream was real or whether it was the product of a literary fiction is put aside, one can see that the inclusion of the dream in the account is the product of a 'formula of priority' within the recensions of Aššurbanipal which has reinterpreted the events of the past. This formula of priority has two components: a historical-circumstantial component and ideological one which is tributary and interpretive of the former. Since the role of the formula of priority is legitimation of the royal aspirations, it has utilized the genre of the dream to an apologetic function as political propaganda for the legitimation and guarantee of the continuance of the dynasty ('La Délégation Envoyée par Gygès', in *ARINH*, pp. 203-224, esp. pp. 212-214, 223). Gelio is undoubtedly correct that the dream had an ideological function in the Assyrian texts. But this does not negate its pragmatic function in the transmission code of the historical narrative.

13. Prism A: II.111-125. Translation follows Cogan and Tadmor, pp. 65-84. Concerning the chronology, Millard states: 'c. 665 BC Gyges of Lydia solicited aid against Cimmerian invaders and repulsed them, then forfeited his claims on Assyria by helping Psammetichus of Egypt, and fell to Dugdamme [the Cimmerians' leader], c. 652 BC' ('The Scythian Problem', in *Glimpses of Ancient Egypt: Studies in Honour of H.W. Fairman*, p. 121).

14. While a ruse is not necessarily present, the thrust of a plea for mercy can be seen in the Annals of Aššur-nasir-pal II where we read: 'I approached the city of Suru which belongs to Bit-Halupe. The awe of the radiance of Aššur, my lord, overwhelmed them. The nobles (and) elders of the city came out to me to save their lives. They seized my feet and said: "If it pleases you, kill! If it pleases you, spare! If it pleases you, do whatever you will!"' (I.79-81). See: *AKA*, pp. 281-282; Grayson, *ARI* II, p. 124.

15. Goetze, *Die Annalen des Muršiliš*, pp. 66-73.

16. Col. IV.28-37. For the text, see A. Goetze, *Die Annalen des Muršiliš*, pp. 139ff. See also Col. III.43-51 and R. de Vaux, *The Early History of Israel*, p. 624.

17. See E. von Schuler, *Die Kaškäer. Ein Beitrag zur Ethnographie des Alten Kleinsasien*, pp. 28ff.

18. In this regard the loyalty oath (*adû*) to the Assyrian monarch is informative. The Assyrians often did not maintain control by stationing large garrisons, but relied on an efficient intelligence network. The same seems to be the case with the Gibeonite vassalage to Israel. Cf. Malbran-Labat, *L'armée et l'Organisation Militaire de l'Assyri*, pp. 31-40.

19. *KRI* V, pp. 58-66 (lines 38, 52).

20. Translation follows Kitchen, 'Egypt, Ugarit, Qatna and Covenant', *UF* 11 (1979): 453. See also Edgerton and Wilson, *Historical Records of Ramses III*, pp. 82 and 85.

21. M. Noth understood the narrative as an etiological 'Überlieferung' (*Das Buch Josua*, pp. 53-55). R.G. Boling argues that: 'There can be no doubt about the historicity of a treaty with the Gibeonites' (*Joshua*, p. 262).

22. Text: Goetze, *Die Annalen des Muršiliš*, pp. 156-159 (lines, III.11-40) + Ten Cate, *JNES* 25 (1966): 162-191. Translations: Gurney, *The Hittites*, p. 109.

23. See: Ten Cate, *JNES* 25 (1966): 168, 177 and 184.

24. On these phenomena in ancient Near Eastern and biblical texts, see now the fine work of M. Weinfeld, 'Divine Intervention in War in Ancient Israel and in the Ancient Near East', in *HHI*, pp. 121-147.

25. Cf. our presentation in chapter 3, pp. 125-27.

26. Hittite: *para ḫandandatar*. HW defines as 'göttliches Walten, Wunder'. A. Goetze notes that the phrase is peculiar to supernatural phenomena of salvation by the gods (*Kleinasien*², pp. 146, 148).

27. There is still uncertainty concerning the meaning of the term $^{\text{GIŠ}}$*kalmišana-*. *HW* defines the word as 'Donnerkeil' ('Thunderbolt') which it very well may be; although many interpreters prefer 'meteor'. Weinfeld prefers thunderbolt and attempts to trace its relation to the same in Ugaritic (see 'Divine Intervention in War', p. 139, and n. 34).

28. H. Wolf, *The Apology of Hattušiliš*, p. 34. Cf. also M. Weinfeld, 'Divine Intervention in War', p. 139, n. 93.

29. Although this is not explicitly stated, the fact that the 'meteor' struck the land and specifically the capital city, Apasa, it seems very probable that there were casualties.

30. Text: W. Mayer, *MDOG* 115 (1983): 82-83, lines 141-152.

31. *AHw*, p. 911-912, s.v. *qatû* 'vernichten'.

32. Cf. Millard's discussion, *TB* 36 (1985): 61-77, esp. pp. 74ff.

33. This calls into question the understanding of L. Roussel who felt that the account was a legend inspired by scattered large stones so that the miracle was 'très folkorique' (*Le Livre de Josué*, pp. 97-98).

34. For example, A.G. Auld states: 'Verses 12 to 14 <chapter 10> seem to be a separate piece of information. They read rather like an appendix, but what they report is far from peripheral. In fact it is rather like an alternative account. In verse 11 God's weapons are great hailstones; in verses 12-14, a stopping of sun and moon in their tracks ... we are dealing here with alternative memories of divine action ...' (*Joshua, Judges, and Ruth*, pp. 69-70). Cf. Butler, *Joshua*, p. 111; and Boling, *Joshua*, p. 282.

35. See M. Cogan and H. Tadmor, 'Ahaz and Tiglath-Pileser in the Book of Kings: Historiographic Considerations', in *EI* 14 (1978): 55-57 <Hebrew>.

36. For a similar example of flashback introduced by אז, see: 10:33.

37. For example, P.F. Ceuppens states: 'L'arrêt du soleil et la prolongation du jour ne constitueraient donc pas des faits historiques, mais serviraient uniquement d'ornement poétique pour illustrer le caractère merveilleux de la victoire de Josué' (*Le Miracle de Josué*, p. 16). Hence, the account in Joshua 10:12-13a is 'passage essentiellement poètique' and is simply following the tradition of 'les poètes orientaux' (pp. 16-17). For an earlier discussion using this type of argument see A. Schulz, *Das Buch Josua*, p. 41.

38. J. Bright, 'Joshua', in *IntB*. R.B.Y. Scott suggests that it is a request that the clouds hold (Josh. 10:11) in order that the heat of the day not interfere with the pursuit of the enemy ('Meteorological Phenomena and Terminology in the Old Testament', *ZAW* 64 (1952): 19-20).

39. See J.F.A. Sawyer, 'Joshua 10:12-14 and the Solar Eclipse of 30 September 1131 B.C.', *PEQ* 104 (1972): 139-146. F.R. Stephenson, 'Astronomical Verification and Dating of Old Testament Passages Referring to Solar Eclipses', *PEQ* 107 (1975): 119.

40. Dus, *VT* 10 (1960): 353-374; and J. Heller, 'Der Name Eva', *ArOr* 26 (1958): 653-656.

41. R. de Vaux, *The Early History of Israel*, p. 634.

42. Holladay, *JBL* 87 (1968): 169-170.

43. *Ibid.*, p. 176. If the sun stood still over Gibeon and the moon over Aijalon, then the time of day could only have been morning which fits

the context very well since Joshua is supposed to have marched all night in order to arrive and attack the enemy 'suddenly' (10:9). If this were the case, Joshua would have had a full moon to aid his march to Gibeon.

44. R. Campbell Thompson, *The Reports of the Magicians and Astrologers of Nineveh and Babylon in the British Museum*, no. 124 (obv 5b-9).

45. *Ibid.*, no. 127 (rev. 1-2).

46. *Ibid.*, no. 120.

47. *Ibid.*, no. 157.

48. Halpern, 'Doctrine by Misadventure Between the Israelite Source and the Biblical Historian', in *The Poet and the Historian*, p. 55. Others have argued along similar lines. For example, J.A. Bewer also argued that the narrator who quoted the poem interpreted it prosaically (hence misinterpreting it) as a stupendous miracle (*The Literature of the Old Testament*, p. 5). Partly behind this is the assumption that the poem is older than the narrative in which it is embedded. This assumption is, of course, not necessarily true.

49. R. de Vaux, *Early History of Israel*, p. 634.

50. P.D. Miller, *The Divine Warrior in Early Israel*, p. 126.

51. *Ibid.*, p. 126.

52. M. Weinfeld, 'Divine Intervention in War', in *HHI*, p. 146.

53. *Ibid.*, p. 146.

54. *Iliad* II:412-415. F.M. Abel has pointed out a number of examples of this nature from classical antiquity (*Bible de Jérusalem*, pp. 12ff). R.K. Harrison argues along these same lines stating, 'Other aspects of Joshua can also be paralleled from the eastern Mediterranean cultures, such as the standing still of the sun and moon in order to assure the victorious conclusion of the fight, since in antiquity battles normally ended at sunset each day, regardless of the outcome (*Iliad* XVIII:239ff)' (*Introduction to the Old Testament*, p. 674).

55. Another illustration that helps understand the language utilized here comes from the American Civil War. On September 17, 1862 during the battle of Antietam, the Federals repeatedly attacked General Lee's lines and by the narrowest of margins repeatedly failed to break though. The fighting was so intense that one confederate soldier wrote: *'The sun seemed almost to go backwards, and it appeared as if night would never come!'* (see: D.S. Freeman, *Lee's Lieutenants: A Study in Command*, II, p. 224).

56. Tadmor, 'History and Ideology', in *ARINH*, p. 17.

57. *Ibid.*, p. 17, n. 13.

58. Text: V. Scheil, *Mémoires de la Délagation en Perse*, 14, p. 9ff. Translation: E. Sollberger and J.-R. Kupper, *Inscriptions royales sumeriennes et akkadiennes*, p. 126.

59. Sollberger and Kupper comment: 'The assertion does not have to be taken literally. It is even probable that several campaigns are alluded to here; cf. Hinz, *CAH* I/2 p. 652ff' (p. 126, n. 1). Cf. also the *Concise Annals of Hattušili I* (see: pp. 132-136).

60. 1st Beth-Shan Stela of Seti I (*KRI* I 12, 1-15; Wilson, *ANET*, p. 253).

61. Translation is that of K.A. Kitchen, *Pharaoh Triumphant*, p. 22. See also A. Spalinger, 'The Northern Wars of Seti I: An Integrative Study', *JARCE* 16 (1979): 31. Concerning the identification of the cities here see Wilson, *ANET*, p. 253, n. 6; for Yenoam see now N. Na'aman, *Tel Aviv* 3-4 (1977): 168-177, who argues for a location east of the Jordan at Tell esh-Shihab.

62. Soggin, *Joshua*, p. 123.

63. J. Friedrich made a comparison between the phenomenon described in the Annals of Muršili and the Gebel Barkal Stela of Thutmose III, see *OLZ* 39 (1936): 135ff. M. Weinfeld discusses this text, but in relation to Judges 5, not Joshua 10 ('Divine Intervention in War', pp. 125-127).

64. Lines 33-36. W. Helck, *Urkunden der 18. Dynastie*, pp. 1238-1239; Reisner, *ZÄS* 69 (1933): 35-36.

65. *bi(')yt* = 'miracle' *CDME*, p. 80.

66. Following W. Helck, *Übersetzung*, p. 10.

67. *wnwty* = 'hour-watcher, astronomer' *CDME*, p. 61. See *AEO* I, pp. 61-62.

68. See: Helck, *Übersetzung*, p. 10, n. 7.

69. *r-'k'* = 'on a level with' *CDME*, p. 50. Following Helck, (*Übersetzung*, p. 10), we translate 'from its position' which fits the context better.

70. Again following Helck's reconstruction and translation, *Urkunden*, p. 1238, and *Übersetzung*, p. 10.

71. There is an obvious parallel here to the 'stars fighting' in Judges 5:20 against Sisera. See Weinfeld, 'Divine Intervention in War', *HHI*, pp. 125-128.

72. Lines 5-6; Helck, *Urkunden*, pp. 1229-1230.

73. *sšd* = 'thunderbolt' according to *CDME*, p. 249. However, Shirun-Grumach argues that '*sšd* describes the activity of the star in analogy with the numinous appearance of Pharaoh on the war chariot (cp. *WB* IV, 300 10-12)'. She feels that through a comparison of *sšd* here and

in the poetical stela (*Urk.* IV 615, 13 = line 15), one can see that the meaning is brightness not thunderbolt or flash ('Die poetischen Teile der Gebel-Barkal Stele', p. 128, n. 53).

74. Cp. the Poetical Stela (line 15): *Urk.* IV, pp. 610-619:

I came to make you trample the eastern land,
as you trod down those in the regions of god's land;
I caused them to see your majesty as the radiant splendor of a star.
(as one) that scatters its flame in the fire as it sheds its flame.

75. P.D. Miller, p. 127.

76. *Ibid.*, p. 128.

77. For example, Noth, *Das Buch Josua*, pp. 60-67. See also J. Gray, *Joshua, Judges, and Ruth*, pp. 104-107.

78. Noth, *Josua*, pp. 60ff; and 'Die fünf Könige in der Höhle von Makkeda', *Palästinajahrbuch* 33 (1937): 22-36. Also see Elliger who argues along similar lines ('Josua in Judäa', *Palästinajahrbuch* 40 (1934): 47-71). Interestingly, Elliger divided chapter 10 into three main sections (1-15; 16-27; 28-43), whereas Noth felt that there were only two main sections (1-15; 16-43). He felt that the story in 16-43 was 'ausgesprochen ätiologisch, wie ganz abgesehen vom Inhalt selbst die Schlussworte in 27 deutlich zeigen; und zwar handelt es sich auch hier um eine Ortsätiolgie' (p. 60). He saw verses 28-43 as a continuation of the etiological story in verses 16-27. He derived the number 'five' etiologically from the five trees at Makkedah on which the kings were supposed to have been hung. Hence the number of the kings was determined by the number of the trees, and the cities to which the kings belonged were simply chosen from among those in the neighborhood of Makkedah. In order to maintain this theory he eliminated verses 28 and 33 as glosses. Gray thinks that 'the number five may have been suggested by the five trees at Makkedah to the aetiological tradition was attached, or the number five in both cases may have had a mnemonic value in folk-narration, like the five kings in Gen. 14' (*Joshua, Judges and Ruth*, p. 103). Gottwald distinguishes only two main sections for the chapter (1-15; 16-43), although he argues that 'the lack of homogeneity between vss. 16-27 and vss. 28-43 is evident on closer inspection' (*Tribes of Yahweh*, pp. 49, 552-554). But cf. note 87 below.

79. Noth, pp. 60ff; and 'Die fünf Könige in der Höhle von Makkeda', pp. 22-36. Also see Elliger pp. 47-71. However, there are significant difficulties with verse 15. See Appendix, note 23. Cf. also, G.E. Wright, *JNES* 5 (1946): 112; and Halpern, *CBQ* 37 (1975): 307.

80. Butler, *Joshua*, pp. 111-112.

81. W. Mayer, *MDOG* 115 (1983): 82-83, lines 150-151.

82. Prism A (Rassam). Col. V.11-14.

83. Prism A (Rassam). Col. IX.38-41.

84. Poetical Stela: *Urk.* IV, 610.7-9.

85. G.A. Gaballa, *JEA* 55 (1969): 82-88. Fig. no. 5.

86. Interestingly, the action of the Israelite chiefs in placing their feet on the neck of the enemy kings (10:24) is found in the Annals of Tukulti-Ninurta I: 'I captured Kaštiliaš, king of the Kassites (alive). I trod with my feet upon his lordly neck as though it were a footstool' *TN*, p. 12, ll. 60-63.

87. Annals of Thutmose III, lines 86-89: *Urk.* IV, pp. 657-658.

88. The practice is also observed in Egypt. For example Merenptah states: 'They (the Libyans) are cast to the ground by hundred-thousands and ten-thousands, the remainder being impaled (put to the stake) on the South of Memphis' (*KRI* IV, 34/13-14).

89. B. Halpern feels that there are three objections to an etiological argument. 'First, Noth is unable to demonstrate that the etiological factor is determinative in the story of the pursuit to Makkedah (vss. 16-27); recent scholarship has emphasized, this is a *sine qua non* of the etiological principle, since the tale of the stone may very well have been secondarily attached to a local narrative ... Second, the battle account of 10:1-14 locates Joshua at Makkedah (vs. 10) ... Third, it seems likely that the southern hill cities are not presented in a random order. Depending on the location of Makkedah, the Shephelah campaign has a regular, logical north to south sequence in vss. 28-39' (*CBQ* 37 (1975): 307-308).

90. Shalmaneser I. See: *IAK*, pp. 111-126: lines 11-13. Memorial mounds are even much earlier than this as the inscription of Enmetena of Lagash demonstrates: 'Enanatum, ruler of Lagash, fought with him (Ur-Lumma) in the Ugiga-field, the field of Ningirsu. Enmetena, beloved son of Enanatum, defeated him. Urluma escaped, but was killed in Umma itself. He had abandoned sixty teams of asses at the bank of the Lumagirnunta-canal, and left the bones of their personnel strewn over the plain. He (Enmetena) made five burial mounds (heaps) there for them'. Note the use of the number 'five'. For text, see: E. Sollberger, *Corpus des inscriptions royales présargoniques de Lagaš*, Ent. 28-29. For translations, see: J. Cooper, *SARI*, p. 55; E. Sollberger and J.-R. Kupper, *Inscriptions Royales Sumeriennes et Akkadiennes*, p. 72 and note e; S.N. Kramer, *The Sumerians*, p. 314; and Willem H.Ph. Römer, *TUAT*, 1/4, p. 310.

91. Letter to the God (lines 300-302). Cf. Joshua 8:29 which states: 'He hung the king of Ai on a tree and left him there until evening. At sunset, Joshua ordered them to take his body from the tree and throw

it down at the entrance of the city gate. And they raised a large pile of rocks over it, which remains to this day'.

92. The Walters Art Galley (lines 108-112): Grayson, *AfO* 20 (1963): 94-95. In addition to this heap, Sennacherib claims to have set up a stela to memorialize his victory over the Elamites at Halule (lines 113-114).

93. While many OT scholars have thought that the formula עד היום הזה 'until this day' is the sign *par excellence* of the etiology, Childs argues that the formula 'seldom has an etiological function of justifying an existing phenomenon, but in the great majority of cases is a formula of personal testimony added to, and confirming a received tradition' ('A Study of the Formula, "Until This Day"' *JBL* 82 (1963): 279-292). Also, the formula can be used in a non-etiological way expressing only the *terminus a quo* for a particular text.

94. *Urk*. IV 662.5-6. The translation follows Lichtheim, *AEL* II, p. 33. She also notes that this 'leather scroll' is a reference to the campaign diary.

95. The Definition of an etiology according to M.P. Nilsson, *Geschichte der griechischen Religion*², I, p. 25.

96. Cf. Childs' discussion, 'The Etiological Tale Re-examined', *VT* 24 (1974): 392.

97. See Boling, p. 152. And also Childs, *JBL* 82 (1963): 292. Childs correctly concludes: 'extreme caution should be observed in assuming an inferential model of etiology which implies that the link between cause and effect is artificial and unhistorical. Only in those cases in which elements of mythical causation can be clearly demonstrated is there an adequate warrant for such a move' (*VT* 24 (1974): 397).

98. Soggin, *Joshua*, pp. 127-128.

99. For this type of symmetric structure, see: S. McEvenue, *The Narrative Style of the Priestly Writer*, p. 29, n. 18; and R. Boling, *Joshua*, p. 294.

100. See the discussion in chapter 2. White argues that the historian 'fashions' his material and that this fashioning is a 'distortion' of the whole factual field of which the discourse purports to be a representation [*History and Theory* 14 (1975): 59].

101. M. Fishbane, 'I Samuel 3: Historical Narrative and Narrative Poetics', in *Literary Interpretations of Biblical Narratives*, p. 203.

102. Text: Helck, *Urkunden der 18. Dynastie*, Vol. 17, pp. 1228-1243; Reisner, *ZÄS* 69 (1933): 24-39.

103. Text: *KRI*, IV, pp. 12-19.

104. The Egyptian *tm wn* is literally ‘did not exist’ or ‘non-existent’. It is equivalent to Hebrew אין in Isaiah 41:11 (ואבדו אנשי ריבך יהיו כאין :: ‘those who oppose you will be as non-existent ones and perish’); and Isaiah 40:17 (כל הגוים כאין נגדו :: ‘All the nations are as nothing before you’). In the context of Joshua 9-12, such terms as אבד, השמיד, לא נותר, etc. are also semantically the same. Cf. also the Libyan War Inscription (Karnak) of Merenptah which states: ‘and none of them (the Libyans) escaped’ (*KRI* IV 6/2-3).

105. Text: M. Lidzbarski, *Handbuch der nordsemitischen Epigraphik*, plate I; *KAI* I, no. 181; *SSI* I, pp. 71-83. Lines 7, 11-12, 14-17.

106. G. Ryckmans identified the term רית as a cognate to South Arabic *ryt* ‘offering’ [*JEOL* 14 (1956): 73-84, esp. p. 81]. S. Segert has endorsed this suggestion (‘Die Sprache der moabitischen Königsinschrift’, *ArOr* 29 (1961): 244). Gibson’s objection is unconvincing (*SSI* I, p. 79). Röllig translates as ‘Darbringung’ (*KAI* p. 175).

107. Chicago-Taylor Prism, Col. I.58 (see Borger, *BAL*[2] p. 70).

108. See Goetze, *Die Annalen of Muršiliš*, pp. 78-81.

109. Text: *KAI*, #202; *SSI* II, pp. 6-17. Concerning the ‘Heilsorkal’, see: J.C. Greenfield, ‘The Zakir Inscription and the Danklied’, in *Proceedings of the Fifth World Congress on Jewish Studies*, pp. 174-191. Concerning the name, see: A.R. Millard, ‘Epigraphic Notes, Aramaic and Hebrew’, *PEQ* 110 (1978): 23-26.

110. Cf. the list of kings in the Zakkur inscription.

111. Chicago-Taylor Prism (II. 37-60a); *BAL*[2], I p. 73.

112. For the text, see A.K. Grayson, *AfO* 20 (1963): 83-96.

113. Also see: Esarhaddon: *Nin.A* IV. 62-69; and Tukulti-Ninurta I: *TN* #16 (lines 69-87), pp. 26-29.

114. See Gardiner, *The Kadesh Inscriptions of Ramesses II*, pp. 14-15; and also Spalinger’s discussion *Aspects*, p. 164. It is just like a listing of the Allies in an account of World War II in which usually the Big Three are mentioned; but sometimes, depending on contributions, others might be listed (e.g., Canadians, Poles, etc.). Another ANE example can be seen in the *Concise Annals of Hattušili I* (see: pp. 132-136).

115. R. Mond and O. Myers, *The Temples of Armant*, p. 139.

116. Shils, p. 72.

117. *Ibid.*, p. 72.

118. W.T. Pitard, ‘Amarna *ekemu* and Hebrew *naqam**’, *Maarav* 3 (1982): 24.

119. *Ibid.*, p. 17. Pitard’s study calls into question Mendenhall’s understanding of the term נקם. Mendenhall believes that נקם is

a technical covenantal term which meant 'the executive exercise of power by the highest political authority for the protection of his own subjects' (*The Tenth Generation*, p. 78). It was the power used by a sovereign to correct a situation of danger for the sovereign's faithful vassals when all regular and normal legal processes to clear up the danger had been tried and had failed. He sees the term as connoting extralegal but legitimate intervention by YHWH during a crisis in his vassal territory, Israel (*The Tenth Generation*, pp. 76-82). Pitard shows that the root *nqm** did not have this meaning in Hebrew or in the cognate languages.

120. Shils, p. 67. Such an understanding would appear to support a revolt theory concerning the origins of Israel. Of course, one must assume that the ideology arose in opposition to the 'establishment'—i.e., the rulers of the city-states. But there are indications that the ideology has not developed internally, but externally. The difference between the Israelite ideology in Joshua 9-12 and other ancient Near Eastern conquest accounts may be more apparent than real. The differences, for example, in religious outlook—and we must emphasize that we are only speaking with regard to Joshua 9-12—are not very great. Here it is YHWH rather than Aššur, Amun, the Sun-goddess of Arinna, or Kemoš who is the deity who actively intervenes on behalf of his people.

121. One has to admit the possibility that the biblical writer has cast the account in this ideological mode. We cannot pursue this question more fully since we do not know enough about the 'historical context' from which the text arose.

122. In Exodus 23:23-30 the promise of YHWH to drive out the inhabitants of the land gradually seems to imply that there was a policy of selectivity even in this policy of the חרם. See also *Theological Wordbook of the Old Testament*, s.v. חרם, pp. 741-742.

123. For text and bibliography, see section *10:28–42* (pp. 226-28 above) and note 105 above.

124. I.106-110. See *AKA*, pp. 291-292; and Grayson, *ARI* II, pp. 125-126.

125. For a jural ideology of war in the Old Testament, see R.M. Good, 'The Just War in Ancient Israel', *JBL* 104/3 (1985): 385-400. In the context of the ancient Near East, see G. Furlani, 'Le guerre guali giudizi di dio presso i babilonesi e assiri', in *Miscellanea Giovanni Galbiati*, pp. 39-47.

126. Cf. Gen. 15:16 which states: 'for the sin of the Amorites has not yet reached its full measure'. Hence the biblical view is that YHWH is judging and driving out the Amorites because of their sin (עוֹן —'crime, perversion').

127. F.N.H. Al-Rawi, 'Nabopolassar's Restoration Work on the Wall 'Imgur-Enlil' at Babylon', *Iraq* 47 (1985): 1-13. Lines I.24-II.5. Cf. also the similar phrase in the Meša Inscription: 'Omri, the king of Israel, had oppressed Moab many days because Kemoš was angry with his land' (line 5). Moreover, note the meoisis in the Nabopolassar text: 'I, the weak, the powerless ...'

128. Cf. also the prisms of Aššurbanipal: Prism T (V.9-32) (R. Campbell Thompson, *The Prisms of Esarhaddon and Ashurbanipal*, pp. 29-36), and Prism F (V.72-VI.11) (J.M. Aynard, *Le Prisme du Louvre AO 19.933.*) in which 'the goddess Nana, who for 1635 years had been angry and had gone to live in the midst of Elam, a place not proper for her', chose Aššurbanipal to deliver her and bring her back to her proper abode.

129. L.W. King, *Babylonian Boundary Stones*, no. VI (pp. 29-36).

130. J.J.M. Roberts, 'Nebuchadnezzar I's Elamite Crisis in Theological Perspective', pp. 183-187.

131. King, *Babylonian Boundary Stones*, p. 33.

## NOTES TO CHAPTER SIX
(pp. 241-263)

1. Obviously, the writer utilized source material (war reports, diaries(?), the Book of Yashar, etc.) so that in one sense separate accounts were collected (just like Assyrian annals were probably constructed from a collection of campaign reports). But this is quite different from the notion of most biblical writers who speak of Joshua 9-12 as a composite of various different *traditions* which accrued over a long time period.

2. For example, Butler states concerning the nature of chapter 10: 'the chapter contains a holy war narrative, a poetic fragment transformed into a secondary etiology to illustrate holy war technique, a typical conquest itinerary, and a theological summary' (*Joshua*, p. 112). And Miller and Tucker: 'separate traditions have been combined and edited to comprise the narrative' (*Joshua*, p. 89).

3. Cf. Sh. Yeivin, *The Israelite Conquest of Canaan*, p. 3.

4. Childs, *An Introduction to the Old Testament as Scripture*, p. 247.

5. G.F. Moore, *Judges*, p. 8. Compare this recent comment of Auld: 'There is an ambivalence in the Book of Joshua over just how complete Israel's conquest was ... In Judges 2 and 3 we shall find two "divine" reasons to justify a less than complete conquest' (pp. 78-79).

6. Childs, *Introduction*, p. 249.

7. The notion of 'a single campaign' (פעם אחת) must be understood figuratively. For example, Tiglath-Pileser claims to have 'plundered from the edge of the land of Suhu to Carchemish of Hatti-land in a single day (*ina ištēn ūme*)'. Furthermore, the term '*girru* :: campaign' has a wide semantic range (*CAD* G p. 138) and the Hebrew פעם אחת may have a similar range of meaning. Furthermore, at the end of each year of Muršili's Annals this syntagm occurs: *nu ki-i I-NA* MU 1.KAM *i-ya-nu-un* :: 'And I did (all) this in one year'. Muršili's accomplishments (whether always done in a single year) are, nevertheless, narrated using this idiomatic expression.

8. The term conquest means 'act or *process* of conquering' <emphasis mine> according to *Webster's New World Dictionary*, p. 311. The synonyms 'subdue' and 'subjugate' have connotations of completeness that we believe the Hebrew terms for 'conquer' in the context of Joshua לכד and לקח lack. 'To subdue' means 'to defeat so as to break the spirit of resistance'. And 'to subjugate' is 'to bring under complete subjection'.

9. The Akkadian verb *kašādu*, in this instance, is the semantic equivalent of the Hebrew verbs לכד and לקח.

10. M. Noth ascribes the description of the 'land that remains' (vv. 2-6) to the hand of a 'supplementer' who erroneously thought that the reference in verse one that 'there are still very large areas of land to be taken over' was to the territory which had not yet been conquered. In reality, Noth argues, the meaning of the reference in verse one is that until then the Israelites had established themselves only in the area 'around Gilgal' where the camp was, and now they had to settle in the rest of the land as well. He states: 'Der Satz <1bβ> besagt also, dass nach den vorausgegangenen Feldzügen, nach denen man immer wieder nach Gilgal zurückgekehrt war, das Land nun wirklich erst in Besitz genommen, d.h. von den Stämmen besiedelt werden müsse—allerdings nicht im ganzen, sondern nur noch „in sehr weitem Umfang", da man ja wenigstens um Gilgal herum sich schon festgesetzt hatte. *Der Ergänzer von 2-6 aber hat das fälschlich dahin verstanden*, dass ein Teil des Landes noch unerobert sei; das veranlasste ihn, „das übrig gebliebene Land" nun sekundär noch genau festzulegen' (*Das Buch Josua*, pp. 73-74) [emphasis mine]. Y. Kaufmann violently objected to this understanding of Jos. 13:1-6: 'This interpretation is illogical. How could it be said of "all the Land", apart from the camp area, that "very much" of it remained? And what sense then do the opening words make: "Thou art old, advanced in years"? The meaning of this introduction is plain: thou art old and therefore cannot complete the conquest, cf. Jos. 23:2-14; Deut. 31:2-3. But the essential point is that 13-19 speak of the distribution of "remaining" territory. These chapters assume that, before the allocation of portions, there was no settlement anywhere, not even "around Gilgal",

seeing that the settlement was by tribes. Hence, if, *before* the distribution, the phrase "remaining territory" is used, it can only mean the territory which remained unconquered' (*The Biblical Conquest of Palestine*, p. 58, n. 56). While there appears to be a discrepancy between the opening words of 13:1-6 and the description of the territorial distribution, Boling is probably right when he states concerning verses 2-6: 'This most extravagant description of the extent of the Israelite conquest is perhaps to be recognized as hyperbole ...' (*Joshua*, p. 337).

11. By hyperbole, we mean the use of exaggerated terms for the purpose of emphasis or heightened effect; more is said than is literally meant.

12. A. Goetze, *Die Annalen des Muršiliš*.

13. Gardiner notes that 'the swearing of an oath to declare that one has spoken the truth goes back to the Middle Kingdom, e.g. *Inscriptions of Sinai*, ed. Čern , pl. 17, no. 53; in historical texts of Dyns. 18th and 19th' (*The Kadesh Inscription of Ramses*, p. 34).

14. *KRI* II, pp. 119-124. Translations: Gardiner, *The Kadesh Inscriptions of Ramses II*, p. 30; Lichtheim, *AEL*, II, p. 62.

15. Another hyperbole in the biblical narrative is encountered in Joshua 10:2 ('all of its men were heroic warriors').

16. *KRI* IV, pp. 12-19. Since there is no reference to an Asiatic campaign in the O.T., some scholars doubt the historicity of Merenptah's claims. However, the war scenes at Karnak on the south approach, west wall may indicate that Merenptah did in fact campaign in Canaan. While these scenes have usually been attributed to Ramesses II, the oldest readable cartouches in the scenes are those of Merenptah—never Ramesses II. One of the scenes may even represent Merenptah's action against Israel. See: F. Yurco, *SSEAJ* 8 (1978): 70; L. Stager, *EI* 18 (1985): 56-64; and Williams, *DOTT*, p. 137.

17. *šrm* is a transliteration (not a translation) of the Canaanite שלום.

18. *fk.t* is an old perfective (See Černý and Groll, *Late Egyptian Grammar*, pp. 196-197 (paradigm 2). Yurco points out that the determinative for Israel is not a haphazard designation. It means that the Egyptians did not regard them as a city-state with fixed borders like e.g., Gezer. In this phrase Israel is understood to be a collective, a distinct people, not named after any particular territory or city. In Egyptian, the names of countries, cities, and provinces are fem. (see *Gram*, pp. 66, 92). But the masc. pron. is used with Israel which possibly indicates an identity with a male deity or eponymous ancestor (*SSEAJ* 8 (1978): 70). 'Since Israel is here made parallel with Hurru, we may surmise that the former was not an insignificant tribe, but an important and strong people by this time' (Williams, *DOTT*, pp. 140-

141). Finally, Stager remarks: 'Thus, the Egyptian account, although couched in poetic and rhetorical forms, preserves some interesting and very specific details about Merenptah's enemies' (*EI* 18 (1985): 61).

19. The poem is beautifully structured. *šrm* and *ḥtpw* are a pair which help form an inclusio (lines 1a-1b and 5a-5b). The enemies are clustered in a 3 (countries) + 3 (cities) + 2 (countries). The last pair forms the relationship: Israel (as husband) and Hurru (as wife/widow).

20. L.D. Levine points out that a 'campaign', as reported in the annals of Sennacherib, does not necessarily end with the events described in the original document; and that it was possible to produce an account of a campaign before that campaign had been completed. Furthermore, events in the campaign were assigned to that particular campaign because of the writer's point of view rather than any strict chronological grounds ('Preliminary Remarks on the Historical Inscriptions of Sennacherib', in *HHI*, pp. 72-73).

21. On Joshua's selective strategy, see Y. Yadin, *Military and Archaeological Aspects*, pp. 6-8.

22. *AKA*, p. 83. Cf. also Muršili II's Annals, Thutmose III (Amant Stela), etc. mentioned in our discussion of Joshua 12 in the previous chapter.

23. Auld, *Joshua, Judges and Ruth*, p. 72.

24. Gray, *Joshua, Judges and Ruth*, p. 40. Noth theorized a pan-Israelite redaction which was the work of the *Sammler* (*Das Buch Josua*, pp. 35-45).

25. Miller and Tucker, *Joshua*, p. 14.

26. Hamlin, *Joshua: Inheriting the Land*, p. 93.

27. Noth, *Josua*, pp. 12-13; 60-67.

28. Col. III.47-52: *AKA*, pp. 53-54.

29. See Stager's discussion concerning this in *EI* 18 (1985): 56-64.

30. A. Graeme Auld, *Joshua, Judges, and Ruth*, p. 4.

31. Miller and Tucker, *Joshua*, p. 12.

32. F.T. Miller, *The Complete History of World War II*. Chicago, 1945.

33. *Ibid.*, p. 5.

34. A. Danto, *Analytical Philosophy of History*, pp. 149-151.

35. As Pfeiffer put it (*Introduction to the Old Testament*, pp. 27-29).

36. Miller and Tucker, *Joshua*, p. 73.

37. Throughout this discussion the adjectives artificial, synthetic, simulated and representative are used neutrally.

38. Miller and Tucker, *Joshua*, p. 92. Along similar lines Auld argues: 'At first hearing the opening of Joshua 11 makes a rather similar impression to the opening of chapter 10. Both start with the initiative of an apparently prominent king, here Jabin, king of Hazor, there Adonizedek, king of Jerusalem. In each case reports of Joshua's prowess prompt the king in question to organize an anti-Israelite alliance. But to the attentive listener these two stories have a somewhat different ring. While Hazor, like Jerusalem, Lachish and Eglon, will reappear in Biblical history, the towns to which Jabin sends are known only in the town lists of Joshua 12 and 19. Only one of the kings is named (contrast 10:3), and after mention of three minor places the report turns to generalities' (p. 76). Does Auld really think that the towns mentioned and the kings named make such a great difference in the two accounts?

39. *Ibid.*, p. 90.

40. Noth, *Das Buch Josua*, p. 12.

41. Butler, *Joshua*, p. 113.

42. Col. VI.39-54; VIII.39-44. See: *AKA*, pp. 82-84, 104; and Borger, *AfO* 25 (1974-77): 164.

43. This questions the statement of Miller and Tucker that 'pursuit of the fleeing enemy is a consistent element of holy war accounts' (*Joshua*, p. 93).

44. R. Mond and O. Myers, *The Temples of Armant*, p. 139.

45. Gottwald, *Tribes of Yahweh*, pp. 552-554. See also G. Mendenhall, 'The Hebrew Conquest of Palestine', *BA* 25/3 (1962): 66-87.

46. While still arguing for a peasant revolt model of the conquest, M. Chaney admits that this passage is 'the product of royal functionaries and/or priestly elites' from the period of the 'Josianic reform' who 'could not be expected to transmit traditions of peasant uprisings in a sympathetic and unrefracted form'. Instead, the events were interpreted 'in terms of Deuteronomistic ideology'. In fact, so 'heavily and repeatedly redacted' is the prose of Joshua that the evidence is 'more ambiguous than a modern historian might wish' and hence only 'circumstantial' in its support of the revolt model. He feels that the Song of Deborah is more direct evidence for a revolt model ('Ancient Palestinian Peasant Movements and the Formation of Premonarchic Israel', in *Palestine in Transition*, pp. 67, 69-70). We would agree that Joshua 9-12 may be 'the product of royal functionaries', although its date of origin is uncertain. From the evidence of our research, it seems that the passage exhibits all the trademarks of an imperialistic ideology. While this does not 'disprove' the revolt model—such is beyond the scope of this study—, it questions whether Joshua 9-12 really supports this model.

47. Sennacherib's campaign against the people of Bit-Yakin is a prime example (Col. IV.32-46).

48. Syntagms like $^{KUR}$*X dan-na-at-ta-aḫ-ḫu-un* ('I made Mt. X empty (of humanity') and *ú-šam-qit-ma e-du ul e-zib* ('I slaughtered and not one escaped') are directed at city populations as well as kings and their armies. Since these are semantically the same as ויחרם אותה ואת כל הנפש אשר בה and השאיר לא שריד בה it would follow that these too can be directed at the urban populations. Moreover, there are not 'two different historical horizons in the traditions about the aftermath of the battle of Gibeon'. One point which many biblical scholars (including Gottwald pp. 253-54 above) seem not to be able to comprehend is that it is possible to have a battle in the open field, a king flee (not necessarily to his own city), and then to have a siege of that city. There is a difference between a siege and an open field battle! E.g., Sargon defeats Rusa in a battle in a ravine in the mountains of Urartu during which Rusa flees on the back of a mare. Rusa hides in a mountain cave while Sargon sieges, captures and destroys Rusa's cities (narrated basically one at a time). Or consider the campaign of Shalmaneser III against Hazael. Shalmaneser defeats Hazael in open battle and then sieges and captures Damascus (but not Hazael). Such enumeration could continue. But hopefully the point is clear that the biblical text is well within the transmission code of ANE conquest accounts.

49. Another powerful argument of Gottwald is the analogy of premonarchic Israel to segmentary lineage systems. J. Rogerson has recently argued that pre-monarchic Israel was not a segmentary lineage society but an association of small chiefdoms. After a thorough analysis of the arguments concerning segmentary lineage systems, Rogerson concludes: 'Although the negative direction of this article is much greater than its positive suggestions, it will have succeeded if it serves to warn all those interested in the sociological study of the OT against an over-hasty and superficial equation of pre-monarchic Israel with segmentary lineage societies. Although parallels can indeed be found between aspects of segmentary societies and passages in the Old Testament, it is necessary to relate those aspects of the segmentary societies to their structure and function as a whole. *If this is done, the analogy with the Old Testament is hardly persuasive*' <my emphasis> (*JSOT* 36 (1986): 17-26).

50. W. Brueggemann, *Revelation and Violence: A Study in Contextualization*.

51. *Ibid.*, pp. 10-15.

52. *Ibid.*, pp. 37-38.

53. *Ibid.*, pp. 38, 38, n. 55, 47, and 48.

54. See Boling, *Joshua*, p. 316.

55. A. Spalinger, 'The Northern Wars of Seti I', *JARCE* 16 (1979): 30. Also see Y. Yadin, *The Art of Warfare in Biblical Lands* I, p. 230. Moreover, the scene indicates that the Shasu lacked the strength to capture any of the key cities held by the Egyptians or their allies because they are not pictured as being in the city of Gaza, only outside (see Spalinger's discussion).

56. *Ibid.*, p. 31. Some scholars have equated the Shasu with the ancestors of the early Hebrews [e.g., M. Weippert, 'Semitische Nomaden des zweiten Jahrtausends: Über die Š'sw der ägyptischen Quellen', *Biblica* 55 (1974): 265-280, 427-433; and D. Redford, 'An Egyptological Perspective on the Exodus Narrative', in *Egypt, Israel, Sinai*, p. 151]. This view is most often (though not always) connected with the 'infiltration theory' of Israelite origins. For the most recent delineation of this view, consult V. Fritz, 'Conquest or Settlement?', *BA* 50/2 (1987): 84-100. However, see: M. Chaney, 'Ancient Palestinian Peasant Movements and the Formation of Premonarchic Israel', in *Palestine in Transition*, pp. 42-44.

57. *Ibid.*, p. 35.

58. The lack of chariots and horses continued in underdeveloped militaries and can be seen in the Arab wars of Assurbanipal. The Arabs lacked chariots and horses and used camels for their calvary. This is very clearly the case as seen in the Arab contingent at the battle of Qarqar. See I. Eph'al, *The Ancient Arabs*, pp. 76, n. 230 and 85, n. 261. Superior technology does not guarantee victory [e.g., the U.S. defeat in Southeast Asia and the Soviets defeat in Afghanistan].

59. I. Finkelstein, *The Archaeology of the Israelite Settlement*. Jerusalem: Israel Exploration Society, 1988. See the review of D. Esse, *BAR* 14/5 (1988): 8ff.

Finkelstein's theory is based on the archaeological studies of the Iron I settlement process. Finkelstein believers that the Iron I settlers were formerly pastoral nomads who had had prolonged contact with the LBA Canaanite culture. He calls them 'sedentarizing pastoralists'.

While nomadic groups are notoriously difficult to detect archaeologically, Finkelstein believes that sanctuaries and cemeteries away from the centers of settled population point to the existence of such groups during the LBA, and he tentatively identifies them with the *shasu / sutu* referred to in a number of ancient (most Egyptian) texts.

The three main aspects of the material culture that Finkelstein uses for his 'sedentarizing pastoralist' model are:

a) Pillared four-room houses. Finkelstein believes that this house is a successful adaptation to its environment, both socially and naturally, from the Bedouin tent. Hence, he sees this as evidence for pastoral sedentarization. But while the house is a successful adaptation, architectural form are generally linked with their environments, and the origins of the four-room house should be sought in developments within rural village life rather than from Bedouin/pastoralist antecedents [So argues Esse, *BAR* 14 (1988), p. 10].

b) Proliferating use of silos for grain storage. Finkelstein argues that 'a proliferation of silos generally characterizes groups in the process of sedentarization or societies organized in local rural frameworks' (Finkelstein, p. 266). Esse disagrees:

> The large number of modest size silos are typical of small-scale rural production, however, in contrast to the more developed redistributive network evident from the large-size communal silos at sites from the time of the monarchy. The combination of four-room houses, small 'family' silos and a limited ceramic repertoire illustrate the rural foundation of Israelite society and its successful adaptation to its ecological niche. The presence of such silos need not imply a group of pastoralists in the process of 'sedentarization,' however [Esse, *BAR* 14 (1988): 10].

c) Elliptical settlement compounds. Finally, Finkelstein argues that the occurrences of elliptical settlement compounds reflect the intermediate stage between pastorialism and rural village life, i.e., the process of pastoralists settling down. But they might also reflect simply functional requirements rather than a process. These compounds may illustrate specialized architecture for the pastoralist end of the continuum, contemporary with the four-room house construction of the village end of the continuum [Esse, *BAR* 14 (1988): 10].

60. N.P. Lemche, *Early Israel* [VTS 37] (Leiden: E.J. Brill, 1985), pp. 411-435. A more popular form in his theory can be see in his *Ancient Israel: A New History of Israelite Society* (Sheffield: JSOT Press, 1988), pp. 85-90, 100-102.

61. R.B. Coote and K.W. Whitelam, *The Emergence of Early Israel in Historical Perspective* (Sheffield: Almond Press), pp. 117-138.

62. J.A. Callaway, 'A New Perspective on the Hill Country Settlement of Canaan in Iron Age I,' in *Palestine in the Bronze and Iron Ages: Papers in Honour of Olga Tufnell*. Ed. by J.N. Tubb, pp. 31-49. London: Institute of Archaeology, 1985.

Callaway has put forward arguments against semi-nomadic origins for the Iron I settlers, preferring to view them as Canaanite villagers displaced from the coastal plain and the Shephelah. To him the cause for these refugees' movement was pressure and conflict as the result of the arrival of the Philistines and other 'sea peoples'. These highland settlers eventually emerged as Israel, so that Israel's origins must ultimately be sought in the Canaanite villages of the plains and lowlands.

If the Iron I villagers were refugees from the coastal plain and the Shephelah, moving inland under pressure from the Philistine invasion, one would expect them to encounter a number of early Iron Age settlements in the highlands of Judah, but this is not the case.

63. R.B. Coote and K.W. Whitelam, *The Emergence of Early Israel in Historical Perspective*, p. 136.

64. J. Gray, *Joshua, Judges, and Ruth*, p. 107. See also G. von Rad, *Der heiligen Krieg im alten Israel*[3]; R. Smend, *Jahwekrieg und Stämmebund*[2]; F.M. Cross, Jr., 'The Divine Warrior in Israel's Early Cult', in *Biblical Motifs*; P.D. Miller, *The Divine Warrior in Early Israel*.

65. *Ibid.*, p. 107.

66. Butler, *Joshua*, p. 115.

67. D.J. McCarthy, 'Some Holy War Vocabulary in Joshua 2', *CBQ* 33 (1971): 228. He also discussed אימה (2:9), מסס (2:11), and מוג and concludes that these are all words 'show clearly the intertwining of the vocabularies of the holy war and of the theophany, or perhaps better because broader, the divine visitation' (pp. 228-230).

68. See for a few examples, Weinfeld, 'Divine Intervention in War', pp. 124-136.

69. Gebel Barkal Stela 6-11.

70. We are translating the *sḏm.f* here as past tenses. Cf. M. Lichtheim, *AEL* II, p. 38, n. 1.

71. H.-P. Müller, '*Ḥmm*', in *TDOT*, 3:420-421; and M. Weippert, '"Heiliger Krieg" im Israel und Assyrien', *ZAW* 84 (1972): 460-493.

72. Miller and Tucker, *Joshua*, p. 55.

73. The policy was continued during the monarchy (cf. David with the Urim and Thummim and Ahab and Jehosaphat in I Kgs. 21).

74. On a number of these themes see M. Weippert, *ZAW* 84 (1972): 460-493.

75. Butler, *Joshua*, pp. xxiii, 111-119.

76. Tadmor, 'Autobiographical Apology', in *HHI*, pp. 42-43. It is worth repeating the words of Liverani at this point: 'The 'holiness' of a war cannot result from an analysis, since indeed there cannot be a 'lay' war. The war is always a holy one if fought by us, always a wicked one if fought by the enemy; therefore, 'holy' means only that it answers our social values, it means Assyrian' ('The Ideology of the Assyrian Empire', p. 301). Finally, M. Weippert argues that it is not possible to speak of 'holy war' as a distinctively Israelite special 'sacral institution' of the 'amphictyony' [as von Rad, *ZAW* 84 (1972): 460-493].

77. H. Eberhard von Waldow, 'The Concept of War in the Old Testament', *Horizons in Biblical Theology* 6 (1984): 36-37.

78. P.C. Craigie, *The Problem of War in the Old Testament*, p. 49.

79. Hamlin, *Joshua: Inheriting the Land*, pp. 92-93.

80. Casualties of the enemy (often inflated) do occur. Casualties of one's own army are uncommon. One clear exception is the casualty list at the end of Sargon's Letter to the God. The purpose of this document as part of a public ceremony explains this innovation. Even then it hardly represents the actual casualties of Sargon's eighth campaign: eight persons! Note that the casualty list at the end of Sargon's Letter is identical with that at the end of Esarhaddon's Letter! (see: R. Borger, *Die Inschriften Asarhaddons Königs von Assyrien*, pp. 102-107).

81. In fact, the expression 'teaching material' is very inadequate. One could reasonably argue that a great deal of ancient Near Eastern history writing was in some way didactic.

82. J. Van Seters, *In Search of History*, pp. 322-331, esp. 330-331.

83. *Ibid.*, pp. 330-331.

84. For some of these, cf. H. Tadmor, 'Aramaization in the Assyrian Empire', *Assyrien und seine Nachbarn*, pp. 550-561.

85. Col. III.64-65: *AKA*, p. 365; See also, A.K. Grayson, *ARI*, II, p. 141.

86. Michel, *WO* 1 (1949): 458:42 (and passim).

87. E. Unger, *Reliefstele Adadniraris III. aus Saba'a und Semiramis*, 13, cf. 1R 30 iv 9.

88. The Sheikh Hammad Stele. A.R. Millard and H. Tadmor, 'Adadnirari III in Syria', *Iraq* 35 (1973): 57-64.

89. For a listing see: *CAD* M II, p. 70.

90. Karnak: *Urk*. IV, 1310.18 and 1311.1-2. The scribe of this stela has mistakenly repeated the war diary twice.

91. Memphis: *Urk*. IV, 1302.7. Of the two versions, the Memphis Stela is the more reliable according to Spalinger, *Aspects*, pp. 147-148.

92. While the text of Joshua 9-12 cannot be identified as any particular genre *per se*, the analysis of the ancient Near Eastern material has improved the over-all understanding of the biblical narrative. For example, while the biblical text may be geographically arranged like an Assyrian Summary text which telescopes the material, it also evinces the episodic nature and syntagmic structure of the Annalistic texts. The biblical account's 'mixed nature' means that we can benefit only from a thorough comparison with other ancient Near Eastern conquest accounts in terms of the interpretation, and not from genre classification. So, to categorize this narrative as a Summary text and to draw certain conclusions from that classification would cause innumerable problems. But by analyzing texts from many different genres within the general 'open' category of 'conquest accounts', it is

possible to gain a much better understanding of the biblical conquest account as a whole.

## NOTES TO CONCLUSION
(pp. 265-266)

1. Spalinger, *Aspects*, p. 239. One always receives conflicting information concerning the numbers killed in wars. In recent years, one thinks especially of the conflicting numbers in the Vietnam War and the Iran-Iraq War.

2. For an application of this method to the narrative of 1 Kings 1-11, see our article: 'The Figurative Aspect and the Contextual Method in the Evaluation of the Solomonic Empire (1 Kings 1-11)', in *The Bible in Three Dimensions*, pp. 142-160.

# BIBLIOGRAPHY


Abel, F.M. *Bible de Jérusalem.*[2] Paris, 1958.

Abercrombie, N., Hill, and Turner, N. *The Dominant Ideology Thesis.* London, 1984.

Abou-Assaf, A., Bordreuil, P. and Millard, A.R. *La Statue de Tell Fekherye et son inscription bilingue assyro-araméene.* Etudes Assyriologiques. Paris: Editions Rescherche sur les Civilisations, 1982.

Aharoni, Y. 'Some Geographical Remarks Concerning the Campaigns of Amenhotep II'. *JNES* 19 (1960): 177-183.

Al-Rawi, F.N.H. 'Nabopolassar's Restoration Work on the Wall 'Imgur-Enlil' at Babylon'. *Iraq* 47 (1985): 1-13.

Albrektson, B. *History and the Gods: An Essay on the Idea of Historical Events as Divine Manifestations in the Ancient Near East and in Israel.* Lund, 1967.

Albright, W.F. 'The Israelite Conquest of Canaan in the Light of Archaeology'. *BASOR* 74 (1939): 11-23.

Alt, Albrecht. 'Josua'. *BZAW* 66 (1936): 24-26.

Alter, Robert. *The Art of Biblical Narrative.* London and Sydney, 1981.

Althusser, L. 'Ideology and Ideological State Apparatuses'. In *Lenin and Philosophy.* New York, 1971.

Apter, David L. 'Ideology and Discontent'. In *Ideology and Discontent.* Ed. David L. Apter, pp. 1-17. New York, 1964.

Archi, A. 'The Propaganda of Hattusili III'. *Studi Micenei ed Egeo Anatolici* 14 (1971): 185-216.

___ 'La storiografia ittita'. *Athenaeum* NS 47 (1969): 7-20.

Auld, A. Graeme. 'Textual and Literary Studies in the Book of Joshua'. *ZAW* 90 (1978): 412-417.

___ *Joshua, Judges, and Ruth.* [The Daily Study Bible]. Philadelphia: The Westminster Press, 1984.

___ 'Joshua: The Hebrew and Greek Texts'. *VTS* 30 (1979): 1-14.

Aynard, J.-M. *Le prisme du Louvre AO 19.939.* Paris, 1957.

Badalì, E. et al., 'Studies on the Annals of Aššurnasirpal II: I. Morphological Analysis'. *Vicino Oriente* 5 (1982-83): 13-73.

Barnes, Barry. *Scientific Knowledge and Sociological Theory.* London and Boston, 1974.

Barr, J. 'Story and History in Biblical Theology'. In *Scope and Authority of the Bible.* pp. 1-12. = *JR* 56/1 (1976): p. 5.

Barthélemy, D. *Critique textuelle de l'Ancien Testament: 1. Josué, Juges, Ruth, Samuel, Rois, Chroniques, Esdras, Néhémie, Esther.* [Orbis Biblicus et Orientalis, 50/1]. Göttingen, 1982.

Barthes, R. *Eléments de Sémiologie.* Paris, 1964.

___ *La Plaiser de Text.* Paris, 1971.

___ *S/Z*. Paris, 1970.
Bauer, Th. *Das Inschriftenwerk Ashurbanipals*. 2 Vol. Leipzig, 1933.
Baumgartner, W. *OLZ* 27 (1924): 313-318.
Beckman, G. 'The Hittite Assembly'. *JAOS* 102 (1982): 435-442.
Bewer, J.A. *The Literature of the Old Testament*. Rev. Ed. New York, 1947.
Billerbeck, A. and Delitzsch, F. 'Die Palasttore Shalmanassars II von Balawat'. *Beiträge zur Assyriologie und semitischen Sprachwissenschaft* 6 (1908): 129-155.
Blenkinsopp, J. *Gibeon and Israel*. Cambridge, 1972.
Bodine, W.R. *The Greek Text of Judges: Recensional Developments*. [Harvard Semitic Monographs, 23]. Chico, California, 1980.
___ 'KAIGE and other Recensional Developments in the Greek Text of Judges'. *Bulletin of the International Organization for Septuagint and Cognate Studies* 13 (1980): 45-57.
Boling, Robert G., and Wright, G. Ernest. *Joshua: A New Translation with Introduction and Commentary*. [Anchor Bible Commentary]. Garden City, New York, 1982.
Borger, R. *Die Inschriften Asarhaddons Königs von Assyrien*. [AfO Beiheft 9]. Graz, 1956.
___ *Babylonisch-Assyrische Lesestücke*. 2nd Edition. 2 Vol. Rome, 1979.
___ *Einleitung in die Assyrischen Königsinschriften*. Vol. I. Leiden, 1961.
___ *AfO* 25 (1974-1977): 161-165.
___ 'Gott Marduk und Gott-König Sulgi als Propheten: Zwei prophetische Texte'. *BiOr* 28 (1971): 3-24.
___ Editor. *Historisch-chronologische Texte*. [Texte aus der Umwelt des Alten Testaments]. Vol. 1, part 4, pp. 284-450. Gütersloher, 1984.
___ 'Die Inschriften Asarhaddons (AfO Beiheft 9)'. *AfO* 18 (1958): 113-118.
Braudel, F. 'The Situation of History in 1950'. In *On History*. Trans. S. Matthews. Chicago, 1980.
Breasted, J.H. *Ancient Records of Egypt*. 5 Vols. Chicago, 1906-1907.
Brett, M. 'Literacy and Domination: G.A. Herion's Sociology of History Writing'. *JSOT* 37 (1987): 20-24.
Bright, J. 'Joshua'. In *The Interpreter's Bible*. 12 Vols. Nashville, 1951-57.
___ *Early Israel in Recent History Writing*. 1956.
Brinkman, J.A. 'Merodach-Baladan II'. In *Studies Presented to A. Leo Oppenheim*. pp. 31-35. Chicago, 1964.
___ 'Additional Texts from the Reigns of Shalmaneser III and Shamshi Adad V'. *JNES* 32 (1973): 40-46.
___ *A Political History of Post-Kassite Babylonia 1158-722 B.C.* Rome, 1968.

___*Prelude to Empire: Babylonian Society and Politics, 747-626 B.C.* [Occasional Publications of the Babylonian Fund, 7]. University Museum, 1984.

Brooke, Alan England, and Norman McLean, with Henry St. John Thackeray for Vols. II and III. Editors. *The Old Testament in Greek According to the Text of Codex Vaticanus, Supplemented from Other Uncial Manuscripts, with a Critical Apparatus Containing the Variants of the Chief Ancient Authorities for the Text of the Septuagint*. Vol. I: *The Octateuch*. Vol. II: *The Later Historical Books*. Vol. III, Part 1: *Esther, Judith, Tobit*. Cambridge, 1906-1940.

Brueggemann, Walter. *Revelation and Violence: A Study in Contextualization*. <The 1986 Père Marquette Theology Lecture>. Milwaukee: Marquette University Press, 1986.

Bull, L. 'Ancient Egypt'. In *The Idea of History in the Ancient Near East*. ed. by R.C. Dentan, pp. 1-34. New Haven and London, 1955.

Burrows, M. 'Ancient Israel'. In *The Idea of History in the Ancient Near East*. ed. by R.C. Dentan, pp. 99-131. New Haven and London, 1955.

Butler, Trent. *Joshua*. <Word Biblical Commentary>. Waco, 1983.

Callaway, J.A. 'A New Perspective on the Hill Country Settlement of Canaan in Iron Age I'. in *Palestine in the Bronze and Iron Ages: Papers in Honour of Olga Tufnell*. Ed. by J.N. Tubb, pp. 31-49. London: Institute of Archaeology, 1985.

*Cambridge Ancient History*, 3rd. ed. Vol. 2, pt. 1: History of the Middle East and Aegean Region c. 1800-1380 B.C., ed. by I.E.S. Edwards, C.J. Gadd, N.G.L. Hammond, and E. Sollberger. Cambridge, 1973.

*Cambridge Ancient History*, 3rd. ed. Vol. 2, pt. 2: History of the Middle East and Aegean Region c. 1380-1000 B.C., ed. by I.E.S. Edwards, C.J. Gadd, N.G.L. Hammond, and E. Sollberger. Cambridge, 1975.

Cancik, H. *Grundzüge der hethitischen und alttestamentlichen Geschichtsschreibung*. Wiesbaden, 1976.

___*Mythische und historische Wahrheit*. SB 48. Stuttgart, 1970.

Carr, E.H. *What is History*? 1961.

Cassuto, U. 'The Rise of Historiography in Israel'. In *Eretz-Israel* 1 pp. 85-88. <Hebrew>.

___'The Beginning of Historiography among the Israelites'. In *Biblical and Oriental Studies*, ed. U. Cassuto. Vol. 1, pp. 7-16. Jerusalem, 1973.

Ceram, C.W. *The Secret of the Hittites*. [Trans. by R. and C. Winston]. New York, 1955.

Černý, J. and Groll S. *A Late Egyptian Grammar*.$^{2}$ Rome, 1978.

Černý, J. 'Stela of Ramesses II from Beisan'. *EI* 5 (1958): 75-82.

Ceuppens, P.F. *Le Miracle de Josué*. Paris, 1967.

Chaney, M. 'Ancient Palestinian Peasant Movements and the Formation of Premonarchic Israel'. In *Palestine in Transition: The Emergence of Ancient Israel*. [SWBAS, 2]. ed. by D.N. Freedman and D.F. Graf, pp. 39-90. Sheffield, 1983.
Childs, B.S. 'A Study of the Formula "Until This Day"'. *JBL* 82 (1963): 279-292.
___ *VT* 24 (1974): 385-397.
___ *Introduction to the Old Testament as Scripture*. Philadelphia, 1979.
Çilingiroğlu, A.A. 'The Eighth Campaign of Sargon II'. *Anadolu Araştirmalari* 4-5 (1976-1977): 252-269.
Clements, R. 'History and Theology in Biblical Narrative'. *Horizons in Biblical Theology* 4-5 (1982-83): 51-55.
___ *Isaiah and the Deliverance of Jerusalem* [JSOTS, 13]. Sheffield, 1980.
Coats, G.W. *Genesis*. [FOTL Vol. 1]. Grand Rapids, 1982.
Cogan, M. and Tadmor, H. 'Gyges and Ashurbanipal: A Study in Literary Transmission'. *Or* 46 (1977): 65-85.
___ 'Ahaz and Tiglath-Pileser in the Book of Kings: Historiographic Considerations'. In *Eretz-Israel* 14 (1978): 55-57 <Hebrew>.
Coggins, R.J. 'History and Story in Old Testament Study'. *JSOT* 11 (1979): 36-46.
Cohen, Ralph. 'History and Genre'. *New Literary History* 17 (1986): 204.
Colie, R.L. 'Johan Huizinga and the Task of Cultural History'. *AHR* 69 (1963-64): 607-630.
Cook, Albert. '"Fiction" and History in Samuel and Kings'. *JSOT* 36 (1986): 21-35.
Cooper, Jerold S. *Sumerian and Akkadian Royal Inscriptions: Presargonic Inscriptions* Vol. I [American Oriental Society Translation Series, 1], New Haven, 1986.
Cooper, Alan. 'The Life and Times of King David According to the Book of Psalms'. In *The Poet and the Historian: Essays in Literary and Historical Biblical Criticism*. [HSS, 26]. Ed. by R.E. Friedman. pp. 117-132. Chico, California, 1983.
___ 'On Reading the Bible Critically and Otherwise'. In *The Future of Biblical Studies*. Ed. by R.E. Friedman and H.G.M. Williamson. pp. 61-79. Atlanta, 1987.
Coote, R.B. and Whitelam, K.W. *The Emergence of Early Israel in Historical Perspective*. Sheffield: Almond Press, 1986.
Craigie, P.C. *The Problem of War in the Old Testament*. Grand Rapids, 1971.
Cross, F.M. 'The Divine Warrior in Israel's Early Cult'. In *Biblical Motifs*. Ed. by Alexander Altmann. Cambridge, Mass., 1966.
___ *Canaanite Myth and Hebrew Epic: Essays in the History of the Religion of Israel*. Cambridge, 1973.
Cuddon, J.A. *A Dictionary of Literary Terms*. Revised Edition, 1979.

Danto, A. 'Mere Chronicle and History Proper'. *Journal of Philosophy* (1953): 39-50.
___ *Analytical Philosophy of History*. Cambridge, 1965.
Davies, P.R. *JTS* 36 (1985): 168-172.
de Filippi, W. 'The Royal Inscriptions of Aššur-Nasir-Apli II (883-859 B.C.)'. *Assur* 1/7 (1977): 123-169.
Dentan, R.C., ed. *The Idea of History in the Ancient Near East*. New Haven and London, 1955.
Derrida, Jacques. 'The Law of Genre'. *Critical Inquiry* 7/1 (1980): 64-65.
de Sélincourt, Aubrey. Translator. *Herodotus: The Histories*. Baltimore, 1954.
de Vaux, R. *The Early History of Israel*. 2 Vols. London and Philadelphia, 1978.
Dietrich, M., Kümmel, H.M., Loretz, O., and Otten, H. *Historisch-Chronologische Texte*. [Texte aus der Umwelt des Alten Testaments]. Vol. 1, part 5, pp. 452-520. Gütersloher, 1985.
Dray, W.H. 'On the Nature and Role of Narrative in Historiography'. *History and Theory* 10 (1971): 153-171.
Driver, S.R. *An Introduction to the Literature of the Old Testament*. 8th Edition. [International Theological Library]. Edinburgh, 1909.
Dus, J. 'Gideon—eine Kultstätte des Šmš und die Stadt des benjaminitischen Schicksals'. *VT* 10 (1960): 353-361.
Ebeling, E., Meissner, B., and Weidner, E.F. *Die Inschriften der altassyrischen Könige*. [Altorientalische Bibliothek 1]. Leipzig, 1926.
Eco, Umberto. *The Role of the Reader*. Bloomington, 1982.
___ *Semiotics and the Philosophy of Language*. Bloomington, 1984.
___ *A Theory of Semiotics*. Bloomington, 1976.
Edel, E. 'Die Stelen Amenophis II aus Karnak und Memphis'. *ZDPV* 69 (1953): 98-176.
Edgerton, W.F., and Wilson, J.A. *Historical Records of Ramses III. The Texts in Medinet Habu*. [OIS, 12]. Chicago, 1936.
Edzard, D.O. 'Königsinschriften. A. Sumerisch'. *RLA* 6 (1980): 59-65.
Egan, Kieran. 'Thucydides, Tragedian'. In *The Writing of History: Literary Form and Historical Understanding*. Ed. by R.H. Canary et al., pp. 78-82. Madison, 1978.
Elliger, K. 'Josua in Judaea'. *Palästinajahrbuch* 30 (1934): 47-71.
Ellis, M. de J., ed. *Essays on the Ancient Near East in Memory of Jacob Joel Finkelstein*. Memoirs of the Connecticut Academy of Arts and Sciences, December, vol. 19. Hamden, Conn., 1977.
Eph'al, Israel. *The Ancient Arabs: Nomads on the Borders of the Fertile Crescent 9th-5th Centuries B.C.*. Jerusalem, 1982.
Evans, C.D., Hallo, W.W., and White, J.B. *Scripture in Context: Essays on the Comparative Method*. [Pittsburgh Theological Monograph Series 34]. Pittsburgh, 1980.

Fales, F.M. 'The Enemy in Assyrian Royal Inscriptions: "The Moral Judgement"'. In *Assyrien und Seine Nachbarn*. Vol. II, pp. 425-435. Berlin, 1984.

___ 'A Literary Code in Assyrian Royal Inscriptions: The Case of Ashurbanipal's Egyptian Campaigns'. In *ARINH*. Ed. by F.M. Fales. pp. 169-202. Rome, 1981.

___ Editor. *Assyrian Royal Inscriptions: New Horizons in Literary, Ideological and Historical Analysis*. [Orientis Antiqvi Collectio, 17]. Rome, 1981.

Fensham, F.C. 'The Treaty Between Israel and the Gibeonites'. *BA* 27 (1964): 96-100.

Field, Frederick. Editor. *Origenis Hexaplorum quae supersunt sive veterum interpretum Graecorum in totum Vetus Testamentum fragmenta*. 2 Vols. Oxford, 1875.

Finkelstein, I. *The Archaeology of the Israelite Settlement*. Jerusalem: Israel Exploration Society, 1988.

Finkelstein, J.J. 'Mesopotamian Historiography'. In *Proceedings of the American Philosophical Society* 107 (1963): 461-472.

Finley, M.I. *The Use and Abuse of History*. New York, 1975.

Fishbane, M. 'I Samuel 3: Historical Narrative and Narrative Poetics'. In *Literary Interpretations of Biblical Narratives*. Vol. 2. Ed. by Gros Louis, pp. 191-203. New York, 1982.

Frandsen, Paul John. 'Egyptian Imperialism'. in *Power and Propaganda: A Symposium on Ancient Empires*. [Mesopotamia 7]. ed. by. M.T. Larsen. pp. 151-165. Copenhagen, 1979.

Freeman, D.S. *Lee's Lieutenants: A Study in Command*. 3 Volumes. New York: Charles Scribner's Sons, 1943.

Frei, Hans. *The Eclipse of Biblical Narrative*. New Haven, 1974.

Friedman, Jonathan. 'Ideology'. In *The Social Science Encyclopedia*. Ed. by Adam Kuper and Jessica Kuper. pp. 375-376. London, Boston, and Henley, 1985.

Friedrich, J. *Hethitisches Wörterbuch*. [Indogermanische Bibliothek 2]. Heidelberg, 1952.

Fritz, V. 'Conquest or Settlement?' *BA* 50/2 (1987): 96-97.

___ 'The Israelite "Conquest" in the Light of Recent Excavations at Khirbet el-Meshâsh'. *BASOR* 242 (1981): 71.

Furet, François. 'Quantitative History'. In *Historical Studies Today*. Ed. by F. Gilbert and S.R. Graubard. pp. 54-60 New York, 1972.

Furlani, G. 'Le guerre guali giudizi di dio presso i babilonesi e assiri'. In *Miscellanea Giovanni Galbiati*. pp. 39-47. Milan, 1951.

Gaballa, G.A. 'Minor War Scenes of Ramesses II At Karnak'. *JEA* 55 (1969): 82-88.

Gadamer, Hans-Georg. *Truth and Method*. New York, 1978.

Gadd, C.J. *Ideas of Divine Rule in the Ancient East*. London, 1948.

___ 'Inscribed Prisms of Sargon II from Nimrud'. *Iraq* 16 (1954): 173-201.

Garbini, G. *History and Ideology in Ancient Israel*. New York, 1988.

Gardiner, Sir A.H., Peet, T.E., and Čern , J. *The Inscriptions of Sinai.* 2 Vols. London, 1952-55.
Gardiner, Sir A.H. *Ancient Egyptian Onomastica.* 3 Vols. London, 1947.
___ *Egypt of the Pharaohs: An Introduction.* Oxford, 1961.
___ *The Royal Canon of Turin.* Oxford, 1959.
___ *Egyptian Hieratic Texts.* Vol. I Leipzig, 1911.
___ *The Kadesh Inscriptions of Ramesses II.* Oxford, 1960.
Garstang, J. and Gurney, O.R. *The Geography of the Hittite Empire.* London, 1959.
Geertz, Clifford. 'Ideology as a Cultural System'. In *Ideology and Discontent.* Ed. by David E. Apter. pp. 47-76. New York, 1964.
Gelio, R. 'La Délégation Envoyée par Gygès, Roi de Lydie: un Cas de Propagande idéologique'. In *Assyrian Royal Inscriptions: New Horizons.* pp. 203-224. Ed. by F.M. Fales. Rome, 1981.
Gerhart, M. 'Generic Studies: Their Renewed Importance in Religious and Literary Interpretation'. *JAAR* 45/3 (1977): 309-325.
Gese, H. 'Geschichtliches Denken im Alten Orient und im Alten Testament'. *ZThK* 55 (1958): 127-145. Translated by J.F. Ross as 'The Idea of History in the Ancient Near East and the Old Testament'. *Journal for Theology and the Church*[2] (1965): 49-64.
Gibson, John C.L. *Syrian Semitic Inscriptions.* 3 Volumes. Oxford, 1971-1982.
Girndt, Helmut, and Simons, Eberhard, and Habermas, Jürgen. 'Zum Problem der Legitimation politischen Handelns—Eine Auseinandersetzung mit Jürgen Habermas'. In *Legitimationsprobleme politischer Systeme.* Ed.by P.G. Kielmansegg. Opladen: Westdeutscher Verlag, 1976.
Giveon, R. *The Impact of Egypt on Canaan.* [Orbis Biblicus et Orientalis, 20]. Vandenhoeck & Ruprecht, 1978.
Goedicke, H. *The Report about the Dispute of a Man with his Ba.* Baltimore, 1970.
___ *The Report of Wenamun.* Baltimore and London, 1975.
___ 'Some Remarks Concerning the Inscription of Ahmose, Son of Ebana'. *JARCE* 11 (1974): 31-41.
Goetze, A. *Die Annalen des Muršiliš.* Hethitische Texte in Umschrift, mit Übersetzung und Erläuterungen. Vol. 6. MVAG 38. Leipzig, 1933.
___ *Kleinasien.* 2nd ed. Munich, 1957.
Goldwasser, O. 'Hieratic Inscriptions From Tel Sera' in Southern Canaan'. *Tel Aviv* 11/1 (1984): 77-93.
Goldwitzer, H. 'Historischer Materialismus und Theologie'. In *Traditionen der Befreiung.* ed. W. Schottroff and W. Stegemann. Munich, 1980.
Good, R.M. 'The Just War in Ancient Israel'. *JBL* 104/3 (1985): 385-400.

Goody J.R. and Watt, I. 'The Consequence of Literacy'. *Comparative Studies in Society and History* 5/3 (1963): 304-345.

___ 'The Consequences of Literacy'. In *Literacy in Traditional Societies*. ed. by J.R. Goody, pp. 27-68. Cambridge, 1968.

Gottwald, N.K. *Tribes of Yahweh*. New York and London, 1975.

Gould, Julius. 'Ideology'. In *A Dictionary of the Social Sciences*. pp. 315-317. Ed. by Julius Gould and William L. Kolb. New York, 1964.

Grapow, H. *Studien zu den Annalen Thutmosis des Dritten und zu ihnen verwandten historischen Berichten des Neuen Reiches*. Berlin, 1947.

Gray, J. *Joshua, Judges, and Ruth*. [New Century Bible]. Grand Rapids, 1986.

Grayson, A.K. 'Histories and Historians of the Ancient Near East: Assyria and Babylonia'. *Or* 49 (1980): 140-194.

___ 'Studies in Neo-Assyrian History: The Ninth Century B.C'. *BiOr* 33 (1976): 134-145.

___ 'Assyrian Royal Inscriptions: Literary Characteristics'. In *Assyrian Royal Inscriptions: New Horizons*. pp. 35-48. Ed. by F.M. Fales. Rome, 1981.

___ 'Assyrian and Babylonian King Lists: Collations and Comments'. *Lišan mitḫurti. Festschrift W. von Soden*. [AOAT 1]. pp. 265-277. Neukirchen-Vluyn, 1969.

___ *Assyrian Royal Inscriptions*. 2 Vols. Wiesbaden, 1972-76.

___ 'Problematical Battles in Mesopotamian History'. In *Studies in Honor of Berno Landsberger on his Seventy-Fifth Birthday*. [Assyriological Studies, 16]. Chicago, 1965.

___ 'The Walters Art Galley Sennacherib Inscription'. *AfO* 20 (1963): 83-96.

___ *Assyrian and Babylonian Chronicles*. Locust Valley, N.Y., 1975.

Greenspoon, L. *Textual Studies in the Book of Joshua*.

Greenstein, E.I. and Marcus, D. 'The Akkadian Inscription of Idrimi'. *JANES* 8 (1976): 59-96.

Gressmann, H. *Die älteste Geschichtsschreibung und Prophetie Israels*. SAT II/1. Göttingen, 1910; 2nd ed., 1921.

Grintz, J.M. 'The Treaty of Joshua with the Gibeonites'. *JAOS* 86 (1966): 113-126.

Groneberg, B. *Répertoire Géographique des Textes Cuneiformes*. Wiesbaden, 1980.

Guidi, Ignazio. 'L'historiographie chez les Semites'. *RB* 15 (1906): 509-519.

Gunkel, H. 'Geschichtsschreibung im A.T.' *RGG*, Vol. 2, pp. 1348-1354. *RGG*², Vol. 2, pp. 1112-1115.

___ 'Die israelitische Literatur'. In *Die Kultur der Gegenwart: Die orientalischen Literaturen*.

___ *Genesis, übersetzt und erklärt*. HKAT I/1. Göttingen, 1901; 3rd ed., 1910.

___ *The Legends of Genesis*. Translated by W.H. Carruth. Chicago, 1901. Reprinted with a new introduction by W.F. Albright. New York, 1964.
___ 'Die Grundprobleme der israelitischen Literaturgeschichte'. In *Reden und Aufsätze*, pp. 29-38.
Gunn, B. *Studies in Egyptian Syntax*. Paris, 1924.
Gunn, D.M. *The Story of King David: Genre and Interpretation*. JSOTS 6. Sheffield, Eng., 1978.
___ 'New Directions in the Study of Biblical Hebrew Narrative'. *JSOT* 39 (1987): 65-75.
Gurney, O.R. 'The Hittite Empire'. In *Power and Propaganda: A Symposium on Ancient Empires*. [Mesopotamia 7]. ed. by. M.T. Larsen. pp. 151-165. Copenhagen, 1979.
___ *The Hittites*. 3rd ed. London, 1961.
Güterbock, H.G. 'Hittite Historiography: An Introduction'. In *History, Historiography and Interpretation*. Ed. by H. Tadmor and M. Weinfeld. pp. 13-29. Jerusalem, 1983.
___ 'Sargon of Akkad Mentioned by Hattušili I of Hatti'. *JCS* 18 (1964): 1-6.
___ 'The Deeds of Suppiluliuma as Told by His Son, Muršili II'. *JCS* 10 (1956): 41-50; 59-68; 75-85; 90-98; 107-130.
___ 'Die historische Tradition und ihre literarische Gestaltlung bei Babyloniern und Hethitern bis 1200'. *ZA* 42 (1934): 1-91 and *ZA* 44 (1938): 45-149.
___ 'The Hittite Conquest of Cyprus Reconsidered'. *JNES* 26 (1967): 73-81.
Habermas, Jürgen. 'Legitimationsprobleme im modernen Staat'. In *Legitimationsprobleme politischer Systeme*. Ed. by P.G. Kielmansegg. Opladen: Westdeutscher Verlag, 1976.
___ *Knowledge and Human Interests*. Boston, 1971.
___ *Theorie und Praxis: Sozialphilosophie Studien*. Neuwied, 1963.
Hall, Emma Swan. *The Pharaoh Smites His Enemies*. [Münchner Ägyptologische Studien, 44]. Deutscher Kunstverlag, 1986.
Hallo, W.W. 'Assyrian Historiography Revisited'. In *Eretz-Israel* 14 (1978): 1-7.
___ 'Sumerian Historiography'. In *History, Historiography and Interpretation*. Ed. by H. Tadmor and M. Weinfeld. pp. 1-12. Jerusalem, 1983.
___ 'Biblical History in its Near Eastern Setting: The Contextual Approach'. In *Scripture in Context: Essays on the Comparative Method*. Ed. by Carl D. Evans, W.W. Hallo, and John B. White. pp. 1-12. Pittsburgh, 1980.
Halpern, B. 'Gibeon: Israelite Diplomacy in the Conquest Era'. *CBQ* 37 (1975): 303-316.
___ *The Emergence of Israel in Canaan*. [SBL Monograph Series, 29]. Chico, California, 1983.

___ 'Doctrine by Misadventure Between the Israelite Source and the Biblical Historian'. In *The Poet and the Historian: Essays in Literary and Historical Biblical Criticism*. [HSS, 26]. Ed. by R.E. Friedman. pp. 41-74. Chico, California, 1983.
___ 'Biblical or Israelite History?' In *The Future of Biblical Studies*. Ed. by R.E. Friedman and H.G.M. Williamson. pp. 103-139. Atlanta, 1987.
___ *JBL* 104/3 (1985): 506-509.
___ *The First Historian, The Hebrew Bible and History*. San Francisco, 1988.
Hamlin, E.J. *Joshua: Inheriting the Land*. [International Theological Commentary]. Grand Rapids, 1984.
Harrison, R.K. *Introduction to the Old Testament*. Grand Rapids, 1974.
Hawkins, J.D. 'Hatti'. In *RLA* 4 (1972-75): 152-159.
Hayes, W.C. *The Scepter of Egypt*. New York, 1953.
Hecker, K. *Untersuchungen zur akkadischen Epik*. Neukirchen-Vluyn, 1974.
Hegel, G. *Vorlesungen über die Philosophie der Geschichte*. Frankfurt am Main, 1970.
Heidel, A. 'A New Hexagonal Prism of Esarhaddon'. *Sumer* 12 (1956): 9-37.
Helck, W. *Urkunden der 18. Dynastie*. [Urkunden des ägyptischen Altertums]. Berlin, 1955.
___ 'Überlegungen zur Geschichte der 18. Dynastie'. *OA* 8 (1969): 281-327.
___ *MDAIK* 28 (1972): 101-102.
___ *Die Beziehungen Ägyptens zur Vorderasien im 3. und 2. Jahrtausand v. Chr.*[2] Wiesbaden, 1971.
___ *Geschichte des alten Ägypten*. [Handbuch der Orientalistik]. Leiden, 1968.
___ *Untersuchungen zu Manetho und den ägyptischen Königslisten*. Berlin, 1956.
___ *MDOG* 92 (1960): 5
___ 'Die Sukzija-Episode in Dekret des Telepinus'. *WO* 15 (1984): 103-108.
Heller, J. 'Der Name Eva'. *ArOr* 26 (1958): 636-656.
Herrmann, A. *Die ägyptische Königsnovelle*. Leipziger ägyptologische Studien 10. Glückstadt-Hamburg-New York, 1938.
Herrmann, S. '2 Samuel VII in the Light of the Egyptian Königsnovelle—Reconsidered'. In *Pharaonic Egypt: The Bible and Christianity*. Ed. by S. Israelit-Groll. pp. 119-128. Jerusalem, 1985.
___ 'Die Königsnovelle in Ägypten und in Israel'. *Wissenschaftliche Zeitschrift der Karl-Marx Universität Leipzig* 3/1 (1953/54): 51-62.
Hirsch, E.D. *Validity in Interpretation*. New Haven, 1967.
Hoffman, I. *Der Erlass Telipinus*. Heidelberg, 1984.

Hoffmeier, James K. 'Some Egyptian Motifs Related to Warfare and Enemies and Their Old Testament Counterparts'. In *Egyptological Miscellanies: A Tribute to Professor Ronald J. Williams*. Ed. by J.K. Hoffmeier and E.S. Meltzer, pp. 53-70. [Ancient World VI]. Toronto, 1983.

Hoffner, H.A., Jr. 'Histories and Historians of the Ancient Near East: The Hittites'. *Or* 49 (1980): 283-332.

——— 'Propaganda and Political Justification in Hittite Historiography'. In *Unity and Diversity: Essays in the History, Literature, and Religion of the Ancient Near East*. Ed. by H. Goedicke and J.J.M. Roberts, pp. 49-62. Baltimore and London, 1975.

——— 'Review of *Der Anitta-Text*, by Erich Neu'. *BASOR* 226 (1977): 78.

Holladay, J.S., Jr. 'The Day(s) the Moon Stood Still'. *JBL* 87 (1968): 166-178.

Holmes, Samuel. *Joshua: The Hebrew and Greek Texts*. Cambridge, 1914.

Hornung, E. *BiOr* 45 (1988): 108.

——— *Der Eine und die Vielen: Ägyptische Gottesvorstellungen*. Darmstadt, 1973.

Houwink ten Cate, Philo H.J. 'Muršiliš' Northwestern Campaigns—Additional Fragments of His Comprehensive Annals'. *JNES* 25 (1966): 162-191.

——— 'A New Fragment of the "Deeds of Suppiluliuma as Told by His Son, Muršili II"'. *JNES* 25 (1966): 27-31.

——— 'The History of Warfare According to Hittite Sources: The Annals of Hattušiliš I (Part 1)'. *Anatolica* 10 (1983): 91-109; (Part 2). *Anatolica* 11 (1984): 47-83.

Huizinga, J. 'De Taak van Cultuurgeschiedenis'. In *Verzamelde Werken*. ed. by Leendert Brummel et al. Vol. 7, pp. 45ff. Haarlem, 1948-1953. 9 Volumes.

——— 'A Definition of the Concept of History'. in *Philosophy and History: Essays Presented to Ernst Cassirer*. Ed. by R. Klibansky and H.J. Paton, pp. 1-10. <Dutch original 1928; translated by D.R. Cousin in 1936>. Cambridge, 1936.

Iggers, Georg G. *New Directions in European Historiography*. London, 1985.

——— *The German Conception of History: The National Tradition of Historical Thought From Herder to the Present*. Middletown, Connecticut, 1968.

Imparati, F. and Saporetti, C. 'L'autobiografia di Hattušili I'. *Studi Classici e Orientali* 14 (1965): 40-85.

Israelit-Groll, S. Editor. *Egyptological Studies*. [Scripta Hierosolymitana 28]. Jerusalem, 1982.

——— Editor. *Pharaonic Egypt: The Bible and Christianity*. Jerusalem, 1985.

Jacobsen, T. *The Sumerian King List*. Assyriological Studies 11. Chicago, 1939.

Jameson, Fredric. *The Political Unconscious*. Ithaca, 1981.

Jepsen, A. 'Ein neuer Fixpunkt für die Chronologie der israelitischen Könige?' *VT* 20 (1970): 359-361.

Johnson, Harry M. 'Ideology and the Social System'. In *International Encyclopedia of the Social Sciences*. Vol. 7, pp. 76-85. Ed. by David L. Sills. New York, 1968.

Kallai, Z. 'The Wandering-Traditions from Kadesh-Barnea to Canaan: A Study in Biblical Historiography'. *JJS* 33 (1982): 175-184.

___ 'The Boundaries of Canaan and the Land of Israel in the Bible'. In *Eretz-Israel* 12 (1975): 27-34 <Hebrew>.

Kammenhuber, A. 'Die hethitische Geschichtsschreibung'. *Saeculum* 9 (1958): 136-155.

Katz, Ronald C. *The Structure of Ancient Arguments: Rhetoric and Its Near Eastern Origin*. Shapolsky/Steimatzky, 1986.

Kaufmann, Y. *The Biblical Account of the Conquest of Palestine*. Jerusalem, 1953.

Kearney, P.J. 'The Role of the Gibeonites in the Deuteronomic History'. *CBQ* 35 (1973): 1-19.

Kemp, Barry J. 'Imperialism and Empire in New Kingdom Egypt (c. 1575-1087 BC)'. In *Imperialism in the Ancient World*. Ed. by P.D.A. Garnsey and C.R. Whittaker. Cambridge, 1978. pp. 8-20; 43-57.

Kempinski, A. 'Tell el 'Ajjul Beth-Aglayim or Sharuhen'. *IEJ* 24 (1974): 145-152.

___ 'Some Observations on the Hyksos XVth Dynasty and Its Canaanite Origins'. In *Pharaonic Egypt: The Bible and Christianity*. Ed. by S. Israelit-Groll. pp. 129-137. Jerusalem, 1985.

Kempinski, A. and Košak, S. 'CTH 13: The Extensive Annals of Hattušili I (?)'. *Tel Aviv* 9 (1982): 87-116.

Kessler, K. *Untersuchungen zur historischen Topographie Nordmesopotamiens in neuassyrischer Zeit*. Beiheft zum TAVO Band 26. Wiesbaden: Harrassowitz, 1980.

Kielmansegg, Peter Graf. Editor. *Legitimationsprobleme politischer Systeme*. [Politische Vierteljahresschrift, Sonderheft 7/1]. Opladen: Westdeutscher Verlag, 1976.

King, L.W. and Budge, E.A.W. *Annals of the Kings of Assyria* I. London, 1902. [no subsequent volumes appeared].

King, L.W. *Babylonian Boundary Stones and Memorial Tablets in the British Museum*. London, 1912.

Kinner-Wilson, R. 'The Kurba'il Statue of Shalmaneser III'. *Iraq* (1962): 96-115.

Kitchen, K.A. *Ancient Orient and the Old Testament*. Downers Grove, Illinois, 1966.

___ 'Interrelations of Egypt and Syria'. In *La Siria nel Tardo Bronzo*. [Orientis Antiqvi Collectio, IX]. Ed. by M. Liverani. Rome, 1969.

___ 'Egypt, Ugarit, Qatna and Covenant.'. *UF* 11 (1979): 453-464.

___ *The Third Intermediate Period in Egypt (1100-650 B.C.)*. Warminster, 1973.

___ *Pharaoh Triumphant: The Life and Times of Ramesses II*. Warminster, 1982.

___ *Ramesside Inscriptions, Historical and Biographical*. Oxford, 1961-.

Klatt, Werner. *Hermann Gunkel: Zu seiner Theologie der Religionsgeschichte und zur Entstehung der form-geschichtlichen Methode*. Berlin, 1972.

Klein, Ralph W. *Currents in Theology and Mission* 12 (1985): 123.

Knudsen, E.E. 'Fragments of Historical Texts from Nimrud—II'. *Iraq* 29 (1967): 49-69.

Knudtzon, J.A. *Die El-Amarna Tafeln*. 2 Vols. Leipzig, 1915.

Košak, Silvan. 'The Rulers of the Early Hittite Empire'. *Tel Aviv* 7 (1980): 163-68.

Kramer, S.N. *From the Tablets of Sumer*. Garden City, N.Y., 1956.

___ *History Begins at Sumer*. Garden City, N.Y., 1959.

Krecher, J., and Müller, H.-P. 'Vergangenheitsinteresse in Mesopotamien und Israel'. *Saeculum* 26 (1975): 13-44.

Kümmel, H. 'Hethitische Texte'. In *Historisch-Chronologische Texte*. ed. by M. Dietrich, H.M. Kümmel, O. Loretz, and H. Otten. [*TUAT* 1/5]. pp. 452-480. Gütersloher, 1985.

LaCapra, Dominick. 'Comment'. *New Literary History* 17/2 (1986): 221.

Ladurie, E. LeRoy. *The Mind and Method of the Historian*. Translated by Siân Reynolds and Ben Reynolds. [*Le territoire de l'historien*. Vol. 2, 1978]. Chicago, 1981.

Lambert, W.G. 'Destiny and Divine Intervention in Babylon and Israel'. *OTS* 17 (1972): 65-72.

___ 'History and the Gods: A Review Article'. *Or* 39 (1970): 170-177.

___ 'Tukulti-Ninurta I and the Assyrian King List'. *Iraq* 38 (1976): 85-94.

Landsberger, B. Sam'al. *Studien zur Entdeckung der Ruinenstätte Karatepe*. 1 Liefg. Veröffentlichungen der Türkischen Historischen Gesellschaft VII. Serie Nr. 16. Ankara, 1948.

Laroche, E. *Catalogue des Textes Hittites*. Paris, 1971.

Lasine, S. 'Indeterminacy and the Bible: A Review of Literary and Anthropological Theories and Their Application to Biblical Texts'. *Hebrew Studies* 37/1 (1986): 48-80.

Le Goff, Jacques. 'Is Politics Still the Backbone of History?' In *Historical Studies Today*. Ed. by F. Gilbert and S.R. Graubard. p. 340. New York, 1972.

Le Gac, I. *Les Inscriptions D'Aššur-Nasir-Aplu III*. Paris, 1906.

Lee, Dwight E. and Beck, Robert N. 'The Meaning of "Historicism"'. *American Historical Review* 59 (1954): 568-577.

Lemche, Niels Peter. *Early Israel: Anthropological and Historical Studies on the Israelite Society Before the Monarchy*. [VTS 37]. Leiden, 1985.

___ *Ancient Israel: A New History of Israelite Society*. Sheffield: JSOT Press, 1988.

Lévi-Strauss, C. *The Elementary Structures of Kinship*. London, 1969.
___ 'Reciprocity and Hierarchy'. *American Anthropologist* 46 (1944): 266-268.
Levin, D. In *Defense of Historical Literature*. New York, 1967.
Levine, L.D. 'Preliminary Remarks on the Historical Inscriptions of Sennacherib'. In *History, Historiography and Interpretation*. Ed. by H. Tadmor and M. Weinfeld. pp. 58-75. Jerusalem, 1983.
___ 'Sennacherib's Southern Front: 704-689 B.C.' *JCS* 34 (1982): 49-51.
___ 'The Second Campaign of Sennacherib'. *JNES* 32 (1973): 312-317.
___ 'Geographical Studies in the Neo-Assyrian Zagros,—II'. *Iran* 12 (1974): 99-123.
Levy, F.J. 'Editor's Foreword'. To *The Theory and Practice of History*, p. vi.
Lichačov, D.S. *Poetika Drevnerusskoi Literatury*. Moscow, 1979. [Russian].
Lichtheim, George. 'The Concept of Ideology'. *History and Theory* 4/2 (1965): 164-195.
Lichtheim, Miriam. *Ancient Egyptian Literature: A Book of Readings*. 3 Vols. Berkeley, Los Angeles and London, 1973-1980.
Liddell, H.G. and Scott, R. *A Greek-English Lexicon*. New York, 1878.
Lidzbarski, M. *Handbuch der nordsemitischen Epigraphik*. 2 Volumes. Weimar, 1898.
Lie, A.G. *The Inscriptions of Sargon II, King of Assyria*. Part 1: The Annals. Paris, 1929.
Lipiński, E. 'Etymological and Exegetical Notes on the Mesha Inscription'. *Or* 40 (1971): 325-340.
Liver, J. 'The Literary History of Joshua IX'. *JSS* 8 (1963): 227-243.
Liverani, M. 'Critique of Variants and the Titulary of Sennacherib'. In *Assyrian Royal Inscriptions: New Horizons*. Ed. by F.M. Fales. pp. 225-258. Rome, 1981.
___ 'Storiografia politica Hittita—I. Šunaššura, ovvero: della reciprocita'. *OA* 12 (1973): 267-297.
___ 'Storiografia Politica Hittita—II. Telipinu, Ovvero: Della Solidarietà'. *OA* 16 (1977): 105-131.
___ 'Contrasti e confluenze di concezioni politiche nell 'età di el-Amarna'. *RA* 61 (1967): 1-18.
___ 'Un nuovo modo di lettura delle lettere di el-Amarna: Le lettere del faraone a Rib-Adda'. *OA* 10 (1971): 253-268.
___ 'Memorandum on the Approach to Historiographic Texts'. *Or* 42 (1973): 178-194. Reproduced in *Approaches to the Study of the Ancient Near East*. Ed. by G. Buccellati. Rome, 1973.
Long, B.O. 'On Finding the Hidden Premises'. *JSOT* 39 (1987): 10-14.
___ *I Kings with an Introduction to Historical Literature*. [FOTL Vol. 9]. Grand Rapids, 1984.
Loretz, Oswald. *Habiru-Hebräer: Eine sozio-linguistische Studie über die Herkunft des Gentiliziums ʿbri vom Appellativum habiru*. [Bei-

heft zur Zeitschrift für die alttestamentliche Wissenschaft, 160]. Walter de Gruyter, 1984.
Luckenbill, D.D. *The Annals of Sennacherib*. [OIP 2]. Chicago, 1924.
___*Ancient Records of Assyria and Babylonia*. 2 Vols. Chicago, 1926-1927.
Lukács, G. *Geschichte und Klassenbewusstsein: Studien über marxistische Dialektik*. Berlin, 1923.
Machinist, P. 'Assyrians and Hittites in the Late Bronze Age'. In *Mesopotamien und Seine Nachbarn*. Ed. by H.J. Nissen, and J. Renger. pp. 266-269. Berlin, 1987.
Maisler, B. 'Ancient Israelite Historiography'. *IEJ* 2 (1952): 82-88.
Malamat, A. 'Doctrines of Casuality in Hittite and Biblical Historiography: A Parallel'. *VT* 5 (1955): 1-12.
Malbran-Labat, Florence. *L'Armee et l'Organisation Militaire de l'Assyri: d'Apres les Lettres des Sargonides Trouvées à Ninive*. Ecole Pratique des Hautes Etudes IV Section, Sciences historiques et philologiques, 2. [Hautes Etudes Orientales, 19]. Librairie Droz, 1982.
Mandelbaum, M. 'A Note on History as Narrative'. *History and Theory* 6 (1967): 414-419.
Mannheim, K. *Ideology and Utopia*. London, 1936. 2nd Edition, 1960.
Marazzi, Massimiliano. 'Überlegungen zur Bedeutung von pankuš in der hethitisch-akkadischen Bilinguis Hattušilis I'. *WO* 15 (1984): 99.
Margolis, M.L. 'Specimen of a New Edition of the Greek Joshua'. *Jewish Studies in Memory of Israel Abrahams*. pp. 307-323. New York, 1927. = reprint, Sidney Jellicoe, Editor. *Studies in the Septuagint: Origins, Recensions, and Interpretations*. pp. 434-450. New York, 1974.
Margolis, M.L. *The Book of Joshua in Greek*. Paris, 1931.
Mayer, W. 'Sargons Feldzug gegen Urartu—714 v. Chr. Eine militärhistorische Würdigung'. *MDOG* 112 (1980): 13-33.
___'Die Finanzierung einer Kampagne'. *UF* 11 (1979): 571-595.
___'Sargons Feldzug gegen Urartu—714 v. Chr. Text und Übersetzung'. *MDOG* 115 (1983): 65-132.
McCarter, P.K. *I Samuel* [The Anchor Bible]. Garden City, N.Y., 1980.
___'Yaw, Son of Omri: A Philological Note on Israelite Chronology'. *BASOR* 216 (1974, erch. 1975): 5-7.
McCarthy, D.J. 'Some Holy War Vocabulary in Joshua 2'. *CBQ* 33 (1971): 227-228.
___*Treaty and Covenant*. AnBib 21. Rome, 1963.
McCullough, W.S. Ed. *The Seed of Wisdom: Essays in Honour of T.J. Meek*. Toronto, 1964.
McEvenue, Sean. *The Narrative Style of the Priestly Writer*. Analecta Biblica 50. Rome: Pontifical Biblical Institute, 1971.
Meissner, B. 'Die Eroberung der Stadt Ulhu auf Sargons 8. Feldzug'. *ZA* 34 (1922): 113-122.

Melchert, H. Craig. 'The Acts of Hattušili I'. *JNES* 37 (1978): 1-22.
Mendenhall, G.E. *The Tenth Generation: The Origins of the Biblical Tradition*. Baltimore and London, 1973.
___ 'Law and Covenant in Israel and the Ancient Near East'. *BA* 17 (1954): 26-46; 49-76.
Michel, E. 'Die Aššur-Texte Salmanassars III. (858-824)'. *WO* 1/4 (1949): 265-268; *WO* 2/1 (1954): 27-45; *WO* 2/2 (1955): 137-165; and *WO* 2/3 (1956): 221-241.
Millard, A.R. 'Review of A.K. Grayson's Assyrian and Babylonian Chronicles'. *JAOS* 100/3 (1980): 364-368.
___ 'The Old Testament and History: Some Considerations'. *FT* 110 (1983): 34-53.
___ 'The Scythian Problem'. In *Glimpses of Ancient Egypt: Studies in Honour of H.W. Fairman*. pp. 119-122. Ed. by J. Ruffle, G.A. Gabella, and K.A. Kitchen. Warminster, 1979.
___ 'Sennacherib's Attack on Hezekiah'. *TB* 36 (1977): 61-77.
___ 'Adad-Nirari III, Aram, and Arpad'. *PEQ* 105/2 (1973): 161-164.
___ 'Fragments of Historical Texts from Nineveh: Ashurbanipal'. *Iraq* 30 (1968): 98-111.
Millard, A.R. and Tadmor, H. 'Adad-Nirari III in Syria: Another Stele Fragment and the Dates of His Campaigns'. *Iraq* 35 (1973): 57-64.
Miller, P.D. *The Divine Warrior in Early Israel*. Cambridge, Mass., 1973.
Miller, J.M. and Tucker, G.M. *The Book of Joshua*. [The Cambridge Bible Commentary]. Cambridge, 1974.
Miller, J.M. and Hayes, J.H. *A History of Ancient Israel and Judah*. London, 1986.
Miller, J.M. 'The Moabite Stone as a Memorial Stela'. *PEQ* 104 (1974): 9-18.
Miller, F.T. with a Board of Historical and Military Authorites. *The Complete History of World War II*. Chicago: Readers' Service Bureau, 1945.
Mindell, M., Geller, M.J. and Wansbrough, J.E. Editors. *Figurative Language in the Ancient Near East*. London: School of Oriental and African Studies, 1987.
Mink, Louis O. 'The Autonomy of Historical Understanding'. In *Philosophical Analysis and History*. Ed. by William H. Dray. pp. 160-192. New York and London, 1966.
___ 'Narrative Form as a Cognitive Instrument'. In *Literary Form and Historical Understanding*. Ed. by R.H. Canary, and H. Kozicki. Madison, 1978.
Möhlenbrink, K. 'Die Landnahmesagen des Buches Josua'. *ZAW* 56 (1938): 238-268.
Momigliano, A. 'The Origins of Universal History'. In *The Poet and the Historian: Essays in Literary and Historical Biblical Criticism*. [HSS, 26]. Ed. by R.E. Friedman. pp. 133-148. Chico, California, 1983.

Mond, R., and Meyers, O.H. *Temples of Armant, A Prelimary Survey: The Text*. Translated by M.S. Drower. London, 1940.
Moore, George F. *A Critical and Exegetical Commentary on Judges*. [ICC]. New York, 1895.
Morenz, S. *Egyptian Religion*. Trans. by A.E. Keep. London, 1973.
Mowinckel, S. 'Israelite Historiography'. *ASTI* 2 (1963): 4-26.
___ 'Die vorderasiatischen Königs- und Fürsteninschriften eine stilistische Studie'. In *Eucharisterion, Festschrift Hermann Gunkel dargebracht*. Vol. 1. FRLANT 19, pp. 278-322. Göttingen, 1923.
Müller, H.-P. 'Ḥmm'. In *TDOT*. Vol. 3, pp. 420-421.
Murnane, William J. *The Road to Kadesh: A Historical Interpretation of the Battle Reliefs of Sety I at Karnak*. [SAOC 42]. Chicago: The Oriental Institute of the University of Chicago, 1985.
Na'aman, N. 'Two Notes on the Monolith Inscription of Shalmaneser III from Kurkh'. *Tel Aviv* 3 (1976): 89-106.
___ 'Sennacherib's 'Letter to God' on His Campaign to Judah'. *BASOR* 214 (1974): 25-39.
Nash, Ronald H. *Christian Faith and Historical Understanding*. Grand Rapids, 1984.
Neu, E. and Otten, H. *Indogermanische Forschungen* 77 (1972): 181-190.
___ *Der Anitta-Text*. Studien zu den Bogazkoy-Texten 18. Wiesbaden, 1974.
Nissen, Hans Jörg, and Renger, Johannes. Editors. *Mesopotamien und Seine Nachbarn: Politische und Kulturelle Wechselbeziehungen im Alten Vorderasien Vom 4. Bis 1. Jahrtausend v. Chr*. [Berliner Beiträge zum Vorderen Orient, 1]. Dietrich Reimer, 1987.
Noth, M. 'Die fünf Könige in der Höhle von Makkeda'. *Palästinajahrbuch* 33 (1937): 22-36. = *Aufsätze zur biblischen Landes- und Altertumskunde*. Ed. by H.W. Wolff. Vol. I, pp. 281-293. Neukirchen-Vluyn, 1971.
___ 'Die Annalen Thutmose III. als Geschichtsquelle'. *ZDPV* 66 (1943): 156-174.
___ *Das Buch Josua*. [HAT 7]. 3rd ed. Tübingen, 1971.
___ 'Geschichtsschreibung im A.T.' In *Die Religion in Geschichte und Gegenwart*. 3rd ed. Vol. 2, pp. 1498-1504. Ed. by K. Galling. Berlin, 1957-62.
___ *Überlieferungsgeschichtliche Studien*. Tübingen, 1943. Partly translated as *The Deuteronomistic History*. JSOTS 15. Sheffield, 1981.
Oded, Bustenay. *Mass Deportation and Deportees in the Neo-Assyrian Empire*. Reichert, 1979.
Oden, R.A., Jr. 'Hermeneutics and Historiography: Germany and America'. In *Seminar Papers of the SBL*. 1980.

___ 'Intellectual History and the Study of the Bible'. In *The Future of Biblical Studies*. Ed. by R.E. Friedman and H.G.M. Williamson. pp. 1-18. Atlanta, 1987.

Olmstead, A.T.E. *JAOS* 41 (1921): 345-382.

___ *JAOS* 38 (1918): 209-263.

___ 'Assyrian Historiography'. The University of Missouri Series, Social Studies Series II/1. Columbia, Mo., 1916.

Oppenheim, A.L. *Ancient Mesopotamia: Portrait of a Dead Civilization*. Chicago and London, 1964.

___ 'The City of Aššur in 714 B.C.' *JNES* 19 (1960): 133-147.

___ *Interpretations of Dreams in the Ancient Near East*. [TAPS 46/3]. Philadelphia, 1956.

Oren, E.D. 'Governors' Residencies in Canaan under the New Kingdom: A Case Study of Egyptian Administration'. *JSSEA* = [*Journal of the Society for the Study of Egyptian Antiquity*] 14/2 (1985): 35-50.

___ 'The "Ways of Horus" in North Sinai'. In *Egypt, Israel, Sinai: Archaeological and Historical Relationships in the Biblical Period* (Ed. by A.F. Rainey. Tel Aviv, 1987), pp. 69-119.

Orlinsky, H.M. 'The Hebrew *Vorlage* of the Septuagint of the Book of Joshua'. *VTS* 17 (1968): 187-195.

Orsini, G.N.G. 'Genres'. In *Princeton Encyclopedia of Poetry and Poetics*. Ed. by A. Preminger. pp. 307-309. Princeton, 1967.

Otten, H. *Die Apologie Hattušiliš III. Das Bild der Überlieferung*. [StBoT 24]. Wiesbaden, 1981.

___ 'Aitiologische Erzählung von der Überquerung des Taurus'. *ZA* 21 (1963): 160ff.

___ 'Neue Fragmente zu den Annalen des Muršili'. *MIO* 3 (1955): 153-179.

Otto, E. 'Geschichtsbild and Geschichtsschreibung in Ägypten'. *WO* 3/3 (1964/1966): 161-176.

___ *Die biographischen Inschriften der ägyptischen Spätzeit*. Leiden, 1954.

Page, S. 'A Stela of Adad-Nirari III and Nergal-Ereš from Tell Al Rimah'. *Iraq* 30 (1968): 139-153.

Paley, Samuel M. *King of the World: Ashur-nasir-pal II of Assyria 883-859 B.C.* Brooklyn, N.Y., 1976.

Percy, W. 'Metaphor as Mistake'. *The Sewanee Review* 66 (1958): 79-99.

Pfeiffer, Robert H. *Introduction to the Old Testament.*[2] New York, 1948.

Piepkorn, A.C. *Historical Prism Inscriptions of Ashurbanipal*. [Assyriological Studies, 5]. Chicago, 1933.

Pitard, Wayne T. 'Amarna *ekemu* and Hebrew *naqam**'. *Maarav* 3/1 (1982): 5-25.

___*Ancient Damascus: A Historical Study of the Syrian City-State from Earliest Times Until its Fall to the Assyrians in 732 B.C.E.* Winona Lake, 1987.
Polzin, R. 'HWQY' and Covenantal Institutions in Early Israel'. *HTR* 62 (1969): 233-240.
Posener, G. *Littérature et politique dans L'Égypte de la XII^e dynastie.* Paris, 1956.
Press, Gerald A. *The Development of the Idea of History in Antiquity.* Kingston and Montreal, 1982.
Pritchard, J.B. *Ancient Near Eastern Texts Relating to the Old Testament.* 3rd ed. with supplement. Princeton, N.J., 1969.
Puhvel, Jaan. *Hittite Etymological Dictionary.* [2 Vols. in 1]. Paris, 1984.
Rad, G. von. *Der heiligen Krieg im alten Israel.*[3] Göttingen, 1958.
___'The Beginnings of Historical Writing in Ancient Israel'. In *The Problem of the Hexateuch.* pp. 166-204. 1944.
Rainey, Anson F. Editor. *Egypt, Israel, Sinai: Archaeological and Historical Relationships in the Biblical Period.* Tel Aviv University, 1987.
Ranke, G. von. *Entstehung des Historismus.* Munich, 1936.
Redford, D.B. *History and Chronology of the Eighteenth Dynasty of Egypt: Seven Studies.* Toronto, 1967.
___'Studies in Relations between Palestine and Egypt during the First Millennium B.C. Pt. 1: The Taxation System of Solomon'. In *Studies in the Ancient Palestinian World.* Ed. by D.B. Redford and W.J. Wevers, pp. 141-156. Toronto, 1972.
___*Pharaonic King-Lists, Annals and Day-Books: A Contribution to the Study of the Egyptian Sense of History.* SSEA, IV. Benben, 1986.
___'The Hyksos Invasion in History and Tradition'. *Or* (1970): 1-51.
___*Akhenaten: The Heretic King.* Princeton, 1984.
___'An Egyptological Perspective on the Exodus Narrative'. In *Egypt, Israel, Sinai: Archaeological and Historical Relationships in the Biblical Period.* ed. by A.F. Rainey, pp. 137-161. Tel Aviv University, 1987.
Reisner, G.A. 'Inscribed Monuments from Gebel Barkal'. *ZÄS* 66 (1931): 89-100.
Reisner, G.A. and Reisner, M.B. 'Inscribed Monuments from Gebel Barkal. Pt. 2: The Granite Stela of Thutmose III'. *ZÄS* 69 (1933): 24-39.
Renger, J. 'Königsinschriften. B. Akkadisch'. *RLA* 6 (1980): 65-77.
Ricoeur, P. 'Explanation and Understanding: On Some Remarkable Connections Among the Theory of the Text, Theory of Action, and Theory of History'. In *The Philosophy of Paul Ricoeur.* Ed. by C.E. Reagan and D. Stewart. Boston, 1978.
Rigg, H. 'Sargon's "Eighth Military Campaign"'. *JAOS* 62 (1942): 130-138.

Roberts, J.J.M. *The Princeton Seminary Bulletin* 5/3 (1984): 250-251.
___ 'Myth versus History: Relaying the Comparative Foundations'. *CBQ* 38 (1976): 1-13.
___ 'Nebuchadnezzar I's Elamite Crisis in Theological Perspective'. In *Essays on the Ancient Near East in Memory of J.J. Finkelstein*. Ed by M. de Jong Ellis, pp. 183-187. Hamden Conn., 1977.
Roccati, A. *La Littérature historique sous l'ancien Empire égyptien*. [Les Éditions du Cerf, 29]. Paris, 1982.
Rogerson, J.W. *JTS* 37/2 (1986): 451-454.
___ *Anthropology and the Old Testament*. Sheffield, 1984.
___ 'Was Early Israel A Segmentary Society?' *JSOT* 36 (1986): 17-26.
Rokeah, D. 'Speeches in Thucydides: Factual Reporting or Creative Writing?' *Athenaeum* 60 (1982): 386-401.
Röllig, W. 'Zur Typologie und Entstehung der babylonischen und assyrischen Königlisten'. *Lišan mitḫurti. Festschrift W. von Soden*. AOAT 1, pp. 265-277. Neukirchen-Vluyn, 1969.
Roussel, L. *Le Livre de Josué: Chapitres 1-12 texte, Traduction, Commentaire*. [Publications de la Faculté des Lettres de l'université de Montpellier, 8]. Nimes, 1969.
Rowton, M.B. 'War, Trade and the Emerging Power Center'. In *Mesopotamien und Seine Nachbarn*. Ed. by H.J. Nissen, and J. Renger. pp. 140-143. Berlin, 1987.
Ryckmans, G. 'Het Oude Arabië en de Bijbel'. *JEOL* 14 (1956): 73-84.
Safar, F. 'A Further Text of Shalmaneser III from Assur'. *Sumer* 7 (1951): 3-21.
Saggs, H.W.F. 'Assyrian Warfare in the Sargonid Period'. *Iraq* 25 (1963): 145-160..
___ *The Encounter with the Divine in Mesopotamia and Israel*. London, 1978.
___ *The Might That Was Assyria*. London, 1986.
Sawyer, J.F.A. 'Joshua 10:12-14 and the Solar Eclipse of 30 September 1131 B.C'. *PEQ* 104 (1972): 139-146.
Scheil, V. *RA* 14 (1917): 159-160.
Schneidau, Herbert. *Sacred Discontent*. Baton Rouge, La., 1977.
Scholes, Robert. *Semiotics and Interpretation*. New Haven, 1985.
Schrader, E. *Zur Kritik der Inschriften Tiglath-Pileser II*. [Abh. d. Kön. Akad. d. Wiss. zu Berlin]. Berlin, 1880.
Schramm, W. *Einleitung in die Assyrischen Königsinschriften*. Vol. II. = [Handbuch der Orientalistik (Ed. by B. Spuler), 1. Abteilung Der Nahe und der Mittlere Osten, Ergänzungsband Fünf, 1 Abschnitt. Leiden, 1973.
Schuler, E. von. *Die Kaškäer. Ein Beitrag zur Ethnographie des Alten Kleinsasien*. Berlin, 1967.
Schulz, A. *Das Buch Josua*. Berlin, 1924.
Schumpter, J.A. *Imperialism and Social Classes*. Oxford, 1951. [Translation of *Zur Soziologie der Imperialismen*. (1919)].

Scott, R.B.Y. 'Meteorological Phenomena and Terminology in the Old Testament'. *ZAW* 64 (1952): 19-20.
Seeligmann, I.L. 'Aetiological Elements in Biblical Historiography'. *Zion* 26 (1961): 141-169 <Hebrew>.
Segert, S. 'Die Sprache der moabitischen Königsinschrift'. *ArOr* 29 (1961): 231-259.
Sethe, K. *Urkunden der 18. Dynastie, historisch-biographische Urkunden*. IV. 2nd Ed. Leipzig, 1927-1930.
Shaw, Harry. *Dictionary of Literary Terms*. 1972.
Shils, Edward. 'The Concept and Function of Ideology'. In *International Encyclopedia of the Social Sciences*. Ed. by David L Sills. Vol. 7, pp. 66-76. New York, 1968. 17 Volumes.
Shirun-Grumach, I. 'Die poetischen Teile der Gebel-Barkal-Stele'. In *Egyptological Studies*. [Scripta Hierosolymitana 28]. Ed. by S. Israelit-Groll. pp. 117-186. Jerusalem, 1982.
Smart, Ninian. *Beyond Ideology: Religion and the Future of Western Civilization*. San Francisco, 1981.
Smend, R. *Jahwekrieg und Stämmebund.*² [FRLANT 84]. Göttingen, 1966.
Smith, Morton. *JAAR* 53 (1985): 133.
Soggin, J.A. *Joshua*. Tr. R.A. Wilson. [OTL]. Philadelphia, 1972.
___ 'Ein ausserbiblisches Zeugnis für die Chronologie des Jᵉhô'aš/Jô'aš, König von Israel'. *VT* 20 (1970): 366-368.
Sollberger, E. and Kupper, J.-R. *Inscriptions Royales sumeriennes et akkadiennes*. [Littératures anciennes du Proche-Orient]. Paris, 1971.
Sommer, F. and Falkenstein, A. *Die hethitisch-akkadische Bilingue des Hattušili I*. Abh. der Bayerischen Akad. der Wiss., Phil.-hist. Abt., N.F. 16. Munich, 1938.
Spalinger, A.J. *Aspects of the Military Documents of the Ancient Egyptians*. [Yale Near Eastern Researches, 9]. New Haven and London, 1983.
___ 'The Northern Wars of Seti I: An Integrative Study'. *JARCE* 16 (1979): 29-47.
___ 'A New Reference to an Egyptian Campaign of Thutmose III in Asia'. *JNES* 37 (1978): 35-41.
___ 'A Critical Analysis of the "Annals" of Thutmose III (Stucke V-VI)'. *JARCE* 14 (1977): 41-54.
___ 'Some Notes on the Battle of Megiddo and Reflections on Egyptian Military Writing'. *MDAIK* 30 (1974): 221-229.
___ 'Aššurbanipal and Egypt: A Source Study'. *JAOS* 94 (1974): 316-328.
___ 'Egyptian-Hittite Relations at the Close of the Amarna Period and Some Notes on Hittite Military Strategy in North Syria'. *BES = Bulletin of the Egyptological Seminar* 1 (1979), pp. 73-88.
Speiser, E.A. 'Geschichtswissenschaft'. In *RLA* 3 (1956): 216-220.

___ 'Ancient Mesopotamia'. In *The Idea of History in the Ancient Near East*. Ed. by R.C. Dentan, pp. 35-76. New Haven, 1955.

___ 'The Biblical Idea of History in Its Common Near Eastern Setting'. In *Biblical and Oriental Studies*. Ed. by J.J. Finkelstein and M. Greenberg. pp. 187-210. Philadelphia, 1967.

Stager, L.E. 'Merenptah, Israel and Sea Peoples: New Light on an Old Relief'. In *Eretz-Israel* 18 (1985): 56-64.

Stambovsky, P. 'Metaphor and Historical Understanding', *History and Theory* 27 (1988): 125-134.

Stark, Werner. *The Sociology of Knowledge*. London, 1958.

Starke, F. 'Der Erlass Telipinus'. *WO* 16 (1985): 100-113.

___ 'Halmasuit im Anitta-Text'. *ZA* 69 (1979): pp. 47-120.

Stephenson, F.R. 'Astronomical Verification and Dating of Old Testament Passages Referring to Solar Eclipses'. *PEQ* 107 (1975): 117-120.

Sternberg, Meir. *The Poetics of Biblical Narrative: Ideological Literature and the Drama of Reading*. Bloomington, Indiana, 1985.

Stol, M. *On Trees, Mountains, and Milestones in the Ancient Near East*. [Mededeelingen en Verhandelingen van het Voorziatisch Egyptisch Genootschap 'Ex Oriente Lux', 21]. Leiden: Ex Oriente Lux, 1979.

Streck, M. *Assurbanipal und die letzten assyrischen Könige bis zum Untergange Niniveh's*. [VAB, 7]. Leipzig, 1916.

Sturtevant, E.H. and Bechtel, G. *Hittite Chrestomathy*. Philadelphia, 1935.

Tadmor, H. 'The Aramaization of Assyria: Aspects of Western Impact'. In *Assyrien und seine Nachbarn*. II, pp. 449-470. Berlin, 1987.

___ 'The Autobiographical Apology in the Royal Assyrian Literature'. In *History, Historiography and Interpretation*. Ed. by H. Tadmor and M. Weinfeld. pp. 36-57. Jerusalem, 1983.

___ 'Observations on Assyrian Historiography'. In *Essays on the Ancient Near East in Memory of J.J. Finkelstein*. Ed. by M. D. Ellis, pp. 209-213. Hamden, Conn., 1977.

___ 'Assyria and the West: The Ninth Century and Its Aftermath'. In *Unity and Diversity: Essays in the History, Literature, and Religion of the Ancient Near East*. Ed. by H. Goedicke and J.J.M. Roberts, pp. 36-48. Baltimore and London, 1975.

___ 'The Historical Inscriptions of Adad-Nirari III'. *Iraq* 35 (1973): 141-150.

___ 'Introductory Remarks to a New Edition of the Annals of Tiglath-Pileser III'. In *Proceedings of the Israel Academy of Sciences and Humanities*. Vol. II, No. 9, pp. 1ff. Jerusalem, 1967.

___ 'The Inscriptions of Nabunaid, Historical Arrangement'. *Assyriological Studies* 16 (1965): 351-364.

___ 'The Last Three Decades of Assyria'. In *The Proceedings of the 25th International Congress of Orientalists*. Moscow, 1962. <Russian>.
___ 'Que and Muṣri'. *IEJ* 11 (1961): 143-150.
___ 'The Sin of Sargon'. *Eretz-Israel* 5 (1958): 150-163.
___ 'The Campaigns of Sargon II of Aššur: A Chronological-Historical Study'. *JCS* 12 (1958): 22-40; and 77-100.
___ 'History and Ideology in the Assyrian Royal Inscriptions'. In *Assyrian Royal Inscriptions: New Horizons*. Ed. by F.M. Fales, pp. 13-34. Rome, 1981.
Talmon, S. 'The Presentation of Synchroneity and Simultaneity in Biblical Narrative.' In *Scripta Hierosolymitana* 28 (1978): 9-26.
___ '*Har* and *Midbar*: An Antithetical Pair of Biblical Motifs'. In *Figurative Language in the Ancient Near East*. Ed. by M. Mindell, M.J. Geller, and J.E. Wansbrough, pp. 120-140. London, 1987.
Tanner, J.R., Previté-Orton, C.W. and Brooke, Z.N. Editors. *The Cambridge Medieval History*. Vol. 5. Cambridge, 1926.
Thackeray, H. St. John. 'New Light on the Book of Jashar (a Study of 3 Regn. viii 53$^b$ LXX)'. *JTS* 11 (1910): 518-532.
Thiele, E.R. 'An Additional Chronological Note on "Yaw, Son of Omri"'. *BASOR* 222 (1976): 19-23.
Thompson, R.J. *Moses and the Law in a Century of Criticism Since Graf*. Leiden, 1972.
Thompson, R. Campbell. *The Reports of the Magicians and Astrologers of Nineveh in the British Museum*. 2 Vols. [AMS reprint of 1900 edition], 1977.
___ *The Prisms of Esarhaddon and of Ashurbanipal*. London, 1931.
___ 'The British Museum Excavations at Nineveh (1931-32)'. *AAA* 20 (1933): 79-127.
Thompson, Kenneth. *Beliefs and Ideology*. London and New York, 1986.
Thureau-Dangin, F. *Une Relation de la Huitième Campagne de Sargon*. TCL 3. Paris, 1912.
___ *Die sumerischen und akkadischen Königsinschriften*. Berlin, 1907.
Trigger, B.G., Kemp, B.J, O'Connor, D., and Lloyd, A.B. *Ancient Egypt: A Social History*. Cambridge, 1983.
Trompf, G.W. 'Notions of Historical Recurrence in Classical Hebrew Historiography'. *Studies in the Historical Books of the Old Testament*. [VTS 30]. Ed. by J.A. Emerton. pp. 213-229. Leiden, 1979.
Twaddle, Michael. 'Imperialism'. In *The Social Science Encyclopedia*. Ed. by Adam Kuper and Jessica Kuper. pp. 377-379. London, Boston, and Henley, 1985.
Unger, E. *Reliefstele Adadniraris III. aus Saba'a und Semiramis*. Leipzig, 1913.
Ungnad, A. 'Datenlisten'. In *RLA* Vol. 2, pp. 131-194.
___ 'Eponym'. In *RLA* Vol. 2, pp. 412-457.

___ 'Jaua, Mâr Ḫumri'. *OLZ* 9 (1906): 224-226.
van der Toorn, Karel. *Sin and Sanction in Israel and Mesopotamia: A Comparative Study*. [Studia Semitica Neerlandica, 22]. Assen/ Maastricht: Van Gorcum, 1985.
Van Seters, John. *The Hyksos: A New Investigation*. New Haven, 1966.
___ 'Histories and Historians of the Ancient Near East: The Israelites'. *Or* 50 (1981): 137-185.
___ *In Search of History: Historiography in the Ancient World and the Origins of Biblical History*. New Haven and London, 1983.
Waldman, M. *Toward A Theory of Historical Narrative: A Case Study in Perso-Islamicate Historiography*. Columbus: Ohio State University Press, 1980.
Waldow, H. Eberhard von. 'The Concept of War in the Old Testament'. *Horizons in Biblical Theology* 6 (1984): 36-37.
Walsh, W.H. *An Introduction to the Philosophy of History*. London, 1951.
Weber, Max. *Wirtschft und Gesellschaft: Grundriss der verstehenden Soziologie*. 4th Edition. Vol. 1, pp. 758-778 Tübingen, 1927.
*Webster's 3rd New International Dictionary*. Vol. I. s.v. 'historiography'. p. 1073.
Weidner, E.F. 'Bruchstücke assyrischer Königsinschriften'. *AfO* 22 (1968-1969): 75-77.
___ 'Die Annalen Königs Aššurdân II. von Assyrien'. *AfO* 3 (1926): 151-161.
___ 'Die Kämpfe Adadnarâris I. gegen Hanigalbat'. *AfO* 5 (1928-1929): 89-100.
___ 'Neue Bruchstücke des Berichtes über Sargons achten Feldzug'. *AfO* 12 (1937-1939): 144-148.
___ *Die Inschriften Tukulti-Ninurtas I*. [AfO Beiheft, 12]. Graz, 1959.
Weinfeld, M. '"Justice and Righteousness" in Ancient Israel against the Background of "Social Reforms" in the Ancient Near East'. In *Assyrien und Seine Nachbarn*. II. pp. 491-519. Berlin, 1987.
___ 'The Loyalty Oath in the Ancient Near East'. *UF* 8 (1976): 379-414.
___ 'The Period of the Conquest and of the Judges as Seen by the Earlier and the Later Sources'. *VT* (1967): 93-113.
___ 'Freedom Proclamations in Egypt and in the Ancient Near East'. In *Pharaonic Egypt: The Bible and Christianity*. Ed. by S. Israelit-Groll. pp. 317-327. Jerusalem, 1985.
___ 'Divine Intervention in War in Ancient Israel and in the Ancient Near East'. In *History Historiography, and Interpretation*. Ed. by H. Tadmor and M. Weinfeld. pp. 121-147. Jerusalem, 1983.
Weinstein, J.M. 'The Egyptian Empire in Palestine: A Reassessment'. *BASOR* 241 (1981): 1-18.

Weippert, M. 'Jau(a) Mār Ḫumrî—Joram oder Jehu von Israel?' *VT* 28 (1978): 113-118.
___ 'Die Kämpfe des assyrischen Königs Aššurbanipal gegen die Araber'. *WO* 7 (1973): 39-85.
___ '"Heiliger Krieg" in Israel und Assyrien: Kritische Anmerkungen zu Gerhard von Rads Konzept der "Heiligen Krieges im alten Israel"'. *ZAW* 84 (1972): 460-493.
___ *The Settlement of the Israelite Tribes in Palestine*. [Studies in Biblical Theology, 21]. London, 1971.
___ 'Semitische Nomaden des zweiten Jahrtausends: Über die Š'św der ägyptischen Quellen'. *Biblica* 55 (1974): 265-280, 427-433.
Welleck R. and Warren, A. *Theory of Literature*. New York, 1956.
White, H. *Tropics of Discourse*. Baltimore and London, 1978.
___ *Metahistory, The Historical Imagination in Nineteenth-Century Europe*. Baltimore and London, 1973.
___ 'The Question of Narrative in Contemporary Historical Theory'. *History and Theory* 23 (1984): 2-42.
___ 'Historicism, History, and the Figurative Imagination'. *History and Theory* Beiheft 14 (1975): 48-67.
Whitehead, A.N. *Adventures of Ideas*. New York, 1971.
Whitelam, K.W. 'Recreating the History of Israel'. *JSOT* 35 (1986): 45-70.
Whybray, R.N. *The Succession Narrative*. SBT 2/9. London, 1968.
Williams, R.J. 'Egypt and Israel'. In *Legacy of Egypt*. Ed. by J.R. Harris (1971), pp. 262ff.
___ 'Literature as a Medium of Political Propaganda in Ancient Egypt'. In *The Seed of Wisdom: Essays in Honour of T.J. Meek*. Ed. by W.S. McCullough, pp. 14-30. Toronto, 1964.
___ 'The "Israel Stele" of Merenptah'. In *Documents from Old Testament Times*. pp. 137-141. Ed. by D. Winton Thomas. New York, 1958.
Wise, Gene. American *Historical Explanations*. Homewood, Ill., 1973.
Wiseman, D.J. *Chronicles of the Chaldean Kings (625-556 B.C.) in the British Museum*. London, 1956.
___ *The Vassal Treaties of Esarhaddon*. London, 1958.
___ 'Historical Records of Assyria and Babylonia'. In *Documents from Old Testament Times*. pp. 46-83. Ed. by D. Winton Thomas. New York, 1958.
Wolf, H.M. 'The Apology of Hattušiliš Compared with Other Political Self-Justifications of the Ancient Near East'. Dissertation,
Brandeis University, 1967.
Woudstra, Marten H. *The Book of Joshua*. [NICOT]. Grand Rapids, 1981.
Wright, G.E. 'What Archaeology Can and Cannot Do'. *BA* 34/3 (1971): 70-76.
___ 'The Literary and Historical Problem of Joshua 10 and Judges 1'. *JNES* 5 (1946): 105-114.

Wyatt, N. 'Some Observations on the Idea of History among the West Semitic Peoples'. *UF* 11 (1979): 825-832.

Yadin, Y. *The Art of Warfare in Biblical Lands: In the Light of Archaeological Study*. 2 Vols. Trans. by M. Pearlman. New York, 1963.

___ *Military and Archaelogical Aspects of the Conquest of Canaan in the Book of Joshua*. [El Ha'ayin, 1]. Jerusalem, 1965.

Yeivin, S. *The Israelite Conquest of Canaan*. Istanbul: Nederslands Historisch-Archaeologisch Institut in Het Nabije Oosten, 1971.

___ 'A New Egyptian Source for the History of Palestine and Syria'. *JPOS* 14 (1934): 194-229.

Younger, K.L., Jr. 'Panammuwa and Bar-Rakib: Two Structural Analyses'. *JANES* 18 (1986): 91-103.

___ 'A Critical Review of John Van Seters, *In Search of History*'. *JSOT* 40 (1987): 110-117.

___ 'The Figurative Aspect and the Contextual Method in the Evaluation of the Solomonic Empire (1 Kings 1-11)'. In *The Bible in Three Dimensions*. Ed. by D. Clines, S. Fowl, and S. Porter (Sheffield: Sheffield Academic Press, 1990), pp. 142-160.

Yurco, F. 'Merenptah's Palestinian Campaign'. *JSSEA* 8 (1978): 70.

Zaccagnini, C. 'The Enemy in the Neo-Assyrian Royal Inscriptions: The "Ethnographic" Description'. In *Assyrien und seine Nachbarn*. Vol. II, pp. 409-424. Berlin, 1987.

___ 'An Urartean Royal Inscription in the Report of Sargon's Eighth Campaign'. In *ARINH*. Ed. by F.M. Fales. pp. 260-264. Rome, 1981.

Zimanksy, Paul E. *Ecology and Empire: The Structure of the Urartian State*. [Studies in Ancient Oriental Civilization, 41. The Oriental Institute, 1985.

# APPENDIX

## JOSHUA 9-12

### *Text, Translation, Notes and Syntagmic Analysis*

This appendix offers a syntagmic identification and analysis as well as a selective presentation of particular issues concerning textual transmission and other important exegetical points.

The MT and the Greek version of the book of Joshua do not coincide at every point (this is surely litotes!). Fortunately, Max L. Margolis turned his attention to Joshua in order to present a text as close as possible to the original form of the Old Greek.[1] His methodology was, by and large, sound and the results have stood the test of time.[2] However, his assessment that the OG translator utilized a text almost identical to the MT, which he then modified in the direction of a general curtailment, cannot be sustained. It appears that H.M. Orlinsky was correct in his arguments that the translator of the OG of Joshua was faithful to his text; that the differences between the OG and the preserved Hebrew are due to the fact that behind the OG of Joshua lay a different Hebrew *Vorlage* from that of the preserved Hebrew; and that the difference between these two texts are such that a third text must be assumed.[3]

### *The Syntagms of Joshua 9-12*

The following is a list of the Hebrew syntagms which occur in Joshua 9-12. One should compare the listing of Assyrian syntagms, especially in the case of the connotations and extensions (pp. 72-78).

A — *Spatio-Temporal Coordinates*

This function typically includes syntagms like:

$A^2$: ויהי כשמע אדני צדק מלך ירושלם;
$a^{1,2}$: ויעבר יהושע וכל ישראל עמו מלבנה לכישה;
$A^2$: ואת מקדה לכד יהושע ביום ההוא.

B — *Disorder*

This represents the breakdown of order caused by the enemy often communicated in the form of a report:

וישלחו אנשי גבעון אל יהושע אל המחנה הגלגלה ואמר.

C — *Divine Aid*

Here the two most common syntagms are:

$C^2$ (the oracle) :: ויאמר יהוה אל יהושע;

$C^4$ the divine intervention :: ויתן יהוה גם אותה ביד ישראל.

Extensions used with this function are:

$C^{\aleph}$ — אל תירא מהם;

${}^{C}L^{\aleph}$ — כי בידך נתתים.

E — *Move from place to place*

Two common syntagms used in this function are:

$E^{12}$ — ויעל יהושע מן הגלגל

$E^{\xi}$ — ויבא אליהם יהושע פתאם

F — *Presence*

The function is expressed in the narrative by the syntagm: ויחנו עליה :: "and he took up positions against it."

G — *Flight*

Like in the Assyrian syntagms, this function is connotated by either $^{-}$ or $^{\Delta}$. Hence,

$G^{\Delta 1}$ is: ויראו מאד;

$G^{-2}$ = ויאספו ויעלו חמשת מלכי האמרי ..... הם וכל מחניהם;

$G^{-3}$ — ויחנו על גבעון וילחמו עליה.

H — *Pursuit*

The pursuit of the enemy is an important syntagmic function in the narrative: וירדפם דרך מעלה בית חורן.

L — *Outcome of the Combat*

Like the Assyrian syntagms, this function is divided into two areas: destruction ($L^1$) and acquisition ($L^2$). Common syntagms include:

$L^{1\aleph\beta}$ — ויכם עד עזקה ועד מקדה

$L^{1\beth\zeta}$ — החרם אותה ואת כל הנפש אשר בה

$L^{1\eta}$ — לא השאיר שריד

$L^{2\aleph\zeta\alpha}$ — וילכדו אותה ואת מלכה

A list of conquered cities is represented by $L^{\circ\chi}$.

M — *Submission*

Seen in the syntagms: ויעש להם יהושע שלום and ויכרת להם ברית לחיותם.

N — *Exemplary Punishment*

Often expressed by the following syntagm: ככל אשר עשה ללבנה.
But also connotated [n] וישמו אבנים גדלו על פי המערה.

O — *Consequences*

These syntagms represent this function:

$O^6$ — ויתנה יהושע לנחלה ישראל רמחלקתם לשבטיהם;
$O^7$ — והארץ שקטה ממלחמה.

Q — *Return*

Obviously used in this regard is: וישב יהושע וכל ישראל עמו אל המחנה הגלגלה.

## *Text and Translation*

### *Chapter Nine*[4]

$A^2$ [1]ויהי כשמע כל המלכים אשר בעבר הירדן בהר ובשפלה ובכל חוף
הים הגדול אל מול הלבנון החתי והאמרי הכנעני הפרזי
החוי היבוסי
$G^2$ [2]ויתקבצו יחדו להלחם עם יהושע ועם ישראל פה אחד

1. When all the kings west of the Jordan who were in the hill country, the Shephelah, and all along the sea coast of the Great Sea as far as Lebanon—the Hittites, the Amorites, the Canaanites, the Perizzites, the Hivites, and the Jebusites—heard about these things,
2. they came together and united to fight against Joshua and Israel.

$A^2$ [3]וישבי גבעון שמעו את אשר עשה יהושע ליריחו ולעי
$G^{-5}$ [4]ויעשו גם המה בערמה
U וילכו ויצטירו
ויקחו שקים בלים לחמוריהם
ונארות יין בלים ומבקעים ומצררים
[5]ונעלות בלות ומטלאות ברגליהם ושלמות בלות עליהם
וכל לחם צידם יבש היה נקדים
[6]וילכו אל יהושע אל המחנה הגלגל
ויאמרו אליו ואל איש ישראל
מארץ רחוקה באנו
ועתה כרתו לנו ברית

[ [5] ]

3. But When the inhabitants of Gibeon heard what Joshua had done to Jericho and Ai,
4. they also[6] resorted to shrewd trickery.
   They went as a delegation[7]
   after they had loaded on their donkeys worn-out sacks and worn-out wine-skins, tattered and mended.
5. And they wore worn-out and patched sandals on their feet.

And all the bread of their provision was dry and mouldy.

6. Then they went to Joshua in the camp at Gilgal;
and they said to him and to the men of Israel:
'We have come from a distant land;
make a treaty with us.'

V 7 ויאמרו איש ישראל אל החוי
אולי בקבי אתה יושב
ואיך אכרות לך ברית
8 ויאמרו אל יהושע
עבדיך אנחנו
ויאמר אלהם יהושע
מי אתם
ומאין תבאו
9 ויאמרו אליו
מארץ רחוקה מאד באו עבדיך לשם יהוה אלהיך
כי שמענו שמעו
ואת כל אשר עשה במצרים
10 ואת כל אשר עשה לשני מלכי האמרי אשר בעבר הירדן
לסיחון מלך חשבון ולעוג מלך הבשן אשר בעשתרות
11 ויאמרו אלינו זקינינו וכל ישבי ארצנו לאמר
קחו בידכם צידה לדרך
ולכו לקראתם ואמרתם אליהם
עבדיכם אנחנו
ועתה כרתו לנו ברית
12 זה לחמנו חם הצטידנו אתו מבתינו ביום צאתנו ללכת אליכם
ועתה הנה יבש והיה נקדים
13 ואלה נארות היין אשר מלאנו חדשים
והנה התבקעו
ואלה שלמותינו
ונעלינו בלו מרב הדרך מאד

7. The men of Israel said to the Hivites:
'But perhaps you live near us.
How then can we make a treaty with you?'

8. And they said to Joshua:
'We are your servants!'
But Joshua said to them:
'Who are you?
And where do you come from?'

9. And they said to him:
'Your servants have come from a very distant land because of the fame of YHWH your God.
For we heard of his reputation,
and all that He did in Egypt,

10. and all that He did to the two kings of the Amorites east of the Jordan:

to Sihon, king of Heshbon and Og, king of Bashan, who (reigned) in Ashtaroth.

11. Moreover, our elders and all the inhabitants of our land[8] said to us:
"Take provisions for your trip;
go and meet them and say to them:
'We are your servants;
make a treaty with us'.
12. This bread of ours was hot when we packed it at our homes
on the day that we left to go to you.
But now look it is dry and mouldy.
13. And these wine-skins which we filled with wine were new;
and look (now) they are cracked.
These our clothes and sandals are worn out by the very long trip'".

W [14]ויקחו האנשים מצירם
ואת פי יהוה לא שאלו
M [15]ויעש להם יהושע שלום
ויכרת להם ברית לחיותם
וישבעו להם נשיאי העדה

14. The men[9] (of Israel) sampled the provisions;
But they did not inquire of YHWH.
15. Then Joshua made peace with them;
and he made a treaty with them to let them live;
and the leaders of the congregation ratified it by oath with them.

X [16]ויהי מקצה שלשת ימים אחרי אשר כרתו להם ברית
וישמעו כי קרבים הם אליו ובקרבו הם ישבים
E [17]ויסעו בני ישראל
ויבאו אל עריהם ביום השלשי ועריהם גבעון והכפירה ובארות
וקרית יערים
L$^{1-x}$ [18]ולא הכום בני ישראל כי נשבעו להם נשיאי העדה ביהוה
אלהי ישראל

16. Three days after they had made the treaty with them,
they heard that they were neighbors, living near them.
17. Then the Israelites set out;
and on the third day came to their cities: Gibeon, Kephirah, Beeroth, and Kiriath Jearim.
18. But the Israelites did not attack them because the leaders of the congregation had sworn an oath to them by YHWH, the God of Israel.

Y$^{1}$ וילנו כל העדה על הנשיאים
[19]ויאמרו כל הנשיאים אל כל העדה
אנחנו נשבענו להם ביהוה אלהי ישראל
ועתה לא נוכל לנגע בהם
[20]זאת נעשה להם
והחיה אתם ולא יהיה עלינו קצף על השבועה אשר נשבענו להם

[21]ויאמרו אליהם הנשיאים
יחיו ויהיו חטבי עצים ושאבי מים לכל העדה

Then the entire congregation murmured[10] against the leaders.
19. But all the leaders said to the entire congregation:
'We have sworn an oath to them by YHWH, the God of Israel;
and we can not injure them now.
20. This is what we will do to them:
We will let them live so that wrath will not be upon us for breaking the oath which we swore to them'.
21. And the leaders said to them:
'Let them live, but let them be woodcutters and water-carriers for the entire congregation'.

Y$^{2}$ כאשר דברו להם הנשיאים
[22]ויקרא להם יהושע וידבר אליהם לאמר
למה רמיתם אתנו לאמר
רחוקים אנחנו מכם מאד
ואתם בקרבנו ישבים
[23]ועתה ארורים אתם
ולא יכרת מכם עבד וחטבי עצים ושאבי מים לבית אלהי

When the leaders had spoken to them,
22. then Joshua summoned them and spoke to them saying:
'Why did you deceive us by saying:
"We live a long way from you";
when you actually live near us?!
23. You are now under a curse:
You will never cease to serve as woodcutters and water-carriers for the house of my God'.

Y$^{3}$ [24]ויענו את יהושע ויאמרו
כי הגד הגד לעבדיך את אשר צוה יהוה אלהיך את משה עבדו לתת
לכם את כל הארץ
ולהשמיד את כל ישבי הארץ מפניכם
ונירא מאד לנפשתינו מפניכם
ונעשה את הדבר הזה
[25]ועתה הננו בידך
כטוב וכישר בעיניך לעשות לנו עשה

24. They answered Joshua saying:
'Because your servants were clearly told that YHWH your God had commanded his servant Moses to give you all the land,
and to wipe out all of the inhabitants of the land from before you,
we feared for our lives because of you.
So we did this thing.
25. We are now in your hands.
Whatever seems good and just to do in your eyes do to us'.

M [26]ויעש להם כן ויצל אותם מיד בני ישראל
ולא הרגום

[27]ויתנם יהושע ביום ההוא חטבי עצים ושאבי מים לערה
ולמזבח יהוה
ער היום הזה אל המקום אשר יבחר [יהוה]

26. Thus he did to them and rescued them from the hand of the Israelites.
27. And on that day Joshua made them woodcutters and water-carriers for the congregation and for the altar of YHWH:
until this day at the place which YHWH chooses.[11]

## *Chapter Ten*

[1]ויהי כשמע ארני צרק מלך ירושלם $A^2$
כי לכר יהושע את העי ויחרימה כאשר עשה ליריחו ולמלכה כן עשה
לעי ולמלכה
וכי השלימו ישבי גבעון את [יהושע את] ישראל
ויהיו בקרבם
[2]וייראו מאר $G^{\Delta 1}$
כי עיר גרולה גבעון כאחת ערי הממלכה
וכי היא גרולה מן העי וכל אנשיה גברים
[3]וישלח ארני צרק מלך ירושלם אל הוהם מלך חברון ואל פראם $G^{-2}$א
מלך ירמות
ואל יפיע מלך לכיש ואל רביר מלך עגלון לאמר
[4]עלו אלי
ועזרני ונכה את גבעון
כי השלימה את יהושע ואת בני יעראל

1. Now when Adoni-Zedek,[12] king of Jerusalem, heard
that Joshua had captured Ai and had totally destroyed it, as
he had done to Jericho and its king,
and that the inhabitants of Gibeon had made peace with Joshua[13] and Israel,
and (that) they (Joshua and Israel) were in their midst,
2. they very afraid[14]
because[15] Gibeon was an important city like one of the royal cities;
and because it was larger than Ai and all its men were warriors.
3. So Adonizedek king of Jerusalem, sent to Hoham king of Hebron, Piram[16] king of Jarmuth, Japhia king of Lachish, and Debir king of Eglon, saying:
4. 'come up to me,
and help me to attack Gibeon;
because it has made peace with Joshua and the Israelites'.

[5]ויאספו ויעלו חמשת מלכי האמרי מלך ירושלם מלך חברון מלך $G^{-2}$
ירמות מלך לכיש מלך עגלון הם וכל מחניהם
ויחנו על גבעון $G^{-3}$
וילחמו עליה

5. Then the five kings of the Amorites—the king of Jerusalem, the king of Hebron, the king of Jarmuth, the king of Lachish, and the king of Eglon, joined forces and came up—they and all their armies.

They took up positions against Gibeon;
and attacked it.

B [6]וישלחו אנשי גבעון אל יהושע אל המחנה הגלגלה לאמר
אל תרף ידיך מעבדיך
עלה אלינו מהרה
והושיעה לנו
ועזרנו כי נקבצו אלינו כל מלכי האמרי ישבי ההר

6. Then the inhabitants of Gibeon sent to Joshua in the camp at Gilgal saying:
'Do not abandon your servants.
Come up to us quickly,
and rescue us!
Help us, because all of the Amorite kings have joined forces against us'.

$E^{12}$ [7]ויעל יהושע מן הגלגל הוא וכל עם המלחמה עמו וכל גבורי החיל
$C^{2}$ [8]ויאמר יהוה אל יהושע
$C^{\aleph}$ אל תירא מהם
'$L^{\aleph}$ כי בירך נתתים
N לא יעמד איש מהם בפניך

7. So Joshua went up from Gilgal, he and all the people of his army and all of the elite warriors.
8. And YHWH said to Joshua:
'Do not be afraid of them;
I have delivered them into your hand.
Not one man of them will be able to withstand you'.

$E^{\xi}$ [9]ויבא אליהם יהושע פתאם
כל הלילה עלה מן הגלגל
$C^{4}$ [10]ויהמם יהוה לפני ישראל
$L^{1\chi\beta}$ ויכם מכה גדולה בגבעון
H וירדפם דרך מעלה בית חורן
$L^{1\chi\beta}$ ויכם עד עזקה ועד מקדה
$G^{\Delta 3}$ [11]ויהי בנסם מפני ישראל הם במורד בית חורן
$C^{4}$ ויהוה השליך עליהם אבנים מן השמים עד עזקה
N וימתו רבים אשר מתו באבני הברד מאשר הרגו בני ישראל בחרב

9. Joshua came upon them suddenly,
by having marched up all night from Gilgal.[17]
10. YHWH threw them into confusion before Israel,
who[18] smote them in a great victory at Gibeon,
and who pursued them on the road of the ascent of Beth Horon,[19]
and who smote them up to Azekah and up to Makkedah.
11. Then during their flight from Israel on the descent of Beth Horon to Azekah,
YHWH hurled stones[20] down on them from the sky,
and more of them died from the hailstones than were killed by the swords of the Israelites.

$a^2$ 12אז ידבר יהושע ליהוה ביום תת יהוה את האמרי לפני
בני ישראל
$C^4$ ויאמר לעיני ישראל
N שמש בגבעון דום   וירח בעמק אילון
13וידם השמש   וירח עמד   עד־יקם גוי איביו

הלא היא כתובה על ספר הישר
ויעמד השמש בחצי השמים
ולא אץ לבוא כיום תמים
14ולא היה כיום ההוא לפניו ואחריו
לשמע יהוה בקול איש
כי יהוה נלחם ישראל

Q [15וישב יהושע וכל ישראל עמו אל המחנה הגלגלה]

12. At that time, on the day that YHWH gave the Amorites[21] over to Israel,
Joshua spoke to YHWH;
and said in the presence of Israel:

'Sun, stand still over Gibeon,   Moon, over the valley of Aijalon',
13. So the Sun stood still,   and the moon stopped,
until the nation avenged itself on its enemies.

Is it not recorded in the Book of Yashar?[22]
So the sun stopped in the middle of the sky;
and delayed going down about a complete day.
14. There has never been a day like that day before or after,
(a day) when YHWH listened to a man.
Surely YHWH fought for Israel!

[Then Joshua and all Israel with him returned to the camp at Gilgal.][23]

$G^{\Delta 3}$ 16וינסו חמשת המלכים האלה
$G^{\Delta 4}$ ויחבאו במערה במקדה
$L^{2\alpha}$ 17ויגד ליהושע לאמר
נמצאו חמשת המלכים נחבאים במערה במקדה
18ויאמר יהושע
גלו אבנים גדלות אל פי המערה
והפקידו עליה אנשים לשמרם
H 19ואתם אל תעמדו
רדפו אחרי איביכם
וזנבתם אותם
אל תתנום לבוא אל עריהם
$C^4$ כי נתנם יהוה אלהיכם בידכם

16. Now these five kings had fled,
and they had hidden in the cave at Makkedah.
17. It was related to Joshua:
'we have found the five kings hiding in the cave at Makkedah'.
18. Joshua said:
'Roll large stones up to the mouth of the cave,
and post some men there to guard it.

19. But do not stay there.
Pursue after your enemies,
and cut off their retreat!
Do not let them enter their cities,
for YHWH your God has given them into your hand'.

L[1] [20]ויהי ככלות יהושע ובני ישראל להכותם מכה גדולה מאד עד תמם
G[Δ3] והשרידים שרדו מהם
G[Δ4] ויבאו אל ערי המבצר
Q [21]וישבו כל העם אל המחנה אל יהושע מקדה בשלום
[ ] לא חרץ לבני ישראל לאיש את לשנו

20. Now as Joshua and the Israelites[24] victoriously finished exterminating them completely,
although the survivors ran away from them
and entered their fortified cities.
21. All the army returned safely to the camp[25] to Joshua at Makkedah.
No one uttered a word against the Israelites.[26]

N [22]ויאמר יהושע
פתחו את פי המערה
והוציאו אלי את המשת המלכים האלה מן המערה
[23]ויעשו כן ויציאו אליו את חמשת המלכים האלה מן
המערה את מלך ירושלם את מלך חברון את מלך ירמות את מלך לכיש
את מלך עגלון
[24]ויהי כהוציאם את המלכים האלה אל יהושע
ויקרא יהושע אל כל איש ישראל
ויאמר אל קצינ י אנשי המלחמה ההלכוא אתו
קרבו שימו את רגליכם על צוארי המלכים האלה
ויקרבו וישימו את רגליהם על צואריהם

22. Joshua said:
'Open the mouth of the cave,
and bring those five kings out to me'.
23. Thus they did, bringing out these five kings out from the cave—the king of Jerusalem, the king of Hebron, the king of Jarmuth, the king of Lachish, and the king of Eglon.
24. When they had brought these kings to Joshua,
Joshua called all the men of Israel[27]
and said to the chiefs of the army who had come with him:
'Come near and place your feet on the necks of these kings'.
So they came near and placed their feet on their necks.

[25]ויאמר אליהם יהושע
אל תיראו
ואל תחתו
חזקו ואמצו
כי ככה יעשה יהוה לכל איביכם אשר אתם נלחמים אותם
L[1צα] [26]ויכם יהושע אחרי כן
L[1כα] וימיתם

N ויתלם על חמשה עצים
ויהיו תלוים על העצים עד הערב

25. Joshua said to them:
'Do not be afraid;
do not be discouraged.
Be strong and courageous.
Because this is what YHWH will do to all the enemies you are going to fight'.

26. Then Joshua struck them,
and put them to death.
And he hung them on five trees;
and they were left hanging on the trees until evening.

$N^{g}$ [27]ויהי לעת כבוא השמש צוה יהושע
וירידום מעל העצים
$N^{f}$ וישלכם אל המערה אשר נחבאו שם
וישמו אבנים גדלות על פי המערה עד עצם היום הזה

27. At sunset Joshua gave the command,
and they took them down from the trees,
and threw them into the cave where they had been hiding.
And they placed large[28] stones (back) over the mouth of the cave which are there until this selfsame day.

$A^{2} + L^{2א\zeta}$ [28]ואת מקרה לכד יהושע ביום ההוא
$L^{1צ\zeta\alpha}$ ויכה לפי חרב ואת מלכה
$L^{1ב\zeta}$ החרם אותה ואת כל הנפש אשר בה
$L^{1\eta}$ לא השאיר שריד
N ויעש למלך מקרה כאשר עשה למלך יריחו
$a^{1,2}$ [29]ויעבר יהושע וכל ישראל עמו ממקדה לבנה
$L^{1\zeta}$ וילחם עם לבנה
$C^{4}$ [30]ויתן יהוה גם אותה אותה ביד ישראל
$L^{2א\zeta}$ ו[ילכדו אותה ו]את מלכה
$L^{1צ\zeta}$ ויכה לפי חרב ואת כל הנפש אשר בה
$L^{1\eta}$ לא השאיר בה שריד
N ויעש למלכה כאשר עשה למלך יריחו
$a^{1,2}$ [31]ויעבר יהושע וכל ישראל עמו מלבנה לכישה
F ויחן עליה
$L^{1\zeta}$ וילחם בה
$C^{4}$ [32]ויתן יהוה את לכיש ביד ישראל
$L^{2א\zeta}$ וילכדה ביום השני
$L^{1צ\zeta}$ ויכה לפי חרב
$L^{1ב\zeta}$ ו[יחרם אותה ו]את כל הנפש אשר בה
N ככל אשר עשה ללבנה
$a^{2} + G^{-3}$ [33]אז עלה הרם מלך גזר לעזר את לכיש
$L^{1צ\alpha\beta}$ ויכהו יהושע ואת עמו
$L^{1\eta}$ עד בלתי השאיר לו שריד
$a^{1,2}$ [34]ויעבר יהושע וכל ישראל עמו מלכיש עגלנה
F ויחנו עליה

| | |
|---|---|
| וילחמו עליה | $L^{1\zeta}$ |
| [35]ו[יתן יהוה את ביד ישראל] | $C^{4}$ |
| [ו]ילכדוה ביום ההוא | $L^{2\text{א}\zeta}$ |
| ויכוה לפי חרב ואת כל הנפש אשר בה ביום ההוא | $L^{1\text{צ}\zeta}$ |
| החרים | $L^{1\text{ב}\zeta}$ |
| ככל אשר עשה ללכיש | N |
| [36]ויעל יהושע וכל ישראל עמו מעגלונה חברונה | $a^{1,2}$ |
| וילחמו עליה | $L^{1\zeta}$ |
| וילכדוה | $L^{2\text{א}\zeta}$ |
| ויכוה לפי חרב ואת מלכה ואת כל עריה ואת כל הנפש אשר בה | $L^{1\text{צ}\zeta\alpha}$ |
| לא השאיר שריד | $L^{1\text{ח}}$ |
| ככל אשר עשה לעגלון | N |
| ויחרם אותה ואת כל הנפש אשר בה | $L^{1\text{ב}\zeta}$ |
| [38]וישב יהושע וכל ישראל עמו דברה | $a^{1,2}$ |
| וילחם עליה | $L^{1\zeta}$ |
| [39]וילכדה ואת מלכה ואת כל עריה | $L^{2\text{א}\zeta\alpha}$ |
| ויכום לפי חרב | $L^{1\text{צ}\zeta}$ |
| ויחרימו את כל נפש אשר בה | $L^{1\text{ב}\zeta}$ |
| לא השאיר שריד | $L^{1\text{ח}}$ |
| כאשר עשה לחברון כן עשה לדברה ולמלכה וכאשר עשה ללבנה ולמלכה | N |

28. On that day Joshua took Makkedah.
He put the city and its king to the sword,[29]
and he destroyed it and everyone in it;[30]
He left no survivors.[31]
and he did to the king of Makkedah as he had done to the king of Jericho.
29. Then Joshua and all Israel with him moved on from Makkedah to Libnah.
He attacked Libnah;
30. and YHWH gave it into the hand of Israel too.
[and they took it and its king.][32]
And he (Joshua) put it and everyone in it to the sword.
He left no survivors there.
And he did to its king as he had done to the king of Jericho.
31. Then Joshua and all Israel with him moved on from Libnah to Lachish.
He took up positions against it;
and attacked it.
32. YHWH gave Lachish into the hand of Israel;
and he took it on the second day.
He put it to the sword,
and [he destroyed it] and everyone in it.[33]
according to all that he had done at Libnah.
33. At that time, Horam king of Gezer had come up to help Lachish;
but Joshua smote him and his army;
until no survivors were left.
34. Then Joshua and all Israel with him moved on from Lachish to Eglon.
They took up positions against it;
and attacked it.

35. And [YHWH gave it into the hand of Israel;][34]
[and] they took it on the same day.
And they put it to the sword and everyone in it on that day.
They completely destroyed them.
according to all that they had done to Lachish.
36. Then Joshua and all Israel with him marched up from Eglon[35] to Hebron.
And they attacked it.
37. They took it;[36]
and they put it and its king and all of its towns[37] and everyone in it to the sword.
They left no survivors;
according to all that they had done to Eglon.
They completely destroyed it and everyone in it.
38. Then Joshua and all Israel with him turned around;
and attacked Debir.
39. They took it and its king and all its villages;
and they put them to the sword.
They completely destroyed everyone there;
they left no survivors;
As they had done to Hebron so they did to Debir and its king like they had (also) done to Libnah and its king.[38]

| | |
|---|---|
| L[1צג] | [40]ויכה יהושע את כל הארץ ההר והנגב והשפלה והאשרות<br>ואת כל מלכיהם |
| L[1ח] | לא השאיר שריד |
| L[1כג] | ואת כל הנשמה החרים |
| C[4] | כאשר צוה יהוה אלהי ישראל |
| L[1צג] | [41]ויכם יהושע מקרש ברנע ועד עזה ואת כל ארץ גשן<br>ועד גבעון |
| L[2אקג] | [42]ואת כל המלכים האלה ואת ארצם לכד יהושע פעם אחת |
| C[4] | כי יהוה אלהי יערצל נלחם לישראל |
| Q | [[43]וישב יהושע וכל ישראל עמו אל המחנה הגלגלה] |

40. Thus Joshua smote the whole region, (including) the hill country, the Negev,[39] the Shephelah, and the mountain slopes, together with their kings.
He left no survivors.
He totally destroyed all who breathed,
just as YHWH the God of Israel had commanded.
41. Joshua smote them from Kadesh-Barnea, to Gaza, and from the whole land of Goshen to Gibeon.
42. All these kings and their lands Joshua conquered in a single campaign.
because YHWH the God of Israel fought for Israel.

[43. Then Joshua returned with all Israel to the camp at Gilgal.][40]

*Chapter Eleven*

$A^{2}$ [1]ויהי כשמע יבין מלך חצור
$G^{-2\aleph}$ וישלח אל יובב מלך מרון
ואל מלך שמרון ואל מלך אכשף [2]ואל המלכים אשר מצפון בהר
ובערבה נגב כנרות ובשפלה ובנפות רור מים [3]הכנעני ממזרח
ומים והאמרי והחתי והפרזי והיבוסי בהר והחוי תחת חרמון
הארץ המצפה
$G^{-2}$ [4]ויצאו הם וכל מחניהם עמם עם רב כחול אשר על שפת הים
לרב וסוס ורכב רב מאר
$G^{-3}$ [5]ויוערו כל המלכים האלה
ויבאו ויחנו יחרו אל מי מרום להלחם עם ישראל

1. Now when Jabin king of Hazor heard of this,
he sent to Jobab king of Madon, to the king of Shimron, to the
2. king of Acshaph, and to the kings who were from the northern hill country, and in the Arabah south of Kinnereth,[41] and in the Shephelah and in Naphath Dor[42] on the west, to the Canaanites in the east and on the west the Amorites,[43] the Hittites, the Perizzites, and the Jebusites in the hill country; and to the Hivites below Mt. Hermon in the region of Mizpah.
4. They came out and all their armies with them and a large number of horses and chariots—a huge army, as numerous as the sand on the sea-shore.
5. And all these kings joined together;
and they came and made camp together at the Waters of Merom, to fight against Israel.

$C^{2}$ [6]ויאמר יהוה אל יהושע
$C^{\aleph}$ אל תירא מפניהם
'L' כי מחר כעת הזאת אנכי נתן את כלם חללים לפני ישראל
N את סוסיהם תעקר ואת מרכבתיהם תשרף באש

6. YHWH said to Joshua:
'Do not be afraid of them,
because by this time tomorrow I will hand all of them over to Israel, slain.
You are to hamstring their horses and burn their chariots'.

$E^{\xi}$ [7]ויבא יהושע וכל עם המלחמה עמו עליהם על מי מרום פתאם
$L^{1\beta}$ ויפלו בהם
$C^{4}$ [8]ויתנם יהוה ביר יעראל
$L^{1\aleph\beta}$ ויכום
H וירדפום עד צירון רבה ועד משרפות מים ועד בקעת מצפה
מזרחה
$L^{1\aleph\beta}$ ויכם
$L^{1\eta}$ עד בלתי השאיר להם שריד
$C^{2}$ [9]ויעש להם יהושע כאשר אמר לו יהוה
N את סוסיהם עקר ואת מרכבתיהם שרף באש

7. So Joshua and his entire army came against them suddenly at the Waters of Merom;
and attacked them.
8. And YHWH gave them into the hand of Israel,
and they smote them;
and pursued them as far as Greater Sidon and Misrephoth Maim,[44] and the Valley of Mizpah on the east,
and they smote them
until there were no survivors left.
9. So Joshua did to them as YHWH had said:
He hamstrung their horses and burned their chariots.

| | |
|---|---|
| a^2 | 10 וישב יהושע בעת ההיא |
| L^{2אζ} | וילכד את חצור |
| L^{1צα} | ואת מלכה הכה בחרב |
| | כי חצור לפנים היא ראש כל הממלכות האלה |
| L^{1צζ} | 11 ויכו את כל הנפש אשר בה לפי חרב |
| L^{1בζ} | החרם |
| L^{1η} | לא נותר כל נשמה |
| L^{בזζ} | ואת חצור שרף באש |

10. At that time: Joshua turned back;
and captured Hazor.
He put its king to the sword,
because Hazor had been the head of all these kingdoms.
11. They put everyone in it to the sword;
They totally destroyed them;
not sparing anything that breathed.
And they burned Hazor.

| | |
|---|---|
| L^{2אζα} | 12 ואת כל ערי המלכים האלה ואת כל מלכיהם לכד יהושע |
| L^{1צζα} | ויכם לפי חרב |
| L^{1בζ} | החרים אותם |
| C^2 | כאשר צוה משה עבד יהוה |
| L^{1-גζ} | 13 רק כל הערים העמדות על תל[י]ם לא שרפם ישראל |
| L^{בזζ} | זולתי את חצור לבדה שרף יהושע |
| L^{2ב&} | 14 וכל שלל הערים האלה והבהמה בזזו להם בני ישראל |
| L^{1צζ} | רק את כל האדם הכו לפי חרב |
| L^{1η} | עד השמדם אותם |
| L^{1η} | לא השאירו כל נשמה |
| C^2 | 15 כאשר צוה יהוה את משה עבדו |
| | כן צוה משה את יהושע |
| | וכן עשה יהושע |
| | לא הסיר דבר מכל אשר צוה יהוה את משה |

12. Joshua took all these royal cities and their kings.
And he put them to the sword.
He totally destroyed them,
as Moses the servant of YHWH had commanded.
13. Yet Israel did not burn any of the cities on their mounds.[45]

except Hazor which Joshua burned.
14. The Israelites carried off for themselves all the plunder and livestock of these cities,[46]
but all the people they put to the sword,
until they had exterminated them,
not sparing anyone who breathed.
15. As YHWH had commanded Moses his servant,
so Moses commanded Joshua;
and so Joshua did.
He left nothing undone of all that YHWH had commanded Moses.

| | |
|---|---|
| 16 ויקח יהושע את כל הארץ הזאת<br>ההר ואת כל הנגב ואת כל ארץ הגשן ואת השפלה ואת הערבה<br>ואת הר ישראל ושפלתה 17 מן ההר החלק העולה שעיר ועד<br>בעל גד בבקעת הלבנון תחת הר חרמון | $L^{2\text{ב}\zeta}$ |
| ואת כל מלכיהם לכד | $L^{2\text{א}\alpha}$ |
| ויכם | $L^{1\text{צ}\alpha}$ |
| וימיתם | $L^{1\text{נ}\alpha}$ |
| 18 ימים רבים עשה יהושע את כל המלכים האלה מלחמה | $L^{1\text{ו}}$ |
| 19 לא היתה עיר אשר השלימה אל בני ישראל | $G^{-6}$ |
| בלתי החוי ישבי גבעון | $G^{\Delta 6}$ |
| את הכל לקחו במלחמה | $L^{2\text{ב}\zeta}$ |
| 20 כי מאת יהוה היתה לחזק את לבם לקראת המלחמה<br>את ישראל | $C^{4}$ |
| למען החרימם לבלתי היות להם תחנה | $\cdot L^{1\text{נ}}$ |
| כי למען השמידם | $\cdot L^{1\text{ח}}$ |
| כאשר צוה יהוה את משה | $C^{2}$ |

16. So Joshua seized this entire land:
the hill country, all the Negev, the whole region of Goshen, the Shephelah, the Arabah, and the mountains of Israel with
17. their foothills, from Mount Halak, which rises towards Seir, to Baal Gad in the Valley of Lebanon below Mount Hermon.
He captured all their kings,
and he smote them,
and put them to death.
18. Joshua made war on all these kings for a long time.
19. There was not one city which made peace with the Israelites,
except for the Hivites, the inhabitants of Gibeon.
They took them all in battle.
20. For it was YHWH himself who hardened their hearts to make war against Israel,
in order that He might destroy them completely without mercy being shown to them,
in order that he might exterminate them,
as YHWH had commanded Moses.

| | |
|---|---|
| 21 ויבא יהושע בעת ההיא | $a^{2}$ |
| ויכרת את הענקים מן ההר מן חברון מן ענב ומכל הר יהודה | $L^{1\text{ה}}$ |

ומכל הר ישראל
עם עריהם החרימם יהושע L[1β]
[22]לא נותר ענקים בארץ בני ישראל L[1η]
רק בעזה בגת ובאשדוד נשארו L[1-η]

21. At that time: Joshua went,
and destroyed the Anakites from the hill country: from Hebron, Debir and Anab, from all the hill country of Judah, and from all the hill country of Israel.
Joshua totally destroyed them and their towns.
22. No Anakites were left in Israelite territory;
only in Gaza, Gath, and Ashdod did any survive.

[23]ויקח יהושע את כל הארץ L[2λ]
ככל אשר דבר יהוה אל משה C[2]
ויתנה יהושע לנחלה לישראל כמחלקתם לשבטיהם O[5]

והארץ שקטה ממלחמה O[7]

23. So Joshua took all the land,
just as YHWH had said to Moses.
And Joshua gave it as an inheritance to Israel according to their tribal divisions.

Then the land had rest from war.

## *Chapter Twelve*

[1]ואלה מלכי הארץ אשר הכו בני ישראל L[1ξα]
וירשו את ארצם בעבר הירדן L[2η]
מזרחה השמש מנחל ארנון עד הר חרמון וכל הערבה מזרחה

1. These are the kings of the land which the Israelites smote.
And they dispossessed their lands over east of the Jordan: from the Arnon Gorge to Mount Hermon, including all the eastern side of the Arabah:

[2]סיחון מלך האמרי היושב בחשבון L[°x]
משל מערוער אשר על שפת נחל ארנון ותוך הנחל וחצי הגלעד
ועד יבק הנחל גבול בני עמון
[3]והערבה עד ים כנרות מזרחה ועד ים הערבה ים המלח מזרחה
דרך בית הישמות ומתימן תחת אשדות הפסגה
[4]וגבול עוג מלך הבשן
מיתר הרפאים היושב בעשתרות ובאדרעי
[5]ומשל בהר חרמון ובסלכה ובכל הבשן עד גבול הגשורי
והמעכתי וחצי הגלעד גבול סיחון מלך חשבון

2. Sihon, king of the Amorites, who reigned in Heshbon.
He ruled from Aroer on the rim of the Arnon Gorge—from the middle of the gorge—to the Jabbok River, which is the border of the Ammonites—including half of Gilead.

3. (He also ruled) over the eastern Arabah from the Sea of Kinnereth to the Sea of the Arabah—the Salt Sea—, to Beth Jeshimoth, and then southward below the slopes of Pisgah.
4. And the territory of Og king of Bashan,
one of the last of the Rephaites, who reigned in Ashtaroth and Edrei.
5. He ruled over Mount Hermon, Salecah, all of Bashan to the border of the people of Geshur[47] and Maacah, and half of Gilead to the border of Sihon king of Heshbon.

L[ix] [6]משה עבד יהוה ובני ישראל הכום
O[6] ויתנה משה עבד יהוה ירשה לראובני ולגדי ולחצי שבט המנשה

6. Moses, the servant of YHWH, and the Israelites conquered them.
And Moses the servant of YHWH gave their land to the Reubenites, the Gadites, and the half-tribe of Manasseh to be their possession.

L[ix] [7]ואלה מלכי הארץ אשר הכה יהושע ובני ישראל בעבר הירדן ימה
מבעל גד בבקעת הלבנון ועד ההר החלק העלה שעירה
O[6] ויתנה יהושע לשבטי ישראל ירשה כמחלקתם
[8]בהר ובשפלה ובערבה ובאשדות ובמדבר ובנגב
החתי האמרי והכנעני הפזי החוי והיבוסי

7. These are the kings which Joshua and the Israelites smote on the west side of the Jordan:
from Baal Gad in the Valley of Lebanon to Mount Halak, which rises towards Seir.
Joshua gave it to the tribes of Israel as an inheritance according to tribal allotments.
8. —the hill country, the western foothills, the Arabah, the mountain slopes, the desert and the Negev—(the lands of) the Hittites, Amorites, Canaanites, Perizzites, Hivites and Jebusites:

| | | | | |
|---|---|---|---|---|
| אחר | מלך העי אשר מצד בית אל | אחר | [9]מלך יריחו | L[x] |
| אחר | מלך חברון | אחר | [10]מלך ירושלם | |
| אחר | מלך לכיש | אחר | [11]מלך ירמות | |
| אחר | מלך גזר | אחר | [12]מלך עגלון | |
| אחר | מלך גדר | אחר | [13]מלך דבר | |
| אחר | מלך ערד | אחר | [14]מלך חרמה | |
| אחר | מלך עדלם | אחר | [15]מלך לבנה | |
| אחר | מלך בית אל | אחר | [16]מלך מקדה | |
| אחר | מלך חפר | אחר | [17]מלך תפוח | |
| אחר | מלך לשרון | אחר | [18]מלך אפק | |
| אחר | מלך חצור | אחר | [19]מלך מדון | |
| אחר | מלך אכשף | אחר | [20]מלך שמרון מראון | |
| אחר | מלך מגדו | אחר | [21]מלך תענך | |
| אחר | מלך יקנעם לכרמל | אחר | [22]אחר קדש | |
| אחר | מלך גוים לגלגל | אחר | [23]מלך דור לנפת דור | |
| | | אחר | [24]מלך תרצה | |

כל מלכים שלשים ואחד

| | | | | |
|---|---|---|---|---|
| 9 | king of Jericho | 1 | king of Ai (near Bethel) | 1 |
| | king of Jerusalem | 1 | king of Hebron | 1 |
| | king of Jarmuth | 1 | king of Lachish | 1 |
| | king of Eglon | 1 | king of Gezer | 1 |
| | king of Debir | 1 | king of Geder | 1 |
| | king of Hormah | 1 | king of Arad | 1 |
| | king of Libnah | 1 | king of Adullam | 1 |
| | king of Makkedah | 1 | king of Bethel | 1 |
| | king of Tappuah | 1 | king of Hepher | 1 |
| | king of Aphek | 1 | king of Lasharon | 1 |
| | king of Madon | 1 | king of Hazor | 1 |
| | king of Shimron Meron | 1 | king of Acshaph | 1 |
| | king of Taanach | 1 | king of Megiddo | 1 |
| | king of Kedesh | 1 | king of Jokneam in Carmel | 1 |
| | king of Dor in Naphoth Dor[48] | 1 | king of Goyim in Gilgal[49] | 1 |
| 24 | king of Tirzah | 1 | | |

thirty-one kings in all.

## *Notes To Appendix*

1. Max L. Margolis, *The Book of Joshua in Greek*. Paris, 1931.

2. L.J. Greenspoon, *Textual Studies in the Book of Joshua*, p. 1.

3. H.M. Orlinsky, 'The Hebrew "Vorlage" of the Septuagint of the Book of Joshua', *VT* 17 (1968): 187-195. Also S. Holmes argued for this understanding (*Joshua: The Hebrew and Greek Texts*, pp. 3-6). See also A.G. Auld, 'Joshua: The Hebrew and Greek Texts', *VTS* 30 (1979): 1-14.

4. The functions occurring in this section are: U = the preparation of the deception; V = the execution of the deception; W = the result of the deception (i.e., the fall, etc.); X = the discovery of the truth; Y = the consequences [it is divided into three sub-functions: $Y^1$ = the decided action in response to the deception; $Y^2$ = the confrontation; $Y^3$ = the revelation of the cause of the deception].

5. OG inserts 8:30-35 here. Boling states: 'It is not impossible that the LXX is correct in reading 8:30-35 next. As it stands, however, the unit poses the sharpest possible contrast with the resourceful response of the Gibeonite dwellers' (pp. 261-262). On the other hand, while the MT probably preserves the correct order, if the Greek *Vorlage* is maintained, then the stress would be on the Canaanite kings immediate response to the destruction of Ai in 8:28-29; as well as an emphasis on the 'aliens who lived among them' (8:35b) which is immediately followed by the story of how the 'alien' Gibeonites came into the Israelite camp (9:3ff).

6. In the expression גם המה, there is a reference implied to what Joshua had done at Jericho and Ai so that there is an ironic twist. The Israelites, who

had used trickery and deception to conquer Jericho and Ai, are themselves now the victims of deception.

7. We understand the verbs וילכו ויצטירו as a hendiadys. The textual problem here is difficult. There are three positions which scholars have taken on the problem in the past:

A). The reading ויצטירו is favored. E.g., Gesenius favored ויצטירו stating: 'HITHPAEL הצטיר Josh. 9:4, may be "they betook themselves to the way." But no other trace of this form and signification is either found in Hebrew, or in Aramaean, and the ancient interpreters have all given it as צטירו "they furnished themselves with provisions for the journey," as in ver. 12, which appears to me preferable' [*Gesenius' Hebrew and Chaldee Lexicon*, (trans. S.P. Tregelles), p. 709]. See also: Margolis, *The Book of Joshua in Greek*, p. 151).

B). The Hebrew text should be restored ויצטירו ויצטירו. Boling feels that this reading is reflected in the 'LXX, where 'ἐπεσιτίσαντο και ἡετοιμάσαντο' seems to reflect a Hebrew text that has been obscured by haplography: וריטשיו וריטשיו. A few manuscripts read only the first verb, whereas major Hebrew witnesses read only the second verb. The latter occurs nowhere else in Scripture' (*Joshua*, p. 257).

C). The reading of the MT's ויצטירו is favored. E.g., Woudstra, *The Book of Joshua*, p. 155, n. 8. Some of the proponents of this argue that the reading ויצטירו is only a conjecture of the translators of the ancient versions. Barthélemy hesitantly favors the MT; see: *Critique textuelle*, p. 14.

8. The OG reads: ἀκουσάντες. Boling feels: 'ἀκουσάντες probably reflects a converted imperfect (as at the beginning of 2:11) lost by haplography in MT: *wy*[*šm'w wy*]*'mrw*' (*Joshua*, p. 258). Margolis stated: 'apparently read וישמעו and ואמרו (*Joshua in Greek*, p. 157). However, it is also possible that the term was added to continue the thought started in v. 10. While many of the differences between the Greek and MT must be attributed to the Greek translators using a different *Vorlage* then the MT, this is certainly not the explanation in every instance. There are other places where the Greek has added in order to amplify the text (see for example 9:27 below).

9. Boling argues that the OG (οἱ ἄρχοντες) reflects הנשיאים and is a 'scribal anticipation of their pivotal role and the repeated references to this group in the remainder of the chapter' (*Joshua*, p. 258; see also, Margolis, *Joshua in Greek*, p. 159). But Barthélemy points out that נשיאים is not employed in this narrative without the determinative of the genitive העדה (vss. 15 and 18) or in the immediate context of the word (vss. 19 and 21) (*Critique textuelle*, p. 15). Hence the implication is that האנשים is the better reading.

10. The verb לון meaning 'to murmur against' (*KBL* p. 477) occurs only in Ex. 15-17; Num. 14-17; Ps. 59:16 and here. It is reminiscent of the Exodus and Numbers contexts in which the people of Israel murmured against the leaders

of the nation. Again, note the irony. Immediately after their great victories at Jericho and Ai and after the covenant renewal in the midst of the promised land the people murmur.

11. The OG has a lengthy addition at this point (see: Margolis, pp. 167-168 and *B-McL*, p. 709). Margolis gave the best explanation for this lengthy phrase: 'The plus was introduced by the Greek translators to mitigate the zeugma' (*Joshua in Greek*, p. 167). The final [κύριος] has the overwhelming support of the Versions and should be included. The beginning of the next chapter has ויהי which could have easily confused the reading of יהוה at this point.

12. OG: Αδωνιβεζεκ MT: אדני צדק. The OG here and in verse 3 reflects אדני בזק in its Hebrew *Vorlage* (Margolis, p. 168, *B-McL* p. 709). The same spelling is encountered in the MT and LXX in Judges 1:5-7. M. Noth felt that this reflected the original in Joshua 10. He argued that אדני צדק was a later attempt to adapt this tradition to Jerusalem ('Jerusalem und die israelitische Tradition', in *Gesammelte Studien*², p. 172; see also, Soggin, *Joshua*, p. 119). However, G.E. Wright argued that the original form of this name may well be preserved in the MT of Joshua since Judges 1 is full of difficulties. Furthermore, 'from no other source do we know of a town named Bezek in southern Palestine. More serious is the name of the king itself. The second element according to ancient nomenclature should be either the proper name of a god or an appellative of such a god; and 'bezek' does not seem to meet these requirements. In addition, Adoni-bezek sounds very much like Adoni-zedek in Joshua 10. For these reasons it is commonly thought that the two were one and the same. If that is the case, then Joshua may preserve not only the original reading of the name but perhaps also a more reliable tradition regarding the incident itself. As recounted in Joshua, the event bears all the marks of verisimilitude' (*JNES* 5 (1946): 108). Boling adds that 'Adonibezeq is most likely a title, not a name' (p. 275). While Wright's argument concerning the sounds of Adonibezeq and Adoni-zedeq could go either way, we believe that he is correct concerning the second element of the name.

13. Boling feels that the MT has sustained a haplography so that the text should read: את [יהושע ואת] ישראל (p. 275). The analogies of 9:2 and 10:4 and the plural ויהיו seem to indicate that this is correct.

14. See: Barthélemy, *Critique textuelle*, p. 17. The plural reading would be further supported by the suffix on the last word of verse 1 (בקרבם).

15. While Boling sees a haplography in the MT, we feel that the Greek witnesses an amplification of the text (Margolis, p. 170).

16. OG: φεδων MT: פראם. See Margolis (p. 171) and esp. Greenspoon (p. 68).

17. כל הלילה עלה מן הגלגל is a noun clause used in an adverbial accusative of manner (Williams, *Syntax*, p. 81).

18. We are understanding the subject of the three 'waw'-clauses as 'Israel'.

19. The OG reflects חורנים or a similar form in its Hebrew *Vorlage*. Soggin argues that this is 'improbable since it introduces a town which is found only in Moab in the OT and on the Mesha stele, lines 31-32. Perhaps the Hebrew text of LXX had a 'mem' enclitic which was no longer understood as such' (*Joshua*, p. 119). But Boling argues: 'Here and in the next verse LXX reads "Horonaim," which need not be the Transjordan town of that name. The ending is dual and may be taken as referring to the two (Beth)-Horons, upper and lower' (p. 276).

20. OG: λίθους χαλάζης. According to Margolis, χαλάζης is for גדלות by interpretation from what follows (p. 177). However, it is unlikely that the OG translator would have failed to translate גדלות had it been present in his Hebrew *Vorlage*. Greenspoon argues that it is probable that in the text underlying both the OG and MT traditions 'stones' stood unmodified at this point. In the OG *Vorlage* 'stones' became 'hailstones' (χαλάζης) drawn from a clause later in this same verse (ברד). Both the OG and the MT readings arose from marginal glosses (see, *Textual Studies*, pp. 69-70).

21. The OG adds significantly to the text. While Holmes and Soggin argue for the originality of the OG (*Joshua: The Hebrew and Greek Texts*, p. 50; *Joshua*, p. 119), Boling opts not to restore this to the text and/or translation (p. 276). To us the Greek seems to be amplifying.

22. Concerning הלא, Soggin states that the translation should be 'Surely'. He argues: 'instead of translation "h$^{a}$lo" by the rhetorical question, 'Is it not written?', it seemed better to translate it as a 'lamed' affirmative' (*Joshua*, p. 119). But Boling objects stating: 'Soggin revowels as 'lamed' affirmative and translates 'Surely,' but he does not explain the prefixed interrogative particle' (Boling, p. 285). We agree with Boling and retain the rhetorical question (note: whether a rhetorical question or statement, the meaning is still the same: namely, that the quote comes from the Book of Yashar).

The Book of Yashar probably comprised an ancient national song-book that may have originated as early as the period of the Wilderness wanderings (Thackeray, *JTS* 11 (1910): 518ff; C.F. Kraft, *IDB* II, p. 803). It was not an anthology in which poetic compositions by David and Solomon were included and must be regarded as pre-monarchic (see R.K. Harrison, *Introduction to the Old Testament*, p. 670).

23. Verses 15 and 43 are missing in the best witnesses to the OG (See Margolis, pp. 181 and 205, and S. Holmes, *Joshua*, p. 4). While a translation is lacking in the OG, one is found in B$^{b}$(?)$^{c}$(?)Gθcgiknoqrv(mg)x y$^{a}$(?)z(mg)ȺɆ$^{f}$$. However, וישב is translated ἐπέστρεψεν in 10:15, but ἀπέστρεψεν in 10:43 in Gbcxz(mg)ȺɆ$^{c}$$ (sub x G$).

A number of scholars have concluded that the verses are not original. E.g., Boling argues: 'The statement is probably a gloss that seeks to understand where Joshua received the report with which the next unit begins. The glossator did not recognize the digressionary character of vv 12-14' (p. 277). While this is certainly a possibility for the insertion of the verse, there are also two others. First, verse 15 could be a part of the quote from the book of Yashar (the quote = 12-15). Hence the literal repetition of verse 15 in verse 43 anticipates the literal course of events (Delitzsch, *Joshua*, pp. 108-109). Second, the return of the Israelites to Gilgal may be a type of resumptive repetition. This is a narrative technique whereby the narrative can convey somewhat simultaneous events. Hence the purpose of the second of the repeated phrases is to return the reader to the scene in which the first phrase occurred. This is necessary because in the interlude the reader was taken to a different scene. Now he returns to his original point, to see what was happening there at roughly the same time as the intervening events. Along these lines one might then see the two verses functioning as an inclusio which sets off the section (16-42), and emphasized to the ancient reader that he was entering a digressionary, roughly simultaneous section (see: S. Talmon, 'The Presentation of Synchroneity and Simultaneity in Biblical Narrative', in *Scripta Hierosolymitana* 28 (1978): 9-26; and A. Berlin, *Poetics and Interpretation of Biblical Narrative*, pp. 126-129). This seems to be the most likely explanation in our opinion for verses 15 and 43. Another example of resumptive repetition in Joshua can be seen in the phrase found in 11:23b and 14:15b: והארץ שקטה ממלחמה :: 'then the land had rest from war'. The section preceding both verses (i.e., 11:21-23 and 14:6-15) narrates events that are roughly simultaneous [the former emphasizing Joshua's role (as primary) and the latter Caleb's role (as secondary) in the conquest of the Anakites]. Such a technique may be involved in the scribal repetition of the return voyage of Pharaoh in *Stücke* V-VI of Annals of Thutmose III.

24. See Greenspoon, *Textual Studies*, pp. 70-71.

25. LXX[AB] lack an equivalent for אל המחנה. Boling sees this as haplography (p. 277).

26. חרץ לשון is literally 'sharpen the tongue against' (*KBL* p. 336). The same idiom is found in Ex. 11:7a 'But among all the Israelites not a dog will bark at any man or animal'.

27. The OG translator probably did not read איש in his Hebrew *Vorlage* here; and wrote πάντα ισραηλ.

28. The OG lacks a translation of גדול, although it is found in the asterisked addition of Origen.

29. Soggin argues that ואת מלכה is missing in the LXX and 'from the stylistic point of view is an addition in the Hebrew. Here and in the verses that follow, LXX has the verbs in different persons, and a complete formulation where this is not so in MT' (*Joshua*, p. 120). Boling, however, argues that while the equivalent for ואת מלכה is lacking in LXX[AB] and may be secondary, there is a chiastic pattern in the 1st half of the verse (direct object :: verb :: temporal phrase :: verb :: direct object) which argues the contrary (p. 290).

30. Read אותה (OG has ἐν αὐτῇ) instead of MT אותם (Margolis, p. 190). Some have argued that the MT is the 'lectio difficilior' and hence retain the reading אותם. E.g., E. Merrill argues that the 'waw' on ואת should be understood as a 'waw explicativitum' (*GKC* @ 154a) so that the plural MT is preferable; thus the meaning is: 'he put them (the population and king) under

the ban; that is, every person in it—he left no survivor' (*GTJ* 3 (1982): 14, n. 16). While this is a possible explanation, the syntagmic structure seems to argue for the singular (Cf. 10:37e: ויחרם אותה ואת כל הנפש אשר בה!). Thus the singular seems preferable. Cp. also 10:30c and 10:39c.

31. OG adds καὶ διαπεφευγῶς (see Joshua 8:22). See Margolis, p. 191; Soggin, p. 120; and Boling, 290.

32. This sentence fell out through haplography as Boling suggests (p. 290). For the OG see: *B-McL* p. 714 and Margolis, p. 192. This syntagm is evident in almost every episode of this section. It is probably best to see it as original (see chart, pp. 205-206 above).

33. The MT and OG *Vorlage* evince contrasting omissions (Boling, p. 290):

MT: ו[יחרם אותה ו]את כל הנפש אשר בה
OG: ויחרם אות[ה ואת כל הנפש אשר ב]ה
:: καὶ ἐξωλέθρευσαν αὐτὴν

In light of the structure, the verse should be restored (see chart, pp. 203-206 above).

34. Restored from the OG after an obvious haplography (so Boling, p. 290; see: *B-McL* p. 715; Margolis, p. 196). Hence we read: ו[יתן יהוה את כיר ישראל].

35. OG lacks מעגלונם as the result of inner-Greek halpography involving ἐ[κ ....ε]ις (cf. Boling, p. 290).

36. Lost by haplography in LXX^AB (cf. Boling, p. 290).

37. Orlinsky argued that the phrase ואת מלכה ואת כל עריה was lacking in the Hebrew *Vorlage* to the OG and was a later post-LXX accretion in the Hebrew text (*JAOS* 59 (1939): 22-37 and *VT* 17 (1968): 192). He saw this as a dittography 'only after original (ואת מלכה ואת כל) חצריה (LXX τὰς κώνας αὐτῆς = חצריה!—had become corrupted into preserved עריה)' (*VT* 17 (1968): 192). Thus 'Unlike the capital cities Jerusalem and Samaria (which may be treated as synonymous with their respective countries, Judah and Israel), to no city (such as Debir in v. 39) are other cities attributed in the Bible; it is 'settlements' (חצריה), not 'cities' (עריה) that are thus associated. (Cf. Debir and ten other cities in xv 48-51 'and their settlements' (וחצריהן)' (*ibid*., p. 192).

Quite simply Orlinsky is wrong! Three examples will demonstrate: First, in II Chron. 14:14 (MT v. 13) we find:

MT: ויכו כל הערים סביבות גרר
OG: ἐξέκοψαν τὰς κώνας αὐτῶν.

Thus the city of Gerar (which is not one of the two capitals) is attributed with ערים. Second, in Isa. 42:11 we are told that the desert has ערים:

MT: ישאו מדבר ועריו
OG: εὐφράνθητι ἔρημος καὶ αἱ κῶναι αὐτῆς

Third, in Jos. 13:30 we see that עיר can be the equivalent of 'settlement':

MT: וכל חות יאיר אשר בבשן ששים עיר
OG: καὶ πάσας τὰς Κώμας Ιαΐρ αἵ εἰσιν ἐν τῇ Βασανίτιδι ἑξήκοντα πόλεις

Cp. also I Chron. 27:25 and Jer. 19:15. Thus the usage of עיר in the context of Jos. 10:37 is within its semantic range, and Orlinsky's 'supposed corruption' is mythical. Boling rightly understands there to be a sizeable halpography. 'This is far more plausible than the argument that the longer reading is secondary and based on a supposed but unattested prior corruption which must be posited' (p. 290).

38. וכאשר עשה ללבנה ולמלכה is lacking in LXX[B] and thus is often considered to be secondary (e.g., Margolis, 201). However, it is attested in numerous Greek manuscripts (according to *B-McL* p. 716): AGGKNΘabcghijkp stv-$b_2$ $, Armenian, and Coptic (Sahidic[c]). Boling argues in favor of retaining it as original: 'But this is the last of six victories (seven including the Gezer force); we should expect special treatment. The phrase is thus retained, especially in view of the frequency with which LXX[A] is proving now to be the carrier of superior readings' (p. 291).

39. והנגב. See Boling (p. 296) and Greenspoon (pp. 42-43).

40. See our discussion of this verse in note 23 above.

41. Boling believes the LXX anticipation of 'Greater Sidon' in v. 8 and a loss of one letter, 'ayin, triggered this development which ends with 'Rabbah opposite Kinnereth' (p. 301). Barthélemy argues similarly: 'Ici, "la Araba, au sud de Kinerot" a donc bien des chances de désigner la même dépression, située également par rapport à (la mer de) Kinerot' (p. 20).

42. See Soggin's discussion of נפות דור (*Joshua*, p. 134).

43. Boling correctly notes the chiastic pattern (Canaanites: east :: west: Amorites) which is obscured by the misdivision in the LXX (where both groups are 'on the west') (p. 301).

44. Concerning משרפות מים, see: Barthélemy, *Critique textuelle*, p. 20.

45. Boling correctly points out the reading should be 'tells' or 'mounds' following the plural in the LXX as opposed to the MT's תלם (p. 303).

46. 'Livestock of these cities'. This is lacking in the LXX and Syriac.

47. For גבול הגשורי see Boling, p. 321.

48. See the discussion at 11:2.

49. See Greenspoon, p. 190, n. 285.

# INDEX

## AUTHOR

Abel 314
Abercrombie 284
Aharoni 171, 172, 301
Al-Rawi 321
Albrektson 277, 279
Alt 310
Alter 39, 40, 188, 272
Althusser 276
Apter 47, 275
Archi 269, 292
Auld 247, 313, 321, 324, 325, 377
Aynard 321
Barnes 33, 271
Barr 37-39, 272
Barthélemy 378, 379, 383
Barthes 56, 278-281
Baumgartner 280
Beck 270
Beckman 269, 294
Bewer 314
Billerbeck 288
Boling 310, 312, 313, 318, 323, 326, 377-383
Borger 280, 284-286, 288, 290, 319, 325, 330
Braudel 271
Breasted 301
Brett 274
Bright 212, 313
Brinkman 287-289
Brueggemann 254, 255, 326
Bull 165-167, 298, 308
Burrows 278
Butler 220, 251, 258, 260, 313, 316, 321, 325, 329
Callaway 328
Cancik 54, 55, 126, 141-145, 278, 292, 293, 297, 298
Carr 32, 33, 271
Cassuto 277
Ceram 292
Černý 303, 308, 323
Ceuppens 313
Childs 242, 243, 247, 318, 321
Çilingiroğlu 289
Clements 38, 39, 272
Coats 26, 31, 32, 34, 267, 270
Cogan 311, 313
Coggins 272
Cohen 28, 29, 269
Colie 268
Cook 272
Coote 256, 257, 328, 329
Craigie 329
Cross 34, 329
Cuddon 29, 269
Danto 40, 41, 273, 324
de Vaux 212, 214, 312-314
de Filippi 290
Delitzsch 288, 381
Derrida 28, 269
Dray 274
Dus 212, 313
Eco 49, 71, 275, 276, 278-280, 282, 284
Edel 305
Edgerton 312
Edzard 280
Egan 37, 272
Elliger 316
Eph'al 327
Fales 56, 64, 67-71, 278, 282-284
Fensham 310
Finkelstein, I. 256, 327, 328
Finkelstein, J.J. 61, 62, 280
Finley 25, 267
Fishbane 227, 318
Frandsen 185, 306-308
Freeman 314
Frei 272
Friedman 275, 276
Friedrich 296, 297, 315

Fritz 327
Furet 281
Furlani 320
Gaballa 317
Gadamer 269
Gadd 311
Garbini 267, 275, 276
Gardiner 172, 179, 300, 301, 303, 308, 319, 323
Geertz 48-50, 275, 276
Gelio 311
Gerhart 269
Gese 165, 279, 298
Gibson 319
Giveon 306
Goedicke 305
Goetze 128, 293, 294, 296, 297, 312, 319, 323
Goldwasser 307
Goody 274
Gottwald 253, 254, 316, 325, 326
Gould 275
Grapow 171, 299, 300, 302, 308, 309
Gray 223, 247, 258, 316, 324, 329
Grayson 69, 79, 311, 318-320, 330
Greenspoon 377, 379-381, 383
Gressmann 32, 271, 310
Grintz 310
Guidi 271
Gunkel 32, 268, 280
Gurney 128-130, 294, 295, 297, 312
Güterbock 125, 128, 130, 131, 136, 280, 292, 295-297
Habermas 48, 271, 275
Hall 215
Hallo 52-53, 268, 275-277, 280, 310
Halpern 213, 267-269, 273, 310, 314, 316, 317
Hamlin 248, 249, 260, 261, 324, 330
Harrison 314, 380
Hayes 306
Hecker 283
Hegel 268
Helck 168, 299, 301, 304, 305, 307, 315, 318
Heller 212, 313
Hirsch 269
Hoffmeier 178, 298, 303, 309
Hoffner 30, 125, 126, 131, 137, 144-145, 269, 279, 292, 295-297
Holladay 212-214, 313
Holmes 377, 380
Hornung 176, 190, 299, 303, 305
Houwink ten Cate 296
Huizinga 26, 27, 268, 280
Iggers 267, 268, 270
Imparati 296
Jameson 28, 269
Jepsen 291
Johnson 48, 67, 275, 276, 283
Kammenhuber 125, 292, 295
Kaufmann 225, 322
Kearney 310
Kemp 298, 308
Kempinski 137, 296, 305
King, 321
Kinner-Wilson 288
Kitchen 177, 276, 303, 307, 312, 315
Košak 137, 296
Kramer 317
Krecher 279, 281
Kümmel 295, 297
Kupper 315, 317
LaCapra 29, 269
Ladurie 281
Lambert 281
Landsberger 271
Le Gac 286, 290
Lee 270, 314
Lemche 256, 257, 328
Lévi-Strauss 283
Levin 41, 42, 273, 293
Levine 34, 72, 271, 284, 288, 289, 324
Lidzbarski 319
Lie 61
Liver 310

Liverani 61-67, 126-128, 279, 282-288, 292-294, 307, 329
Lloyd 298
Long, B. 277
Luckenbill 283, 288, 289
Lukács 48, 275
Machinist 298
Maisler 277
Malamat 279
Malbran-Labat 312
Mandelbaum 274
Mannheim 48, 275, 276
Marazzi 294
Margolis 359, 377-383
Mayer 289, 313, 316
McCarter 287
McCarthy 258, 329
McEvenue 318
Meissner 289
Melchert 296
Mendenhall 242, 319, 325
Michel 286-288, 330
Millard 34, 271, 272, 277, 282, 288, 291, 311, 313, 319, 330
Mink 273
Mink 42
Möhlenbrink 310
Mond 319, 325
Moore 243, 247, 321
Morenz 175, 302, 303
Mowinckel 52, 53, 277, 280
Müller 258, 279, 281, 329
Na'aman 287, 288, 315
Nash 33, 271
Neu 130, 295, 296
Noth 171, 201, 220-223, 249-251, 274-277, 300, 310-317, 322-325, 379
O'Connor 178, 298, 303
Oden 32, 33, 57, 267, 269, 271, 278
Olmstead 66, 280-282, 290
Oppenheim 64, 281, 289, 311
Oren 306
Orlinsky 359, 377, 382, 383
Orsini 269
Otten 129, 294, 296, 297
Otto 167, 168, 298, 299
Page 290, 291
Paley 290
Percy 276
Pfeiffer 40, 273, 324
Piepkorn 311
Pitard 234, 291, 319-320
Press 128, 180, 279, 328
Puhvel 297
Rainey 306
Redford 299, 300, 305, 306, 327
Reisner 309, 315, 318
Renger 280
Ricoeur 269, 271, 272
Rigg 289
Roberts 53, 236, 274, 277, 321
Rogerson 270, 293, 326
Rokeah 37, 271, 272
Röllig 280, 319
Roussel 313
Rowton 283
Ryckmans 319
Safar 286
Saggs 66, 283
Saporetti 296
Sawyer 212, 313, 229, 236, 237
Scheil 315
Schneidau 39, 272
Scholes 56, 278
Schrader 290
Schramm 286, 288, 290
Schulz 313
Scott 313
Segert 319
Sethe 308
Shaw 30, 269
Shils 319, 320
Shils 49, 232, 233, 275, 276
Shirun-Grumach 173, 302, 315
Smart 283
Smend 329
Soggin 217, 225, 291, 310, 315, 318, 379-383

Sollberger 315, 317
Spalinger 55, 168, 170-174, 182-183, 278, 299-305, 308-309, 315-319, 327, 330, 331
Speiser 278, 281, 292
Stager 323, 324
Stambovsky 199, 274, 310
Starke 294, 295
Stephenson 313
Sternberg 43, 269, 273
Streck 310
Tadmor 39, 53, 79, 215, 260, 272, 277, 281-286, 290, 291, 311-314, 329, 330
Talmon 274, 381
Thackeray 380
Thiele 287
Thureau-Dangin 289
Toorn 277
Trigger 188, 298, 306, 307
Trompf 270
Tucker 248-251, 321, 324, 325, 329
Twaddle 282
Unger 330
Ungnad 287
Van Seters 26, 27, 29-31, 53, 54, 131, 165-168, 261-262, 267, 268, 270, 271, 274, 277, 279, 280, 292, 293, 295, 298, 299, 305, 308, 330
Waldman 31, 270, 272
Waldow 260, 329
Watt 274
Weber 275
Weidner 286, 289
Weinfeld 214, 272, 307, 312-315, 329
Weinstein 305
Weippert 287, 327, 329
White 35, 38, 44, 45, 181, 234, 267, 271-274, 278, 318
Whitehead 273
Whitelam 256, 257, 271, 328, 329
Whybray 36, 37, 271, 272
Williams 166, 298, 323, 379
Wilson 288, 298, 300, 304, 305, 308, 312, 315
Wise 36, 55, 277, 282, 308
Wiseman 287, 288
Wolf 209, 269, 312
Woudstra 378
Wright 246, 316, 379
Wyatt 279
Yadin 324, 327
Yeivin 321
Yurco 323
Zaccagnini 63, 67, 281, 283, 290

## SUBJECT

administration of ideology 65, 185-189
annalistic texts 68, 72, 79-115, 263, 279, 330
Assyrian ideology 64-69, 72, 283
'Complete Conquest' 241-247
contextual approach/method 52-55
date of composition 261, 302
depictive imagery 199, 274
direct speech 36-37, 198, 272
Display Texts—see: Summary Texts
distortion 47-51, 67, 276, 282, 318
Egyptian genres 168-175
Egyptian ideology 169, 170, 175-189, 194, 234, 308
'Enemy' 67-69, 177-185
eyewitness 40-41, 250
false consciousness 47-51, 275, 276, 282
figurative account 45, 193
generic approaches 61, 62, 292
genre 61, 62, 79, 128, 168, 174, 268, 269, 279, 280, 311, 330

German historiographic tradition 267
*girru* 123, 283, 322
Greek historiography 53-55
Gyges 201, 202, 311
Habermas 271, 275
hailstones 208-211, 219, 313, 380
*Ḫerem* 135, 227-228, 235-236
high-redundance message 71, 72, 123, 170, 184, 189, 194, 226, 253, 300
historicism 268, 270, 278
Hittite ideology 128-130
Hittite syntagms 132-136
holy war 220, 235-236, 258-260, 321, 325, 329
hyperbole 190, 192, 212, 216, 219, 228, 234, 243-245, 251, 253, 323
'ideas of history' approaches—see: 'sense of history'
Ideal Chronicle 40-41, 250
ideology 62, 64-68, 71-73, 76, 123, 128-130, 169, 170, 175, 177, 184, 185, 189, 194, 232-237, 253, 255, 267, 275, 276, 282-284, 290, 295, 300, 308, 314, 320, 325, 329
impartial 126
imperialism 65-66, 129, 130, 282, 294, 306-308
intentionality 273
Israelite ideology 232-234, 253, 320
iterative scheme 223-228
*iw.tw* texts 168-170, 175, 184, 191, 194, 296, 300
jural aspect 236, 253
*Königsnovelle* 168, 299
*Letters to the God* 72, 115-119, 263, 279
Marxist 275, 276, 282
Metonymy 192, 193
*Nḫtw*: the Literary Reports 172-173
*Nḫtw*: the Daybook Reports 170-172
objectivity 271
*panku* 128, 269, 294
parataxis 277
*pišnadar* 136, 302
political history 167, 268
Protector of Egypt 176, 177
reconstruction of Israelite history 279
reconstructional approaches 61
royal ideology 73, 175, 177, 300
semiotics 275, 276, 278, 280, 282
'sense of history' 62, 125-128, 167
Shasu 255, 256, 327
'story' 37-45
Summary Texts 72, 120-122, 124, 290
suspension of disbelief 55-56
Syntagms of the Assyrian Texts 72-79
Syntagms of the Hittite Texts 132-135
*Tagebuchstil* 171
Thucydides 37, 271, 272
*umma* formula 128
vengeance 129, 130, 214, 215, 234, 295
veracity 64, 204, 265, 281, 282

SCRIPTURE

## *Joshua*

2-11 247
9 197, 198, 200-202, 204, 205, 207, 211, 229, 230, 237, 244, 245, 251, 254, 258, 259, 268, 270, 271, 274, 279-281, 287, 288, 292, 295, 296, 298, 308, 309, 310, 314, 317, 319-322, 325, 329, 330, 377-379, 381, 384
9:1 251
9:1 197, 198
9:1-2 197
9:3 197, 200
9-12 197-199, 200, 228, 233-236, 237, 241, 243, 251, 253, 255, 263, 265, 266, 279, 319-321, 325, 330
10 197-202, 204-209, 211-215, 218-223, 225-229, 232, 234, 236, 237, 241, 242, 244, 247, 248, 251-253, 258, 261, 263, 268, 270-272, 274, 281, 286, 292, 295-298, 303, 304, 307, 309, 310, 313-317, 320-323, 325, 326, 378-380, 382, 384
10:10 205, 211
10:11 209, 313
10:11-15 208
10:12-14 313
10:12-13a 313
10:12-14 211, 212, 215, 236
10:12b-13a 212
10:13 215, 234, 295
10:14 218
10:16-27 220, 222, 225
10:16-43 253
10:28-39 261, 227
10:28-42 226, 320
10:29 248
10:40-42 211, 241, 251
10:42 209
10:8 229
10-11 244, 249, 253
11 197, 199-201, 204-207, 209, 226, 228, 229, 237, 242, 244, 246, 251, 254, 268, 271, 272, 279, 281, 286, 288, 289, 292, 293, 299, 303-305, 307, 308, 311-313, 317, 319, 321, 323, 325, 329, 331, 378-382, 384
11:1 197, 200
11:1-15 251
11:18-19 246
11:6 229
12 197, 198, 200, 212, 214, 230-232, 237, 244, 247, 268, 275, 279, 281, 289, 290, 292, 293, 298-300, 304-306, 308, 309, 311, 313, 315, 317-321, 323-325, 330, 378, 379, 381
12:2-5 230
12:7 198
12:7a 230
12:7b-8 230
12:9-24 230
13:1b-2a 244
13:30 383
15:63 244, 247
16:10 242, 244, 247
17:12 244, 247

## *Deuteronomy*

17:14-20 255

## *Judges*

1 198, 242, 243, 246, 253, 379
5:20 218, 315

## *1 Samuel*

14:23-24 215

*2 Samuel*

21:1-14 200

*Isaiah*

42:11 382

*Habakkuk*

3 218

*2 Chronicles*

14:13 382

## ANCIENT TEXTS

*Assyrian*

Shalmaneser I 224, 285, 317
Tukulti-Ninurta I 285, 286, 317, 319
Annals of Tiglath-Pileser I 79-89, 215, 223, 310
Ashur-Dan 90-94
Aššur-nasir-pal 72, 94-99, 236, 282, 311
  Standard Inscription 120-121
  Annals 94-99
Shalmaneser III 99-110, 244, 262, 282, 286, 288, 326
Adad-nirari III 121, 281, 290, 291, 330
  Tell Al Rimah Stela 121-122
  Sheikh Hammand Stele 330
Samsi-Adad V 262
Sargon II 115, 262, 289, 290
  Letter to the God 115-119
  Annals 262
Sennacherib 221-224, 228, 230, 231, 283, 284, 288, 289, 318, 324, 326
  Walters Art Galley 230-231
  Annals 111-115
Esarhaddon 39, 221, 260, 262, 319, 321, 330
Aššurbanipal (Prisms A, F, T) 39, 70, 71, 201, 221, 262, 310, 311, 321

*Hittite*

Anitta Text 130-132
Proclamation of Telipinu 30, 127, 128, 293
Hattušili I 137-140
  Concise Annals 137-140, 315, 319
  Extensive Annals 137, 296
CTH 9:6 137
Suppiluliuma 126, 130, 292, 293, 295, 297
  Deeds of Suppiluliuma 160-163, 297
  Suppiluliuma's Treaty with Mattiwaza (BoST 8, 14:46) 122
Muršili II 126, 132, 198, 202, 203, 207-209, 228, 244, 245, 248, 297, 312, 315, 319, 322-324
  Detailed or Comprehensive Annals 140, 144, 158-160
  Ten Year Annals of Muršili II 140-158, 244
Hattušili III 30, 260
  Apology 29, 30, 269, 272, 277, 312, 329

*Egyptian*


Admonitions of Ipuwer 177
Amenemope 301
Merikare 177
Kamose 173, 179, 299, 300, 304-306
Tomb biography of Ahmose son of Ebana 171
Tel Sera' Hieratic Ostraca 307
Tombos Stela of Thutmose I 173
Thutmose II 168, 183, 304, 309
Hatshepsut 302, 309
Thutmose III
  Annals 55, 169-174, 176, 178, 183, 187, 189, 190, 192, 217, 221, 222, 224, 227, 232, 252, 256, 258, 272, 299-303, 305, 308, 309, 315, 317, 324
  Stück I 171, 174, 183, 301, 302, 305
  Stück V 183, 302
  Stücke V-VI 173, 174, 301-303, 381
  Armant Stela 172-175, 232, 252, 308
  Gebel Barkal Stela 173, 178, 302, 304, 305, 307-309, 315, 329
  Poetical Stela 192, 258, 302, 303, 316, 317
  Dedication Inscription: Urk. IV, 758.7 183
  List of Southern Lands 309
Amenhotep II 171, 172, 176, 263, 301, 309
  Memphis and Karnak Stelae 171
  Great Sphinx Stela at Giza 303
Thutmose IV 304
Amenhotep III 171, 190, 304, 309
  Bubastis Fragment 171
  Assuan Philae Road Stela 304
Amenhotep IV 304
Seti I 173, 216, 217, 255, 256, 304, 315, 327
Ramesses II 169, 171-174, 176, 183, 191, 204, 221, 231, 245, 279, 301, 303, 304, 308, 309, 319, 323
  Kadesh Inscription 169, 171, 172, 231, 301, 319, 323
  Undated War Scene: KRI II, 154.3 183
  Undated War Scene: KRI II, 166.14 183
  Beth-Shan Stela 303, 308, 315
Merenptah
  'Israel' Stela 173, 174, 188, 190, 227, 245, 249, 309, 323, 324
  Karnak War Inscription 177, 180, 181, 317, 319
  Athribis Stela 173
Ramesses III 169, 173, 174, 188, 191, 193
  Medinet Habu 169, 191, 204, 304, 309
Piye Stela 300, 309
Psammetichus III Stela 304


*Other*


Bar-Rakib 272
Enmetena 317
Herodotus 53, 165, 298
Iliad 215, 314
Josephus 287
Meša Inscription 227, 235, 321
Nabopolassar 236, 321
Nebuchadnezzar I 321
Quintilianus 25
Puzur-In-Sušinak 216
Samsu-iluna 122
Thucydides 37, 271, 272
Zakkur 229, 319